AUTOCOURSE

THE WORLD'S LEADING GRAND PRIX ANNUAL

HAZLETON PUBLISHING

the success formula

F1, F3, F3000, Prototype Sports – whatever the formula it's a racing certainty that Lucas will be an important ingredient. Which is not surprising because Lucas equipped cars can be relied upon to keep going when the going gets tough.

Our high standards are achieved with innovation and leading-edge-technology. At a time when keeping pace with accelerating change is a continuous challenge.

But our support for the sport is not confined to world champions. Our nationwide network of dealers – The Lucas Special Section – is there to help competitive motorists at all levels. Lucas – the formula for success.

Lucas Electrical

For information write to
Lucas Electrical Ltd., Great Hampton Street,
Birmingham B18 6AU, or telephone 021-236 5050.

CONTENTS

Autocourse is published by Hazleton Publishing, 3 Richmond Hill, Richmond, Surrey TW10 6RE. Printed in Holland by drukkerij de lange/van Leer bv, Deventer. Typesetting by C. Leggett & Son Ltd, Mitcham, Surrey. Colour reproduction by Adroit Photo Litho Ltd, Birmingham.

ISBN: 0-905138-44-9

UK distribution by
Osprey Publishing Limited
12/14 Long Acre
London WC2E 9LP

United States distribution by
Motorbooks International
Publishers & Wholesalers Inc.
Osceola, Wisconsin 54020, USA.

Photographs in *Autocourse* 1986-87 have been contributed by:
Bernard Asset/Agence Vandystadt, Patrick Behar, Malcolm Bryan, Diana Burnett, Paul-Henri Cahier, Mark Clifford, John Colley, Daytona International Speedway, Juta Fausel, Geoff Goddard, Lukas Gorys, David Hutson, International Press Agency, Joseph Jiran, Brendan McFarlane, Steve Small, Graham Smith, Nigel Snowdon, Keith Sutton, Steve Swope, John Townsend, Andrew Whyte.

ACKNOWLEDGEMENTS

The Editor of *Autocourse* wishes to thank the following for their assistance in compiling the 1986-87 edition:
Canada: Canadian Automobile Sports Club. **France:** AGS, Automobiles Ligier (Danny Hindenoch), Renault Sport (Jean Sage). **Germany:** BMW GmbH (Uwe Mahle), Zakspeed Racing (Jonathan Palmer). **Great Britain:** Arrows Racing Team (Pierre Van Vliet), Benetton Formula Ltd (Rory Byrne, Peter Collins, Pat Symonds and Nigel Wollheim), Cosworth Engineering (Geoff Goddard and Dick Scammell), Barry Griffin, Brian Hart, Team Haas (Tyler Alexander, Neil Oatley and Sophie Sicot), Edgar Jessop. Team Lotus (Ann Bradshaw and Peter Warr), McLaren International (Ron Dennis), Motor Racing Developments (Herbie Blash), Tyrrell Racing Organisation (Brian Lisles, Maurice Phillippe, Stuart Sykes and Ken Tyrrell), Dave Wass, Williams Grand Prix Engineering (Frank Dernie, Patrick Head and Peter Windsor). **Italy:** Ferrari SpA SEFAC (Harvey Postlethwaite and Brenda Vernor), Minardi Team, Giorgio Piola, Pirelli. **Switzerland:** Kaspar Arnet, Marlboro Motorsport (Agnes Carlier and Sally Doodson), Olivetti/Longines. **United States of America:** Championship Auto Racing Teams, Daytona International Speedway, International Motor Sports Association, NASCAR News Bureau, Sports Car Club of America, United States Auto Club.

PUBLISHER
Richard Poulter

EDITOR
Maurice Hamilton

EXECUTIVE PUBLISHER
Elizabeth Le Breton

ART EDITOR
Steve Small

PUBLISHING ASSISTANT
Jane Payton

HOUSE EDITOR
S.G. Spark

SECRETARY
Jane Doyle

ASSISTANT
Joss Hobbs

RESULTS AND STATISTICS
John Taylor

LAP CHARTS
Angela Poulter

TECHNICAL CORRESPONDENT
Giorgio Piola

FRENCH EDITOR
José Rosinski

UNITED STATES EDITOR
Gordon Kirby

CHIEF PHOTOGRAPHER
Nigel Snowdon

The dust-jacket photograph was taken by Mark Clifford and depicts 1986 World Champion, Alain Prost, at the wheel of his Marlboro McLaren MP4/2C.

Title page photograph
The reigning World Champion strengthens the late defence of his title with a win in Austria.
Photo: Lukas Gorys

Grand Prix title page photograph
Alain Prost and the McLaren MP4/2C at Monza.
Photo: Paul-Henri Cahier

The choice of the world leaders

Everyone knows I am a great collector of statistics, so that will tell you how proud I am to have joined the ranks of double World Champions. Also, in winning my 25th Grand Prix in Adelaide I have equalled the number of victories won by Jim Clark and my friend Niki Lauda.

This year, the outcome of the championship was decided at the last Grand Prix and, this time, events turned in my favour. In similar circumstances I failed in 1983 and 1984 and I have now been repaid after such a bitter experience. I know how the losers felt – Nigel in particular, who was in a position to win the championship for the first time. I honestly hope that he will quickly overcome his disappointment and I'm sure he will be one of my most serious rivals in the 1987 Championship.

The Marlboro McLaren team has achieved an unprecedented feat in the history of the championship by taking one of their drivers to the title for three consecutive years. It is proof of the exceptional quality of their organisation and the outstanding attributes of the men who form the team. To be honest, what other team would have overcome the temptation to rest on their laurels after two successful years in 1984 and 1985 and survived the departure of their technical director just as the battle for the title reached its climax? But the team spirit that exists at McLaren enabled them to negotiate the problem by closing ranks and reacting marvellously in very difficult circumstances. I am happy to be able to pay a well-deserved tribute to them in this *Autocourse* foreword.

In 1987 I shall need the team's support more than ever as I try to equal or, if possible, even to beat the current record of 27 Grand Prix victories held by Jackie Stewart – hopefully on my way to achieving a hat-trick of World Championships. You can see that the objectives I have set myself are ambitious, but with the assistance of this first-class team, nothing is impossible . . .

That day even more people

appreciated Shell Oils.

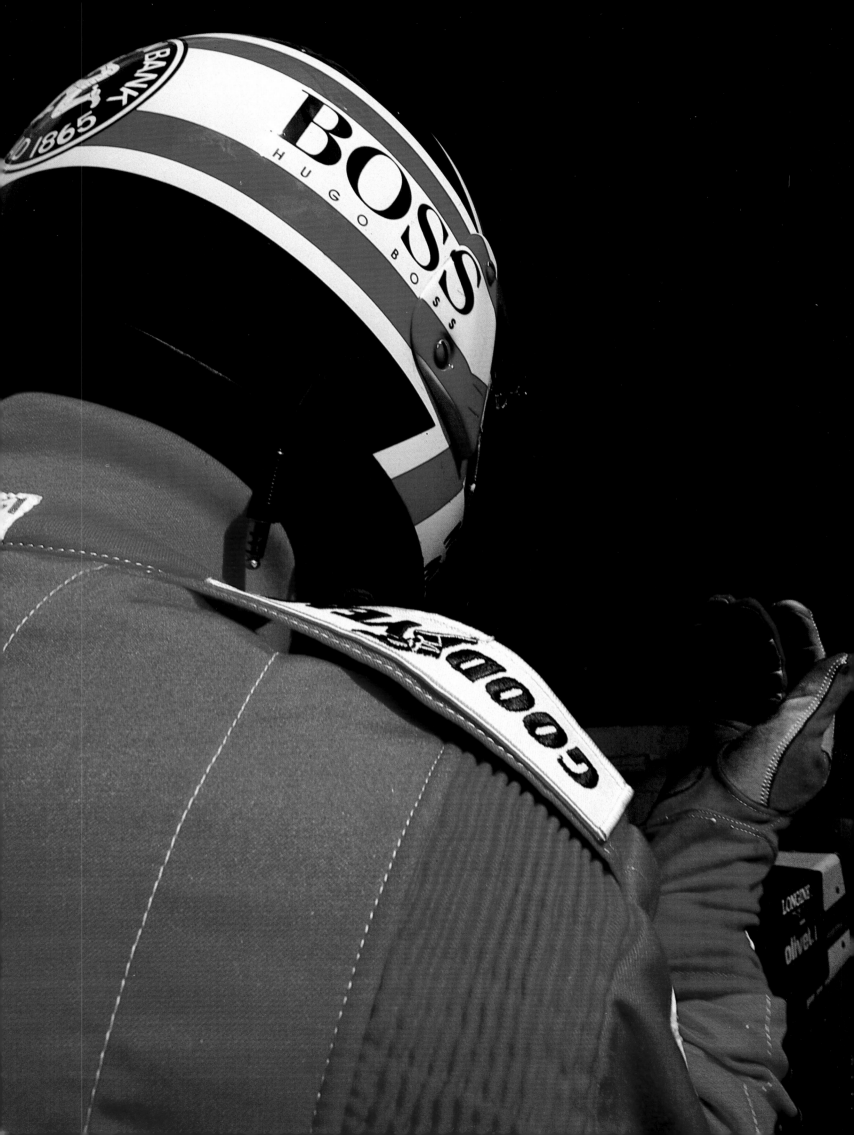

INTRODUCTION

'What do I have to do?'
The World
Championship turned
its back on Nigel
Mansell fifty miles from
the end of a dramatic
season.

If proof were needed of the demands imposed by a gruelling season of sixteen races, then you needed to look no further than Nigel Mansell's ashen face in Adelaide as he left the paddock, carrying nothing but his helmet bag.

The championship battle, a tremendously absorbing affair which had started with a clash of wheels in Rio de Janeiro 32 weeks previously, had taken the teams to North and South America, Europe, Mexico and, finally, Australia. There, we had three drivers with an excellent chance of taking the title. Events during that 82-lap race went beyond even the most imaginative script-writer but, at the end of the day, there could only be one winner.

First among equals in 1986 was Alain Prost. *Autocourse* salutes the Frenchman, not only for becoming the first driver in 26 years to win back-to-back championships, but also for the example he set as reigning champion in 1986. Diplomatic – but candid when necessary – out of the cockpit, the McLaren driver's aggressive form at the wheel has provided a yardstick for future champions, in any category of the sport, to measure themselves by.

If Mansell had to lose the title fifty miles from the chequered flag, then he gave way to the most complete driver of the current generation. The tragedy is that he had to lose under such spectacular circumstances; a straight defeat or, indeed, an error on Mansell's part would have been more acceptable to the Englishman.

It may not have been much consolation to Nigel at the time, but he had played a major part in rekindling enormous interest in motor racing in Britain. How else do you keep the nation from its bed at three o'clock on a Sunday morning? What other explanation can there be for a portrait of a racing driver at the top of the front page of *The Times* the morning after Mansell had won in Portugal? Somehow, the Bulldog Drummond climax to the saga gave the nail-biting story added poignancy.

Certainly, the last episode was relayed with superb clarity by the engineers of Australia's Channel 9 television network and their efforts with the onboard cameras introduced viewers to a new world which can only enhance the sport's appeal in the future.

Looking back, it is a pleasure to present a record of such a dramatic season and we hope this book serves as a continual reminder of a year when sportsmanship, intrigue and close competition ousted politics from the driving seat.

There were, however, moments of great sadness and we pay tribute to Elio de Angelis; one of the few serious accidents of the year depriving Grand Prix racing of a man who epitomised such valuable qualities as skill, glamour and gentlemanly behaviour.

Away from the race track, but none the less deeply affecting the sport, a major accident left Frank Williams with severe paralysis and it said much for the man that his well-drilled team was able to carry off the Constructors' Championship with nine victories. That they should lose the ultimate prize to McLaren with the last throw of the dice was the story of the season, detailed and examined in the following pages by the top writers in the sport.

We also mark a major political milestone as the world of Formula 1 set up its extravagant camp for the first time inside the Eastern Bloc. The Hungarian Grand Prix was an outstanding success, even matching the competent arrival of the Australian Grand Prix at the end of the previous year.

Apart from one or two reports of over-zealous officials, the return to Adelaide did little to change our opinion that the Australians have set new standards, not just for street racing but for motor sport as a whole. Keke Rosberg won the inaugural event in 1985 and for 55 laps in October the Finn looked like bowing out of Grand Prix racing in the best possible way.

Unfortunately, like Niki Lauda the previous year, he finally vacated the cockpit while the car was parked by the trackside rather than in the winner's enclosure. Keke's outspoken comments on page 26 illustrate just why such a colourful character will be missed, both on and off the track.

Talking of colour, we take great pleasure in introducing even more superb colour photographs culled from the work of the best motor sport lensmen in the world. Colour photography now illustrates the Top Ten, a feature which remains the most contentious – not to mention the most difficult to write – section of the book.

You may agree with the choice; on the other hand, you may not. What is certain is that motor sport owes each driver a debt of thanks for providing such a wonderful season and a vast pool of material for use in *Autocourse 1986/87,* one of the few motor sport annuals unaffiliated to any organisational body within the sport.

We remain, we hope, first among equals.

Maurice Hamilton
Ewhurst, Surrey
November 1986

Although
the Grand Prix
winners over the
last 20 years have
had countless tyre
changes, the name has
remained the same ▦
They've all banked on
Goodyear ▦ Jack Brabham
turned to Goodyear in 1966 and

184 GRAND PRIX VICTOR

promptly won the driver's champio
The incredibly successful Tyrrell
Goodyear in the early seventie
going ▦ Nothing succeeds like
reputation won us a place
on the rostrum) ▦ And
performance of their
Goodyear were first
first over the line. So to
particularly exciting one
and Goodyear ▦ A partner
doesn't end at the finish.
Nigel drives Goodyear home
as well ▦ Even though the name
has stayed the same for the last 20
years, the tyres haven't. It is our constant
research and improvement that makes sure one
thing doesn't change. Goodyear keep on winning ▦

L E A D I N G   T H E   W O R L D

...IES ON THE SAME TYRES.

...nship 🏁

...eam stuck with

...nd won almost everything

...uccess and in the 77–78 season our

...on the new Lotus (and won Lotus a place

...when Ferrari wanted a tyre to match the

...new turbo-charged car,

...choice and Ferrari were

...he 86 season and a

...or Nigel Mansell

...hip that

...IN TYRE TECHNOLOGY

GOOD/YEAR

OUR GRIP TOOK

HIM TO THE TOP.

Alain Prost got to the top on skill and determination.

And on Goodyear Eagle F1 tyres.

You, too, can have the grip and performance of a world champion.

Because many of the lessons we learn on the racetrack, we put into the development of our Eagle NCT and GT road tyres.

In the race for tyre technology there's only one winner.

Eagle F1 Rain-Racing   **Eagle NCT**   **GT**

N T Y R E T E C H N O L O G Y

1 *Alain Prost*

1
ALAIN PROST

2
NIGEL MANSELL

3
AYRTON SENNA

4
NELSON PIQUET

5
GERHARD BERGER

6
STEFAN JOHANSSON

7
MICHELE ALBORETO

8
KEKE ROSBERG

9
RENÉ ARNOUX

10
RICCARDO PATRESE

THE EDITOR'S EVALUATION OF THE LEADING GRAND PRIX DRIVERS OF 1986

Paul-Henri Cahier

An almost faultless year but, significantly, one which did not suffer from the pressures and self-esteem attached to the office of reigning World Champion. After struggling for so long to take the title, Prost would have been forgiven for allowing himself a marginal reduction in pace. Not a bit of it. If proof of his remarkable commitment is necessary, then look no further than Spa-Francorchamps. This daunting circuit presented Alain with no fears despite the Frenchman having to cope with a car which had bent engine mountings and buckled suspension – anathema to such a perfectionist. More to the point, he had no hope of winning and sixth place was, on the face of it, a poor reward. But, had the championship been won by one point instead of two, then he would have deserved it for that drive alone. It almost seems carping to mention the shunt during practice in Detroit but if that was the height of his indiscretions then we have witnessed a season of outstanding all-round ability.

2 *Nigel Mansell*

Paul-Henri Cahier

3 *Ayrton Senna*

Paul-Henri Cahier

In the aftermath of the Adelaide disaster, during conversations about a championship lost, it was easy to forget that he had won five Grands Prix. Each victory was the result of hard graft; an extension, you might say, of his motor racing career in general. If Mansell was the most improved driver of 1985, then he continued that trend in 1986, his performances being rounded off by a blend of clean, tactical and very fast driving. Of course, he had the equipment to do the job but the revelation of the past season has been the manner in which he demolished Nelson Piquet's reputation. Startline luck at Brands Hatch notwithstanding, Mansell's drive that day swept away any lingering doubts that a truly world class driver had finally emerged from the wreckage of a hitherto controversial career. The British Grand Prix was perfection and a suitable antidote for the gaffe in Rio and, more significantly, the fumbled start in Mexico. That, rather than the blow-out in Adelaide, probably contributed towards his failure to take the title. But, even so, the championship would have been a fitting end to a year in which Nigel Mansell was the pacesetter more often than not. Losing it will make him stronger still.

Eight pole positions and two wins scarcely begin to tell the story, the statistics fading into insignificance when you stand at any corner and watch this man at work. The speed and control exercised by the Brazilian are simply breath-taking but, as the results indicate, his equipment was frequently unable to match such exceptional pace. At Estoril, he kept in touch with the Williams-Hondas in a car which clearly was not as easy to drive, yet he showed intelligent use of the back-markers to keep Piquet at bay. Elsewhere, the pacing of his race at Jerez took advantage of a tactical error by the Williams team and, overall, the pole-position laps were quite staggering and indicative of an almost error-free year. The acquisition of Honda power for 1987 may prove to be his equal. On the other hand, the mating of the new engine to the Lotus may not be as simple as it seems. If Ayrton Senna has a shortcoming, then it will be his reaction to a failure to achieve the success he richly deserves.

Paul-Henri Cahier

Nigel Snowdon

Keke Rosberg and Michele Alboreto
promised much but Alain Prost
dominated the contribution made by
members of the Marlboro World
Championship Team.

ARN LA BRUN
IDUM T.F. GHI
SENBER DAN
PIQ JON PAL
MA TAM STR
ROS PAT BOL
PROST

5 Gerhard Berger

Paul-Henri Cahier

In truth, the Austrian should not be as high as number 5 but in many ways this sums up the gap between the top four and the rest. The move to Benetton and the tutelage of team manager Peter Collins proved as fortuitous for Berger as the rapidly developing potential of the car put at his disposal. Unfortunately, it took some time to achieve the race reliability to match his frequently stunning practice performances, something which the win in Mexico helped to compensate. Some of the misfortune during the races was of Berger's own making as he threw caution to the wind in an effort to create an impression by running at the front. He would argue that the Ferrari contract for 1987 proves this tactic paid off but the Italian team, while having a future champion on their hands, may not tolerate such unfettered skill at the expense of a measured performance. On the other hand, it may be just what Enzo Ferrari thinks he needs in order to return the Prancing Horse to the winner's circle.

6 Stefan Johansson

Keith Sutton

Ferrari have never worked with anything approaching logic when it comes to hiring and firing drivers and the dismissal of Johansson at the end of 1986 is a case in point. Agreed, his practice performances have been poor and, as a result, Johansson became embroiled in first-lap incidents. But Ferrari, surely, can not blame Johansson for the mechanical mayhem which was usually exacerbated by the non-availability of the spare car? (At Monza, in Alboreto's absence and with the T-car at his disposal, Johansson showed what was possible.) For sheer tenacity (Imola, Monaco, Austria, Monza, Mexico and Adelaide), Johansson deserves credit but then that would require Ferrari to admit they had frequently given him a difficult car in the first place . . .

Paul-Henri Cahier

4 Nelson Piquet

A myth exploded? We said last year that the comparison between Mansell and Piquet would be an interesting one; a euphemism for the belief that the Brazilian would turn out to be the dominant force at Williams. How wrong can you be? The way in which Piquet, matched by Mansell during qualifying, was generally overshadowed in the races, has been one of the most fascinating aspects of the season. It raises the interesting point that, apart from his early days with Lauda, Nelson has never before had a truly competitive team-mate to work with – or against. Yet the superb car control seen in Hungary proves that the genuine flair remains although his season was peppered with fundamental mistakes. It was also riddled by a series of minor mechanical flaws, the broken undertray during practice in Portugal, for instance, costing him dearly. It has been a difficult year for Piquet but he will surely bounce back; his natural talent is too great to suggest otherwise. A myth exploded? It's too early to agree with that.

7 Michele Alboreto

A disastrous year in many ways but, throughout, Alboreto's underlying flair continued to show. There were occasions, such as Monza, when the stirring chase of the Williams-Hondas was bound to end in mechanical failure but Michele's frustration after a summer of negligible results was understandable. There could be no argument, however, over his dazzling display during practice at Monaco where control of the car counted for more than the performance it had to offer. There were one or two unnecessary collisions which perhaps reflected a loss of interest and enthusiasm and Alboreto, in urgent need of race wins, must now hope for salvation from the drawing board of John Barnard.

Paul-Henri Cahier

8 Keke Rosberg

Diana Burnett

More subdued, both in and out of the cockpit, following the switch from Williams to McLaren. The MP4/2C either did not suit – or was not tailored to suit – Keke's flamboyant, darty style of driving and it was not until Brands Hatch and Hockenheim that adjustments were made which allowed the McLaren number 2 to fly. Before that, a memorable drive at Monaco had defied predictions about the outcome of his untidy efforts but, elsewhere, a mixture of technical problems and a press-on style in the softly-softly world of 195 litres contrived to keep him away from the podium. The swansong at Adelaide had about it all the fire and thunder we had been expecting all year; the hasty departure from the cockpit being indicative of an unfortunate mental conditioning that something was bound to go wrong. A win would have been just reward and a suitable end to a career which has brought such pleasure to spectator enclosures the world over.

9 René Arnoux

Keith Sutton

The familiar mixture of brilliance and sheer hooliganism maybe, but Arnoux deserves a mention simply because of his remarkable form after a year's lay-off. Always in contention, frequently running in the top six, he surpassed himself in Rio, Jerez, Imola and Monaco, although the latter performance scarcely made up for a silly accident during practice. Despite a complete lack of development on the Ligier during the second half of the season, he still managed to qualify in the top six in Adelaide. He also contrived to behave like an idiot from time to time (Detroit, Hungary, Italy and Mexico) but, overall, a worthy return to the Formula 1 scene. Some of his colleagues, however, might not agree . . .

Paul-Henri Cahier

10 Riccardo Patrese

A new man this season due, possibly, to the absence of Piquet's dominant presence at Brabham. Showing more resolve than during his past three seasons put together, Patrese capitalised on superb natural skill which has been wasted during a long and largely unproductive career in Formula 1. He helped carry the team through the post-de Angelis gloom and a finish in the points in Mexico would have been well-deserved and equally well-received. Unfortunately, he reverted to type and spun it away, strengthening the belief that he may never be a truly complete driver. None the less, both Patrese and Derek Warwick deserve credit for persevering with a problematical car during such a dismal season for the Brabham team.

Thierry Boutsen and Jonathan Palmer were worthy of inclusion in the Top Ten. Once again, Boutsen showed remarkable determination with an uncompetitive car, his practice performance at Monaco ranking alongside his efforts in Montreal, Detroit and Monza. His persistence has been justifiably rewarded by the Benetton contract; a Grand Prix win is overdue.

Just as deserving when it comes to receiving the attention of a top team, Jonathan Palmer has shown his worth as a driver by hurling the recalcitrant Zakspeed around Monaco to earn a place on the grid. When it rained during practice in Montreal, ability counted for more than the usual technical shortcomings. A deserving but elusive place in the points in Mexico should have nicely rounded off a season which suffered immeasurably from the team's need to run a second car for financial reasons.

The restrictive nature of the Monte Carlo streets also gave Martin Brundle the opportunity to show a degree of natural flair in a season hamstrung by a car and engine combination which was short of pace. Brundle had much to prove during 1986 and the results he needed were not forthcoming, although bringing the Tyrrell into the points without the benefit of fifth gear in Hungary was indicative of a sensitive and sympathetic touch. A question mark, however, still hovers over a driver who has earned an unfortunate reputation among his colleagues for excessive aggression, which is a shame, since there is a great deal of untapped talent remaining.

Philippe Streiff, perhaps too serious for his own good, did little to enhance his standing although, in fairness, driving the second Tyrrell was not exactly a passport to success during 1986. Even so, he spun a lot and there are few hints, at this stage, of an outstanding performer.

Derek Warwick, in the same category when it came to the machinery at his disposal, nevertheless grasped his opportunity after a brief absence. Bravery and resilience are the attributes which spring to mind at the end of a wretched season, one which made the barren 1985 season look like a year of champagne and caviar. Even so, his cheerful presence did much for flagging morale within the struggling Brabham team and it is to be hoped that such a competitive racer will not be overlooked simply because of the unbelievable trials and tribulations he experienced during the past season.

Hats off to Johnny Dumfries. A potential World Champion he may not be but the manner in which he handled the media hostility surrounding his arrival at Lotus, and the ever-present pressure within the team, went a long way towards silencing his critics. Dumfries never complained and simply got on with the job and it was only cruel luck which robbed him of points first time out. He may have been out of his depth at times but the Scotsman earned respect from the team (a notable achievement which says much about the man) and he definitely deserved a second year in which to settle down and learn from his mistakes.

We knew from experience what Alan Jones was capable of – which is why his performances were disappointing. The political and technical shortcomings within the Haas-Lola team aside, the former champion showed a lack of interest in working hard for a minor placing. But there were occasions when the hard-nosed racer in him reappeared, particularly if there was a chance of success.

Jones was overshadowed during the first eight races or so by Patrick Tambay and one of the season's great imponderables is 'what might have happened had Patrick not been eliminated at the first corner at Spa?'. Inconsistent lap times hinted at a loss of motivation during the latter half of the year although he proved capable of producing a quick lap during practice with a car and engine combination which proved to be as disappointing as the Frenchman's results.

Christian Danner's raw enthusiasm led to the sluggish Osella being committed to spectacular angles during the first few races and the ability to keep pace with Boutsen from time to time hinted at skills which were, perhaps, hidden by the inadequacies of the Arrows-BMW.

Teo Fabi, the most enigmatic of all the drivers, showed a remarkable discrepancy between his best performances, which were very impressive indeed, and his worst drives, which totally lacked interest and commitment. He started the season on a promising note, fast lap times in Rio and Jerez indicating what might have been had he not been delayed by mechanical problems, but mid-season he may as well have stayed at home. The move to the fast circuits, where precision and neatness were paramount, rekindled his interest, however. While his talent may be brilliant, if illusive, a consistent cutting edge was frequently blunted by simple mistakes.

Rating the Osella drivers, Piercarlo Ghinzani and Allen Berg, is like examining artists who are attempting to work with blunt pencils and watered-down paints. At least the Minardi drivers, Andrea de Cesaris and Alessandro Nannini, had potentially useful equipment and, on the rare occasions when the cars ran without an accompanying haze of smoke, Nannini demonstrated a considerable flair which deserves the close attention of team managers. Certainly, he showed up de Cesaris as completely indifferent and it is unfortunate and inappropriate that Nannini should end such a promising year parked so comprehensively against the wall in Adelaide.

A Top Ten drawn up before the British Grand Prix would surely have included Jacques Laffite. Perhaps spurred on by Arnoux, Jacques showed commendable speed in Rio and Jerez, followed by the usual understated self-control and coolness at Monaco and excellent form in Detroit, where he actually led the race. Had it not been for a catalogue of problems during practice at Brands Hatch, then he would have been further up the grid and probably clear of the accident which removed one of the sport's great competitors – hopefully only on a temporary basis.

Laffite was replaced by Philippe Alliot, the Frenchman proving faster than his drives with RAM had suggested although frequent incidents and spins showed he was almost too anxious to succeed. If Huub Rothengatter drove as expressively as he speaks then he would have won several races by now, but at least the Dutchman's work with the Zakspeed, while suffering from the inevitable shortcomings of being the number 2 in a small team, was businesslike if eventually fruitless.

Of the occasional drivers, Alex Caffi and Ivan Capelli did not have competitive equipment but the Italians demonstrated commendable common sense and track manners while running in such elevated company. A one-off drive for Eddie Cheever in Detroit was as impressive as any performance from the American in the past. His was the name on everyone's lips – until the next race. Such are the fickle ways of Formula 1.

Jacques Laffite

Keith Sutton

Thierry Boutsen

Paul-Henri Cahier

Lukas Gorys

Patrick Tambay

Keith Sutton

Teo Fabi

Diana Burnett

Alessandro Nannini

EVERYONE KNOWS THE WINNING

A fantastic season for the Williams team. Their victory was achieved through consistent high standards. The best talent, the best teamwork and the best technology.

Mobil are part of their winning formula. Our advanced synthetic oils and greases are now proven leaders in the toughest engineering environment there is.

SECRET OF WILLIAMS FORMULA

After powering through a gruelling Formula One season, Mobil will continue to set the standards in lubricant technology. Remember, we backed the winner on the nose.

Mobil

HONDA

Progress with Distinction

1986 Constructor's World Championship

It's now history that the Williams-Honda team wiped the floor with the combined might of their Grand Prix competitors.

Indeed, the Formula One Constructor's Championship was wrapped up for Williams-Honda with three races still to go: a tribute not only to the machinery, but to the skills of Piquet and the most successful English driver for a decade, Nigel Mansell.

But does this have any bearing on the real world of traffic jams, motorways and petrol prices?

If you're fortunate enough to drive a

POWERED BY HONDA

Honda, the answer's yes.

We don't spend millions a year simply for the thrill of the chequered flag. Our Formula One engine is designed within

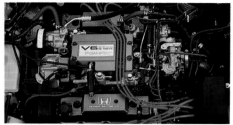

V6 2.5L. 24 Valve

the disciplines of achieving ultimate performance backed up by reliability and economy.

Which are much the same disciplines that guide the building of all our cars. Any successful developments on the race track, therefore, can be a source of inspiration in the manufacture of our entire range.

The new Legend, for instance, sports a completely new 2.5 litre engine. It's no coincidence that it is a 4 valve per cylinder V6, just like the Formula One car.

Another track bred innovation is the

programmed fuel injection (PGM-FI) which adds precision and punch to our engines in the Prelude, CRX, Accord and the Legend.

In fact, it's fair to say that making our racing cars better makes our road cars better.

And you can hardly make better racing cars than the best in the world.

(H) HONDA

Honda (UK) Ltd, 4 Power Road, Chiswick, London W4 5YT

KEKE ROSBERG

Keke Rosberg is quite emphatic about it: he decided at the end of 1984 that he would retire at the end of the 1986 season. Typically, he doesn't mince words on what amounts to an extremely contentious subject.

'I started being fairly fed up at around that time when the Honda engine blew up around my ears every weekend', he insists unequivocally. 'And the fact was – and still is – that I wanted to change teams and Frank Williams wouldn't let me go. He forced me to sit out my contract. There was nothing wrong with that in itself, but in '84 I found Patrick Head impossible to work with. I don't really know why, but there was no worthwhile communication between us at all. So I decided that I would leave when my contract was up.

'Then, in 1985, Patrick was back to his old self, so I was happy that our last season together was a pleasant one.'

Those remarks put Rosberg's character into pin-sharp focus. Aside from his considerable talent behind the wheel of a Grand Prix car, he is devastatingly open and candid when it comes to speaking his mind. However, coupled with this tendency to shoot from the hip, Keke is imbued with unmistakable honesty and sense of fair play. Almost uniquely, at least amongst Formula 1 drivers, he is prepared to admit that he can be wrong.

When the news broke that Nigel Mansell would be joining the team as his partner for 1985, Keke was beside himself with sheer indignation and annoyance. He didn't want Nigel in the team because he didn't like what he had heard about him. There was also a rankling suspicion that Williams had been talking about swapping Rosberg for Mansell at the end of 1982, Keke's Championship year. But now he admits he was wrong about Mansell.

'Nigel was one of the reasons that I wanted to leave Williams', says Keke directly, 'but I was completely wrong about him. His reputation was not correct. It was wrong, completely wrong. It must have made him very wary when he arrived in a new team to hear his team-mate saying "well, I don't want him here". It took us four or five months to work it out, but now we're very good friends. I based my feelings about him on what I heard from other people, not my personal knowledge. And obviously I got a lot of reports about him from Elio de Angelis as I was very close to him.'

On the other hand, when Patrick Head tried to talk rationally, and in detail, about why he should abandon his deliberately oversteering style, Keke would have none of it. 'Until somebody can prove to me that my way's wrong, I'll keep doing it my way, thank you!' was his crisp rejoinder.

Towards the end of the 1985 season one sensed ever so slightly that Keke might have liked to change his mind and stay with the Williams-Honda squad. But, professional that he always has been, he made his decision to drive for

McLaren International and he entered into that commitment with enthusiasm. Never once, as he saw Piquet and Mansell run riot through the results with their FW11-Hondas, did Keke confess to even a twinge of regret. Always his own man, he resolutely maintained that he was delighted with the McLaren deal.

Behind the scenes, however, he was worried. Not until the pre-British GP Brands Hatch test did he get the MP4/2C handling to his personal preference. 'After two years of the car being set up by Prost and Lauda, it was perhaps obvious that I might have different tastes', he admits. 'But when I was talking about getting rid of a lot of understeer, I meant a lot. They were thinking in terms of the fine adjustments they were used to talking about with Niki and Alain. It took some time to get the message across . . .'

When it came to the Brands Hatch race, Keke was competitive, but it was pole position at Hockenheim after a battle with team-mate Prost that brought home to everyone that Rosberg had hit the pace again. And with a splendid sense of irony, it was the race at which he announced his intention to retire.

This marked the final few pages of a book whose leading character had started with kart racing in the mid-1960s. There was no stopping him, despite the protestations of his father Lars, a veterinary surgeon and amateur rallyist who felt that Keke should pursue a more conventional career as a dentist. Keke was on his way, first in karts, later in Formula Vee and F2.

Trouble was, from the outset Keke liked to travel first class, although in those early years he often lacked the price of a ticket. That is not to say he was a spendthrift; far from it. He is, and always has been, shrewd with his money. Close might be a better expression. He doesn't stint himself on Ferraris and Learjets, but once you try to get him to buy you pie and chips in the Silverstone café you have a problem on your hands. If he wasn't such a lovely bloke, I'd call him tight!

Whether racing Super Vees over the limit or competing all over the world in Fred Opert's F2/Atlantic/Pacific Chevrons in 1978, Keke was prepared to work, both on and off the circuits, but he insisted on being paid the rate for the job. In the spring of 1978 he speedboated to victory in the non-title International Trophy race at Silverstone, handling Teddy Yip's bulky Theodore with rare natural skill on the near-flooded track surface. But it was not until James Hunt decided to retire mid-season in 1979 that Keke became a fully fledged member of the F1 fraternity, driving for Walter Wolf.

At the end of '79, Wolf and Fittipaldi amalgamated and Keke signed for another two seasons. It cost him a lot of his F1 momentum as the programme got bogged down through lack of money and technical resources. But he never stopped trying. Even when he failed to qualify for the 1980 British GP at Brands

continued on page 28

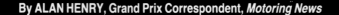

By ALAN HENRY, Grand Prix Correspondent, *Motoring News*

Hatch, he tried so desperately hard that he had a blinding headache for a week. 'That's the frustrating thing', he shrewdly observed, 'being in a slow car. In a competitive car, it would have been easy. That sort of effort would have translated into worthwhile results.'

Keke was to get his opportunity at the end of 1981. His partnership with Fittipaldi dissolved as the team headed for oblivion, but Rosberg was soon under consideration for a Williams seat. Alan Jones had retired, leaving a vacant cockpit in one of the prestige teams of the time. At his first Paul Ricard test session Keke was right on the pace. Frank didn't hesitate, signing him immediately.

Initially taken on as number two to the enigmatic Carlos Reutemann, Keke found himself promoted to the status of team leader when the Argentinian retired after a mere two races. He accepted the challenge with relish, although there were those who said he demonstrated more extrovert enthusiasm than inherent skill. Keke just saw it as doing his job; getting on with things and 'pressing on'. He wiped those critics in the eye by winning his first Grand Prix at Dijon-Prenois (the Swiss) and plucked the World Championship from beneath the noses of Prost, Lauda and Watson.

Slow onto the turbo bandwagon, Williams laboured for most of 1983 with Cosworth V8-engined cars, only fielding the prototype Honda-propelled machines at the end of the year. But the FW09 and its derivatives were distinctly canine machines, condemning Keke and team-mate Jacques Laffite to a tiring, frustrating season in 1984.

Notwithstanding the FW09's poor track manners – and Keke's habit of publicising them (a trait which consistently irritated Patrick Head) – Rosberg scored the best single F1 victory of the year. Handling his machine with deft flair on the crumbling Dallas track surface, he dodged every pitfall to win splendidly. It was a success which underlined his strength as a great improvisor. Throw all the balls in the air, make everything unpredictable, and Keke would excel.

Despite his success in taking two victories in 1985 with the new FW10/10B, Keke had a somewhat complex relationship with the Williams team to the end of his time with them. He was perhaps only partly joking when he remarked that, 'they've never really forgiven me for not being Alan Jones.' Truth be told, anybody who had turned up in Jonesey's wake was going to have problems with the team. The team revolved around Jones, was identified with him. Now they were landed with this moustachioed, chain-smoking little man who, on first glance at least, had a fairly firm idea of his own importance. It was a bit of a culture shock for the Williams lads.

Keke never conformed. He would only go so far down the road towards what he regarded as Frank's obsessively committed involvement towards motor racing. It was always clear to Keke that there was life after Formula 1 and he intended to plan for it while he was still earning the big money.

Of course, his acumen as a businessman was quite remarkable. He loved the wheeling and dealing involved in getting all his sponsorship contracts together. In his Williams days his bright yellow overalls resembled a millionaire's patchwork quilt, making it all the more surprising to some that he made the move to the monotone red livery of a Marlboro-McLaren driver. But he knew perfectly well what he was doing!

Describing Keke as 'flashy' would almost certainly please him. He has always revelled in a brashly extrovert personal style. What other driver would have a stained glass window depicting his helmet in his own home, as Keke did when he lived in England at Cookham Dean?

What other driver could name his pink-liveried high-speed motor cruiser *Wet Dream* and then wonder, in all honesty, why the British Register of Shipping declined to accept it? Or have his helmet colours painted onto the tail of his aircraft? In many others, these peacock qualities would be accompanied by an aloof snobbery. Keke, mercifully, has a keen sense of humour and a capacity to laugh at himself, inviting one to accept all these excesses with equanimity.

What will he miss most about life out of a racing car? 'It's difficult to say what that could be because I've not yet retired', he replied with a twinkle in his eye. 'I also don't know what I *won't* miss, although I've a pretty shrewd idea. Perhaps I'll miss the travelling. On the other hand, perhaps I'll find that I can't get used to being in one place. It's a no-man's land. But I will miss the competition . . .'

Then we asked him how he would like to be remembered, in pure motor racing terms. 'I really don't know. Really I don't.' He was thoughtful. 'I suppose it would be nice to be recalled as a driver who tried all the time; for people to think, well, he was always working as he was supposed to work.

'But my history is so small, I'm hardly likely to go down in many record books. I haven't exactly set the world alight, have I? But it's been a lot of good fun. It still is. In five years' time nobody will remember that I was there.'

Those who were at Monaco '83, Dallas '84 or Adelaide '85, to mention but a few memorable races, would take serious issue with Keke over that last remark.

THEY CAME, THEY SAW, THEY CONCURRED.

When we unveiled the new Pirelli P700 last summer, we made some exceptionally immodest boasts on its behalf.

We said it marked the birth of the second generation of ultra-low profile tyres.

And claimed that a radical new approach, to both design and materials, had resulted in a tyre superior in every dimension even to the P7.

(Which itself is the low profile tyre that everyone has been trying to beat for the past decade.)

The facts and figures from our testing supported our claims, but naturally we didn't expect the hard-bitten gentlemen of the world's motoring press to be so easily convinced.

So we invited them to try the P700s for themselves.

We put the tyres on a selection of the most powerful production cars around.

We put the cars on a very demanding track (Jarama, near Madrid), which we'd made even more interesting with the addition of an irrigated slalom section and a flooded hairpin.

Then the journalists put them through their paces.

With many of our guests navigating the harsh gradients and unnerving bends of Jarama as if they had urgent deadlines to meet, what followed turned out to be no mean test. Even for the world's finest high performance tyre.

We're just pleased that, when they came to write about their experiences and impressions, the praise was as unrestrained as the driving.

And now for sump thing completely different…

QXR is a totally new kind of oil from Duckhams, specially developed for high performance engines — and high performance drivers.

QXR is the outcome of a unique refining process that "cracks" the molecular structure of the base oil giving it a purity and a viscosity index conventional technology could never achieve (and a price conventional oils could never justify).

As a result, QXR has better cooling properties at higher temperatures than ordinary oils, and doesn't break down under the stress of continuous hard driving. At the same time it has a low-drag formulation that protects your engine at low temperatures and during cold starts.

QXR has been tested on and off the track and in all kinds of engine. In one torture test generating turbo temperatures of 900° centigrade, QXR maintained higher oil pressures than any other leading mineral or synthetic oil tested.

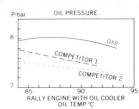

P/bar — OIL PRESSURE
QXR
COMPETITOR 1
COMPETITOR 2
85   90   95
RALLY ENGINE WITH OIL COOLER
OIL TEMP °C

So if you have a high performance engine, or just an active right foot, get some QXR under the bonnet. Fast.

HIGH PERFORMANCE ENGINE PROTECTION

an ordinary oil,

down

DUCKHAMS

QXR

THE WINNERS WHO LOST

We didn't know it at the start of the year, but 1986 was destined to go down in F1 history as one of the sport's great turning points, the end of a golden era. Barely a year after the final 3-litre Cosworth DFV derivative had been pensioned off into retirement, FISA decided to execute a massive U-turn, setting the Grand Prix business firmly back in the direction of naturally-aspirated engines. It may have been sudden, but, in reality, the sport's governing body was simply addressing a serious problem which had been allowed to snowball for too long.

Unquestionably, F1 turbo racing '86 style was a terrific success. We had a great World Championship struggle and some superb individual Grands Prix. Yet, if the serious student of motor racing examined the scene under a microscope, there were some disturbing cracks beginning to develop in the F1 fabric. The racing itself took place against a background of increasing concern

over the way in which the sport was evolving.

It wasn't simply a question of speed and safety; it was also the expense and technical relevance which was worrying team owners, engine manufacturers and FISA alike. Turbo F1 technology appeared to be rushing into an esoteric blind alley, crammed with massively expensive computer-age equipment. Given impetus by a few well-heeled manufacturers, headed by Honda, the high-tech tide threatened to leave F1 beached above the financial high-water mark once the surge of unlimited expenditure finally receded.

The start of the year marked another step in FISA's short-term efforts to keep the lid on performance as permitted fuel capacity was slashed from 220 to 195 litres. But while that went some way towards containing racing lap speeds, it did nothing to stop the prohibitive cost of qualifying with special high-boost 'sacrificial' engines brought into action simply to guarantee a

competitive grid position. This appeared to have all the symptoms of financial and technical insanity so, after toying with a revised qualifying procedure, FISA finally blew the whistle on turbo development as from the start of 1987.

Beginning with the introduction of pop-off valves to restrict turbo boost pressure at the start of next season, turbochargers will be phased out over a two-year period. By 1989, F1 will cater only for 3·5-litre naturally-aspirated engines, with a maximum of 12 cylinders. At the stroke of a pen, the old order changeth . . .

However, these major rule changes merely rumbled on the horizon like distant thunder when the 1986 Championship chase got under way in Brazil in the middle of March. On the strength of the last few races of 1985, Williams-Honda and McLaren-TAG were going to monopolise the action centre stage, while the brilliant Ayrton Senna would be ploughing a lonely furrow at

Paul-Henri Cahier

insisting on its exclusive availability.

The Mansell critics, believing that Nigel would continue true to his generally perceived form, nodded sagely when he speared his FW11 into the barrier at Rio, attempting to dislodge Senna from the lead midway round the opening lap. Would he never learn?

Those critics were in for a surprise at Jerez, the brand new venue for the Spanish Grand Prix hosting the second round of the championship. Not only did Mansell match Piquet's pace with no apparent trouble, but demonstrated how well he could channel his determination by gobbling up Senna's advantage in the closing stages of the race, after a dramatic pit stop for fresh tyres. Lotus and Williams crossed the line as one in the closest F1 finish for more than a decade.

Rivalry at Williams ran deep. It had originally been intended that engineer Sergio Rhineland should preside over Mansell's FW11 with the more senior Frank Dernie, WGPE's aerodynamicist, looking after Piquet's machine. But when Rhineland left the team before the start of the season, Patrick Head assumed his duties in the field. Thus, to the casual observer who didn't know the details, it seemed as though the team's number two driver was being cossetted by the Chief Designer. In turn, there was no doubt that Dernie developed a passionate zeal for 'his man' to beat 'the other bloke'.

Piquet's failure to win the championship had its roots firmly embedded in an arrogant over-confidence. That win in Brazil lulled this old professional into a false sense of security. By the middle of the season he was locked into an indifferent run of mediocre performances and, privately, he even confessed that he'd 'let things slip quite badly'.

His first lapse had been at Monaco, where a preference for the social life conspired with an unsuitable final-drive ratio to produce a lacklustre seventh on race day. He perked up to lead at Spa before his retirement, was outclasssed by Mansell at Montreal and then evened the score for 'silly shunts' by wiping off a wheel at Detroit. He was off the pace again at Paul Ricard.

By contrast, Nigel inheritied a good win at Spa, then triumphed convincingly at both Montreal and Paul Ricard. Even when he was not winning, Mansell looked the more convincing performer. At Monaco, he concentrated well to finish fourth and notched up an equally impressive, brake-troubled fifth at Detroit.

Brands Hatch was unquestionably the high spot of the season as Mansell capitalised brilliantly on an unexpected helping of luck. As his FW11 broke a driveshaft c/v joint accelerating into Paddock Bend, so a multiple pile-up in his wake immediately caused the race to be red-flagged. He took the spare FW11 for the restart and beat Nelson in a straight fight for an emotional victory in front of an ecstatic Brands Hatch crowd. It was only sad that the price of Nigel's second chance was that Jacques Laffite's Ligier slammed into the barrier at the top of Paddock, the popular veteran Frenchman sustaining leg injuries which kept him out of the cockpit for the remainder of the season.

Team Lotus at the head of what amounted to a one-car team, in terms of winning potential. Ferrari and Benetton-BMW were poised in the wings, possible winners on long odds, while the striking lowline Brabham BT55 encouraged some intriguing speculation.

In the event, it was Williams Grand Prix Engineering which grasped the mantle of McLaren International in mastering the art of going quickest for longest with the most economical rate of fuel consumption. The technical merits of the Williams-Honda FW11 package are examined elsewhere in *Autocourse*, but they only formed part of the championship-winning package. It was the personal chemistry of the Williams-Honda set-up which attracted the most attention, revolving around the personal relations between the two drivers. In a nutshell, neither could stand the sight of the other. No 'media gossip' here; they were quite open about it. This

was an inescapable fact and the Williams operation simply had to work round it, a task aided, one may say, by the fact that both men are highly professional racing drivers.

During the summer of 1985, immediately after Keke Rosberg announced his impending switch to McLaren, Frank Williams signed Nelson Piquet on a highly lucrative two-year contract. This was at a time when Nigel Mansell was finding his feet with the Williams team, working up a level of confidence which was eventually to produce his first Grand Prix victory at Brands Hatch in October. By that time the ink was long dry on Piquet's contract as his team-mate.

Although Piquet was recruited as number one, it was initially agreed that the use of the spare car would alternate between the two drivers from race to race. Yet it was an indication of the potential personal tensions simmering beneath the surface that, within two or three races, Piquet was

Steve Hallam, Ayrton Senna and Gérard Ducarouge study lap times at Hockenheim. Eight times out of sixteen, the Brazilian was top of the list (right).

Ron Dennis and Alain Prost (below). It proved a sometimes turbulent year for the McLaren boss but ultimately a successful one for the reigning World Champion.

Lukas Gorys

This defeat really irked Piquet and he turned his fortunes round magnificently to win in fine style at Hockenheim, the inaugural championship in Hungary and at Monza. But the pendulum swung back in Mansell's favour at Estoril, the peak of the Englishman's season where he beat Prost, Piquet and Senna in a straight fight. It was his most commanding victory of all. Then came the knife-edge result at Mexico leading up to that last-moment disappointment in Adelaide where both Williams drivers found themselves outfumbled by circumstance, allowing the title to pass to Prost at the very last throw of the dice.

Irrespective of the outcome of the title chase, Mansell had won more races than any other driver (five) during the season, his march to F1 maturity having speeded up dramatically during his two years with Williams. The Didcot-based team generally provided him with more tranquil and congenial surroundings than he had known at

Team Lotus, despite a mid-season flirtation with Ferrari which resulted in a decision to stay where he was for 1987 and '88.

Luck played a part in the fortunes of each of the 'top three', but Mansell did as much as possible to manoeuvre himself into a championship-winning position. True, he failed to get his Williams into first gear in Mexico, but he was driving a perfect race in Adelaide before tyre failure intervened to send his championship aspirations out of the window.

Putting Nigel's performances throughout the year into perspective, he got to within a sniff of the title not only by being at the wheel of the best car, but also by driving better than his rivals for much of the time. He suppressed his wilder instincts, concentrated unerringly and generally kept out of trouble. He matured into an accomplished professional and, irrespective of his failure to take the title, scaled fresh heights of achievement which

his critics found difficult to believe. Either way, his 1986 season represented a superb act of self-justification after all those years in the wilderness.

Notwithstanding the achievements of the two Williams teamsters, it would have been a brave gambler ever to have bet against Alain Prost, as became plain in Adelaide. The 1985 World Champion never once displayed a trace of 'post-championship blues' and played a central role in every race of the year. Like Mansell, the true index of his quality could be seen in his capacity to come to terms with difficult situations. So, while his crushing victory at Monaco ranked as one of the very best wins of '86, his fights through the field from positions of adversity at Spa and Monza showed Alain's greatness in its true light. The fact that he also became the first driver to win the championship 'back-to-back' since Jack Brabham (1959 and 1960) proved almost incidental. Quite simply, he was the best . . .

Of the other race winners, Ayrton Senna demonstrated a magical flair and unfettered brilliance – whenever the Lotus-Renault package permitted him to do so. Team Lotus had been battered by the storms of hostile press reaction after declining to take Derek Warwick onto its strength as Senna's number two, largely on the Brazilian's insistence. At one point he threatened to go to Brabham if Warwick was signed and many people felt that Peter Warr should have called his bluff. Had Senna defected thus, he would, as things turned out, been consigned to the wilderness. There was a feeling that Ayrton may have been just 'trying it on'; if he was, he must have been amazed at the way in which the Lotus management capitulated.

In the event, even Senna's brilliance could not cope consistently with the Williams-Hondas, particularly in races where fuel consumption was marginal, and Lotus's star performer failed in his

37

Choosing the correct gear ratios proved to be the least of their worries for Riccardo Patrese and the Brabham team

René Arnoux bounced back after a year's absence from Grand Prix racing (below).

bid to take the title. Unquestionably he is one of the most complete performers of all – second only to Prost – yet such a towering egocentric that one wonders whether he will ever quite be able to string together a championship-winning run.

Only one new face appeared on the winner's roštrum in 1986 and that was really no great surprise. When Gerhard Berger found his Benetton-BMW's Pirelli tyres were letting him run non-stop through the Mexican Grand Prix, he scored a long overdue triumph for the former Toleman équipe, which had been hovering on the brink of success for some time. Benetton made far better use of BMW power and Pirelli rubber than the high-priced Brabham team ever looked likely to do, much to Bernie Ecclestone's exasperation. Berger, Ferrari-bound for '87, always fought like a tiger, no matter what the circumstances.

Of the supporting cast, Keke Rosberg was the biggest disappointment, the Finn temperamentally unsuited to the artificial and absurd disciplines of fuel consumption racing. Time and again, in the early part of the year, Keke would use more boost than was prudent to catch Prost, only to drop back to a crawl in the closing stages as he eked out his 195 litres of Shell to get to the finish. He couldn't handle the McLaren chassis on Prost's settings, his personal anathema being understeer, and despite a good second behind Alain at Monaco and a pole-winning show at Hockenheim, the genial Finn was generally no match for the Frenchman. Then, in his very last race before retirement, he clicked brilliantly and proved to us that the old flair was lurking close beneath the surface. In Adelaide, he was, quite simply, the class of the field.

Ferrari's twosome grappled with the indifferent F1/86 as best they could, Stefan Johansson scoring more points than Michele Alboreto – which achievement brought him dismissal by the rather contrary powers-that-be at Maranello. Pit-lane gossip whispered that his days were numbered after he passsed Alboreto at Spa against team orders, but Ferrari's loss will undoubtedly be somebody else's gain.

It was a shame that the Brabham BT55 turned out to be such a lemon, for it not only resulted in the break-up of the Ecclestone/Gordon Murray partnership after 14 years, but also failed to do justice to any of its drivers. Riccardo Patrese, anxious to re-establish his reputation after two years in the Alfa Romeo doldrums, appeared in the Brabham camp as a reformed personality. Serious-minded, committed and very professional in his outlook, F1 racing's former *enfant terrible* emerged from 1986 with a much-changed reputation. He drove some fine races, but the record book hardly indicates that fact accurately.

Of course, the Brabham squad was sent reeling by the fatal accident which deprived the Grand Prix scene of that charming and courteous gentleman, Elio de Angelis. His place was taken by Renault refugee Derek Warwick, but it seemed something of an uphill struggle for the Englishman. Although his ability and tenacity in the cockpit were undimmed, the frustrations inherent in the whole programme got him down. It was all enough to get anybody down, so Derek's occa-

sional moments of depression hardly came as a surprise.

René Arnoux's much-heralded return to the F1 scene for Ligier never quite gelled; Laffite often had the measure of him prior to his Brands Hatch shunt, and René's erratic style was as unreliable as ever. Ligier, along with Tyrrell, had a hard time as Renault-engined also-rans, most of the *Régie's* attention, quite understandably, being lavished on the dynamic Senna/Lotus partnership.

Of the new boys on the scene, Johnny Dumfries and Alessandro Nannini turned more than a few heads. The Scottish earl suffered somewhat from 'market resistance' amongst the media in the early weeks of the season, coming as it did after the Warwick/Lotus controversy, but although lack of testing miles handicapped his performance quite dramatically in the first races, he gathered speed towards the end of the summer and developed into a very respectable performer. It is an interesting testimony to the crucial importance of testing and circuit knowledge that Dumfries's best result, fifth place, was at the Hungaroring, a circuit where everybody started equal with no prior knowledge. Team Lotus rather squandered his talent, to be honest, and then threw him out for 1987 when Honda made it plain that Lotus would have to take Satoru Nakajima – if they wanted Honda engines!

Nannini, Andrea de Cesaris's Lancia WSC partner, now found himself ranged against his fellow Italian in the two-car Minardi set-up. The new boy from Siena frequently ran in front of his considerably more experienced colleague, always looking cool, controlled and confident. By the end of the season the big teams were showing interest. . .

Amongst the old boys, Laffite looked a possible Grand Prix winner on a couple of occasions, proving that life begins at forty, whilst Alan Jones put in some gritty drives for Team Haas, but eventually lost interest when he saw it was making little firm progress. Patrick Tambay's level of accomplishment was patchy but he could still turn in some quite stylish performances on his day.

Lukas Gorys

Hamstrung by less than competitive machinery, Martin Brundle, Jonathan Palmer and Thierry Boutsen failed to make much progress throughout the year, but most observers know them to be better than their cars. Christian Danner arrived in the second Arrows mid-season after Marc Surer had been badly injured in a rally accident, while Huub Rothengatter bought a drive in the second Zakspeed, a move which produced little apart from added pressure on Palmer's racing programme. Osella struggled on gamely, but had nothing to show for efforts backed by minuscule budget.

Taking a wider view, F1 popularity seemed to continue its upward spiral in 1986. The World Championship celebrated its first Grand Prix behind the Iron Curtain when Hungary staged its maiden post-war event of any significance on a splendid, purpose-built facility near Budapest. The track configuration was not perfect, but the facilities were up-to-the minute and the organisational arrangements superb. The Spanish GP returned to the calendar after a five-year absence with an event at the new Jerez track, while Mexico came back into the fold after 16 years away. There was no GP of Europe, either in Britain or at the new Nürburgring, and prospects for a Japanese event seemed as distant as ever.

Was it a healthy season? On balance yes. There were some positively dismal races, notably at the Österreichring where Prost's ailing McLaren lapped everybody else running at the finish, but the splendid British, Spanish, Portuguese, Italian and Mexican events made up for the low moments. Yet it was not *simply* a healthy season from the point of view of the actual racing.

Above all, 1986 will be remembered as the year when FISA and the constructors agreed to a sea change, a major directional rethink. Turbo technology was showing all the signs of running away with its own expense and complexity; the whole business of forced-induction engines was turning into a monster whose appetite could be sated only by serving up ever-increasing helpings of money. At one point it threatened to devour the sport, but now it has been caged – and a death sentence hangs over its head.

We have enjoyed the turbocharged era, for it has produced some truly great racing. It did so, on some occasions, in 1986. Race speeds and performances may be little changed in 1987 under the 4-bar rule, and there are signs we may witness one more year of memorable competition. But the writing is on the wall. Qualifying speeds will be reduced and, in 1988, turbos will have their final curtain call as the restrictions squeeze even more tightly.

FISA has had the good sense to clear the shelves before the shop went bust. More hearteningly, the switch to naturally-aspirated engines has received almost unanimous support from all participating teams.

That, in itself, made history . . .

39

24 VALVES, 1974.

24 VALVES, 1978.

As BMW discovered years ago, when you need extra power from an engine (on the race track for instance), just double the valves per cylinder.

The extra valves mean that the cylinders can take in more air and fuel on each stroke, burn it more efficiently and expel it quicker.

So much so, that six cylinders with four valves can produce more power than twelve cylinders with two.

Take the three cars above, developed by BMW Motorsport.

THE LATEST IN A SHORT LINE OF SUPERCARS.

24 VALVES, 1986.

The 3.5 litre CSL, affectionately known as the Batmobile, won the first of many races at the Salzburgring in 1974, beating a 7 litre Camaro in the process.

A 192 mph version of the M1, driven by Nelson Piquet, won at the Nurburgring in 1981. And for the last three years running it's won its class at Le Mans.

The M635CSi, however, is merely a luxury road-going coupé. Although it's capable of 158 mph, it hasn't won a thing. Except praise.

THE ULTIMATE DRIVING MACHINE

FAST

It's not fair. But then anybody who knows anything about motor racing in general, and Formula 1 in particular, will already know that there's nothing fair about Grand Prix racing. What's more, there never has been.

All other things being equal, by the end of each season the Haves shall have more, and the Have-nots will have less. But this is not an immutable law of nature.

We should specify what the Haves must have, for in one particular case a leading team which seemed to have everything has this year fetched up amongst the Have-nots. The prerequisites to success (in alphabetical order rather than order of importance) are: a good budget, a good chassis, a good driver or drivers, a good engine, good team organisation and good tyres. There's also another vital ingredient to mix in with all these and that's good luck, which in many ways the best teams will make for themselves.

The most significant rule-change affecting the 1986 Championship season was the reduction in race-distance fuel allowance from 220 litres to just 195, placing more emphasis than ever before upon crucial fine balance in power-versus-economy. This posed a nice engineering problem which demanded commitment, investment, inspiration and perspiration to unlock. The season's end result reflects who did it best.

The Constructors' Championship became effectively a three-horse race between teams which embarked upon their programme equipped with all the above. They were of course Williams-Honda, McLaren-TAG Turbo and Lotus-Renault, and where winning was concerned they left the rest for dead.

Tyres are heated during qualifying in Hungary to help cope with the effects of prodigious power from the Honda V6 *(above right).*

McLaren: John Barnard parted company with the team towards the end of yet another successful season for the MP4 concept *(right).*

A choice of micro-chips for the TAG turbo *(top right).*

By DOUG NYE

BUT FRUGAL

WILLIAMS/HONDA

From late-1985, Williams Grand Prix Engineering took a near stranglehold on Formula 1 with their Honda V6-engined cars. As installed in the new '195-litre regulation' FW11 chassis, Honda's 1986 F-Type engine consistently demonstrated the best power/fuel economy/reliability factors.

Patrick Head's FW11 design was very much a state-of-the-art, high-tech car, carrying that twin-turbocharged 4-cam 80-degree V6 engine plus a mass of electronic micro-processing equipment to handle its boost, ignition and injection requirements, in addition to driver-to-pit radio communications and car-to-pit in-race telemetry which enabled the pit crew to 'watch the gauges' while also monitoring their driver's reaction (or obedience) to radioed instructions and advice. 'The driver', said Patrick, with just a trace of mischievous relish, 'can no longer tell us lies . . .'

His champion car uses a moulded carbon-Kevlar-aluminium composite chassis, the finished vehicle being exquisitely crafted, beautifully made in all respects. Merely the fit between engine cover and mechanicals beneath had to be seen to be believed, clearance being barely measurable in millimeters in some crucial areas. This was evidence of the investment Williams had put into advanced computer-aided design/computer-aided manufacture (CAD/CAM) techniques, an expensive General Electric CALMA system.

The FW11 design was very much an evolutionary development of 1985's sometimes-troubled, subsequently dominant FW10-series, which was itself Patrick Head's first attempt at moulded carbon-composite chassis construction.

He and WGPE composites specialist Brian O'Rourke worked out the design and methodology between them in the winter of 1984/85, when Patrick had decided he needed a chassis of the greatest possible cross-section. Logically, it should form the outer periphery of the body, and logically that meant moulding it in composite.

That initial FW10 was successful, especially in late-season 1985 FW10B form, and this past season's champion FW11 design has been superficially very similar. Both used laminated carbon/Kevlar double skins sandwiching Nomex (a material like stiff brown paper) honeycomb. Where in the FW10 the two small bulkheads sandwiching the inboard-mounted front springs and dampers were machined from aluminium, in the FW11 they were instead carbon/Kevlar mouldings. The FW11 tubs incorporated no aluminium bulkheads at all and were considerably lower and a little longer than those used in their predecessors.

Unlike the FW10's tubular bolt-on roll-over bar, the '11 used a composite base-pyramid moulded into the chassis with a steel hoop tailored to the height of the individual driver for whom the tub was intended.

The smaller fuel cell enabled Williams, like other teams, to lay their drivers back into a less-forward driving position; in the FW11 that meant lowering his head fully 4 inches, permitting an even lower bodyline. The toluene-based 'funny fuel' was also accommodated lower. The 1986 tub emerged some 1.5 inches longer than an FW10's while the new F-spec – 'F for Frugal' – Honda engine was also slightly longer than its E-Type predecessor, so the FW11's wheelbase was 112 in. against FW10's 109.5 in.

Suspension was pretty much as for the late-season 1985 FW10B, excepting a 2-inch wider rear track and a better-integrated six-speed gearbox casing to support it all.

Normally Williams ran French-made lightweight SEP carbon brake discs, clasped by carbon pads within AP aluminium calipers with titanium pistons. But there was extensive experimentation with an Automotive Products carbon twin-disc system, offering roughly twice the friction and cooling area of a single-disc plus other 'interesting characteristics'.

Three FW11s – all using F-Type engines from the start – were ready in time for Brazil, where Piquet won after Mansell's first-lap collision with Senna's Lotus had terminated a rare outing with AP's twin-disc brakes.

The Williams-Hondas rapidly became the cars to beat. Although both Senna of Lotus and Prost of McLaren did just that, it was very much WGPE's season, with Mansell versus Piquet for the Drivers' title and the Constructors' Championship sewn up in Portugal.

Pondering the season in August, Patrick Head considered 'Brands Hatch has been probably our best race, our only 1-2 so far, and a race run at enormous pace, continually setting new lap records and with both cars handling pretty well and neither driver complaining of anything; both in good nick after the finish. We controlled the turbo boost they could run, using the radio from the pits. We instructed them to use the lower race boost setting and the data we received in the pits told us that they were using it.'

The drivers had a four-position boost selector: position '1' was a fuel conservation mode, '2' and '3' race boosts on higher or lower levels, and '4' providing an extra 50 to 60 bhp overtaking boost for very limited use only! It was not available to the drivers at every race. Of the two alternative race boost positions, '2' burned slightly too little fuel, hence producing less than optimun power, over race distance, while '3' used slightly too much; the drivers normally juggled between these two.

The actual telemetry processing and transmitting box on the cars, which kept the pit informed of so many parameters, was no bigger than a Swan Vestas matchbox and weighed mere ounces, belying its usefulness when combined with the two-way radio link in race strategy. Formula 1 today embodies genuine team effort. No longer is the driver on his own once those lights go green.

The worst race was in Monaco where Williams's preferred, more reliable, longer final-drive ratio of the two available proved not low enough with the second new chicane now in place. The Hondas were knocked down to around 4000 rpm, way off the cam; both there and at Rascasse, pick-up and response were 'terrible', and the drivers had no chance. Patrick had to admit 'Sorry, we just haven't got the bits'. Thereafter new CWPs were cut by a different supplier to produce a lower final-drive which proved fine, as at Detroit.

There, other pressures caused Mansell's front brake calipers to be undercooled in the race, provoking his boiling-fluid problem.

Changes to the FW11s were mostly in detail only, primarily to the water and turbocharger cooling systems. Various very sophisticated tweaks were developed, and some fitted, but we don't talk about those. Incidentally, there was no substance in the stories of some diff skulduggery on Piquet's part in Hungary; Mansell had tested all available diffs previously at Croix-en-Ternois and all race set-up choices in Hungary were made in open discussion with everybody present, whatever the media might prefer to believe to the contrary. (Indeed, with hindsight, the assumptions made in the Grand Prix report on page 154 may not be totally accurate. None the less, it is believed that Piquet was less than frank when discussing the value of the differential in question. Whether it is reasonable to expect him to have been more open about his discovery is another question entirely. Editor.)

Preventive reinforcement was necessary in certain areas, while Mansell's British GP first-start transmission failure centred upon an overloaded standard Lobro Porsche or BMW M1-type CV joint, whose cage exploded under the Honda engine's startline torque. WGPE began making their own redesigned CV joint cages at that point, but then one failed in Austria. Third time lucky . . . those CV joints lead a hard life. Also in Austria, Piquet's air inlet temperature control failed, allowing the log temperatures to soar, causing pre-ignition which in turn destroyed a piston. That was the first time in fourteen races that Williams-Honda had failed to score.

Other significant incidents included the chest-strap of Mansell's harness – an item requested by Piquet earlier in the year and adopted subsequently by Nigel – working loose and bothering him at Monza. Perhaps more significantly, his front tyres were worked too hard and overheated late in that race. Then at Estoril Piquet's poor grid position was caused by a stay attaching his car's undertray to the tub becoming insecure in qualifying, creating oversteer, the cause not being located in time to save his chances. This left him trapped behind Senna in the race. Possibly his front brakes were also overcooled that day, contributing to the spin which seriously compromised his World title hopes.

Seven cars were used during the season, a spare being provided at last for Mansell come Portuguese GP time, with the Constructors' title about to be won and only the Drivers' crown to worry about. The season which had been so overshadowed at its beginning by Frank Williams's accident, was to end in (qualified) triumph . . .

McLAREN-TAG TURBO

After five-and-a-half successful seasons as technical director of McLaren International, John Barnard's MI career reached its end. In August he was gone, off to brainstorm a new Ferrari for 1988. He left the team midway through their spirited defence of the Constructors' title which had been their own in 1984/85.

43

John Barnard tucked the turbos on the TAG-Porsche engine closer to the block to improve inlet airflow.

The remarkably compact Ford-Cosworth turbo engine tucked in the back of the Haas-Lola.

MI's 1986 MP4/2C cars looked superficially little changed from 1985's '2Bs or even 1984's supreme MP4/2s. They didn't even look far removed – unless you stood them side-by-side – from Barnard's original carbon-composite MP4/1s of 1981.

At least John could joke about this long-lasting family resemblance, secure in its success having proved the quality of his basic concept; 'I now know, I'm absolutely convinced, that provided you put your finger on the right bits and pieces you can design a chassis which will go on for *years*!', he told me.

Where others, like Williams and Ferrari, used their chassis outer skin as an external body surface, John preferrred a straight-edged tub extensively cowled-in by separate body panels. This gave his team total aerodynamic flexibility as changing the external shape did not mean producing an entirely new chassis moulding. Conversely, one was not restricted in aerodynamic terms by the tub's external shape.

However, this past season's McLaren '2C tubs were modified in detail from the 1985 '2Bs, largely to take advantage of the new 195-litre fuel cell restriction. The driver was seated lower, less upright than before, enabling subtle aerodynamic improvements which, coupled with a rear suspension change plus repositioning of the turbochargers to improve inlet air flow, made for a faster car. The gearchange went inside the tub instead of its earlier position where it came over the top of the tub's right-hand side at a 15-degree angle, which the drivers had never really liked. John had to put it inside the tub to arrange the revised turbo inlets as he wanted.

This was actually the TAG Turbo V6's third turbocharger location; in-line, with the axis of the turbo fore-and-aft, drawing air from up front near the side pod radiator inlets. This change gave MI the space to incorporate Bosch's latest engine management system air-sensing units, which measured actual mass-flow instead of volume alone, thereby monitoring changes in air density – a vital factor.

In theory this is the perfect way of regulating fuel supply. Once MI's latest Bosch Motronic MP1:7 management system computer had been told what air–fuel ratio was required, its new sensors could then tell it the mass-flow of air at any given moment. That enabled it to compute the amount of fuel needed to be mixed with that mass-flow to meet the required ratio. This was a continuous adjustment which promised the ultimate in best horsepower-cum-fuel economy under all conditions. The system would compensate automatically for changes of altitude, humidity, barometric pressure, everything. But for much of the year it was not raced, simply because its reliability compared to the old system was not yet proven. Nevertheless, as McLaren recovered from their mid-season dip, Bosch produced some definite management system improvements which triggered the resurgence at Hockenheim. But there the fuel level computer readout went haywire instead. Who said this game was fair?

The four new '2C tubs for '86 were all moulded at McLaren's Woking factory, using raw material supplied by their former sub-contractors, the Hercules Corporation of Salt Lake City, USA.

A six-speed gearbox, based on the old five-speeder with a revised end-plate assembly, became standard because terminal speeds were becoming so high that some rev jumps were too big to keep within the TAG Turbo engine's most effective rev band. These modifications also allowed the gearbox to accommodate both reverse and an improved oiling system.

The Porsche-engineered TAG Turbo engines themselves had been little modified. I believe only five new engines were produced to complete MI's float of around 25, most changes being to the Bosch electronics although some improved turbo compressors came along which offered more boost without the old penalty in back-pressure.

When Rosberg, with his vast Honda engine experience, first tried the TAG Turbo, he declared there was little difference in mid- to low-range torque, but at high revs the Honda seemed a lot stronger.

The '2Cs were indeed another stride forward from the twin-championship winning '2s and '2Bs, and until Detroit McLaren went swinging along without any major problems.

Prost was just being his usual astonishingly competent, cheerful self – arguably the most complete driver in the business – but Rosberg's substitution for the Prost-like, smooth-driving Lauda caused some headaches. He quickly exhibited a problem with which the team eventually sympathised. Barnard: 'I don't think he realised how different a McLaren was going to be to drive compared to what he'd had before because our car didn't respond to his driving style in the way the Williams had.'

John would not compromise his car to suit the Finn's rugged driving style until after Monaco, when his car's set-up was altered for him. 'It wasn't just oversteery . . . there's all sorts of degrees of entering a corner, how fast you apply the lock and how much weight transfer that application induces . . . he was then much happier with the car' and took the lead in Canada.

This wide new disparity between set-ups caused considerable difficulties with the spare car; no longer was it speedily adaptable to either driver.

Meanwhile, MI hit a mysterious mid-season slump. In Canada, Williams demonstrated a sudden edge on fuel consumption, and Detroit was a poor McLaren race, 'but we couldn't really see why'. The cars ran well at Ricard but had to back-off to finish, while at Brands Hatch, despite being set up precisely in successful test-session form, they suddenly would not handle. The only possible reason appeared to be some tiny external change, probably in the tyres. Race engineers Steve Nichols and Tim Wright set to work on the problem with Barnard. They would maintain the momentum most competently after he had left.

Best race was clearly Monaco; most frustrating must have been Hockenheim where the remapped engines flew on Porsche's home ground only for that computer glitch to leave the cars out of fuel. The worst race was undoubtedly Spa where the engine situation was doubtful. They had run new fuel after Imola, which appeared to avoid an

Paul-Henri Cahier

engine-destructive problem, but it reappeared at Spa. After being delayed at the first corner Rosberg boosted his engine to oblivion regardless!

John was fulsome about the plus from Spa: 'Alain's comeback drive there was quite something; it was amazing, because after that first-corner shunt, the stop to fit a new nose and losing a lap he was blindingly fast *even with a bent engine mount*.

'When we got his car back here the top right-hand engine plate was bent like a banana . . . you can't bend one engine plate and leave the rest straight. The whole engine must have been skewed, which means his car was literally bent in the middle!'

Despite all that, Prost's post-race engine read-out revealed normal race boost throughout. Even in that situation the current master had taken his lap times out of himself, not his car. The sign of real, pure, class . . .

LOTUS-RENAULT

Team Lotus aimed high, anxious to provide Ayrton Senna with his first World Championship title.

Gérard Ducarouge's new Lotus Type 98T abandoned Team's original 'folded-up Kellogg's packet' form of carbon-composite chassis construction in favour of an integral unified moulding. Like his Type 96 Indy and 97T 1985 Formula 1 tubs, aluminium foil was used as the void-filling sandwich between the 98T's moulded composite skins. Its bulkheads were machined from solid aluminium. The smaller fuel cell reduced tub height behind the cockpit, enabling the management system black box to be mounted there, giving easier access and simplifying the wiring loom. For the first time Lotus had a continuously-monitoring fuel-level readout dash display.

Their Renault V6 engines were prepared and

45

PIZZA, BR
OR NOUVEL

V6 turbo

THE RENAULT GTA V6 TUF

ATWURST
LE CUISINE?

30. 200 bhp. 155 mph. BON APPETIT.

Once Rory Byrne became accustomed to the characteristics of the upright BMW engine, the Benetton began to show its class.

Renault's innovations proved notably effective and reliable.

Keith Sutton

rebuilt by Renault Sport themselves at Viry-Châtillon, whereas the other client teams – Ligier and Tyrrell – drew their engines from Mecachrome in Bourges.

Renault Chief Engineer Bernard Dudot's new weapon for 1986 was the EF15*bis* engine, which inevitably became known popularly as the 'EF15B'. It was available in two forms, standard or DP, which stood for *Distribution Pneumatique*. A small pressure vessel within the vee acted as a compressed-gas reservoir, piped down into the valvegear. Each valve was manufactured with an integral flange around its stem to act as a piston, running within a tiny gas-filled cylinder. The flange compressed the gas on each down-stroke, to be returned against the retreating cam-follower by its subsequent expansion. This elegantly obviated all the age-old problems and limitations of metal valve springs, saving weight and preventing surge. The air springs were both naturally self-damping and rising-rate, and the DP engine also included a weight-saving new ignition system in which each spark plug was fitted with its own tiny individual ignition coil, buried in each plug-well, each coil being triggered on command from the central computer.

These innovations proved remarkably effective and reliable. The Renault engine in this form was lighter, less complicated and lower than before, its rev limit soared from 11,000 to 12,500 rpm, and it offered a wider spread of useable power. Most EF15*bis* engines were constructed initially with conventional valvegear heads, but the DP equipment was progressively incorporated when possible.

The combination of DP valvegear and revised ignition saved 5.51 lb in the upper part of the engines, while the induction logs and pipes on top were lowered and curved inwards to allow a neater, lower or tighter body-panel shape in this crucial area.

While the EF15*bis* – DP-spec or otherwise – was intended for economic racing, the older high-boost EF4*bis* was no longer compatible with the 1986 chassis; it was too big, so EF15s with water injection and no wastegates were used instead.

However, when Senna finished at Rio in Round One on near-dry tanks, Piquet's Williams-Honda won easily with fuel to spare. The writing was clearly on the wall.

To give the Brazilian every possible advantage short of a Honda engine, Ducarouge developed a low-ground-clearance, high-download qualifying ploy which helped pop Senna onto pole at Jerez and Imola, creating a terrific stir which Colin Chapman himself would have *relished*. At Imola a bad UJ batch ruined Lotus hopes, and at Monaco Senna had to settle for third behind the uncatchable McLarens.

On circuits where consumption was no problem, like Detroit, Senna could shine, and did. At that point he still led the Driver's Championship, and a further improved C-spec engine emerged with a redesigned lean-burn top end for more economical power.

Team hoped to compete again in the horse-power-versus-fuel economy battle, but at Brands Hatch the new engine misfired and they had to race the old one. At Hockenheim the new engine ran well but Piquet's Williams-Honda ran better. In Hungary the new engine again misfired and by running the old type, Senna inevitably used all his fuel again. This misfiring problem intruded intermittently (when it mattered most) in Austria and only extensive testing subsequently traced its certain cure to careful, painstaking selection of all-compatible electrical components. There was no apparent difference between them; simply some would work in harmony and others would

The BMW M12/13/1 engine: advantages were offset by numerous problems.

not. It was only by trial and error that a misfire-free set could be matched.

For Monza they at last felt confident they had gripped this problem. They had – so a bad clutch batch bit them instead . . . Who said this game was fair?

Peter Warr: 'By this time it was the last chance to keep our championship hopes alive. Renault's onboard computer had been superb, very accurate, all season, until in Portugal Ayrton had 1.4 laps still showing on his gauge when the engine stopped a third of the way round the last lap, 2.5 litres short . . . He was rightly deeply disappointed after driving what he felt was the race of his life.'

Through the season Team had deployed only their normal complement of four chassis, Gérard's aerodynamic package basically remaining very stable all season although continuous suspension development made the cars better latterly on rear-tyre consumption. In the interests of reliability, Senna used the five-speed gearbox while the troublesome six-speed unit accounted for Johnny Dumfries retirement on more than one occasion.

The qualifying ploy seemed to reappear with knobs on at Estoril, but the key to Senna's startling closing-minutes charge onto pole was the fitting of an experimental turbocharger pair half an hour earlier. They had been run only on a Viry-Châtillon dyno but showed considerable extra power, so Team took the gamble . . . and it paid off.

It was another moment which, as Peter Warr said, 'the Old Man would have loved . . .'

BENETTON

After 14 races, during which they had shown an increasingly powerful competitiveness, the Benetton (née Toleman) team won a Grand Prix in convincing style. Initially the short notice and minimum testing time of the change from Hart to upright BMW M12/13 power created problems. Engineer Rory Byrne: 'We only started designing this year's car in the last week of October '85 – wind tunnel research, everything.' The early part of the season was devoted merely to making sufficient parts to go racing, while the cars ran as built until after Ricard.

The powerful, top-endy BMW's demands on the chassis were quite new, as evidenced at Rio where the cars were quickest on the straight, but only mid-fielders on lap time. They have exclusive use of the MoD wind tunnel at Shrivenham, and a subtle but total reworking of chassis and aerodynamic configuration evolved there. Only then could aerodynamic and fundamental set-up changes be phased in – new underbody, front and rear wing systems, and front and rear suspensions were all redesigned to harness Bee-Emm's power; and it was not until the Austrian GP that they could all be combined into one complete package.

There Benetton could at last use all BMW's power, their Pirelli tyres proved best and at last a Rory Byrne Formula 1 design really showed its class.

They seemed set for a stunning 1-2 until Fabi ran over a bump out of the chicane, his rear wheels bounced and the engine over-revved. Then Berger

agonisingly suffered a battery fault due to porosity in a connection between a battery plate and terminal. In contrast, their least competitive race was Montreal.

Seven tubs were built, '04 being written off at Montreal, two others being rebuilt after serious damage, one in a fire at Silverstone and the other brake-testing at Croix.

With Brabham crippled, Benetton carried Pirelli hopes high. The Italian company's preseason testing was wrecked by Brabham's problems and Benetton's lateness, but the Witney team caught up fast. Pirelli were competitive early on, and Rory feels that if his chassis had been sorted out as early as they could have done really well. The Pirellis were most effective on rough surfaces; smooth tracks were not their *forte*. But Pirelli made fine constructional changes to assist Benetton's escape from handling problems, and while some problems were experienced in providing sufficient tyres to service the team's needs. Finally, though, they proved their point by helping Benetton to a very convincing win in Mexico. Pirelli's farewell season in Formula 1 saw them perform very well . . . for the wrong teams. Who said Formula 1 was fair?

THEY ALSO SERVED

The season saw FERRARI struggling. In hindsight it seems as if at least 80 per cent of their problem stemmed from the failure to invest in their own wind tunnel four years earlier. Only as I write, in October 1986, is the Fiorano tunnel entering commission. The alloy-block 120-degree '032'-series engines have, they believe, been very competitive, but throttle response remained mediocre until the end of the year. The faster the circuit, the better the Ferraris showed, but the overall package was clearly deficient in 1986 company. The 1986 chassis were demonstrated better than '85, but the opposition had progressed so rapidly they were still not good enough.

In search of more reliable braking, Ferrari replaced proprietary Brembo brake calipers with a new design of their own early in the season, but after two hydraulic leaks – one which caused Johansson's crunching head-on shunt at Jerez – it was set aside and Brembos re-adopted. At Rio a disc bell failed, while other problems came from a variety of sources. Eight cars were built, numbers '087' to '094', of which three were lost in crashes: '087' at Jerez, '090' at the Österreichring and '091' at Montreal – all with the unfortunate Johansson at the wheel.

For BRABHAM, of course, 1986 became a nightmare. De Angelis's fatal testing accident deeply affected Gordon Murray, and the production of his lowline BT55 with its 72-degree lay-down BMW M12/13/1 engine became a case of too many eggs being jeopardised in one basket. Pre-season testing was grossly disrupted by problems with the new Weismann transmission and chassis, which left team, BMW and Pirelli alike all in trouble. Under calendar pressures they could not catch up, and Elio's death – the first driver Brabham have ever lost – was an extra, crippling blow.

In retrospect, Brabham had suffered most from

the loss of rear-wing sidestep winglets when they were banned for 1985. The quite tall upright BMW engine masked the rear wing centre, so something had to be done to clear airflow to the wing. Gordon's lay-down engine idea was intended to achieve this, while also slashing frontal area and lowering the centre of gravity. It should have worked.

But back in 1958 Colin Chapman had laid the Climax 4-cylinder engine on its side in his first Formula 1 Lotus 16 and it too encountered problems, winding its own oil round in the crankcase and letting it pool in the head and cam-box. Similar maladies beset the Bee-Emm; scavenging had to be improved to release power otherwise being absorbed, and its induction also seemed constricted. All season it ran very hot indeed. All these difficulties offset the advantages of the lowline BT55's low frontal area. BMW could not improve their engine while chassis problems masked evidence of progress. Reclining the engine dictated bevel-drive transmission, which made the car long and thus compromised nimble response in search of straightline speed. It was consistently slow out of corners, yet was often fastest by the end of the straight. It was dogged all season by this poor traction.

By British GP time when Patrese drove an upright-engine BT54, Brabham were happy to go all-upright but BMW lacked the engines, being fully committed to Mader for Benetton and Arrows.

Two major rear suspension revisions were made in search of traction, and the front suspension was reworked to move the wheels rearwards, so applying more weight to the rears. Rising-rate changes were also made, but Brabham were so far behind it proved impossible to close the gap mid-season. They were on the treadmill where so many others had suffered before. Yet morale within the team remained remarkably high in the face of such adversity.

Several BT55s were built, each tub being slightly different in carbon lay-up, but having started with such a radically different car they were crippled once problems interrupted the development programme.

LIGIER fared better until Laffite's accident, while of the supporting cast most interesting was the HAAS-LOLA team, introducing the Cosworth-produced Ford V6 turbo engine (of which I am told 30 were built during the season). Ford had little choice of teams, and in this first year the Haas-Lola outfit was largely untried and fairly ineffective. The engines were run in very conservative tune which made them mechanically reliable but never competitive. The cars worked best on medium-speed circuits, would always lose time out of second- or third-gear corners, and the Hungaroring suited them perfectly, which explains their better showing there.

But overall, Ford were in a quandary, with their new engine's Formula 1 life rapidly running out and no top team available to make the most of whatever Keith Duckworth's latest creation may have to offer under their name.

It was the story of 1986: nothing is fair in Formula 1.

1.6 LITRE FUEL INJECTED ENGINE – 115 B.H.P.   TOP SPEED – 122 M.P.H.   0-60 M.P.H. I

TOP SPEED: 122 MPH; 0-60 MPH: 8.6 SEC (CAR MAGAZINE)

1986 WORLD RALLY CHAMPIONS

IT'S A PUSSYCAT
UNTIL YOU STEP ON IT.

205 GTI

WHISKER OVER 8 SECONDS.

PEUGEOT 205 GTI

THE LION GOES FROM STRENGTH TO STRENGTH.

ONE PLUG OVERSHADOWS ALL OTHERS.

Throughout the 1986 Grand Prix season the Honda-Williams team relied on NGK Spark Plugs. Naturally, they won the World Constructors Championship. **NGK Copper Core Excellence.**

THE CARS

Williams Grand Prix Engineering won the Constructor's Championship, thanks to nine victories and the all-round competitiveness of the team throughout the year.

McLaren International kept pace with Williams until mid-season, when a series of problems for Rosberg began to affect the team's points-scoring potential, effectively reducing it to one car.

Team Lotus, third in the Constructor's table, showed no interest in this aspect of the championship by relying solely on the efforts of Ayrton Senna who, for all his skill, could not hope to match the combined driving force of Mansell and Piquet with the Williams-Hondas.

Alfa Romeo, Renault and RAM no longer entered cars, while Toleman were bought by Benetton and the Beatrice title was removed from the Lola team once the American sponsor had lost interest.

AGS moved into Formula 1 after competing in F2 and F3000, the French team taking part in two races at the end of the European season.

THE ENGINES

Honda dominated the results with nine wins, compared to four by TAG, two by Renault and one for BMW.

Benetton (née Toleman) switched to BMW from Hart, the British engineering manufacturer maintaining a presence with Lola until the arrival of the Ford-Cosworth turbo engine at the end of April.

Alfa Romeo supplied Osella with their ageing V8s; BMW also continued with Arrows while designing a 'lay-down' version of the four-cylinder M12/13 for Brabham, whilst Renault's presence in Formula 1 was restricted to the supply of engines for Lotus, Ligier and Tyrrell.

Motori Moderni, in their second year of Grand Prix racing, did business with Minardi as usual, as well as catering for the late arrival of the AGS team. Zakspeed continued to design and build a four-cylinder engine for the German team's exclusive use.

Renault, solely through the efforts of Senna, claimed eight pole positions. Honda won four, while TAG and BMW managed two apiece. Honda dominated the fastest laps with a total of eleven, BMW taking three and TAG two.

Note: The details in the tables which follow were supplied by the respective teams and manufacturers, to whom *Autocourse* offers its sincere thanks.

	BMW M12/13 Turbo	Ferrari F1/86 Turbo	Ford F1 Turbo	Hart 415T Turbo	Honda RA166-E Turbo
No. of cylinders	4 in-line	V6 (120°)	6	4 in-line	V6
Bore and stroke	89·2 mm × 60 mm	81 mm × 48·4 mm	—	88 mm × 61·5 mm	—
Capacity	1499 cc	1496·43 cc	1497 cc	1496 cc	1500 cc
Compression ratio	7·5:1	7·5:1	7·5:1	7:1	—
Maximum power	800–900 bhp (1050–1100 bhp in qualifying)	851 bhp	900 bhp	760 bhp at 10,500	—
Maximum rpm	11,200	11,500	11,500	11,000	—
Valve sizes	—	—	—	35·0 mm - inlet / 30·0 mm - exhaust	—
Valve lift	—	—	—	10·5 mm	—
Valve timing	—	—	—	—	—
Block material	Cast iron	Aluminum alloy	Aluminium	Aluminium	Cast iron
Pistons and rings	Mahle/Goetze	Mahle	Mahle/Goetze	Mahle	Honda
Bearings	Glyco	Clevite	Vandervell	Vandervell	—
Fuel injection	Bosch	Weber/Marelli	Ford EEC IV	Zytek/Hart	Honda/PCM-FI
Ignition system	Bosch	Marelli	Marelli	Marelli	Honda
Turbocharger(s)	Garrett	2 × Garrett	2 × Garrett	Holset	2 × IHI
Weight (less intercooler)	165 kg	—	128 kg	294 lb	—

	Motori-Moderni V6 Turbo	Renault EF15B Turbo	Renault EF15C Turbo	TAG PO1 (TTE PO1) Turbo	Zakspeed 861 Turbo
No. of cylinders	V6	V6	V6	V6	4 in-line
Bore and stroke	80 mm × 49·7 mm	80·1 mm × 49·4 mm	80·1 mm × 49·4 mm	—	90·4 mm × 58·25 mm
Capacity	1498·9 cc	1494 cc	1494 cc	1496 cc	1495 cc
Compression ratio	7:1	7:1	7·5:1	—	7·5:1
Maximum power	—	—	—	—	800–1100 bhp
Maximum rpm	12,000	12,000	12,000	—	11,000
Valve sizes	—	31·6 mm/26·75 mm	31·6 mm/26·75 mm	—	—
Valve lift	—	9·4 mm/8·5 mm	9·4 mm/8·5 mm	—	—
Valve timing	—	316°/300°	316°/300°	—	—
Block material	Aluminium alloy	Aluminium	Aluminium	Aluminium alloy	Aluminium
Pistons and rings	Mondial/Goetze	Mahle/Goetze	Mahle/Goetze	Mahle/Goetze	Mahle
Bearings	Clevite	Glyco	Glyco	Glyco	Glyco
Fuel injection	Weber Marelli Electronic	Bendix/Renault Sport	Bendix/Renault Sport	Bosch Motronic	Bosch Motronic
Ignition system	Marelli Electronic Raceplex	Renault Sport	Renault Sport	Bosch Motronic	Bosch Motronic
Turbocharger(s)	2 × KKK	2 × Garrett	2 × Garrett	2 × KKK	KKK
Weight (less intercooler)	154 kg	140 kg	140 kg	—	160 kg

The most moving moment in our Supra will not come as you're slipping along the autobahn at 138 miles per hour.

(Thrilling the natives with your perfect aero-dynamic body.)

The moment is more likely to arrive as the ventilated disc brakes, with Anti-Lock Braking System, bring you to an effortless stop.

You have reached the end of the road without your cool being lost or your comfort disturbed.

To hand, you have had thermostatically controlled air-conditioning.

To bottom, a sports seat with electrically controlled lumbar and side supports.

THE NEW TOYOTA SUPRA. EVEN STATIONARY IT HAS

TOYOTA

D800 GWN

The uni-directional tyres and the double-wishbone suspension system have carried you safely, cushioning every bump.

The fuel-injected 3-litre engine, aired by no less than 24 valves, has been smooth and responsive.

(Even producing, as it does, the combined power of 201 horses.)

As you switch off the ignition and regard the most lavishly equipped dashboard you have ever set eyes on, you will be aware your journey is over.

Most importantly, perhaps, you will know you have arrived.

SUPRA: £15,849 (MANUAL). PRICE CORRECT AT TIME OF GOING TO PRESS INCLUDES CAR TAX AND VAT BUT NOT DELIVERY AND NUMBER PLATES. DOT FUEL CONSUMPTION FIGURES: URBAN CYCLE 21.6 MPG (13.1L/100KM): CONSTANT 56 MPH, 36.7 MPG (7.7L/100KM): CONSTANT 75 MPH, 29.7 MPG (9.5L/100KM).

THE POWER TO MOVE YOU.

AGS JH21C

Arrows A8

Arrows A9

Benetton B186

Brabham BT55

Brabham BT54

1986 F1 CAR SPECIFICATIONS

	AGS JH21C	Arrows A8	Arrows A9	Benetton B186	Brabham BT54	Brabham BT55
Sponsor/s	Charro	Barclay/USF&G	Barclay/USF&G	Benetton SPA/Sisley/ Riello/Flying Tigers/ EUROBAGS/Frizerca	Olivetti	Olivetti/ Armani
Designer/s	Christian Vanderpleyn	Dave Wass/ Dave Nielson	Dave Wass	Rory Byrne	Gordon Murray/ David North	Gordon Murray/David North/ Peter Weismann
Team Manager/s	Frederic Dhainaut	Alan Rees	Alan Rees	Peter Collins	Herbie Blash	Herbie Blash
Chief Mechanic/s	Jean-Claude Silant	—	—	John Mardle	Charlie Whiting	Charlie Whiting
No. of chassis built	1	6	1	7	2	8
ENGINE						
Type	Motori Moderni V6	BMW M12/13	BMW M12/13	BMW M12/13	BMW M12/13 Turbo	BMW M12/13/1
Fuel and oil	—	BMW/Castrol	BMW/Castrol	BMW Wintershall/Castrol	—/Castrol	—/Castrol
Sparking plugs	Champion	Champion	Champion	Champion	Champion	Champion
TRANSMISSION						
Gearbox (speeds)	Hewland DGB (5/6)	Arrows/Hewland FGB (6)	Arrows/Hewland DGB (6)	Benetton (6)	Hewland/Weismann/ Brabham/Getrag (5/6)	Brabham/Weismann transverse (5/6/7)
Driveshafts	Löbro	Arrows	Arrows	Benetton	Brabham	Brabham
Clutch	AP	AP	AP	AP	Borg & Beck	Borg & Beck
CHASSIS						
Front suspension	Double wishbones, pushrods	Double wishbones, pushrods	Double wishbones, pushrods	Double wishbones, pullrods	Double wishbones, pushrods	Double wishbones, pullrods
Rear suspension	Double wishbones, pushrods	Double wishbones, pushrods	Double wishbones, pushrods	Double wishbones, pushrods	Double wishbones, pushrods	Double wishbones, pullrods
Suspension dampers	Koni	Koni	Koni	Koni	Koni	Koni
Wheel diameter	front: 13 in. rear: 13 in.	front: 13 in. rear: 13 in.	front: 13 in. rear: 13 in.	front: 13 in. rear: 13 in.	front: 13 in. rear: 13 in.	front: 13 in. rear: 13 in.
Wheel rim widths	front: 12 in. rear: 16·5 in.	front: 11·75 in. rear: 16·375 in.	front: 11·75 in. rear: 16·3 in.	front: 12 in. rear: 16·25 in.	front: 12 in. rear: 16 in.	front: 12 in. rear: 16 in.
Tyres	Pirelli	Goodyear	Goodyear	Pirelli	Pirelli	Pirelli
Brakes	SEP	AP/SEP	AP/SEP	SEP/AP/Brembo	SEP/Brabham/Girling	SEP/Brabham/Girling
Brake pads	SEP	AP/SEP	AP/SEP	SEP/AP	SEP	SEP
Steering	Renault	Arrows	Arrows	Jack Knight/Benetton	Brabham	Brabham
Radiator/s	Secan	Behr/Unipart	Behr	Behr	Unipart/Llanelli/Behr	Unipart/Llanelli/Behr
Fuel tank	—	ATL	ATL	ATL	ATL	ATL
Battery	Magneti Marelli	Varley	Varley	Hitachi	Yuasa	Yuasa
Instruments	—	VDO	VDO	Yamaha	Bosch	Bosch
DIMENSIONS						
Wheelbase	113 in./2873·5 mm	111 in./2819 mm	115 in./2921 mm	108 in./2743 mm	119 in./3023 mm	120 in./3048 mm
Track	front: 71·26 in./1810 mm rear: 65·11 in./1654 mm	front: 71·75 in./1822 mm rear: 66 in./1676 mm	front: 71·75 in./1822 mm rear: 66 in./1676 mm	front: 71·5 in./1816 mm rear: 66·25 in./1683 mm	front: 69 in./1753 mm rear: 65 in./1651 mm	front: 70 in./1778 mm rear: 65 in./1651 mm
Gearbox weight	—	105 lb/48 kg	100 lb/45 kg	130 lb/59 kg	110 lb/50 kg	123·45 lb/56 kg
Chassis weight (tub)	—	88 lb/40 kg	71 lb/32 kg	88 lb/40 kg	93 lb/42 kg	81·57 lb/37 kg
Formula weight	1191 lb/540 kg	1201 lb/545 kg	1190 lb/540 kg	1208 lb/548 kg	1190 lb/540 kg	1232 lb/559 kg
Fuel capacity	43 gal./195 litres	42 gal./193 litres	42 gal./193 litres	42·9 gal./195 litres	48·3 gal./220 litres	42·9 gal./195 litres
Fuel consumption	4·5 mpg/63 litres/100 km	4·5 mpg/63 litres/100 km	4·5 mpg/63 litres/100 km	3·8-4·2 mpg/67-74 litres/100 km	3·5-4·5 mpg/63-80 litres/100 km	3·5-4·5 mpg/63-80 litres/100 km

Ferrari F1/86

Lotus 98T

	Ferrari F1/86	Ligier JS27	Lola THL-1	Lola THL-2	Lotus 98T
Sponsor/s	Agip/Fiat/ Goodyear/Marlboro	Loto/Gitanes/Elf	Beatrice/BP/ Ford/Champion	Beatrice/BP/ Ford/Champion	Imperial Tobacco Co./ DeLonghi/Elf
Designer/s	Ferrari Gestione Sportiva	Michel Têtu/ Michel Beaujon	Neil Oatley/Ross Brawn/ John Baldwin	Neil Oatley/Ross Brawn/ John Baldwin	Gérard Ducarouge Martin Ogilvie
Team Manager/s	Enzo Ferrari	Guy Ligier/ Gérard Larrousse	Teddy Mayer/ Tyler Alexander	Teddy Mayer/ Tyler Alexander	Peter Warr
Chief Mechanic/s	Scaramelli/ P. Corradini	Jean-Pierre Chatenay	Harold Mendel	Harold Mendel	Bob Dance
No. of chassis built	7	5	3	6	4
ENGINE					
Type	Ferrari F1/86 '032'-series	Renault EF15	Hart 415T	Ford TEC V6	Renault EF15
Fuel and oil	Agip	Elf	BP	BP	Elf
Sparking plugs	Champion	Champion	Champion	Champion	Champion
TRANSMISSION					
Gearbox (speeds)	Ferrari	Ligier/Hewland	Force/Hewland (6)	Force/Hewland (6)	Lotus (5/6)
Driveshafts	Löbro/Ferrari	Löbro	Force	Force	Löbro/Lotus
Clutch	AP	AP	AP	AP	AP
CHASSIS					
Front suspension	—	Double wishbones, pushrods	Double wishbones, pushrods	Double wishbones, pushrods	Double wishbones, pullrods
Rear suspension	—	Double wishbones, pushrods	Double wishbones, pushrods	Double wishbones, pushrods	Double wishbones, pullrods
Suspension dampers	Marzocchi	Koni	Koni	Koni	Koni
Wheel diameter	front: 13 in. rear: 13 in.	front: 13 in. rear: 13 in.	front: 13 in. rear: 13 in.	front: 13 in. rear: 13 in.	front: 13 in. rear: 13 in.
Wheel rim widths	front: 11 in. rear: 16-3 in.	front: 12 in. rear: 16-12 in.	front: 12 in. rear: 16-3 in.	front: 12 in. rear: 16-3 in.	front: 11-5 in. rear: 16-25 in.
Tyres	Goodyear	Pirelli	Goodyear	Goodyear	Goodyear
Brakes	Brembo/SEP	Brembo/SEP	AP/SEP	AP/Alcon/SEP	Brembo/SEP
Brake pads	SEP	SEP	Ferodo/SEP	Ferodo/SEP	SEP
Steering	Ferrari	Ligier	Force	Force	Lotus/Knight
Radiator/s	Valeo/IPRA	Secan	Secan/Llanelli	Secan	Secan/IPRA
Fuel tank	Pirelli/ATL	ATL	ATL	ATL	ATL
Battery	Yuasa	Yuasa	Gates	Gates	Yuasa
Instruments	Magneti Marelli	Brion Leroux	VDO/Silverstone Electronics	VDO/Silverstone Electronics	Mors/Brion Leroux
DIMENSIONS					
Wheelbase	110-9 in./2816 mm	112 in./2835 mm	110 in./2794 mm	104 in./2642 mm	107 in./2720 mm
Track	front: 70-7 in./1795 mm rear: 65-5 in./1663 mm	front: 70-5 in./1790 mm rear: 65-4 in./1662 mm	front: 71 in./1803 mm rear: 64 in./1626 mm	front: 71 in./1803 mm rear: 64 in./1626 mm	front: 70-9 in./1800 mm rear: 63-7 in./1620 mm
Gearbox weight	—	141 lb/64 kg	—	—	99 lb/45 kg
Chassis weight (tub)	—	75 lb/34 kg	—	—	81-61 lb/37 kg
Formula weight	1191 lb/540 kg	1201 lb/545 kg	1190 lb/540 kg	1190 lb/540 kg	1190 lb/540 kg
Fuel capacity	42-9 gal./195 litres	43 gal./195 litres	42-9 gal./195 litres	42-9 gal./195 litres	42-9 gal./195 litres
Fuel consumption		4-6 mpg/61 litres/100 km	4-5 mpg/62 litres/100 km	4-5 mpg/62 litres/100 km	4-3 mpg/65 litres/100 km

Ligier JS27

Lola THL-2

Lola THL-1

	McLaren MP4/2C	Minardi M/85B	Minardi M/86	Osella FA1F	Osella FA1G	Osella FA1H
Sponsor/s	Marlboro/Shell/ Saima/Boss/ Segafredo/Goodyear	Simod/Gilmar/Resta/ Roltra/Eclat/Reporter/ Biopoint/CMC Monoceram/ Computervision	Simod/Gilmar/Resta/ Roltra/Eclat/Reporter/ Biopoint/CMC Monoceram/ Computervision	Landis & Gyr	Landis & Gyr	Landis & Gyr
Designer/s	John Barnard	Giacomo Caliri	Giacomo Caliri	Giuseppe Petrotta	Giuseppe Petrotta	Giuseppe Petrotta
Team Manager/s	Ron Dennis	Giancarlo Minardi	Giancarlo Minardi	Enzo Osella	Enzo Osella	Enzo Osella
Chief Mechanic/s	Dave Ryan	Ermanno Cuoghi/ Bruno Fagnocchi	Ermanno Cuoghi/ Bruno Fagnocchi	—	—	—
No. of chassis built	5	2	1	2	2	2
ENGINE						
Type	TAG (TTE PO1)	Motori Moderni V6	Motori Moderni V6	Alfa Romeo V8	Alfa Romeo V8	Alfa Romeo V8
Fuel and oil	Shell	Agip	Agip	Agip	Agip	Agip
Sparking plugs	Bosch	Champion	Champion	Champion	Champion	Champion
TRANSMISSION						
Gearbox (speeds)	McLaren International (5)	Minardi (5)	Minardi (5)	Osella/Hewland FGB	Osella/Hewland FGB	Hewland DGB
Driveshafts	McLaren International	Minardi	Minardi	Osella	Osella	Osella
Clutch	Borg & Beck	AP	AP	Borg & Beck/AP	Borg & Beck/AP	Borg & Beck/AP
CHASSIS						
Front suspension	Double wishbones, pushrods	Double wishbones, pullrods	Double wishbones, pushrods	Pushrods	Pushrods	Pushrods
Rear suspension	Double wishbones, pushrods	Double wishbones, pushrods	Double wishbones, pushrods	Pushrods	Pushrods	Double wishbones, pullrods
Suspension dampers	Bilstein	Koni	Koni	Koni	Koni	Koni
Wheel diameter	front: 13 in. rear: 13 in.	front: 13 in. rear: 13 in.	front: 13 in. rear: 13 in.	front: 13 in. rear: 13 in.	front: 13 in. rear: 13 in.	front: 13 in. rear: 13 in.
Wheel rim widths	front: 11·75 in. rear: 16·3 in.	front: 12 in. rear: 16·5 in.	front: 12 in. rear: 16·5 in.	front: 11·5 in. rear: 16·5 in.	front: 11·5 in. rear: 16·5 in.	front: 11·5 in. rear: 16 in.
Tyres	Goodyear	Pirelli	Pirelli	Pirelli	Pirelli	Pirelli
Brakes	SEP	Brembo	Brembo	Brembo	Brembo	Brembo
Brake pads	SEP	Ferodo	Ferodo	Ferodo	Ferodo	Ferodo
Steering	McLaren	Minardi	Minardi	Osella	Osella	Osella
Radiator/s	Unipart/McLaren	IPRA/Behr	Valeo/Behr/Secan	IPRA/Secan	IPRA/Secan	IPRA/Secan
Fuel tank	ATL	Pirelli/Sekur	Pirelli/Sekur	Pirelli	Pirelli	ATL
Battery	RS	Yuasa	Yuasa	Magneti Marelli	Magneti Marelli	Magneti Marelli
Instruments	Bosch/Contactless	Digitek/Contactless	Digitek/Contactless	VDO	VDO	VDO
DIMENSIONS						
Wheelbase	110 in./2794 mm	105 in./2670 mm	107 in./2708 mm	108·46 in./2755 mm	111·42 in./2830 mm	112 in./2850 mm
Track	front: 71·5 in./1816 mm rear: 66·0 in./1676 mm	front: 71·4 in./1813 mm rear: 65·4 in./1661 mm	front: 72 in./1813 mm rear: 65 in./1661 mm	front: 68·11 in./1730 mm rear: 63 in./1600 mm	front: 70·9 in./1800 mm rear: 63 in./1600 mm	front: 70·8 in./1800 mm rear: 65·7 in./1670 mm
Gearbox weight	125 lb/57 kg	121 lb/55 kg	99 lb/45 kg	83·7 lb/38 kg	83·7 lb/38 kg	92·6 lb/42 kg
Chassis weight (tub)	78 lb/35 kg	99 lb/45 kg	82 lb/37 kg	81·57 lb/37 kg	81·57 lb/37 kg	77 lb/35 kg
Formula weight	1191 lb/540 kg	1278 lb/580 kg	1234 lb/560 kg	1256 lb/570 kg	1267 lb/575 kg	1267 lb/575 kg
Fuel capacity	43 gal./195 litres	43 gal./195 litres	43 gal./195 litres	48·1 gal./219 litres	48·1 gal./219 litres	44 gal./200 litres
Fuel consumption	—	4·3 mpg/65 litres/100 km	4·5 mpg/63 litres/100 km	—	—	—

Minardi M/86

Osella FA1F

McLaren MP4/2C

SIERRA BY

THE SIERRA RS COSWORTH. 2·0 LITRE, TURBOCHARGED, FUEL-INJECTED, 16 VALVE, TWIN CAM COSWORTH ENGINE. CHASSIS DEVELOPED BY FORD SPECIAL VEHICLE ENGINEERING. EQUIPMENT INCLUDES RECARO FRONT SEATS, SUNROOF, ELECTRIC FRONT WINDOWS, ELECTRICALLY OPERATED HEATED DOOR MIRRORS, CENTRAL LOCKING, POWER STEERING, ELECTRONIC STEREO SYSTEM. TAKES FIVE IN COMFORT. LARGE BOOT. PERFORMANCE? MAX. POWER 204 PS, MAX. SPEED 149 MPH,† 0·60 MPH 6·5 SECONDS,† AND THAT'S JUST THE ROAD GOING VERSION.   †FORD COMPUTED FIGURES.

COSWORTH OUT OF SPECIAL VEHICLE ENGINEERING. *Ford*

	Tyrrell 014	Tyrrell 015	Williams FW11	Zakspeed ZAK861
Sponsor/s	Data General	Data General	Canon/Mobil/ICI/ Denim/Honda/ Calma	West
Designer/s	Maurice Phillippe/ Brian Lisles	Maurice Phillippe/ Brian Lisles	Patrick Head/ Frank Dernie	Paul Brown
Team Manager/s	Ken Tyrrell	Ken Tyrrell	Frank Williams/ David Stubbs	Helmut Barth
Chief Mechanic/s	Roger Hill	Roger Hill	Alan Challis	Peter Krumbein
No. of chassis built	3	5	6	4
ENGINE				
Type	Renault EF15	Renault EF15	Honda RA166-E	Zakspeed
Fuel and oil	Elf	Elf	Mobil	Shell
Sparking plugs	Champion	Champion	NGK	Champion
TRANSMISSION				
Gearbox (speeds)	Tyrrell/Hewland (6)	Tyrrell/Hewland (5/6)	Williams (6)	Zakspeed/Hewland (6)
Driveshafts	Tyrrell	Tyrrell	Williams	GWV
Clutch	AP	AP	Borg & Beck	AP
CHASSIS				
Front suspension	Double wishbones, pullrods	Double wishbones, pushrods	Double wishbones, pushrods	Double wishbones, pullrods
Rear suspension	Double wishbones, pullrods	Double wishbones, pushrods	Double wishbones, pullrods	Double wishbones, pullrods
Suspension dampers	Koni	Koni	Penske	Koni
Wheel diameter	front: 13 in. rear: 13 in.	front: 13 in. rear: 13 in.	front: 13 in. rear: 13 in.	front: 13 in. rear: 13 in.
Wheel rim widths	front: 12·25 in. rear: 16·3 in.	front: 12 in. rear: 16·3 in.	front: 12 in. rear: 16·5 in.	front: 11·5 in. rear: 16·25 in.
Tyres	Goodyear	Goodyear	Goodyear	Goodyear
Brakes	AP	AP	AP Lockheed/SEP	AP
Brake pads	Ferodo·Hitco	Hitco/SEP	SEP	Ferodo
Steering	Tyrrell	Tyrrell	Williams	Zakspeed
Radiator/s	Llanelli/Secan	Llanelli/Secan	Secan	Behr
Fuel tank	ATL	ATL	ATL	ATL
Battery	RS	RS	RS	Bosch
Instruments	Brion Leroux	Brion Leroux	Honda	Bosch
DIMENSIONS				
Wheelbase	108·5 in./2756 mm	108·5 in./2756 mm	112 in./2855 mm	111 in./2820 mm
Track	front: 69·5 in./1765 mm	front: 69·5 in./1765 mm	front: 72 in./1829 mm	front: 70·8 in./1800 mm
	rear: 64·5 in./1636 mm	rear: 65·0 in./1651 mm	rear: 66 in./1676 mm	rear: 63 in./1600 mm
Gearbox weight	115 lb/52 kg	115 lb/52 kg	—	—
Chassis weight (tub)	78 lb/35 kg	70 lb/32 kg	—	62 lb/28 kg
Formula weight	1190 lb/540 kg	1190 lb/540 kg	1191 lb/540 kg	1224 lb/555 kg
Fuel capacity	42·9 gal./195 litres	42·9 gal./195 litres	42·9 gal./195 litres	42·9 gal./195 litres
Fuel consumption	4·5-5·0 mpg/ 63·0-56·7 litres/100 km	4·5-5·0 mpg/ 63·0-56·7 litres/100 km	4·4 mpg/ 64 litres/100 km	—

Tyrrell 015

Zakspeed ZAK 861

Williams FW11

ELIO DE ANGELIS

by Derick Allsop, Motor Racing Correspondent, *Daily Mail*.

For once he didn't appear quite so well-groomed, quite so sophisticated, and he had distinct problems negotiating the lingual chicanes. He spread himself across a corner of the motorhome, his race suit half open, and declared a little belatedly: 'Tonight I think I get drunk'. Except that he didn't say 'drunk'.

This was Elio de Angelis's way of enjoying victory, the second of his Formula 1 career, at Imola. It was, alas, to be his final victory and we were to enjoy his driving and his company for just one more year. He died, after a terrible crash in testing, at the Paul Ricard circuit in May.

Perhaps if he had won more of his 108 races some of the uninhibited fun might have evaporated from his hour of triumph. I like to think not. Elio had an insatiable appetite for the good things in life and nothing exceeded his delight in success.

It can be claimed – with a degree of justification – that he didn't chase that success as forcefully as some. If the machinery met his requirements he would push himself to the limit; if it didn't he would not attempt to defy logic or the odds. Consider that philosophy and his intense dislike of testing, and you have the wretched irony of his death.

But there were always those who underestimated de Angelis, those who were reluctant to acknowledge his quality. His arrival in Formula 1 as another rich kid was not calculated to smooth his path. Suspicion and envy find fertile ground in this game.

I believe he was, at critical points in his career, a victim of circumstances and misfortune. When he joined Lotus the great team was in decline anyway, but his anxiety was compounded by the emergence of Nigel Mansell as a declared challenger to his Number One status and the death of Colin Chapman.

The renaissance of Lotus gave him fresh optimism and eventually Mansell departed to make way for Ayrton Senna. That was, however, the beginning of the end of his association with the Norfolk camp.

By the time of that 1985 San Marino Grand Prix win, Senna had spelled out his own ambitions and the Latin cocktail proved an impossible mix. Although de Angelis led Senna for much of the Championship he was soon informed that the young Brazilian would be team leader for '86. 'I don't think it is fair but what can I do?' Elio would

ask. There was, of course, only one answer and he left Lotus after six years with the team.

Again he was to sign for a team with a glorious past but an uncertain future. Brabham were on the downward curve and a new car faced inevitable testing problems. He had four races with Brabham, all without scoring, before his fatal accident.

Yet above the ill-luck and the political in-fighting rose a rare man, a rare driver, and the legacy of his memory is one we should cherish. Modern sport has a way of draining the colour and substance from its exponents. De Angelis's resistance to such a threat provided a marvellous exception. The driving reflected the man. It had style, charm; it was easy, natural; it was unhurried, uncomplicated.

De Angelis was a Roman, a fiercely proud Roman, of wealthy stock. He had the looks of a young Brando and the charisma, too. The debonair Elio didn't, however, take kindly to anyone ramming the silver spoon down his throat. 'That makes me angry', he would say.

When Elio was angry the glossy image cracked. He could remonstrate, gesticulate and sulk in true Italian tradition. But mostly we saw another Elio; a warm, wholesome, intelligent, perceptive human, with a glint in his eye and a devastating smile. He would engage you in frank, fascinating conversation on a range of subjects, then have you reeling in laughter at his jokes. Even in English, he was the most captivating of raconteurs.

He was a multi-talented man. During the drivers' South African sit-in of 1982, Elio helped buoy morale with a splendid performance

of classical music on the piano. He once told me: 'Some day, when I finish racing, I will settle down, have a family and play my piano.'

He was a versatile sportsman. He loved skiing and tennis and, as a player or spectator, had a ferocious passion for football. But more than anything he craved speed, an obsession he inherited from his powerboat racing father Giulio.

Elio, the eldest of four children, raced with his father and had a few 'character-building' mishaps along the way. He decided to seek fame on dry land. He began racing karts at the age of 14 and was European champion at 18. He moved on to cars and swiftly advanced through F3 and F2. He had his F1 baptism with the Shadow team in 1979 and impressed sufficiently to earn his chance with Lotus the following season, as partner to Mario Andretti.

His first Grand Prix success, at the Österreichring in 1982, was one of the most thrilling in the history of the World Championship. He managed to fend off Keke Rosberg's Williams and take the decision by inches. Amid the chaos and confusion and celebration that followed, he virtually ran down Chapman. The party spilled into the night and into Italy, but victories were not to flow as readily as the champagne.

Instead, de Angelis was to develop a reputation as a consistent finisher and points scorer. He came third, behind the irresistible McLarens, in the 1984 Championship and, when he achieved his second win the following spring, glimpsed the prospect of the title itself. 'Then we will have a REAL party', he promised.

It was never to be. Elio died in a Marseilles hospital on 15 May 1986, aged 28. His car had cartwheeled over a barrier, landed upside down and burst into flames. Approximately eight minutes elapsed before he was released and then there was a lengthy wait for a helicopter.

His death weighed heavily on the sport's conscience. There were sudden pledges of improved safety standards for testing, of a reduction in power, of modifications to the Ricard circuit.

I, for one, though, will remember Elio for much more than the tragic circumstances in which he died. You see, he really did give us so much to savour and to celebrate, after all.

DROIT DU SEIGNEUR

On the eve of his retirement race, Keke Rosberg considered his career, and the men against whom he had raced. How did he rate them?

'Oh, it's not a matter of rating them', he replied at once. 'I mean, there's Prost and then the rest. And I don't think that – I *know* it. He's the best I've ever known, no question about it.

'As an all-round race driver he's head and shoulders clear of anyone else, because he's brilliant in every department: fast circuits, slow, qualifying or race, wet or dry . . . Also he's an honest man and has a sense of humour.' Rosberg paused before the ultimate driver's accolade: 'And he's *bloody* quick, I can tell you.'

In the normal course of events a Grand Prix driver will chew on a razor blade before speaking of one of his fellows in this style. Oh, they all said that about Moss, about Clark, but the world was far less paranoid then. You could safely admit the superiority of another without being labelled a loser. Even in Stewart's time there was general accord that he was the best.

JYS himself says this of Prost: 'I used to think he and Piquet were on a par, but not now. Unlike Nelson, Alain doesn't make unnecessary mistakes. He's an extremely nice guy, but undoubtedly he has the killer instinct all the great ones have to have. He can be ruthless when he needs to be.'

No doubting that. At Spa, a race he believes he would have won without problem, Prost was delayed by a first-corner accident started by Senna. Working on the principle of 'don't get mad, get even', he kept his anger to himself, channelled it into perhaps the best drive by anyone in 1986. Next on the calendar was Montreal.

Early in the race Mansell was away into the lead, and Senna, second, was holding up a bunch led by Prost. A faint heart never got by Ayrton Senna, and there was a degree of *Droit du Seigneur* in the way Alain dealt with him. Into the flat-out right-left-right swerves after the pits the McLaren was alongside the Lotus, and through the first part nosed ahead. Before the left-hander Prost simply chopped across to claim the line, obliging Senna to lift, flick sideways, put two wheels on the grass.

Throughout the manoeuvre Alain's head never moved. There was no glance in the mirror, nothing. It was a matter of 'I'm coming through – make your arrangements', as cold-blooded a pass as any you will ever see. Intimidation, it said, is a game we can all play.

'Was it close?' Alain innocently asked afterwards. 'Really?' Surely, I said, that had been your purpose? Prost said nothing, answered with the flicker of a grin.

Months later he, like Mansell and Piquet, went to Adelaide to decide the World Championship, and his mood on arrival was not good. Jet-lagged, and wondering where his luggage had got to, he went off to play golf. He shares Mansell's passion for the game, if not his ability, and afterwards felt much better.

'It's a long way down here, huh? Without still having a chance in the championship, I would have dreaded the flight, but if I'm honest about it there is only a small chance for me and Piquet. Nigel is going into the last round of the Open with a six-stroke lead . . .'

Consider the elements which had Alain in contention for the title during which the overall supremacy of Williams-Honda was unquestioned. Consider that, while Senna was sometimes a threat, Rosberg occasionally so, only Prost regularly disturbed Mansell and Piquet. Consider, too, that he did it as reigning World Champion, that men in this position habitually – if unconsciously – relax a fraction during the following season.

At Rio, the opening race, Alain felt more relaxed than for months, 'back in a car again, the only place I can get away from all the bullshit'. There was no Brazilian hat-trick for him, but the

number 1 McLaren led a while before retiring. Into its third season of Grands Prix, John Barnard's miraculous MP4/2 could still do the job. And Prost knew that nothing within himself had changed. What he still wanted more than anything was to win – *here, today, now*. He is possessed by the thought of more victories, of passing Stewart's 27.

Becoming World Champion eased a lot of the tensions within him. 'I am much more relaxed this year', he said. 'Retiring in the first race would have worried me a lot before, but now I think "So what?" – I have 15 more chances to win. Plenty of time for the others to have problems.'

Imola he won by intelligence and discipline. No-one hates the fuel limit regulations more than Alain, but, as Jimmy Durante used to say, 'Dese are de conditions dat prevail'. You must, in other words, play by the house rules, and, whatever they may be, Prost will adapt and win. While others in the San Marino Grand Prix veered between charging and cruising, the World Champion drove on his instruments, running dry literally as he crossed the line.

'Alain', Nigel Mansell remarked, 'is a great driver, the rival I most admire. But he's also a great *manager* of a car. He'll race as hard as anyone, believe me but only if he knows he can – if the fuel readout is giving him the right message. There's no percentage in running out two laps from the end.'

His victory in Monte Carlo was a straightforward *tour de force*, making everyone else look flat-footed and clumsy. You watched his serene progress, noted that he was using minimal revs, changing up early, never clipping a kerb, let alone a barrier, and you started to believe you could do it yourself. It was some of the others – those bouncing uncertainly from one apex to the next – who made it look difficult.

In its way, perhaps more significant was that Alain took his third Monaco pole in four years. As usual, others bitched about 'traffic', said they were on real screamer until René de Patrese blocked them. 'It is difficult finding a clear lap', Prost agreed, before adding a fine throwaway line: 'It was like that for me one year . . .'

His drive at Spa, though, was mesmeric in a different, way. Blamelessly delayed by the antics of Senna and Berger at La Source, the first hairpin, he drove a slow, punctured, lap back to the pits. After the McLaren had been checked over he came back to sixth from the very tail of the field, having driven the fastest race of the afternoon.

'Not only that', John Barnard said, 'he did it in a damaged car. We were satisfied it was safe when he pitted, but it certainly wasn't in A1 condition – we knew that when we found bent engine mountings afterwards. The thing was like a banana!' Alain, it transpired, had needed an eighth of a turn of lock in a straight line.

'Not only that', Barnard added, 'he never touched the boost, even though the temptation must have been tremendous'. This the team knew, for there is effectively a 'tachograph' in the Bosch engine management system. 'People say he's lucky', John concluded, 'but that's not so: he's intelligent.

'The other thing about Alain is that when he says "That's it – that's as fast as I can go", you know that *is* it. He puts his thumb under his chin, pushes his head back, and that means he's been right on the edge. There's been no-one like him in my experience.' Barnard is not known for his frivolous distribution of compliments to racing drivers.

After that drive in Belgium, Prost quietly pointed out that maybe that single point would be crucial at season's end. He said the same after Hockenheim where the fuel readout played him false. If we needed proof of the man's competitive spirit we saw it there as he jerked forward in the cockpit, urging the car

onward. Then he got out, began shoving it towards the line.

'I knew it wasn't allowed', he remarked, 'but I thought it would be good for the TV cameras to see the absurdity of the rules in Formula 1. Probably a lot of people thought we had not put enough fuel in . . . Impossible to race like this. Crazy.'

Jean-Marie Balestre doesn't care for comments like that. Any remarks derogatory to FISA – in other words, suggestive of the governing body's fallibility – were to be punished, he told the drivers at mid-season. Accordingly, when Prost gave forth with a few well-chosen words at Monza, he was fined. Alain's relationship with Balestre has never been a close one, and he was understandably incensed in Italy when allowed to run 'thumb under chin' for nearly half the race before being black-flagged for an infringement before the start. The fine, sense be praised, was later rescinded.

The most demoralising race of the season for Prost was the British Grand Prix, strictly a two-car battle between Mansell and Piquet. At Brands Hatch, one of Alain's favourite circuits, he was obliged to run minimum boost all the way simply to make it to the flag. Third, *lapped*, he suggested afterwards that the World Championship was now between the Williams drivers.

In Austria, though, he nursed a stricken car to victory once more, and began cautiously to hope once again. In Portugal his iron self-discipline kept him from hustling Senna and Piquet: no fuel, no finish. And when Nelson obligingly spun, and Ayrton ran dry, Alain was in there for another six points.

Mexico brought more of the same. On five cylinders for the last third of the race, Prost was careful not to hurt his tyres because he dared not stop, for fear of losing the engine. Thus, he made it through on two sets, Mansell taking three, Piquet an extraordinary four.

For these reasons, Alain was still in the game when they headed for Australia. 'I don't know who'll be champion', Rosberg murmured in practice, 'but I guarantee Prost will win the race.' McLaren engineers Steve Nichols and Tim Wright said the same: 'We know Alain will do his part, but . . .'

His drive in Adelaide was Prost pure. While Senna, Piquet and Rosberg treated the first lap like the last, Alain took a seat in the stalls, looked on from a distance. Inexorable is how he is in a race, and he was just so this day. Despite a puncture and a long stop, he was up with the leaders again when Mansell's tyre blew, when Piquet was called in.

Afterwards, in victory, he was remarkably gracious. 'I would like to say how sorry I feel for Nigel. Twice I lost the title at the last race, and I know how he must feel. He deserved to be World Champion this year.'

The two men are good friends – close enough for Mansell to have joined in the laughter at the driver's meeting in Mexico, where the Englishman suffered unpleasantly from a visit by Montezuma. Any questions? they were asked at the end. Silence. Then a lone, deadpan, voice: 'Excuse me, 'ave you a brown flag for Nigel . . .?'

Three years ago, at Spa, Alain spoke of Villeneuve as the sport's last superstar. 'The rest of us', he said, 'I think are a bunch of good, professional drivers. But there is no-one really exceptional'.

He has now distanced himself from the rest, moved into the sphere of the great. 'What pleases me this year', he said after Adelaide, 'is that I cannot remember making any big mistake anywhere.' He made one, in fact. During qualifying at his hated Detroit, he hit the wall. A few minutes after he walked in, the McLaren was brought back, dangling from a breakdown truck. At this, there was something close to shock in the pits. And it probably pleased the other drivers to be reminded that Prost, like them, is not infallible. *That* is how good he has become.

By NIGEL ROEBUCK, Grand Prix Editor, *Autosport*

It's about to put the skids under its rivals.

The new Vauxhall Carlton will, we suspect, find much favour amongst drivers.

But it could cause feathers to be ruffled amongst the makers of its rivals.

For here is a car that embodies so many advances, it suddenly makes the others seem decidedly dated.

The Carlton's new suspension is a case in point. We call it Advanced Chassis Technology, or ACT.

Drivers will call it nothing short of remarkable.

Our engineers, you see, have come up with a cunning new geometry design which automatically compensates for the forces caused by sudden braking or steering movements.

Thus an emergency high-speed lane change that would have the back of other cars slewing out, can be accomplished with ease in the Carlton.

A corner tight enough to cause violent steering

The dash is totally new. So too are the seats.

The driver's seat is height adjustable on all models and has twin lumbar support controls on the GL and CD.

Other luxury features are there in abundance.

All 8 saloons and 8 estates have power steering, tinted glass, high-security central locking with deadlocks, even heated washer nozzles.

And the security-coded stereo system has not two, not four, but *six* speakers.

GL models also have a sliding, tilting glass sunroof with blind, and electric door mirrors. (Heated of course.)

And the top of the range CD models not only have electric windows and alloy wheels, but a cruise control too.

So what else is new about the new Carlton?

In 2 words, practically everything.

There are new engines. (Including a 115 bhp fuel-injected 1.8i.)

There is a new engine management system on the 2.0i models. (The very latest state-of-the-art Bosch ML4 Motronic.)

There are new brakes. (Discs all round. And the option of the new second generation ABS.)

There is a new 5-speed gearbox. There is a new 4-speed automatic.

And there is more, much more.

But the new Carlton is essentially a driver's car. We therefore urge you to take a test drive.

changes when you lift your right foot in rival cars, should cause no white knuckles in the Carlton.

And neither should slamming on the brakes when one side of the car is on slush and the other is on dry road.

Whereas most other cars will veer suddenly to one side, the Carlton will stop in a straight line.

But the Carlton isn't just a source of great comfort in an emergency.

Those smoothly-rounded lines and flush windows do more than give it a class-leading drag co-efficient of 0.28.

They also give a better combination of head and leg room than any rival can offer.

The new Vauxhall Carlton.

B E T T E R .   B Y   D E S I G N .

HONDA V6 - HONOURABLE

The Honda V6; around 1200 bhp from just 1.5 litres.

WORLD CHAMPIONSHIP ENGINE

Paul-Henri Cahier

It was clear after their hat-trick of victories in the final three Grand Prix races of 1985 that Williams-Honda were in the box seat for the coming season. As the 1986 World Championship series developed, McLaren-TAG Turbo and Lotus-Renault put up strong resistance but Williams-Honda generally dominated.

The Japanese twin-turbocharged 4-cam V6 engines maintained a consistent edge in terms of horsepower, reliability and fuel economy combined, and for Honda R&D at Wako, just outside Tokyo, this real success in Formula 1 justified a long and occasionally troubled V6 racing engine programme which had begun six years earlier in 2-litre unblown Formula 2.

Honda R&D has made a terrific commitment to turbocharged 1500 cc Formula 1, and it has paid off handsomely, not only in promotable success on circuit but also in research and development areas which have always been Wako's prime concern. When Honda first returned to European road racing in 1981 with Ron Tauranac's Ralt Formula 2 team, they were reviving an old partnership which had dominated 1-litre Formula 2 in 1966 with Ron's Brabham-Honda cars. The modern Ralt-Hondas won the European Formula 2 title in 1981 and 1983, while the Spirit Racing team ran this same Honda 'RA263-E' engine more successfully during Ralt's poor 1982 season.

At that time Ralt's star seemed to have been eclipsed and for 1983 it was Spirit who managed to talk Honda into Formula 1 using a turbocharged 1500 cc short-stroke version of the basic iron-block 80-degree V6. Engineer Nobuhiko Kawamoto — who in 1966 had been a Brabham-Honda mechanic — was now President of Honda R&D, and he won Board approval for Spirit to take Honda back into Formula 1 with this rather untidy hybrid engine.

Honda had already discussed Formula 1 with Tauranac, but he recommended they should tackle American Indycar racing instead. 'Formula 1's a hard nut to crack', he reasoned. 'With Indy racing you'll start out as a bigger fish in a small pond. In any case America is one of your biggest markets so an Indy programme seems to make more sense as a first move out of Formula 2.'

Indy V8 plans were laid, based upon an alternative DFV-like engine designed for naturally aspirated Formula 1, and perhaps yet to form the basis for a 1989 3·5-litre engine? But through 1983 Ralt-Honda concentrated upon another F2 Championship while Spirit carried Honda back into Formula 1.

And, as Tauranac had predicted, they discovered just how hard it could be.

Their short-stroke 'RA163-E' F1 V6, had been quietly unveiled at the Geneva Motor Show that year, just thirty minutes before TAG Turbo engines introduced their Porsche-engineered McLaren-bound engine amidst enormous razzmatazz.

Whereas the German engine was a masterpiece of packaging to suit McLaren's design strictures, the 'freelance' Japanese V6 was very much an engine-man's engine, designed with more thought for how it would mount on a dyno than in a racing car!

Its wide-spaced overhead camshafts suggested either a wider-than-fashionable included angle between the twinned inlet and exhaust valves, or a very large cylinder bore. Camshaft gear-drive ran up the front of the block, twin distributors drove from the inlet camshaft tails and the mock-up's makeshift twin KKK turbochargers fed clumsy induction logs high on top.

The whole operation was shrouded in corporate secrecy, funded by Honda R&D with press information by MI5. Wako's people were only interested in learning and proving more about advanced high-output engine technology. Not even fake bore and stroke dimensions were published and none have been confirmed since.

However, there is evidence that the F1 V6 inherited a 90 mm bore from the 2-litre F2, and adopted the tiny stroke of just 39.2 mm in contrast to the F2's alleged 52.3 mm, to form a very over-square unit displacing 1495.52 cc against the F2's 1995.29 cc. Under the approved FISA capacity formula (bore × bore × stroke × 0.785 × number of cylinders), a 39.3 mm instead of 39.2 mm stroke would still produce the legal capacity of 1499.33 cc.

This believed F1 stroke:bore ratio of 0.44 presented the expansive piston area of 381.7 cm^2 compared to the believed 82 mm × 47.2 mm TAG Turbo V6's 316.9 cm^2. The original unblown F2 Honda V6 had developed at best around 175 bhp per litre, and at 3.5 ata boost the F1 version was now said to aim at 760 bhp, at 4.0 ata 860 bhp and at 4.5 ata around 960 bhp.

Initially nothing like 3.5 ata would be attempted, and at Geneva Honda merely claimed 600 bhp with twin KKK turbocharging, although Japanese IHI (Ishikawajima-Harima Industries) turbos were soon to replace the German units. As the project developed, so improved versions of engineer Kitamoto's V6 and its tailor-made IHI turbocharging system would be developed in close co-operation. Similarly, the Honda Kikaki carburetion and fuelling section was creating a completely new all-electronic engine management system for the new Grand Prix engine.

For the short-term, Stefan Johansson did his best with the F2-based Spirit-Hondas in Formula 1, making their debut in the Race of Champions at Brands Hatch on 10 April 1983. They entered the World Championship in the British GP at Silverstone.

This low-budget programme merely gave Honda a toe in the water. Discussions between Williams and Honda during the previous winter had already suggested a joint development car, building towards full collaboration in 1984, but this idea had been filed as the Spirit developed. By the time Spirit staged Honda's World Championship comeback at Silverstone, negotiations had advanced between WGPE and Honda R&D.

Johansson, ironically, made Honda's first finish, 12th in Austria, where Kawamoto and Frank Williams announced their agreement for 1984, Honda to supply engines FOC. Williams had already been given the go-ahead to design a Honda-powered car. Spirit's involvement was under review. At Zandvoort Johansson finished seventh, just out of the points. The Patrick

69

The modern design equipment installed at Williams enabled aerodynamicist Frank Dernie to encase the Honda V6 in a snug-fitting engine cover.

Head-designed prototype Williams-Honda FW09 then tested at Donington just before the Italian GP, in which the first pukka F1 Spirit-Honda 101 broke after only four laps. The European GP at Brands Hatch was to be Spirit's last Honda-powered race, Johansson placing 14th.

Meanwhile, although there had been no intention to race the new FW09 that year, at Monza it had become clear to Patrick Head and Frank Williams that if they were to challenge seriously for the 1984 World title they should go in at the deep end with one car, maybe two, for the South African GP.

A telex zinged away to Honda asking sanction for the entry and supply of race engines. Japanese decision-making typically takes time. Kawamoto was to agree but by that time Williams had already started work on the new cars . . .

They qualified well at Kyalami, but had insufficient intercooling capacity to run as much boost as the team would have liked. Both drivers, Rosberg and Laffite, initially liked the new cars' handling. They raved about Honda's albeit peaky power but into 1984 they found their chassis dogged by massive and apparently incurable initial understeer. These handling problems were exacerbated by the Japanese V6's narrow rev band and explosive power. It came in with a stupendous BANG, which both threatened the structural integrity of the chassis and triggered lurid terminal oversteer as a postcript to that gross initial understeer . . . a combination that was neither pleasant nor quick.

Team forethought and sheer car control enabled Rosberg to break Honda's modern F1 duck by winning the mid-season 1984 Dallas GP, but as designer Kitamoto and development engineer Hagi sought more power in a wider band from the

V6, a series of spectacular mechanical failures, usually piston-initiated, wrecked their first full season. When they persuaded the engines to last race distance, fuel-thirst made survival impossible. The second half of '84 saw the Williams-Honda finish only once from 14 starts.

Essentially that 1984 'D-spec' engine was still merely a short-stroke F2 unit and once it had been turbocharged for Formula 1 it suffered all the internal cooling problems one would expect from an engine suddenly asked to produce double its original designed horsepower.

Kawamoto – the Boss – attended the Dutch GP and recognised that both the engine itself and Honda's contemporary approach to Formula 1 were inadequate. Building a workable relationship of mutual trust between two cultures takes time. Now WGPE and Honda were getting there . . .

In Holland Kawamoto saw Rosberg run as high as third early on, driving ferociously hard, but his fuel readout was soon signalling danger and he was forced progressively to turn down the boost, ending up on minimum but running out regardless before the finish. Team-mate Laffite ran sixth until his engine exploded under Kawamoto's gaze, so little of it remaining in the car that Patrick Head remarked 'It's a good job that it won't make the finish. It would be disqualified for being underweight . . .'

Some of the FW09s' handling problems were attributed to flexure within the monocoque-engine assembly and the V6's mounts, its basically F2 crankcase and block apparently inadequate for the power, torque and chassis loads it was

now being asked to handle.

Thus far, with the Dallas win to their credit, Kitamoto and Hagi had worked miracles in achieving so much with what was really an inadequate compromise hybrid engine.

Now Kawamoto put together a substitute F1 R&D team headed by engineer Ichida. In effect, they were to take over the baton first from Kitamoto, then in the middle of last year from Hagi. Original engine designer Kitamoto was able to bequeath a wealth of experience and information upon which Ichida's team could build. Local cooling hot-spots were blamed for the crippling series of piston collapses, and soon Ichida had revised, stiffened, external coolant-piped 'E-spec' units under development.

For the start of 1985, the first carbon-composite Williams FW10 chassis were introduced, powered by modified 'D-spec' engines while Ichida's replacement tailor-made 'E-spec' was being finalised. Honda wanted a more useable power curve, better mechanical reliability and improved structural rigidity within the basic iron-block. It is possible that a less radical stroke:bore ratio was adopted, nearer TAG Turbo's alleged 82 mm × 47.2 mm which is a ratio of 0.57:1. Honda unlocked a lot of power, around 810 bhp in the race at Silverstone '85 and over 1070 bhp for qualifying there, figures which the team confirm as being 'about right'.

This past season BMW have reputedly been running around 1350 bhp for qualifying, so Honda must have been producing around 1200. With good reason these engines have been described as bombs kept just this side of exploding by their management systems.

Honda have seemed able to run their engines very hot and at high turbo boost, ceramic

The cool crisp taste of
Martini Extra Dry shines through.
Once found, never lost.
It's there to be discovered.

*Martini and M&R
are registered Trade Marks.*

It's easy to produce a vehicle, cram it with extras, and then pretend it's luxurious.

It's an entirely different matter, however, to design, engineer and build what is uncompromisingly a luxury car, from the ground up.

JAGUAR
JAGUAR CARS LIMITED, ENGLAND

The new Jaguar XJ6 is that car.

Turn the key, and up to seven on-board computers inform you of all major functions, via a unique mix of traditional instruments and a multi-symbol dot matrix display.

The 2.9 litre electronically fuel injected engine demonstrates Jaguar's mastery of all-alloy technology. It reaches 60mph in 9.6 seconds, and achieves an unruffled 120mph*. The 3.6 litre 24 valve twin cam is even more potent.

Transmission is via a 5 speed Getrag gearbox —as

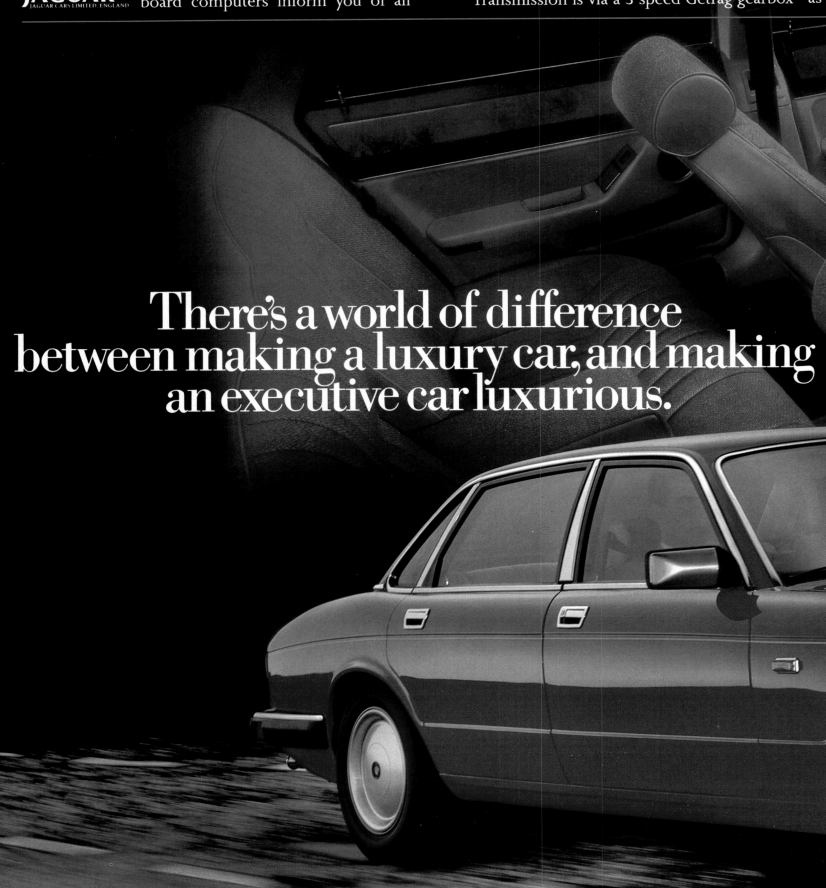

There's a world of difference between making a luxury car, and making an executive car luxurious.

used in the XJ-S. A new 4 speed automatic is an option.

The legendary ride is enhanced by anti-dive, anti-squat suspension geometry. An advanced self-levelling system and 'anti-yaw' ABS braking are options.

Refinement, however, is Jaguar's true luxury.

The uncanny silence comes solely from painstaking engineering and attention to detail. Not the simple expedient of adding sound-deadening material.

Instead, we take time to perfect each XJ6. Craftsmen carefully match walnut veneers. The upholstery is hand sewn. And every car is comprehensively roadtested.

Yet all this is achieved from only £16,495.

Not an unusual price, for an executive car. But for luxury like this, the difference is unparalleled.

THE NEW JAGUAR XJ6 FROM £16,495

Combined technology. The Honda V6 was carefully mated to the Williams chassis – and vice versa. The IHI turbocharger with its conical air filter is clearly shown, with the intercooler to its right and the water radiator beyond that.

turbocharger internals being suggested as the way to maintain very close – high-boost – tip clearances against the compressor casings.

What we do know for sure is that the early-1985 interim D engines used the improved engine mounts of the forthcoming Es to match the new FW10 carbon chassis, and were further modified to sidestep early IHI turbocharger problems. A new, more robust six-speed gearbox was developed by Williams to suit.

Ichida's E-spec engines emerged in Montreal '85, where Rosberg finished second after two stops – one after losing boost due to an electrical problem, then a puncture. Mansell had a boost problem and ran a race which burned only 185 litres of fuel instead of his permitted 220 . . . Next race, Detroit, Keke won.

The FW10-Honda Es were mechanically satisfactory at Ricard for the French GP but the heat and speeds there simply aggravated their already rampant hunger for tyres. A spell of unreliability followed, stemming from the car at Silverstone and largely the engine bottom-end thereafter. Ichida fixed it, helping Mansell to finish second, Rosberg fourth, at Spa.

Williams had been nagging at Honda to reduce the engine's overall height, and lower inlet manifolding finally arrived in time for Brands Hatch, enabling a lower engine cover to be adopted. This improved airflow under the rear wing and with revised rear suspension the FW10B could handle Honda's now-reliable power. Mansell won the European GP with Rosberg third, again at Kyalami with Rosberg second, and then Rosberg won the season finale in Australia as Mansell was sidelined by Senna and his own impetuosity.

Since the introduction of the FW10B coincided with the team's hat-trick of victories, most pundits assumed that this new version must have been appreciably quicker than the preceeding '10A, but at Spa for the Belgian GP the '10As had already been very competitive but WGPE hadn't got their balance 'quite right enough to win'. Earlier, in the Italian GP at Monza, the '10As had been the fastest cars running until Mansell had an ignition system problem, after which he lapped as quickly as Rosberg until both cars stopped near the finish with mechanical malfunctions.

Most significantly, the '10B might not have been much quicker than the '10A, but it was very much kinder on its tyres when setting similar lap times. The '10A had always been hungry, a tyre destroyer. This was in fact much of the reason for WGPE's pit crew becoming such tyre-change champions, as they demonstrated in Adelaide that year when winner Rosberg changed tyres no less than three times – and that was on the kinder '10B.

The Honda-powered '10As had already won at Detroit and taken a strong second place at Ricard in the French GP before Rosberg took pole position for the British GP. So the '10A model was working most effectively at that time but at Silverstone WGPE 'didn't quite get the balance of the car right in the race'. Not Honda's fault. At the *ersatz* Nürburgring, the '10As were again very quick 'but we had a tyre damaged by the car's hunger,

Keke had a brake-seal problem in a caliper and Nigel an exhaust problem, so that was two races lost with chassis-related mechanical problems.' Not Honda's fault.

Three races followed in a row – Austria, Holland and Italy – each spoiled for Williams by Honda engine bearing failures after running competitively each time. But Honda R&D's engineers were now reacting much more quickly and were able to fix their bearing problems in the revised top-end E-Type engines presented at Brands. Thereafter in the FW10Bs they not only ruled the waves, it looked as if they could walk on them . . .

Into the winter of 1985/86, the latest Honda engines were second only to BMW's staggering stock-block M12/13 4-cylinder units for outright power but quite unlike the Bee-Emm they had also become fabulously reliable.

Undoubtedly Mobil's fuel research and development had played its part in unlocking such dependable power. BMW had led the way into controversial 'funny fuels' in 1983-84, reasoning that with a 220-litre race allowance on its way, one should obtain better value from each individual litre. Accordingly they adopted special 'high-aromatic' hydrocarbon fuel brewed to their requirements by the BASF chemical company, and now Honda had followed their lead with the help of Mobil's chemists.

High-aromatic fuels, like toluene (derived commonly from tar process residue) are extremely dense, having available within a given volume the maximum amount of hydrogen and carbon atoms for burning with oxygen. Their density poses problems being slow-burning and difficult to ignite – hence the F1 cars' black smoke-trails in cold temperatures when the inlets and logs run too cool for the fuel to vapourise adequately.

Fuel apart, Honda Kikaki unlocked more power through painstaking development of their all-electronic engine management system to improve its distribution and combustion. In effect, each electrically timed and tailored squirt through one of the variable-size injector nozzles mixes globules of fuel with molecules of air. Each fuel globule with its attached air molecules is then ignited; if distribution is poor and combustion inefficient only the outside of the fuel globule burns, leaving its core unconsumed, whereupon the residue gets blown out of the exhaust, its potential energy going to waste.

Much of Honda's advance in power has come from persuading the injection to atomise its fuel more thoroughly, ensuring rapid evaporation as it picks up heat on entering the combustion chamber, dispersing into the oxygen available there so it burns completely and none gets wasted.

The geographic gulf between Didcot and Wako which had delayed development reaction times was plugged in June '85 when a lavishly equipped Honda-run engine shop adjoining the Williams factory was commissioned. Honda's Wako engine rebuild turn-round times were still far longer than Williams's old DFV norm – in part meaning more engines were needed to keep the team supplied – so although all race engines up to the 1986 Brazilian GP were Japanese-built, subsequent engines were rebuilt and serviced at Didcot.

Formula 1 R&D meanwhile proceeded at Wako while Honda R&D has been moving to the Tochigi centre with its test-track complex some sixty miles due north of the Tokyo waterfront. Their F1 standard-setting V6 engines remained a curious mixture of the beautifully hand-finished and the untidily conceived near-volume production design.

For this past season's 195-litre race-distance fuel restriction, Ichida's group introduced the further developed 'F-spec', or reportedly 'RA166-E', V6 variant – 'F for frugal' they say – with still-lower induction logs on top.

Rio is not very heavy on fuel because so much of the circuit is negotiated on part throttle, but in January/February the team completed considerable development work there in two seven-day two-car test periods, 28 car-days of work. The FW11 promptly became Patrick Head's first design to win on its debut, as did Ichida's latest F-spec engine, also a first for Honda R&D. The

first Rio test session had seen the first run of the 195-litre fuel restriction F-Type engine, mounted in an adapted FW10B.

Honda R&D had few F-spec engines available at that time, and the Rio test '10Bs both wore the taller '10A bodywork because the team had a new and bigger ECU central programming unit for the Honda engine's fuel injection plus a revised tank-top position for the capacitor-discharge ignition box, moved from above the gearbox. Combined with the tall original 220-litre '10A tank, this demanded more room within the bodywork, so the old '10A engine cover was used to suit. 'We knew therefore that we were running slower than we could do, but we knew roughly by how much.'

In the subsequent February session at Rio, WGPE ran one of these '10Bs with '10A bodywork but using the F-spec engine for tyre testing. The first of the brand new FW11s made its debut there as all these winter developments were brought together at last.

The rest of the story you will already know or will find elsewhere in these pages.

Honda R&D's 1986 Formula 1 engine programme has been co-ordinated by engineer Sakurae who attends the great majority of races, while engine design chief Ichida-*San* normally concentrates on the work back home. Engineer Goto ran the engine shop adjoining WGPE's factory at Didcot and accompanied the team to every race.

One cannot overstate the brilliant no-holds-barred job which Honda R&D have done in Formula 1, especially considering the rather untidy 2-litre Formula 2-based V6 engine with which they first entered the fray in 1983-84. The natural questions are: how powerful and how fast?

With a turbocharged engine, in which ultimate power output is dependent upon boost pressure chosen, output varies from one circuit to another, and also of course between qualifying and the race. Boost pressures are rumoured to run at around 5 ata (qualifying) and 4 ata (race). Honda F-Type outputs computed from outside observation include a low of 1051 bhp – from only 1.5-litres, remember! – in qualifying at Rio, adjusted to 906 bhp for the race. Qualifying peak pre-Monza seems to have been around 1130 bhp at Hockenheim, and 963 bhp for the race there, which with appropriate gearing for the fast circuit gave a top speed of 332.5 km/h (206.6 mph) in qualifying, and 324 km/h (201.3 mph) in the race. These are unconfirmed figures however; Williams-Honda play their cards very close to their chest.

With the Williams team, Honda have now achieved enormous success amongst the fiercest opposition the racing world can offer. Next year their engines will be powering Lotus chassis and I presume Honda R&D's learning curve will begin to rise even more steeply. Hard on the opposition, maybe, but so, so majestic . . .

THE FIRST RANGE OF
THE DIFFERENCE

SUPREME
FOR HIGH PERFORMANCE ENGINES

*If all cars
on the road were
standard, a standard oil
would be fine.
But a Porsche is not a Princess
is not a Sierra is not a Lada. And a quick look at the
handbook of different cars will tell you the manufacturers demand different specifications of oil for their engines.*

THE RIGHT OILS ————————— **BECAUSE YOUR HANDBOOK**

OILS TO RECOGNISE BETWEEN CARS.

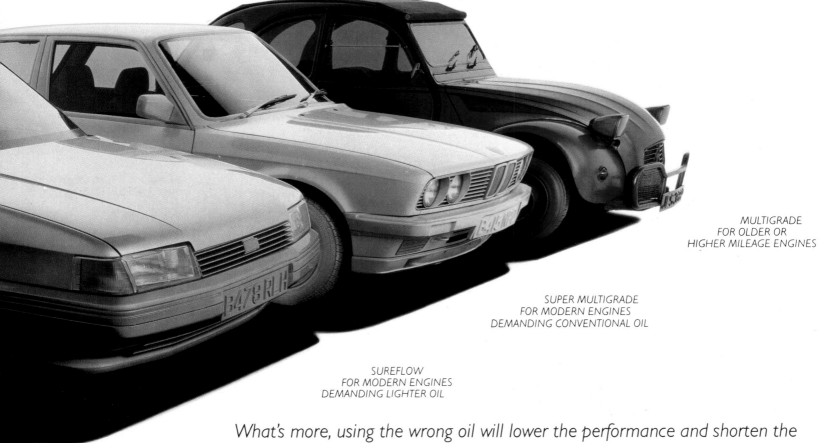

MULTIGRADE
FOR OLDER OR
HIGHER MILEAGE ENGINES

SUPER MULTIGRADE
FOR MODERN ENGINES
DEMANDING CONVENTIONAL OIL

SUREFLOW
FOR MODERN ENGINES
DEMANDING LIGHTER OIL

What's more, using the wrong oil will lower the performance and shorten the life of an engine. (Think about it, would you put 2 star petrol in a 4 star engine?)

Now with a range of 4 superb oils Unipart have made it easy to get the right oil in the engine no matter what the specification. On the front of each Unipart pack is a coloured roundel – red or grey or yellow or green. On the back of each can is a chart which colour-codes all makes of cars in red or grey or yellow or green.

Match your car to the pack with the right coloured roundel and you've got the right oil. This, for the first time, makes it easy for the motorist to get the right oil in his car.

Consumer advertising and in-store sales aids will ensure The Right Oils is an enormous success. To make sure that you benefit, telephone your Unipart wholesaler now.

SAYS SO

Hazleton Securities Ltd

JACKIE STEWART'S PRINCIPLES OF PERFORMANCE DRIVING

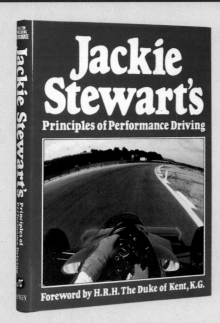

Jackie Stewart's name became a legend in Grand Prix racing when he retired in 1973 with three World Championships and a record of 27 Grand Prix wins to his credit.

Now, in conjunction with Alan Henry, he shares his own personal insights into the essential skills needed to become a champion driver, although this is more than just a 'how to race' book. Share the Stewart philosophy – not only behind the wheel but also in his approach to business and life in general.

29 colour and 120 black & white photographs
ISBN: 0 905138 43 0
Price: £14.95

THE ART & SCIENCE OF MOTOR CYCLE ROAD RACING

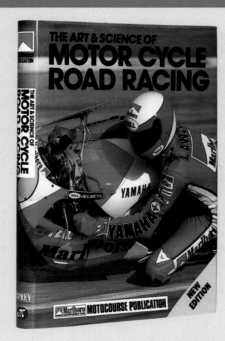

by Peter Clifford

The second edition of this best-selling book has been acclaimed as the most accurate and authoritative account of the skills and principles involved in motor cycle road racing. Cornering, engines, steering, suspension, frames, tyres – all are explored in detail, and now a completely new chapter covers the latest technical innovations and how these affect the rider.

20 colour and 80 black & white photographs
ISBN: 0 905138 35 X
Price: £12.95

McLAREN: *The Grand Prix, Can-Am and Indy Cars*

by Doug Nye

From the early days of McLaren Cars in 1963 to Emerson Fittipaldi's first World Championship title for the team in 1974. Two years later James Hunt did it again, winning his historic season-long battle with Niki Lauda.

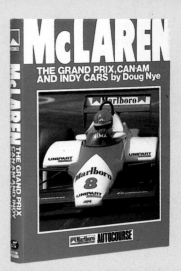

20 colour and over 90 black & white photographs

ISBN: 0 905138 28 7
Price: £12.95

BRABHAM: *The Grand Prix Cars*

by Alan Henry

The story of the Brabham Grand Prix team from its early pioneering days in the Sixties through to the takeover of the team by Bernie Ecclestone in 1972 and Nelson Piquet's World Championship titles in 1981 and 1983.

28 colour and 145 black & white photographs

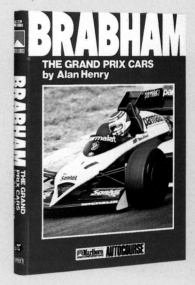

ISBN: 0 905138 36 8
Price: £14.95

FERRARI: *The Grand Prix Cars*

by Alan Henry

The history of the most famous racing marque of them all from its first hesitant steps on to the Grand Prix stage in the early post-war years through to Lauda's two World Championship titles in 1975 and 1977 and the highly specialised world of the turbocharged engines of the Eighties.

35 colour and over 100 black & white photographs

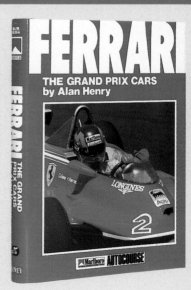

ISBN: 0 905138 30 9
Price: £14.95

AUTOCOURSE
1986-87

The 1986-87 edition of *Autocourse* will be the most colourful and lavish in its 36-year history with over 100 photographs in superb colour and over 150 excellent black-and-white shots from the very best motor sport photographers. It contains complete coverage of the 1986 Formula 1 season plus full reviews of sports car and US racing, Le Mans and Formulas 3 and 3000 in a new and exciting 272 pages. A major issue – engines – is covered by Doug Nye, while Alan Henry's in-depth feature on Keke Rosberg and a comprehensive results and statistics section complete this collector's edition.

ISBN: 0 905138 44 9
Price: £19.95

MOTOCOURSE
1986-87

All the action and excitement of the 1986 World Championship season is here in a new, top-quality package featuring 50 per cent more spectacular colour.

As well as his original Grand Prix reports, editor Peter Clifford takes an exclusive look behind the scenes at Michelin and holds an in-depth interview with Mike Trimby who acts on behalf of the riders. Lively coverage of the US scene, Isle of Man TT, detailed statistics and much more makes *Motocourse* a must for all motor cycle enthusiasts.

75 colour and 130 black & white photographs
ISBN: 0 905138 45 7
Price: £17.95

RALLYCOURSE
1986-87

The fifth edition of *Rallycourse* focuses on the atmosphere and action of a controversial season in World Championship rallying. The story unfolds through the lively reports of editor Mike Greasley, with over 100 dramatic colour photographs from the inimitable Reinhard Klein. A special feature on the Hong Kong–Beijing rally, full results, maps, stage times and much more, make this annual an essential record of the rallying year.

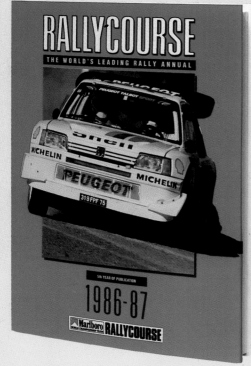

110 colour and 40 black & white photographs

ISBN: 0 905138 46 5
Price: £17.95

THE AUTOCOURSE HISTORY OF THE GRAND PRIX CAR 1966-85

by Doug Nye

This detailed, well-illustrated historical survey spans the era from the 350-horsepower tube-framed cars to the nearly 800-horsepower turbocharged carbon-composite cars of 1985. Follow the fortunes of the great teams and the not-so-great as Doug Nye reveals the inside technical story of the cars and human story of the men who devised, designed and developed them.

This major production is essential reading for all Formula 1 enthusiasts and an important collector's item.

50 colour and 130 black & white photographs plus 60 line drawings and unique factory blueprints

ISBN: 0 905138 37 6
Price: £19.95

Published by Hazleton Publishing, 3 Richmond Hill, Richmond, Surrey TW10 6RE.
Distributed by Osprey Publishing Ltd and available through your local or specialist bookshop.

THOROUGHBREDS USE THE THOROUGHBRED PLUG.

CHAMPION®

The Power Plug

Grande Prêmio do
BRASIL

Nelson Piquet gave the Williams-Honda team an excellent start to the season by scoring maximum points in Rio.

Before the race, Nelson Piquet considered the main threat would come from within his own team. At no point did he even mention Ayrton Senna, the man on pole position. Whether this was a strategical bluff in Nelson's game of wits with his fellow-countryman was not clear but, at the end of the warm-up on race morning, Ayrton actually agreed with Piquet's forecast.

The JPS Lotus-Renault, maintained Senna, would be unable to match the Canon Williams-Honda in this fuel consumption-related formula. And so it proved.

A scuffle on the first lap saw Nigel Mansell spin his Williams as he tried to snatch the lead from a resolute Senna. Watching from a distance, Piquet knew the race would be his and, within two laps, he was in front, the Williams only losing the lead briefly during the delay caused by two planned pit stops for tyres.

In between, there was a brief intrusion by Alain Prost, the World Champion climbing from 13th place at the end of lap 1. It was an impressive drive which saw the Marlboro McLaren lead for seven laps, the result of a one-stop-only ploy which did not look like coming off. In any case, that would remain pure speculation since Prost's TAG engine failed at half-distance, a similar problem having sidelined Keke Rosberg's McLaren.

On 23 March, Williams and Honda were unbeatable and, by common consent, the clear favourites to take the title.

ENTRY AND PRACTICE

Practice was a promoter's dream. Slogging it out were two Brazilians, Ayrton Senna and Nelson Piquet, and their pace was such that Piquet spun and Senna produced one of his mesmeric laps to claim pole position for his home Grand Prix. Before that, however, the result could have gone either way.

Senna celebrated his 26th birthday on the opening day of practice but Piquet had no intention of making a gift of the overnight pole. The Lotus driver had set the ball rolling with a 1m 27.893s lap but, less than a minute later, Piquet had claimed 1m 26.878s. Then there was a lull while both sides took stock.

Eight minutes before the end of the session, Piquet reappeared and sliced another half-second off his time. Senna responded a few minutes later with a 1m 26.983s; sufficient to take second place from Mansell but not good enough to cope with his fellow-countryman.

Senna had completed more laps than anyone else on Friday morning and when he switched to the spare car for the afternoon he found the handling was less than perfect. There was, of course, another hour on Saturday.

This time, instead of the hot but sultry conditions which had attended practice on Friday, the sun beat down fiercely as battle was joined once again. On this occasion Piquet was out first. Within seven minutes he had recorded 26.755s, but he was not satisfied since he had needed to avoid Marc Surer's Arrows crawling back to the pits at about 10 mph. Senna, with 27.403s, was still unhappy with his car and he returned to the Lotus garage to consider minor changes to the settings.

In an effort to put pole beyond reach, Piquet set off on his last set of tyres. Lining up for a fast left-hander, the Brazilian put his right-rear tyre on the grass and, in an instant, the 1100 Japanese bhp had snapped the car sideways. Piquet spun across the track, the kerb at the exit of the corner launching the Williams into the air.

For a brief instant it seemed Piquet would land on his head but the FW11 eventually crashed back onto its wheels in a cloud of dust. Apart from a bruised wrist Piquet was unhurt, but practice, as had been the norm in the event of any incident during the two days, was stopped immediately.

By the time the circuit had been cleared there were eight minutes remaining. And Piquet still held pole. Senna remained in his car, helmet in place, his eyes fixed intently on the Longines monitor. A nod to Lotus engineer Steve Hallam and the V6 was fired into life. With less than one minute of practice remaining, Senna began his last lap.

It was one of those devastating displays where you could see the Lotus was being pushed to its very limit, the driver using all the track. And, at the end of the back straight, he put his right-front wheel onto the grass to obtain a faster line through the left-hander. All this at about 180 mph . . . The result: 1m 25.501s and pole position.

Piquet maintained his place on the front row since a succession of minor problems prevented Nigel Mansell from offering a challenge. On Friday he had experienced difficulties with the turbo boost and incorrect gearing which caused the Honda to hit the rev-limiter, while on his final run on Saturday a wayward Minardi took the edge off his best lap of the weekend.

None the less, second and third on the grid was a good result for Williams and the time sheet was sent immediately by facsimile to London, where Frank Williams was recovering from massive injuries received in a road accident a few weeks previously. Doubtless this news gave the team boss a boost when he needed it most.

The Lotus and the Williams duo filling the first three places on the grid was expected; the appearance of the Gitanes Ligiers in fourth and fifth places was something of a surprise. Here we had René Arnoux, making his Formula 1 comeback after a year's absence, and Jacques Laffite, the oldest man in the field and, supposedly, a poor qualifier.

Apart from an outing at Macau the previous November, Arnoux had done very little driving but it was scarcely obvious as the little Frenchman applied his familiar head-down style. Arnoux's practice was disrupted by a turbo fire on Friday morning, forcing René to use the T-car to record tenth-fastest time in the afternoon. On Saturday, he might have gone even quicker had he not been delayed by Piquet's accident.

'What time did Keke do in the McLaren?' was Laffite's mischievous rejoinder as he climbed from his car on Saturday afternoon. Jacques, of course, knew the 'Fastest man in the World' was back in seventh place and it was his way of cocking a snook at those of us who doubted the Frenchman's commitment during qualifying. He then rubbed it in by adding that he had made a small mistake during the lap which otherwise would have been good enough for fifth place . . .

Little had been expected of the Ferrari team in the light of their poor performances in the second half of 1985 but the Italians arrived in Rio with a new car which had been the subject of many detailed changes. Even more impressive was the Ferraris' high position on the list of straightline

A troubled practice and a short race for Alessandro
Nannini in the Minardi.
Photo: Nigel Snowdon

speeds, coupled with the fact that Michele Alboreto had set his practice time using the 1985 model.

The Italian had suffered a rash of breakages to the fuel pump drive and the shortage of laps on Friday meant he ran one set of race tyres and one set of qualifiers in the afternoon. Saturday got off to a bad start when he collided with Tambay's Beatrice-Lola. The car was rebuilt from the rear of the monocoque to the tip of the gearbox but another pump failure meant Alboreto was in the spare once more. Stefan Johansson was two places behind his team-mate, the Swede spinning on Friday afternoon and losing his best chance on Saturday when the Piquet accident interrupted his final lap.

The fastest McLaren, then, belonged to Rosberg, the former Williams driver splitting the Ferraris. Like Alboreto, Rosberg ran just one set of qualifiers on Friday afternoon thanks to a restricted practice in the morning. A seized turbo delayed the sorting of his new car and he switched to the spare for a while in the afternoon. There were no major problems on Saturday, the Finn simply requiring more miles and a little time to settle into his new environment.

As for Alain Prost, he had been fourth on Friday but slipped five places during the final session. Revised turbos failed to give the anticipated response and wasted the first set of qualifiers. Switching to his race car, Prost then came across the Piquet incident and, by then, the tyres had lost their edge. A return to the pits for a mixture of the best qualifying tyres produced his best but nevertheless unsatisfactory lap of the weekend. Still, a place away from the front of the grid was not entirely new to Prost.

Checking through the comprehensive catalogue of changes which had been made at the last minute to the new Brabham, it was hard to believe that the Olivetti-sponsored team had had four months to prepare for the new season. The BT55 had been more or less redesigned, from the position of the ancillary equipment to alterations to the dash panel and brand new internals for the seven-speed gearbox.

The cars looked impressive but their straight-line speed, the *raison d'être* for all this low line design, was certainly not. The shortfall in power was caused by a problem with the electronic components but Patrese's tenth-fastest time said much for the cornering speed of the cars. Patrese had lost most of the afternoon session on Friday when his car stopped on its first lap. De Angelis, back in 14th place, spun on Friday and an off the following morning forced him to use the spare car for the rest of the day.

Johnny Dumfries, the man chosen eventually to replace de Angelis at Lotus, played himself into Formula 1 with a very sensible performance throughout the two days. The young British driver had an eventful start when an oil scavenge pump failure caused a fire in the undertray of the 98T. With the T-car earmarked for Senna, Dumfries was relegated to the role of spectator and it was difficult to see an established driver such as Derek Warwick (heavily favoured for the job by everyone but Senna) accepting such a

situation so readily.

Dumfries's problems did not end there. A broken turbo meant it was necessary to use race tyres in the afternoon in order to gather more miles with his car but the one run on qualifying tyres was good enough for ninth place. He did improve on Saturday but an indiscriminate piece of driving by de Cesaris and the Piquet incident were enough to see Dumfries slip to 11th.

Teo Fabi and Gerhard Berger were disappointed to be 12th and 16th for Benetton although the team was not dispirited since the problems had been restricted to a number of minor ailments. An electrical misfire and then an exploding plenum chamber hampered Fabi while a down-on-power engine and gearbox trouble prevented Berger from exercising his usual exuberant talent.

The Haas team arrived with three Hart-engined cars and Patrick Tambay's progress was indicative of the work which had been carried out on the chassis and engine alike – despite the team's continuing development schedule with the Ford-Cosworth turbo. Tambay was completing a full tank test on Saturday morning when he had his misunderstanding with Alboreto while being passed by the Ferrari, but at least the damage was confined to one corner of the Lola. In the afternoon, Patrick was badly baulked on his first run but he found an improvement on his final set of qualifiers.

Alan Jones, weighing in at 90.7 kilos to win the dubious honour of being the heaviest driver in the field by a considerable margin, bore the brunt of most of the team's problems. The Australian lost 500 revs on Friday afternoon; on Saturday morning he was stranded out on the circuit with an engine failure and, in the afternoon, he had chronic gearbox trouble.

Down at the Barclay Arrows pit, the list of

The Brabham BT55: a revolutionary concept which got off to a troubled start *(left)*.
Photo: Nigel Snowdon

The Williams mechanics played their part in Piquet's victory by executing a faultless tyre change *(below)*.
Photo: Paul-Henri Cahier

Thinking about what might have been. Nigel Mansell tangled with Ayrton Senna while disputing the lead during the first lap *(bottom)*.
Photo: Paul-Henri Cahier

problems seemed to be evenly distributed. Thierry Boutsen started the ball rolling with a turbo fire ten minutes into the first practice session, a feat he repeated on Saturday morning (a fuel line this time). That meant he had to qualify the T-car. As for Marc Surer, he was plagued throughout by fuel metering unit problems which, at their peak, caused the Arrows to crawl round the circuit at walking pace. Apart from Piquet, Surer was the only driver not to improve his time in the final session.

The circuit, of course, was making its own demands as practice took place in debilitating temperatures. And for Martin Brundle, who had not completed a single mile of testing throughout the winter, the sudden return to the cockpit called for constant neck massages from his wife Liz. At least, that was his excuse . . .

But there did seem cause for concern since a severe lack of downforce on the Data General

Tyrrells made Brundle and new recruit Philippe Streiff work very hard for times which did not mirror their effort.

At least Brundle knew what was in store on the predominantly left-handed circuit. Jonathan Palmer had never raced at Jacarepaguá before and his discomfort was exacerbated by ten stitches in his left thigh, the visible result of an attack on the Englishman in one of Rio's seedier areas earlier in the week. A piston failure on Friday morning forced Palmer to switch to the spare car and he stuck with this brand new chassis for the rest of the weekend, an overheating battery causing an annoying misfire. Then a screw dropped out of the wastegate on his quick lap and that left room for improvement on Saturday.

The all-Italian rear section of the grid was filled, predictably, by the Minardi and Osella teams, each accompanied a list of problems which did not really excuse lap speeds ten seconds slower than

TECHNICAL FILE

ARROWS
Three 1985-spec A8s. No changes except for new duct for oil radiator.

BENETTON
Third new car completed a few days before Rio and tested by Maurizio Sandro Sala at Silverstone. Chassis number two built specially to accommodate Berger since he did not fit the original B186 properly and blew an engine during testing as a result. Cars heavier than planned because one or two pieces used to stiffen suspension not made to the final specification. Ran with carbon-fibre brakes for the first time; Brembo calipers at the front, AP at the rear. Detailed attention paid to engine installation; the chassis tapered around fuel tank to improve location of intercooler. Section cut under fuel tank area to accept mounting point which stiffened engine fixing. Fuel tank height remained similar to 1985 rather than follow popular trend of reducing height. This allowed airflow to sweep inside and away from rear tyres. Gearbox casting carefully sculpted to permit extraction of air underneath.

BRABHAM
Revolutionary new car with 'lay-down' BMW engine, purpose-built to reduce centre of gravity and overall height of car. Driving position lower and more reclined than before giving chassis a slab appearance to help cut drag and achieve a clean airflow to rear wing. Testing at Rio revealed inadequacies with cooling system. Three cars, now totally revised, brought for race. Side pods now wider and taller at inlet. Positions of water and oil radiators changed (oil now in front; water at rear). Modified position of intercooler in left-hand side pod with side exit rather than top exit. Bigger oil cooler for gearbox. Changes to Weismann-inspired seven-speed gearbox; de Angelis car fitted with bevels made by Renk (a German company manufacturing tank transmissions). Changed back to Weismann internals for race. Windscreen and roll hoop over driver's knees raised to conform with regulations forbidding protrusion of driver's head through a line between rear roll-over bar and roll hoop.

FERRARI
Completely new car. Contrary to impression created by taller engine cover, this car much lower than 1985 156/85 model. Roll-over bar enclosed in rear bodywork but 16 cm lower; cockpit 10-12 cm lower; side pods 8-10 cm lower; nose cone not raked so steeply. The foregoing gave the impression of the car being wider than before but this was not so. Carbon-fibre chassis built in two pieces but with floor section and main tub (similar to Williams) rather than half and half as before. Front suspension: dampers mounted horizontally. New digital instrument panel with horizontal rev-counter incorporating colour sections. Almost identical engine installation to 156/85. Revised gearbox casting to cope with new fixing points on top for shock absorbers mounted at 45 degrees. Longer and lower engine cover. New brake calipers made by Ferrari with Brembo components. Top rear aluminium wishbone fitted with carbon-fibre skin for aerodynamic reasons. New underbody with a longer profile. Rear wing centrally mounted on two carbon-fibre plates. Spare car: 156/85 but with revised front uprights from F1/86 and modified front suspension.

HAAS-LOLA
Used 1985 cars some of which had revised installation to accept 1986-spec Hart engines featuring half-inch reduction in length and different exhaust system.

LIGIER
New cars based on 1985 design but reduced in size around fuel tank, allowing smaller and lower engine cover. Pushrod suspension replaced rocker arms at the rear. Aerodynamics refined; new rear wings.

LOTUS
Three new cars. One-piece chassis with reduction in size around fuel tank area due to 195-litre capacity limit. Looked similar to 1985 car but smaller and more refined. Front suspension almost identical to 97T but aerodynamics revised. Rear suspension completely changed; new upright with upper and lower suspension arms changing places (triangular wishbone now on top). Ran vertical front aerofoils on Friday only. Brembo calipers mounted at front of discs.

McLAREN
Three new chassis. Lower driving position allowed roll hoop above driver's knees to be mounted 12 cm lower. Shallower windscreen, cut to give unobstructed vision of mirrors. Instrument panel contained rev-counter and digital computer readout only. Gear linkage now mounted inside chassis. Revised inlet duct for turbo, now running from front of side pod, changing from triangular to square then circular section. Revised position of turbo (closer to and mounted at 90 degrees to engine) allowed a shallower sweep to rear bodywork 'Coke-bottle' shape. Revised geometry to rear suspension. Six-speed gearbox. New underbody and new rear wing.

MINARDI
Brought two chassis, similar to 1985 models but reduced in size around fuel tank. Able to use Weber/Marelli electronics thanks to assistance from Ferrari. New geometry for front suspension; revised fixing points for top wishbones and different pullrod linkages. Radiator positions in side pods changed; water radiator now in front and intercooler (which also cools oil) mounted vertically.

OSELLA
Old car for Ghinzani; more recent car for Danner.

TYRRELL
Waiting for completion of new car. Revised position for turbo inlet duct; moved away from edge of side pod. Streiff's car fitted with Hitco carbon-fibre brakes.

WILLIAMS
Three new chassis. Shallower nose cone (although taller at mounting points for top wishbones). Pushrod front suspension (similar to 1985). Revised positions for radiators and intercoolers (now with side exits). Car narrower and lower in fuel tank area. Close liaison with Honda concerning engine installation saw revisions to ancillary equipment on top of V6 to allow smaller section to rear of tub and lower and narrower fitting for engine cover. Side pods also lower than before. Changes to gearbox casing giving a lighter installation. Revised rear uprights. New underbody with longer profile. Double rear wing to improve air extraction. New support for rear wing. Tried twin carbon-fibre discs by Hitco with AP calipers (raced by Mansell). During testing, tried water-cooled variable turbo.

ZAKSPEED
Two completely new cars, similar to but smaller and lighter than 1985 chassis. Radiator positions angled in similar fashion to Toleman layout. New air duct for revised turbo installation. Revised electronics by Bosch. New suspension, heavily revised at rear with new exhaust system. Vertical fins placed before rear tyres to improve airflow.   G.P.

NEW FOR 1986

ARROWS
Marc Surer joins after occasional races with Brabham in 1985.

BENETTON
Toleman bought out by Benetton. Switch from Hart to BMW engines. Gerhard Berger joins from Arrows as part of BMW package.

BRABHAM
Piquet leaves after seven years. Elio de Angelis moves from Lotus; Riccardo Patrese, made redundant by disbanded Alfa Romeo team, rejoins the team he raced for in 1982 and 1983.

FERRARI
No change.

HAAS-LOLA
Team in difficulties thanks to withdrawal of Beatrice sponsorship and late arrival of Ford-Cosworth turbo engine. Use Hart engine in the interim. Patrick Tambay (ex-Renault) joins Jones.

LIGIER
René Arnoux, out of work since being ejected from Ferrari in early-1985, makes comeback to join Laffite.

LOTUS
After a hectic off-season of bargaining, Lotus acquiesce to Senna's demands and decide against Derek Warwick (out of work thanks to Renault withdrawal) in favour of Johnny Dumfries. De Longhi replaces Olympus sponsorship; additional support from Reporter.

McLAREN
Lauda retires; replaced by Rosberg.

MINARDI
Pierluigi Martini replaced by Andrea de Cesaris (fired by Ligier during 1985). Alessandro Nannini makes Minardi a two-car team for the first time.

OSELLA
Run two cars, Christian Danner joining Ghinzani who goes back to the team with which he made his Grand Prix debut. Use Alfa Romeo engines while waiting for Motori Moderni units.

TYRRELL
Philippe Streiff joins Martin Brundle. Sponsorship from Data General.

WILLIAMS
Nelson Piquet replaces Rosberg.

ZAKSPEED
Take on a full season for the first time.

As if they didn't have enough trouble . . . Elio de Angelis three-wheels the 'lowline' Brabham BT55 back to the pits but he subsequently registered a finish against all expectations *(right)*.

Ayrton Senna holds his nose while Johnny Dumfries grits his teeth as the stink over the choice of the second Lotus driver begins to die down. Senna caused a furore in the British press by effectively putting the block on Derek Warwick as his team-mate. Dumfries, unlikely to make waves, made a very respectable debut at Rio and would have finished in the points but for an electrical problem *(left)*.

René Arnoux made a sparkling return to Formula 1, the Ligier driver finishing fourth *(below)*.

pole. Andrea de Cesaris had clutch, exhaust and halfshaft trouble while electrical trouble for Alessandro Nannini thoroughly disrupted his practice. He took his place at the back behind the Osellas of Piercarlo Ghinzani and Formula 3000 Champion, Christian Danner.

RACE

By 9.0 a.m., four hours before the start, the grandstands were packed with chattering, enthusiastic locals. A home win was on the cards here and that was the signal for high spirits and a high turn-out as temperatures headed towards the upper eighties.

Senna and Piquet may have earned places on the front row but there was a familiar look about the lap times during the 30-minute warm-up. Fastest, with a time of 1m 33.230s, the McLaren of Alain Prost. That was disturbing for the World Champion's rivals since lap times in the 35s, the 34s at best, was the pace they had come to expect. Prost may have been in ninth place on the grid but clearly that meant nothing.

Of more importance perhaps was an electrical problem which had forced Prost to switch to the spare car – and that was found to have a leaking header tank. The men in red and white were in for a busy few hours and, in the event, the race car was satisfactorily repaired.

Fabi switched to his spare car thanks to an electrical problem; Senna, 10th in the warm-up, tried both cars, settling for the designated race chassis; Tambay reported his engine was 500 revs short; Jones had a wheel bearing problem; Mansell was startled to see very high fuel consumption figures on his onboard computer, while Piquet, sixth-fastest, had nothing to report other than a strapped wrist, the result of his crash during practice.

As the cars formed on the grid, the team principals gathered around Piquet's car to display a message for the Williams boss: 'Don't worry Frank – we are minding the store' was an adequate summary of the feelings of the entire pit lane.

Sentiment was put to one side as the cars took the green light. As Senna fish-tailed into the centre of the track, Piquet made a hesitant start while Mansell, timing it perfectly, aimed for the gap between the two. Senna held his ground through the first right-hander but the Williams was right there. Rather than sit and watch the Brazilians have each other off on the first lap, Mansell found himself confronted by Senna, a familiar first-lap senario at the end of 1985. On each occasion, Mansell had lost out. What would he do this time?

The Williams was clearly the better car and Mansell could not resist the temptation as he pulled from the slipstream of the Lotus as the two cars, heavy with fuel and showering sparks from the skid plates, rushed into the braking area for the fast left-hander at the end of the back straight.

There is no question that Mansell was alongside as they began to turn in. But Senna was not about to chance the slippery outside line and he was determined not to alter course despite the presence of a Williams front wheel by his left

shoulder. Mansell then hesitated slightly as he was forced to take to the edge of the circuit. With Senna remaining resolute, there was nowhere to go. When Mansell backed off completely, the balance of the car was upset and the Williams went sideways before mounting the kerb and charging towards the armco lining the inside of the corner. As Senna kept his slithering car under control, the Williams thumped the barrier, tearing off the left-front wheel. Senna 3; Mansell 0.

Who was to blame? Opinions were sharply divided. Senna was clearly risking his own race, never mind Mansell's, by refusing to back off. Mansell, technically, was in the right. It could be argued, too, that Senna should not be allowed to get away with gross intimidation. But moral stand-offs do not win races. Mansell knew Senna's mentality better than anyone else and, since he had the superior car, it would, perhaps, have been wiser to wait rather than attempt a move in the highly charged opening moments of the race. Then he could have dealt with Senna conclusively – as Piquet was about to demonstrate.

The incident had given Senna the feeling that he may have picked up a puncture and, as he blasted down the main straight for the second time, he waved his arm in the air, a vain attempt

to warn his team, watching from the pits, that a change of tyres might be necessary.

Before the start, Piquet reckoned that Mansell would be his only opposition. It was clear, therefore, that a pecking order had yet to be established within the team and the unexpected bonus of finding himself challenging for the lead may have prompted Mansell's disastrous course of action. Whatever the reason, Nelson knew he simply had to bide his time. He took a look at the Lotus on lap two. On lap three, he ducked swiftly out of the slipstream and chopped firmly across Senna's bows once he had established the lead as they reached the end of the straight. After that, Piquet began to pull out about one second a lap. Barring either a mechanical failure or bungled pit stops, the race would be his.

And, for a while, Senna seemed assured of second place. Arnoux was third but the Ligier was offering no threat since he was about to be passed by Alboreto's Ferrari. Rosberg was fifth but that would be a temporary affair since a piston in the TAG engine was about to destroy itself thanks to a programming problem with the electronic box causing the incorrect mixture to reach the cylinder in question.

As for the other McLaren, Prost had made a

January
Lotus sign Johnny Dumfries after protracted negotiations with Derek Warwick and Mauricio Gugelmin.

Robin Herd, Director of March Engineering, awarded CBE in New Year Honours.

Niki Lauda accepts post as 'official adviser' to BMW.

Henri Toivonen (Lancia Delta S4) wins Monte Carlo Rally.

February
Bertrand Fabi killed while testing Ralt Formula 3 car at Goodwood.

Derek Warwick and Eddie Cheever sign for Jaguar.

Beatrice withdraw sponsorship from Haas Indycar and Formula 1 teams.

Ford-Cosworth turbo engine tested in Haas-Lola at Boreham.

March
Four spectators killed on Portuguese Rally; leading drivers pull out.

Frank Williams seriously injured in road accident while returning from test session at Paul Ricard.

Proposal to restrict Formula 1 qualifying to one day does not receive unanimous approval from constructors.

FISA fine Brazilian Grand Prix organisers $50,000 as punishment for Brazilian government officials stopping practice on Friday when their demands for free tickets were not met.

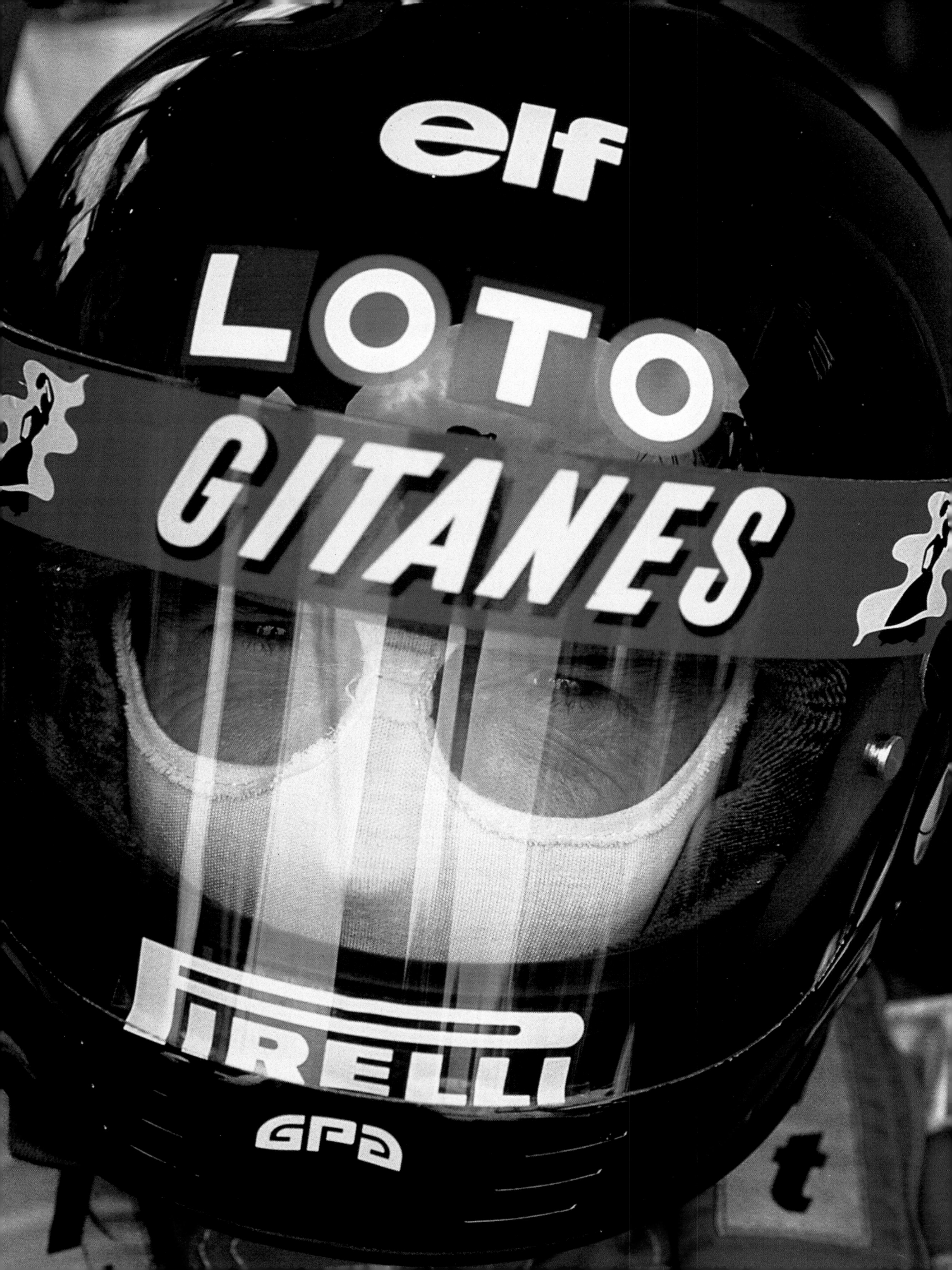
elf
LOTO
GITANES
PIRELLI
GPA

Jacques Laffite: four points for the oldest man in the race *(left)*.

Home win. Ayrton Senna helps Nelson Piquet wave the Brazilian flag after the Williams-Honda had outstripped Senna's Lotus-Renault *(right)*.

reasonable start but he then hesitated long enough to allow a handful of cars push him down to 13th place at the end of the first lap. He was into his stride now and moving towards seventh place behind Patrese's surprisingly rapid Brabham.

Matching Prost's progress, but a few places down the order, Andrea de Cesaris was driving a Minardi like it had never been driven before. By the time the Italian had hurled his car into seventh place on lap 15, the team had given the game away. The haze of fuel vapour emerging from the back of the car suggested a less than circumspect turbo boost setting and it was clear that the team had no intention of reaching the finish – assuming the fuel tank was full in the first place. The news that the car eventually coasted to a halt on lap 17 with 'turbo/engine trouble' was difficult to take seriously.

By lap 14, Piquet led Senna by 10 seconds. Alboreto's third place was coming under attack from Prost, the McLaren making a serious attempt at overtaking the Ferrari at the end of the back straight. Alboreto gave Prost the 'Senna treatment' and the Frenchman wisely backed off in time. On the next lap, he gathered more momentum and claimed the inside line a little earlier.

At about the same time, the pit stops began, de Angelis coming in first on lap 14. The Tyrrell team had decided to make an earlier stop since the tyre wear would be at its heaviest while running a full fuel load and Brundle duly made his stop on lap 15. Johansson lost sixth place when he stopped a lap later and the pit lane really came alive two laps later when Piquet, Alboreto and Patrese peeled off for fresh tyres. Everything went according to plan – which was more than could be said for Brabham as de Angelis reappeared on three wheels, his left-front having detached itself after it had been incorrectly seated during his stop a few minutes earlier.

Up at the front, Prost had caught Senna and it was clear from the sliding Lotus that the Brazilian's stop was overdue. Senna offered no resistance when Prost assumed the lead on lap 20 and, a lap later, the Lotus was in the pits.

As the race began to settle down, it was obvious that McLaren were attempting to get by with just one stop. Prost was leading with Piquet a distant second but, with the Williams gaining at least three seconds a lap, it was clear that the McLaren tactic was not working. By lap 27, Piquet was leading once more.

Prost was in for his tyres a lap later. He rejoined in third place behind Senna but, two laps later, he was back in the pits for good with an engine failure similar to Rosberg's.

Lap 31: Piquet led Senna by 25 seconds. Arnoux was 40 seconds behind the Lotus but the Ligier driver was about to be caught by his team-mate to inject some life into what was becoming a tedious race. A steady drive by Dumfries, helped by Tambay's retirement with a flat battery caused by a broken wire from the alternator, saw the Lotus move into fifth place at the expense of Martin Brundle, but the Lotus driver's excellent debut was about to receive a setback due to an unfortunate series of events.

An electrical problem caused the Renault V6 to lose power and when Dumfries called unexpectedly in the pits, he caught the Lotus mechanics by surprise. They were prepared for Senna's stop and, in a moment of confusion, Ayrton's tyres were being bolted onto the wrong car when someone spotted the error. Eventually, the tyres were fitted since both drivers were using the same compound but, by now, Senna was due and Dumfries was hustled out of the pits without having the original problem sorted out! And, the stop had taken 39 seconds.

Dumfries completed a slow lap with the misfiring engine, during which time Senna passed him and headed for the pits. That stop went according to plan and once Senna had been dispatched, the team were able to attend to Dumfries's problem. He rejoined to find his car running strongly enough to enable him to set fourth-fastest lap of the race. Ninth place would be an inappropriate reward for a drive which should have earned championship points.

Senna, meanwhile, was second once more and although he closed to the gap to 14 seconds, his fastest lap was bettered almost immediately by Piquet. From that point on, Senna cruised home since he was in no immediate danger from the battling Ligiers. Arnoux's heavy demands on his fuel and tyres began to tell in the closing stages and he had no option but to allow the crafty Laffite into third place with ten laps remaining. Brundle, a lap down and having difficulty with fifth gear, had moved steadily into fifth place and, at last, he

would score championship points – officially. (His previous points had been wiped out by the disqualification dramas of 1984.)

Gerhard Berger, his Benetton carrying racy pastel colours on the sidewalls of his Pirellis, took sixth place as the Austrian nursed the car home with the same electrical complaint which had caused team-mate Fabi to make an early and time-consuming pit stop. The little Italian returned several laps down though there was a taste of what might have been when he set second-fastest lap.

Philippe Streiff took a steady seventh while Elio de Angelis was as surprised as anyone when the Brabham actually managed to finish, albeit lacking second and fifth gears. Patrese had retired at half-distance when a water hose broke and the field was depleted further when the Ferraris retired, Alboreto breaking another fuel pump drive and Johansson becoming stuck in the sandy run-off area after his car had run out of brakes.

As Ferrari and TAG suffered a negative return on their weekend's work, the Renault engines never missed a beat, all six finishing a race which had wiped out half of the field. And Senna had run the latest EF15 with the pneumatic valve gear although, at the end of the day, the Lotus-Renault package was about a second-a-lap off the Williams-Honda pace. Senna had predicted as much before the start. 'I think I have done all that I can here this weekend', he said before the start. Nelson Piquet would agree with that; Nigel Mansell had other ideas.   M.H.

89

Gran Premio
TIO PEPE de
ESPAÑA

The Spanish Grand Prix returned to the calendar for the first time in five years and, although the Jerez circuit did not prove popular with spectators, the race provided a dramatic finish between Ayrton Senna *(right)* and Nigel Mansell *(below)*.

'I just did it . . . didn't I?' A sweat-stained Nigel Mansell climbed from the cockpit to claim what he thought might be a brilliant last-ditch victory – but it turned out to be second place by 0.01s! That was the unbelievable, wafer-thin margin by which his charging Williams-Honda FW11 had failed to snatch victory in the inaugural Spanish Grand Prix at Jerez from the clutches of Ayrton Senna's Lotus 98T. What had started as a low-speed procession of a race involving six cars, erupted into a spine-tingling two-car chase highlighted by Mansell's stupendous haul back into contention after pitting for fresh rubber with only eight of the 72 laps left to run. What looked like a demonstration run for pole-man Senna suddenly turned into one of the most dramatic, heart-stopping chases of recent years as the Englishman brought the crowd to its feet in a storming side-by-side finish to round off the contest. The McLaren-TAGs of Alain Prost and Keke Rosberg finished third and fourth, their drivers duped into believing they were in dire fuel consumption trouble, but in reality hamstrung by faulty cockpit readouts, while the reliable Benetton B186s of Teo Fabi and Gerhard Berger completed the top half-dozen. The previous Spanish Grand Prix had seen the late Gilles Villeneuve beat a four-car bunch of rivals across the line by the margin of just over a second – but that was kid's stuff compared with Formula 1's first visit to Jerez. It was a classic, by anybody's standards!

Keith Sutton

ENTRY AND PRACTICE

After an absence of five years, Spain finally rejoined the World Championship calendar with a race at the brand new Jerez autodrome near Seville, leaving Jarama, its former Grand Prix venue just outside Madrid, as a footnote in the pages of Formula 1 history. It was a little hard to understand the economics and finances behind building this superbly equipped new circuit in the heart of Spain's sherry-producing country. Despite the circuit's up-to-the-minute specification and facilities, it was difficult to see how the promoters could be expected to make much of a profit on the gate. Although the stage was set for one of the closest F1 finishes, the serried ranks of grandstands remained, for the most part, empty throughout the weekend. If ever one needed proof that modern-day Grand Prix racing is a child of the television age (and little else) then Jerez provided a copybook demonstration of that adage.

The customary organisational hiccups which seem inevitably to bedevil fledgling Grands Prix hampered the Jerez organisers on the first practice day. Problems with marshals' passes resulted in a badly delayed schedule for which FISA, rather unsympathetically, fined the organisers 50,000 dollars a couple of weeks later. Most people felt that the problems of running a new Championship race were quite demanding enough without such a flagrantly uncharitable piece of posturing on the part of the sport's governing body, which is itself hardly a fine example of efficient bureaucracy.

The circuit was adjudged quite satisfactory by the drivers, if rather on the bumpy side. Although computer predictions suggested lap times in the 1m 52s bracket, pole position turned out to be half

a minute faster as Ayrton Senna demonstrated that the track might have been tailor-made for his Lotus 98T with its powerful hydraulic valve-lift Renault qualifying engine. Bottoming out in spectacular clouds of sparks all round the circuit, Senna underlined his brilliance with a 1m 21.605s on Friday afternoon. This was not only good enough for pole, but so comfortably dominant a performance that Senna could afford to spectate for much of Saturday qualifying, displaying an almost insolent confidence which must have driven his rivals mad with frustration. Only when it seemed that fellow Brazilian Nelson Piquet was getting uncomfortably close with his Williams-Honda did Ayrton relinquish his place against the spectator fence and strap himself into the cockpit.

He need not have bothered; Piquet barely came within 0.6s of the Lotus team leader's best time and Senna was quicker than the Williams in that second session anyway. It was the Lotus marque's 100th pole position since Stirling Moss started the habit at Monaco in 1960 with Rob Walker's private Lotus 18.

However, there was rather more to it than simply Senna's excellence behind the wheel, a punchy engine and a superb Ducarouge chassis. The fact that the spare qualifying spec 98T scraped its belly on the track far more than any of its contemporaries put rivals in a suspicious mood.

April

Shah Alam and Surfers Paradise withdraw from 1986 FIA Sports Prototype World Championship.

Plans for Grand Prix circuit in Barbados unveiled.

There were dark rumours that the Hethel car's side pods were flexing, allowing the underside, protected by stellite rubbing strips, to touch the track and develop ground effect in a manner not envisaged by the spirit of current flat-bottom regulations. Certainly the Lotus was very stiffly set up, raising depressing echoes of the absurd 1982 'go-kart' era. Such was the pummelling Ayrton received over the Jerez weekend that he immediately took off to Austria for a secret physiotherapy session with Niki Lauda's mentor Willi Dungl in order to soothe the aches and bruises in his neck and back.

Ayrton, whose mechanics had worked flat-out to replace an engine after an oil-line came adrift during Friday's untimed session, was suitably coy about his whole Friday performance, although the frustration he reflected had a curiously pre-planned ring to it. 'The car was too hard for me today, wrongly set up; we were running too low and bottoming out everywhere. But it was worth it . . .' It was also *intended!*

That notwithstanding, the Brazilian worked out his qualifying tyre combination to perfection. The Jerez track surface threw up a performance peculiarity which had been encountered by many teams the previous summer in Montreal: soft race tyres seemed to give more grip than out-and-out qualifiers. Ayrton opted for 'B' compound fronts, but complemented them with soft 'E' compound rears. It proved to be the perfect balance.

Piquet, who had spun off attempting to challenge Senna for pole in Brazil, had a similarly trying time at Jerez. During Friday morning's untimed session he slid his Williams FW11 across one of the circuit's murderously serrated kerbs, inflicting considerable damage to the underside of its monocoque. The chassis had to be stripped

91

Elio: deep in thought with the BT55.

down for repair overnight, so Nelson transferred to the spare FW11 for the rest of the weekend. He used this to set his best time on Saturday afternoon and join Senna on the front row, his 1m 22.431s best achieved despite running wide at the pits hairpin on this quickest lap.

Nigel Mansell exuded a mood of controlled competitiveness from the start of the meeting, determined not to be lured into what he considered the trap Senna had set for him at Rio. He survived a slightly worrying moment during Friday qualifying when former team-mate Keke Rosberg misjudged the speed at which Nigel's Williams was catching his McLaren coming up past the pits: Rosberg moved over on him and the Englishman got into a huge fishtail as he was edged off-line onto the dust. Keke came over and apologised quite sincerely after the session.

On Saturday morning Nigel briefly tried Nelson's rebuilt race car which was now the designated team spare, finding that it 'felt OK, but there's still a slight aerodynamic imbalance there somewhere'. In final qualifying he switched back to his race car and managed 1m 25.576s for third place on the grid, despite getting tangled up in traffic on both his runs.

The McLaren International squad felt guardedly confident about its Jerez prospects, having pinpointed a programming problem with the onboard computer which had been responsible for the piston failures on both MP4/2Cs at Rio. Both World Champion Prost and his partner Rosberg complained of a touch too much understeer for their preference, but wound up qualifying solidly fourth and fifth, confident about their prospects for the race.

'I reckon we're qualifying nearer the times that we can produce in the race than most others', grinned Prost. 'I think I'm really starting to get the hang of the car now', added Keke, 'although some of these quick corners are a bit like trying to thread the eye of a needle!'

Riding the crest of a wave of confidence following their strong 3-4 finish in Brazil, Ligier twins Jacques Laffite and René Arnoux came to Spain fresh from a productive test session at Nogaro. The destiny of the team's sole hydraulic valve-lift race Renault V6 was settled in Jacques' favour by the spin of a coin, although Arnoux qualified sixth on 1m 24.274s on Saturday after his Friday efforts were frustrated by electrical problems and he had to wait until Laffite had finished with his race car before he could set a time. Laffite wound up eighth on 1m 24.817s which he set on Friday.

Cast in the Team Lotus supporting role as usual, Dumfries unfortunately damaged the undertray of his Lotus 98T over a kerb during pre-practice testing on Thursday, slightly damaging a radiator mounting in the process. The car was repaired for Friday morning, but then a gearbox input shaft failed and he was late out for first qualifying with a replacement gearbox fitted. The undertray had to be wired up as it failed to fit properly, so Johnny's Friday efforts were thwarted when it dropped down midway through his quickest lap. On Saturday he sliced four seconds off to qualify on row five, then stopped

with a broken driveshaft on his second run.

The Benetton-BMW équipe stopped off at Jarama for a day's chassis testing on the way down to Jerez, the B186s now able to run qualifying rubber effectively now that Pirelli had come up with a stiffer sidewall construction which better suited Rory Byrne's chassis design. On Friday Teo Fabi was baulked on his best run and felt unsettled by an excessively long brake pedal movement, while Gerhard Berger continued to complain of poor engine response out of the corners.

Fresh engines were fitted to both Benettons for second qualifying and although neither driver managed to improve, Berger qualified an impress-

ive seventh, two places ahead of his Italian colleague.

Over in the Ferrari camp, Michele Alboreto and Stefan Johansson were hardly suffused with delight by the lively ride their F186s were producing over the Jerez bumps. The most famous of Italian teams arrived in Spain in a somewhat up-tight mood as Andrea de Cesaris's Minardi-MM had just completed a testing stint at Fiorano during which a high-boost run on super sticky rubber had sent the Commendatore bellowing for his men to sally forth and restore the team's honour. This sort of time-wasting morale boosting is precisely the attitude which undermines Ferrari's serious F1 efforts, and it left both drivers in

bad moods as they wrestled their mounts over those tarmac ripples.

Both drivers agreed that the cars needed more downforce. 'It's OK going into the corner', said Johansson, 'but the moment you get hard onto the power it just washes out into massive understeer'. After surviving a brief petrol fire in the engine bay, Stefan qualified 11th with his team-mate two places further back after breaking two driveshafts on Friday whilst experimenting with a new differential.

Martin Brundle was looking forward to racing the new Tyrrell 015 for the first time in Spain, but spun into the guard rail behind the paddock – in full view of the Data General guests – during his first run with qualifying boost and soft rubber. 'I started out using the race engine which we'd employed for the preliminary test at Silverstone', explained Martin rather ruefully, 'then we put the Q-engine in for Saturday and now this happens. I must have gone too hard too soon, cooked the rear tyres and then lost grip. A shame, because although we're a long way off giving Lotus and Williams anything to worry about, it's a chassis with great potential.'

The front of the 015 monocoque was badly rumpled so Martin had to race the spare 014, although his Friday best in the new car prior to the crash earned him 11th place on the grid. Team-mate Philippe Streiff actually spun his 014 on the same corner as Martin's indiscretion, pirouetting to within a couple of lengths of the abandoned car, but he was able to resume unscathed. He finished 20th on 1m 27.637s.

Despite an intensive programme of development testing since their abortive Rio debut, the lowline Brabham BT55s were hardly yet a credit to Gordon Murray's reputation. Despite the incorporation of redesigned intercoolers, revised gearbox cooling and new rear suspension geometry (to rectify a factory drawing office error on the original components!) the BT55s simply staggered out of the tight corners so slowly that they could hardly get out of their own way.

On Friday the team got down to the task of working out suspension settings for the first time, but it made little overall improvement. Patrese qualified 14th on the strength of his Friday best after a misfire intervened to spoil final qualifying, and a dejected de Angelis was right behind him.

Right behind the Brabhams was an elated Jonathan Palmer, the Zakspeed équipe having made a lot of progress on throttle response in the three week break since Rio. Avoiding any recurrence of the turbo surge he encountered at Rio, the Doc kept out of trouble and turned a 1m 26.918s to line up just ahead of the Team Haas Lola-Harts.

Smaller turbos for improved throttle response had been fitted to Brian's 415T engines for Jerez, but a progressively slipping clutch hampered Alan Jones's efforts on Friday. The following afternoon he qualified an encouraging 17th, while Patrick Tambay lined up alongside him after a qualifying run which included 'passing a Benetton, Dumfries's Lotus and Streiff's spinning Tyrrell'. He was pretty happy with that.

A spate of BMW engines damaged against the rev limiters as the rear wheels bounced over the bumps spoiled everything for Arrows teamsters Thierry Boutsen and Marc Surer, 19th and 22nd respectively by the end of qualifying, while the gutless Osella-Alfas vied with the unreliable Minardis in an all-Italian battle for the last four positions in the line-up.

RACE

Sunday dawned cold and bright, making it difficult for the cars to work their tyres up to the correct temperatures during the half-hour warm-up session. McLaren prospects looked good with Prost and Rosberg at the top of the lists and Goodyear's 'B' compound was chosen for the race by all the Akron runners. Berger switched to the spare Benetton after suffering a misfire on his race car while both Tyrrells were showing a worrying tendency to pump most of their oil out into the breather tanks, so these breathers were re-routed back into the main tank before the start of the race.

Going out on the parade lap Piquet was amazed to find his FW11 understeering wildly. 'I don't know what's happened to it since the warm-up', he told Patrick Head on the grid, 'but the front wheels don't feel as though they are connected to the rear'. He would just have to make do, for there was no time left to change anything. Senna led everybody off on the parade lap, briefly paused under the starting gantry and then made a copybook getaway to lead into the first right-hander.

Piquet, still constrained by the BMW four-cylinder starting technique, in which touching the rev limiter was usually fatal, fluffed his start and Mansell took a long look up the inside into the opening corner. However, he wisely thought twice about anything so ambitious, dropping in behind the other FW11. At the end of the opening lap it was Senna pursued by the two Williams cars, then Rosberg, Prost, Arnoux, Laffite, Dumfries, Johansson, Alboreto, Brundle, Berger, Tambay and the rest of the bunch. Fabi came trailing into the pits to have his Benetton's nose section replaced after touching Laffite on the first corner, while Jones's Lola had collided with Palmer's Zakspeed midway round the lap and the Team Haas car lay abandoned on the dusty outfield with a rear wheel hanging off. Palmer managed to limp back to the pit entrance where he retired with a well-mangled right-hand side pod.

Nannini's Minardi broke its transmission before the race had begun and de Cesaris's sister car succumbed to a similar fate second time round. Senna led the field confidently, holding down the pace to suit his fuel consumption readout, while Piquet was unable to pose much of a challenge thanks to that understeer problem. Mansell, worried about his own initial fuel readout, conservatively dropped back to fifth and took it relatively easily for a while, allowing Rosberg into third. An indication of the relatively leisurely pace was the fact that both Ligiers were hanging on at the back of the bunch and the Ferraris, Johansson heading Alboreto, were closing in gradually.

By the end of lap 11 Stefan was lining up Laffite's seventh-place Ligier in his sights, but that was the last we saw of the Swede's Ferrari.

TECHNICAL FILE

ARROWS
Tested Dunlop carbon-fibre discs.

BENETTON
Used BMW engine with long intake trumpets; had room inside bodywork to deal with this. New pick-up points for rear suspension. Used carbon-fibre cover, closely fitting rear discs.

BRABHAM
Continued with long list of modifications, the most important being to the rear suspension. Drawing office error resulted in incorrect machining of components. New position for larger radiator for gearbox. Larger Behr intercooler; water supply for intercooler spray system carried in deformable nose structure. Fuel system modified by BMW. Engines fitted with long trumpets to give better torque at low revs.

FERRARI
New chassis for T-car meant the 1985 156/85 could be dispensed with. Little change to cars since Brazil except for revised front anti-roll bar and stronger fixing plates for disc brakes. Continued to use Ferrari manufactured calipers. Ran revised turbo, along with modification to transmission. On Saturday, Johansson's car fitted with double rear wing; both cars had this arrangement for the race. Tried Marzocchi gas-filled shock absorbers during the two-hour practice session on Thursday.

LIGIER
Tested new rear wing with additional top plate to give extra downforce for slower circuits. Wing tested at Nogaro and fitted to Laffite's car for the race.

LOLA
New brake ducts (tall and thin, similar to McLaren) front and rear. Smaller Holset turbo to give more progressive response.

LOTUS
Only team to use new airbox for Renault engine as, unlike Ligier and Tyrrell, 98T bodywork could accommodate it. In the event, only used by Senna. Ran front vertical fins.

McLAREN
Fine-mesh grille fitted to turbo inlet duct.

MINARDI
Worked on revised gearbox in search of reliability. Race cars fitted with different rear wing arrangements.

OSELLA
Nothing new.

TYRRELL
New 015 for Brundle. Chassis similar to 014 but lower in fuel tank area; chassis generally more rounded. Engine cover enclosed the entire engine. Longer underbody. Inboard rear brakes dispensed with. Pushrod suspension front and rear. New casting for gearbox. The only car to have radiators exiting through top of side pod.

WILLIAMS
New brake ducts at rear. Double discs fitted to front of T-car. Piquet's race chassis damaged on kerbing on Friday; floor panel repaired but car put to one side for emergency use only.

ZAKSPEED
New airbox, following problems in Rio. Revised front wing with new side plates. New rear suspension with additional anti-squat due to different angle of top wishbone.

G.P.

Midway round the 12th lap the brake pedal simply plunged to the bulkhead and the Fl/86 ploughed straight off into tyre-lined guard rail, bouncing back again after a shuddering impact which left the monocoque destroyed and Johansson badly shaken and bruised. He staggered from the cockpit and collapsed by the side of the circuit, from whence he was transported to the circuit medical centre in such precarious fashion that he reckoned he'd had more chance in the Ferrari's cockpit! Subsequent detailed examination of the Fl/86 revealed a brake bleed nipple to have become unscrewed, allowing all the brake fluid to leak away.

Patrese's Brabham BT55 was an early casualty with gearbox failure while both Osellas succumbed to engine failure. Senna edged away a length or so from lap 13 onwards, but Piquet clawed back that minuscule advantage four laps later, in part aided by de Angelis's Brabham trying to push Senna off the circuit when the Lotus lapped Elio's BT55 shortly after it resumed following a tyre stop at the end of lap 16!

By lap 19 Mansell's fuel readout was bang on target again, so Nigel sprinted through to take fourth place from Prost. Arnoux and Laffite were next in line from Alboreto, Berger and Dumfries, with Brundle's Tyrrell hauling in the Scot's 98T.

Streiff was the next casualty with a Renault engine that seemed to have pumped out all its lubricant, notwithstanding those earlier modifications, while Alboreto coasted slowly in to complain of a very peculiar feeling from the front of his Ferrari. Detailed examination revealed that a wheel bearing was breaking up, so he unbuckled his harness and climbed from the cockpit, his work over for the afternoon.

Lap 24 saw Arnoux drop from the fray, stopping to investigate an irritating misfire: he lost several laps having the trouble sorted out, resuming at the tail of the field only to be sidelined with driveshaft failure a few laps later.

Mansell was getting very charged up for a lead challenge and dived inside Piquet to take second place at the start of lap 34 and Prost, not wanting to be left behind, displaced Keke to take over fourth spot as the contest began to pick up pace. Six laps later Piquet's Williams-Honda expired in an expensive cloud of smoke, so now Prost had a clear run at the leaders.

As Nelson's FW11 pulled off just beyond the pits, Mansell did a good job wiping out Senna against Brundle as the leading duo came up to lap the Tyrrell, a perfect manoeuvre which seemingly left the Englishman in great shape. He had no worries about fuel consumption and, once ahead, drove his own race at his own unflustered speed. Within a few laps he had opened a 3.5s advantage over the Lotus and it looked as though he had taken command for good.

Further down, fortunes were mixed. Rosberg, who had earlier turned up the boost and grained his tyres, was now paying the apparent penalty of that earlier enthusiasm in terms of reduced grip and worrying fuel readout figures. He relinquished any hope of staying with the leaders and began to drop away. On the other hand, Brundle had the old Tyrrell 014 well tanked up and had

Never a dull moment. No matter which way you looked, there was something of interest during the Spanish Grand Prix *(left)*.

Mansell eases ahead of Senna moments after they have crossed the line to record one of the closest finishes in Grand Prix racing. Senna won by 0.014 seconds *(below)*.

pushed Dumfries out of sixth place before a death rattle from the camshafts announced the engine's demise due to lack of lubricant.

Just when it looked as though Mansell had it in the bag, he began to realise he had a problem. He could feel the rear end sliding round more than it ought to be and he was gradually losing grip. The rear diffuser panel was becoming detached and a rear tyre had picked up a bit of debris and was now losing pressure. Senna gradually came back at him as the Williams pit monitored Nigel's progress over the radio link and it was made clear to Mansell that pre-heated new tyres were all ready for him the moment he wanted to come in. By lap 66 Prost had closed in to make the leading bunch a threesome, Senna saw a gap and dived through midway round lap 68 and Nigel headed for the pit lane at the end of that lap.

What followed was an absolute classic of a chase. Everybody held their breath as the Williams lads slapped on four fresh Goodyears in less than ten seconds and Mansell erupted back into the race to record a 1m 29s lap from a standing start: his fastest flying lap was a mere 1.3s quicker!

There were eight laps to go now and Nigel was third behind Prost, some 19.4s behind the leading Lotus. Then it was 15.3s, 12.8s, 8.67s . . . all on successive laps! Now he was on Prost's gearbox, but there was no simple way past. For half a lap he struggled to find the right moment before bursting through the McLaren cordon and streaking off after Senna.

The odds were impossible. On lap 70 Mansell was 5.3s adrift. It was unthinkable! On lap 71 he was 1.5s behind. It was amazing! By now Senna was driving on his consumption gauge and his mirrors and, coming down into the final hairpin, the Williams came surging onto his tail, lining up for a final sprint to the line. Out of the corner and

Senna weaved uncharitably; but this was the last lap and Mansell wasn't to be intimidated. He hurled the Williams alongside the Lotus as they catapulted towards the chequered flag and took the lead a millisecond after they crossed the timing line!

It had been the closest Grand Prix finish since pint-sized Peter Gethin pipped Ronnie Peterson at Monza 15 years earlier, Senna's official winning margin being one-hundredth of a second. The fact that Dumfries had retired with gearbox trouble, or that Tambay's Lola had been delayed with a misfire and a pit stop to sort out a guide which was fouling its brake pedal, or even that the McLaren's potential victory run had been stymied by an inaccurate computer readout, were all interesting asides, but very much by-the-by . . .

Senna had calculated the win perfectly; but Mansell, at last, had calculated how to handle Senna . . .   A.H.

Gran Premio di
SAN MARINO

At Imola in 1986, the efficiency of the fuel metering unit bolted to the engine turned out to be more important than the prowess of the man strapped to the driving seat. Electronic wizardry may have ultimately given Alain Prost victory but it also caused the McLaren driver some desperately anxious moments during the last lap.

In 1985, Prost had run out of fuel after taking the flag (only to be disqualified at the post-race check). In 1986, he ran out of fuel *before* the finish but, on this occasion, he stuttered across the line, his car this time conforming to the 540-kg minimum limit.

Fortunately for the Frenchman, Nelson Piquet was not nearby as the McLaren driver swung his car from side to side, forcing the last drops into the fuel system. The Williams driver had gone through his particular form of fuel abstinence earlier in the race as he heeded dire warnings from his computer. With the miles-per-gallon recovering to a healthy average, Nelson put the hammer down in the last ten laps. But, at the end, he was 7.6 seconds too late. With Keke Rosberg having run out of fuel and second place two laps earlier, anything resembling a motor race at Imola on 27 April was purely accidental.

Last gasp. Alain Prost creeps across the line, his McLaren out of fuel. Gerhard Berger makes what could have been a serious tactical error by holding back to prevent unlapping himself, the Benetton driver taking third place *(below)*.

ENTRY AND PRACTICE

Journalists preparing their practice stories at Imola probably wished they had brought a carbon copy of their report from Jerez and, for that matter, Rio. Quickest, yet again: Ayrton Senna. Second fastest: Nelson Piquet. Third: Nigel Mansell. Just as it had been in Brazil and Spain. And, following the usual script, no-one had even looked like approaching Senna's incredible pace.

As in Spain, Senna set his best time on the first day although he was far from happy with his car or his driving. Saturday, he said, would see an improvement but, unlike the majority of his rivals, Ayrton did not do better in the final session. He was the fastest, yes, but even he could not repeat the blindingly fast lap of the previous day as the 98T darted and pattered across the bumps, its suspension stiff, the ride height low enough to cause sparks to fly – in every sense of the expression.

There were muttered accusations from rival designers that the Lotus was creating a form of ground effect, an assumption fuelled by sparks cascading from the sides of the car rather than from the middle. 'How can a supposedly flat-bottomed car be doing this?' they wanted to know. Nevertheless, no-one actually laid a protest; to clear the air, FISA inspected the car, along with three others, and declared it legal.

While Ayrton blamed traffic on Saturday, team-mate Johnny Dumfries had a more serious problem to contend with. Eleventh-fastest on Friday, Dumfries had to wait helplessly on Saturday and watch his name slide to 17th spot while his mechanics attempted to complete an engine change in time. They finished with four minutes remaining – just enough time for Johnny to get comfortable before the chequered flag came out.

There was never any question of Dumfries

having the spare car since this was for Senna's exclusive use. Dumfries maintained a polite silence and, it was at times like this that the wisdom of not signing another top-line driver to partner Senna was apparent. It would have been difficult to imagine Derek Warwick, say, standing idly by under similar circumstances . . .

Any plans Williams may have had for tackling Senna were swiftly disrupted when Piquet had an engine blow on Friday morning and Mansell was delayed by a misfire. Nigel opted to run a set of Cs to check the engine in the afternoon before running qualifiers (Es). On Saturday he moved from fifth to third on the grid; good, but not as quick as his team-mate.

Nelson lost 20 minutes of the Friday qualifying session as the engine change was completed and he eventually set second-fastest time on his third run, using a mixed set of Es. Clearly, there was a margin for improvement. Another engine failure on Saturday morning, however, meant it would have to be attempted in the T-car.

A missed gearchange at the end of his first run lost valuable tenths but the second run was an improvement. He followed this with a third on mixed tyres; then a fourth. On this last lap, Piquet used every ounce of his considerable talent to persuade the car to stay on the track when, judging by the opposite lock required, the tyres had long since submitted to the searing Honda horsepower. 1m 25.569s, almost two-tenths quicker than his second run, was a remarkable achievement, worthy of second place on the grid.

Matching Piquet's spectacular style, but not, unfortunately, his lap time, Keke Rosberg adopted lines and angles which were uncommon for a McLaren driver. Alain Prost, as usual, was deceptively neat and it was the Frenchman who finished the quicker of the two despite problems working his front qualifying tyres to a temperature to match the rears. There were the usual quietly voiced complaints about a shortage of horsepower in qualifying and it was in this area that Rosberg certainly missed the benefit he had enjoyed with Honda in 1985.

So far, the grid was following the form dictated in Brazil and Spain – with one exception. Splitting the McLarens, much to the delight of the partisan spectators, was the scarlet Ferrari of Michele Alboreto. Ferrari had carried out a lengthy and worthwhile test at Imola and their aim, at the very least, was to score championship points (their first of the season) on home ground.

The drivers reported that the balance of the F1/86 was much improved and certainly, judging

The compact dimensions of the Ford turbo are clearly evident.

by the lurid slides, there was plenty of horsepower available during qualifying. The speed trap figures backed this up but, of course, the race would be a different story. There were continuing worries about the brakes, for example; not a comforting thought for the drivers as they rushed into Tosa or down the hill to Rivazza. Indeed, Stefan Johansson suffered a recurrence of this problem during his first run on qualifiers. A slow puncture on his second run kept him in seventh place more than half a second behind Rosberg.

René Arnoux, in eighth position, was the quickest Pirelli runner which said much for the Frenchman's skill since the Ligier team reckoned the Italian rubber was better suited to the Benettons of Gerhard Berger and Teo Fabi, ninth- and tenth-fastest. Major changes to the set-up of the Ligiers were required to make the most of the Pirellis during qualifying, the drivers opting for different solutions. Arnoux favoured less wing while Jacques Laffite preferred more downforce, the latter being held up badly by de Cesaris as he tried to improve on 14th place in the final session.

The Benetton drivers' practice was hampered by engine misfires and fuel pick-up problems. The delay was so great that on Saturday morning Fabi spent his time working on a full-tank set-up for the race while Berger concentrated on a quick combination for the final practice session. Then, the engine problems returned . . .

A piston failure on Friday morning caused Patrick Tambay to miss most of the afternoon session while the Hart engine in his Haas Lola was changed. The following day, however, a combination of smaller turbos and the latest-spec Hart engine saw the Frenchman take an excellent 11th place, something which pleased Tambay greatly in the light of the attention being showered on the Ford-Cosworth powered Lola of Alan Jones in the garage next door.

This, in fact, was to be Brian Hart's last race for the forseeable future and the irony was that his four-cylinder motor had never run better thanks, in part, to the late discovery of an installation problem on the FORCE-designed and prepared car. The British engine company had certainly learnt a lot since their debut at the same circuit five years earlier.

Looking back on lessons learned in 1985, when Thierry Boutsen finished second at Imola, the Arrows team switched their A8s back to the same set-up as 12 months previously after both Thierry and Marc Surer had complained about unpredictable handling. The change obviously worked as Boutsen claimed a worthy 12th place – despite the usual carelessness shown by de Cesaris while being lapped – in the final session, while the hard-working Surer, one of his runs spoiled by a misfire, was 15th.

The Tyrrell team had worked hard to repair Martin Brundle's 015 after the damage incurred during practice at Jerez but the resulting lack of testing with the new car was reflected by 13th place for the Englishman. Apart from a reluctance to change direction at the chicanes, the Tyrrell-Renault became breathless after 10,700 rpm and a cure could not be found. In addition a leak from the water injection system in the nose of the car gave

TECHNICAL FILE

ARROWS
No change.

BENETTON
Ran revised rear suspension as tested by Fabi at Vallelunga; different fixing points for top wishbones to increase anti-squat. Ran BMW engines with longer trumpets.

BRABHAM
New rear suspension geometry with different length for pushrod. Ran vertical front wings with three-piece winglets mounted on side pods.

FERRARI
Had tested a smaller one-piece airbox and a four-piece exhaust system exiting beneath revised undertray but none of these items appeared at Imola. New chassis for Johansson featured a different fixing point for top wishbone and other small changes. Revised profile for rear wing. Completely new fuel system after pipes leading to electronic injector had leaked and caused a fire at Jerez.

LIGIER
Race cars ran Renault engines with revised plenum chambers; engine covers modified to suit. New position for wastegate exhaust.

LOLA
Ran Ford engine in THL-2 chassis – 15 cm shorter than THL-1 due to reduced dimensions of V6 compared with the Hart 415T. Fuel tank lower but otherwise chassis and aerodynamics more or less the same. Used AP calipers with Hart-engined car while Ford Chassis used new calipers made by Alcon. THL-2 ran an intercooler in each side pod; THL-1 continued with one radiator on right-hand side for water and oil. Replaced electronic box on top of engine with a smaller version mounted on fuel tank.

LOTUS
The subject of speculation over methods used to achieve ground effect during practice. Titanium rubbing strips placed on underbody, just ahead of rear tyres. Used a hydraulic set-up pioneered by Brabham on the BT49 at the time of the rigid side skirts. Hydraulic jacks could be seen on top of the shock absorbers with pipes connected to a box mounted in front of steering, the aim being to run the car as close as possible to the ground and gain additional ground effect, even with a flat bottom. Did not run vertical front wings and fitted larger brake ducts and a double rear wing.

McLAREN
No change.

MINARDI
De Cesaris's car fitted with airbox similar to Ferrari. One large side exit for radiator instead of two. Bodywork three kilos lighter.

OSELLA
Unveiled an unfinished chassis with new suspension (pullrod) and revised aerodynamics and bodywork.

TYRRELL
015 damaged in Spain now repaired. Engine cover modified to accept Renault engines with revised plenum chambers.

WILLIAMS
Problems with rear underbody in Spain led to stiffer fixing points. T-car ran twin discs at the front during practice; other chassis used the larger of two AP calipers available. Enriquez Scalabroni, an Argentine ex-Dallara engineer responsible for the revised suspension and bodywork on the FW10 in 1985, present at a race for the first time; spent most of the weekend monitoring the Lotus pit.

ZAKSPEED
Ran new electronic control, regulating air to the turbo through a butterfly system similar to McLaren.

G.P.

Stefan Johansson was hardly jumping for joy at the end of a difficult drive with his brakeless Ferrari. Michele Alboreto had little to be pleased about either, the Italian losing a steady fourth place (which might have been third) with a turbo failure (left).

Alessandro Nannini cancelled an impressive performance during practice by crashing his Minardi on the first lap (below).

Erich Zakowski entered a second Zakspeed for Huub Rothengatter, a move which meant Jonathan Palmer no longer had a spare car. Rothengatter's return to Formula 1 was understandably lacklustre (bottom).

Brundle's feet a continual soaking. Philippe Streiff, of course, had to persevere with the older 014 and he damaged a rear corner when he spun off in the closing minutes of practice on Saturday morning. The mechanics did well to repair the car in time, Streiff running a set of Cs before an abortive attempt on qualifiers to improve his previous best.

The Tyrrell team's misfortunes were doubly significant since they had secured additional sponsorship from the Italian Kelémata company. But if Tyrrell were vexed by their problems, they were operating with cheerful optimism when compared to the turmoil in the Brabham pit. Playing before the Olivetti and Pirelli principals, the lowline BT55s were abysmally slow out of the corners, so much so that they barely managed to stagger through the speed trap ahead of an Osella. By the end of the straight, however, speed trap readings showed the blue-and-white cars to be among the quickest.

Hampering progress was a series of gearbox problems and leaking clutches which required the removal of the gearboxes to effect repairs. The net result was a late appearance by both drivers in the final session and marginal improvements worth 16th and 19th on the grid. Mr Ecclestone's team had enjoyed happier days.

Boosted by a win for Lancia at Monza the previous weekend, Alessandro Nannini and Andrea de Cesaris flung their Minardis around Imola in a haze of high boost from the MM motors and, surprisingly, it was the former who set by far and away the best time, Nannini taking 18th place on a circuit he knows well. De Cesaris, by contrast, was the more untidy of the two and distinguished himself by blocking other drivers, his best effort being a second slower than his team-mate.

A tight-lipped Jonathan Palmer maintained a diplomatic silence when questioned about the Zakspeed team's decision to run a second car for Huub Rothengatter. Palmer's feelings could be imagined when his car developed a severe misfire on Friday morning and he had to sit out most of the session. With the spare car now Rothengatter's race car, Palmer had no option. In the afternoon, Palmer was baulked – by, among others, Rothengatter – but progress was made on Saturday. Then, just as he was completing a quick lap in the final session, the left-rear suspension broke, spinning the Englishman to a harmless but infuriating halt.

Bringing up the rear were the Osella drivers, the financial crisis within the Italian team being illustrated by welding on the cylinder heads of the Alfa Romeo engines and the appearance of a half-finished version of a new car. This did nothing to raise the morale of either Christian Danner or Piercarlo Ghinzani, and the latter managed just half a lap on Sautrday before his engine failed.

RACE

Rain during the night left an overcast sky and the threat of a wet race. The warm-up, run on a damp track, did not allow the teams to learn much although Laffite discovered that his pneumatic Renault V6 was sufficiently down on power to warrant changing to a more conventional 'valve spring' engine for the race. Rosberg and Prost, first and third-fastest, were split by Senna but, of more significance, the Ferraris were down in ninth and 12th places while Berger was fourth and Tambay eighth.

As the pit lane opened at 2.0 p.m., a light shower doused the track, the drivers cautiously setting off on their warm-up laps. Prost completed two laps in his spare car before stopping for a planned change to his race car, which he preferred. As the World Champion left the pits, he met Martin Brundle, running in with the unenviable task of explaining to Ken Tyrrell how the 015 Tyrrell had left the track and crashed heavily into the barrier about half a mile from the pits. Still searching for a cure to the performance problems with the Renault engine, Brundle had been keen to pack in a few laps and check the value of one or two last-minute changes. Now, for the second race in succession, he would revert to the 014 model; only, on this occasion, Brundle had not driven the older car for a single lap during the previous two days.

Fortunately, the rain had stopped by the time the cars left the grid for the final parade lap. For the second year in succession at Imola, Jonathan Palmer was destined not to take the start from his grid position, this time because the Zakspeed's engine would not fire.

Marshals had just managed to push the Zakspeed to the pit lane exit when Senna led the field onto the grid. On the green, the Lotus made a perfect start which was matched by Piquet. Mansell, the first indications of an engine misfire bogging the Williams down, was slow to get away; an unfortunate occurrence from Alboreto's point of view since he had shot off the line only to be forced to back off as he tried to squeeze between Mansell and Prost.

By the time they had reached Tosa, Piquet had powered past Senna while Rosberg had taken advantage of Mansell's problem to slot into fourth behind Prost. Further back, Nannini threw away all his hard work during practice by colliding with another car and wrecking the left-front suspension on the Minardi, the Italian retiring on the

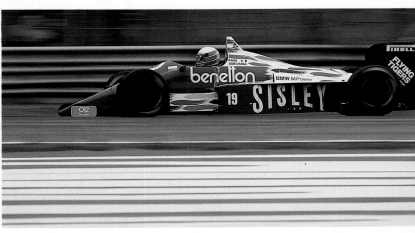

Patrick Behar

spot.

As Piquet began to pull away, Mansell fell further behind and, at the end of lap three, he was in pits to see if anything could be done about the electrics. The black box was changed but, two laps later, the Williams stopped for good with a blown engine.

The fourth lap had seen a change to the leader board as Prost passed Senna on the run to Tosa, Rosberg pushing the Lotus down to fourth at the exit of the corner. Bearing in mind that Senna had run out of fuel while leading the previous year's race, it was reasonable to assume that he was playing a cautious game. In fact, Ayrton's somewhat tardy performance was being governed by a vibration from the back of the car.

Patrick Tambay felt a vibration of a different kind when his Hart engine cried 'Enough!' on lap six, thus ending, for the time being, Brian Hart's participation in Formula 1, exactly five years after

making his debut with Toleman. For Monaco, Tambay would have a Ford engine similar to the one in the back of Jones's car, currently lying in 13th place.

While the winner of the 1983 San Marino Grand Prix climbed from the Lola, Keke Rosberg made clear his views about winning in 1986 as he overtook his team-mate and claimed second place. Prost made use of the fuel-conserving draught provided by Rosberg's car as they ran in tandem but it was soon evident that they were making little impression on Piquet, the gap being 5.6 seconds after nine laps.

At the end of that lap, Dumfries arrived in the pit lane to report a problem at the rear of the car, which was a pity since the Scotsman had made a good start from 17th place on the grid and had been lying 13th at the time. He returned for one more lap but it was no good. As Dumfries arrived back in the pit lane he found Senna stationary

with exactly the same problem; a broken right-wheel bearing. This was later attributed to the machining of a flange to the incorrect tolerance; the first of a new batch had been fitted to each car as part of the pre-race preparation so the problem had not occurred during practice. Other sources, however, suggested that the uprights may have been flexing.

That lack of quality control removed Senna from the permutation of likely winners and, around this time, Piquet's hopes of carrying on to the chequered flag took a sharp knock. His monitoring device showed he was using more fuel than he should have been and, as he backed off, the McLarens closed to within a second. Alboreto was ten seconds away in fourth while the Benettons of Fabi and Berger had displaced Johansson, the Ferrari driver having been forced to pump his brakes from as early as lap four.

Jacques Laffite, making his usual rapid prog-

The pace of the San Marino Grand Prix was dictated by the dashboard-mounted fuel consumption monitor *(far left)*.

The Benettons of Gerhard Berger and Teo Fabi ran in tandem for many laps. Fabi *(left)* retired when a missed gearchange caused a broken valve on the BMW but Berger *(below left)* scored points yet again by finishing third.

Alan Jones renewed his association with Ford at Imola *(right)*.

Lukas Gorys

ress during the race, had also caught and passed the Ferrari to take eighth place but then his Renault engine began to lose boost and, after two stops, he called it a day. Arnoux, up to fifth once Senna had retired, had been in for tyres much earlier and was now in ninth place and closing on the Brabham of Patrese.

Around lap 26, the leaders began to make their pit stops, the Ferrari team sending Alboreto out in just 8.4 seconds to allow the Italian to maintain his fourth place ahead of Berger and the flying Arnoux, the Ligier having dispatched Patrese and capitalising on subsequent pit stops by Fabi and Johansson. The main interest, though, lay in how Piquet, Rosberg and Prost would fare when they made their stops.

Piquet was first. The wheel-change seemed reasonable but Nelson was slow to get away and, all told, the stop took 13.29 seconds. One lap later and Prost came in for an 8.62-second stop, good enough to put him ahead of Piquet on the road and in a position to take the lead once Rosberg had made his stop on lap 33.

This was a near-disaster: Rosberg and Ron Dennis suffered a breakdown in communications which saw Keke remove his foot from the brake before the left-rear wheel nut had been tightened. By the time the McLaren was back on the ground, 14.8 seconds had gone by, Keke rejoining in second place, some way behind his team-mate but ahead of Piquet who was continuing to cruise, as per instructions from the computer.

Lap 35: Prost led Rosberg by nine seconds with Piquet a further seven seconds behind and dropping back, thus allowing Alboreto to nibble at an 11-second deficit, much to the approval of the crowd. Half a minute behind the Ferrari, Arnoux continued his vigorous drive, with Patrese, enjoying an excellent run on hard Pirellis, not far behind in sixth place. Both the Ligier and the Brabham had overhauled Berger as the Benetton driver nursed his car along without a clutch, anxious not to abuse the gearbox unnecessarily. All three, of course, were the sole representatives for their respective teams; Laffite having retired not long before de Angelis went out with a blown engine and Fabi stopped with a broken valve on his BMW, the direct result of a missed gear-change.

During lap 45 Prost, using his brakes and gearbox rather than the retardation from the TAG, had managed to pull further away from Rosberg who, in turn, was 17 seconds ahead of Piquet, the Williams driver now having his mirrors full of red Ferrari. Then, with about ten laps remaining, Piquet received permission from his onboard controller to take off. The fuel consumption figures were now making sensible reading after his enforced economy.

Sadly, Arnoux retired at this point when, of all things, a wheel came off, the little Frenchman parking himself out of points after another impressive drive. That let Patrese into fifth place with Johansson sixth and Berger seventh. With the knowledge that he had fuel in hand and that his gearbox was standing the strain of clutchless changes, Berger closed on the Ferrari as Stefan continued to struggle with his almost brakeless

car. On lap 54, they came across Brundle (lying 10th) who was closing on Ghinzani (a couple of laps behind and about to run out of fuel). As Brundle nipped past the Osella, Berger took the opportunity to trap Johansson and power past the Ferrari. Berger then almost fell over Brundle and Johansson replied immediately as they rushed down the hill towards Ravazza. In the end, the thought that the Ferrari might not stop at the bottom of the hill settled the issue in Johansson's mind and Berger was away after some pretty desperate weaving on his part.

Lap 57 saw another change to the leader board as Alboreto relinquished fourth place and rolled into the pits, the tips of the turbine wheel on the Ferrari having broken. This was the result of attempting to run a leaner fuel mixture in the interests of economy.

Now there are just three laps to go and Piquet is right with Rosberg. The Williams has just set the fastest lap but Rosberg, having measured his fuel carefully, feels he can hold Nelson off.

Then the McLaren runs out . . . Rosberg's shrug of despair as he climbs from the cockpit says all you need to know about onboard computers which give incorrect readings.

Two laps to go, and Patrese, having just taken a remarkable fourth place with the Brabham, coasts to a halt. All this helps elevate Berger to third place, a lap behind Prost who, in turn, is nearly half a lap ahead of Piquet. With the computer showing 3 litres of fuel in hand, Prost confidently, if carefully, sets off on his last lap. Accelerating out of Rivazza, the TAG coughs and almost dies . . .

There is about a mile to go. Prost desperately swings the McLaren from side to side. The engine picks up fuel and propels the car forward. At Variante Bassa the engine stutters again. More urgent sawing at the wheel is followed by a final burst of power – good enough to carry Prost onto the pit straight for a gentle coast to the line. Seven-point-six seconds later, Piquet and his Williams-Honda blast across the line. Had he begun his late charge half a lap earlier . . .

Berger takes third, the Benetton catching the struggling McLaren of Prost at the final corner. Thinking quickly, Berger backs off and decides not to unlap himself since that would mean another lap with a clutchless car which might run out of fuel.

Berger subsequently received wide acclaim for his cool approach. In fact, it was the wrong move. Piquet, for all Berger knew, could have run out of fuel on his last lap, in which case Berger would have taken second place. And what if Berger had run out? It would have made no difference; he would still have finished third, since Johansson, the next man through, would have taken the chequered flag a lap behind.

Such complicated equations, easy to evaluate away from the tension of the race track, summed up the San Marino Grand Prix and the fuel capacity restrictions of 1986. It wasn't *racing* by any stretch of the imagination. But these were the rules and all the teams had to play by them. And, in that context, Alain Prost did a better job than anyone else – convincingly so. M.H.

FORD RETURN

It was natural, if inappropriate, to recall the debut of the Ford-Cosworth DFV in 1967. That, after all, was a major milestone in the history of Formula 1 when the V8 took pole position and went on to win the Dutch Grand Prix with Lotus. Now, in 1986, we had the latest Ford engine: the turbocharged V6, designed by Keith Duckworth to allow Ford to pick up where they had left off after 155 Grand Prix victories with the DFV.

No one, least of all the Ford personnel, honestly expected a repeat of that remarkable performance at Zandvoort 19 years previously. Formula 1 had changed beyond recognition and the mood within the Haas-Lola team was one of caution.

For a start, the long-awaited 120° unit, remarkably compact in the back of the THL-2 chassis, would not enter the high-boost qualifying race necessary for a favourable grid position. The emphasis in this low-key operation was on gradual learning; with that in mind, the team was well-satisfied with 21st place on the grid for Alan Jones.

The only problem during Friday's qualifying had been a slight oil leak from the gearbox bell-housing followed by a vibration, traced eventually to the left-rear brake caliper fouling the inside edge of the wheel rim. Jones had qualified 17th but he was unable to improve in the final session when his first run on qualifying tyres was spoiled by traffic. During the second and final run, the exhaust manifold cracked and that was that.

In typical fashion, Jones did not hang about at the start of the race, the 1980 World Champion working his way into ninth place by lap 14. Then the rather convoluted gear linkage worked loose and required a pit stop. Ten laps later, a manufacturing fault on the water radiator put Jones in for a lengthy halt while the radiator was changed. Unfortunately, it was not bled properly and the Lola retired eventually with overheating.

It may not have been Zandvoort 1967 but it was an encouraging debut, Jones commenting that the V6 was progressive, the smooth power delivery making the car easy to drive. Certainly, Ford had done enough to warrant goodwill visits from various team principals, anxiously casting an eye to the future.

April

Eden Donohue, widow of Mark Donohue, receives $9.6m in an out-of-court settlement with Goodyear and Penske, following Donohue's fatal accident at the Austrian Grand Prix meeting in 1975.

FISA fine organisers of Spanish Grand Prix $50,000 for organisational shortcomings at Jerez.

Grand Prix de MONACO

Well-deserved applause for Prost after a faultless drive *(right)*, Rosberg's second place took McLaren to the top of the Constructor's Championship *(below right)*.

'All that hard work – and he beats me by four-tenths of a second.' Nigel Mansell, a non-qualifier on Thursday, examines the lap times after Prost had eased the Williams driver off pole position in the final minutes on Saturday *(below)*.

It was not an enthralling race by any means. In fact, it was the usual procession headed, once again, by Alain Prost, although that understates the McLaren driver's brilliance. Prost did not dominate simply by preventing others from overtaking; he scored his second win in as many weeks by taking an impressive pole position and then disappearing into a world of his own where the only worry would be maintaining concentration for almost two hours. The closest anyone got to the World Champion was when they were being lapped.

Keke Rosberg's vigorous charge into second place injected an element of – whisper it – overtaking! Ayrton Senna, his Lotus no match for the McLarens, hung on to finish third, the Brazilian in turn getting the better of Nigel Mansell's sluggardly Williams-Honda.

Finishing was the prime objective here, 12 of the 20 starters achieving their aim. It might have been 14 at the chequered flag had Patrick Tambay and Martin Brundle not ended a lengthy battle for eighth place when the Lola and Tyrrell collided, Tambay completing a spectacular aerial roll. Neither driver was injured but Brundle's helmet carried a tyre mark as a graphic reminder of the special demands of racing at Monte Carlo. And, for the third year in succession, it was Prost who mastered them with deceptive ease.

ENTRY AND PRACTICE

The race, we knew, would prove little. The highlight of this overblown spectacle would undoubtedly be the qualifying sessions on Thursday and Saturday as the drivers earned the right to take part in Sunday's parade. With 26 drivers going for 20 places on the grid, the struggle among the lower order would be just as intense as the battle for a place at the front. With overtaking being severely limited, a prime position would have increased significance.

In fact, overtaking proved extremely difficult during practice itself, each driver explaining away his grid position by shrugging and saying 'Traffic'. Each driver, that is, except Alain Prost.

The secret this weekend lay in looking after your tyres. A set of well-managed qualifiers could see you through four or five laps – take Prost's final session as an example.

Thursday had been a bit of a disaster for the World Champion despite having set the fastest time during the unofficial session in the morning. In the first qualifying period Prost clipped a barrier, a rare error which forced him to switch to the spare car and accept fourth-fastest time. He had everything to go for on Saturday.

Waiting for a fuel leak to be rectified, Prost then ventured out at the half-hour mark and improved his previous best by almost two seconds. Traffic had been the problem, of course, so he returned ten minutes later with his second set of qualifiers. Cruising just off the pace, he put in four laps, all the while assessing the situation; a slow car here, one just leaving the pits there. Then, with eight minutes left, the road ahead was clear and his tyres were still in good shape. With finger-tip precision, he lapped the track at just over 90 mph

to snatch pole from Nigel Mansell, the lap being so smooth that those watching knew nothing about it until the times were announced.

Spectators, on the other hand, had a fairly shrewd idea that Mansell would be among the fastest, the Williams skimming the armco at the exit of Casino Square lap after lap. On his quickest run, the Williams actually brushed the barrier for about 25 metres, the driver never dreaming of lifting off . . .

In the space of half an hour or so, Mansell had not only secured a place at the front of the grid, he had ensured that he would have something to do on Sunday afternoon. Before the start of the final session, Mansell, the man who had started from the front row during the previous three Grands Prix at Monaco, had been a non-qualifier.

This had been brought about by a fundamental error in the programming of the engine management systems. On Thursday, Honda had suffered no less than four engine failures and, halfway through the first qualifying session, they simply

ran out of cars. Nelson Piquet had been rather more fortunate than Mansell since he had managed to put in a time good enough for 13th place; it may not have been brilliant but at least he was in the race. If it rained in the final session, Mansell, 22nd-fastest, would be a spectator.

Fortunately, the fine weather which attended the entire weekend ensured that the final session would not be disrupted but, even so, Piquet had troubles of his own, a down-on-power engine forcing a switch to the spare car and subsequent gear selection trouble keeping him in 11th place. He would pay for it dearly in the race.

So, Mansell was on pole, only to be demoted by a 1m 22.627s from Prost. Where was Senna while all this was going on? Quickest on Thursday, Senna revealed his hand during the closing minutes of the unofficial session on Saturday by recording a staggering 1m 22.340s. No-one, surely, could match that? No-one did. And neither could Senna when it really mattered.

The final session started off well enough when Ayrton, one of the first out on the track, recorded 1m 23.538s to consolidate pole. Then came a lull as marshals cleared away the pool of Agip dumped at Tabac by de Cesaris's Minardi. While the men in orange suits massaged the oil with cement dust, the clock kept ticking, leaving about thirty minutes of good running time. When Mansell took pole with 1m 23.047s, Senna returned to improve his time still further – but it was not enough. He kept circulating but each lap was spoiled by slower cars, the entire pit lane seemingly on the track at once. On one occasion he made a stunning exit from Casino, only to find Berger and Tambay motoring slowly and gesticulating at each other. The man who considered pole to be his property reluctantly returned to the pits where he

described the situation to the man from *Autocar* as 'stressing' . . .

For Johnny Dumfries, practice was a disaster. He had experience of Monaco thanks to an undistinguished Formula 3 outing in 1984 but that was no substitute for packing in as many laps as possible in the Lotus. And, from that point of view, he did himself no good by locking a brake and charging the barrier at Massenet on his second flying lap on Thursday morning. That meant no further laps until the plunge straight into qualifying. The understandable lack of confidence and commitment showed as he steered away from the walls until the crown wheel and pinion broke after 11 laps. On Saturday, gearbox trouble impeded his progress further and, despite a seven-second improvement, he was a non-qualifier in a car which, in theory, was capable of winning the race.

Joining the other Lotus on the second row was Michele Alboreto, this due solely to the efforts of the driver. The Ferrari danced and pattered across the bumps as Michele converted the inherent understeer into oversteering slides by heavy applications of throttle. His one banzai lap was a full second quicker than anything he had done before, which says much about his bravery and the fact that all four wheels of the F1/86 were damaged at the end of it!

Poor Stefan Johansson was in another race, the Swede taking 15th place after the most frustrating practice session imaginable. *Every* time he appeared in Casino Square, he was baulked, de Cesaris being the culprit on at least two occasions. Having slipped from 10th, Johansson rounded off a miserable final session by being the unwitting party in a nasty incident in the pit lane. As the Ferrari driver entered the pits, he clipped Jean

Sage with a rear wheel, throwing the Renault man into the air. Fortunately, what at first looked like serious head injuries for Sage turned out to be mild concussion and a broken shoulder.

Gerhard Berger continued to confound everyone by looking as though he was about to hit the barrier at any minute and yet he contrived to remain in complete control. Fifth-fastest was a fine reward for a spectacular effort, all his troubles being confined to an engine fire on Thursday morning and a misfire on Saturday morning.

Indeed, the Benetton team's problems lay with Teo Fabi's race car which had developed a nasty tendency to bounce at the front end and drag the Italian towards the barrier. No immediate cure could be found and he switched to the spare car to find another three seconds and move from 19th to 16th spot on Saturday.

Before Monaco, the betting was that Benetton and Ligier would fight for the honour of being the best Pirelli runner. Brabham, on their Imola showing, did not merit a mention. However, since the San Marino Grand Prix there had been considerable activity in Chessington and Munich as the engineers searched for improved traction and bottom-end power from the lay-down engine. To that end, much of the hardware of the side pod had been moved further back and the engine men had discovered that much of their trouble lay in the exhaust configuration. This was changed and the results were dramatic, Riccardo Patrese holding second place on the grid until the final 15 minutes. Even so, he was pleased with sixth place. Elio de Angelis, on the other hand, just scraped onto the back of the grid, a misfire ensuring that he was one of three drivers who failed to improve their time in the final hour.

In fact, had justice been done – a rare thing during practice in Monte Carlo – René Arnoux would have topped Benetton and Brabham. The little Frenchman was on sparkling form, urging the Ligier into third place on Thursday. He was all set to at least hold that place on Saturday when he became involved in a contretemps with Mansell during the closing stages of the morning session. According to the Williams driver, he had been blocked by the Ligier on a number of occasions and, when Mansell found car 25 in his way while the Williams was equipped with a set of qualifiers,

enough was enough. The two made contact, Arnoux's car becoming airborne before thumping the barrier on the approach to Rascasse. The JS27 was badly damaged and Arnoux was consigned to the spare, which happened to be fitted with a race engine. He finished the day in 12th place, two rows behind team-mate Laffite. Jacques, seventh-quickest on the first day, held that place despite spoiling a run by failing to warm his qualifiers properly. None the less, he was poised for a typical Laffite run into the points.

There were Ford engines for both Tambay and Jones at Monaco, relegating Brian Hart to the role of an interested spectator. And Hart was the first to concede how quick Tambay looked as he confidently hurled the Haas Lola through Casino, the lack of explosive qualifying power from the turbo not mattering quite so much on this circuit. The frustrations of trying to find a clear lap had reduced Tambay to a spark-spitting fury on Thursday but he made amends in the final session

by working his way into 11th place, despite warming a set of qualifying tyres too quickly. For Alan Jones, it was a complete reversal of fortune, the Australian basking in sixth place on Thursday but dropping to 18th on Saturday when a front wishbone broke as he tried to find a clear lap.

Row five: Keke Rosberg and Martin Brundle. Thursday had seen the McLaren take second-fastest time with a typically lurid Rosberg lap, the antithesis of Prost's stealthy style. Keke continued his energetic progress to improve by a second in the final session but it was only good enough for ninth place at the end of a final session bedevilled with traffic.

On Thursday, Brundle had been the only British driver to qualify, and that was thanks to a carefully calculated lap on rapidly deteriorating qualifying tyres at the end of the session. During the 48-hour break, serious thought was given to the handling and, by Saturday, the 015 Tyrrell looked much more impressive as Brundle thor-

oughly enjoyed a clear lap and his car's dramatic improvement. Philippe Streiff, having the benefit of an 015 for the first time, made little progress on the first day when a broken oil-line caused a gearbox failure. On Saturday, though, a superb effort in a basically unfamiliar car saw Streiff move from non-qualifier to 13th-fastest.

As ever, the Arrows drivers had to work very hard with their elderly cars, the narrow power band of the BMWs making each lap a furious mixture of rapid gearchanging and sawing at the wheel, Boutsen qualifying half a second quicker than Surer. That left Jonathan Palmer as the final qualifier to share the back row with de Angelis, Palmer's Zakspeed cutting a spectacular lap which saw him take Casino on the very limit and run flat-out round the outside of a slower car in the tunnel.

Palmer's team-mate, Huub Rothengatter, never looked like qualifying but the same could not be said for the unfortunate Piercarlo Ghin-

René Arnoux made a nonsense of the belief that overtaking is difficult at Monaco, the Ligier driver charging into fifth place after a troubled practice.

Nigel Snowdon

zani, the Italian taking the Osella by the scruff of its untidy neck and just failing to make the cut by less than a tenth of a second. Christian Danner could not be accused of failing to try although each ragged lap gave the impression that it would be his last. And right at the bottom of the list came the Minardis, neither Andrea de Cesaris nor Alessandro Nannini managing to record a single quick lap on Saturday thanks to engine and turbo failures.

RACE

Although spectators were reported to be thinner on the ground than in recent years, there was no shortage of pomp and ballyhooo as the start time approached. The serious business of the morning had seen Prost fastest in the warm-up. That came as no surprise. However, the same could not be said for the second-quickest runner, one Riccardo Patrese in the hitherto troublesome Brabham. And, to show the revival was no fluke, Elio de

Angelis was fifth, the BT55s separated by René Arnoux and Keke Rosberg. Bearing in mind the grid positions, it was significant that Mansell was eighth, two places behind Senna.

Worries about tyre choice rose in accompaniment with the track temperature, the sun shining for the fourth day in succession. Goodyear advised their runners to plan a pit stop while Pirelli took the opposite point of view but, as the cars formed on the grid, Tambay began to believe he would not start, never mind reach the point where a tyre change would be necessary.

An oil leak from a cam-box cover necessitated a hurried switch to the spare car which, unfortunately, had been set up for Jones. This meant removing bits and pieces from Patrick's car as it was wheeled away and, when that was done, it was then discovered that the turbocharger was dripping oil and this, too, had to be changed. Meanwhile, a water leak on Laffite's car led him to swap to the spare chassis and Jacques was not amused to find the field leaving the grid for the final parade lap while he was still in the process of putting on his gloves and helmet. He had no option but to start from the back, a dreadful handicap at a circuit such as this.

Making sure of his pole position advantage, Prost was the first to reach Ste Devote, a corner where it was confidently predicted at least two or three cars would end their race against the barrier. In fact, it was incident-free, Senna having nipped ahead of Mansell on the run in. Capitalising on the gap left by Laffite, Rosberg had made a storming start, the McLaren having moved from ninth to fifth by the time the field had reached Mirabeau! At the end of the lap, Prost led by two car lengths while, at the back of the field, Fabi crept into the pits to attend to a fuel injection lead which had blown off. The Benetton returned some time later out of the hunt and, eventually, out of the race with brake trouble.

Alan Jones, on the other hand, was shortly to retire with a perfectly sound car and, curiously enough, the trouble could be attributed to broken boltheads on the left-rear caliper of Philippe Streiff's Tyrrell! That problem had occurred during the warm-up and the Tyrrell team decided to switch Streiff's car from carbon to cast-iron brakes as a precaution. Going into Tabac on lap 3, the Frenchman, still getting used to the longer brake pedal, stopped a little sooner than Jones expected just as the Australian was having a run down the inside. The two cars touched and spun, Streiff managing to get going again without too much difficulty.

For Jones, it was a different story, the Lola now pointing in the wrong direction. With the leaders about to bear down on him at any moment, Jones wisely decided a three-point turn was out of the question and he motored back towards the escape road at the chicane where, he reasoned, he could turn round in safety. Such logic obviously escaped the man controlling the exit of the escape road and he steadfastly refused to let Jones back out! One very angry Australian but, one needless retirement.

After ten laps, Prost led Senna by five seconds, the Lotus driver barely able to hang on to the McLaren. Mansell had stayed with Ayrton for

TECHNICAL FILE

ARROWS
No change.

BENETTON
Both race cars had modified rear uprights to accept Brembo rather than AP calipers (AP mounted below disc; Brembo at the rear). Side plates to front wings had spring-loaded pivots to prevent excessive ground contact under braking. FISA scrutineer called for a stronger fixing. Both drivers used cast-iron brakes in race.

BRABHAM
Major changes to BT55. Hardwear in side pods pushed back approximately 40 cm to change weight distribution. New position for intercooler did away with long pipes which contributed to poor engine response. Turbo also moved back and placed at a different angle. Exhaust pipe now much shorter. Fire extinguisher, previously under the driver's legs, mounted in rear of right-hand side pod. Tank for water spray (used during qualifying) moved from nose to back of gearbox. Front deformable structure a different design with four mounting points instead of two.

FERRARI
Brought fourth chassis which was not completely finished. As usual, ran engines with more torque at low revs. Used smaller turbos incorporating butterfly assembly, operated mechanically and linked to throttle, to improve engine response. Used Brembo calipers all round. Fitted new rear brake ducts. For Monaco, the step under the front of the chassis filled in. Ran double rear wing.

LIGIER
Ran rear wing with additional top-mounted blade (as seen in Spain).

LOLA
All three cars with Ford engines. T-car featured a different airbox. Ran double rear wings.

LOTUS
Continued with hydraulic system which could be adjusted by driver to affect ride height front and rear. Ran double rear wings and vertical front wings.

McLAREN
John Barnard not present in Monte Carlo. Porsche believed to be working on major modifications which would allow engine to be mounted lower in the chassis.

MINARDI
No change.

OSELLA
No sign of new car. Plans for use of Motori Moderni engine appeared to have fallen through.

TYRRELL
015 for Streiff. Both drivers used thicker carbon-fibre discs but Streiff forced to race with cast-iron brakes.

WILLIAMS
Four chassis available, Mansell's T-car being the chassis damaged by Piquet in Spain (design of tub allowed floor pan to be replaced). Winglets, fitted to side pods during testing at Ricard, not used at Monaco. Small alteration to rear of underbody. T-car fitted with double front discs for Thursday practice only.

ZAKSPEED
Third chassis, lighter and with the facility to run carbon-fibre brakes, now available. Tried double rear wing and winglets at rear of side pods. Longer intake trumpets meant revision to engine cover on Palmer's car.   G.P.

Ayrton Senna blasts out of the tunnel at 170 mph.

May
John Paul Jnr unable to take part in Indy qualifying due to imposition of five-year sentence for racketeering and holding a false passport.
Henri Toivonen and co-driver Sergio Cresto killed on Tour de Corse.
Yannick Dalmas (Martini-VW MK49) wins Monaco Formula 3 race.
Audi Sport pull out of World Rally Championship.

several laps but it was soon apparent that the Honda engineers had not catered for the slow corners, the V6 engine stammering in a manner which had not been obvious during the hectic practice laps as they dealt with other, more pressing problems at the time.

As Mansell began to fall away, there was little danger of the Williams being passed by Alboreto since the Ferrari driver was too busy fending off Rosberg. Patrese, living up to the warm-up promise, had just moved into sixth place ahead of Gerhard Berger while Brundle, after a good start, was coming under pressure from Tambay and Piquet (also in trouble with a reluctant Honda V6 on the exit of slow corners). Behind them, and gaining rapidly, was Arnoux, the Ligier driver clearly annoyed about the injustice of his grid position while, three places behind, came team-mate Laffite, also on the boil because of his starting position. By lap 13, Jacques would have passed Surer, Boutsen and Johansson to take 12th place while René would have moved into 10th spot, ahead of Piquet.

This was running against the expected form since overtaking was supposed to be limited, but one thing was sure – Rosberg would soon pass Alboreto even if it meant climbing over the top of the Ferrari. Energetic as always, Keke made a powerful exit from Rascasse at the end of lap 15, the McLaren running round the outside of the Ferrari and continuing to do so as Michele made life difficult by leaving the minimum amount of room. But it was enough and Rosberg took fourth place as they braked for Ste Devote.

By lap 20, Rosberg had caught Mansell, the Williams then setting the fastest lap so far as he reacted by closing the gap on Senna. Prost, of course, was continuing his serene progress, about 12 seconds ahead of the Lotus. Further back, Patrese still held sixth place although the Brabham was coming under pressure from Berger. Then there was a gap to a bunch of cars led by Brundle with Arnoux next, the Ligier having passed Tambay, who still had Piquet snapping at his heels. About to join this foursome was Laffite, the Ligier having got the better of Johansson as the Ferrari driver struggled not only with terrible handling but also with the additional problem of a broken gear lever on a circuit where the gearshift is used every few seconds. Boutsen and Surer, 14th and 15th, were about to be lapped, while at the back Palmer and Streiff were engaged in their own little battle. The Tyrrell and the Zakspeed were well clear of an unhappy de Angelis as the Brabham driver struggled with low boost, a big disappointment after his encouraging perform-ance in the warm-up.

Mansell, too, was disappointed by his lack of competitiveness. No sooner than Rosberg had taken third place from him on lap 26 the Williams went into the pits for tyres, rejoining in fifth place behind Alboreto. Michele moved into third place when Rosberg made his stop and, at the same time, Patrese brought the Brabham in for fresh Pirellis. The Italian stalled as he attempted to leave his pit and this effectively removed him from the leading contenders, the BMW engine soon to quit out on the circuit.

Lukas Gorys

Stefan Johansson cranks on the lock as he guides his Ferrari through the new chicane leading onto the waterfront.

Philippe Streiff and Martin Brundle prepare for battle, the Tyrrell drivers qualifying comfortably. Streiff went on to finish 11th while Brundle ended an excellent drive under pressure when he and Tambay collided while disputing eighth place.

Arnoux, now into sixth place, having passed Brundle and Berger, was not expected to stop so the Frenchman was poised to make the most of any problems the Goodyear runners might have when they made their stops. Prost was next to come in, the McLaren being dealt with in the usual efficient manner. However, by the time he rejoined, Senna was in the lead, Prost closing quickly as he made the most of his fresh rubber. Getting past, of course, would be another story but Prost knew Senna would be stopping soon. Even so, he seemed to be taking a long time about it and for two laps the slithering Lotus held the McLaren at bay. While all this was going on, Prost became acutely aware that Rosberg was reeling them both in. Prost was also aware that team orders were non-existent . . .

The matter was resolved when Senna peeled into the pits at the end of lap 42 and, from that point on, Prost began to gradually extend the ten-second gap over his team-mate. Senna rejoined just ahead of Mansell, the Williams pressuring the Brazilian for a couple of laps before deliberately dropping back, Mansell's helmet liberally coated in hot Elf sprayed from the back of the Lotus.

By half-distance only four of the twenty starters had retired but that was about to change. Alboreto crawled into the pits with a broken turbo at the end of lap 39 and, four laps later, Berger stopped for tyres only to find that the drive-pegs on his left-rear hub had broken. Nothing could be done and he lost the opportunity of becoming the only driver to score points in each race held so far.

The Brundle-Tambay-Piquet trio had been broken up during their pit stops but, as though pre-ordained, they were running in formation again by lap 54, Brundle leading the group and holding seventh place behind the Ligiers of Arnoux and Laffite.

Ten laps later and they were still together, Piquet breaking rank on lap 68 by passing Brundle on the charge up the hill to Casino. Sensing that Brundle would have been unsettled, Tambay decided to overtake on the approach to Mirabeau but the Tyrrell driver had recovered his composure. Darting from behind the Tyrrell, Tambay found that there was the minimum of room on the bumpy inside line and, almost inevitably, the two cars made contact as Brundle turned into the corner. Wheels interlocked, sending Tambay's Lola into the air where it

completed a somersault before glancing off the barrier on the outside of the corner. The car crashed back onto the three wheels which had remained attached firmly to the chassis and Tambay was able to step from the wreckage. Brundle tried to limp back to the pits but a steering arm, bent during the impact, finally broke as he reached Rascasse. A tyre mark on Brundle's helmet revealed how fortunate both drivers were to emerge unscathed.

Mansell, waiting to lap the pair of them, had a ringside view of the shunt and he managed to pick his way through. Prost, arriving not long after, was confronted by a single yellow flag and he just managed to scrape past the remnants of an incident which merited a more vigorous use of the warning flags.

Having survived that hazard, Prost continued his exemplary drive to the chequered flag, the World Champion motoring quickly but with a minimum of revs and fuss. It was the perfect illustration of how to win at Monte Carlo – by driving as slowly as you dare. Rosberg's flushed features and Senna's glazed expression as they stood on the podium suggested the pace of the McLaren had been too quick by far . . .

THE PRICE OF PROGRESS

How much did it cost to keep pace with Formula 1 technology in 1986? The going rate, according to the organisers of the Monaco Grand Prix, was just under £1m. That was the figure needed to pay for modifications which allowed the AC de Monaco to tailor their circuit to suit the cars.

The tangible result of the reconstruction programme was a concrete extension grafted onto the quayside at the site of the chicane, the object being to do away with the left-right flick in favour of a more pedestrian left-hander, followed by a right leading onto the quay.

Certainly, there had been cause for concern the previous year, drivers saying the chicane had become nothing more than a blur at around 160 mph. A sheer rock face prevented a diversion inland, leaving the construction of an extension into the harbour as the only alternative if the circuit was not to become obsolete.

There were complaints that the new corners, taken in second gear, were too slow, but generally the drivers approved of the modification which added 16 metres to the length of the circuit. It was difficult to gauge the increment in lap time since the levelling of bumps, particularly at the entrance to the pit straight, had speeded things up but, overall, about four seconds had been added.

It was thought that the new chicane would at least provide a much-needed overtaking point after the 175 mph dash through the tunnel. This was not to be, the adverse camber on the inside making such a move treacherous and consigning the cars to the queue which has become the hallmark of Grand Prix racing at Monaco.

A new chicane leading onto the harbour-front prevented the Monaco circuit from becoming obsolete.

Grand Prix de BELGIQUE

Nigel Mansell experienced both ends of the motor racing spectrum at Spa-Francorchamps. His entire weekend had been tinged with thoughts of Elio de Angelis, a soul-mate since the time Nigel had left Lotus after a fraught five-year period together. Now Mansell was enjoying the fruits of his association with Williams but his one regret was that Elio was not there to see it. The Englishman, overcome with emotion, dedicated the third win of his career to the memory of the Italian, fatally injured during a test session a few days previously.

Mansell's victory was thanks to a brilliantly executed pit stop and an intelligent drive thereafter. With careful use of the boost control, he defeated his only rival, Ayrton Senna, the Lotus driver eventually settling for second place and the six points which would move him to the top of the championship. Of the rest, Nelson Piquet seemed set for an easy win until sidelined by a turbo boost control failure, while Alain Prost, caught in a first-corner pile-up, showed what might have been by setting fastest lap on his way to a lonely sixth place.

There must have been times during the weekend when Mansell privately questioned the reason for it all but, in the event, not even a potentially disastrous spin would prevent him from experiencing one of the high points of a sometimes cruel sport.

Pause for thought. Nigel Mansell spares a moment in victory for Elio de Angelis, his former team-mate, after a well-judged win at Spa.

ENTRY AND PRACTICE

The commentator was running through his familiar discourse during the closing minutes of practice. The first day had been the usual battle between Williams, McLaren and Lotus and it seemed that Piquet had just pipped the reigning World Champion for the overnight pole. Nothing new there.

Suddenly, he interrupted his calm statement of facts with a terse announcement: 'Berger on pole!' And then, as though not believing the time which had flashed before him, he repeated the message.

The news came as no surprise to anyone watching out on the circuit. The Austrian had taken the Benetton to the very limit and it was clear that his saloon car experience had given him an intimate knowledge of the sweeps and undulations of this superb track. The question was, could anyone match that time on Saturday and, if so, could Berger find yet more speed from the nimble chassis?

It was not until the last ten minutes of the final hour that Nelson Piquet's name jumped to the top of the list. He had spent Friday at the wheel of the spare Williams since he felt the handling of his race car was not consistent and he would return to that chassis the following morning when his race car stopped with a broken driveshaft. Running a set of race tyres, Nelson was following the theory that qualifiers were barely able to last a lap but, in the end, he did try the softer rubber for that one quick lap – and this in the race car since the T-car had suffered an engine failure, possibly caused by lack of fuel and the subsequent detonation.

He had beaten Berger's time by one-tenth of a second and it was conceivable that the Benetton driver could muster a reply. Berger had already been out but a slight misfire had cost him at least half a second. By now, Piquet had done his best although the Benetton team were to cut it too fine since, by the time Berger completed his warm-up lap, the session had ended just five seconds before, denying him the chance of a final run.

Nigel Mansell, fourth-fastest on Friday, was also looking for an improvement in the final session and he felt confident after setting a 1m 54.5s on race rubber. Switching to the softer Es, he came across René Arnoux halfway through his quick lap. Clearly, the incident between the two at Monaco had not been forgotten as they held each other up, Mansell claiming that Arnoux deliberately slowed in front of him. Whatever the cause, it meant Mansell had to accept fifth place.

In the light of his dominant performance during practice the previous year, third-fastest was something of a disappointment for Alain Prost. On Friday, he had been caught by traffic and, on his last lap, the World Champion found oil unexpectedly at the Bus Stop chicane. On top of that, the car was not as he would have liked it – which is to say, it was not absolutely perfect – but, for the final session, the handling had been improved. He ended the day a couple of tenths slower than Piquet, a discrepancy accounted for by a minor turbo problem which needed attention, but not before he had taken the competitive edge off his set of qualifying tyres.

Keke Rosberg had a more serious problem on Friday afternoon when his turbo suddenly lost boost as he accelerated down the hill towards Eau Rouge. With great presence of mind, Rosberg just managed to stop the car in time to allow him to pull off the track; had he crossed the bridge, there would have been no alternative but to attempt to complete the full lap. As it was, he was in a position to return to the pits on foot and his mechanics were able to retrieve the qualifying

tyres from the abandoned car.

The brake-locking moment had taken its toll however and he found the tyres were finished before the end of his flying lap. On his second run, Rosberg came across Senna on the climb from Eau Rouge and there was little he could do but lift off. Saturday brought no further problems, except that the improvement in his lap time did not keep pace with those around him and Rosberg slipped to eighth place. He was not unduly worried, however, since overtaking would not be a problem at this track.

The same thought probably occurred to Ayrton Senna as he considered starting his second race in succession away from his coveted pole position. In truth, the Lotus never looked capable of carrying the brilliant Brazilian to the front of the grid, a return to the old-style rear suspension (in the interests of avoiding wheel-bearing failures which occurred at Imola) upsetting the balance of the 98T considerably. The black car showered sparks from the rear of the side pods as usual but any advantage this offered was clearly outweighed by the drag penalty, Senna being 19th-fastest through the speed trap at the top of the hill. Rain, perhaps, would be his only saviour in the race although Ayrton could never be discounted, particularly when he casually announced that the car had popped out of third gear a couple of times during his fastest lap . . .

After the dramas with the six-speed gearbox at Monte Carlo, Lotus had switched Johnny Dumfries back to five speeds and, apart from a minor hitch with the detent spring on third gear, he had no problems. Certainly, the fast sweeps of Spa suited the Englishman more than the cramped confines of Monaco and his time, 13th-quickest, resulted from a particularly smooth lap on qualifiers which had passed their best.

Ermanno Cuoghi (left) works on the Minardi of
Andrea de Cesaris but the Italian team was destined
to have another miserable weekend.

Moment of anticipation. Patrick Tambay and
Jonathan Palmer prepare to lead the field onto one
of the most charismatic and challenging Grand Prix
circuits in the world.

Paul-Henri Cahier

Nigel Snowdon

Martin Brundle ended an encouraging performance in the Tyrrell-Renault with gearbox trouble.

May
Elio de Angelis fatally injured during test session at Paul Ricard.
John Foulston buys Brands Hatch, Oulton Park and Snetterton for £5.25m to guarantee future of motor sport at the British circuits.
FOCA sign deal with Silverstone to run British Grand Prix for five years.
FISA announce plans to curb F1 power.
Derek Warwick signs for Brabham.

Teo Fabi was sixth, a performance which would have been considered quite respectable had it not been for the other Benetton parked on the front row. To be fair, it was Fabi who seemed to be carrying the team's troubles for the second race in succession. On Friday morning, for example, he took his brand new car out, only to have the turbo blow up in the biggest possible way, the turbine wheel punching its way through the exhaust and landing in the spectator enclosure! In the afternoon, driving the T-car of course, Fabi had the intercooler fail and he returned to the pits on the back of a motor cycle. With Friday's plans shot to pieces, it was not surprising to find a major improvement in the final session.

René Arnoux's plans received a setback on Saturday morning when an electrical problem sidelined his brand new Ligier. The previous day, both he and Jacques Laffite had been unhappy with the Pirelli qualifiers on the dusty circuit although heavy rain overnight did little to improve things. Arnoux just managed to beat Rosberg's time but, for Laffite, 17th place summed up a final session in which he had a broken gearbox and then a misfire when he switched to the spare car.

Twelve months previously, Ferrari had come away in high spirits from the abandoned meeting at Spa, Michele Alboreto having been among the quickest in the one qualifying session we had seen. Now they were ninth and eleventh, the drivers saying the cars had never been worse. The problem, as ever, was a mixture of understeer and a severe lack of traction, something which revised rear suspension did not seem to cure. True, Alboreto was the fastest (199.667 mph) through the speed trap at the top of the hill in the last session but, elsewhere, the red cars bounced and jumped in an alarming fashion.

Not so, the red cars of Team Haas. Patrick Tambay, tenth-fastest, revelled in the handling of the Lola as he flung it through Eau Rouge, the Frenchman finding that the chassis made up for the lack of qualifying boost on the Ford engine. Indeed, there was drama in that department on Saturday morning when an oil leak caused a fire, the subsequent engine change costing Tambay 15 minutes of the final session. As for Alan Jones, he never seemed to manage a clean run. On Thursday, fourth gear kept jumping out while, in the final session, a broken throttle sensor meant he had to park the Lola near the bus stop chicane – but not before he had managed 16th-fastest time.

Martin Brundle and Ken Tyrrell were pleased with their day's work on Saturday as the Englishman registered ninth-fastest time with a car which was giving the driver great confidence. Then, in the final few minutes of practice, the sun disappeared and Tambay and Johansson pushed Brundle down to 12th! A gap of six places to Philippe Streiff's Tyrrell did not do the Frenchman justice even though he spun his 015 more than once. Streiff put the problem down to an inconsistent brake pedal but Ken Tyrrell was less than willing to accept such an excuse!

Thierry Boutsen's handicap was obvious as he struggled with the old Arrows A8 although a heroic effort on his home circuit was worth 12th

Overnight hero. Gerhard Berger became the man of the moment when he set the fastest time during the first day's practice. He eventually started from second place on the grid, only to become involved in the first-corner shunt *(right)*.

Patrick Tambay, poised to run competitively, got no further than the first corner, his Lola-Ford wiping off the left-front wheel against the Benetton of Teo Fabi *(far right)*.

Stop-Go-Stop. Alan Jones ran strongly until the Lola-Ford, its onboard computer out of action, ran out of fuel in the closing stages *(below)*.

place on Friday. He was set to improve even further with an engine which felt particularly strong but, ironically, the BMW blew up when Thierry tried running more boost in the final session. Marc Surer, meanwhile, was down in 21st place after managing just one quick lap on Saturday afternoon before a valve broke.

Understandably downbeat, the Brabham team busied themselves with one car for Riccardo Patrese. Fastest through the speedtrap on Friday, the BT55 was not putting down the power elsewhere and, to add to the team's difficulties, an engine blew and Riccardo inadvertently over-revved the engine in the spare car when the wheels unexpectedly left the ground. In the final session he encountered an oily track and electrical problems and the only thing remarkable about his time was the fact that it was identical, to the third place of decimals, to that set by Boutsen.

Andrea de Cesaris was the last driver to break the two-minute barrier and team-mate Alessandro Nannini might have joined him had it not been for a turbo fire. Jonathan Palmer, the Zakspeed driver working hard as he struggled with a lack of downforce, tried carbon-fibre brakes for qualifying and although 20th-fastest time was nothing to shout about, the Englishman was pleased with the progress that had been made since they last appeared at Spa. Time had been spent experimenting with different turbochargers to improve throttle response on Palmer's car, leaving team-mate Huub Rothengatter to qualify 23rd, ahead of the Osella team. Christian Danner had a new car at his disposal although it was burdened by an Alfa Romeo engine rather than the Motori-Moderni which the team had planned to run – but could not afford. The ancient V8s gave the usual amount of trouble, particularly during the final session when Ghinzani did not manage a flying lap.

RACE

Patrick Tambay had said all along that he was confident about a competitive race with the Lola-Ford and, sure enough, on race morning he was fifth-fastest behind the McLaren and the Williams teams. Alan Jones, by contrast, was 24th having failed to manage a single timed lap. Time was lost initially with a gear selection problem and then the engine refused to run cleanly, this the result of the faulty master switch. Once the offending part had been traced, the 30-minute session was over and there had been no time to calibrate the cockpit readout for the fuel consumption computer.

If Jones's half-hour had been action-packed, consider the catalogue of disasters which attended Jonathan Palmer's efforts to run the Zakspeed for more than two laps. The boost gauge fell out of the dashboard and a faulty alternator meant the engine would not rev over 6000. Switching to the spare car, he was faced with a broken rev-counter, a sticking throttle and, finally, a piston failure! Elsewhere, de Cesaris and Ghinzani had engine failures and fuel-feed problems meant Danner never left the pits.

In fact Danner, along with Patrese, returned to the pit lane at the end of the final parade lap and,

in retrospect, this was probably the safest place from which to start the race. The tight hairpin at La Source was to cause mayhem as the field jostled for position.

Piquet made a perfect start, as did Prost, the McLaren slotting in behind the Williams on the inside line. Berger took a second or two to get going and, when he did, the Benetton squirmed its way to the right, effectively blocking a charge by Senna. Undaunted, Ayrton moved left to run round the outside of the Austrian as he, in turn, formed up beside Prost under braking for La Source. The three cars were side-by-side as they rounded the corner, Senna's line being, perhaps, a mite optimistic since he clearly intended to emerge in front of Berger, if not Prost.

Prost suddenly found he had nowhere to go and, in an instant, he was a mere passenger as the McLaren and Benetton locked wheels, both cars turning sharp left, Prost then becoming airborne before crashing nose-first onto the kerbing on the outside of the corner. This effectively blocked the way for the rest of the field and cars were going in every direction as drivers tried to avoid instant retirement.

Fabi had been slow off the line, causing Rosberg to take to the grass on the outside. That little diversion over, Keke then made another change to his plans as he took to the escape road to avoid the chaos, the McLaren completing a complete 360-degree turn before picking a way through. Fabi had come to rest alongside his team-mate and the right-rear corner of Teo's car was to snare Tambay's Lola as the Frenchman tried to squeeze through on the inside. Tambay's hopes of a competitive race were smashed – along with the left-front suspension. Prost and Berger, on the other hand, managed to get going even though the front of both cars would need attention.

Piquet, of course, knew nothing of all this as he sped up the hill towards Les Combes, and Senna, in close pursuit, had little notion of pandemonium which he had unintentionally sparked off! As ever, there were one or two drivers who benefited from all this. Mansell, fortunately as it turned out, had been bogged down at the start when his engine hesitated briefly as this allowed him to find a way through to third place. Into fourth came Johansson, followed by Dumfries (from the sixth and seventh rows of the grid!) with Jacques Laffite a handy sixth. His Ligier team-mate, however, had been delayed and Arnoux came through in 12th place behind the Tyrrells of Brundle and Streiff.

Streiff's car was carrying a camera which had given a driver's eye view of the dust and damage at La Source. As the field headed into the country on their second lap, Prost and Berger reached the pits where the McLaren mechanics changed the nose cone and gave the car a quick check-over before sending the World Champion on his way, not long before Piquet arrived at the end of his second lap. Berger was in deeper trouble still, the Benetton team changing a steering arm although they could do nothing about a bent right-front wishbone. He would rejoin two laps down, his high hopes reduced to aiming for a finish at best.

Rushing past the old pits at the start of lap 3, Mansell took second place from Senna to give the Williams team a healthy grip on this race, Piquet being some six seconds ahead of the Englishman. Johansson was pounding along in the skittish Ferrari, his fourth place being protected by Dumfries as the Lotus driver headed a queue comprising Jones, Laffite, Alboreto (making impressive progress), Boutsen and Rosberg.

Lap 5, and Johansson found himself in third place, the happy benefactor of a spin by Mansell at the bus stop chicane. 'It was entirely my own fault', said Mansell. 'I had been flat-out through the kink before it and I couldn't stop in time. I didn't want to go up the escape road and out the other side since there might have been a penalty imposed for that. So, I had to bounce the car over the kerbs very hard, and that made it jump into a spin. Not very clever, was it? But it said a lot for the car that I was able to continue.'

Piquet now led Senna by 10 seconds and soon Ayrton would become the sole Lotus driver as Dumfries spun off at Stavelot and holed a radiator. He had been under pressure from Alboreto since Jones had dropped back, soon to call at the pits for fresh tyres. With Dumfries gone, the midfield began to spread out a little, Rosberg continuing his climb by taking sixth place from Laffite. That would be as far as he would get, however, the McLaren pulling off with engine trouble, and there was a further retirement when Boutsen, doing great things with the Arrows, suffered an electrical problem which caused the BMW to cut out.

By lap 10 Piquet was leading Senna by 8.2 seconds. Johansson was third with Mansell making a strong recovery and soon to take the Ferrari under braking for Les Combes. Alboreto held fifth place and Arnoux was now sixth although his stirring drive was due to be cut short by a broken mounting to the rear wing, possibly the legacy of the first-corner shunt. With nothing to lose, René rejoined to run for five laps with the Renault engine cranked at full boost. Not surprisingly, the V6 blew apart after 21 miles of fairly furious motoring . . .

Nelson Piquet was also running on maximum boost, although not by choice. Cruising easily, the Brazilian suffered a failure on the electronic boost control and, although he tried to continue, it soon became clear that it was a hopeless cause. Switching off, he coasted into the pits at the end of lap 16, an almost certain nine points lost through no fault of his own.

That left Senna in charge although Mansell was closing on the Lotus, and by lap 19 they were less than two seconds apart. The pit stops, due any minute, would be critical.

Mansell came in first and, the way things turned out, that proved to be the best move from a psychological point of view. Senna, the pressure removed, relaxed to the tune of a couple of seconds a lap; vital seconds in fact. Then the Lotus crew, placed next door to Williams, had a grandstand view of a superb 7.9-second pit stop for Mansell. When Ayrton came in at the end of the next lap, the men in black and gold knew they would need to show exceptional dexterity to beat that time.

In the event, they didn't and Ayrton rejoined just as Mansell, his tyres working perfectly,

TECHNICAL FILE

ARROWS
Nothing new.

BENETTON
Switched from Brembo calipers on rear to AP. Front wing side plates still not completely rigid despite stronger fixings. Longer trumpets on BMW engines. Distributor location altered by 45 degrees to avoid problem with engine cutting out.

BRABHAM
Only one car entered after Elio de Angelis's fatal accident during testing at Ricard. No modifications, apart from a return to the narrower entrance to side pods.

FERRARI
First official appearance of Garrett turbos on Ferraris (T-car retained KKK). All cars returned to KKK on Friday and Saturday because Garrett not yet ready for qualifying. Revised rear suspension with new top mounting point for pushrod. New fabricated uprights in one piece (previously part machined). Removed butterfly arrangement from turbo duct (as seen in Monte Carlo). Nose of Alboreto's car had underside step filled in.

LIGIER
Plans to run hydraulic system on suspension shelved after insufficient testing.

LOLA
New chassis for Jones. Ran tall front brake ducts like McLaren. Five engines available incorporating modifications.

LOTUS
Due to wheel-bearing problem in San Marino GP (thought to have been caused by insufficient stiffness in upright), returned to 1985-spec rear suspension. As a result, hydraulic systems could not be fitted and handling appeared to suffer. Mini-skirts fitted to front wing side plates. Used vertical aerofoils behind front wheels.

McLAREN
New chassis (T-car). Recent test session spent working primarily on engine management system.

MINARDI
No further development with present chassis while waiting for new car.

OSELLA
Danner used older chassis in preference to new car which was completely unsorted. New car fitted with rear suspension similar to Lotus's 1985 specification.

TYRRELL
Extra duct on engine cover of 015 to help cool electronic box. Brundle's car fitted with double carbon-fibre discs front and rear (as tested at Ricard).

WILLIAMS
Angular mini-skirts fitted to lower edge of end plates to front wings. Fitted intercooler bypass, operated by air pressure and temperature to send air, under certain circumstances, direct to turbo in order to improve throttle response. T-car fitted with twin discs.

ZAKSPEED
Tried carbon-fibre brakes on T-car.

G.P.

blasted past the Lotus on the run down to Eau Rouge to take second place.

In the lead, we had Stefan Johansson. It was a rather artificial situation since the Ferrari would stop a few laps later and rejoin in fourth place behind team-mate Alboreto – not planning to change the harder B compound tyres he had chosen, as opposed to the Cs favoured elsewhere. Laffite was fifth but Brundle was about to lose an excellent sixth place when the gearbox broke, elevating Jones into the points. After a stop for tyres, Prost continually broke the lap record to haul in the Lola at 3s per lap. After a struggle to pass Berger (a lap behind in any case) the issue was settled when the Australian made a second stop for tyres on lap 32.

The leaders had no intention of stopping again and it was a question of playing a tactical game governed by the amount of fuel remaining. Senna had reduced the gap from four seconds to 0.983 seconds on lap 26, whereupon Mansell turned up his boost for a lap and immediately opened the

Jacques Laffite follows a trail of sparks laid by Johnny Dumfries through Eau Rouge. Keeping pace with the Ligier driver are Boutsen, Jones, Alboreto, de Cesaris and Brundle *(left)*.

Alain Prost makes his way back to the pits after the first-corner incident. The World Champion showed remarkable commitment by racing into a lonely sixth place with a car which was later found to have bent engine mountings and damaged suspension *(bottom)*.

FISA ATTEMPT TO BOLT THE STABLE DOOR

In the light of FISA's hasty and far-reaching reaction to Henri Toivonen's fatal accident in the Tour de Corse Rally, it was no surprise to find Jean-Marie Balestre introducing a parcel of reforms at Spa, a week after the death of Elio de Angelis at Paul Ricard.

The FISA President did not hold a press conference as such and the journalists and team managers present were not given the opportunity to ask questions. Instead, M. Balestre read a prepared statement, the most important points of which are listed below.

1. Six members of the FISA Executive Committee had demanded, on a future date, an extraordinary meeting of the committee to take the necessary decisions for the limitation of engine power in Formula 1.

2. It was intended to apply, as soon as possible (by 1 February 1987 at the latest), for new regulations to limit engine power, during practice and the race, to 600 bhp.

3. All the teams, as well as members of the FISA Drivers' Council, had agreed unanimously to the idea.

4. There was no indication of exactly how the power would be limited although it was believed that either air restrictors or pop-off valves would be investigated.

M. Balestre also announced that the Paul Ricard circuit would be reduced in length in time for the French Grand Prix on 6 July. The revision would do away with the Verrerie left-right flick after the pits, the high-speed complex where de Angelis's Brabham crashed during the test session of 14 May. No mention was made of the apparent lack of safety features at the time of the accident.

gap. Senna, setting his fastest lap of the race, had tried to keep pace but the gap increased. It was then that Senna decided to settle for a safe six points. The gap went from 1.5s to 1.7s to 2.0s and then 2.8s in successive laps. By lap 38, with five to go, Mansell led by five seconds and the race, effectively, was over.

There was, however, a scrap going on for third place, albeit between two cars from the same team! Alboreto, struggling with his harder tyres, had been caught by Johansson on lap 36 and the Swede made it clear that he wanted to get by. A 'Slow' sign from the Ferrari pit must have escaped Stefan's attention as he moved ahead on lap 38. 'Signals!' he grinned afterwards. 'I didn't see any signals . . .'

As for Jones, he had no fuel consumption readout to look at and the lack of such vital information told when the Ford engine coughed its last as he accelerated from La Source three laps from the end. Mansell, of course, needed no reminding of the perils of using too much fuel in

the closing stages and he had Patrick Head's booming voice echoing the thought over the pit-to-car airwaves. In the end, the Williams weighed in 8 kg over the limit, suggesting there was more than enough Mobil in the tank. As for Senna, the 98T tipped the scales a mere 2 kg on the credit side to support the Brazilian's decision to back off during the last ten laps.

'I had big understeer all through the race, so the car was very hard on the front tyres', declared Ayrton. 'I was worried about the fuel but I knew that only Mansell, of all the championship contenders, was in a good position for points. Therefore I decided to have six points rather than risk having nothing.'

It almost went without saying that Mansell and Senna knew that, had Prost not been the innocent victim of the first corner shambles, the McLaren driver would have been on course for his third win in succession. As it was, Prost had shown remarkable commitment in a car which he knew may have been damaged in that shunt. Fastest lap

and one championship point was a poor reward. Berger must have had similar feelings as he came home tenth, his tyres in tatters since a broken clutch meant he could not contemplate stopping for fresh Pirellis.

Jonathan Palmer, on the other hand, had been a frequent visitor to the pits as a slack alternator belt caused havoc throughout the race. A similar problem ended a spirited drive by Rothengatter, the Dutchman running in 12th place in the early stages. The final visitor to the pits turned out to be Marc Surer, the Arrows tricycling to a halt after the right-front wheel had fallen off, conveniently, at the corner before the pits!

There had been a time when that sort of incident seemed to be the prerogative of Nigel Mansell. Perhaps, as he listened to the British National Anthem, he had time to reflect on his chequered career. Certainly, he found time to remember Elio de Angelis as he dedicated this splendid victory to his former team-mate.

M.H.

Grand Prix
LABATT du
CANADA

Harmonious relationship. Patrick Head and Nigel Mansell worked out the perfect set-up for Montreal.

From the fourth pole position of his career, Nigel Mansell made it clear that he was a firm World Championship contender with a brilliantly mature drive to win the Canadian Grand Prix at the Circuit Gilles Villeneuve. Traditionally a race whose length makes fuel efficiency every bit as crucial to success as driving flair, the Mansell/Williams-Honda partnership was in a class of its own. Balancing speed and restraint to perfection, Nigel's Montreal success was easily the best of his four GP victories to date. What's more, the results sheet bore testimony to the quality of the opposition he had defeated in a straight fight. Second, World Champion Alain Prost's McLaren-TAG; third, Nelson Piquet in the other Williams; fourth, Keke Rosberg's McLaren-TAG. The rest had been lapped. Truly a flawless performance!

ENTRY AND PRACTICE

The three-week breathing space between Spa and Montreal might have suggested a mid-season slackening of the F1 pace, but merely consulting a calendar did not provide the full story. Not only did the teams have to prepare their machinery for a gruelling two-week North American tour during that break, but there were test sessions at both Brands Hatch and Hockenheim to be dealt with as well. Nevertheless, the well-oiled FOCA system ensured that everybody was ready to go at the start of the first practice session for the Canadian Grand Prix, held as usual at the Circuit Gilles Villeneuve on Ile Notre Dame, a subway ride away from downtown Montreal.

Torrential rain greeted the F1 competitors as they edged out onto the circuit for Friday morning's untimed session – soaking both expensive equipment and long-suffering mechanics in the makeshift, uncovered pit lane – and although the track dried up substantially for the first timed session it was not until Saturday morning that the weather took a definite turn for the better. Thus Friday's best times, around 4s off the bone-dry Saturday pace, were only of academic interest.

One factor which was destined to remain consistent, however, was the struggle for supremacy between Nigel Mansell's Williams FW11 and Ayrton Senna's Lotus 98T. Right at the end of Friday afternoon Senna slotted in a 1m 28.889s best just as the chequered flag came out, but the Englishman paid him back and firmly grasped pole on Saturday.

Not that Nigel's efforts were without drama. On his first Saturday run he was edged onto the kerb coming out of one of the chicanes by Thierry Boutsen's Arrows, the Williams's consequent excursion on the rough clearly looking a lot more spectacular from the outside than it did to the man in the cockpit. Mansell trailed into the pit lane where clods of earth and grit were cleaned out of the radiator ducting before he continued with the job in hand!

Senna set the ball rolling with an energetic 1m 24.188s almost before most drivers had climbed into their cockpits. Having set this base time, Ayrton retired to the seclusion of the pit lane where he carefully monitored the progress of his rivals, the Brazilian feeling that there was still scope for personal improvement as he had locked

up a couple of times and did not feel totally happy with the balance of his chassis.

Both Williams-Hondas were afflicted with a slight high-speed misfire, but the Honda engineers were not unduly concerned and it did not adversely affect their lap times. Nelson Piquet came close to grabbing pole, but it was eventually Mansell who made the best use of his Goodyear E qualifiers to record a shattering 1m 24.118s and settle the argument for good.

Senna responded with a untypically frantic kerb-hopping, opposite-lock counter-attack, but proved unable to match his earlier time, let alone beat the Englishman, while Piquet ended up tucked in tightly behind his team-mate with a 1m 24.384s, third-quickest. This was a fine effort on a third run with 'best of what's left' part-worn rubber after his first two attempts had been spoiled by driver error and traffic respectively.

In the McLaren International camp Alain Prost was hoping that revisions to the fuel management systems of the TAG V6 would keep him out of trouble on this traditionally fuel-marginal race, but he was plagued with an irritating engine pick-up problem on his race car throughout practice. 'The revs are dropping so low at the hairpins that the engine is almost dying on me', reported the World Champion.

The dry conditions on Saturday revealed another problem in the form of a tiresome degree of understeer. Despite this and continuing signs of that engine response gremlin, Prost did superbly well to qualify fourth on 1m 25.533s. Keke Rosberg, who hates understeer in any shape or form, wrestled his way round to a slightly disappointed sixth place on 1m 25.533s.

Splitting the two McLarens was René Arnoux's Ligier JS27, the Frenchman only being demoted from the second row by Prost in the dying moments of the second session. The World Champion also featured in Jacques Laffite's best qualifying effort. 'Alain was doing a slow lap warming up his tyres when I was going really hard and he lost me a few tenths, but it wasn't his fault', trilled the irrepressible Jacques after clinching eighth place on the grid.

Gerhard Berger salvaged the Benetton-BMW team's honour with a promising seventh-fastest 1m 26.439s, the B186 not quite living up to the Austrian's expectations in the dry. Teo Fabi, meanwhile, had dropped a rear wheel onto a damp

patch right in front of the pits during Friday qualifying, his Benetton snapping away from him and smacking the pit wall head-on before bouncing back to rest on the opposite side of the track.

Within minutes team manager Peter Collins was on the phone to the team's Witney, Oxfordshire, factory requesting that the test car be flown straight out to Montreal on the first available flight. It eventually arrived in time to do service as spare on race day, so Teo had to rely on the original spare for the rest of qualifying, eventually lining up a distant 15th on 1m 26.439s after being plagued with a misfire throughout the Saturday session.

Over in the Brabham camp Derek Warwick was making his F1 return as successor to the late Elio de Angelis. The Englishman, in a buoyant optimistic mood despite having written off a BT55 during his first test run at Donington Park, threw himself back into the cauldron of F1 qualifying with enormous zest.

Both Derek and Riccardo Patrese had a hard time at Montreal. The BMW engine's narrow rev band and poor weight transfer left them struggling for grip out of the two tight hairpins. Altering the rear suspension geometry made little difference to the problem. After experiencing difficulty engaging first gear on Friday, Derek switched to the spare car for the rest of qualifying and recorded a 1m 27.413s to line up tenth, the BT55 rounding off the second session by rolling to a halt on the circuit with loss of fuel pressure.

Patrese squeezed in one place ahead of the Englishman, but he ran out of cars on Saturday when his own suffered engine failure and Derek's discarded race car lost turbo boost when he had a try in that. He was waiting for Warwick to return in the original spare when that too expired, so any prospect of his further improvement vanished.

Michele Alboreto and Stefan Johansson had stormed to a convincing 1-2 success for the Prancing Horse 12 months earlier, so the two Ferrari drivers were in a guardedly optimistic mood at the start of qualifying. But this was soon dashed on Friday by no fewer than five major turbo malfunctions, a quality control problem and a build-up in exhaust back pressure (created possibly by the revamped undertrays they were trying) causing the turbine thrust bearings to fail one after another.

Johansson, a great improvisor on such bumpy

TECHNICAL FILE

ARROWS
No change.

BENETTON
Still working on semi-flexible fixings for front wing side plates with mini-skirts. BMW had revised position for injectors as seen on Patrese's Brabham in Belgium.

BRABHAM
Had tried modifications to the side pods at Donington, designed to shift weight to the rear of the car. Had hoped to revise layout of radiators and intercoolers but the cooling was not as efficient. Warwick wrote off a car at the end of his Donington test. New chassis in Montreal with revised dash panel to give more leg room. On Friday, Warwick's car had new front suspension with narrower angle wishbones. Both cars fitted with this suspension for the race although a revised rear geometry was abandoned. Tried running a rear anti-roll bar (mounted on top of castings for shock absorbers) on Saturday but this was not a success. Also tried McLaren-style front brake ducts.

FERRARI
Revised underbody with separate exhaust pipes (as introduced by Renault in 1983). Upper rear wishbones machined instead of being fabricated. Different fixing to upright to increase rigidity. One-piece rims by Speedline. Engineer Enea Spallanzani present to look after engines. Five turbos failed (four on cars with new exhaust configuration). Garrett brought additional turbos on Saturday and Ferrari also reverted to older system of oil cooling for turbos. All three cars had revised exhausts and underbody configurations on race day.

LIGIER
New car for Arnoux. Race cars featured smaller water radiators. Did not bring chassis number 4, as seen during testing with hydraulics on suspension.

LOLA
Small deflectors on inner face of rear wing side plates. Tried skirts on front wings. Only six engines available here. Tambay's car written off during warm-up on race morning.

LOTUS
Senna's car fitted with 1986 rear suspension again which allowed a return to the hydraulic control system. Dumfries had the old style rear suspension.

McLAREN
Porsche introduced a new fuel-feed system for the TAG engine, the fuel pump being modified to run a separate feed to each bank of cylinders rather than a single run as before. This development, in the interests of improved economy, was seen on three engines on Friday. On Saturday, seven engines were so equipped.

MINARDI
Engine supply reduced to four.

OSELLA
Did not use new car.

TYRRELL
Philippe Streiff relegated to the 014 following his shunt in an 015 during testing at Brands Hatch (to ensure a full complement of the latest car for Detroit). 015s had double carbon-fibre discs. Revised engine cover on one car to suit new plenum chamber on Renault V6.

WILLIAMS
Upper rear wishbones oval (rather than circular) construction in the interests of improved aerodynamics. Williams, in keeping with the majority of the leading runners, fitted mini-skirts to the front wings.

ZAKSPEED
One car fitted with experimental engine running three injectors per cylinder.

G.P.

John Townsend

The absence of Marc Surer, seriously injured during a rally in Germany, was another blow during an increasingly sad summer for motor sport.

Italian knees-up. Riccardo Patrese reclines in the cockpit of the BT55 during a difficult two days of practice with the Brabham-BMW.

May
Bobby Rahal (March Cosworth 86C) wins Indy 500.
June
Jo Gartner killed at Le Mans.
Marc Surer seriously injured when his Ford RS200 crashed during the Hessen Rally in Germany.
Ayrton Senna visits Maranello.

and demanding tracks, was briefly third behind Senna and Piquet on his first Friday run, but the F1/86 proved almost unmanageable over the bumps in the dry and the Swede slumped to a disappointing 18th when the grid was published.

The original underbodies were refitted on Friday night following this spate of turbo trouble, but Alboreto could only salvage a lowly 11th place on the grid after this débâcle. He lined up just behind the two Brabhams and ahead of Thierry Boutsen in the lone Arrows A8 racing that weekend. A deal to obtain Christian Danner's services as stand-in for the injured Marc Surer was thwarted when the formalities of his release from Osella were not completed in time, so the reigning Formula 3000 champion had to wait another week until Detroit before joining the Arrows line-up.

The Team Haas Lola-Ford duo proved well matched with Alan Jones recovering from a suspension-damaging slide into a tyre barrier during Friday's wet untimed session to pip team-mate Patrick Tambay for 13th place. Jones used Goodyear E compound qualifiers to set his time while Patrick used harder Cs to do his time, the Frenchman concluding that Jones had taken the correct route. Both men complained of a difficult gearchange and Patrick lost two nose cones on Saturday morning due to a failure in their carbon-fibre bonding. They were bolted directly to the front of the monocoque for race day to prevent a recurrence of this trouble.

Behind Fabi in 16th place came Johnny Dumfries, the Scot still running a 1985 rear end on his Lotus 98T owing to a shortage of the redesigned rear uprights that had been produced in the wake of the Imola wheel-bearing failures. The Lotus Number Two admitted that he failed to get the best out of his qualifying rubber and complained of poor engine response out of the hairpins during Saturday qualifying.

Over at Tyrrell, Philippe Streiff was paying the penalty for writing off the latest 015 chassis at the Brands test, the lanky Frenchman confined to an 014 for Montreal as Uncle Ken was anxious to keep the two remaining new cars intact for their appearance in front of the team's sponsors in Detroit. It was with some irony, then, that Streiff qualified the older car 17th, two places in front of a troubled Martin Brundle in the newer machine.

On Friday, Martin suffered a fuel pick-up problem during the morning, then slid off the track at the pits hairpin during first qualifying thanks to a rear caliper first overheating and then failing. On Saturday, his Renault 'pneumatic' qualifying V6 dropped its valves after a leak in the air pressure activation system, so he had to switch to his other car which was already fitted with a race engine in preparation for Sunday. Following a further brief delay with a quick-release fuel cap jamming open, he just managed to squeeze in one run on qualifiers close to the end of the day.

Completing the top 20 was Nannini's Minardi ahead of team-mate de Cesaris. Then came Palmer, thwarted by lack of boost and a major engine blow-up in the Zakspeed, while the two Osellas of Ghinzani and Danner sandwiched Rothengatter's Zakspeed right at the back.

RACE

The weather on race morning was absolutely perfect with temperatures in the mid-seventies and a cooling breeze coming off the St Lawrence River, so a huge crowd poured onto Ile Notre Dame to prepare for the unusually early start (noon), dictated by the American Open Golf Championship which was also to be televised later in the day.

The half-hour race warm-up saw Rosberg and Prost first and second, but poor Tambay was written out of the script when his Lola crashed heavily at the esses beyond the pits, bouncing off both walls after a possible track rod failure. The Frenchman survived intact, but his feet were badly bruised and lacerated in the impact, so there was no question of his starting the race. He was taken away to hospital where he remained for a couple of days.

Other problems included Dumfries taking the spare Lotus after his own suffered an engine failure in the warm-up, Palmer's Zakspeed resolutely failed to fire up for the parade lap and was pushed to the side of the circuit while Danner's Osella was still in the pit lane having an oil leak quenched when the starting light blinked green and the pack got away.

Mansell accelerated off the line superbly, easing ahead of Senna through the esses while Prost was already harrying the Lotus from third place. Down to the first hairpin and all the way round that first lap, Nigel was being handed a major bonus on a plate as it became clear that Ayrton was bottling up the rest of the competition.

At the end of lap 1 Mansell swept through with a commanding 3.1s advantage over Senna with Prost, Piquet, Rosberg, Arnoux, Berger, Patrese, Alboreto, Laffite, Warwick, Jones, Boutsen and the rest of the field in hot pursuit. By the end of lap 2 Nigel was out of sight with 5.5s in hand over the Brazilian. Already it looked as though the race was in the bag.

However, Prost was in a serious mood. Keke had moved onto his tail by lap 3 and at the start of lap 4 he had a long look inside Senna going into the fast esses, decided that was where he would pass the Lotus and mentally filed it for next time round. Into the pits hairpin at the end of that lap Rosberg locked a front wheel and oh-so-nearly hit his team-mate up the gearbox. Then Alain ousted Senna from second place with a brilliantly decisive lunge round the Lotus at the fast esses, the Brazilian getting into a big slide on the inside apex kerbing as Alain slammed the door very firmly in his face.

This lost Senna so much momentum out onto the following straight that Rosberg immediately hauled by into third place and, by the end of the fifth lap, Ayrton had dropped back to sixth.

As the race at the head of the field settled into a secure pattern, so a spate of problems began to hit several cars further down the field. Danner's Osella succumbed to turbo failure on lap 7, Jones lost a wheel balance weight and came in to change tyres on the Lola, while Patrese spun his BT55 at the pits hairpin and chopped back into the traffic right in front of his team-mate. Palmer was now

'What do we do next?' Michele Alboreto, Stefan Johansson and Harvey Postlethwaite appear to have run out of ideas when it comes to curing the handling problems on the Ferraris.

The damp conditions proved to be a great equaliser during practice on Friday, Jonathan Palmer setting a very competitive time. In the dry, however, it was a return to the familiar struggle . . .

Musical cars. Christian Danner was selected by Arrows to replace Marc Surer, seriously injured in a rally accident. Danner's debut with the British team (*right*), lasted about 25 metres, the German getting no further than the end of the pit lane. The late nomination by Arrows and contractual difficulties with Osella meant Danner had to return to the Italian team for the rest of the weekend (*far right*).

Derek Warwick, re-united with John Gentry his former engineer at Toleman and Renault, had a brief race when he returned to Formula 1 with Brabham (*below right*).

running in close company with team-mate Rothengatter, the big Dutchman keeping ahead by dint of running far too much boost pressure for the good of his fuel consumption figures.

A binding rear brake was hampering Piquet's progress in fourth place while Arnoux's Ligier was having a real dust-up with Senna for fifth. Fabi's Benetton was out after 13 laps with electrical failure, Nannini's Minardi expired with an ominous looking turbo fire, while both Ferraris were beginning to get into their stride, Johansson now running seventh ahead of Alboreto and heading towards the Championship points.

Up at the front Rosberg now decided to make a bid for the lead. He eased past Prost, the Frenchman keeping a wary eye on his fuel consumption, and closed in on the leading Williams. By lap 16 he was sitting right on Mansell's gearbox and ran round the outside of the FW11 to take the lead into the pits hairpin at the end of that lap. Mansell stayed with him for a couple of laps, then eased back a few lengths in order to keep the Honda fuel consumption readout on schedule.

This little sprint had put Rosberg's overall fuel consumption figures 4 litres into deficit, but the Finn remained convinced that he could get the consumption figures balanced towards the end of the race. Mansell began to come back at the McLaren after four laps or so, the leading trio closing up into tight formation as Prost stepped up the pressure once more. At the start of lap 22 this leading group came up to lap Jones, fresh from another stop prompted by a blistered rear tyre.

At the hairpin on the outward leg Rosberg left a little too much room inside him and Mansell dived through to retake the lead, squeezing between the McLaren and lapped Lola with a superb sense of

opportunism. From that moment onwards, Mansell's victory was never really in question.

Johansson's fine effort for Ferrari was destined to come to a spectacular end on lap 31, just when it seemed as though the Swede would be a comfortable top six finisher. Sweeping through the esses beyond the pits Stefan found Dumfries's Lotus, fresh from a pit stop, right on the racing line. He moved his Ferrari to the right to overtake, just as Johnny moved the same way, intending to make room for Johansson on the left.

The Ferrari ran straight into the back of the Lotus, both machines being eliminated from the race on the spot, much to Stefan's ill-concealed annoyance. Alboreto had to spin wildly in avoidance, the Italian banging his right leg very painfully against the underside of his Ferrari's steering rack as he did so. In considerable pain, quite shaken from his close escape and later to lose

the use of a couple of gears, Michele's challenge was spent and he faded quickly after this dramatic moment.

Mansell stopped for fresh tyres at the end of lap 30 and, with Prost (who had retaken Rosberg for second) stopping next time round, Nigel relinquished his advantage for only a single lap. But while Mansell has a very slick tyre change, Prost was delayed by a sticking front wheel nut and dropped back to fifth behind Senna by the time he resumed. Ayrton made his routine stop at the end of lap 34, so now the order was Mansell, Piquet, Rosberg and Prost.

Piquet dropped to fourth behind Prost when he stopped on lap 36, changing his C front/B rear tyre choice to Cs all round. Arnoux was now fifth (running non-stop on his Pirellis) with Senna all over him, the Brazilian not getting the same level of grip from his replacement set of tyres.

Mansell by now had the race in the bag, consolidating his advantage to 20s over Prost by the chequered flag, the chances of a Williams 1-2 being spoiled when Piquet made a second stop to change blistered rear tyres ten laps from the finish. Rosberg backed off dramatically to preserve his fuel supply, paying the penalty for running too hard early on, and was the last unlapped runner in fourth place.

Senna had finally slipped by Arnoux for fifth when Mansell lapped them both. René later commented that he drove the entire race with one eye on his fuel-monitoring readout. 'The only exciting part was the last lap when the computer told me I had no fuel left. Wondering whether I would run out was the most interesting moment of the race', he grinned.

Jacques Laffite finished a good seventh ahead of the cruising Alboreto and Brundle's Tyrrell, the Englishman delayed by a slow routine tyre change (a wheel nut jammed) and a later stop with a punctured tyre. Jones struggled round to 10th with Streiff's old Tyrrell 014 11th and Rothengatter, who had to crawl round gently for the last 15 laps to pull back a 14-litre fuel deficit, the last runner in 12th spot.

Both Brabhams failed to last the distance, the BT55s succumbing to engine trouble, while Berger joined Fabi in retirement with a turbo failure after an earlier spin. Boutsen suffered electrical failure, yet again, de Cesaris broke the Minardi's transmission and Ghinzani's gearbox failed.

As the mechanics loaded up for the trip to Detroit, the drivers returned to their hotels wondering just how they could stem the progress of the Mansell victory bandwagon.

A.H.

UNITED STATES
Grand Prix
DETROIT

The uncovered pits may not have found favour with the teams but they did present the basis for this stunning rooftop picture.

Early in the race, Ayrton Senna picked up a puncture and slipped from first to eighth place. Coming seven days after a distant fifth place in Montreal, it seemed as if this heralded a serious decline for the Brazilian and John Player Special Team Lotus. In fact, it was the beginning of a triumphant comeback.

Slicing through the field – a difficult task on the bumpy, angular street circuit – Senna claimed nine points to give himself and Lotus a boost when they needed it most. Now he led the championship once more and, in a complete reversal of fortune, it was Nigel Mansell who came home fifth this weekend, his Williams hobbled by a brake problem from as early as lap 5 – just after he had taken the lead.

True, Senna had been aided by his rivals' misfortunes. These included an intermittent cut-out problem on Alain Prost's Marlboro McLaren; Nelson Piquet had crashed; and René Arnoux, inheriting the second place vacated by the Williams driver, had driven into the wreckage a few laps later, leaving his Ligier team-mate, Jacques Laffite, to collect a worthy six points. But at the end of a race where his rivals ran into either hard luck or the wall nothing could detract from a drive of sustained speed and brilliance by Senna.

ENTRY AND PRACTICE

It was, perhaps, appropriate that Detroit, with its 73 floors of glass-sided Renaissance Center, should witness a scene which typified the attitude of the sportsperson in the Eighties. The 'Ren-Cen', to give it the snappy title which actually helps to disguise the paradox of such a dreamy, highly inefficient hotel and office complex, is but a step away from the track. It was not too much to expect, therefore, that the pole-position winner should attend the post-practice briefing which the American media expect and enjoy in other sports. On Friday, for example, the provisional pole-sitter, Nigel Mansell, arrived with such haste in the media centre that he caught the pressmen by surprise.

On Saturday, the journalists were ready and the surprise this time came in the form of Ayrton Senna's disembodied voice trotting out his comments from a tape recorder held by a hapless and highly embarrassed PR lady. Ayrton, it seemed, was a few floors up, tuning his television set to the World Cup football. The news that France had beaten Brazil was later received with sardonic smiles by the bemused media . . .

Ill manners aside, Ayrton had been at his best earlier in the day. Practice had boiled down to a battle between Senna and Mansell with the contest, won by the Englishman on Friday, being fought all over again as the track, now coated with rubber, became faster in the second official session.

The problem on Friday had been deciding on the right tyre for the 'green', dusty streets. Mansell had settled for a mixture of soft race rubber and a set of qualifiers while Senna had stuck with the latter. Qualifiers were perhaps the fastest, but not by much. Mansell's times proved that race tyres were the best compromise since they allowed the opportunity to find a clear lap but, even so, his one run on qualifiers produced a lap which was faster than Senna's. Saturday, though, made all this irrelevant.

Again, Mansell chose a set of Cs and a set of the softer Es. He produced a 1m 40.244s, completed a slow lap and then went for a time. This lap, much quicker than the previous one, was spoiled near the end as Rothengatter wandered into the path of the flying Williams. Never mind, Mansell still had a set of qualifiers.

Senna was onto the track immediately. Running a set of Es, he produced a stunning 1m 38.301s to claim pole. Mansell returned on his qualifiers. This would be worth watching.

Indeed it was. But Mansell got no further than turn four, where he suddenly backed off. An urgent radio message from the pits informed him that Prost had crashed into the wall at the exit from the chicane. The red flag was out. The damage had been done in more ways than one.

Once the wrecked McLaren had been cleared, Mansell returned but, as expected, the qualifying tyres had lost their edge. He did manage to get to within half a second of Senna's time and, since there was no-one else remotely in touch with these two protagonists, Mansell was at least assured of a place on the front row.

With seven minutes remaining, Senna completed his second run and the fact that he was almost a second slower than before was immaterial. He had secured pole position and now he could nip off to watch his beloved country play football.

Nelson Piquet did not have quite the same urge to support his home team, but perhaps the Brazilian had other things on his mind. Like the speed of his team-mate, for instance. For the second weekend in succession, Nelson was overshadowed by Mansell and, as a result, an uncharacteristic desperation crept into his driv-

ing. Then he crashed at the chicane on Saturday morning. That meant he had to switch to the spare car (set up for him in any case) in the afternoon and he chose two sets of race tyres (one of which turned out to be unbalanced). It was not until a superb effort on his 18th and final lap that he got to within three-tenths of Mansell's time to take third place.

Fourth, the Ligier-Renault of René Arnoux. The Frenchman really attacked the street circuit and his enthusiasm on Friday led to a brush with the wall during one of his fastest laps. René was unhappy with the handling of his car but improvements by Michel Tétu on Saturday filled Arnoux with renewed confidence although his time (1m 39.689s) was not his best since he had passed a handful of slower cars during that lap. Making it two Ligiers in the first six, Jacques Laffite jumped from 12th to sixth in the final session, the Frenchman also finding his JS27 'undriveable' on Friday. On Saturday, he was caught out by Prost's accident and could not find a clear lap thereafter.

The most heroic, if not spectacular, effort came from Stefan Johansson. Conceding that the only way to overcome the dreaded understeer on the Ferrari was to pitch the car into oversteer, the result made excellent viewing as the F1/86 bucked and bounced over the bumps. Stefan had been fourth-fastest on Friday but he managed to find a reasonably clear lap the following day to maintain a place in the top five. Michele Alboreto could not match this extrovert performance, partly because of the Ferrari's inability to cope with the merest ripple but largely because of stabbing pains in his legs. The Italian had bashed his shins against the steering rack while spinning to avoid the Dumfries/Johansson tangle in Montreal and now the streets of Detroit were exacerbating the injuries.

June
FOCA discuss possibility of running Grand Prix at Laguna Seca.
Cheever replaces injured Tambay at Lola.
Danner takes over Surer's seat at Arrows; Berg joins Osella.

Stefan Johansson (right), forced the understeering Ferrari around Detroit in the most spectacular manner. He qualified an excellent fifth but retired from the race.

Gerhard Berger and Teo Fabi (below) had a troubled weekend as the Benetton team struggled to make their cars competitive on the streets of Detroit.

Alain Prost's opinion of Detroit as a race track was not helped by the uncharacteristic shunt and in many ways it simply summed up an unhappy time for the team in general. For reasons which escaped them, the MP4 never had worked satisfactorily here and, it seemed, never would. On Friday, the lack of grip was so severe that they even resorted to carrying additional fuel to prevent the rear wheels from spinning. Things improved slightly with the application of more rubber to the track surface on Saturday and Prost was just beginning his one lap on Es when the car got away from him as he powered through the chicane. At least it was a short walk across the road to his pit . . .

Keke Rosberg, the winner of the previous year's race, was an unhappy ninth with a similar tale to tell about the lack of traction. Splitting the two McLarens was the Brabham of Riccardo Patrese. The Italian was agreeably surprised since the lowline car was something of a handful over the bumps and the chance of a smooth lap was ruled out completely by the violent throttle response from the BMW engine. Like McLaren, the Brabham team found their car to be more stable with about 30 gallons on board but the nervousness in qualifying trim prompted Derek Warwick to try fitting a rear anti-roll bar for the final session. It was the first time such a device had been seen on a Brabham since 1982 – and Warwick soon found out why. He dropped from 11th to 15th place.

Warwick was as delighted as anyone to find his Jaguar team-mate, Eddie Cheever, in the pit lane on Friday morning. Eddie, wearing a pair of Alfa Romeo overalls with the badges torn off, had been in Rome on Wednesday when he received a call from Teddy Mayer, asking him to jump on the first plane to Detroit where he would act as a stand-in

for Patrick Tambay. The Frenchman was hobbling around the pits, the bruising to his feet and ribs from his shunt in Montreal precluding further work at the wheel, particularly at a track as bumpy as this.

Mayer and Haas had originally tried to place Michael Andretti in the seat but FISA would not grant the American a Superlicence. That might have been understandable had the less experienced Allen Berg not been climbing into a Formula 1 car for the first time in the next pit! FISA's political in-fight with CART notwithstanding, E. Cheever was jet-lagged, but back in Formula 1. Bearing in mind that he had not sat in the car until Friday morning, Eddie did a superb job. Gradually playing himself in, and with the benefit of sleep on Saturday, he took tenth place although, characteristically, he was not pleased with himself. The time had been set on Cs and when the American went for a quick run on qualifiers he slid on oil and brushed a wall. Even so, he was eleven places ahead of Alan Jones.

Differential trouble on Friday had kept the Australian off the pace and a brush with de Cesaris in the final session scuppered his one lap on qualifiers but Jones was honest enough to admit that, these troubles apart, he was deeply dissatisfied with his performance.

Twelfth place for Gerhard Berger should not have pleased the Austrian either in the light of recent performances but there was no denying that Detroit did not suit the Benettons. Berger didn't help by tapping a wall so hard on Friday that he knocked a couple of teeth off the steering rack but, otherwise, he drove with his usual verve and enthusiasm. Teo Fabi, two seconds slower, showed even less interest than usual.

If anyone had a right to be dejected, then it should have been Thierry Boutsen as he soldiered

on with the now ancient Arrows A8. The Belgian driver's talent is such, however, that he carried that car, with its volatile engine response, into 13th place. Joining him at last, following a contractual settlement with Osella, Christian Danner had to acclimatise himself to both a new car and a new circuit (not to mention qualifying tyres which were a rare commodity in the Osella pits) and he did well to take a place just two seconds off Boutsen's time.

Johnny Dumfries, learning the circuit but very much under scrutiny after his débâcle on the streets of Monaco, was 14th – and he genuinely felt he should have been higher. He set his time on Cs and, just as he was starting a run on Es, fourth gear stripped. The lull as Prost's car was scooped up allowed time for repairs. Unfortunately, Johnny spoiled an impressive two days by clouting the wall.

If Dumfries was disappointed, Martin Brundle

was boiling with frustration over 16th place on a circuit which he knows and enjoys. The gamble of running race and qualifying tyres on Saturday failed to pay off when, during his all-important lap on Es, Martin was blocked three times. Philippe Streiff, relegated to the 014 on Friday to preserve the 015s for final practice and the race, suffered the same frustrations and finished two places behind his team-mate – disappointing performances all round since the Tyrrells had looked remarkably neat and tidy compared to some.

Friday's practice had been a waste of Jonathan Palmer's time, the Zakspeed driver managing a total of 17 laps due to trouble with the crown wheel and pinion on one car and a blown turbo on the spare. Saturday was better although Palmer had a lot of sorting to do in the limited time available. Huub Rothengatter was one of two drivers who failed to improve, gearbox problems confining the Dutchman to the pits in the final session.

That left the Osellas and the Minardis, Piercarlo Ghinzani heading the group in 22nd place. To be fair, the impressive Alessandro Nannini, faster than Andrea de Cesaris in the first three sessions, did not manage a lap on Saturday due to engine trouble with his Minardi. Berg, replacing Danner at Osella, had the unenviable task of learning about Formula 1 on a tricky circuit and in an infinitely more difficult car. He avoided contact with the walls to earn a set of qualifiers on Saturday and reduced his time considerably.

RACE

Life in the Renaissance Center can become excessively wearisome as pop groups thump out music which, judging by the excessive amplification, is expected to reach those asleep 650 feet above. By Sunday morning, the combination of over-priced wine and underscored music can have a strange effect – but was that really Nigel

Mansell I saw go by just then – in a Ferrari? It was tempting to go back indoors again and lie down, except that the lifts (sorry, elevators) were jammed with corporate partygoers rocketing skywards for an afternoon of revelry.

The explanation was simple enough. Stefan Johansson reached the pits for the warm-up only to find that his helmet was missing. The loan of Mansell's back-up crash-hat solved the problem until Stefan's helmet could be found. That wine was not so bad after all . . .

Neither was Mansell's Williams in race trim, although judging by the Englishman's soaking tee-shirt after just 30 minutes at the wheel the sultry conditions were going to make this one of the toughest races of the season. At least he was starting from the front row. The worry, though, was second-fastest time in the warm-up for Arnoux and the perky little Frenchman would be starting from the second row.

Paul-Henri Cahier

Nigel Snowdon

Wearing his Ford hat . . . Eddie Cheever, called up at the last minute to deputise for the injured Patrick Tambay, did an excellent job for Haas and Ford at Detroit *(above)*.

No place for a new boy. Allen Berg *(left)*, was thrown in at the deep end when he joined Osella to drive a Formula 1 car for the first time on a difficult and unfamiliar circuit.

After the disappointment of Monaco, Johnny Dumfries set the record straight by taking an excellent finish on a day when over half the field retired.

Jacques Laffite led a Grand Prix for the first time in three years. The Ligier driver took an eventual second place *(below)*.

The concrete walls of Detroit were waiting to catch the unwary, but Ayrton Senna did not put a wheel out of place during a remarkable comeback drive to take his second win of the season *(far right)*.

Photo:

Nelson Piquet worked the Williams-Honda into the lead at one stage but destroyed his chances and his car against the wall.

Sure enough, as the field charged into the first left-hander, Arnoux's Ligier locked up and almost went straight on as he narrowly avoided contact with the back of Mansell's Williams. For the remainder of the lap, Arnoux harrassed Mansell who, in turn, was looking for a way past Senna.

Ayrton gave Nigel the opportunity he had been waiting for when the Lotus driver missed a gear at the end of lap 2. Mansell seized the moment, leaving Senna to deal with Arnoux while the Williams pulled away at around a second a lap. At this rate of going, a third win in succession looked as though it would be a formality. Until lap 5.

Mansell suddenly became aware that his rear brakes were not working efficiently. This should not have been a surprise on a circuit which punishes brakes but the novelty in this instance was the fact that the rear carbon-fibre discs were running too *cool*. As Mansell wound the brake balance to the rear in an effort to generate more

heat, so Senna reeled the Williams in, thus wiping out the tyre advantage Mansell should have had in the early laps.

Senna had gone against the popular belief that Cs were the tyres to have, the Lotus driver, along with Rosberg and Prost, opting for the harder Bs.

'I spent a lot of time trying both in practice', said Senna. 'There was no doubt that the Cs gave better grip for a few laps. After that, though, they started to go off and then we got a big understeer problem – which is our main problem with the Lotus anyway. I knew we would lose out on grip initially, but I still thought my car was better balanced on the Bs; that it would be the best compromise for the whole race.'

Compromise or not, Senna now had Mansell under pressure as the Williams brake pedal showed an alarming inconsistency on a circuit such as this. Lap 8, and Senna slipped neatly by under braking. Within the space of another few

laps, Mansell was down to fourth behind the Ligiers of Arnoux and Laffite and only marginally ahead of Prost and Piquet. Out of the race were Rosberg, having stopped for tyres early on before retiring with broken transmission; Berger, with electrical trouble; and then Brundle with a similar ailment. In the case of the Tyrrell driver, the problem was caused by an overheating electronic control box (mounted, it was pointed out by Renault, in a poor position) which caused the engine almost to die. Brundle wisely parked the car before the tunnel rather than try to crawl through the darkness but it was a disappointing way to end a race which had promised much as he lay in a handy 12th place.

It was shock rather than disappointment which affected the leader as his Lotus suddenly began to squirm sideways under power on lap 12. Realising he had punctured a rear tyre, Senna headed for the pits where the JPS crew had him under way in

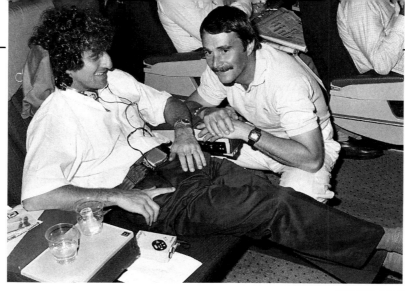

Alain Prost and Nigel Mansell, relaxing on the flight home, were happy to have scored points after a difficult race in Detroit.

11.67 seconds. But, during that time, seven cars had gone by and the race was now being led by the Ligier team!

Mansell was third and, confusing the issue, he set the fastest lap of the race so far as he closed on Laffite. Prost was running easily in fourth with Piquet not far behind but attention now centred on Senna as he passed Johansson and then closed on Alboreto in sixth place. Lap 19 and Senna was through while, at the front, Jacques Laffite had muscled his way past his team-mate to lead a Grand Prix for the first time in three years. Not only that, he set fastest lap as he pulled away!

Arnoux, who had started on softer rear tyres than Laffite, was now paying the price as he held up Mansell, Prost, Piquet . . . and Senna. The Ferraris were dropping back while Eddie Cheever held an excellent ninth place, the Lola under no threat from Patrese as the Brabham driver made the most of a narrow rear Pirelli which, surprisingly, offered more grip. Boutsen was 11th and Dumfries, having made a cautious start, overtook Jones (who had made his usual storming start) to take 13th.

The Lolas, however, were destined to retire with, the official bulletin said, broken drive pegs. Whether, in the case of Cheever, this happened before or after he tapped the wall because of broken rear suspension is not clear . . . Whatever the cause, it was the end of three days' work by the American which had impressed everyone in the team.

By lap 27 Laffite still led from Arnoux although the second Ligier was the first car to make a scheduled stop for tyres. The rest followed in the order, Johansson, Prost, Laffite – leaving Piquet in the lead, followed by Senna and then Mansell. The Brazilian driver waited for another eight or nine laps before coming in and it was at this point that the race took a dramatic turn.

Ligier, not so accustomed to pit stops as the Goodyear teams, had been rather slow and this put Laffite and Arnoux out of the picture for the time being. Piquet's stop, however, took 18 seconds thanks to a sticking right-front wheel (Mansell, ironically, had suffered a similar problem). But when Senna stopped at the end of the next lap, the Lotus crew had him away in 8.28 seconds, effectively giving Ayrton an advantage of 10 seconds – and the lead.

Piquet, realising this would be the case, went flat-out from the minute he left the pits and immediately cut a lap of 1m 41.233s, about a second quicker than anything which had been recorded before. On the next lap, he crashed.

Turning into the final left-hander before the pits chicane, Nelson clipped the apex, the impact throwing the Williams across the track and into the outside wall where the right-front suspension was destroyed. Piquet, hopping from the car, admitted his mistake. The same could not be said for the inefficient marshals after the event.

The Williams, stuck at the exit of a blind corner, needed to be removed quickly. The marshals dithered and waved their arms, and for some reason the crane on the opposite side of the track was not brought into action for quite some time. Inconsistent flag-waving confused the issue

further and, after four laps, the warning flags disappeared. Assuming the wreck had been removed, Senna took his normal line through the corner – and narrowly missed the Williams. Arnoux, now in second place, was not so lucky.

René did not actually hit the Williams but, instead, glanced the wall, breaking his right-front suspension. Reversing out from behind Piquet's car, Arnoux compounded his error by driving straight into Boutsen as the hapless Arrows man made his way by. Both were to join Piquet in the short walk along the riverfront to the pits. Both Arrows were now out, Danner's hopes of finishing a race for the first time being dashed by a metering unit failure.

(Later, the officials defended themselves by quoting the regulations which stated that yellow flags need not be waved after four laps since the obstruction is then considered part of the course. Maybe so . . . but at the exit of a blind corner? Surely common sense should have prevailed here.)

As a result of Arnoux's departure, Senna was now 30 seconds clear of Prost but the Frenchman was being caught by his business partner, Jacques Laffite. Prost was suffering from that curious cut-out problem which had afflicted the TAG engine from time to time and he put up little resistance when the Ligier went by with eight laps to go. There was a danger of Laffite catching Senna and, in a complete reversal of the Canadian Grand Prix, the Brazilian was about to lap Mansell.

Concentrating on keeping his car away from the walls while pumping his brakes, Mansell was caught out momentarily. His visit to an escape road was enough to let Alboreto, still suffering from painful legs, into fourth place. Patrese, in brake trouble, was soldiering on take a hard-earned point for sixth position while, against all odds, Johnny Dumfries and Jonathan Palmer were showing every sign of finishing a race which was to eliminate 10 of the 25 starters (the 26th, Rothengatter, did not make the grid due to an electrical failure on the warm-up lap). Palmer was struggling without a clutch while Dumfries was lucky to survive a brush with a wall which did no more than puncture a tyre. Streiff would be ninth while Warwick, an early visitor to the pits to change tyres, then had the additional complication of no clutch and an inoperative bottom gear. But at least he finished and, overall, created a favourable impression with his new team.

A decent result for Dumfries rounded off the Lotus team's day but, more than anything else, the nine points for Ayrton provided a shot in the arm after the disappointment of Montreal. It was also a boost for the noisy pocket of Brazilian supporters in the public enclosure, Senna stopping to collect a green-and-yellow national flag on his slowing-down lap.

It was, in many ways, an uncomplicated victory since the drivers did not need to worry about fuel lasting for a mere 157 miles. Stamina, brakes and those menacing concrete walls were the deciding factor here and, in that respect, Senna did an excellent job and thoroughly deserved to be leading the championship once more.   M.H.

TECHNICAL FILE

ARROWS
No change.

BENETTON
Chassis number 4 badly damaged in Canada; brought chassis 2 to Detroit for Fabi. Scrutineers checked side plates to front wings. The single forward fixing was made up of two tubes, the outer attached to the wings, the inner attached to side plates. Benetton said it permitted adjustment; rivals claimed pressure of air on shaped rear outer edge of wings created a torsion bar effect on tubes. Gabriel Cadringher, FISA Scrutineer, made no comment other than to recommend a more secure fixing.

BRABHAM
Race cars fitted with revised front suspension tested in Canada.

FERRARI
Built up chassis 89 to replace Johansson's car damaged in Montreal. New lubrication system for turbo with revised shaft. Fitted twin brake system with additional pipes running to calipers from twin pumps, requiring additional vent in nose; designed to avoid overheating. This system not tested beforehand. All three cars fitted with same multiple exhaust system seen in Canada. Only the T-car remained with old style top rear wishbones.

LIGIER
Laffite's car fitted with a smaller water radiator.

LOLA
Chassis 1 brought from England to replace Tambay's wrecked car from Montreal. Ran side plates to rear wings incorporating small flaps.

LOTUS
No change.

McLAREN
No change.

MINARDI
No change.

OSELLA
No change.

TYRRELL
Removed double discs tested in Belgium and Canada. Vertical wings mounted behind front wheels on Brundle's car.

WILLIAMS
Gauze grille fitted to mouth of side pods to prevent rubbish from collecting and causing overheating. Only the T-car so equipped during practice but race cars were modified later. Fitted additional oil radiator on top of left-hand side pod, complete with duct, to T-car for Friday's practice.

ZAKSPEED
No change.   G.P.

131

Grand Prix de FRANCE

It was a gamble, no question of that, but Patrick Head had worked it all out in minute detail and reckoned it was worth trying. He scheduled two tyre stops apiece for the Williams-Honda FW11s in the French Grand Prix at Paul Ricard, calculating that the advantage the cars would gain on fresh rubber would significantly outweigh the delays involved in stopping. His theory was correct and, aided by fine team work in the pits and Nigel Mansell's latest display of superbly controlled flair behind the wheel, the team notched up its fourth win of the year. More importantly, it was Nigel's third success of the season – one memorable for his expert success over Alain Prost's McLaren-TAG (which made only one tyre stop) and which brought him to the verge of the World Championship lead as he headed home for the British Grand Prix the following weekend.

Nigel Mansell's successful gamble of two pit stops for tyres enabled him to dominate at Paul Ricard, the scene of past unhappy experiences for the Englishman.

Ayrton Senna, caught out by oil in the early laps, crashed and failed to finish in the points for just the second time in eight races.

Alain Prost and the McLaren-TAG had to take second place to the Mansell/Williams-Honda combination – again.

Paul-Henri Cahier

Designers' Silly Season. Adrian Newey, very much in demand in CART circles, left March to join the Haas team *(right)*.

Renault introduced a revised engine, used exclusively by Ayrton Senna at Ricard.

ENTRY AND PRACTICE

The French Grand Prix returned to Paul Ricard for the second successive year and was scheduled to remain at the venue just north of Bandol for the next four. However, in the wake of Elio de Angelis's fatal testing accident during the week immediately following the Monaco Grand Prix, the FFSA decided to speed up plans to shorten the circuit, surfacing a link road connecting the start-and-finish straight at a point just before the daunting Verrerie S-bend with the Mistral straight about halfway down towards the challenging Signes right-hander. This reduced the circuit length from 3.6 to 2.36 miles and most drivers considered the modifications to be a major improvement, although the track surface on the new link proved slippery from the word go.

As if to emphasise the track's revamped image, some 20 tons of blue paint were liberally applied to the kerbing and run-off areas adjoining the circuit, the organisers explaining that it was intended to produce a 'visual shock' for the spectators. Unquestionably, that aim was achieved . . .

If the FFSA had expected all this 'window dressing' to produce a slick new public profile, then it was to be swiftly disabused. Many aspects of the organisation looked somewhat dilatory and FISA severely censured the French national sporting authority before the first session had started. A mobile television crane, locked up and parked on the circuit, caused a delay to the Friday schedule. For that, the FFSA received a fine of $20,000, shortly followed by a further $15,000 fine for failing to provide adequate radio commentary facilities. This was all rounded off with a firm warning that if the circuit authorities failed to tighten up their act speedily then they could forget any plans for staging the French GP in 1987.

The two days of qualifying followed the familiar pattern evolved in North America as Ayrton Senna's Lotus 98T and Nigel Mansell's Williams FW11 contended for pole position. Renault, mindful of just how effective the Honda V6 had become as a race engine, was anxious not to let the grass grow under its feet and produced a revised specification race engine at Ricard. Dubbed EF15C, the modified power unit incorporated a new cylinder head design with reprofiled ports and smaller wastegates for improved response.

'The intention is to provide a unit which offers an improved performance/fuel consumption equation which will prevent us from encountering Montreal-type consumption problems at high-revving circuits like Hockenheim', explained Gérard Ducarouge. Senna ran the new engine for 40 laps in Friday's untimed session before switching to his qualifying spare for the afternoon.

The Brazilian set his pole time on the first day, failing to improve on his 1m 6.526s the following after both Andrea de Cesaris's Minardi and Thierry Boutsen's Arrows had blown their engines and dropped oil over a considerable portion of the circuit.

'The car didn't feel ideally balanced on Friday', Senna explained, 'and I was hoping to go quicker, because the track felt as though it had more grip

on Saturday before that oil went down, although it was slightly hotter and we were running into a bit of a head wind on the back straight.'

Mansell traded fast times energetically with Senna throughout Friday qualifying, eventually losing out by a scant 0.2s. 'Two of my runs were spoiled by traffic', said Nigel, 'particularly when I had to squeeze past one of the Minardis on the tight infield section before the pits. I was also impressed with the straightline speed of the Ferraris. Michele came past me, when I was running qualifying boost, on the back straight and it seemed as though I was tied to a post!'

On Saturday came the drama with the oil slick, which Nigel met on his first attempt when he found marshals in the middle of the track attempting to clear it up – without warning flags – on the main straight. Then he suffered a major engine failure on the Mistral straight on his second run. Still, he was happy enough.

Nelson Piquet had a brand new FW11 chassis (05) to replace the one he had rattled off the walls in Detroit. The Brazilian was happy with its handling and, despite a slight fuel cut-out problem on Friday, he posted third-quickest time. His first Saturday run was spoiled when a hose connecting a turbo to its intercooler became dislodged, and the oil had gone down before he could do his second.

Over in the Ligier camp there was a highly optimistic feeling in view of Laffite's recent second place in Detroit. But it was René Arnoux, winner here for Renault in '82, who was right on the pace during Ricard qualifying. He set fifth-fastest time in the JS27 on Friday – 'but I was baulked by Alboreto' – and then emerged as one of the few drivers to improve on the second day, winding up fourth overall. 'I think I could have gone even quicker and pushed Mansell off the front row if

Jacques hadn't held me up inadvertently at one point', enthused René. Jacques himself finished 11th-quickest, failing to improve on his Friday best after trying for a quick time just after the oil had gone down.

McLaren International's two drivers were suffering from their usual lack of qualifying horse-power and World Champion Alain Prost also complained about poor throttle response for much of qualifying. He still managed fifth-quickest time on Friday, though, and improved marginally to hold his position the following day.

On Saturday afternoon Prost got involved in a slight collision with Alboreto's Ferrari, the Italian machine's right-rear wheel glancing the McLaren's left-front on one of the slow infield loops. Prost admitted that he may have lifted off rather abruptly in response to the oil flags, Michele being forced to weave round his McLaren. The Ferrari was launched over a low kerb and came fishtailing back on the track beyond the apex of the corner, both cars then crawling into the pits to change bent wheels.

Alboreto's sixth position was achieved with an F1/86 featuring a slightly longer wheelbase, this being but one element in a series of modifications intended for incorporation into a revised Ferrari later in the season. Team-mate Johansson managed tenth-best time, although an electronic error deep within the Olivetti/Longines briefly raised his hopes by proclaiming him second only to Senna at one point on Saturday afternoon! Sadly, Stefan's elation was shortlived and the fictitious time was erased from the list almost before it had been recorded. 'Still, I suppose we've got less understeer than I'd expected', reflected the Swede ruefully.

Keke Rosberg managed seventh in his McLaren immediately ahead of Benetton's Gerhard Berger,

Johnny Dumfries takes to the dirt after his coming-together with Rothengatter's slow Zakspeed. The Lotus driver, having made a good start, retired eventually with engine trouble.

A troubled weekend for Alboreto. The Ferrari driver tangled with Prost during practice and then stalled on the starting grid. He recovered to finish a distant eighth. Piquet, troubled by oversteer and a piston which was on the point of failure, follows to finish third.

the Austrian recording this time despite a slight misfire in his B186. His team-mate, Teo Fabi, was right behind in ninth spot and, impressively, the compact Italian's best time was set after the oil had been dropped.

Johnny Dumfries had also obviously been heartened by his run to seventh place in Detroit and looked more confident than hitherto behind the wheel of the second Lotus 98T. He spoiled things a bit on Friday by locking up his qualifiers going into the first tight right-hander, but went out shortly before the end of Saturday's session to improve from 15th to 12th, barely two seconds slower than his team leader.

After being obliged to miss the two North American races following his accident during the race morning warm-up in Montreal, Patrick Tambay was back in harness once more, although on Friday he admitted he was suffering slightly as the Lola's seat harness chafed on his bruised rib cage. 'I think the car is probably better than I am today', confessed the genial Frenchman. He managed 13th-quickest time on Friday and held that position the following day, lopping a further half-second off his quickest time. 'I nearly went off on Boutsen's oil', he admitted, 'so I did my best time on my third run which quite pleased me.' Tambay had a new Lola chassis (005) at his disposal and tried a revised Ford V6 with smaller turbo compressors, all part of the ongoing Ford development programme.

Alan Jones found his car weaving disconcertingly under hard braking during Friday's untimed session, rather taking the edge off his confidence. He qualified 19th on Friday, but slipped a further place the following afternoon, his Lola suffering from a fuel leak into the cockpit for much of Saturday's two sessions, making life pretty uncomfortable for the Australian.

Both Brabham BT55 drivers were complaining of excessive understeer, particularly on the 'new link' section. Added to that, the BMW engine response out of the corners was as bad as ever and the lowline cars proved frustratingly slow in a straight line. Derek Warwick ended up 14th, grappling with fluctuating turbo boost pressure throughout the Saturday session. Riccardo Patrese had to switch to the spare car for second qualifying after his race chassis developed gearbox trouble. Then he was badly baulked on his first run and the oil went down before he could salvage anything worthwhile from his second. He finished up an angry 16th.

Martin Brundle was optimistic about race prospects for the Tyrrell 015 which he reckoned was 'as fast as anything through the tight infield section.' He did a promising 12th-quickest time on Friday, but found himself stranded out on the circuit the following afternoon with a seized front brake. With no spare 015 available, there was no option but for Martin to sit out the remainder of second qualifying. He dropped to 15th as a result.

Philippe Streiff survived a minor collision with Alboreto's Ferrari to qualify 17th ahead of Christian Danner's Arrows A8, the German having to ease off his BMW's qualifying boost pressure in order to prevent the rev-limiter from cutting in abruptly on the back straight.

To the thinly veiled annoyance of Andrea de Cesaris, his Minardi team-mate Alessandro Nannini qualified 19th, almost two seconds faster than the former Ligier driver. Andrea suffered turbo failures in both qualifying sessions and asked to borrow Sandro's machine to see if it was any quicker. It wasn't, leaving Andrea simmering quietly back in 23rd place.

Jonathan Palmer's biggest problem with the Zakspeed was a steering vibration so severe that

TECHNICAL FILE

ARROWS
No change.

BENETTON
Two race cars fitted with larger heat exchangers for oil systems on Saturday. Brakes not so critical at Ricard; returned to AP calipers.

BRABHAM
Patrese tested nose configuration similar to that seen in Brazil. Tried front wings with wider plane and smaller rear flaps. All three cars had front suspension tried in Canada. BMW tested new injection pump. Sergio Rinland (ex-Williams and RAM) now at Brabham.

FERRARI
Revised front suspension on race cars increased wheelbase by 45 mm because wishbones angled forward (with front wings cut to suit). Tested at Imola new rear end made up of suspension from 1984 C5 (the pushrod variety introduced in Holland). Car tested was 10 cm shorter due to omission of the bell-housing between engine and gearbox. Louvred ducts to top and sides of side pods to assist turbo cooling.

LIGIER
New wastegate and new electronic mapping made available by Renault – but not the latest engine.

LOLA
New chassis for Tambay, who worked with new recruit, Adrian Newey.

LOTUS
Senna given the latest Renault engine (EF15C) featuring new heads, fuel system, wastegate and electronic mapping. Only two EF15Cs available. Senna completed 40 laps during practice with no problems and raced the other engine (briefly). Main advantage: improved fuel consumption. External difference: location of fuel-feed pipe outside, instead of inside, vee; different trumpets and injectors. Senna's car fitted with Brembo calipers while Dumfries given 1985 Brembo/Lotus calipers.

McLAREN
Secret test at Silverstone to try small side skirts (similar to Williams). Ran these at Ricard. Fitted flexible skirts to front wing side plates on Saturday. Complied with Scrutineer's wishes for more rigid fixing.

MINARDI
Nannini's car fitted with new Brembo calipers giving a weight saving of 6 kg – represented a saving of £4000 per weekend, a good solution for a team unable to afford carbon-fibre discs. Revised differential fitted to Nannini's car on Friday; de Cesaris's car so equipped on Saturday.

OSELLA
Ghinzani raced new car.

TYRRELL
Revised electronic mapping but none of the other Renault modifications made available. Small deflectors fitted to side plates of rear wing.

WILLIAMS
New, lighter chassis for Piquet to replace car damaged in Detroit. Fitted skirt with 1 cm vertical edge to side plates of front wings for Saturday morning practice only.

ZAKSPEED
No change. G.P.

Christian Danner finished a Grand Prix for the first time. Forced to switch to the spare Arrows at the last minute, Danner stalled on the grid but, once under way, took a careful eleventh place *(right)*.

René Arnoux spent a large part of his birthday on the first day of practice driving the spare Ligier to test various settings for the race. Diligent work by the French team allowed Arnoux to hold second place before making the first of two stops for tyres. He finished an eventual fifth.

International Press Agency

June/July
FISA announce controversial proposals governing qualifying procedures at Grands Prix and changes to the engine formula.
March designer Adrian Newey joins Haas Formula 1 team.
BMW decide to quit Formula 1 at the end of 1986.
Cosworth produce 400th DFV engine.

the task of reading the cockpit instruments was rendered almost impossible! On Saturday he used the spare 861 with a double rear wing, but the higher ambient temperatures knocked the edge off the engine's performance. He was disappointed to emerge 22nd on the grid only two places ahead of plodding team-mate Huub Rothengatter. The final row was occupied by the Osellas of Ghinzani and Berg, the young Canadian having a particularly torrid time with two fires caused by ruptured fuel filters.

RACE

After both days of qualifying had taken place in absolutely sweltering conditions, race morning dawned slightly overcast with a very real chance of rain threatening. Rosberg's McLaren produced the quickest time in the half-hour warm-up, in which Johansson's Ferrari suffered a spectacular turbo failure in front of the pits and Berger's Benetton needed an engine change as it was suffering from a serious misfire.

The last few moments before the start were to prove hectic for the Benetton lads. Berger went out on the warm-up lap in his race car, but immediately radioed in that the engine was awful and that he wanted to switch to the spare. He did just that, then found that the spare would not pull sufficient boost pressure, so the Austrian tore back into the pits for a second time and switched back to the race car. He just managed to squeeze out a minute or so before the pit lane closed, leaving his belts to be done up on the grid where the rear body section was also fitted. Meanwhile, Fabi's B186 suffered a brief turbo fire which was quickly extinguished and everybody prepared for the start.

Alboreto and Danner stalled their engines just before the green light came on, but the Ricard startline is sufficiently wide to ensure that everybody else avoided them as the pack sprinted off down to the first tight right-hander. Mansell made an excellent start, moving sufficiently clear of Senna to pull across the Lotus's bows and swing into the turn without any dramas.

Down the back straight, through the infield twists and out onto the start-and-finish straight to complete lap 1, Mansell led from Senna, with Arnoux third ahead of Berger, Prost, Dumfries (a fine start), Piquet and Rosberg. Warwick's Brabham had bumped a rear wheel of Fabi's Benetton in that first-lap traffic jam, so they both trailed into the pits at the end of the first lap, Derek for a replacement nose, Fabi with a punctured rear Pirelli.

With Mansell easing away all the time, Senna really had his hands full keeping the Williams-Honda in sight on this difficult circuit, but the whole complexion of the Championship battle was altered as early as lap 4. On the preceding lap, de Cesaris's Minardi blew up in a big way, the inconsiderate Italian cruising round the infield section on the racing line as lubricant spewed out of his Motori-Moderni V6.

Alan Jones promptly spun off on this treacherous slick and most of the field confessed to having major difficulties, made all the more unexpected by the apparent lack of oil flags warning of the

137

The officials at Paul Ricard displayed an alarming degree of ineptitude, particularly in the light of de Angelis's fatal accident two months before. Philippe Streiff directs an ill-equipped marshal as a fire, caused by a broken injector on his Tyrrell-Renault, takes hold. Streiff, it should be said, did not help matters by leaving the fuel pump switched on.

Jacques Laffite: another consistent drive into the points *(below)*.

hazard. On lap 5 Mansell survived a severe slide on the slippery surface, but Senna went skating off into the tyre barrier on a fast right-hand kink, removing a front wheel from his Lotus and writing himself out of the equation very firmly. To his considerable credit, he went straight back to the pits and apologised to his mechanics.

This celebrated retirement took the heat off Mansell slightly, only Arnoux looking like any sort of threat to the Williams at this stage in the game. Berger was fending off both the McLarens from third place, while Piquet was now sixth ahead of Laffite and Dumfries. Rothengatter stopped early to change a deflated tyre, Johansson's Ferrari broke a turbo on lap 6 and Fabi's Benetton misfired into retirement two laps later.

The two McLarens quickly moved ahead of Berger and on lap 11 the Benetton was chopped badly by Danner's Arrows as Gerhard came up to lap it, the B186 losing its nose section as it slewed over one of the A8's front wheels. The impact also damaged the gearbox, so although Berger resumed after stopping for a fresh nose section to be fitted, he eventually retired with gear selector trouble on lap 23.

Meanwhile, Prost was putting everything he'd got into a challenge for the lead. 'Almost from the start my fuel gauge told me that the engine was consuming fuel at a far heavier rate than during practice', explained the World Champion, 'so I had to run the absolute minimum boost pressure settings and try and make up the deficit as much as I could out of the chassis.'

The Williams team strategy was something of a gamble, calling for both cars to make two routine tyre stops. On the one hand, there was the risk that a fumbled wheel change might cost a lot of time. On the other hand, if it worked, Patrick Head had calculated that the FW11s would be in really good shape. The concept worked perfectly!

By lap 19 Prost was less than five seconds behind the leading Williams and, when Nigel got badly held up trying to lap Palmer, the McLaren ace took another couple of seconds out of his advantage. Piquet made his first stop on lap 21, dropping from fourth to fifth, while Mansell changed tyres on lap 25, dropping back to third behind the two McLarens.

Prost waited until the end of lap 36 to make his one tyre stop of the race, allowing Mansell back into the lead with Piquet now third and Rosberg fourth ahead of Arnoux and Laffite. On lap 35 Dumfries's Lotus was savaged from behind by Rothengatter's Zakspeed going into the first right-hander beyond the pits: the German car broke its left-front suspension in the impact, but Dumfries continued after a precautionary pit stop, the Lotus eventually seizing its engine on lap 57.

On lap 44, Streiff's Tyrrell rolled to a halt just before the pit lane entry, its engine compartment billowing smoke and flame after a fuel line had become disconnected and pumped 102RON Elf onto a hot turbo. Philippe quickly vacated the cockpit, but unfortuantely forgot to turn off the electric fuel pump – which went on feeding the fire until the battery flattened itself!

The result was a spectacular conflagration and one can only rejoice that there was no driver

The hand of friendship and the grim face of power. Alain Prost offers warm congratulations to Nigel Mansell after a drive which left the World Champion's McLaren-TAG struggling. Jean-Marie Balestre, weakened by the effort of introducing another series of unpopular reforms, contemplates a holiday.

THE RACE TO BAN QUALIFYING TYRES AND ENGINES

In the week preceding the French Grand Prix, the FISA Executive Committee issued a series of controversial changes to the Grand Prix qualifying procedures, due to come into effect in 1987. The main points of the communiqué were:

Friday: untimed practice for one hour in the morning followed by a further one and a half hours in the afternoon.

Saturday: half an hour of untimed practice in the morning. In the afternoon, a qualifying session over a distance of 25 per cent of the length of the race on Sunday with a quantity of fuel allocated in proportion to the 195 litres allowed for the race.

The drivers to take the start of this 'session' in grid formation, the positions being determined on the basis of the results obtained by the drivers in the previous Grand Prix and their classification in the current World Championship.

Sunday: half-hour warm-up in the morning. The grid for the race to be determined by parameters, 30 per cent of which shall correspond with the results of the qualifying session on Saturday afternoon and 70 per cent on the results obtained by the drivers in the previous Grand Prix and their classification in the current World Championship (the precise details were due to be finalised at a later date).

The purpose of the regulations was the banning of qualifying tyres and engines, which would almost certainly be the case. In return, however, the teams and drivers would be faced with two starts, and the accompanying dangers, in the course of the weekend. Regardless of the dubious phraseology used by FISA, the 'qualifying session' would be a race in everything but name.

The proposals caused immediate resentment among the drivers since they had not been consulted at any stage.

New Formula 1 from 1989

The FISA Executive Committee also decided on major changes for 1989, the aim being to reduce engine power to 600 bhp by one of the following means:

1. Reduction of cubic capacity to 1100 or 1200 cc; or

2. The compulsory use of normally aspirated engines with a maximum capacity of 3500 cc.

The latter alternative seemed to gain most favour among the teams when questioned by *Autocourse* at Paul Ricard.

trapped in the Tyrrell because the circuit fire marshals' efforts to extinguish the flames were pure slapstick comedy. The whole affair was highlighted by a giant fire tender moving the *wrong way* down the pit lane in an attempt to extinguish the blaze, a task which took far, far too long and made one wonder just how much progress the circuit had made on safety facilities since the unfortunate de Angelis accident.

Lap 53 saw Prost back in the lead as Mansell stopped for his second tyre change, but Nigel now had fresh rubber and plenty of fuel with which to come back at the World Champion. On lap 58 he tore past the McLaren as they went across the start-and-finish line and, for the remaining 22 laps, had no problem controlling the race.

Nigel did admit that Prost kept him on his toes for longer than he had expected, but towards the end Alain had to ease off quite dramatically to conserve his precious remaining fuel. The winning margin was just over 17 seconds at the flag.

Piquet, troubled by low-speed oversteer and a piston in his Honda engine which, it was later established, was on the verge of breaking up, brought his Williams FW11 home third, slipping past Rosberg in the closing stages. Keke admitted, 'I lost a lot of time at the first corner where I was

almost forced to stop in the traffic. From that moment on I was at a fuel disadvantage as compared with Alain because I'd got that deficit to claw back in addition to making the race distance. It was all very frustrating.'

Keke was the last unlapped runner, the Ligiers of Arnoux and Laffite both making two tyre stops apiece to complete the top six, while Patrese worked hard to take seventh in his BT55. Eighth was Alboreto, the Italian climbing back doggedly after stalling on the line, while Warwick passed Brundle in the closing stages when the Tyrrell lost fourth gear. Derek drove most of the race having to hold third gear in place, as his bruised hand testified!

Danner finished a solid 11th ahead of Boutsen, the Belgian delayed by several stops to patch up disintegrating bodywork. Tambay's Lola looked a possible candidate for sixth place, but a seized front brake caliper sidelined him with 15 laps to go, while Palmer suffered an engine failure in his Zakspeed.

For Mansell, however, there was nothing to complain about. As he aimed for Brands Hatch – and a home crowd – his feet were planted firmly on top of the world.

A.H.

SHELL OILS
B R I T I S H
Grand Prix

The Williams-Honda team totally dominated the British Grand Prix *(main picture)* and Nigel Mansell convincingly crushed his team-mate Nelson Piquet despite being forced to race the spare car.

Brabham brought their BT54 out of retirement, Riccardo Patrese running strongly before retiring *(above right)*.

Thierry Boutsen *(top right)* celebrated his birthday by making the headlines for all the wrong reasons. After causing the first-lap accident, the Belgian driver was able to switch to his spare car but the Arrows-BMW was plagued by a misfire.

An angry Derek Warwick ran out of fuel a few yards from the line and dropped from sixth to eighth place after an excellent drive in the difficult BT55 *(below right)*.

There was a point, five seconds after the start, when it looked as though it would be a tedious race: no happy ending for the capacity crowd, nothing to say. At the finish, it was difficult to know where to begin describing one of the most remarkable days in the history of the British Grand Prix.

Nigel Mansell won his fourth race of the season to move to the top of the championship. He did it after a race-long battle with his Williams team-mate Nelson Piquet; he did it in a car which he had been reluctant to drive all weekend and, along the way, he lapped the third-place McLaren of Alain Prost. But, more than that, Mansell had no right to be in the race in the first place.

Within 15 metres of the start, a broken driveshaft meant that Mansell's race was run. Victory for Piquet became a foregone conclusion. Within 100 metres of the start, a multiple accident caused the race to be stopped and the subsequent delay allowed Mansell the luxury of restarting with the back-up car.

The spare FW11 had been set up for Piquet and the Brazilian was to witness its effectiveness when Mansell took the battle to him – and won. Convincingly, for there was no-one else in the contest. And the only black spot in an otherwise perfect day at Brands Hatch was the leg and pelvic injuries suffered by Jacques Laffite in that highly significant first-lap accident.

International Press Agency

A miserable weekend for Jacques Laffite began when his Ligier caught fire during practice on Friday. He collided with Rosberg later in the day but that was to be a minor problem when compared to his misfortune in the race. The innocent victim of the first-lap accident, Laffite suffered injuries to his legs and pelvis just after he had started what should have been his 175th Grand Prix.

ENTRY AND PRACTICE

For once, practice was not about the man on pole; the high point was seeing the owner of his team.

Frank Williams made a welcome and, at times, emotional return to the Grand Prix paddock when he came to Brands Hatch to see his cars in action. More than that, he faced the press and the standing ovation gave an indication of the appreciation of this brave act and the esteem which the Formula 1 world held for the team boss as he continued to make a long and slow recovery from his road accident.

Frank refused to take credit for the success enjoyed by his team. It was a well-oiled, highly motivated operation and proof of this was an all-Williams front row by 2.0 p.m. on Saturday. Moving on from the obvious delight shared by everyone for Frank, the internal political implications of this were interesting: Nelson Piquet was the faster of the two Williams drivers, and had been throughout practice.

It was good to see that Nelson had no intention of being cowed by Mansell's recent success and Nelson was the only driver to break the 1m 7s barrier. Mansell, for once, seemed to be receiving most of the team's misfortune but there could be no getting away from the fact that Nelson had shown all his old flair as he went to work on this difficult circuit.

Make no mistake, Mansell wanted pole more than anything and, indeed, his desire at times seemed to be ruling his head, particularly during a ragged lap on Saturday as he tried to make up for problems the previous day. That was when a water leak had called for a switch to the T-car while the engine was changed. The spare car, in fact, was no answer since there was a problem with the turbo wastegate and by the time qualifying came round in the afternoon, Mansell was not as prepared as he would have liked.

Not having had the chance to run qualifiers, Mansell ran a set of Cs and then a set of the qualifiers (Es). He held pole briefly but when Piquet responded on his qualifiers, Mansell's lap on Es was blighted by a high-speed misfire. Saturday was not much better, traffic barring the way on his first set of qualifiers. On his second, the high-boost misfire returned and, just as he was fiddling with the boost control *and* trying to negotiate Stirlings Bend *and* keep an eye on two cars in front, he ran wide and that was that. Piquet, meanwhile, had calmly produced his scintillating lap with no trouble at all.

Things were not so straightforward at Lotus. Generally, the track conditions were slower and more slippery than expected although no-one could pinpoint the reason. Ayrton Senna, who we had expected to see on the front row at the very least, had great difficulty in coaxing the correct temperature into his Goodyears and, additionally, there was a misfire on his race car. Ayrton alone had the use of the latest Renault engine, the EF15C, and he took time out to run the race car on Saturday afternoon to see if the misfire had been cured by a change of wiring loom. On top of that, the handling did not allow the usual flowing style from Senna and, although there was an improve-

July

Lotus rumoured to be switching from Renault to Honda engines.

Ligier announce deal with Alfa Romeo.

Ferrari, among others, approach Mansell for 1987.

Frank Williams made a most welcome return to the Formula 1 scene. He was treated to pole position, the first two places and fastest lap in the race, results which were bound to bolster his determination to recover from a road accident earlier in the year.

ment on Saturday, he spoiled his best lap with a missed gearchange.

It was a blown engine which would mar Gerhard Berger's day on Saturday. The Austrian had taken his Benetton around Brands on the very limit to set an excellent second-fastest time on Friday but that time remained his best when the subsequent switch to the spare in the final session put him a second off the pace. Berger's extrovert style proved too much for Teo Fabi although it was the Italian who had to make use of his spare (there was one for each driver) on Friday after encountering engine trouble on his regular car.

The Benettons were well-suited to the fast sweeps of Brands; that was more or less expected. So, too, was the fact that the McLaren drivers would find difficulty in tuning their cars to this circuit. Prost had come across that problem during the European Grand Prix the previous October and things were no different nine months on. Oversteer on the bumps made the car almost undriveable and a stiffening of the front end suited Rosberg more than Prost. For once, Keke was able to fling the car around and his progress through Graham Hill Bend was a reminder of his days with Williams.

Keke, quickest at one stage on Friday, failed to put in a lap on his second set when his car was savaged by Laffite, the Frenchman having left his braking too late going into Druids. For Saturday, Rosberg was again the quicker of the two and, as ever, the McLaren drivers were more confident about the race than practice.

One of the highlights of the European Grand Prix had been the performance of the Ligiers and the French were therefore disappointed to find themselves struggling. René Arnoux complained of poor balance and no grip, the little man with the punk crew-cut resorting to soft race tyres to set eighth-fastest time, a respectable position but, by all accounts, hard work.

René, though, was lucky. Poor Laffite, the lap record holder, was down in 19th place. The incident with Rosberg aside, he had already walked back to the pits earlier on Friday after a fuel injection pipe had come adrift and set fire to the rear of his car. On Saturday, the engine kept cutting out – all of which meant Jacques was actually slower in practice than he had been in the race the previous year! And, in retrospect, this lowly grid position was a catastrophy.

Ninth: Derek Warwick. This, too, was a surprise but for the opposite reason. No-one expected the cumbersome BT55 to be that competitive, least of all the man wrestling with the steering wheel. A switch to the spare car combined with a brave effort made up for the appalling lack of power and grip out of the slow corners. Brabham, meanwhile, took a couple of steps backwards to make one step forward. How? By producing a couple of 1985 BT54s for Riccardo Patrese.

In this public back-to-back test, it was clear that the lowline BT55 was marginally the better of two very mediocre cars and it was questionable whether the massive logistical problem of bringing two totally different chassis and their spares had been worthwhile. Patrese was not helped by a

boost problem which obliged him to switch to his spare chassis on Saturday afternoon. He was 15th, one second slower than Warwick who, in turn, was three seconds off the required pace.

Warwick headed a pocket of British drivers in the middle of the grid, Johnny Dumfries taking 10th place ahead of Martin Brundle's Tyrrell. This was the closest Dumfries had been to Senna since the start of the season and it was the result of a confidence imbued by driving on a circuit he knew and liked. Indeed, Dumfries would have been higher still had it not been for a moment on oil on his first set and a wayward Benetton while running his second set. Dumfries tried a third run but without improvement. Nevertheless, his Friday time remained a respectable achievement.

Brundle, on the other hand, did manage to quicken his pace on Saturday, which was just as well since aerodynamic adjustments were worth over a second and at least six places on the grid. Brundle was looking for a further improvement when he came across blue smoke hanging in the air at Graham Hill Bend. Suspecting that there might be oil lurking on this tricky fifth-gear left-hander, he backed off fractionally and that was enough to add a second to what should have been another fast lap.

The culprit had been Michele Alboreto, the Ferrari driver having pulled off to enable the efficient marshals to deal with a turbo fire. It summed up a troubled two days of understeer and lack of traction over the bumps, although the red car had not been short on power when it came to rushing through the speed traps (the Benetton-BMWs also being among the quickest). With the pits a step away, Alboreto returned to take over the spare car . . . only to find Stefan Johansson sitting patiently at the wheel.

The Swede had suffered an engine failure (causing a harmless spin at Druids early in the final session) and he had stepped into the T-car. Finding oil on the track, Stefan returned to the pits to wait for a more opportune moment. Alboreto's arrival on foot ended that idea. Johansson was ordered out of the spare and stood idly by while Alboreto, on his last lap, improved by over a second. Johansson, now almost speechless with rage, had not completed a single quick lap and he dropped from 10th (a place higher than Michele on Friday) to 18th.

The furious schedule of four races in five weekends had played havoc with the Arrows team's plans to finish their new car in time for Brands Hatch. As a result, Thierry Boutsen was yet again back in the elderly A8 and doing his usual competent job. Christian Danner had a more trying time, his engine being down on power on Saturday morning. The replacement was no better and the German was restricted to three cylinders and Friday's time at the end of the final session.

Ford produced a revised-specification engine for Brands Hatch but a water leak (believed to have been caused by a loose water cap) meant Tambay didn't get far with the V6 on Friday morning. A return to the old-spec engine compounded problems with understeer and he was 17th. Alan Jones, on the other hand, had a revised Ford for

the final session, the Australian reporting that the higher compression improved the response. For once, Jones had a relatively trouble-free practice and he took 14th place, an encouraging performance since the Fords were continuing to run at race boost during qualifying.

Philippe Streiff's Tyrrell had been repaired following the fire at Ricard – which was just as well since the team were short of 015s. The Frenchman tangled with Boutsen at Druids on Friday afternoon and a pick-up problem with the fresh Renault V6 for Saturday meant he only found an extra couple of tenths in the final session.

Alessandro Nannini once again qualified ahead of Andrea de Cesaris, the Minardis beating the Zakspeed of Jonathan Palmer in both sessions. Nannini, relying on Friday's time, had turbo trouble in the final hour and Palmer was similarly afflicted, the German four-cylinder refusing to run high boost at a time when, according to Palmer, the chassis was working efficiently.

Not working efficiently in the eyes of the scrutineers on Friday was the fire extinguisher on Huub Rothengatter's Zakspeed. A leaking valve had been the culprit but the team was fined £2000 and the times deleted. On Saturday, Rothengatter could only manage a lap ten seconds off pole to split the Osellas of Ghinzani and Berg, the young Canadian having to sit out the final session after crashing earlier in the day.

RACE

There were an estimated 120,000 people crammed into Brands Hatch and it must have been unnerving for poor Piquet to know that the majority of them wished him ill in the nicest possible way.

He must have been even more disturbed when a turbo fire caused him to pull up suddenly on the main straight during the morning warm-up. The flames were soon dealt with but, meanwhile, Mansell was second-fastest, splitting the McLarens of Rosberg and Prost.

The good news was that the car was repairable and the Brazilian would have no need of the spare car. Which, in retrospect, was just as well . . .

Senna was fourth-fastest, two-tenths quicker than Riccardo Patrese, although this encouraging performance by the Italian was marred by an engine failure which forced him to take the spare BT54 for the race. Before the day was out, spare cars would be in common use all round but, in the meantime, all eyes were on the start.

Piquet may have held pole but Mansell, quite literally, was in a better position since the sloping track surface usually worked in favour of the man on the outside of the front row. And, if he was to win this race, Mansell needed to beat his team-mate away from the lights.

As far as Mansell was concerned, everything seemed to be going according to plan – at least for the first 15 metres or so. The Englishman had edged alongside but, as he snatched second gear, an explosion at the rear of the car announced the failure of the left-hand driveshaft coupling.

As Mansell crept slowly up the hill towards Druids, he radioed to the Williams pit that his race

The most crucial few seconds of the British Grand Prix. Thierry Boutsen's wayward Arrows collects several cars at the entrance to Paddock Hill Bend as Jacques Laffite, forced to the right, heads towards the waiting armco. The race was stopped, allowing Nigel Mansell to take the restart – and win.

was over. And, to his great surprise, black flags informed him that the race was momentarily at an end for the rest of the field as well.

As the rear half of the grid had rushed towards Paddock, Thierry Boutsen suddenly lost control of his Arrows. The cream-and-brown car had careered from right to left, bouncing off the barrier on the outside of the track before spinning into the path of at least nine cars as they crested the rise.

Johansson, confronted by the Arrows (now dragging an advertising banner with it), swerved to the right, forcing Laffite, running alongside the Ferrari, to do the same. As they took to the sloping grassy surface on the inside of the corner, Johansson just clipped the edge of the barrier surrounding the mouth of the tunnel under the track. Laffite, a hapless victim, was about to pay dearly for such a lowly grid position.

The Ligier rammed the barrier head-on and, since the armco was not designed to give at this point, the car took the brunt of the impact. Meanwhile, back on the track, there was chaos as neither Palmer nor Ghinzani could avoid ramming the Arrows and, along the way, Danner, de Cesaris, Nannini, Rothengatter and Berg became caught in the mayhem. The race was stopped immediately.

Palmer, running from the scene, spotted Laffite trapped in his car and immediately rushed to his aid. The doctor was shocked by the state of the Ligier and it took at least 35 minutes to stabilise Jacques and free him from the cockpit. As the officials worked quietly and efficiently, other members of the marshalling force at Brands Hatch did neither themselves nor the circuit any credit by rudely refusing anxious members of the Ligier team access to the scene. Once free, Jacques was taken to a helicopter and flown to hospital in Sidcup where he was found to have injuries to his legs and pelvis.

In all there was a delay of 80 minutes, during which time frantic work saw Nannini's car repaired (although not in time to allow him to take his place on the grid) and Rothengatter's Zakspeed made ready along with Johansson's lightly damaged Ferrari and Warwick's Brabham (the nose of which had been damaged by Dumfries in a separate incident). Danner, Berg and Ghinzani were out for the day, while stepping into T-cars would be Palmer, Boutsen, de Cesaris and, of course, Mansell.

While grateful for this second chance, Mansell nevertheless was pessimistic about driving a car which, as a matter of course, had been set up for Piquet. 'I only drove this car briefly on Friday', said Nigel, 'and it hasn't really worked well all weekend.'

Once the helicopter had returned from Sidcup, the British Grand Prix started from scratch (the rules saying that if the race is stopped within two laps, the first start is null and void). This time, Mansell was not about to try any heroics in a car which was comparatively new to him and, on the green light, he slotted into second place behind Piquet. On the run towards Hawthorn, he dropped to third behind Berger.

ARROWS
Nothing new.

BENETTON
Four cars available. Chassis number 3, damaged during test at Croix-en-Ternois, becomes T-car. Each car now fitted with the larger oil cooler seen at Paul Ricard.

BRABHAM
Two BT54s (one brought from Donington Collection) for Patrese. Gordon Murray wanted to do back-to-back tests with BT55 to check engine response and acceleration on both cars. There was only a small difference in the lap times but the BT55 had better straightline speed, thus pinpointing the poor acceleration from the corners. No work done on the BT54 apart from the introduction of a slimmer front brake duct. No changes to BT55.

FERRARI
All three cars fitted with revised front suspension, first seen at Paul Ricard, and new top rear wishbones introduced in Canada. Wider rear wings with larger side plates. Alboreto's car fitted with a skirt, wrapped around the nose cone, and a double rear wing. Alboreto's car also had stiffer suspension than Johansson's. Ferrari used KKK turbos during qualifying but reverted to Garrett for the race.

LOLA
New Ford engine (revised pistons and higher compression to give better response) for Jones on Friday; Tambay's turn on Saturday. New side plates to rear wing to increase downforce.

LOTUS
New chassis for Senna to replace car damaged at Paul Ricard. Only Senna had use of latest Renault engine, the EF15C. Senna used T-car (lighter and fitted with smaller fuel tank) for qualifying.

McLAREN
Prost tried different front suspension geometry. All three cars fitted with small skirts. Used heated tyres during qualifying for the first time.

MINARDI
Brembo brake calipers for Nannini.

OSELLA
Nothing new.

TYRRELL
Brundle's car fitted with skirt around nose. The sloping bottom to nose cone filled in to create a level surface. Rear wing fitted with the vertical deflectors seen in France. Did not have the latest wastegate used by Lotus and Ligier.

WILLIAMS
Fitted small side skirts to chassis, as seen for the first time at Paul Ricard, even though rear edges destroyed after two or three laps. (Gabriel Cadringher, FISA Scrutineer, held a meeting with team engineers to discuss mini-skirts. It was agreed that side skirts should be banned, as from Hockenheim, and that the skirts on the front wings should be made of the same material as the side plates.)

ZAKSPEED
Engines with three injectors per cylinder available on all three cars. Rothengatter's car, damaged at Paul Ricard, repaired. Carbon-fibre brakes on T-car.

G.P.

After two laps, Mansell felt he had waited long enough. Leaving Surtees, he overtook the Benetton with a display of power which set the tone for the remainder of the race. If the Williams Honda could run at those speeds *and* have fuel remaining, then no-one would have a look in.

By lap 6, Berger had fallen five seconds behind although the gradually increasing gap over Senna's fourth-place Lotus was proof that the Benetton was not hanging around. In fact, Senna was coming under pressure from Rosberg but that spark of interest was to die when Keke retired with gearbox trouble at the end of lap 8. The Finn, who for once had the legs of his team-mate, was bitterly disappointed.

That allowed Prost to take fifth place with Fabi moving into the points ahead of Alboreto and Arnoux. Jones and Warwick were not far behind while Patrese, having dispensed with Dumfries, was catching his Brabham team-mate. Everyone then shuffled forward one place on lap 14 when Fabi, running soft Pirellis on the front and hard on the rear, made an unscheduled stop with a badly delaminating tyre. In the end, the vibrations caused by the out-of-balance tyre were to shake the fuel system apart! It was to mark the beginning of the Benetton team's decline since Berger, running easily in third place, would roll to a silent halt on lap 23. The Austrian walked back to report an apparent engine failure, but when the black box was changed after the race, the BMW burst into life . . .

In the meantime, there had been a further change in the top six on lap 17. To everyone's surprise, Prost headed for the pits and a change of tyres and, indeed, the stop was far from routine since a balance weight had flown off one wheel to cause a severe vibration. Prost collected fresh rubber, no doubt aware that the timing of this incident was very awkward and he would almost certainly have to stop again in any case.

At around the same time, Boutsen made a long stop to cure an electrical problem on the spare, while six laps later Johansson was ended by a holed radiator.

All this went unnoticed, however, for Mansell was sitting on Piquet's tail after setting the fastest lap so far on lap 20. Heading out of South Bank on lap 23, Nelson missed a gear and, instantly, Mansell was ready to snap up such a simple but costly mistake. The public enclosures erupted as he came by in the lead. Next phase of this in-house battle would be the pit stops.

Most certainly, this race was proving a Williams benefit. With Berger's demise, Senna had taken third place but he was some 25 seconds behind the leaders. Realistically, Ayrton knew there was no chance of catching the Williams given the comparative fuel consumption of his Renault engine and the more economical Honda but such arguments became academic on lap 27 when the Brazilian pulled into the pits, fourth gear on the Lotus having broken. Ayrton did one more lap but it was pointless. He retired from the second race in succession.

Two victories in as many weeks for Williams was on the cards. But for which driver? There were no team orders, Patrick Head and Frank

Dernie assiduously giving Mansell and Piquet instructions for identical boost settings. Both men were driving as hard as they could – and there was nothing in it. The pit stops might just decide the outcome of this race.

Piquet came in first. Everything went according to plan, Nelson on the move again after 9.04 seconds. That was at the end of lap 30. Two laps later and Mansell made his stop. Again, near perfection by the Williams crew, this stop taking half a second longer.

As Mansell rocketed up the slope leading onto the track, Piquet was powering onto the pit straight. Mansell was into Paddock first, his heated Goodyears giving him a limited amount of grip – but not as much as Piquet, who was back in the groove and his tyres at working temperature. Sensing it was now or never, Piquet took a look at the inside line going into Surtees. Mansell would have none of it and quickly closed the door. They ran nose to tail for the rest of the lap, Piquet drawing along the outside of his team-mate as they approached Paddock for the 34th time. With Mansell sticking to the inside, Piquet had the momentum for a clean run through Paddock and a run at the inside under braking for Druids. The aerial camera showed it was likely to come off – but Nannini, dutifully staying over to the right, was in the way! Nothing for it but to back off and tuck in behind Mansell once more. By now, of course, Mansell's tyres were working well and he began to reel off a string of quick laps. Piquet responded each time and their pace was such that it was easy to think the drivers had forgotten about fuel conservation.

Over half a minute behind all this, René Arnoux had moved into third place when Alboreto made his stop for tyres. Soon it was René's turn and he collected a hard left-front and three soft race tyres on lap 39. It was a poor choice since he would be back for more of the same 14 laps later! Prost, now third, knew he would need to make his second stop but the combination of comparatively slow work by the Ligier team and an engine failure on Alboreto's Ferrari meant the World Champion was able to stop on lap 50 and yet retain third place.

Arnoux dropped to fifth behind the BT55 of Warwick, the Englishman being the sole surviving Brabham entry. Patrese, after an excellent run which had taken him ahead of his team-mate, retired the BT54 from sixth place with engine failure just before half-distance. Warwick, however, was going superbly although he would have no answer to Arnoux and his second set of fresh tyres. Tambay, sixth, was in the points (Jones having retired his Lola from a creditable seventh place early on) but, closing rapidly on the Frenchman, came Brundle and Streiff followed by Dumfries, troubled with understeer, holding ninth place ahead of Palmer's Zakspeed.

The back-markers had been lapped two or three times and, on lap 51, the Williams duo rubbed in their superiority by putting Prost's McLaren a lap behind.

The pace was unrelenting. On lap 54, Piquet set a new record with 1m 10.089s. Mansell replied with a 1m 09.808s. The leaders had been brought

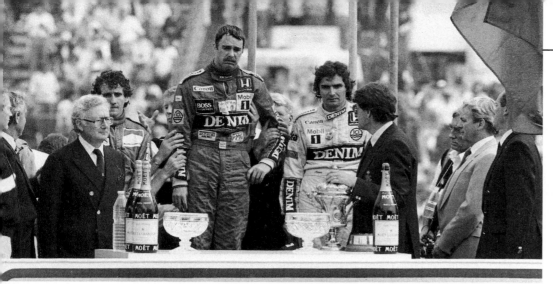

René Arnoux: third before his pit stop and an eventual fourth place.

A dehydrated Nigel Mansell receives support on the rostrum after a physically demanding race run without the aid of a drink bottle in the spare Williams.

Going spare. Mansell and the travel-stained back-up car head towards a rapturous welcome at home.

Philippe Streiff took advantage of Derek Warwick's troubles on the last lap to steal sixth place for Tyrrell.

closer together while lapping Brundle, the Tyrrell driver doing his best to keep out of their way but causing more harm than good in the process.

The gap remained at a couple of seconds, Piquet saving himself for one last fling. On lap 68, he went round in 1m 09.805s. Mansell responded instantly with the new lap record of 1m 09.593s while Piquet's reply was *only* a 1m 09.837s. Next lap Piquet, recorded 1m 10.666s, then 1m 11.367s. Game, set and match to Mansell.

There were now four laps to go and, seeing the gap increase, the crowd sensed victory, Mansell's every move being cheered to the echo. On his penultimate lap, Mansell went round in 1m 10.900s, giving him a clear margin to savour his last victorious lap. A disappointed Piquet took second, with Prost third and one lap down, and Arnoux fourth, two laps behind. Three laps behind came Brundle after passing Warwick four laps from the end. That much Warwick could take,

even though he had run his race with minimum boost and revs to save fuel, but he was infuriated to find his car running out of petrol on the last lap. As he coasted to within a few metres from the line, Streiff and Dumfries roared by as they finalised their own private battle. It was the first point of the season for the Frenchman and well deserved since he had been struggling for the latter part of the race with a loose steering wheel, of all things.

Mansell tottered from the Williams in a thoroughly dehydrated state, the spare car being without the luxury of an onboard drink bottle. It took some time for him to piece togther his version of the race but, in essence, his driving told the story. Under the greatest possible pressure, in a car he was not entirely familiar with, Mansell had beaten Nelson Piquet fair and square. Now he led the championship. There were not many people who, if they were honest, would have bet on either at the beginning of the season.   M.H.

Grosser Preis von
DEUTSCHLAND

Take your partners. Teo Fabi and Stefan Johansson begin the First Corner Waltz – fortunately with less serious consequences than the first-lap accident at Brands Hatch two weeks previously. With Senna and Rosberg already out of sight, the eventual winner, Nelson Piquet, leads the rest of the field.

'I've let things slip recently, but I'm going to get back in the swing of it all now. I feel confident that the championship is still safe.' Thus spoke Nelson Piquet just after the British Grand Prix at Brands Hatch, where he had been beaten into second place by a brilliantly on-form Nigel Mansell. But two weeks later, the Brazilian proved that his mid-season loss of form had been merely an interlude, not a permanent decline. He returned to his winning ways at Hockenheim to take the German Grand Prix in commanding style, although two pit stops for fresh Goodyears guaranteed that he had to keep up the pressure to regain the lead from Keke Rosberg's pole-position McLaren-TAG a mere six laps from the chequered flag. However, that bland fact fails accurately to reflect Nelson's dominance. The combination of his cool, controlled driving style and the ultra-competitive Williams-Honda FW11 ensured that he was the contender by which the pace of the race was measured. When both Rosberg and team-mate Alain Prost ran out of fuel on the final lap, Piquet was left to beat Ayrton Senna's Lotus 98T by just over 15s, Mansell trailing home an unhappy third after a race spent grappling with difficult handling caused by a partially detached rear underbody diffuser panel.

ENTRY AND PRACTICE

Two days of qualifying for the German Grand Prix were dominated by Keke Rosberg. Firstly, the genial Finn announced that he would be following his McLaren predecessor Niki Lauda into retirement at the end of the season. Secondly, he had at last got his McLaren MP4/2C handling to his own personal taste and notched up the first pole position of his brief post-Williams career. After months of discussion and debate, Rosberg had a McLaren that did not understeer.

'Well, I suppose there's a touch of understeer in race trim', admitted Keke, 'but the biggest problem I've had to deal with up to now is an acute "wash-out" understeer where you simply had to back off the throttle to regain grip at the front. Now it's mild by comparison, but the basic problem has been when I have talked about "less understeer", the McLaren engineers have been interpreting in terms of Alain's very fine margins. But I was talking about a very drastic change indeed. Now we're running a lot less rear wing at this circuit and I'm really feeling quite optimistic.'

Not that Keke won pole without something of a scrap, of course. His team-mate Alain Prost was right with him throughout the Saturday session and the World Champion looked as though he had timed things perfectly by setting fastest time a mere ten minutes before the chequered flag. But Keke was really in the mood and stormed straight back onto the circuit, redressing the balance a few minutes from the end.

Although many observers interpreted the appearance of new turbos for the TAG V6 at Hockenheim as a calculated response to Ron Dennis's attempts to woo Honda, they were in fact just part of Porsche's continuing programme of development, these components just having arrived at the end of the Weissach pipeline. They improved the TAG V6's 'driveability' and both

drivers were in a buoyant mood prior to the race, although qualifying had not been without its incidents. On Friday morning Prost had suffered an engine failure, losing him the first 20 minutes of first qualifying while a replacement was installed, and Keke had a nasty moment running round the outside of a slower car at the flat-out Ostkurve. 'It could so easily have been one of those Villeneuve-type situations', he reflected quietly. 'One of those deals where you either back off or close your eyes . . .'

Third place on the grid fell to Ayrton Senna's Lotus 98T, although for a long time it seemed as though the Brazilian might be well out of the picture as far as front-running grid positions were concerned. It was only after some truly heroic work by the Lotus mechanics that Senna was given an outside chance of a decent qualifying run, but, predictably, he grasped it with both hands and rose to the occasion spendidly.

Things went wrong for Ayrton from the word go. On Friday morning his qualifying spare 98T suffered an engine failure on its first lap, obliging him to transfer to his race car and because he racked up more miles than expected it was necessary to make an overnight engine change.

Short of miles in his Q-car, Senna chose a set of C compound Goodyear race tyres for his first Friday run, seeking sanctuary in the pits when a rain shower interrupted proceedings. His second run was fouled up when Allen Berg threw his Osella into the tyre barrier at the Ostkurve chicane, scattering used Pirelli P6s all over the track. That left him eighth at the end of day one.

This was just a preliminary taste of the troubles to follow on Saturday. About ten minutes before the start of second qualifying, the mechanical fuel pump failed on his Q-car as it was being warmed up in the pit garage. Strapped into the cockpit of his race car, Ayrton waited patiently while the mechanics sweated blood removing the Q-car

engine, replacing the offending pump and then reassembling the whole lot. It was touch and go whether they would make it . . .

Ten minutes from the end Senna did one run in the race car, the mechanics putting the finishing touches to his other machine as he hurtled back into the pit lane with less than five minutes to go. He jumped straight out and immediately climbed aboard the rebuilt Q-car, hurtled back onto the circuit once more and just managed to speed into his one flying lap a matter of seconds before the chequered flag appeared at the startline. In that one banzai effort he vaulted from eighth to third, a performance which prompted cheers of delight from the exhausted mechanics.

Senna's team-mate Johnny Dumfries wound up a steady 12th on his debut outing at Hockenheim, admitting that he missed a gear and made several mistakes on his best Saturday lap. On Friday he had been one of many caught out by the changing weather conditions, running out of time on his second set, but keeping out of trouble and further enhancing his reputation.

Underlining his improving form, Gerhard Berger stormed round to set fourth-quickest time in his Benetton B186, joining Senna on the outside of row 2. He had a nasty moment on Saturday afternoon after failing to see Mansell bearing down on him as he went into one of the chicanes, the Austrian losing his car's nose cone over a kerb as he lurched up the escape road to avoid a collision. On his second run he blew a turbo, preventing further improvement. Team-mate Teo Fabi wound up a disappointed ninth after failing to get a clear lap in either session.

High on downforce but short on straightline speed, the Williams-Honda FW11s of Nelson Piquet and Nigel Mansell finished fifth and sixth, the Brazilian revelling in the excellent balance on this fast circuit. Mansell got held up by Senna's Lotus – 'by mistake, I hope' – on Friday and then

found that when he turned up the boost to 'P4' on Saturday it made very little difference.

Experiments with the old Brabham BT54 had come to an end as there was a shortage of 'upright' BMW engines after Brands Hatch, so Riccardo Patrese and Derek Warwick were both back behind the wheels of lowline BT55s for the German race. Despite recent intensive engine development work following a busy Silverstone test, qualifying at Hockenheim proved an enduring nightmare for the two Brabham drivers with virtually everything possible going wrong.

Patrese's car refused to rev properly for much of the two days, but an engine change just prior to the last session seemed to do the trick and the Italian pulled a quick lap out of the bag to line up seventh, topping 211 mph on the fastest straight as he did so.

Warwick, meanwhile, ended up sharing the spare BT55 with his team-mate on Friday, his own machine having suffered turbo surge and stripped seventh gear by the end of the untimed session. By the time 'Del Boy' got his hands on the spare, it was losing power thanks to a split intercooler; on Saturday morning he blew up both the race car and the spare. In the final session the next replacement engine failed to run properly for more than a single lap, so he wound up a fuming 20th, wondering what else fate might have in store for him!

Philippe Alliot joined René Arnoux as the replacement for the injured Jacques Lafitte in the Ligier squad, the former RAM driver starting off in promising style to set seventh-fastest time on Friday. But his lack of familiarity on qualifying rubber saw him drop to 17th overall on Saturday, six places behind his colleague.

Running the Brabham team a close second in the technical disaster stakes at Hockenheim was Ferrari. For this race the team had brought along a spare car with revised weight distribution and altered suspension geometry. Michele Alboreto used it on Friday after breaking the gearbox on his race car: he felt the muletta's new specification was basically an improvement. 'It turns in better than the regular chassis, but then seems to lose grip in the middle of the corner', he reported.

That effort earned the Italian tenth place in the starting line-up, Michele's time almost matched by Stefan Johansson whose F1/86 blew a turbo on its second Friday run after wrecking an engine during the untimed stint. Lack of grip continued to plague him the following day, but he capitalised on the Ferrari engine's blindingly quick straight-line performance to compensate for that shortcoming on the twisty sections. To be so close to his team-mate was praiseworthy under the circumstances.

The Haas Lola-Fords were simply slow in a straight line, reflecting the relative lack of top-end power from their Cosworth-built V6 engines. Throughout both sessions Alan Jones complained of excessive understeer, his problems on Saturday being compounded by a pick-up problem which obliged him to drop to first gear, instead of the more usual second, at the Ostkurve chicane. His disappointed 19th position left him six places behind Patrick Tambay who was late out for

second qualifying following an engine failure in the Saturday untimed session. 'I think I could have been quicker than that if Alliot hadn't held me up at one of the chicanes', Patrick said.

Martin Brundle and Philippe Streiff had three Tyrrell 015s on team strength at last, but the Englishman's two stabs at qualifying turned out to be rather a shambles, his spare car briefly catching fire and stopping out on the circuit during Friday morning's session. That obliged him to take his race car out for first qualifying, but he got caught out by the rain shower and Berg's Osella shunt at the Ostkurve. Despite being messed about by one of the Ferraris during second qualifying, Martin took 15th place, Streiff taking a dissatisfied 18th after grappling with an obscure electrical misfire for most of the two days.

Happy to perform well on Zakspeed's home soil, Jonathan Palmer did a good job to line up a fine 16th overall. Using his spare 861 with its qualifying turbo, he set the time on Saturday before blowing up the engine by over-revving it as he hung on in the slipstream of a faster car. He spent the rest of the session in his race car, fitted with the normal turbo. Team-mate Huub Rothengatter did not have a qualifying turbo fitted to his 861 and failed to break the 1m 50s barrier, lining up a lowly 24th.

The attractive new Arrows A9, with its inboard gear cluster ahead of the differential, made its debut driven by Thierry Boutsen but a host of irritating overheating and minor gear-selection problems hampered his progress and his efforts in second qualifying were finally thwarted when the turbo set light to the snug-fitting rear bodywork. He wound up 21st, four places behind team-mate Christian Danner who heaved the old A8 round to qualify 17th.

In the Minardi camp, Alessandro Nannini squeezed in ahead of team-mate Andrea de Cesaris yet again, taking 22nd place on the grid despite suffering two engine failures on Friday, and the two Osellas shared the last row as was now becoming usual. Piercarlo Ghinzani had to sit out Friday qualifying in order to conserve the team's dwindling supply of engines, while the suspension damage sustained by Berg when he hit the Ostkurve chicane wrote him out of the Saturday equation while the team waited for a new suspension link to be flown in from Italy.

RACE

Riccardo Patrese did a bit of BMW public relations work during the race morning warm-up session, storming round in qualifying trim to post a time three seconds quicker than Mansell's Williams. It

The German Grand Prix was virtually a shakedown test for the new Arrows A9 *(left)*.

Bernie Ecclestone and Carl Haas talk percentages *(below left)* as they discuss a rumoured takeover of the American team by the Brabham boss.

Honda revealed their plans for 1987 by announcing a deal with Lotus to complement their existing arrangement with Williams. Peter Warr and Patrick Head, seated either side of Mr Sakuri, listen intently as the head of Honda R&D makes one of the most eagerly awaited statements of the year *(right)*.

Philippe Alliott – back on the Formula 1 scene as a replacement for the injured Laffite *(below)*.

LOTUS GO EAST; THE REST GO NOWHERE

Peter Warr pulled off a considerable coup by concluding a two-year deal between Team Lotus and Honda. The liaison, announced after final practice at Hockenheim, not only gave Lotus access to the highly competitive V6 engines but, more importantly perhaps, it also ensured Lotus of the continuing services of Ayrton Senna and Gérard Ducarouge. Had Lotus remained with Renault, Senna and the French designer most certainly would have gone in search of a team with Honda horsepower. Renault, meanwhile, were left looking for a top-line team.

Warr's timely negotiations had beaten McLaren to it, Ron Dennis and Alain Prost having made an apparently fruitless trip to Japan the week before the German Grand Prix. Also in Japan, Patrick Head made a lightning visit (thought to have been arranged by Honda once they had decided against McLaren) to reaffirm the Williams-Honda contract. The Japanese company had offered to withdraw preconditions which had forced Williams to reconsider their involvement with Honda and enter serious discussions with Renault for 1987.

Honda had wanted Williams to give their second car to Satoru Nakajima, the local driver entrusted with Honda's test work in Japan. Williams would have none of it and, in the end, Honda found a place for their man alongside Senna at Lotus. Johnny Dumfries, therefore, would be removed from Lotus under similar 'terms of convenience' to the circumstances which had led to his drive in the first place.

The press conference, chaired by Mr Yoshitoshi Sakuri, director of R&D at Honda, was the subject of backstage man-oeuvring. Lotus were ready to announce their plans but Williams went to great lengths to force a cancellation of the briefing. Williams were still in discussion with Mansell over 1987 but Lotus wanted the press conference to go ahead, if only to clear the air and stop Ferrari from constantly pressuring Senna to accept a deal, rumoured to be worth $12m over two years.

Mansell's prevarication, due to a disagreement over his financial worth, proved to be an increasing source of irritation to both sides. Piquet, meanwhile, made capital out of the unease by craftily making it known that he was more than happy to fulfill the second year of his contract with this fine team. Just two weeks before, he had been complaining about supposed favouritism shown by Williams to Mansell and the Englishman's ruthless driving tactics at Brands Hatch . . .

M.H.

---

was not of any significance or consequence, of course, but it made everybody in the Brabham-BMW camp feel a bit better.

When it came to lining up for the race, the Brabham squad was back to its more familiar disorder. Warwick opted to race the spare BT55 but when it was fired up it initially refused to run cleanly. He switched to his original race car, but that ran even rougher and, after hurried debate, he switched back to his first choice. The problem with this car was found to be a speck of dirt blocking one of the fuel injectors, so that was duly rectified and the car readied for the start. Meanwhile, Jones's Lola sprang a water leak and the Australian switched to the spare car, starting the parade lap late and lining up at the back as a result.

Rosberg got bogged down slightly as the starting light blinked to green, Senna leaping through into the lead from the second row, swiping Prost's right-front wheel as he did so. Berger followed through into second place and these two led the field out of the stadium with Rosberg leading the chase. Further back, Alliot's Ligier came tearing down the outside of the grid, pitching Johansson's Ferrari into Fabi's Benetton which, in turn, had been squeezed against the pit wall by Arnoux. Johansson spun in the middle of

the pack, sending Fabi into immediate retirement. Stefan and Alliot trailed round slowly to the pits, requiring attention to a damaged nose section and a punctured tyre respectively.

At the end of lap 1 Senna still led Berger by less than a length, with Rosberg, Piquet, Prost, Mansell, Patrese, Alboreto, Arnoux, Dumfries and the fast-starting Warwick next up. On the second lap Keke nipped through into the lead ahead of Senna with Berger already dropping back slightly, handicapped by fading turbo boost pressure. The next time round saw Piquet up to third ahead of Berger, and Nelson then ducked inside Senna to take second place. At the end of lap 5 Berger came coasting into the pits, the pipe from the intercooler to the engine leaking. He lost two laps while it was fixed.

Rosberg was in fine form at the head of the field, but his McLaren-TAG was no match for a Williams-Honda in race trim at Hockenheim, Piquet catching him easily and slipping by to take over the lead on lap 6. Prost was running third with Senna fourth, Arnoux fifth and a frustrated Mansell sixth, the World Championship points leader already dropping away.

'It felt fine for the first few laps', Mansell explained, 'but then it suddenly started oversteering violently at high speed.' Only detailed

examination after the race would pinpoint the precise problem: the bolts holding the rear underbody diffuser panel had failed and only three of the original ten were still intact at the finish, contributing to an unnerving degree of aerodynamic imbalance. Mansell briefly slipped to seventh behind Alboreto, but moved back to sixth again when the Ferrari's transmission failed on lap 7.

Piquet had originally intended to make just one routine stop for tyres, so the Williams pit was thrown into something of a flap when the Brazilian made an unscheduled visit for fresh rubber at the end of lap 15 – just when everybody expected the troubled Mansell to arrive! Patrick Head screamed through his radio link, telling Nigel to stay out for another couple of laps, so Nelson was despatched back into the race in fourth place, his FW11 fitted with the specially pressured set of Goodyears intended to aid Nigel's handling imbalance!

Everything duly sorted itself out with Rosberg and Prost now running in 1-2 formation ahead of Senna. Johnny Dumfries, doing well in seventh and then eighth place (after being passed by Patrese) came in for fresh tyres on lap 17 but went no further. The Lotus's water radiator had been holed by some flying debris, a tell-tale pool of water beneath the car betraying the cause of its

Patrick Behar

retirement.

Other early departures from the field included Ghinzani's Osella and Alliot's delayed Ligier, both of which succumbed to engine failure. Boutsen pitted for tyres in the new Arrows on lap 10 only to return three laps later with a turbo problem which erupted into a spectacular fire – fortunately one which was speedily quelled.

With Berger now back in the race, but two laps down, the Brabhams were moving into contention, Patrese pulling up to fifth by lap 20 before dropping back to seventh over the next couple of laps and then cruising in to retire with a terminal misfire caused by a broken spark plug electrode. The Italian's demise allowed Warwick to move up to seventh place, the Englishman staying there all the way to the finish to record his best result since joining the team in North America.

Rosberg came in for his sole routine tyre stop on lap 19, briefly promoting Prost into the lead, but

the World Champion was in for fresh tyres himself next time round. Piquet redressed the balance on lap 21 by taking the lead just as Senna came in, the latter dropping from his temporary second back to fourth.

By the end of lap 26 Piquet had slightly more than five seconds in hand over the tenacious Rosberg, but the Williams was going to have to make one more tyre stop. That duly came at the end of the following lap (with 17 to go) and Nelson resumed the chase in third place behind the two McLarens. From now on it was a mathematical certainty that Piquet would regain the lead.

Nelson was well in the swing of things as he completed the 30th lap and Keke, despite trying everything he knew, could not retain the McLaren's advantage. By lap 33 the gap was just under 6s, then Nelson turned in his personal quickest lap of the day and closed to 5.5s. In another two laps the McLaren was less than 3s

ahead, Keke's helmet bobbing from left to right as he tried to keep track of the Williams looming large in his mirrors.

On lap 39 the inevitable came to pass, but Rosberg hung on like the trouper he is and refused to let Nelson off the hook. Sadly, though, it was to be the McLaren-TAG drivers who were to suffer after a couple of excellent drives. As Nelson finished with a spurt, Rosberg felt his engine dying on him as he changed down through the gears for the first chicane on the outward leg of the circuit. Deprived of the engine's braking effect, he wisely steered down the escape road, emerging at the other end of the chicane with the engine running again. But it failed to finish the lap: on the return straight it rolled to a halt, out of fuel, despite the reassuring cockpit messages being imparted by the computer readout!

Prost's indignation was to be made public on the final corner in front of the huge stands when his

152

Keith Sutton

Mr Dejected. Alain Prost's bitterly disappointed pose sums up the fuel capacity restrictions and the failure of his McLaren-TAG to reach the finish. He dropped from third to sixth place in the closing laps.

Keke Rosberg *(left)* hitches a ride on the victorious and more economical Williams-Honda of Nelson Piquet.

TECHNICAL FILE

ARROWS
First appearance of A9 at a race. Gear cluster mounted ahead of the differential to give a more compact and stiffer rear end. Changing of ratios required the removal of the suspension, which was pushrod but of a new design incorporating shock absorbers mounted in Ferrari T3 fashion. Unusual angular shape to front of chassis (with pushrod front suspension). Car had very narrow rear bodywork but otherwise was conventional.

BENETTON
New rear wings for race cars. Fabi had revised fixing point for rear suspension on Friday; Berger had the same arrangement on Saturday.

BRABHAM
Had experimented with a shorter wheelbase by removing a section of the chassis in the fuel tank area and angling rear wishbones. This car tested at Silverstone but not brought to Hockenheim. On race cars, the rear edge of side pods, previously curving down, were levelled to increase exit by 4 cm and improve airflow. BMW tried different turbos along with various experiments to improve acceleration. Race cars ran with less downforce on rear wing and no winglets at rear of side pods to give better straightline performance.

FERRARI
To alter weight distribution, wheelbase on T-car reduced from 2762 cm to 2632 cm by removing bell-housing. Oil tank, previously inside bell-housing, now mounted on top of gearbox, causing a revision of rear suspension in order to relocate shock absorber mountings. Short wheelbase had been tested at Paul Ricard; the modified suspension was based on a geometry tested privately at the Nürburgring in 1984. Now only using the geometry and the rockers; the wishbones and uprights were new. As a result of shorter wheelbase, the bodywork was reduced, leaving insufficient room in the underbody for the separate exhaust pipes; now using single pipe. New rear wing with side plates modified to resemble McLaren. All three cars had front suspension pushed forward by 5 cm. Used new Garrett turbos in qualifying but at least four blew up.

LIGIER
Arnoux used the EF15C for the first time. Ran new brake ducts. Team reduced to three cars following Laffite's accident at Brands Hatch. Laffite replaced by Philippe Alliot.

LOLA
Both drivers had revised Ford engines (seven available). Jones tried new AP calipers.

LOTUS
Senna had three EF15C engines available.

McLAREN
Rosberg tested new KKK turbos and revision to fuel injection system at Silverstone; subsequent power advantage seen during qualifying at Hockenheim. Size of oil radiator in combined water/oil radiator increased. Rosberg and Prost used different suspension geometries. Both cars ran rear wings without lip to top edge in order to decrease drag.

MINARDI
Repaired the cars damaged at Brands Hatch.

OSELLA
Ghinzani's car fitted with the rear suspension and gearbox from new car destroyed at Brands Hatch.

TYRRELL
Three 015s available for the first time. Brundle used the latest car with cooling duct and sleeves for rear shock absorbers. Had latest wastegate but not the EF15C engine. The only team to continue with skirts on front wing side plates.

WILLIAMS
To conform with new regulations, front wing side plates made of uniform material but with wooden rubbing strips. Revised rear wing had three small tubes to improve airflow to lower surface.

ZAKSPEED
Palmer's car and T-car fitted with carbon-fibre rear brakes. T-car had narrower front wing.

G.P.

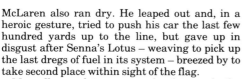

McLaren also ran dry. He leaped out and, in a heroic gesture, tried to push his car the last few hundred yards up to the line, but gave up in disgust after Senna's Lotus – weaving to pick up the last dregs of fuel in its system – breezed by to take second place within sight of the flag.

Mansell, urged to press on hard towards the finish, was the lucky beneficiary of third place ahead of Arnoux's Ligier, the Frenchman complaining of poor grip throughout. The McLarens were classified fifth and sixth, Rosberg ahead of Prost, while the Haas Lola-Fords of Patrick Tambay and Alan Jones were eighth and ninth.

Tambay ran as high as 11th on the opening stages before being forced into the pits on lap 6 when his left-front wheel shed its balance weights. Jones's car was similarly afflicted, but it was also jumping out of third gear from half-distance onwards and the Lola had discarded one of its rear-view mirrors by the time he got to the chequered flag!

Alan just managed to scramble across the line 0.1s ahead of Berger's Benetton, the Austrian setting the fastest race lap during his recovery, while Johansson called it a day four laps from the end when he pitted with a loose rear wing end plate. Stefan was classified 11th ahead of Allen Berg, the Canadian recording his first GP finish, while Danner's Arrows was sidelined by turbo failure four laps from the end.

Both Minardis failed to make it to the finish, gearbox failure claiming de Cesaris, while Nannini blew his engine. Brundle's Tyrrell stopped with an engine fire after a slow start when the Englishman could not select first on the line, followed by a long stop to change the spark box. Palmer's Zakspeed went out seven laps from the end with a major valvegear breakage.

The Williams-Honda success was not news. Piquet's apparent success in shrugging off his mid-season blues was not really a surprise either. Mansell was now on his guard.   A.H.

HUNGARIAN
Grand Prix

Senna appears to be savouring the prospect of trouble at Williams after Piquet had failed to share his secret with Mansell *(right)*.

It was Alain Prost's 100th Grand Prix but it turned out to be a race he would rather forget. The World Champion *(below)* returns to the pits on foot for the second time on race day.

The first Hungarian Grand Prix marked the building of an important sporting link with the Eastern Bloc and possibly the irretrievable breakdown of driver relationships within the Williams-Honda team. Hungary's bold and imaginative move into the world of Grand Prix racing was rewarded by a titanic battle between Nelson Piquet and Ayrton Senna, this second win in succession for the Williams driver moving Piquet to within eight points of his team-mate.

Nigel Mansell maintained his championship lead by finishing third but the fact that he had been lapped by Piquet aggravated an already cool liaison between the two. As Piquet swept by, it was obvious to Mansell that the Brazilian had found a technical advantage and kept it to himself.

It was a matter of Piquet's discretion, of course, but this lack of equanimity threatened to split the compact working relationship of the Williams team. Senna, by finishing second for Lotus, maintained a serious presence in the championship, as did Prost even though the race had been a disaster for the McLaren team. However, 10 August had been anything but a calamity for the proud people of Hungary.

ENTRY AND PRACTICE

From the moment the transporters were waved courteously and efficiently through the Hungarian border it was clear the organisers of the first World Championship Grand Prix in the Eastern Bloc were out to impress. This was a significant event, both politically and from a sporting point of view, and upon arrival at the Hungaroring it became obvious that nothing had been overlooked.

The 2.494-mile circuit, part of the £5m package funding the entire event, had been carefully laid out across a valley near the village of Mogyoród, about 12 miles north-east of Budapest. Safety and medical facilities were up to standard and now it was left to the drivers to pass an opinion as they prepared for an exploratory two-hour practice session on Thursday afternoon.

At 2.0 p.m. precisely, an official announced 'The track is open', before adding in delightfully quaint English, 'please drive your cars.' The session was stopped just once, to allow abandoned cars to be towed in, and at the end of it the drivers were cautious in their judgement. The one drawback was a lack of fast corners, although, in fairness, the plan to have a sweeping downhill section behind the pits had been scuppered by the discovery of an underground spring. There had been no alternative but to introduce a series of tight corners at the point in question.

That aside, there was the usual lack of grip from the fresh surface, the organisers perhaps overcompensating in their bid to avoid a catastrophy similar to Spa in 1985. Without a coat of rubber and oil to work on, qualifying tyres were useless during the first timed practice on Friday, the majority of drivers settling for soft race tyres as Mansell and Piquet set the fastest times.

By Saturday, however, conditions were such that qualifiers offered an advantage – provided

you could find a clear lap. And it was Ayrton Senna who was prepared to bolt on a set of Es and go for it. Waiting until the halfway point in the 60-minute session, the Lotus driver shaved a full second off Mansell's best, which had been set on race tyres in the opening minutes of the final session.

Mansell had been lucky to survive a brush with the barrier earlier in the day when a misunderstanding with Patrese had sent the Williams skating off the track. Apart from a bruised knee and relatively little damage to the car, Mansell had gone as quickly as he could. He had decided to hedge his bets and, with his one set of qualifiers bolted in place, he took to the track the minute Senna had completed his typically spectacular lap. Unfortunately Mansell's efforts were to be wrecked when he came across Warwick and Streiff running side-by-side. And Senna still had one set of qualifiers remaining.

Alain Prost came to within a half-second of Ayrton's time to take second place but Senna knew his main rival would be Piquet, particularly when the Lotus driver spun spectacularly during his second run. Piquet improved – but only enough to take third place – and Senna went out for a final run on a mixture of tyres from both sets of qualifiers . . . and spun again! 'I think I've spun here more times than in the rest of my career!' said Ayrton. 'There's just no grip at all – and if you get off line, it's finished. And because there is so little grip, whatever you do to the car makes no difference.'

Piquet did make one change to his car by winding on even more wing and the additional downforce helped him move into second place in the closing minutes of a practice session run in very humid conditions. That put Prost into third place with Keke Rosberg taking fifth behind a disappointed Mansell.

The McLaren drivers had been hampered by a

comparative lack of downforce, the assiduous Prost working solidly with spring and roll bar changes although his calculations were upset by a mistake with tyre pressures on his first run on Saturday. The lack of downforce also reduced tyre temperatures, something which did not suit Rosberg who lost time on Friday when an engine failure forced him into the spare car for the timed session.

There was a gap of over a second between Rosberg and the next man, Tambay, although the Lola driver was not unduly upset since this represented his best qualifying position of the season so far. The Hungaroring suited the power curve of the Ford engine, the gentle but progressive response from the V6 being just right for such a slippery surface. Equally, the straights were not long enough to allow the lack of top-end power to become a handicap. Tambay had been troubled by brake pad knock-off as well as an incident with Arnoux, while Jones, slipping from sixth to tenth place on Saturday, had too much oversteer and the misfortune to be caught two days running on the oil from a broken Motori-Moderni engine.

The Ferrari drivers, of course, were quite accustomed to poor traction but on this occasion the slow corners merely exaggerated the savage response from the Garrett turbos. By running a huge rear wing and cranking on as much front wing as he dared, Stefan Johansson flung his car into an excellent seventh place with a lap which was worth almost half a second more than anything he had done before. As for Michele Alboreto, down in 15th place, his attention had been diverted by a front wheel which fell off the Ferrari and reflected the Italian's lack of confidence in his team at the time. Michele, on his way to the TAG motorhome to discuss the possibilities for 1987, declared that his car was difficult enough to drive with four wheels, never mind three . . .

The first day of practice had been hard work for

Johnny Dumfries but once a gear-selection problem had been sorted out and the handling improved on Saturday he felt more confident. His last lap of the day was an excellent effort, worth eighth place and much closer to his Lotus team-mate than ever before. As for René Arnoux, the bewildered Ligier driver had been trounced by his team-mate Philippe Alliot on Friday but a complete change to the set-up of his car saw a major improvement to ninth in the final session. Fastest Pirelli runner he may have been but René was convinced he would have been much higher had he not been involved in that incident with Tambay. Arnoux's views, of course, were diametrically opposed to those of Tambay!

Alliot ended practice in 12th place, splitting the Benettons of Berger and Fabi. In truth, neither driver felt at home on this circuit although by the end of practice they could be forgiven for thinking that Huub Rothengatter was out to get them. The Dutchman collided with Fabi as he was on a fast lap and then blew up, spraying oil just as Berger was about to try for a quick lap. Despite this, Berger was fourth-fastest on the first day but failed to improve sufficiently when he spun twice on Saturday. The tight corners were not to his liking and his wistful look suggested he couldn't wait to get to grips with the Österreichring in a week's time.

It was a major achievement for Riccardo Patrese to complete a single lap of practice, never mind take 15th place with the difficult Brabham BT55. The Italian spent the whole weekend suffering from a septic wisdom tooth, a distraction he had to endure since any treatment would have ruled him out of the race. The BT55 was desperately struggling for grip (as demonstrated in several spins) and the poor engine response was a major handicap here. Derek Warwick, a second slower, had the additional excitement of being overtaken by his water tank (a reservoir for the

spray directed onto the intercooler while running qualifying boost) which had dislodged itself from the back of the car as the Englishman braked hard for a tight corner. After trying six different tyre compounds Warwick came to the conclusion that there was simply no grip to be had and 19th place would be the best he could manage.

Sixteenth place was a major disappointment for Martin Brundle since the Tyrrell driver had high hopes of a place in the top ten after successfully fine-tuning his car on Saturday morning. A broken alternator belt put paid to that and the Renault V6 then developed a misfire, added to which Brundle lost one lap arguing with the driver of a slow-moving car. Philippe Streiff had similar problems with traffic when Fabi unintentionally held up the Frenchman during an otherwise trouble-free session.

Minardi brought along their latest car for Andrea de Cesaris but handling problems left him slower than Alessandro Nannini in the older model. In a similar vein, Thierry Boutsen spent Friday's practice with the Arrows A9 before handing the new car over to Christian Danner. That was not the answer to Boutsen's problems however since the A8 blew an engine on Saturday morning. When he took out the spare A8 in the afternoon, the BMW engine lost boost so he switched back to the original, now with a fresh engine – which promptly cut out halfway round the circuit. Danner, meanwhile, had blown up the A9 and he finished the session in the 'low-boost' spare A8. Their 21st and 22nd places summed up the disaster for the team.

That left the Zakspeed and Osella teams at the back of the grid. Ghinzani came off best with the smoking Italian car and at least he had the luxury of a couple of laps on Saturday, Berg being hobbled by a broken transmission at the start of the session. As for Palmer and Rothengatter, they were frustrated by almost non-existent engine

The Hungarians broke all records and motor racing broke through another international barrier when the first Formula 1 car rolled out, exactly on time on 7 August, to start practice for the first World Championship Grand Prix in an Eastern Bloc country.

Formula 1 went east but the impact went beyond mere political boundaries. The Hungarian Grand Prix was watched by 200,000 enthusiastic spectators; the spread of television coverage into Bulgaria, Czechoslovakia, Poland and the USSR raised the worldwide audience towards a staggering one thousand million viewers.

The circuit, constructed in seven months, was tight but of a high standard and the organisation proved capable of promoting a round of the World Championship.

All of this was achieved thanks to the enormous amount of work put in by the Hungarian government and the consortium promoting the event. But none of it would have happened had it not been for the enterprising spirit of Bernie Ecclestone.

The thought of spreading the sport's appeal into communist countries had been with Ecclestone and FOCA for some time. An attempt to raise interest in Moscow got off the ground but was to fail for minor technical reasons. Hungary, with its more liberal attitudes, was the next target once Ecclestone had visited and been impressed by the dignified city of Budapest.

The fundamental requirements were on hand: hotels, an international airport, good communications and an efficient television company. The proposed circuit was to have run through a park at the edge of the city – the scene of the one previous Hungarian Grand Prix in 1936 (won by Nuvolari in an Alfa Romeo). That scheme, intended for 1984, was rejected on environmental grounds.

The concept, however, found many supporters, quick to appreciate the value of Grand Prix racing in terms of promoting both the economy and the overseas view of Hungary, a country hitherto saddled with a grey image and memories of the fearful uprising in 1956.

Tibor Balogh, a motor sports administrator and Hungary's main delegate at FISA, was instrumental in convincing the government of the advantages and persuaded it that a purpose-built circuit would be financially supportable.

A site, near the village of Mogyoród, 12 miles north-east of the capital, was chosen and final approval was granted in January 1985. The financing and operation of the project was handled by Forma-1, a new company consisting of several large businesses, each member contributing 11 million forints (£170,000) to supplement an interest-free loan from the State Development Bank.

The venture cost 340m forints (£5.3m) and, judging by the massive interest shown, Forma-1 were on course to recoup their outlay during the five-year contract with FOCA. It was a brilliantly successful start by any standards.

M.H.

The Hungaroring turned out to be a workmanlike, if not particularly challenging, circuit. Packed spectator enclosures watch Senna lead Piquet in the opening laps. Mansell, already in trouble, keeps Tambay, Prost, Jones and Dumfries at bay.

response out of the corners. As a result, no attempt could be made at balancing the chassis and the only consolation was that, from their positions at the back, some of the potential first-corner accidents in the middle of the grid could be avoided.

RACE

Any doubts that the Hungarians, earning an average of £75 per month, would be able to afford the £13 admission charge were dispelled by the massed ranks of spectators, estimated to be in excess of 200,000, enjoying the sweltering heat. Admittedly, the crowd was swelled by enthusiasts from Austria, East and West Germany and Czechoslovakia but the orderly spectators were a massive vote of confidence for Bernie Ecclestone and the progressive Hungarians.

The warm-up saw the McLarens quickest, followed by the Williams team. The most significant aspect of the half-hour session was a vapour lock which caused a misfire on Senna's Lotus. As a precaution, it was decided to change the Renault engine although it did mean that Senna would not have the use of the latest EF15C, a drawback which was to take the edge off his performance in the race.

Elsewhere, Piquet hopped in and out of his T-car as he tried a differential in the hope of making the car more driveable on the slippery surface. The time sheet, with Piquet slower than Mansell, did not point to an obvious advantage although the sneaky Brazilian, sandbagger extraordinary, knew otherwise. And he wasn't about to share his secret with Mansell.

The warm-up had been a waste of time for Arnoux, his EF15C misfiring to the extent where a change to an EF15B was required, while just before the race Alain Prost had to run back to the pits and changed to the spare McLaren after his engine had died on the warm-up lap. It was to be a bad omen for McLaren.

Prost got away cleanly enough at the start but he was no match for Mansell as the Englishman powered between the McLaren and his Brazilian team-mate to take second place. Nevertheless, there was no doubt about who was leading as Senna began to pull away. Out already, the unfortunate Berg, his ratty Osella trailing smoke along the pit lane at the end of the first lap. After a few more minutes, Rothengatter was in the pits (the Zakspeed's oil cooler having been smashed against a kerb), followed by Arnoux with a broken valve on one of his wheels. All four tyres were changed as a matter of routine and he rejoined in 24th place.

First, and looking comfortable: Ayrton Senna. Second, and not so comfortable as his Williams searched for grip: Nigel Mansell. Third, and very confident: Nelson Piquet. And when, on lap 3, the Williams cars changed places, Mansell could see there was a vast difference between the two of them. For the next three laps, Piquet would be over a second a lap faster and there seemed to be nothing Mansell could do about it.

Tambay, following up an excellent start, held fourth place although he was soon to be passed by Prost and the Lola of Jones. By lap 8, Tambay had

fallen behind the Lotus of Dumfries, the Scotsman capitalising on his starting position to good effect and pulling away from the Ferraris of Alboreto and Johansson into the bargain.

The Italian cars had been split initially by Patrese but now the Brabham driver straddled a kerb after spinning at the exit of the tight left-hander behind the pits. The rear of the BT55 hit the barrier and, once he had stopped spinning his wheels in the vain hope of rejoining, Patrese climbed from the blue-and-white car to leave the marshals with the problem of removing it from a dangerous position. And it was here that the inexperience of the Hungarians was most evident.

The Brabham was undoubtedly difficult to move and after much struggling the marshals succeeded in rolling it onto the track and into the path of oncoming cars. Worse still, when a rescue car took it in tow, the Brabham at one stage veered towards the centre of the track and almost collected Senna.

The Lotus driver was still leading but he now had Piquet in close attendance. Mansell was third but about to be passed by Prost while Jones, running strongly in fifth place, was about to make a reluctant stop to attend to a leaking brake caliper, allowing Rosberg and Dumfries to complete the top six. As the Lola mechanics toiled over a seemingly fundamental failure, Johansson arrived in the Ferrari pit to receive another set of tyres. Since they were Bs, the same compound he had started out with, it made little difference to the skittish handling and it was not until he took on a mixture of Bs and Cs ten laps later that the Swede was to become a serious contender.

There was no doubt about Piquet's competitiveness, though, as he took the lead with relative ease on lap 12 and began to pull away. Senna (with the EF15B, remember) was literally powerless to keep pace on the straight. Indeed, he was under serious threat from Prost as the World Champion settled down with the spare McLaren, fitted, incidentally, with Bs on the front and Cs on the rear.

As Prost got on with his race, the McLaren team were counting Rosberg down to his pit stop and, in due course, an MP4/2C arrived in the pits. It was Prost! Rosberg's tyres were quickly slammed into place but Prost needed more than fresh rubber. As the engine cover was removed to attend to the black box, Rosberg arrived, the mechanics waving him straight through. Keke was peaking in third gear by the time he reached the end of the pit lane! It was a chaotic scene which could have been avoided simply by the use of a radio, something which, curiously, the World Champions had never adopted after pit-to-car communication had come into fashion. Prost lost eight laps while a cure was effected and he rejoined to set his fastest lap before tangling with the infamous René Arnoux.

Rosberg, meanwhile, had returned to the pits the following lap since a rear tyre was losing air. Eight laps later, he had worked his way into sixth place but he was back in the pits with another deflating tyre, caused this time by a faulty valve rubber. Along the way, the rear suspension ride height platform had been knocked out of true and the resultant unpredictable handling persuaded Rosberg eventually to call it a day. By the time the

157

Right: Something to smile about. Alan Jones ran strongly in the Lola-Ford once an elementary brake problem had been sorted out.

Rob Walker *(far right)* records the track temperature for readers of *Road & Track*.

Below: The highlight of the race was a superb battle between Senna and Piquet, the Williams driver engaging in a daring move or two to take the lead. Fabi's Benetton and Ghinzani's Osella lie abandoned in a race of attrition.

mechanics had spotted the easily corrected problem, Keke was changing in the motorhome.

Lap 21, quarter-distance, and Piquet set the fastest lap so far as he maintained a three-second advantage over Senna who, in turn, was 12 seconds ahead of Mansell. Dumfries, soon to be overhauled by Berger, was fourth thanks to Alboreto having lost a place in the top six when he stopped for tyres on lap 19. Michele quickly rejoined and made short work of the Tyrrells before closing on Warwick, now in sixth place following Rosberg's demise. Warwick was working hard just to keep the Brabham pointing in a straight line, a change of turbos for the race having done nothing to improve throttle response. Indeed, it was to be a moment's unexpected hesitation from the BMW engine which would cause Alboreto to ram the rear of the BT55, spinning Warwick into retirement and forcing the Ferrari, its nose irreparably damaged, into the pits.

That let Brundle into sixth, briefly to become fifth when Dumfries made his scheduled stop. Mansell had already been in, hoping to rectify his traction problem, but the new tyres only proved

remedial for about five laps before the lack of grip returned. Piquet naturally had no such problems as he came in at the end of lap 35, the Williams crew getting him away in 8.1 seconds. Senna, now leading of course, stayed out for another seven laps and during that time he put on a remarkable spurt, decreasing his lap times considerably. It was a shrewd ploy and showed the Brazilian's sensitive treatment of tyres which should by rights have been past their best.

When Senna came in at the end of lap 42, the Lotus team took 11 seconds but Senna's tactics had been such that he rejoined a full eight seconds ahead of Piquet. The gap came down by a couple of seconds a lap, Piquet sitting on Senna's tail by lap 53. Starting lap 55, Piquet darted to the right of the Lotus, Senna squeezing his rival into a tight approach under braking. Piquet was actually ahead as he turned into the corner but the downward slope of the corner caused his right-rear brake to lock, Piquet skating momentarily off-line to allow Senna room to slip inside at the apex. The crowd loved it.

Two laps later saw Piquet launch another attack, feinting right briefly but then swooping to

the outside this time, Senna giving him the minimum amount of room as they approached the braking area side-by-side. Undaunted, Piquet swept across the front of the Lotus, the Williams drifting into a lurid slide, held beautifully all the way through the corner. Senna was waiting to take advantage, but this time Piquet remained in command, finding time, indeed, to shake his fist.

Mansell, much to his chagrin, was about to be lapped but at least he could keep the flying Johansson, now in fourth place, at arm's length. The Ferrari driver had gradually worked his way through the field after his second stop for tyres, making ground when Dumfries and Brundle made their scheduled stops just after half-distance. Johansson finally moved into fourth place when Berger, having run comfortably in the top six for quarter-distance, pulled into the pits and jumped out of the Benetton. In fact, a petrol leak ensured that his ride had been anything but comfortable although a broken crown wheel was the cause of his retirement. It was the end of another disappointing day for Benetton, Fabi's spirited drive in the early stages being lost when he spun off and was unable to restart because of a

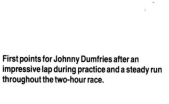

First points for Johnny Dumfries after an impressive lap during practice and a steady run throughout the two-hour race.

broken clutch.

The same could be said for Jones, running strongly after his brakes had been bled. A couple of laps down, the Australian nevertheless showed all his old aggression but broken transmission was to cause yet another retirement. Along the way, Jones passed Tambay as the Frenchman struggled with understeer and a lacklustre drive was capped by a spin at the exit of the right-hander before the pits. He made a quick stop for tyres and the highlight of his final laps was chasing and catching Streiff's Tyrrell for seventh place.

The number one Tyrrell of Brundle, meanwhile, was heading for a well-earned championship point. From the start, the Englishman had insufficient boost to allow him to overtake and his problems were compounded during the last 30 laps by an inoperative fourth gear, Brundle compensating by switching off the rev limiter and running third gear a few hundred revs higher. At the back of the field, Palmer struggled manfully towards a much-needed finish for the Zakspeed team, with his slim chances of a better placing spoiled by a long pit stop to bleed overheating brakes.

With Dumfries having survived a brief off-course excursion to continue his excellent progress in the points, the only Renault runner to have retired was Arnoux, the Ligier driver needing the assistance of his team-mate to notice the spiralling blue smoke as Alliot blasted past on the pit straight.

Senna's Renault V6 was running strongly but lacked that extra surge required to challenge Piquet. None the less, the Lotus driver never gave up as he pushed his tyres to the limit, cutting very fast times before easing off occasionally to allow the Goodyears to recover. Both Lotus and Williams were standing by for another tyre change, Williams deciding that if Senna stopped then Nelson would be called in on the next lap. Neither driver stopped, however, and the final laps were determined by the seconds ticking towards the two-hour mark. It was clear that it would not be possible to run the scheduled 77 laps, and the two hours were up as Piquet headed towards the line on lap 76. It was only in the final three laps that Senna finally reduced his pace, the six points ensuring him second place in the championship table.

Mansell, a lap down, maintained his lead of the championship by taking four points for third place. That was clearly the last thing on his mind as he grimly made his way towards the Williams pit. Why, he wanted to know, had Nelson not shared his advantage? Nelson, if the truth be told, couldn't have cared less.

That was the thorny problem which Frank Williams, a welcome spectator in Hungary, had to tackle before the conflict between the two drivers blew the team's chances apart and allowed Senna and Prost to take advantage. Senna had driven brilliantly and, while it may have been a dismal day for Prost, the World Champion could never be ignored. And Mansell now knew he would need to keep a close eye on the activities of his devious team-mate.

M.H.

TECHNICAL FILE

ARROWS
Boutsen started with A9, now incorporating rear end from A8, before swapping cars with Danner.

BENETTON
All three cars featured revised rear suspension first seen at Hockenheim. T-car fitted with revised pick-ups on gearbox for upper and lower rear suspension. Ran new rear wing, as seen at Hockenheim but with more downforce. Revised exhaust layout raised 4 to 5 cm from underbody. Ran very small vertical fins to underside of rear diffusers. Larger turbo duct inlets.

BRABHAM
Tested three different turbos on the T-car and opted for the middle variety. Patrese's car fitted with revised electronics. Larger oil radiators and double brake ducts front and rear. All three cars fitted with higher rear bodywork to side pods plus revised engine covers incorporating the roll bar. During practice, Patrese's car fitted with a revised airbox with a shorter duct from intercooler to airbox to improve engine response.

FERRARI
Had tested modifications to wastegate, electronics and injection system at Imola but these were not seen in Hungary. Used a revised aerodynamic set-up tested at Imola and the T-car was fitted with the rear wing seen briefly at Hockenheim. This wing required a different mounting to the gearbox. Both race cars fitted with longer side plates to rear wing. T-car fitted with twin brake system first seen in Detroit. By Saturday, Johansson's car also had this revision. Both race cars fitted with bodywork incorporating extra ducts next to turbos. Modifications to turbo shaft in the interests of reliability badly affected engine response.

LIGIER
Arnoux tested Brembo brake system on T-car. Arnoux had EF15C engine.

LOLA
Adrian Newey now in charge of design work at expense of Neil Oatley. Detail changes to mountings for front wings and revised geometry to front suspension to increase anti-dive. Waiting for Secam radiators to improve engine cooling.

LOTUS
Dumfries tested new Brembo brake system.

McLAREN
Flaps to rear wing mounted in a more vertical position. On Saturday, Prost tested titanium vertical fins fitted to underside of rear diffuser (the type of temporary on-site variation normally deplored by John Barnard); all three cars so equipped on race day.

MINARDI
New car for de Cesaris but without the rear suspension seen at Imola (it had failed after ten minutes of testing). New car 18 kg lighter thanks to all-carbon-fibre chassis which did away with the need for aluminium bodywork panels. Absence of bodywork around top of fuel tank meant lower engine cover which improved airflow to rear wing. Wheelbase increased by 5 cm; side pods 10 cm lower. Lower front edge of chassis featured a step similar to that used by Benetton. Symmetrical one-piece machined uprights allowed use on either side of car, thereby saving money.

OSELLA
Modified bodywork and rear aerodynamics to make Ghinzani's car similar to new car destroyed at Brands Hatch.

TYRRELL
Improved cooling system in side pod to increase airflow to gearbox. Small catch tank under gearbox for oil.

WILLIAMS
During practice, race cars fitted with two-piece rear exhaust pipes instead of single (T-car had this modification on Sunday). During qualifying, used spray intercoolers which did away with the need for the intercooler bypass first seen in Belgium. On Sunday, applied more downforce by fitting very steep rear blades to front and rear wings. Piquet set up his race car with a more progressive differential.

ZAKSPEED
Race cars fitted with new front wings. Palmer's car and T-car equipped with carbon-fibre brakes.

G.P.

Nigel Snowdon

ENTRY AND PRACTICE

Coming only a week after the acrobatics of the Hungaroring, most drivers anticipated the wide open challenge of the Österreichring with a sense of exhilaration. The new circuit near Budapest had been interesting enough in its way, but it was hardly one of the classic venues on the championship trail. Now, only four days after the chequered flag had fallen at the end of the first post-war GP to be held in the Eastern Bloc, the sweeping curves and geographical splendour of the Styrian track provided the next contest on the agenda.

The one thing that BMW engines have never lacked is out-and-out power, notwithstanding the response problems that have bugged the specially canted engine installed in the Olivetti Brabham BT55s throughout the season. At last, the lowline cars from Chessington began to show the qualifying form which Gordon Murray was sure they possessed. As if to endorse the correctness of the low frontal area concept, Derek Warwick slammed through the speed trap just before the daunting downhill Boschkurve a shade over 214 mph.

For much of second qualifying it looked as though Riccardo Patrese was in with a very real chance of pole position, so it was supremely ironic to see another BMW customer snatching the premier positions from under the nose of Bernie's fastest runner. Equipped with a conventional 'upright' version of the punchy German four-cylinder, the sleek, stable Benetton B186s proved to be the class of the field, with Teo Fabi just pipping local hero Gerhard Berger for pole position.

The Benetton squad's Mader-prepared 'Bee-Emms' started Friday fitted with qualifying-spec turbos for the first time, but the engines refused to

run cleanly and they were replaced with original-spec turbos midway through the session. In the event, neither Fabi nor Berger was able to make another qualifying run that afternoon. By the time those turbos had been swapped, Warwick's Brabham had been pitched into a massive accident on the climb beyond the pits after the BT55's left-rear Pirelli apparently exploded. Just to be on the safe side, all Pirelli users were advised not to continue running on the latest narrow rear tyres, thereby barring the Benettons from any further mileage until the following day.

Nevertheless, the Rory Byrne-designed machines proved able to sustain their competitive challenge at the front. Despite using the spare car after his race machine developed a misfire, Fabi scorched round to grab pole on his second run, 'although I had to go round the outside of a Minardi on the Rindtkurve, just before the pits, and got into a big understeering slide on the way'. Teo added that he might have been able to go even quicker on a clear lap and also reported that a soft brake pedal had given him a nasty moment at another corner.

Team-mate Gerhard Berger was held up in traffic and had to cope with a slight misfire on his best lap – a scant 0.2s off Fabi's pole – and the Austrian left his second try right to the end of the session in an effort to reverse the front row position. As his Benetton's BMW had lost about 500 rpm at the top end, he was unable to manage it.

Fastest on Friday, overnight pole-winner Keke Rosberg found himself demoted to third place the following afternoon. In first qualifying the McLaren-TAGs had set the pace, Alain Prost holding top slot for much of the time before Keke dislodged him right at the end of the session. This was Rosberg's sole qualifying run of the day, a split intercooler having been diagnosed on his

McLaren at the start of the session, losing the Finn a lot of time while it was fixed.

Notwithstanding his fine performance on the first day, Prost was not satisfied with the over-lively ride on the bumps, and things were not perfect on Saturday either. His race car lost power on the first run, forcing him into the spare for his second. Unfortunately, any attempt at an improvement was thwarted when Riccardo Patrese's Brabham blew up spectacularly and deposited a large oil slick shortly before the Rindtkurve. That left the World Champion a disappointed fifth.

Patrese was feeling a lot better than he had at the Hungaroring the previous weekend. His troublesome wisdom tooth had been extracted in Budapest the day after the Hungarian GP and he really felt optimistic about the BT55's prospects on the super-fast Österreichring, 'where there are no really slow corners to give us any big problems!'

On Friday the Italian managed eighth-quickest time, but when he vaulted briefly into second place on Saturday it began to look as though Gordon Murray's lowline concept was on the verge of a very public vindication. Despite de Cesaris's Minardi lubricating the track with yet another Motori-Moderni failure, Riccardo felt he could go faster. Yet even though he was quickest through the speed traps before the Boschkurve and at the start/finish line, his second attempt went up in smoke – literally! His BT55 suffered such an explosive engine failure that the whole rear end of the car erupted into flames. Although the conflagration was quickly doused, the damage was sufficient to write this spare Brabham out of the equation for the remainder of the weekend.

That drama relegated Patrese to fourth place, but it still represented the best BT55 qualifying position yet. Meanwhile, poor Warwick was brushing himself down after his Friday accident,

Grosser Preis von

ÖSTERREICH

'I just kept hoping that it would last, but I had it in my mind that the race was 53 laps, not 52 and there was no way I could see it was going to manage that.' Alain Prost's delight in victory has not diminished one jot over his illustrious Grand Prix career and the smile of pure pleasure he radiated on the Austrian Grand Prix winner's rostrum was as broad and spontaneous as ever. True, he had been lucky to take this one, but then he deserved some luck after Hockenheim and Hungary. He had last won at Monaco and that was ancient history. He needed another win to boost his championship chances — and the Österreichring provided him with just that. Headed only from the start by the impressive Benetton-BMWs of Gerhard Berger and Teo Fabi, he was perfectly placed to pick up a win when these faster runners faltered. Alain could even take pleasure from the fact that his McLaren had the legs of Nigel Mansell's Williams-Honda (and this on a very fast circuit!), although he was to be very glad that a driveshaft constant velocity joint failure would eliminate the Englishman from second place just after half-distance. If Mansell had been running at the end, the dire engine pick-up problem which Prost suffered in the closing stages might well have cost him the race.

Patrick Tambay completed a memorable day for Haas and Ford by finishing fifth behind Alan Jones to give the Lola team their first points.

the Brabham tottering briefly on two wheels before righting itself and slamming backwards into the guard rail. 'Funnily enough, although my instinctive reaction was to tuck myself down as tightly as possible, in case it went over, the strongest memory of the incident is that I was thinking how well the qualifying engine had been going!' explained Derek casually.

Fighting off an over-enthusiastic marshal who tried to drag him from the Brabham's cockpit without releasing the steering wheel – 'He almost broke my legs with the effort!' – Derek received a standing ovation from the grandstand as he walked back to the pits. The following afternoon Derek only had 'routine' poor response out of slow corners and misfire at high revs to deal with. Considering what he had been through, 10th place on the grid was a fine effort.

In the Williams-Honda camp a rather strained atmosphere could be detected in the wake of Nelson Piquet's Hungaroring gamesmanship where he selected an especially suitable differential and failed to share this information with his team-mate. Happily, Nigel Mansell was feeling pretty philosophical about the whole affair and boosted his self-confidence by out-qualifying his Brazilian team-mate.

On Friday Nigel complained that his so-called qualifying engine felt a bit flat and had poor throttle response. On his best run, de Cesaris blew up in front of him and Saturday began on a poor note when his FW11 broke a driveshaft constant velocity joint, stranding him out on the circuit just before the Glatzkurve.

Because he had lost out in the morning session, Mansell opted for a set of race rubber before switching to qualifiers for the final hour. He confessed to running a bit too hard on full tanks with the race rubber, but was consoled when the run revealed a slight chassis balance problem

which could be corrected overnight and fastest time did not come as a surprise during the race morning warm-up. He then did his one run on qualifiers, ending up sixth-fastest after Patrese's Brabham blew its BMW apart right in front of him.

Piquet had fewer tribulations during qualifying, although his stomach was badly upset on Saturday after he had eaten some wild mushrooms the previous evening. He qualified the spare FW11 as his car race had developed a misfire during the Saturday untimed session and he was cautiously contented with seventh place.

Ayrton Senna was having a rather gloomy time with his Lotus 98T, his Friday qualifying disrupted when the air supply to the pneumatic valvegear failed as mechanics warmed up the car for his first run, pistons making smart contact with the valves in every cylinder. Senna thus had to use Johnny Dumfries's car, the Scot being allowed a single run before Senna took it over for the rest of the session.

Although Johnny failed to get a second attempt, he was heartened to be a mere half-second slower than the Brazilian in the same car, although Ayrton complained that the track surface was rather dirty by the time he went out (Warwick's shunt had scattered a fair amount of dirt around). On Saturday morning Patrick Head warned FISA that he would protest the Lotus-Renaults unless their skid plates were removed and their rear underbody diffuser panels rigidly secured against 'inadvertent' flexing. Lotus complied and Senna wound up a disgruntled eighth, unable to adjust the 98T to his liking. Dumfries had an action-packed second session, getting up to 15th after glancing the Rindtkurve barrier on one run and surviving a huge, grass-cutting slide on his next.

Michele Alboreto was moderately happy with his Ferrari F1/86 on this fast circuit, qualifying

ninth despite a lively ride over the bumps. 'The car feels pretty neutral', he admitted happily, 'but then there are no slow corners to trouble us with understeer'. By contrast, Stefan Johansson's two sessions were an absolute nightmare . . .

On Friday morning he spun off exiting the Hella-Licht chicane, the Ferrari's wayward progress across the grassy infield arrested only when it impaled itself on a steel pole supporting an advertisement hoarding. The pole punched up through the underside of the monocoque, impacting against the bulkhead behind the seat. It was as if Stefan had been hit in the small of the back with a mallet and he was in agony for the rest of the weekend. He used the spare for first qualifying, but a replacement machine was brought in overnight from Maranello ready for the Swede to use on Saturday morning. Its use was shortlived because brake problems spun him backwards into the Rindtkurve guard rail and he had to make do with the spare again for the final session, in which he qualified 14th.

René Arnoux suffered an engine fire on Friday and was never able to string together a really good lap the following day. That left him 12th, one place behind team-mate Philippe Alliot. The Haas Lola drivers found that their Ford V6s proved a bit breathless on this super-fast track, both cars requiring engine changes after the first day when the water temperatures began to rise alarmingly. Tambay wound up 13th in both sessions while Jones managed 16th, convinced that his freshly installed V6 felt more sluggish in the second session than its predecessor had on Friday.

Martin Brundle was disappointed with 17th place in his Tyrrell. 'I drove my rag off all through both days. It's just a question of making the car go quicker on the sections that I know I can.' His team-mate Philippe Streiff had an equally disappointing time, a mysterious electrical gremlin

Right: Ten laps to go and looking good. With Prost's main championship rivals out of the race, Ron Dennis thinks of the points. Ten laps later saw Prost barely managing to creep across the line a few yards ahead of the advancing Alboreto *(below right).*

Gerhard Berger was the centre of attention — some of it more welcome than others.

causing his Renault V6 to cut out intermittently throughout the final session. Despite changing all the electrical ancillaries, Streiff failed to struggle higher than 20th.

Over in the Arrows camp, chief designer Dave Wass had departed and the familiar face of Gordon Coppuck replaced him as technical consultant charged with the job of sorting out the new A9. Thierry Boutsen made some progress with the car, but a blown engine on Saturday morning obliged him to take the spare A8 for second qualifying. That took him to 18th, while Christian Danner, also hampered by engine bothers, was down in 22nd in the other A8.

Andrea de Cesaris swapped about from the new Minardi M/86 to an older M/85B, eventually opting for the latter, but Alessandro Nannini proved much quicker in the new car, much to Andrea's irritation. Nannini qualified 19th, de Cesaris 23rd. Jonathan Palmer found that a new qualifying turbo on his Zakspeed failed to produce the improvement expected, qualifying 21st, three places ahead of team-mate Huub Rothengatter, while Ghinzani and Berg brought up the rear for Osella as usual.

RACE

An unusually small crowd turned out for Sunday's race, despite the presence of an Austrian on the front row of the grid. Niki Lauda, in his role as German television commentator, put this down to many people's short excursion over the border into Hungary the previous week, choosing to watch the Budapest race for its novelty value in preference to Zeltweg. Next year, the rumours went, the positions of these races in the calendar will be reversed so that the Österreichring can take the commercial initiative.

Mansell's Williams was quickest in the half-hour warm-up and most of the talk centred on which compound to run, the spectacular Austrian track being second only to Rio in the abrasiveness of its surface. The Benettons and Brabhams opted for the hardest Pirelli compound, while Goodyear's hardest was fitted to both Williams, although most other Akron runners decided to go slightly softer.

Greater aggravation awaited the Brabham team after the warm-up lap, for Patrese came in complaining that his gearbox was jumping out of second and third. Mechanics on the grid fell on the car, and attempted to change what transpired to be damaged dog rings but there was insufficient time left. With the spare badly fire-damaged by Patrese's trouble the previous day, there was no choice but for Bernie to haul Warwick out of the other BT55 and give it to his faster man. Derek demurred with good grace but Brabham fortunes were to plunge to a fresh nadir when Patrese blew it up on the second lap, changing from sixth to seventh gear on the fastest part of the circuit!

Fluttering against their BMW rev-limiters, the two Benettons sprinted for the first turn side-by-side, Berger just getting the jump on Fabi as they scrambled into the chicane at the top of the hill. At the end of the opening lap Gerhard and Teo slammed through in 1-2 formation, already opening a gap to Prost, Mansell, Piquet, Rosberg, Senna, Arnoux, Alliot, Alboreto and the rest of the pack.

It seemed as though the Benettons were in a class of their own and they quickly pulled out a commanding advantage over their rivals. Fabi dropped back abruptly on lap 5 after running over a kerb, his Bee-Em jumping out of sixth gear, massively over-revving and taking the fine edge off its performance. Teo was now keeping his fingers crossed, privately doubting the engine would last.

Lotus fortunes looked rocky from the end of the opening lap when Dumfries came in for a replacement nose, having wiped off a nose fin against a Ferrari's rear wheel in the first-lap traffic jam. On lap 9 he stopped again to investigate a serious misfire. Senna also called in, first to change a blistered front tyre on lap 8, then pulling in from 17th place with his Renault V6 running roughly as well. After the mechanics had fiddled around with the electrics Senna briefly returned to the fray, but he was soon back for good and retired at the end of lap 12. Meanwhile, a plug change on Johnny's car had gone badly wrong: one of the plugs became cross-threaded as they attempted to remove it and no amount of persuasion would move it one way or another. After some heroic attempts, the task was abandoned and the 98T withdrawn.

Lotus aside, the retirement rate ran at a dramatically high level from the word go, perhaps reflecting that a severely overcrowded international calendar was exacting a toll in mechanical and preparation terms. Berg's Osella blew up on lap 7, Palmer's Zakspeed retired two laps later, and poor Martin Brundle's Tyrrell expired with turbo failure on lap 13. Martin reported that it had been running hot from the word go. Streiff's sister

Thierry Boutsen was reunited with Gordon Coppuck (left) as the Spirit designer joined Arrows on a freelance basis. Christian Danner helped Coppuck celebrate a return to Formula 1 by scoring the first point of the season for Arrows.

Below: Piercarlo Ghinzani (left) and Allen Berg (centre) wait for their Osellas whilst the first practice session gets under way without them.

August
Didier Pironi tests AGS Formula 1 car at Paul Ricard.

Renault delay announcement of their plans for 1987 due to continuing negotiations with McLaren.

TECHNICAL FILE

ARROWS
Gordon Coppuck working with Arrows on a freelance basis for three races; Dave Wass 'relieved of responsibility and considering his future'. A9 appeared with rear end from A8.

BENETTON
Used rear wing similar to type first seen at Hockenheim but with chord 5 cm shorter. Continued with modifications first seen in Hungary. Tried larger turbo. Fabi's T-car fitted with lighter pick-up points for suspension.

BRABHAM
BMW supplied engine with internal modifications to suit fast circuit. Four engines equipped with revised pipes and airbox seen in Hungary. Aerodynamics to suit fast circuit – did not use winglets on rear of side pods, for example. Front and rear calipers with twin coils to cool brake fluid.

FERRARI
Devised new fixing system for nose section (resulting from inability to repair Alboreto's accident damage during race in Hungary). Nose cone, wings and internal mounting tube now in one piece to facilitate easy exchange. This also allowed experiments with different aerodynamic set-ups during practice by simply exchanging nose sections. Modifications to turbocharger included new turbine wheel. Rear wing a mixture of profiles from Hockenheim (rear flaps) and Hungary.

LIGIER
No change.

LOLA
No change.

LOTUS
Dumfries ran six-speed gearbox; Senna used five-speed.

McLAREN
During practice ran small, backward-sloping flap (as opposed to narrow lip normally fitted) on trailing edge of rear wing to improve airflow and reduce drag. Taller trumpets to TAG V6 required raised engine cover.

MINARDI
New car given to Nannini. Removed diffuser since this made setting up the car difficult.

OSELLA
No change.

TYRRELL
No change.

WILLIAMS
Smaller brake calipers, only on Piquet's car. Apart from change to aerodynamics for fast circuit, no other major alterations.

ZAKSPEED
Tried Garrett instead of KKK turbos.

G.P.

Martin Brundle *(right)* urges his Tyrrell through the fast sweeps of the Österreichring but the Renault engine was unable to sustain the pace.

A faulty battery ended Gerhard Berger's dominant run at the front. The Benetton driver returned to set fastest lap, an inadequate consolation for what could have been an easy home win for the Austrian.

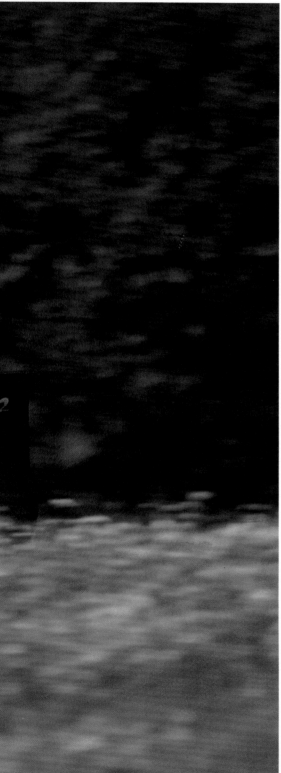

car was already in the pits by this stage, a thin pencil of blue smoke advertising a piston failure at the end of lap 11.

However, up at the front the Benettons looked completely in control. Fabi seemed to be in particularly good shape and hauled up onto Berger's tail going into lap 17. The little Italian neatly towed by into the lead going into the Boschkurve, but his sorely over-taxed BMW expired at almost the precise time he assumed first place. By the exit of the Boschkurve, Berger had swept by once more into the lead.

This left the Austrian playing to his home crowd from a position of strength, but Mansell improved his championship hopes by taking over second when Prost stopped for tyres at the end of lap 21. Then, four laps later, Nigel's Williams surged confidently through into the lead as Berger came in for his routine tyre stop. Or so we thought . . .

On his slowing down lap, Gerhard suddenly became aware of a chronic misfire, reporting it over the radio link to his pit, and the mechanics simply fell on the car as it rolled to a halt. Four fresh Pirellis were fitted, but then the bodywork was lifted off and an agonised groan rose from the grandstands opposite the pits. The problem was a broken battery and by the time it had been replaced Gerhard had lost almost five laps. But he tore back into the contest with great *élan* and immediately began hauling his way back through the depleted field.

Johansson, meanwhile, was having another action-packed day with his Ferrari. Although he thought that 'my brain would explode with all the pain I was going through', Stefan had got up to eighth by lap 26, only to trail into view with his left-front nose wing missing. He had stopped for tyres on lap 22 and was just mentally congratulating himself over the fact that the second set seemed better than the first when WHAM! . . . the left-front fin broke off. It flew back, bounced on his helmet and smashed into one of the rear wing side plates.

The Swede immediately came in for repairs, resumed and found himself grappling with enormous oversteer. 'The engine was really rough as well and the oil light was on for most of the time, so I never thought I'd finish', he reflected later.

Mansell made his routine stop at the end of lap 28, a sticking right-rear wheel nut delaying him more than expected, allowing Prost more than sufficient time to take over in front. He resumed in second, but Piquet had been bothered by ominously rising water temperature for much of the race and crawled slowly into the pits at the end of lap 29. There was nothing that could be done, so he climbed out into retirement.

You could scarcely take breath between retirements! Mansell had just been informed of Piquet's retirement over the radio link when his own FW11 rolled to a halt just beyond the chicane. Another broken driveshaft c/v joint had just sent six crucial points out of the window for the championship leader. 'I don't know whether or not I could have caught Prost', he mused 'but the car felt pretty good and, at the worst, we were going to be second.'

Further 'down the field both Minardis had

expired as usual, de Cesaris's older M/85B succumbing to driveshaft failure, while Nannini's splendid progress with the new M/86 ended when its left-rear suspension broke. The wheel 'tucked under' and the car shot off the track at a suitably accommodating corner which offered a wide run-off and plenty of long grass to stem the wayward machine's wild progress.

All these retirements had suddenly given the front of the field a very familiar 1984 look: both McLarens were cruising round a lap ahead of Alboreto's third-place Ferrari. But Keke was not destined to collect those six points any more than Mansell: with five laps left, the Finn stopped out on the circuit, an electrical short-circuit having rounded off his afternoon's work.

Alain now had it in the bag, his enormous margin over Michele's Ferrari proving extremely valuable when the McLaren began cutting out intermittently with about five laps left to go. 'In places I was freewheeeling, then selecting a gear and trying to jerk it back into life', confessed Prost, 'so I really didn't believe I would make the finish.'

He did, though, with more than a lap in hand over that marauding Ferrari, the Champ thus notching up the 24th victory of his career, only the fourth man ever to achieve this level of success (Stewart, Clark and Fangio being the others).

Behind Alboreto, who had put in one of his typically unobtrusive performances, Johansson finished with a spurt to produce a really worthwhile third place as consolation for all the aggravation he had suffered. By lap 37 he was up to sixth place, but had to work hard dislodging Tambay's Lola which was next on the list. The Ferrari was quicker on the straight but less nimble through the turns. Stefan eventually managed it, but he reserved a very firm piece of his mind for Patrick's driving tactics once the race was over!

Jones's Lola succumbed to the Ferrari's challenge with less of a fight, the Australian having grappled with a slipping clutch almost from the start. 'I couldn't use full throttle and by the end of the race the computer was telling me I had enough fuel for another five laps', joked Alan. The Lolas wound up fourth and fifth behind the Ferraris, the Haas team thus scoring their first points of the season.

Christian Danner's Arrows survived to take sixth, despite an unscheduled stop to sort out a sticking throttle, but Boutsen suffered turbo failure with the new A9, failing to finish. Berger rattled off a whole succession of lap records on his way to a fine seventh, while Rothengatter confounded many observers by lasting the distance to take eighth. Rosberg found himself classified ninth with Arnoux's Ligier tenth, the Frenchman losing a lot of time in the pits sorting out a misfire. Alliot had retired the other JS27 with engine failure on lap 17.

For Prost, this victory represented a long-overdue beacon of hope in his quest for a second straight championship. He and his McLaren had been away from the victory circle since Monaco. Now it seemed that there was life in the old MP4/2C yet. McLaren and TAG might yet make it three titles in a row . . .   A.H.

Gran Premio d'**ITALIA**

Charge! The *Tifosi* go on the rampage. Nigel Snowdon's shot sums up perfectly the Monza atmosphere.

'No problem . . . I tell you, no problem.' Nelson Piquet exuded an air of relaxed confidence as he was filmed by the FOCA television crew prior to the start of the Italian Grand Prix. Nigel Mansell walked by behind him and tried to ruffle his hair. Nelson ducked playfully. It almost seemed, just for a fleeting moment, as if the two Williams team-mates could have been mistaken for friends. Later that afternoon Piquet's prediction came true, his shrewd selection of what appeared to have been a compromise rear wing setting having helped him to mark up a commanding victory over his team-mate. Mansell pulled alongside him on the slowing down lap and applauded him graciously.

Forget the fact that Berger's Benetton used more fuel than was prudent in an outwardly impressive opening charge. Forget that Michele Alboreto kept his Ferrari in touch with the Williams duo. And forget, if you can, the way in which Alain Prost's McLaren was first permitted to start from the pit lane (when it should not have been) and then shamefully black-flagged before it abruptly blew up. All these points were side issues. Monza 1986 was about clearing the decks for a sprint to the title, a sprint between Nelson Piquet and Nigel Mansell. Now the score was even, four wins apiece. And all bets were off . . .

ENTRY AND PRACTICE

The two days of qualifying at Monza, that mecca of motorsport, began on a somewhat confused, mysterious note. When the first untimed Friday morning session began there was only one Ferrari on hand. Specifically, there was only one Ferrari *driver*. Stefan Johansson was firmly strapped into number 28 as usual, parring the volley of press enquiries about his future with the team, but there was no Michele Alboreto to be seen. Panic!

With Ferrari's team leader missing, the Italian press went into top gear, singing along at maximum revs in endless, outlandish speculation. His absence was rumoured to be result of a dislocated shoulder, caused by (a) a fall from his motor cycle, (b) a fall in the shower when he slipped, or (c) a fall in his bathroom when he was suddenly taken ill with food poisoning. Another bizarre theory suggested that he had fallen out with Ferrari and even now was being strapped into the cockpit of a third works McLaren at some suitably secret venue!

Stefan, meanwhile, got on with his own practice efforts, benefiting from Michele's special qualifying engine. This particular Maranello V6 bore little resemblance to anything that had previously been fitted to his car in two seasons, according to the down-to-earth Swede.

Michele, looking rather wan and crestfallen, finally put in an appearance on Saturday morning. Shepherded by Enzo's right-hand man Marco Piccinini, the diplomatic Italian was not keen to discuss the affair. Yes, he had dislocated his shoulder, but his stomach was still rather upset . . . Most people put their money on the motor cycle mishap.

Although Ferrari's efforts were providing the focal point of attention from the madly enthusias-

tic *tifosi*, it was the Pirelli-shod Benetton-BMWs which were really setting the pace during second qualifying. Ayrton Senna's Lotus 98T had topped Friday's qualifying times superbly, but Gerhard Berger and Teo Fabi were right on his tail and took the initiative the following day.

Right in the middle of negotiating his Ferrari contract as Johansson's successor, Berger was in bullish mood from the moment he was first strapped into his B186. A massive engine failure at Parabolica had spiked his final bid for fastest time on Friday, the Austrian's machine pirouetting on its own lubricant as it deposited a swathe of oil which also sent Danner's Arrows straight into the sand trap on the outside. But Gerhard was not to be daunted by a minor incident like that!

On Saturday, the final session turned into a battle of the boost. In the Benetton camp it became a question of who would survive a *banzai* lap on the greatest possible turbo boost pressure. Most observers rocked slightly on their heels when Fabi slammed into his quickest lap at 211.7 mph, but when Berger responded by crossing the timing line at 214.39 mph, it looked as though the Austrian might be on course for his first-ever pole position. Not so. Coming down into Parabolica, the overworked BMW's turbo gave up the ghost, its casing actually split, and he coasted into the pit lane trailing an expensive cloud of smoke. He had to settle for fourth place on the strength of his first Saturday run.

Fabi's efforts earned him the third pole position of his career, but second place in the line-up proved to be a welcome bonus for McLaren International who had hit the headlines the previous week with the departure of designer John Barnard. Prost had won at the Österreichring, but his progress had been bugged by his engine cutting out intermittently during the

closing stages of the race. However, a pre-Italian GP test at Imola confirmed that a revised fuel pick-up system had cured this irritating problem and Alain arrived at Monza in a cautiously optimistic frame of mind.

Although his Friday efforts produced only a lowly ninth place, his progress thwarted by an oil slick at Lesmo laid by Arnoux's expiring Ligier, everything went well for the World Champion the following afternoon. He snatched second place on the grid with a characteristically smooth performance, squeezing the last ounce of potential from that superb chassis, despite being virtually 10 mph down on straightline speed compared to the Benettons.

Relaxed, confident and optimistic, championship points leader Nigel Mansell did well to plant his Williams FW11 on the inside of the second row, third overall. Arnoux's oil spoiled his first Friday run and he had to get badly off-line going into the first chicane after the pits on his second try.

'Jones's Lola was overtaking a slower car and I had to go a long way over to the right in order to nip by them both before the chicane', Nigel explained. 'They didn't really baulk me, but I picked up some dirt on the front tyres which gave me a bit more understeer than I needed through the next right-hander.'

On Saturday, Mansell briefly took pole on his first run, despite a leaking gasket on the Honda V6's left-hand turbo, but he wound off a little too much wing for his second run and slid over the Lesmo kerbing second time out. After that, third place seemed pretty satisfying.

By contrast, Nelson Piquet finished practice a rather disappointed sixth, admitting that he blistered his second set of Goodyears before the end of his second Saturday run. 'I ran a hard

left-rear on my first run', he explained, 'and I now wish I'd stayed with that combination on my second because I think I came out of Parabolica a bit too hard as I went into my quick lap, causing the tyre to overheat'.

Senna felt confident that he could sustain a front-running challenge for Lotus, but dropped to fifth place after a freshly installed Renault V6 blew up on Saturday afternoon. He freewheeled straight back into the pits trailing an ominous haze of blue smoke.

In the Brabham camp a promising Imola test put the team in good heart for Monza, the canted BMW engine's low-speed response seemingly better than ever. On this occasion it was Derek Warwick who came out of the qualifying battle best, yet the catalogue of problems which afflicted him on Friday made his Italian GP weekend seem like an enduring disaster.

Derek blew engines in both his race car and the spare BT55, the first such failure ruining what he felt sure was one of the best single laps of his year. 'I was absolutely storming down towards Parabolica, thinking to myself "right, this will show everybody", when the engine started to hiccup and go flat, but I was so wound up that I just slammed it down into third and kept my foot on the floor . . .'

The spare lasted a few hundred yards down the road after Patrese used it earlier on, but Derek's luck changed during Saturday's untimed session. He managed about thirty trouble-free laps and reaped the benefit of some consistent running by securing an excellent seventh place on the grid.

Warwick had the satisfaction of lining up immediately ahead of McLaren number two Keke Rosberg. The Finn was unexpectedly back in an understeering rut – his old anathema – from which he seemed unable to extricate himself. 'It's

the old story; real front end wash-out', he shrugged, 'the sort of thing which makes it necessary to back off to restore some grip. Can't handle that at all.'

Patrese, meanwhile, blew up the engine in his race chassis and the spare on Saturday, making it a hat-trick when he took over Derek's machine right at the end of the session as that car's engine broke too. Highly disappointed in 10th place on the grid, he was fractionally slower than Alboreto.

Despite his damaged shoulder, Michele reported no problems in the cockpit. 'The harness holds it in place quite well', he stated with a certain lack of conviction. 'It's out of the car that I'm in a fair deal of pain.' His was a fine effort, with or without a special qualifying engine, having missed an entire day's running.

After blowing up his Ligier JS27 on Friday, René Arnoux had a couple of trouble-free runs on Saturday to qualify 11th. Philippe Alliot, evicted from his JS27 to make way for his partner following his lone Friday run, was unable to improve on 14th in the second session when his Ligier suffered a turbo failure as it tore past the pits.

There had been some design department changes in the Arrows camp over the preceding weeks, the most significant being the departure of the long-serving Dave Wass in the wake of the A9's debut. Hardly an unqualified success, the BMW-engined challenger from the Milton Keynes-based team had been transferred into the technical stewardship of freelance consultant Gordon Coppuck. None the less, the new car was only brought to Monza in the role of spare, both Thierry Boutsen and Christian Danner concentrating their efforts on the older A8s.

Boutsen reminded everybody of his considerable talent by qualifying 14th, praising the

performance of the Heini Mader-prepared BMW qualifying engines on this occasion. 'On Friday the car felt really well balanced', he reported, 'but on my second set of qualifiers on Saturday I had such a bad vibration from the rear end that I had to hold onto my helmet in order to focus my eyes in a straight line!'

The ebullient Danner was equally delighted to reach 16th slot, despite that Friday excursion into the Parabolica sand trap and a touch more oversteer than he really wanted on Saturday.

Over at Team Haas, the Lola-Ford THL-2s were much as before, although long-overdue new water radiators were fitted to the two race machines used by Alan Jones and Patrick Tambay. With only race boost pressure settings, it was asking a lot to expect worthwhile grid positions for the Haas entries. Tambay could get no further than 15th, his final attempt spoiled when the engine cut out midway round the lap (the problem was a malfunction in the wiring loom), while Jones was a fuming 18th. The Australian's efforts were thwarted by an oil leak onto the clutch on Friday morning, a replacement V6 which failed to run smoothly and then a water leak on Saturday morning. Once he had completed his two Saturday runs, he changed into civvies and stormed off, well before the end of the session.

Johnny Dumfries did well to slot his Lotus 98T in ahead of Jones in 17th place, despite a sand-scattering moment at one of the chicanes as well as some gear selection problems. He used two sets of qualifying rubber on Saturday, but found both losing grip before the end of his flying lap. 'Some day things go right, some days they don't', he shrugged.

In the Minardi camp things were definitely not going smoothly for nominal team leader Andrea de Cesaris, who found himself upstaged once more

Paul-Henri Cahier

Another anti-climactic end for the Benetton team. Teo Fabi (left) claimed pole position but started from the back of the grid; Gerhard Berger led briefly but could finish no higher than fifth.

Cheers! A welcome drink and third place for the hard-working Stefan Johansson.

Despite missing the first day of practice, Michele Alboreto drove strongly in the race and held on to the Williams-Hondas before retiring.

A rare picture of Andrea de Cesaris enjoying a trouble-free run with the Minardi-Motori Moderni. Needless to say, he failed to finish.

Paul-Henri Cahier

August/September
*Didier Pironi tests Ligier-Renault at Dijon;
may be offered drive for 1987 if Laffite unfit.*

*Kris Nissen (Ralt-VW RT30) wins German
Formula 3 Championship.*

*Peugeot win World Rally Championship for
Manufacturers.*

*Denny Hulme (3.5 Rover Vitesse) wins
Tourist Trophy for the fourth time.*

*Alain Prost fined £5000 by FISA for
criticising the manner of his
disqualification from Italian Grand Prix.*

by the considerably less experienced Alessandro Nannini. On Friday Andrea tried both the new M/86 and the more proven M/85B, switching to the earlier car after a turbo pipe kept blowing off the newer machine. The following day he lost time with a blocked water radiator, eventually taking the M/86 round to qualify 21st, while Nannini used his M/85B to line up two places higher!

Splitting the Minardis was a terribly disappointed Martin Brundle, the Tyrrell driver enduring a couple of really frustrating qualifying sessions. On Friday his first car lost all its gears; he then went out briefly in his race car, switched back to the original machine only for that immediately to stop out on the circuit on its first lap with engine failure. On Saturday he had a disappointing run to 20th place, but at least this was three places ahead of team-mate Philippe Streiff whose 015 suffered a persistent misfire throughout the second session.

Jonathan Palmer tried both his Zakspeeds, to be bugged by a misfire on the first and gear selection trouble with the second during Friday qualifying. The following afternoon he found his rear qualifiers losing grip after less than half a lap. He wound up 23rd, worried about the car's fuel consumption potential.

Huub Rothengatter planted the second Zakspeed on 24th place, the Dutchman lining up ahead of the angular new AGS JH21C which was making its F1 debut in the hands of F3000 leading light Ivan Capelli. Powered by a Motori Moderni V6, this essentially conventional machine had been tested by both Capelli and former Ferrari ace Didier Pironi during the fortnight prior to Monza. It still needed more development running: turbo failure sidelined it on Friday and it blew its engine on Saturday.

Right at the back were the two outclassed Osella-Alfas, Allen Berg's place in the second car being taken on this occasion by Italian F3 exponent Alex Caffi, to satisfy sponsorship considerations. Regular man Ghinzani qualified 26th, but Caffi was allowed to start as a 27th runner as the team is a regular championship contestant.

RACE

As the usual madly enthusiastic crowd took up position at precarious vantage points all round the circuit, Riccardo Patrese raised some cheers by setting fastest time in the half-hour warm-up, although this morale-boosting show was not to be reflected by Brabham team fortunes once the race got under way. By contrast, Warwick's BT55 was suffering with turbo surge from the start and its clutch packed up as well after five laps, so a fresh engine was installed.

The start was something else again. There have been mix-ups in the past, with people in the wrong position, cars late away on parade laps and suchlike, but the Grand Prix World Championship surely notched up another first at Monza when the 1986 Italian GP started without its two front-row cars!

When the time came to fire up engines in preparation for the parade lap, Fabi's BMW blurted into life — and then stalled. Meanwhile, Prost's McLaren had suffered an alternator

malfunction and steadfastly refused to fire up. At the last possible moment (as events would turn out, actually *after* that moment!) Prost hopped out of his stricken machine and ran across to the spare MP4/2C which was waiting at the exit of the pit lane.

A rather surprised Mansell and Berger led the field round the parade lap as Fabi managed to get his Benetton started and chased off after his rivals to start from the back of the grid. An icily under-control Prost sat glowering in the pits waiting to join in after the grid had departed.

This was another fine chance for Berger to display his flair and panache, the Austrian making a brilliant start to lead Mansell down to the first chicane. Senna's Lotus, meanwhile, suddenly slowed and was swamped on all sides as its clutch gave up the ghost, the dejected Brazilian coasting over to the right of the start/finish apron where he promptly abandoned his car.

Aided by a generous helping of boost, Berger flashed through at the end of lap 1 with almost three seconds in hand over Mansell, Piquet, Arnoux, Rosberg, Alboreto, Alliot, Johansson, Warwick, Dumfries, Boutsen, Tambay and the rest of the pack. Gerhard looked absolutely magnificent and fully in command.

Neither Williams driver was unduly concerned by Berger's pace in those early laps, Mansell and Piquet rightly estimating that the battle for victory would be fought between the two of them. Gerhard was punishing his tyres and his fuel consumption mathematics too hard for such an early stage of the race. However, Alboreto quickly picked up the pace, powering past Arnoux's Ligier on lap 3 to take over fourth place, while Prost had joined in at the back and was simply scything through the slower cars, his lap times a model of consistency and speed in the spare McLaren. Meanwhile, a group of officials were locked in debate in the pits over whether or not the World Champion should have been allowed to start . . .

Patrese hauled up onto the tail of Tambay's Lola going into lap 3 and made a bid to get by as the Frenchman entered one of the chicanes. Unfortunately, there was not enough room available and the two cars became firmly interlocked, Tambay rolling to a halt almost immediately, both left-hand tyres deflated. Riccardo coaxed his mount back to the pits, but the right-hand side pod was so badly chewed up that the BT55 was retired on the spot.

Berger eased his pace slightly by the end of lap 4, Mansell, Piquet and Alboreto moving up onto the Benetton's tail to make a tight quartet. Two laps later Nigel was weighing up where and how to pass Berger, finally jumping him on the exit of Parabolica at the end of lap 7. Next time round Piquet and Alboreto followed Mansell through, leaving Berger to contemplate his fuel readout from an increasingly distant fourth place.

With ten laps completed, Fabi had rocketed through to eighth place while Prost was tenth. There had also been plenty of action towards the tail of the field. Streiff's Tyrrell had been in for a replacement nose cone after getting ruthlessly chopped by de Cesaris at Parabolica, while Warwick found his BT55 increasingly troubled by

locking rear brakes, dropping from an initial eighth to eleventh. On lap 17 he spun harmlessly at the first chicane, but in spin-turning the Brabham to rejoin he slid into the guard rail, deranging its rear wing. After that impromptu carnival act, 'Del Boy' was left to walk back to the pits, blushing beneath his balaclava . . .

By lap 12, Mansell, Piquet and Alboreto were running in nose-to-tail formation, but the Englishman was picking his way through the slower traffic with considerable judgement and opportunism, leapfrogging past slower cars just before corners so as to give himself some breathing space over his pursuers.

By lap 18 the astonishing Prost was up to sixth, but by now, almost half an hour into the race, the stewards had decided that he should not have been out there in the first place. By the scant margin of about five seconds, Prost had contravened the rule which states that a driver may not change cars once the green flag has been waved to herald the start of the parade lap, so the black flag, together with his race number, was eventually shown at the startline at the end of lap 26. Incredible as it may seem, Alain had been permitted to battle through the traffic and even to call at the pits to change the car's nose cone (the aerofoil support tube of which had collapsed), yet all for no purpose. Up to this point, no steps to prevent his progress had been taken.

It must have been some small consolation for Prost that he would not have finished the race in any case, as his TAG V6 expired in an expensive cloud of smoke midway round lap 28. Not surprisingly, Alain was extremely angry about the way things had developed and had some pretty choice observations to make on the subject of the stewards' decision. The sport's governing body then responded in its increasingly familiar, impulsive fashion and fined him $5000 for speaking his mind. It also transpired that McLaren International Director Ron Dennis had attempted to persuade the stewards to let Prost race to the finish. Naturally, that was a fact which FISA seized upon with some relish when it announced the penalty.

Meanwhile, the front-running contenders approached the time for their scheduled tyre stops. Piquet pulled in at the end of lap 22, his Williams remaining stationary for over 16 seconds thanks to a grabbing right-front wheel nut. He restarted in fourth place. Mansell then stopped at the end of lap 25, allowing Berger briefly back into the lead, but Nigel went back ahead on lap 27 as the Benetton paused for fresh Pirellis. For two laps Arnoux's Ligier found itself briefly second, until a tyre stop on lap 29 deposed him in favour of Piquet, ahead of Berger and Johansson.

Michele Alboreto, meanwhile, had dropped from contention. On lap 17 he lost control of his Ferrari over a bump coming out of the first chicane whilst hard on Nelson's gearbox. The Italian machine spun wildly, just kissing the right-hand barrier and bending a couple of wheel rims. He stopped for new tyres at the end of the lap, resuming a chastened 11th. He climbed doggedly back to fifth behind his team-mate only for his engine to expire on lap 34.

A touch too much oversteer. Riccardo Patrese *(left)*, struggles back to the pits after an early incident with Tambay's Lola.

Ivan Capelli returned to Formula 1 to give the AGS Grand Prix car its first race *(right)*.

Alex Caffi: a steady, sensible Grand Prix debut with Osella *(far right)*.

As expected, the battle for the lead was now left to the two Williams-Hondas and in the second half of the race it became clear that Nelson's car had a distinct performance advantage. Juggling with rear wing settings, Piquet had been concerned about the potential fuel consumption problems posed by running the same trim as Mansell, so he opted for a wing used at Hockenheim which gave him slightly more straightline speed. In the closing stages of the race he was able to lap over a second faster than Mansell, gobbling up his team-mate's advantage to seize the lead going into Curva Grande on lap 38. For the remaining 13 laps Nelson commanded the race in relaxed style, winning his fourth triumph of the year by fractionally less than ten seconds.

Nigel's progress to second place was also made less comfortable by the fact that an additional chest strap became loosened in his cockpit, fractionally reducing his lateral support. But he applauded Piquet's victory in a sportsmanlike manner which had not always been reciprocated throughout the season up to that point.

In the closing stages of the race, Berger played a tantalising game of cat and mouse with Johansson's Ferrari. 'Every time I got near him, he just streaked away from me', shrugged the Swede. 'Good luck to him if he can run that sort of boost because I can't!' Neither could Gerhard as things turned out. Over the last few laps he had to ease right back to conserve fuel after his earlier extrovert antics. Finally, dirt in a fuel line jammed open one of the injectors to cause a cracked fuel pipe and consequent serious misfire. Stefan breezed past easily to take third place, and the disappointed Berger fell back still further before the finish behind Rosberg's McLaren.

Keke's fourth place was undistinguished and unobtrusive. He had been grappling with understeer throughout the race and also had a fuel consumption problem which ensured he had to drive on his instruments for most of the time.

Seven laps from the finish Alan Jones's Lola relieved Boutsen's Arrows of sixth place, the Australian's progress through the field punctured by two pit stops, one of which had been routine, the other unscheduled after a front wheel balance weight flew off. Boutsen took seventh ahead of team-mate Christian Danner, while the Tyrrells were ninth and tenth, Streiff ahead of Brundle, whose mount developed a misfire in the closing stages.

Alex Caffi deserved praise for keeping out of the way and at least registering a finish, albeit six laps down, but his colleague from the back row, delayed pole-man Teo Fabi, slid off the road with a soft front tyre after making an earlier stop to investigate a misfire.

Other retirements included Capelli's AGS with rear tyre failure, both Minardis with engine and electrical malfunctions, and Ghinzani's Osella which spun before Parabolica after the rear suspension broke. Palmer's Zakspeed broke its alternator, Alliot's Ligier its engine and Arnoux's sister car its gearbox.

Now the two Williams lads were eyeball to eyeball in the victory stakes. Which one would blink first?   A.H.

TECHNICAL FILE

AGS
Appeared at a race meeting for the first time. Used Renault chassis with section removed from top of tub as Renault tub considered to be too high; this necessitated temporary remodelling of top bodywork. Employed Renault front and rear suspension, brakes, intercooler, radiator and gearbox (but not latest model; preferred older gearbox in interest of reliability). Used Motori Moderni engine similar to Minardi except for different airbox and intercooler.

ARROWS
Gordon Coppuck concentrated on A8 and altered rear geometry.

BENETTON
Used BMW engines which gave improved acceleration from slow corners. Blanked off wastegate and fitted megaphone exhaust during qualifying. Did not fit deflectors behind front wheels.

BRABHAM
New chassis for Patrese to replace number 4 burnt out in Austria. Revised rear wings and front wings fitted with side plates with angled lower profiles. Did not use winglets on rear of side pods. All BMW engines now equipped with new inlets as seen in Austria.

FERRARI
Used revised turbos and ancillary ducting as tested at Imola. Intercooler on Alboreto's car set at a different angle. All three cars equipped with a longer and thinner Secam intercooler, designed originally for the short-wheelbase car and found to be more efficient. Race cars fitted with Marzocchi shock absorbers with separate gas cylinders. More competitive form at Monza attributed to improved aerodynamics and chassis tuning, avoiding previous mistakes with incorrect springs for various downforce set-ups.

LIGIER
New chassis for Arnoux. Did not fit vertical deflectors behind front tyres.

LOLA
Revised front suspension and new rear rocker arms with different fixing points for shock absorbers to allow easier access for mechanics. Secam water radiators fitted.

LOTUS
No additional wing at rear, removed vertical deflectors behind front wheels.

McLAREN
Longer trumpets fitted to engines (as seen in Austria). Removed vertical fins from rear diffuser after Friday's practice when they had been causing porpoising. Fitted K27 medium size turbos for the race.

MINARDI
Ran revised rear suspension which allowed various shock absorber positions. Tried a different ducting arrangement for turbochargers on all three cars – NACA duct on top of side pod; snorkle-type duct through centre rather than side of pod (Nannini's car) and side vent similar to arrangement on Williams (T-car). Both race cars then equipped with snorkle duct.

OSELLA
No change.

TYRRELL
New duct arrangements inside side pods on Brundle's car.

WILLIAMS
Strengthened c/v joints (Piquet made three maximum power starts during testing at Imola). Piquet used revised front suspension with different rocker arm as tested at Imola. Boost control modified to overcome inability to generate maximum power during qualifying. Fixing points altered for lower wishbones.

ZAKSPEED
Square-shaped nose fitted to Palmer's car after wind tunnel tests. Altered size and shape of deflector behind front wheels.

G.P.

Grande Premio de
PORTUGAL

When Nigel Mansell is old and grey, sitting at the fireside surrounded by his grandchildren and reminiscing about his Grand Prix heyday in the 1980s, he will be able to show them the results of the 1986 Portuguese Grand Prix at Estoril and chuckle, 'Look at that, kid. Not bad eh? First, Mansell; Second, Prost; Third, Piquet; Fourth, Senna . . .

And that's how it was in the late summer sunshine on 21 September at the challenging little circuit in the scrubland, just a few miles up from the Portuguese resort which gives its name to the circuit. Nigel scored quite the most outstanding victory of his Formula 1 career, leading the final European round of the championship from start to finish in impeccable style at the wheel of his Canon Williams-Honda FW11, convincingly trouncing his three closest rivals in the title chase. They were all in trouble towards the end of the race, but by that time they had been beaten hollow by the moustachioed Englishman on his way to the fifth win of his most successful season by far. At the end of the afternoon it was Prost's McLaren which took second spot, but only after Senna's Lotus 98T had spluttered low on fuel on its final tour and Piquet's Williams had spun with snatching rear brakes a few laps from home. Senna's late-race misfortune also allowed Piquet to make up one more place, so Nelson received a last-minute bonus in his quest to keep on terms with his victorious team-mate in the battle for the championship.

Mansell and his Williams-Honda; a faultless performance.

ENTRY AND PRACTICE

Estoril was preparing to stage its third Grand Prix as the battle-weary Formula 1 teams gathered up their traps and returned to base after the Italian race, but this time the Portuguese event was back to its early autumn slot in the calendar. Two years ago we watched a crushing McLaren-TAG 1-2 secure Niki Lauda's third World Championship title by half a point. Six months later we were back for the first European race of 1985; and in '86 it was the *last* European round on the calendar. But, despite the fact that the Portuguese GP has darted rather uncertainly around the international racing schedule, one common strand of consistency has linked all three races. That factor is Ayrton Senna's sheer brilliance.

In 1984 he finished third behind the McLarens, in a Toleman-Hart TG184. That was the Formula 1 equivalent of taking on Concorde with a Dakota. At the start of '85 he won, superbly, for Lotus in streaming wet conditions. In 1986 he looked as though he might be able to make a last-ditch effort at resuscitating his World Championship dreams when he took a stunning pole position, a full 0.8s faster than his nearest rival.

His fans will tell you that it was classic Senna. Wait until near the end of the session, carefully watch where your key rivals are all round the circuit and, when most of them have retreated to the pits, take advantage of a relatively empty circuit on which to stage your virtuoso performance. Nigel Mansell's Williams FW11 had been fastest during first qualifying on Friday, but the pace of the battle increased considerably during that second crucial hour. First it was Keke Rosberg who stole pole, then Senna (on his first

run), then Mansell, then Berger's Benetton B186. Nigel's second run produced a blistering 1m 17.489s and it looked as though the Englishman just might have had the final word on the subject. But no; Senna put 1m 16.673s under his belt after changing to different qualifying turbos between his two runs.

Of course, if you are less enamoured of Senna and the Lotus *modus operandi*, you would have pointed to the unique qualifying specification in which the Lotus 98T produced that scintillating time. Its special ground-hugging configuration, with side pod securing stays loosened off in order to gain the maximum possible ground effect downforce, ensured that Ayrton's progress on that quickest run was attended by an almost endless shower of sparks as the undertray smashed onto the track surface. In the Williams pit, Patrick Head's face barely betrayed a flicker of an eyebrow. This was something he had warned Lotus about at Österreichring, but no matter. It was Sunday's race that counted.

'It all worked very well for me', said Senna with his customary understatement, 'although I had to wait around a few minutes longer than I would have liked for the track to completely clear.' It was the Brazilian's seventh pole of the season and he was quietly confident about what he could produce when it came to the race.

In the Williams camp there were four FW11-Hondas to be seen, two apiece for championship rivals Nigel Chansell and Nelson Piquet. The team's management was absolutely determined that both men should have complete parity of equipment for the remaining three races on the calendar, a move which enhanced Mansell's cool and collected mood. The only technical changes to

be seen on the cars over the weekend were repositioned cooling inlets for the turbos, mounted vertically atop the side pods. Both men tried them, thought they were a slight improvement, but eventually opted for the original side-mounted ducts as the revised layout had not been sufficiently tested. Everybody was playing safe!

On Friday Nigel tried different set-ups on his two cars during the morning untimed session and, before Jonathan Palmer's Zakspeed blew up and dropped a swathe of oil on the racing line, popped the overnight pole into the bag on hard B compound rubber early in the afternoon. His Saturday qualifying got off to a disappointing start when he was squeezed into the apex of a tight left-hander by Alan Jones's Lola, the Australian simply not seeing him coming. Happily, Nigel was on race rubber, so the resultant half-spin over the kerb cost him only slight damage to a front aerofoil end plate.

On his second run Mansell used qualifiers, gained his front-row position and then, later in the session, had a harmless spin at the bottom of the hill behind the paddock whilst evaluating a different rear wing set-up. He finished the day with a wide grin on his face. He was on row one – and his team-mate was back on row three!

Nelson Piquet came to Estoril fresh from a stunningly quick test session at Silverstone where he had turned a 1m 5s lap on race rubber – and carrying about 60 litres of fuel! 'If I'd been really trying on qualifiers, I reckon that we might have got down into the high 61s bracket', he grinned. 'I mean, can you imagine it? I was slamming through Club corner in fifth, snatching sixth right on the exit . . .' Time was when 65s was a fairly impressive lap time on the *short* circuit, so

An early retirement for Capelli and the AGS.

Nelson's performance seemed a compelling endorsement of FISA's avowed intention of capping the F1 performance spiral dramatically in the near future.

Sadly, Nelson's challenge in second qualifying at Estoril was spoiled when he slid wide over a kerb, slightly dislodging one of the stays locating the outer edge of his FW11's undertray. 'That left him with a slight porpoising problem rather similar to that experienced by Nigel at Hockenheim', explained Patrick Head, 'so he lost some of its downforce.' The Brazilian had to accept somewhat frustrated sixth on the outside of row three.

In the McLaren garage there was a brand new chassis (MP4/2C-5) on hand for the World Champion and TAG Turbo Engines had come up with a revised V6 for the Frenchman to try. This development engine, with revised combustion chambers for improved fuel efficiency, was installed in Prost's new car for Friday's untimed session, but he was not convinced abvout it and switched to his spare chassis for the rest of the day. Alain was in a very withdrawn, subdued mood all weekend, immeasurably saddened by the death of his older brother Daniel who had succumbed to cancer the night prior to first practice in Portugal.

Waiting until the end of the session on Friday, Prost turned third-quickest time of the day on qualifying rubber, and although his first Saturday run was spoiled by a misfire he managed to retain third place with a trouble-free second run on qualifiers. His team-mate Keke Rosberg displayed a more optimistic frame of mind than one might have expected from a man who had only qualified seventh. 'I don't think my grid position is an accurate reflection of the car's true race potential at this track', he declared firmly.

On Friday, Keke's efforts were hampered by a very strange problem indeed. Following a mid-session gear ratio change, he discovered that shifting from fourth to fifth made no difference at all. Most puzzling. It was eventually traced to a touch of 'finger trouble' on the part of the mechanics; they had managed to instal two fourth gears!

On Saturday afternoon Rosberg had to run round the outside of Thierry Boutsen's Arrows A8 on his first run, but waved aside the Belgian's concerned apologies that he might have baulked the McLaren driver. 'Absolutely no problem. I didn't lose any time at all', he told Thierry. His second run was frustrated by a slight engine malfunction. 'One second it's running sweetly, then it's off-song, then it's running sweetly again', he explained.

Despite grappling with excessive understeer, Gerhard Berger and Teo Fabi produced a well-matched performance for the Benetton squad, Gerhard just pipping his colleague for a place on the outside of row two. The Austrian confessed that he had dropped a wheel off the circuit on his best qualifying run, but he broke the 1m 18s barrier to take fourth place. Fabi lined up inside Piquet's Williams on row three, consolidating the team's hope of a good result.

Outside Rosberg on row four was Stefan Johansson, the Swede's days at Maranello now

clearly numbered. However, the genial 'Steven' remained discreet and tactful in his comments about the F1/86's performance on this bumpy track. 'I'm losing quite a bit of time in the slow corners, but otherwise I don't reckon the chassis is too bad at all. Having said all that, though, it is a *very* difficult circuit from the point of view of traffic . . .' There was no concealing the satisfaction he derived from outqualifying Michele Alboreto by five places.

Not that the Italian had an easy time of things, of course. As he leaned into the first right-hander after the pits at the start of his second Saturday qualifying run, the Ferrari's right-front aerofoil began to fall apart! Midway round the lap he found his right-front wheel locking up as it lost downforce and he missed a couple of apexes as a result. Hanging on grimly, he battled round onto the start/finish straight only for the whole nose wing assembly to disintegrate completely as he finished the lap. Debris flew everywhere, puncturing his front tyre and narrowly missing his helmet. Since his first run had been ruined by another Palmer/Zakspeed engine blow-up, a miserable 13th place was all he had to show for his heroic efforts.

Riccardo Patrese produced the best Brabham BT55 qualifying position: ninth, which put him just inside René Arnoux's Ligier JS27. In the final session Riccardo was late out onto the circuit, delayed whilst the inevitable BMW misfire was sorted out, but at least he managed some clear laps without too much in the way of drama. Derek Warwick had been in mechanical trouble from the first session onwards, blowing engines in both the Friday morning and Saturday morning session. He did his best lap on his first Saturday qualifying run, but was unable to improve on 12th overall as his second run ended with the BT55 rolling to a silent stop out on the circuit. The gearbox input shaft had failed.

Arnoux's main claim to fame during qualifying stemmed from a vociferous outburst at the end of the second session. He went on a verbal rampage about the vagaries of the qualifying system: 'It's crazy', he moaned, 'it's almost as important to baulk other people as it is to get a quick lap yourself. Something must be done about it'. Since René himself has a reputation as one of the worst baulkers in the business, this outburst seemed rather ripe, to say the least!

Philippe Alliot lined up right behind Arnoux in 11th place, confident that he could have gone even quicker had not Streiff first held him up in the Tyrrell and then Mansell spun in front of him at the end of the second session. 'Nigel didn't actually get in my way', he confessed', but I was keeping an eye on where he was going to end up and that cost me a couple of tenths.'

In the Haas Lola-Ford camp, it was pretty much 'business as usual' with the agile Neil Oatley-designed chassis handling well through the corners, but losing out quite significantly in the straightline speed stakes. Patrick Tambay ended up a moderately satisfied 14th, just failing to breach the 1m 20s barrier before running out of fuel and rolling to a halt on the circuit during Saturday's session. The Frenchman also suffered

turbo failures in both qualifying sessions and reported a progressively softening brake pedal (caused by pad knock-off) towards the end of his final run.

Tambay had murmured his reservations about the notchy gearchange, but team-mate Alan Jones was more specific in his complaints. 'Every lap I seemed to miss one gear or another', he shrugged, 'but it's quite a good little circuit, although there's not much room on the outside of those fourth-gear turns.' The Australian ended up in 17th place, separated from Tambay by Johnny Dumfries's Lotus 98T and the Minardi M/86 of Andrea de Cesaris.

Johnny's difficult time on Friday left him 18th after finding himself faced with an unenviable decision to make on his best lap. 'I came up behind Johansson and was faced with the choice of trying to outbrake him or aborting my run. I chose the former, but got onto the gravel on the outside of the turn in a big understeering slide.' The following day he improved by three places, running one set of race rubber before switching to qualifiers for his best lap. He had slight problems engaging fourth gear, but he finished heartened by the 98T's race set-up.

De Cesaris got the better of Alessandro Nannini's older Minardi M/85B on this occasion, and his 16th place put him two grid positions ahead of his team-mate. At least he was ahead of both Tyrrell-Renaults, Martin Brundle and Philippe Streiff suffering a truly sickening run of bad luck throughout the two days of qualifying.

On Friday, both Tyrrells succumbed to turbo failure, Brundle's spare 015 briefly catching fire with such ferocity that a rear suspension link retaining bracket – manufactured from aluminium – actually melted. 'The turbo blew, an oil line came off and up it went, all within the space of ten seconds', he shrugged.

That left Brundle lapping at the wheel of his race car for the rest of the session, but any hope of improvement on Saturday was dashed when his engine seized on his first flying lap with B compound rubber. He finished 19th on the grid, 'about half a dozen places further back than we should have been!'

Streiff's first attempt on Saturday was spoiled by heavy traffic, but he reached 23rd place on the grid the second time round. Then, desperately trying to squeeze a third run out his part-worn qualifiers, he spun into the guard rail coming out of a tight hairpin, damaging the rear end of his car.

A couple of engine failures spiked Jonathan Palmer's qualifying efforts with the Zakspeed, but he still managed to squeeze into 20th place, just ahead of the outclassed Arrows A8s of Thierry Boutsen and Christian Danner, both of whom were having a hard time over the bumps and ripples. Piercarlo Ghinzani's Osella was 24th ahead of Ivan Capelli's AGS JH21C (making its second and last 1986 foray after its Monza debut) and Huub Rothengatter's Zakspeed was 26th. Following Alex Caffi's outing in the second Osella at Monza, Allen Berg had managed to come up with some more sponsorship to secure the seat for the balance of the season. Although he qualified

27th, everybody agreed that he could start because Osella was a regular championship contender and he had only been pushed out by Capelli's interloping AGS, just as Caffi had been two weeks earlier.

RACE

In front of a much bigger crowd than was seen at the previous two Portuguese Grands Prix, Alain Prost's McLaren turned the quickest time in the race morning warm-up on Sunday. However, as the track was opened to allow the cars out to cruise round to the starting grid, Alain did one quick lap in his race chassis before driving straight back into the pits and switching to his spare. A fresh engine had been installed in his regular machine after it had developed a misfire during the warm-up, but Alain decided to take the safe route and opt for one which he had tried the previous day. Mansell, meanwhile, took the opportunity to make a last-minute adjustment to the nose wing settings on his Williams. The green flag was waved and the pack was off on its parade lap, dutifully filing round behind Senna's Lotus.

Back on the grid they paused only momentarily, the starting light blinked green and they were off. By the time Senna hit third gear Mansell's FW11 was alongside his Lotus's cockpit and, as they surged down into the first right-hander Nigel pulled clear, cut across onto the racing line and away into a brilliant lead.

From this early stage there was no arguments about who was in charge. Mansell took the race by the scruff of its neck and never looked back. By the end of the opening lap he was a couple of lengths clear of Senna, with Berger already some way further back in third place, pursued by Piquet, Prost, Fabi, Rosberg (whose McLaren sported a distinctive mustard-and-white livery to promote a new low-tar Marlboro cigarette), Johansson, Arnoux, Alboreto, Alliot, Patrese, de Cesaris, Dumfries, Warwick, Jones, Tambay, Brundle, Boutsen, Nannini and the stragglers.

For the first few laps the order did not change very much, although Berger managed to bottle up his pursuers pretty comprehensively, allowing Mansell and Senna to get well clear during that opening sprint. By the time Nelson finally squeezed by into third place on lap 8, he was almost six seconds behind Senna and had plenty of hard work in front of him. Prost followed through to fourth on lap 9 and Rosberg pushed Berger down to sixth next time round.

Early retirements included Capelli's AGS with transmission trouble on lap 7, Rothengatter with similar problems and Ghinzani's Osella with terminal electrical failure, the Italian packing it in after a couple of pit visits failed to rectify the problem.

Down in 15th place, Alan Jones was running just ahead of Patrick Tambay, the Frenchman's Lola already showing the first signs of that pad knock-off gremlin which had plagued him during qualifying. But Jones was just thoroughly browned off by the amount of effort he was having to put in getting nowhere. Braking for an uphill left-hander on lap 11, he simply allowed the Lola to plough slowly off into the sand trap on the

Paul-Henri Cahier

Ayrton Senna prepares for another pole performance. An equally brilliant drive in the race was to be ruined by a faulty fuel consumption readout on the Lotus *(opposite page)*.

Martin Brundle: another frustrating weekend.

Alessandro Nannini made the most of the unreliable Minardi despite a number of pit stops *(above)*.

Keke Rosberg's McLaren received a new colour scheme as Marlboro experimented with a new brand image.

September

Pirelli announce withdrawal from Formula 1 at the end of 1986.

Andy Wallace (Reynard VW 863) wins British Formula 3 Championship.

Renault announce temporary withdrawal from Grand Prix racing after failing to reach agreement with McLaren for the supply of engines.

Ferrari confirm the signatures of Gerhard Berger (to join Michele Alboreto) and John Barnard (as Chief Designer).

Marc Surer, recovering from injuries received in rally accident, decides not to make a comeback to Formula 1.

outside of the turn. He had no more interest in the race and although his departure was officially dressed up as a driver error, he later confirmed that he had deliberately 'parked' the machine out of sheer frustration.

Meanwhile, at the end of the field, Mansell was tightening his grip on the contest. Never looking even slightly under pressure, he gently eased away from Senna, grabbing a tenth here, a couple of tenths there. By lap 14 he was 5.7s ahead, then almost 7s three laps later.

On lap 19 Brundle's Tyrrell, running 18th and trying to get to grips with the obstructive de Cesaris, suffered another engine failure. 'It had been misfiring slightly ever since the start', Martin shrugged on his return to the pits. By that point Streiff's machine was also running hot, destined to succumb to a similar failure ten laps later. 'That's the fifth failure this weekend', winced Ken Tyrrell, 'so I reckon we must have suffered a faulty batch of pistons or liners. The blocks are pressurising so badly that they are actually blowing off the oil lines!'

Approaching the 30-lap mark, shortly before half-distance, all eyes began to watch the pit lane as mechanics prepared for the spate of routine tyre stops. Piquet paused at the end of that lap, briefly promoting Prost to third place, while Keke came in at the same time and dropped to seventh by the end of lap 31.

Senna made his stop at the end of lap 31, just scrambling back into the queue a few crucial lengths ahead of Piquet, while Prost relinquished that briefly held second place at the end of lap 32. Finally, it was Mansell's turn. At the end of lap 33 he was in ... and out again, still 8.4s ahead of Senna and comfortably retaining his lead.

'I didn't really have any problems from that point onwards', Nigel recalled afterwards, 'although I had to concentrate really hard to lap slower cars, a very demanding business on a circuit as tight as this one. Before my pit stop I had one worrying moment when I was forced off-line to get by a slower car and the nose section bottomed out quite badly over the bumps. I started to get a touch of understeer shortly after that and I was concerned that I might have damaged one of the end plates, but there was no big problem. A fresh set of tyres killed that understeer and I didn't have to worry for the rest of the race.'

With Mansell out of sight, the battle for second place really began to hot up. Senna's Lotus was suffering a lot of oversteer in the corners and Piquet was crowding him all the time, willing him to make an error, but on the straights the Lotus had a slight edge. Two or three times Nelson's Honda V6 could be heard fluttering on its rev limiter as he turned up the boost in an effort to draw alongside, but it was to no avail. Ayrton simply doesn't crack under pressure!

Rosberg's run in fifth place ended on lap 42 when his TAG V6 blew up in a massive cloud of smoke after trailing an ominous-looking haze for several laps, while, two laps later, de Cesaris reverted to type and crashed his Minardi quite heavily into the unyielding guard rails. Derek Warwick's Brabham expired on the circuit with apparent electrical failure after misfiring for a

short time and Alliot's Ligier succumbed to an engine breakage.

Rosberg's retirement promoted Berger to fifth place, but Johansson's Ferrari was closing in steadily and it seemed only a matter of time before the Italian car would find a way past. Going into lap 45 Stefan pulled clear on the outside approaching the right-hander after the pits, but Gerhard tried to put two wheels up the inside kerbing in a last-ditch effort to retrieve the place. It all ended in tears with the Benetton launching the Ferrari onto two wheels as it slammed into Stefan's right-hand side pod and the two cars pirouetted to a halt on the sandy run-off.

Johansson kept his engine running and thrashed his way back onto the circuit, gesticulating wildly at the Austrian who was forced to abandon his machine there and then. He had stalled its engine and was unable to restart.

'He slammed into me really hard', Stefan

fumed, 'and damaged the cooling duct to my right-hand turbo. From that point on the throttle response was really lousy!' That little excursion dropped Johansson back to sixth place behind Alboreto and it now seemed as though the top half-dozen would be settled for a smooth run all the way to the finish.

However, as Mansell stroked his way home to a commanding victory – his fifth of the season – the two Brazilians lined up behind him were in for a nasty shock. Piquet's front brakes had not been cooling properly, so he briefly dropped away from Senna to give them the benefit of some clear air. Then, as he closed in on the Lotus again, he suddenly found himself pitched into a spin at the bottom of the hill behind the paddock when the rear brakes momentarily snatched on.

Before Piquet could gather himself up, Prost nipped by into what seemed certain to be third place while Senna, out on his own, appeared to

TECHNICAL FILE

AGS
Fitted mini-skirt to nose.

ARROWS
A9 not developed further; used as T-car.
Gordon Coppuck modified front suspension on
A8 and added new rear wing with second
profile.

BENETTON
New chassis for Berger who qualified with
BMW engine fitted with megaphone exhaust.
Neither driver used wastegate during qual-
ifying. Used AP rear brakes.

BRABHAM
Water tank for intercooler spray moved from
rear of car to front of left-hand side pod.
Revised front wings; ran rear wing introduced
in Hungary. Inverted position of oil radiator on
T-car. Dispensed with rear winglets on side
pods during qualifying.

FERRARI
New chassis (sixth of the series) used as T-car.
Same configuration on all three cars as Monza,
including amended position for intercoolers.
Revised aerodynamics; different front wings
and secondary rear wing.

LIGIER
Nothing new. Ran vertical aerofoils behind
front wheels. Concentrating on new car with
Alfa Romeo engine for 1987.

LOLA
Larger side plates fitted to front wings with
more pronounced angle.

LOTUS
Removed vertical aerofoils behind front
wheels.

McLAREN
New chassis for Prost. Major internal modifications to TAG engines (for Prost and T-car) as
tested at Imola in the week following Monza.
Prost ran this engine on Saturday morning but
raced standard V6 in T-car. Prost also tried an
additional rear wing for a few laps on Friday
morning.

MINARDI
Race cars fitted with new rear suspension and
'snorkle' ducts for turbo; T-car continued with
side duct. Stiffer lower fixing point on chassis
for front suspension – but handling deterio-
rated as a result.

TYRRELL
Larger radiator and longer side pods on
Brundle's car. Revisions to underbody included
less angle on the upward sweep at the rear and
the addition of two vertical fins on the
underside.

WILLIAMS
Spare car for each driver; both spare cars fitted
with radiator made to an earlier manufacturing specification. Tried 'snorkle' ducts for
turbos which improved their efficiency at the
expense of the aerodynamics. Needed to alter
steering geometry because of changed angle
and fixing point for steering rod. Used two
different intercoolers, one without the bypass
system (see Belgian GP, page 115).

ZAKSPEED
New nose available, but not used by either
driver. Both race cars fitted with Garrett
turbos.

G.P.

have second spot all buttoned up. But as Mansell
hammered home to win, Ayrton's mount coughed
and spluttered low on fuel midway round that
final lap, despite its cockpit readout insisting that
there was sufficient fuel in the tank for at least one
more lap!

That allowed Prost, also troubled by marginal
fuel consumption readouts and poor throttle
response out of the corners, to sweep through into
a lucky second place, Piquet also reaping the
benefit by moving up into third. Senna staggered
round that final lap at walking pace to be classified
fourth, but he was not credited with covering the
full race distance as the time he took to complete
his last lap was greater than 110 per cent of the
winner's final tour.

Completing the top six were the Ferraris of
Alboreto and Johansson, while René Arnoux's
Ligier and Teo Fabi's Benetton ran non-stop on
hard Pirellis to take seventh and eighth places.

Dumfries was a steady ninth after a trouble-free
run, while the brake-troubled Arrows A8s were
next up, Boutsen just beating Danner across the
line following a spirited chase.

Palmer was 12th ahead of the plodding Berg,
while Patrese, who retired with only seven laps to
go following a sudden loss of power and engine
failure, covered a greater distance than the
brake-troubled Tambay who was still circulating
slowly at the finish after several abortive pit stops
had failed to rectify his problems.

The day, of course, belonged to Nigel Mansell.
After Piquet's recent run of successes, the
Englishman had proved that he could still regain
the initiative. What's more, he had done so with a
victory even more impressive than at Brands
Hatch. On this particular day he hd been in a class
of his own.

Truly, he looked like a champion in the making.

A.H.

179

Gran Premio de
MEXICO

Gerhard Berger kept a cool head in Mexico, the tactic of running non-stop paying off handsomely.
Photo: Keith Sutton

Peter Collins was in something of a dilemma. An enviable one, certainly, but a dilemma none the less! *Which* national anthem should be played to celebrate the Benetton team's greatest day – Gerhard Berger's superb victory in the Mexican Grand Prix. Pondering the problem, the team manager turned to the team patron; should it be the Italian anthem? Or the national anthem for a car built in Britain? Unhesitatingly, Luciano Benetton made his decision and the British national anthem broke out over the winner's rostrum. It was a great day; a great victory for Berger and the Benetton-BMW équipe which had been knocking hard on the door of success for much of the season. A succession of minor failures had cost the Austrian possible victories in a couple of earlier events, but this time everything worked perfectly. Never running lower than fourth, Berger capitalised on the durability of his Pirelli rubber to speed non-stop throughout the 68-lap penultimate round of the '86 Championship as his Goodyear-shod rivals were delayed by a succession of pit stops for fresh rubber in the sultry, abrasive conditions.

The World Championship battle was not settled, points-leader Nigel Mansell failing to get his Williams FW11 into first gear at the start and trailing away at the tail of the field. An initial battle between Nelson Piquet's Williams and Ayrton Senna's pole-position Lotus 98T was broken up by the tyre wear problems and Alain Prost's McLaren MP/2C eventually wound up second, strengthening the Frenchman's hand in the points chase with only one round left to go. Senna took third with Piquet and Mansell recovering from early delays to finish fourth and fifth. That result left the tussle for the crown tantalisingly in the balance as the circus moved on to Australia.

ENTRY AND PRACTICE

For the penultimate round of the championship struggle, the Formula 1 circus returned to a venue last used some 16 years earlier, the autodrome in Mexico City's Magdalena Mixhuca sports complex. The last Grand Prix to he held on this track witnessed a commanding Ferrari 1-2 for Jacky Ickx and Clay Regazzoni, but unpleasant memories of madly over-enthusiastic crowds swarming all over the circuit before, after and even *during* the event, left deep impressions on those who had been present back in 1970. Those tremors of trepidation amongst the old hands who went back for another look in 1986 as they related their horror stories created a sense of apprehension amongst the current contingent of drivers who had never raced Grand Prix cars there before.

Although the name has changed, to Autodromo Hermanos Rodriguez (the brothers Rodriguez), the track layout itself remains the same. It has been modified here and there, eliminating the hairpin on which Graham Hill's 1964 World Championship chances evaporated at the hands of an over-enthusiastic Lorenzo Bandini, but the famous banked corner before the pits is still present, albeit reprofiled to a slightly shallower angle, offering a spectacular challenge for today's breed of Formula 1 charger.

Unfortunately, although the circuit had been extensively revamped and resurfaced, it was also extremely bumpy. Furthermore, dramatically reduced throttle response is experienced when turbocharged Grand Prix cars are operated 7500 ft above sea level, so the drivers had plenty to keep them occupied. In an attempt to compensate for the thin air at this altitude, most teams came to the race armed with larger turbochargers fed by bigger ducts and bigger radiators as well, all to make the engines breathe and cool as efficiently and effectively as possible.

Most eyes were focused on the battle for the championship, apparently now polarising between Williams-Honda team-mates Nigel Mansell and Nelson Piquet, but Alain Prost was determined not to be left out. Although he was no longer a championship contender, the Mexican GP was just another race for the ultra-competitive Ayrton Senna . . . another race which he might well win.

On the Thursday prior to the race the competitors were allowed an extra couple of two-hour untimed sessions in which to become acclimatised to the Mexican track, Senna making it clear that he was intent on scoring his third win of the year. He established a benchmark time of 1m 19·883s, the best part of a second faster than both the Williams-Hondas, but it was Gerhard Berger who stole the overnight pole on Friday afternoon with a splendid run in the first official qualifying session.

Gerhard looked absolutely frightening as he slammed the Benetton B186 round that daunting 180-degree banked right-hander before the pits, hanging on grimly, but resolutely refusing to lift his right foot. He confessed that the car had been understeering a touch more than he would have liked, but otherwise he felt quite confident that he could sustain his challenge the following day. In truth, that was about all he was able to coax from the B186, so although he sliced a couple of tenths off his best the following afternoon, he slipped to fourth in the overall grid order.

In second qualifying, Senna emerged as the undisputed star of the show. On Friday the Brazilian had complained of a handling imbalance, his Lotus 98T feeling better with a heavy fuel load than with near-empty tanks. In Saturday's untimed session he was getting close to Berger's Friday best, the 98T's Renault EF15C running with revised turbos, the impeller blades of which were adjusted to the requirements of the altitude.

Saturday afternoon saw him follow the classic Senna procedure. He popped one run into the bag early on before retiring to the relative cool of the pits to study the progress of his rivals. His master plan was very nearly thwarted when Rothengatter's Zakspeed crashed heavily coming onto the pit straight, but although the session was stopped, it

was restarted again for a final seven-minute blast a little later.

Senna was now ready to go on his second run on qualifiers and the result was absolutely spellbinding. Never putting a wheel wrong, the Brazilian slammed onto the banking into the last right-hander to complete the lap only for the Lotus suddenly to twitch violently as the 98T hit a notorious bump on the entry. For a split-second, open-mouthed onlookers reckoned disaster was at hand, but then they realised they were watching Senna, not a mere mortal!

With an air of deft contempt, Ayrton controlled the slide superbly, slamming out over the start-and-finish line to stop the clocks one-tenth below the 1m 17s barrier, the only man to get into the 16s! It was a superb virtuoso performance which had little to do with specific chassis set-ups. That particular subject caused Senna and Team Lotus to sound off quite trenchantly during the course of the weekend, both verbally and in print. Anybody wanting to accuse Team Lotus of running a 'cheat' set-up in qualifying sessions should either shut up or put up – and face being sued as a consequence. That was the gist of the message, delivered in typically direct and unsubtle sledgehammer style by the Lotus management. Those who had been casting aspersions went extremely quiet . . . *on the record*, at least.

Meanwhile, the Williams-Honda lads had proved a well-matched pair in the wake of Senna's barnstorming run to pole position. Both men were preoccupied and withdrawn for most to the weekend, brooding on the possible outcome of the intense championship struggle.

Swapping round between their race and spare cars, the two drivers were fractions apart throughout both qualifying sessions, Piquet just slipping ahead to grab the second place alongside Senna on row one. Mansell briefly snatched pole early in the second session with a run on soft C compound Goodyear race tyres, but Piquet responded with a 1m 17·279s. That was good enough for pole until Senna produced his show-stopper right at the end of the session.

Mansell was non-committal about his qualifying performance, trying to keep cool and to avoid worrying about the outcome of the title chase in what was, by any definition, an extremely intense and preoccupying set of circumstances. 'Not happy, not disappointed', was how he described his basic feelings, adding, 'I suppose that we're in the same boat as most other people on this track – our biggest problem being to get the car set up properly to deal with those bumps and undulations. It's been a real challenge, particularly in this heat under that sun.'

With Berger on the outside of Mansell in fourth place, that took care of the first couple of rows. Over in the Brabham camp there were some

bright, smiling faces to be seen as the BT55s produced their best qualifying performances of the season. Riccardo Patrese lined up fifth right on Berger's tail, while Derek Warwick was seventh, World Champion Alain Prost's McLaren splitting the two lowline challengers.

Patrese had a troubled time on Friday, his race car suffering engine failure during the untimed session and the spare dogged by a serious misfire. In first qualifying he was back in his race machine, but he timed things wrongly and got caught out on his first run as the session was red-flagged when Palmer spun in the middle of the circuit and could not restart his Zakspeed. He hit traffic on his second run and wound up 19th, but everything went right the following day allowing him to vault up to seventh with little difficulty.

Similarly, Warwick was suffused with optimism as he anticipated his prospects for Sunday. 'It's terrific on race tyres, really good', he reported, 'but when we try to put on any worthwhile degree of wing, we lose out on the straight. It's hellish over the bumps, but fantastic round that banked right-hander before the pits.' Derek produced ninth-fastest time on Friday and then improved a further two places during that final hour.

Prost's eventual sixth place was something of a disappointment for the McLaren International squad which had been hoping to get the French-man into the top four on the grid for their crucially

No love lost as Senna and Piquet dispute the lead going into the first corner. Piquet came out ahead but Senna finished the race in front of his fellow-countryman *(right)*.

The Mexicans laid on an excellent show against a backdrop of fears over security and a repeat of the chaos which led to the event being struck off the calendar in 1970 *(below)*.

Abandoning a winning ship. Benetton celebrated their first victory knowing that Pirelli were to quit Formula 1, BMW were leaving the team and Gerhard Berger was joining Ferrari *(right)*.

Nigel Mansell; a weekend of pressure *(far right)*.

important race. The Bosch engineers, having concentrated on re-mapping the engine's electronic management system to cope with the unusually high altitude, reaped an early reward in the form of an internal failure in Alain's spare car during Thursday's acclimatisation session.

Alain spent most of Friday working out a satisfactory chassis balance, his afternoon's efforts hampered by Goodyear E qualifiers which lasted less than a complete lap. But by Saturday morning the team was feeling a little more optimistic: 'We're about a day behind schedule', said Ron Dennis thoughtfully.

Keke Rosberg lost much of Friday's timed session when his own car suffered a turbo failure at the end of the untimed stint and the spare, set up for Prost, was out of bounds for the Finn. He had to kick his heels until the closing moments of the first timed hour, only to get carried away with the urgency of the last few minutes, sliding off to the outside of the banked right-hander after trying, by his own admission, to enter it just a shade too quickly!

Unhappy with his MP4/2C's chassis balance, Keke none the less wound up sixth in the untimed warm-up and took 11th slot on the grid with a gritty effort in second qualifying, cursing the time that he had lost with his problems the previous day.

Patrick Tambay took his Haas Lola round to a promising eighth place on the grid, the Ford-propelled machine well ahead of its usual midfield qualifying position. A fresh engine and some aerodynamic changes on Saturday afternoon more than made up for his disappointing showing the previous day when gear-selector problems spoiled his chances with the race car and his spare had engine troubles.

His Lola team-mate Alan Jones started off in buoyant mood on Thursday, but a succession of minor problems sent him sliding back down the grid order to an eventual, frustrated 15th. On Friday his Ford V6 blew a turbo midway through qualifying and although it was changed in double-quick time, his run on E qualifiers was spoiled by Palmer's spin. On Saturday he was less than happy with the Lola's balance on C compound soft race tyres and he failed to break the 1m 20s barrier.

A disappointed Teo Fabi lined up ninth in the other Benetton B186, the little Italian unable to match his team-mate's pace after a troubled couple of days. 'On Friday I had turbo problems and switched to the spare', he explained, 'but I stopped on the circuit with no fuel pressure on Saturday morning and then needed a turbo replaced in final qualifying.' By the time Teo got going again the track was quite oily, so he only improved marginally on his Friday best. He felt pretty dejected with life after that . . .

Philippe Alliot reached tenth and his best time was set using the less powerful EF15B Renault V6. He spun the T-car into the tyre wall coming onto the main straight on Friday morning, resuming work at the wheel of his race car which was later fitted with the rear end of his damaged machine for first qualifying. He improved fractionally from his first day's 11th place to take his

final grid position.

René Arnoux's JS27 race car was fitted with an EF15C qualifying engine on Saturday afternoon but the left-hand turbo did not seem to be giving sufficient boost, so it was changed shortly before the end of final qualifying. On his final run Rothengatter hit the wall right in front of him, so René had to be content with a rather disappointing 13th, splitting the two Ferraris.

If ever there was a circuit tailor-made to aggravate the rough-riding qualities of Maranello's latest F1/86, then this was it! Both Michele Alboreto and Stefan Johansson were really up against it, hanging on for dear life as their charges bumped and twitched over the undulations, the whole picture being made even worse by the now-customary poor throttle response which had bugged them for much of the '86 season.

Michele's Saturday efforts were thwarted by a massive turbo fire on his first qualifying attempt, so he switched to the *muletta* only to have that give up the ghost right at the end of the afternoon with a broken engine. Stefan's suffered engine failure in Saturday's untimed stint, then blew a turbo in final qualifying, so the predominant air in the Ferrari garage was of glumness and gloomy depression. 'The car is *really* bad', shrugged Stefan with an air of masterful understatement.

Martin Brundle came to Mexico in an optimistic mood, the Tyrrell team having the latest-spec Renault EF15C engines available for the first time. However, the Englishman's first crack at qualifying was hampered by a stiff throttle pedal, costing him around 400 rpm at the top end, and he also had to back off suddenly on a quick lap when Rosberg spun in front of him. On Saturday, Rothengatter's Zakspeed imitated Keke's manoeuvre to Martin's cost, spoiling his run on E qualifiers. Finally, Palmer added to his troubles by getting in his way when he went out on C compound rubber. His 16th slot put him three places ahead of team-mate Philippe Streiff.

Johnny Dumfries was right behind the faster of the two Tyrrells, the Scot's best Friday run one of many spoiled by Rosberg's antics on the right-hander before the pits, and that was followed by even worse luck the following afternoon. In the final session Johnny misjudged his entrance to the rather tricky second chicane, bounced over the kerbing and rumbled the undertray severely enough to necessitate a lengthy pit visit. Slightly annoyed with himself, Dumfries had to contemplate the start of the race from 17 places down the grid.

Making it a tight trio of Brits, Jonathan Palmer produced a reasonable 18th place in his Zakspeed, the Doc feeling slightly reassured when it was discovered that a sticking valve in the wastegate was responsible for 'the worst throttle lag I've ever experienced' on Friday. He fell foul of Keke, of course (who didn't), and then his own team-mate's activities thwarted his chances of a decent time on Saturday, Palmer never getting a clear run on qualifying rubber. Huub's shunt appeared to have been caused by a sheared wheel-retaining stud on the left-rear hub. The damage that caused wrote the Dutchman out of the script for the rest of the

weekend as the tiny German team had not brought its spare car out to the Mexican race.

Completing the top twenty was Christian Danner's Arrows A8, the German just pipping team leader Thierry Boutsen by a tenth of a second. Christian had a relatively trouble-free time on Friday, but complained about lack of boost in the final session. The Belgian suffered an engine failure on Thursday and grappled with an irritating lack of boost pressure during Friday qualifying. Things were little improved on Saturday as Thierry stopped on the circuit with metering unit failure during the morning's untimed stint. A replacement Bee-Emm was installed for qualifying, but it was 500 rpm down throughout both his best runs.

In the Minardi camp Andrea de Cesaris was faster than team-mate Alessandro Nannini, but both Motori-Moderni-engined cars were hampered by poor throttle response. The team had been expecting larger turbos to arrive from KKK especially for this race, but because they were not ready in time both drivers simply had to make do with standard equipment. Andrea used the new M/86 to lap a full second quicker than Nannini's M/85B, despite suffering an engine breakage in Saturday qualifying. In their usual positions on the back row were Piercarlo Ghinzani and Allen Berg, both struggling hard with their Osella-Alfas.

RACE

Gerhard Berger gave very public notice of his race-day challenge by winging round to set fastest time in the half-hour morning warm-up, the progress of his Benetton-BMW aided by new Pirelli soft race rubber, several sets of which had been flown in the previous day. Alain Prost was an unobtrusive second ahead of Senna's Lotus, then came Johansson's Ferrari, now in reduced-downforce trim, followed by Mansell, with Piquet down in ninth. A familiar face from the past made a fleeting return to the F1 circuit, albeit for just a brief demonstration run, as Hector Rebaque put in a few laps at the wheel of Patrese's spare Brabham BT55. If the Mexicans couldn't have a local actually competing in the race, then this was probably the next best thing they could expect.

It was very hot and sticky by the time the 25 competitors eased round to take up their positions on the grid, the detailed mathematics of the championship battle being in the forefront of everybody's mind. The cars paused, the starting light blinked red, flashed green and they were away. At least, 24 of them were away! On the inside of the second row Mansell's Williams didn't move an inch, the points-leader swamped by the rest of the pack as Senna and Piquet raced wheel-to-wheel for the first corner at the head of the field.

Mansell, already suffering badly from an attack of the 'Aztec two-step' following dinner with the BBC lads on Friday evening, found himself unable to select first gear as he moved onto his grid position. It was a miracle nobody hit the stationary Williams-Honda and, as the last few rows drew level, he finally managed to stuff it into second and stormed off in hot pursuit. Two days of qualifying effort had gone straight out of the window in about three seconds flat!

RETURN TO MEXICO

Having lost their status as a host nation for the Formula 1 World Championship in 1970, the Mexicans did everything in their power to ensure that the return of Grand Prix racing would not be a temporary one. And, judging by the reaction of the teams, the organisers had achieved their aim at the end of a weekend free from the chaos which had led to the scrapping of the race 16 years before.

In 1970, the enthusiasm of the 200,000 locals lining the Autodromo Ricardo Rodriguez (named in honour of the young Mexican killed during practice for the inaugural race in 1962) had gone unchecked as they climbed the grass banks and sat on the edge of the track. Despite pleas from Jackie Stewart and Pedro Rodriguez (Ricardo's brother), the spectators remained resolute and, fearing a riot if the race was cancelled, the drivers reluctantly set about their work in a circuit lined by human barriers.

Stewart retired when his Tyrrell hit a dog and after 65 laps the chequered flag brought the race to a halt – for ever, it seemed.

Working under the stewardship of a consortium of businessmen, a massive revamp, estimated at US$10m, was put in hand. The circuit, renamed Autodromo Hermanos Rodriguez (to include Pedro, of course), was lined with two layers of fencing, the inner being topped with barbed wire. Seating was provided for 60,000 although, at $115.00 for a three-day ticket, the price seemed beyond the reach of the locals in a city where poverty and social injustice are rampant.

Even so, a well-behaved crowd, estimated at 50,000, was orderly and enthusiastic. The circuit layout was unaltered except for a slow detour to avoid the medium/fast right-hander at the end of the long straight (the necessary run-off area for the old corner being ruled out by the close proximity of the boundary of Magdalena Mixhuca, the municipal park in which the circuit is located). The tight hairpin at the far end of the track was abandoned for similar reasons but the result presented drivers with an excellent challenge, rounded off by that glorious banked 180-degree curve leading onto the pit straight.

The main complaint concerned a bumpy surface as severe as the traditional stomach ailment which afflicts Europeans in a city where the standard of sanitation does not match the smiling enthusiasm of the locals. But they, at least, had no doubts that it was good to be back on the championship trail.

M.H.

TECHNICAL FILE

ARROWS
No A9. Continued work with A8; one vertical aerofoil instead of two behind front wheels, new rear wing with smaller chord, longer and narrower side plates to rear wing plus additional wing, modified underbody with two vertical deflectors, cut bodywork around turbo to allow extraction of hot air.

BENETTON
Filled in the step under nose. Enlarged duct for turbo. Found larger turbo to be only small improvement; raced with standard version. Dispensed with side panel to right side pod to help cooling, particularly the electrics in a bid to stop misfire.

BRABHAM
New chassis (T-car). Revisions to front brake ducts included slats to help disperse heat. Tried using additional oil cooler mounted on existing oil radiator. Patrese tried 'snorkle' air duct on Thursday and Friday; all three cars so equipped by Saturday. Used larger turbos. Gordon Murray not present.

FERRARI
Tried two different Garrett turbos in an attempt to cope with the altitude and a long straight which required full throttle for 12 to 13 seconds. Intercooler (in 'Toleman' position) for Alboreto on Friday and Saturday; all three cars so equipped by Sunday. Fitted new turbos with larger compressor for the race.

LIGIER
Larger water radiator. Revised side plates to rear wing with step – similar to Tyrrell.

LOLA
All three cars fitted with 'snorkle'-style air ducts in place of NACA ducts on top of side pods.

LOTUS
New turbos with larger compressors for Renault engine. Senna's car fitted with tall, thin front brake ducts (similar to McLaren).

McLAREN
Larger compressors on turbos. Used spray for intercooler (for the first time this season). Very little change to chassis.

MINARDI
Position of oil cooler on Nannini's car affected water temperature (M/86 for de Cesaris not affected since this had a larger water radiator). Removed oil radiator and fitted smaller version in each side pod in front of rear tyres.

TYRRELL
Both race cars now fitted with revised underbody and longer side pods with bigger radiators.

WILLIAMS
Prepared for altitude with extensive tests in Japan. Mansell also ran FW11 at Österreichring where he beat Fabi's pole time while running new turbos with 'snorkle' ducts. Fitted front wing side plates with tall profile to help influence flow of thinner air to ducts and side pods. All four cars running revised steering geometry.

ZAKSPEED
Only two cars available. Ran larger Garrett turbos.

G.P.

Senna locked up going into the first right-hander, running sufficiently off-line to leave room for Piquet to nip through into the lead. The two Brazilians were at the head of the field at the end of that jostling opening lap, Williams in front of Lotus, with Gerhard Berger and Alain Prost a menacing third and fourth. Alboreto was fifth ahead of Alliot, Brundle (a fantastic start!), Patrese (caught behind Mansell), Dumfries, Warwick and the rest. Tambay's Lola didn't even make it round a single lap, Patrick being elbowed into a sand trap by one of Arnoux's more outlandish manoeuvres. The Ford-engined car stuck fast, so that was that . . .

From the start, everyone had been keeping fingers firmly crossed on the subject of tyre wear, many of the Goodyear runners being concerned about their prospects. However, Berger had it in his mind that his Pirellis just *might* be able to go the full race distance without a stop, although he, too, felt pretty uncomfortable with a severe bout of tummy trouble.

The opening phase saw the first four cars staying in close company, Piquet running just hard enough to keep control over his pursuers. Prost moved past Berger into third place on lap 7, Alboreto looked secure in fifth and Mansell was keeping his head as he picked off the tail-enders. Fabi's Benetton, which lapsed onto three cylinders on the parade lap, pulled in to retire after five laps, something having gone very badly wrong in the valvegear. Ghinzani was already in the pits with turbo trouble; Streiff's Tyrrell expired with turbo trouble on lap 9 and Alboreto's hopeful run for Ferrari ended in a great gouge of flame two laps later as he too suffered a blown turbo.

Mansell had clawed his way back to tenth place by lap 12, but he had blistered his left-front tyre by his efforts to get through the field and came in for fresh rubber. He resumed in 13th spot, got his head down and began to haul back into contention all over again.

Piquet was still confidently holding sway in the lead with 15 laps run, Senna and Prost shadowing his every move. Berger had dropped back slightly in fourth, although, as things turned out, this would not matter one jot. Johansson at this stage was fifth from Alliot, Rosberg, Brundle and Warwick.

It seemed that the track surface was generating more grip on race day than had been the case throughout qualifying, so most Goodyear runners suddenly found that their oversteer was now turning into a worrying level of understeer. Before half-distance there were already blistered and graining tyres to be seen on the rims of the faster cars' tyres, so pit stops were obviously only a matter of time.

Prost brought his McLaren in at the end of lap 30, dropping back to sixth, while Piquet briefly handed Senna the lead when he stopped his Williams two laps later. Ayrton stayed out until lap 36 before putting the Lotus into the pits for fresh tyres, allowing Berger to wing through into the lead as the Brazilian swung into the pit entrance. The Benetton-BMW was never headed again. Sure enough, Gerhard was going through non-stop.

When the Goodyear runners reappeared after their first stops many expected them to gobble up Berger's advantage, but that simply did not happen. Senna had already recognised the potential problem in the extent of the blistering on his first set. He quickly found that his second set began to blister in the same way, so he realised that there was no chance of catching the BMW-propelled car in the lead. Only if Gerhard's mount failed could the other leading lights expect a fair crack at getting back to first place.

'I wasn't really certain whether I could go the distance on one set or not', grinned Berger afterwards. 'It was only when I got to half-distance and still had pretty reasonable grip that I realised I was in with a chance. From that stage on I concentrated on keeping them in as good shape as possible, knowing that I had quite a cushion over the others.'

Into an eventual second place came the ultra-smooth Alain Prost, the World Champion's superbly sympathetic cockpit technique eking out his second set of Goodyear Cs to the finish. Alain was hampered by an engine which lapsed onto five cylinders midway through the race and he was anxious to avoid a second stop just in case the TAG V6 stalled and might be reluctant to fire up again.

As Berger went on his winning way, Prost took over second place thanks to Senna making a second stop for tyres, and the McLaren moved apart from the Lotus in the closing stages. With Ayrton's badly blistered rubber losing grip it looked as though Johansson's Ferrari might be in with a chance of taking over third place in the dying moments of the contest. But just as the Swede was lining up to have a go at the Lotus, an eruption of white smoke heralded another turbo failure. Stefan pulled off onto the grass, flames licking round the engine bay. There were only three laps left to run . . .

This drama briefly promoted Riccardo Patrese's Brabham BT55 to fourth place, but the Italian slid off after missing a gear and tangling unnecessarily with Boutsen, an error which injected a sense of added urgency to the battle between the next two runners, Piquet and Mansell.

After relinquishing the lead in his first tyre stop, Piquet found himself needing to change twice more before the end, in contrast to Mansell's total of two stops throughout. This allowed the Englishman not only to unlap himself from Nelson, but to make up another full lap and close right in onto his gearbox. Indeed, while they were running sixth and seventh it occurred to Mansell that if he could push Piquet out of sixth place then the Brazilian would be removed from the championship equation. But once Johansson and Patrese had retired such considerations became irrelevant.

Running 4-5 in tight formation, Nelson managed to fend off his team-mate's advances, despite grappling with a broken front brake duct which gave him plenty to think about under harsh deceleration. He crossed the line fourth, Mansell's consequent two points for fifth failing to expand his championship total under the 'best eleven scored' rule.

Philippe Alliot took the first point of his career

Always a threat, Alain Prost gets in among the Williams drivers to strengthen his late bid for the championship by finishing second *(opposite)*.

The best-laid plans of the Williams team were wrecked by unexpected tyre wear. Piquet finished fourth while Mansell, classified fifth, did not help matters by fumbling his start *(centre)*.

Something to smile about at last. Andrea de Cesaris finished a Grand Prix for the first time since Detroit 1985 *(bottom)*.

Keith Sutton

September
Ferrari claims he has a contract signed by Mansell.

October
FISA announce two-year transition from turbos to atmospheric GP engine formula.

Derek Bell and Hans Stuck win 1986 Sports Prototype World Championship for Drivers; Brun Motorsport win Team Championship.

Ivan Capelli (March-DFV 86B) wins Formula 3000 Championship.

Nicola Larini (Dallara-Alfa 386) wins Italian Formula 3 Championship.

with sixth, despite a wild spin, in the Ligier JS27, Boutsen's Arrows being a further lap down ahead of Andrea de Cesaris, the Italian scoring his first race finish for Minardi.

Ninth was Danner, ahead of a disappointed Jonathan Palmer, the Zakspeed driver at one point hauling in Alliot's Ligier hand-over-fist. But just as it seemed as though the Doc might bag a point for sixth, the German car spluttered low on fuel and he dropped back to tenth. 'The computer readout said I'd got 13 litres in hand', shrugged Jonathan ruefully.

Similarly frustrated was Martin Brundle, the Tyrrell driver grappling gamely against making a third tyre stop, although his level of grip had been deteriorating rapidly. 'But my biggest problem was shortly before the end when I saw this red light', he explained sheepishly. 'I thought the race was over, eased off and Danner and Palmer were past before I realised my mistake.' Ken Tyrrell wasn't impressed either but his protest was subsequently rejected by the organisers.

Diana Burnett

Johansson was classified 12th ahead of Patrese, with Nannini 14th and still running at the finish, while Arnoux's Ligier had succumbed to engine failure four laps from the flag. Finally, Berg's Osella continued to trail round, seven laps behind the winner after taking time off for a quick spin. Alan Jones spent much of his race in and out of the pits for fresh Goodyears, eventually dropping out with gear-selection trouble and ominously climbing water temperature.

The day, however, belonged to Berger and Benetton. It was a fine leaving present from the Austrian to the Witney-based team, a portent perhaps of what he will produce for Ferrari. From the team's point of view, it was a long-overdue success to justify all those years of struggle, first under the Toleman banner and more recently flying the colours of the Italian fashion concern.

But it was down to Luciano Benetton himself to make the final gesture which turned a good day into a great one!

A.H.

185

FOSTER'S AUSTRALIAN Grand Prix

Below: **Alain Prost drove another impeccable race and, ironically, an unscheduled stop to replace a punctured tyre may have won the championship for the second year in succession for the Frenchman.**

Out of the race – and out of the championship. **Nigel Mansell** *(above right)* **trudges back to the pits after abandoning his Williams. The Englishman, fortunate to survive a rear tyre failure at over 180 mph, brings his three-wheeling FW11 to a halt as Philippe Alliot rounds the corner at the end of the back straight** *(right).*

Top right: a jubilant Prost takes the chequered flag at the end of a long and difficult season.

It seemed like the ultimate nightmare for Alain Prost. The Australian Grand Prix in the bag, Nigel Mansell out of the race, his second World Championship was beckoning. And now he was going to lose everything – the race win, the title – for a few litres of fuel. 'For the last 15 laps my fuel readout showed that I was five litres short, so I never reckoned there was any chance of making it. In other circumstances I would have eased right back and tried to conserve things, but on this occasion I had to win, so I forced myself to believe that there was something wrong with the computer. I just pressed on and, as it turned out, I finished with it still reading five litres down. Obviously, today the computer was wrong . . .'

Thus spoke Alain Prost, dazed with delight, seconds after becoming 1986 World Champion following an astounding performance in Adelaide. Tyre wear proved to be the crucial factor. Prost's McLaren was forced into the pits on lap 32, and fresh rubber was fitted all round after he punctured a front Goodyear against Gerhard Berger's Benetton B186. Committed to helping his team-mate's championship hopes, Keke Rosberg had stormed into the lead in the opening sprint, intent on handing it to Alain when the Frenchman worked his way steadily through to second place. But a tyre delamination deprived the Flying Finn of that grand gesture and left Nigel Mansell's Williams-Honda running second behind team-mate Nelson Piquet. The Englishman looked as though he had the World Championship in the palm of his hand until a massive tyre failure at 180 mph on the Adelaide circuit's fastest straight hurled him into abrupt retirement. Concern about tyre wear made Goodyear instruct Williams to bring Piquet in, and the delay lost the Brazilian the race lead to Prost's McLaren. Nelson resumed in second but despite shattering the circuit record he failed to make any real impression. Prost cruised home to his 25th Grand Prix triumph, becoming the first man to win the championship 'back-to-back' since Jack Brabham achieved that feat for Cooper in 1959 and 1960!

ENTRY AND PRACTICE

Nerve-wracking wasn't the word for it! Adelaide is a long way to go in order to sort out a World Championship – plenty of flying time for the main contestants to mull over their prospects. Nelson Piquet took his mind off the problem by flying all the way down to Australia in his private Learjet, a multi-thousand dollar extravagance which would obviously be recouped if he won the title. To win the title, he *had* to win the race – and at a rumoured 10,000 dollars a point stipulated in his Williams contract, he was clearly going to be ahead of the game if he buttoned up his third championship!

Nigel Mansell briefly returned home to the Isle of Man after failing to select first gear on the grid at Mexico City, taking as much time off for rest and relaxation as possible. Alain Prost's second place in the penultimate round of the title chase at least gave him a chance in Adelaide: 'I'm happy that I'm going all that way without being completely out of the picture', he grinned. All three were outwardly modest and slightly self-

effacing when it came to discussing their race prospects. The only unequivocal prediction came from Prost's team-mate, Keke Rosberg. Dragging on his umpteenth Marlboro on Thursday afternoon, he stated confidently, 'there's no doubt in my mind that Alain will win the race on Sunday. It's just a question of what the others do if he's going to win the championship.' Prophetic words indeed.

In 1985 Adelaide's first Grand Prix was a rip-roaring success staged in perfect spring weather. Short-sleeved shirts were the order of the day. The F1 fraternity returned to this popular venue twelve months later to find a bitterly cold Antarctic wind blowing up from the south, intermittent rain showers and a lot of thick cloud. And those unpredictable weather conditions played their part during the two days of official qualifying.

Mansell may mathematically have been in with the best chance, but he was certainly not out to drive a tactical race simply to gather the minimum number of points. 'That's just asking for trouble', insisted the Englishman, 'so the only

thing to do is run as hard as possible for another win. If I'm running as hard as I can, I'll be concentrating as hard as I can. It's when you try to ease off and work out where you are relative to your rivals that you run the risk of tripping over a slower car, or making a similar silly mistake.'

Mansell was as good as his word, qualifying on pole position for this final race of the season with controlled yet devastating efficiency. There was no question at all of his cracking under pressure. The Englishman was right on the pace from the start, pipping his Brazilian team-mate to fastest lap in Friday morning's untimed session, despite bending a rear corner on his spare FW11 when it stepped out of line going through the right-hander onto the fast Decquetteville Drive section, the long back straight.

On Friday afternoon first qualifying was effectively halved thanks to a heavy rain shower, while on Saturday the circuit seemed mysteriously to lose grip progressively throughout the session. Almost all the best Goodyear users' times were set on C compound race rubber, a new tyre specially formulated for Adelaide with the intention of

End of term photograph. Back row, left to right: Fabi, Ghinzani, Jones, Brundle, Alboreto, Senna, Johansson, de Cesaris, Berger, Rothengatter, Boutsen, Berg, Nannini (hidden), Palmer and Tambay. Front row, left to right: Alliot, Danner, Streiff, Mansell, Piquet, Arnoux (kneeling in front of Jean-Marie Balestre), Prost, Rosberg, Dumfries, Warwick and Patrese.

A spanner in the works. Keke Rosberg is about to hurl a spanner at his pit crew in indignation after the implement had been left in the cockpit during practice. Rosberg bowed out in spectacular fashion by threatening to influence the outcome of the championship as he led the race for many laps before retiring.

Keith Sutton

minimising the graining problem which Akron's products displayed at the circuit the previous year.

Mansell took the overnight pole, 0.6s faster than the fastest time in 1986, and the following day his efforts proved similarly commanding. He went out early in the final session on Cs, put pole in the bag and retired to the pits. Later he went out again on the same set, but with slightly less rear wing, but that made the FW11 feel too loose and skittish, so he reverted to the original settings and then went for a crack on E qualifiers. He failed to improve his time, in common with most of his rivals. Although partly explicable by Philippe Streiff's Tyrrell having blown its engine exiting the hairpin at the end of the back straight and dropping oil all over the circuit, most front runners agreed that this alone could not account for the sudden loss of a second and a half. It was a real puzzler.

Nelson Piquet lapped 0.3s slower than Mansell to button up the front row for the Williams-Honda brigade, pretty content with his efforts. 'I suppose everything was quite reasonable', he admitted, 'even though we had to dial out an irritating amount of understeer during Saturday's untimed session. In the afternoon it felt quite well balanced and I had no real problems.'

Alain Prost's McLaren-TAG had notched up second place overall in Friday qualifying, so when the reigning champion was quickest on Saturday morning, his team really began feeling cautiously optimistic. Both McLarens were running in very low ground clearance trim and Alain felt certain he could hang onto his front row starting position. But then he fell foul of that dire lack of grip in second qualifying, slumping to fourth behind Ayrton Senna's Lotus 98T.

Alain's team-mate, Keke Rosberg, reported just the same inconsistency, plagued by sudden lack of grip. 'I'll accept that the Tyrrell's oil made some difference, but not enough to make me over a second slower on the same tyre choice I'd used in the morning', he mused. Keke had been fifth on Friday, the sudden rain shower thwarting his

efforts to improve with a second run, but he dropped a couple of places the following afternoon.

His race-winning aspirations in no way blunted since he was written out of the script as a championship contender, Ayrton Senna was out to finish the year on a high note, starting with another pole position. But his Friday efforts were spoiled when he tapped a kerb and spun on his first run, in the dry.

'It was completely my fault', he explained. 'I let it get away from me over the kerb, it spun round and hit the wall, almost head-on.' Fortunately for his mechanics, the damage was confined to a crushed nose box and bent track rod. He was sixth on Friday and then notched up third-quickest time on his first Saturday run. But his final Saturday run, on E qualifiers, was a sight to behold. He was hurling that Lotus round in great opposite-lock slides as if it was a tiny F3 machine, a virtuoso display of car control which was a rare privilege to witness. Straining every rivet and seam in the 98T, his efforts came to nothing at the end of the back straight when he was faced with waving yellow flags; Huub Rothengatter's expiring Zakspeed had just joined Streiff's abandoned Tyrrell on the edge of the circuit. Third was as good as he was going to do.

By contrast, Johnny Dumfries had a rather frustrating time on what was scheduled to be his final outing for Team Lotus. He had a spin, puncturing a tyre, on Friday morning and then managed only one serious run before the rain put paid to things in first qualifying. On Saturday he grappled with gear selection bothers, necessitating a lengthy pit stop, and could only manage 14th overall. 'Things became a bit difficult when that oil went down', he explained 'but we've worked out a reasonable race set-up, so I'm looking forward to the race!'

Slotting in between the two McLarens were Pirelli's fastest contenders, the Ligier JS27 of René Arnoux and Mexican winner Gerhard Berger's Benetton. Arnoux was fourth on Friday, despite being slightly baulked by Dumfries on his quickest run, but then found his engine losing

power after a few laps on Saturday. 'I switched to the spare', he explained, 'but it didn't feel as nicely balanced as the other chassis and I didn't feel quite so happy.' He slipped to fifth as a result.

Meanwhile, Philippe Alliot was putting in a very respectable performance in the other JS27. He lost some valuable time during Friday's untimed stint thanks to a fuel leak sparking off a small fire in its engine bay, but none the less was 11th in the first timed session. He then improved to eighth on Saturday, despite managing only one run on qualifiers. It was a promising time for the former RAM wheelsman.

Despite coming fresh from his Mexican success, Gerhard Berger was very much second in line when it came to using the Benetton team's spare B186. That was the understandable price paid by the Austrian for defecting to Ferrari and Teo Fabi was afforded priority use of the spare car in each of Adelaide qualifying sessions.

The two men encountered mechanical problems in both timed sessions. An engine failure brought Gerhard's efforts to an early end on Friday, Teo having already bagged the spare after his own race machine could not shake off a persistent misfire. On Saturday Berger posted sixth-quickest overall before rolling to a halt with broken transmission.

Returning to the pits on foot, Berger found that Fabi had once more taken the spare car. He had been experiencing a lot of trouble bedding-in his race car's brake pads, so he switched to the spare

Nigel Snowdon

in frustration and then that expired on him after setting a rather disappointing 13th place overall. He went back into the brake-troubled machine, but failed to improve.

Meanwhile, over in the Ferrari camp, the mood was distinctly subdued by the time qualifying had finished. The F1/86s were still proving to be handfuls, but bad luck had really singled out Michele Alboreto and Stefan Johansson for some five-star treatment this particular weekend!

On Friday morning Michele let his mount get away from him, slamming head-on into the wall and writing off its monocoque. A spare monocoque was on hand, so the Ferrari mechanics set about building it up into a new car for Michele to use on Saturday, the Italian qualifying the *muletta* ninth. Then, as that shower of rain eased across the circuit during first qualifying, Stefan arrived on a soaking section of track without warning and spun wildly. He slammed sideways into a very firm concrete retaining wall just behind the paddock and the left-front wheel slammed backwards into the monocoque. Johansson was lucky to stagger away with a badly bruised shin, knee and ankle, but the car was destroyed and for the rest of the weekend he had to use the car originally designated as the spare.

As far as track performance was concerned, the F1/86s were sustaining their customary 1986 form. Both men complained of a rotten ride over the bumps, ceaseless wheelspin, understeer into the corners and oversteer out. Michele and Stefan

qualified ninth and twelfth on the strength of their Friday efforts, neither managing to improve during the final session.

By contrast, the Tyrrell-Renaults looked quite acceptable and Philippe Streiff produced the team's best grid position of the year. The lanky Frenchman's tenth place was the product of an action-packed couple of days. On Friday morning he had been roundly berated by Johansson for allegedly blocking the Ferrari driver through three consecutive corners, but by Saturday afternoon he was basking in the satisfaction of achieving a fifth-row starting position.

With Adelaide's long back straight a crucial component in the equation adding up to a really quick lap, the Tyrrell team gambled on running their 015s with minimal downforce during the final session. As a result, Streiff and Brundle topped the straightline speed stakes at just under 205 mph, vaulting the Frenchman up the grid order. Brundle only got back behind the wheel of his EF15B-engined qualifying spare with about a quarter of an hour left after it had blown up during the untimed stint. But by then the yellow flags were out for his team-mate and for Rothengatter, so he was unable to better 16th overall.

The presence of three new high-compression-spec development Ford V6s for Alan Jones's exclusive use had little effect on Team Haas's downbeat mood. Alan's machine showed a mysterious inclination to lose boost pressure during Friday's untimed session, so the engine was

replaced. However, this task was not completed until the rain arrived midway through the first qualifying. To make matters worse, Alan had no spare car available since Patrick Tambay was strapped firmly into its cockpit, the Frenchman having badly damaged his race chassis when he spun off on a damp patch during the untimed session.

Jones was fed up to the back teeth – and prepared to say so to any pressman who appeared on the scene. The following day's proceedings hardly improved his mood. His race car blew a piston during the untimed session, the replacement 'new-spec' V6 broke a timing chain while being warmed up, and the spare refused to run cleanly over 10,500 rpm. Jones, 26th on Friday, obviously improved (to 15th) on Saturday, but was almost speechless with indignation about the way things had gone. Tambay, two places behind him, was also buttoned up with annoyance because he had not been allocated one of the new-spec engines.

Biggest surprise of the two days was Andrea de Cesaris. The Italian found that the latest Minardi M/86 handled extremely well over Adelaide's bumps and ripples, and the Italian's best qualifying effort of the season brought him into 11th spot. By contrast, Alessandro Nannini found the older M/85B a real pain and took a lowly 18th place on the grid.

Anyone looking for problems needed only to glance into the Brabham garage. The team

189

Martin Brundle's progress into fourth place is monitored by the television camera mounted on the Lotus of Johnny Dumfries. The superb quality of the pictures brought a new dimension to Formula 1 – and caught Dumfries spinning moments after this picture was taken. The Scotsman recovered to finish sixth.

members were not exactly slitting their wrists, but anyone offering a tray of knives might have found more than one taker!

Patrese got no further than 19th after suffering engine trouble on both days, taking over the spare on Friday. Derek Warwick also required its services the following day, while his race car received a fresh engine after a morning failure. The highlight of Derek's Friday qualifying was a trip into a sand trap when he locked the rear brakes going into a tight right-hander. In a well-meaning effort to help him regain the circuit, an adjacent recovery crane briefly winched car *plus* driver up off the ground. This precarious and highly dangerous manoeuvre was to no avail, however, as Del Boy stalled the BT55 just as it was touching down! His meagre reward was 20th.

Behind Warwick was Jonathan Palmer's Zakspeed, the Doc handicapped by poor throttle response and lack of grip. The order continued with Thierry Boutsen's Arrows A8 (the Belgian losing a lot of time on Friday while a brake master cylinder was changed), Rothengatter's Zakspeed (which consumed a couple of engines and gearboxes during the course of the two days) and Christian Danner's Arrows. As in Mexico, the latter car sported a revised livery promoting Megatron, a computer business subsidiary of USF&G, one of the team's prime backers.

And right at the back . . . you've guessed: the dauntless Osella-Alfa squad. Piercarlo Ghinzani just had the edge over Allen Berg by less than a tenth of a second!

RACE

Senna's Lotus was quickest in the untimed race morning warm-up, but Prost was right behind him, ahead of Mansell, Piquet and Berger. Fabi spun and hit one of the concrete walls, wrecking the front end of his Benetton which forced him to take the spare for the race. Confounding the local weather forecasters, the day remained gloomy and overcast with a few spots of rain showing up about twenty minutes prior to the start, to keep everybody on their toes. Local dignitaries, including Prime Minister Bob Hawke and South Australia's Premier, John Banon, took their seats for what promised to be *the* race of the year!

Only 25 cars took the start because, at the end of the warm-up lap, Berg's Osella rushed straight into the pits with turbo failure. Mechanics fell onto the car and began changing the faulty unit, eventually allowing the young Canadian to join in (from the pits) as the leaders were going round on their 10th lap.

Mansell had made a wheel-spinning start to the parade lap, laying down two lines of black rubber so as to give himself a specially 'grippy' piece of track to move off from, once the green light came on. He positioned his Williams precisely on the same spot as he came round to the grid, before catapulting away in the lead down to the first chicane with Senna and Piquet in hot pursuit.

Up the hill into the first tight right-hander, Mansell made room for Senna and Piquet to nip through on the inside, Nigel anxious not to get embroiled in too fierce a battle early on. Rosberg was soon through into third and, as Piquet

outbraked Senna at the end of the back straight, it was Nelson's Williams which led through at the end of the first lap. Further down the field, Arnoux's Ligier had been very slow away and another driver ran up the back of Alboreto's Ferrari. René punctured a front tyre and trailed round for a replacement, but Michele staggered no further than the pits to retire on the spot with damaged suspension.

Mansell pulled back past Senna to take third place on lap 4, the Lotus driver not at all happy with his engine's performance, but Rosberg was the real star of the show. By lap 5 he was right up behind Piquet and tore by into the lead going into lap 7. Prost also moved past Senna, taking over fourth, so the championship confrontation was shaping up nicely. Berger's Benetton led the rest of the field from Johansson, Streiff and Jones's understeering Lola.

Retirements by this stage included, inevitably, Ghinzani with transmission failure, and Nannini's Minardi. The latter crashed his M/85 heavily when he clipped a kerb on the entrance to a fast left/right flick and pitched straight into the opposite wall. Happily, he was not hurt.

Jones's Lola clawed its way up onto Berger's tail, but then blew up at the end of the back straight on lap 16, dropping a swathe of oil on the inside line. Shortly afterwards, Dumfries's Lotus fell foul of this lubricant, its onboard camera recording every detail of a spectacular spin in which he almost collected Brundle's Tyrrell which he was trying to pass.

Prost's progress was now beginning to look remorseless. On lap 12 he took over third place from Mansell and nipped past Piquet nine laps later, just before a spin dropped Nelson's FW11 down to fourth behind his team-mate. With a commanding McLaren 1-2 at the head of the field and Rosberg committed to relinquishing the lead to his partner, Alain's title hopes looked to have an even chance of fulfillment. But Mansell was still tailing them . . .

On lap 32 came the turning point. Lapping Berger's slowing Benetton, one of Prost's front wheels bumped the Austrian's car and the Frenchman raced in to change a deflated Goodyear. He resumed in fourth, leaving technicians from Akron to examine the discarded covers in minute detail. Before the race Goodyear had recommended its users to schedule a routine tyre stop, but the wear rate on Alain's tyres was such that they changed their opinion. Word went out to their teams that a non-stop run looked feasible after all.

On lap 44 Senna's increasingly tired Renault V6 blew up, promoting Johansson to fifth, while at the front of the field Mansell appeared more and more to have it in the bag. Piquet had subsequently retaken him, but Nigel was holding third place with no problem. If he could hang on up to the chequered flag, the Englishman would have done it!

Then came the bitter twist on the final page of the championship story. It started on lap 63 when Rosberg heard an ominous rumbling from the rear end of his McLaren. Convinced the engine had run its bearings, he flicked off the switches and coasted to a halt on the back straight. When he climbed out he realised that it was a tyre problem. The right-rear had started to delaminate and the thumping he had heard had come from flailing strips of rubber hitting the bodywork!

In the pit lane garages there was mounting concern. Piquet and Mansell were first and second, but should they be brought in for new tyres? Nigel's had looked in poor shape for several laps by this stage – but, before anybody could make a decision, Mansell's race came to a spectacular end midway round lap 64.

Storming down Decquetteville Avenue at around 180 mph in sixth gear, Nigel was just edging past Alliot's Ligier when the Williams's left-rear Goodyear simply exploded. Alliot ducked as the debris began flying, the FW11 squatted down on its left-rear corner in a shower of sparks

as the right-front wheel lifted off the track. Fishtailing wildly, Nigel wrestled with the wheel for dear life, successfully aiming the shattered car up the escape road beyond the hairpin where it gently bumped into the wall at walking pace. For a few seconds Mansell sat motionless in the cockpit, getting his breath back after one of the nastiest moments of his career. And with Piquet and Prost running 1-2, his title hopes were almost certainly slipping through his fingers.

'I'm just happy to be alive', he said grimly as he returned to his pit garage where he stayed to watch his rivals' progress on the television monitors. After his disaster, Goodyear advised that Piquet should be called in for a tyre change, promoting Prost into the lead while he was stationary. As soon as Nelson resumed, he began rattling off a whole succession of fastest laps. On the stopwatch it didn't look as though he had a chance. But he could not have known that Alain had his heart in his mouth worrying about that wayward fuel consumption reading. The champion pressed on, believing his hopes were certain to be dashed.

They were not! Over the last few laps he eased back dramatically, adding two and three seconds to his lap times. Yet, suddenly, it was the last lap. For last time he went down the back straight, through the wriggles behind the paddock, out from that final hairpin and up to the flag . . . World Champion for the second year in succession!

Keke had been right. Prost's 25th Grand Prix win brought joy for McLaren and the tiny Frenchman, and made the day one of bleak disappointment for Williams and Honda, in addition to their two drivers. That dejection was doubly upsetting because elderly Mr Sochiro Honda had journeyed from Japan to witness what was to have been a victorious finale to a superb season.

Establishing a new circuit record on the last lap, Piquet had blasted across the line in second place,

while Johansson just managed to scramble back to third at the flag, passing both fuel-starved Tyrrells on the final lap. Brundle staggered home fourth leaving Streiff fifth, out of fuel on the circuit, although Philippe had led Martin by a few lengths throughout up to that point.

Dumfries did well to round off his all-too brief Lotus career with a sixth place, while Arnoux drove flat-out after his first-lap delay to leave him just out of the points in seventh, ahead of team-mate Alliot. Palmer was ninth, hamstrung by heavy fuel consumption and poor throttle response, on top of losing a lap and a half when he was black-flagged to have his Zakspeed's trailing rear underbody secured. 'Apart from that – perfect!' he shrugged.

Fabi's Benetton, delayed by several tyre stops, got no higher than an unimpressive tenth, Berger's sister car having retired with clutch trouble. BMW fared no better on other fronts, with both Brabhams and Arrows failing to complete the event.

Warwick's BT55 wore out its front brakes and Patrese's sister car broke its engine. Amongst the also-rans, de Cesaris accidentally activated the cockpit fire extinguisher as he came in for tyres, the Italian withdrawing from the race doused from head to toe in cold vapour.

After a stop to deal with deranged gear selectors, Patrick Tambay was still running, 12 laps behind after a quick spin, while Berg's Osella was plodding round doggedly trying to keep out of the way but not always succeeding. Neither was classified.

And that's how it was after sixteen races and one of the most nail-biting battles for the World Championship ever witnessed. It would be hard to argue that the best driver had not won at the end of the day, although the margins separating the four or five top drivers of 1986 were clearly minuscule.

Yet Alain Prost fought through and won . . . the best had beaten the rest.   A.H.

TECHNICAL FILE

ARROWS
Unchanged since Mexico except for a return to the larger deflectors behind front wheels.

BENETTON
Race cars set up with Brembo calipers, mounted on trailing edge rather than under discs. Fabi's car fitted with larger AP calipers all round but returned to Brembo for the race. Did not use diffuser under nose.

BRABHAM
Double oil radiator for Warwick's car. Started practice with normal duct for turbo but by Saturday all the cars had 'snorkle' style duct on left side pod. T-car fitted with Brabham-made brake calipers on front; all three cars equipped this way by Saturday.

FERRARI
Following Johansson's practice accident, built up chassis 89 for Alboreto while Johansson took the T-car (94). Race cars fitted with intercoolers in revised position (angled in 'Toleman' style). Johansson's car equipped with twin lines for brake fluid (as first seen in Detroit).

LIGIER
Michel Tétu not present; working on 1987 car. Extra cooling for brakes.

LOLA
Three new engines (with higher compression ratio) for Jones.

LOTUS
Race cars fitted with double brake systems (similar to Ferrari). All three cars equipped with larger front brake ducts.

McLAREN
No major changes to the cars apart from trying different vertical deflectors below rear of underbody. Used the larger turbos during practice and the race.

MINARDI
New car for de Cesaris, fitted with larger and stiffer fixing plate for rear suspension. Nannini's car had additional oil radiator.

OSELLA
No changes. Enzo Osella absent.

TYRRELL
All three cars fitted with longer side pods and revised underbody.

WILLIAMS
Fitted ventilators to wheels to improve brake cooling. Also tried revised brake ducts. Race cars fitted with 'snorkle' ducts during practice on Friday; all four cars so equipped by Saturday. Tried cast-iron brakes on two cars on Saturday but soon dispensed with them.

ZAKSPEED
Nothing new.
                                                              G.P.

October

Gordon Murray leaves Brabham.

Win Percy (3.5 Rover Vitesse) wins FIA Touring Car Championship.

Thierry Boutsen signs for Benetton.

Bernie Ecclestone confirms purchase of Haas-Lola team.

All three works Peugeots excluded from Sanremo Rally.

TEN OUT OF TEN

By GORDON KIRBY

It's all happening at the 70th Indianapolis 500. There are less than three laps to go and fifteen remaining runners are bunched together behind the pace car, drivers' right feet itching at throttles, ready for the race's final restart. Lap 198 and the pace car turns off its lights and dives into the pits.

The place is in pandemonium. 300,000 people are up on their feet, cheering, waving. The noise is unreal. The human roar is actually drowning the sounds from the fifteen screaming turbocharged Cosworth DFXs, each aglow at 12,000 rpm.

Out on the track Bobby Rahal is setting up to outfox leader Kevin Cogan. Neither Rahal nor Cogan have ever won this race of races but they have fought against each other many times in Indycars, and before that in Formula Atlantic. The two men know each other well and they also know that directly behind them in the restart line is Rick Mears, a double winner of this race and the current record-setting pole-sitter.

As the pace car dives into the pits, Cogan, Rahal, Mears and the others are hard on their throttles. The cars are into the fourth turn of the giant, four-cornered oval and the starter is eyeing them, clutching at his flags, holding back on waving the green. But they're already racing and the huge crowd is with the drivers in this dramatic three-way race to the finish.

Thirteen laps earlier, just before this final yellow of the race, Cogan had taken the lead, passing both Mears and Rahal in the space of half a lap as all three leaders fought to lap the slower car of Randy Lanier. Even so, Cogan's car wasn't handling as he would have liked. Twice in the last twenty laps he coped with exciting moments as his car skated out of control into the dusty 'grey' beyond the tyre-blackened 'groove', both times veering perilously close to the wall. Now, with Rahal breathing hard down his neck, Cogan's car ran wide once again. He had to turn the car hard,

fighting the wheel. It was all Rahal needed.

As Cogan's car lost momentum, Rahal pulled onto his tail. Sprinting down to the starter's stand to begin lap 199, Rahal was able to swing inside Cogan. As they crossed the track's triple row of bricks at the start-and-finish line, Rahal was nosing ahead. Going into the first turn he was clear of Cogan, solidly in the lead.

Two laps, flat-out, saw Rahal run his fastest of the day at 209 mph on lap 200. He was the winner, in style, by 1·5 seconds from Cogan. Mears was another half a second back in third place. A furious, exciting finish and a great day for Rahal and the TrueSports/Budweiser team.

It was also a very full taste of the essence of Indycar racing – of speedway or oval track racing in particular. By their very nature, of course, oval tracks encourage wheel-to-wheel racing more than road racing circuits but it shouldn't be forgotten that contemporary Indycar road races

Mid-Ohio: the flourishing Indycar road events have become almost as competitive as the more celebrated oval races.

The incandescent atmosphere and spectacle of the Indianapolis 500 is impossible to capture elsewhere *(left)*.

are very nearly as competitive as the category's more celebrated oval races. The last couple of years have seen many fiercely fought road races with a large number of potential winners and unpredictable results. At the time of writing, seven drivers had won races in 1986 and three or four others had come extremely close to victory.

The race-winners were Rahal (six), Michael and Mario Andretti and Danny Sullivan (two apiece), and Cogan, Johnny Rutherford and Emerson Fittipaldi (each with a single victory). Those who came close included Mears, Roberto Moreno, Roberto Guerrero and Tom Sneva.

Said Fittipaldi after scoring an excellent win in pouring rain at Elkhart Lake, Wisconsin, in early October: 'This is not like Formula 1 where there are usually two or three cars who can win any race. Here there are ten cars that can win any race. You never know who is going to be first or tenth. You can be in one place one weekend and at the other end the next week. It's very competitive.'

What makes Indycar racing so competitive are the tight rules on tyres, turbo boost pressure and aerodynamics. Also, almost the entire field continues to use the Cosworth DFX V8 and the only two competing chassis builders are March and Lola.

Restricted to a single turbocharger and 48 in. Hg (0.65 bar) boost pressure, most DFXs produced between 700 and 730 bhp at 11,500+ rpm. There are seven or eight leading DFX engine builders and after six years of running the same engine formula reliability is excellent.

Last year two fledgling competitors to the DFX appeared. In company with Roger Penske and British-based Ilmor Engineering, Chevrolet produced their own four-camshaft V8, while John Judd developed a destroked turbo version (at 2·65 litres of course) of Honda's F3000 V8. The Ilmor/Chevrolet took a while to come to fruition but in the latter part of the season it was beginning to show its particular mid-range strength as Rick Mears used the engine to qualify on the pole at Sanair. In late-September at Michigan International Speedway, the engine ran a full race distance for the first time and at Elkhart Lake the following weekend Mears and the Ilmor/Chevy finished again, this time in third place. The engine clearly had competitive horsepower and a very wide powerband and looked ready to eclipse the Cosworth in 1987.

The Honda was run by Galles Racing for Geoff Brabham. After missing Indianapolis because of connecting rod problems the Anglo-Japanese V8 subsequently ran in Brabham's car at most remaining races. The engine was competitive and reliable but appeared to be nothing more than that.

English constructors March and Lola continued to dominate the market for chassis. March sold cars to about two-thirds of the field and Lola supplied the rest. A new Eagle appeared at the start of the season but financial troubles sidelined both car and the All-American Racers team until a couple of late-season races. Driven by Jan Lammers the Eagle clearly had potential which hopefully will be revived and possibly even realised in 1987.

March's 86C was a logical development of the previous year's successful 85C and there was real progress on the aerodynamics and weight distribution. A properly de-bugged, rebuilt and developed 86C was a match for Lola's T86/00 at any type of track, whether a Mickey Mouse parking lot circuit or flat-out super-speedway. While Lola's quality control continued to be superior to that at March, both manufacturers lavished a lot of time and money in building cars capable of absorbing energy in 200 mph impacts with the wall. Over the last two or three years March and Lola, working in company with CART, have made some big strides in improving crash safety. Undoubtedly, contemporary Indycars set the standard in crash safety for the rest of motor sport and are well ahead of Formula 1 in this regard, not to mention light years ahead of some well-known Group C constructors . . .

To date, not one Indycar driver has been seriously injured in 1986. Herm Johnson, Randy Lanier and Josele Garza escaped from huge accidents with broken legs – none of them fractures of the multiple or compound type. Also injured were Ed Pimm (broken collarbone in one accident and a broken arm in another) and Al Unser Jnr and Dennis Firestone, both of whom dislocated shoulders. The potentially volatile nature of Indycar racing, with 215+ mph lap speeds and cement retaining walls, makes this an impressive record.

March supplied half a dozen of the top teams with cars while Lola provided only three top teams with chassis and a much smaller percentage of the mid- to backfield. Most of March's engineering support was supplied to the Kraco Stereos team (a single car for Michael Andretti) and to Patrick Racing (two cars for Emerson Fittipaldi and Kevin Cogan). To a lesser extent, TrueSports (Bobby Rahal in the cockpit) were a factory-affiliated

Steve Swope

Mark Clifford

team. Also March-equipped at most races was Penske Racing (Rick Mears, Danny Sullivan and 1985 Champion Al Unser Snr) who were strictly on their own as far as performance development was concerned.

Lola's 'factory' team was of course Newman/ Haas Racing (Mario Andretti at the wheel) and to a lesser degree Team Shierson (Al Unser Jnr in the hotseat). Also Lola-equipped was Rick Galles' ambitious two- and sometimes three-car team (Geoff Brabham, Roberto Moreno and Pancho Carter).

Penske Racing built and ran their own car, designated PC15. Returning as a car constructor after a two-year hiatus, the Penske outfit ran the PC15 only sporadically after the late completion of the first chassis. Nevertheless, progress was made in the latter part of the year and Mears qualified a PC15-Ilmor/Chevrolet on the pole at Sanair in September. By mid-October Penske was about to

decide whether to continue building his own cars next year or become a March customer.

Fought-out over seventeen races, this year's championship was wide open for most of the season. Sponsored for the sixth year by paint and glass manufacturer PPG Industries, the CART/ PPG Indy Car World Series boasted a grand total of more than $15 million in prize money including nearly $4 million at Indianapolis alone. The 1985 Champion, Al Unser Snr, was unable to defend his title, relegated to a third-string role at Penske Racing. He started only four races for the team in what turned out to be an unreliable third car, leaving Penske's defence of the championship in the hands of Rick Mears and Danny Sullivan.

At the start of the season young Michael Andretti set the pace, leading powerfully in the Phoenix season-opener and beating Al Unser Jnr in a magnificent duel at Long Beach. He won again on the one-mile Milwaukee oval the week

Daytona International Speedway

Daytona International Speedway

David Hutson

Joseph J. Jiran

Al Unser Snr, the defending CART champion, handled the third Penske and drove the PC15 Ilmor/Chevrolet during its early stages of development *(top left).*

Emerson Fittipaldi: fully established in CART *(centre top).*

Pit stop for the Darrell Waltrip/Junior Johnson Chevrolet at Daytona *(top right).*

Michael Andretti and the Kraco March took a win at Long Beach before entering a barren mid-season patch, followed by a powerful comeback *(centre).*

NASCAR: a hairy-chested formula which continues to thrive. Geoff Bodine scored a major win at the Daytona 500 *(above).*

Left: **Darrell Waltrip's gnawingly persistent style of driving kept him in contention for the NASCAR title.**

after Indianapolis but in the middle of the summer Michael's early charge dissipated amid reliability shortcomings, a few mistakes of his own and the departure of brilliant young March designer Adrian Newey to Carl Haas's F1 team. Meanwhile, a number of other pretenders to the crown emerged, including Indy winner Rahal and Danny Sullivan who became the first men to win back-to-back races in 1986. Also in the hunt were Mario Andretti and Al Unser Jnr, the two top Lola drivers tending to score more through persistence and reliability compared to sheer speed of the Marches.

It wasn't until September that any one driver was able to put together a string of results. That man was Bobby Rahal, who finally emerged as the dominant Indycar driver of the year with a series of fast, polished performances. At the same time Andretti Jnr began to make something of a comeback and by the middle of October the championship was hanging in the balance between the two friendly, if dissimilar, rivals. Not to be discounted either were seven-time Indycar champions Penske Racing who kept Sullivan in the championship hunt down to the wire.

Rahal and the TrueSports team really came of age in 1986. The combination joined together to go Indycar racing in 1983 and rapidly established themselves as winners in a type of racing that was new to every member of the team. In 1984 and '85 TrueSports operated essentially as March's 'factory' team with Chief Designer Adrian Newey working at the races as the team's engineer. That situation changed last year, however, as True-Sports team owner Jim Trueman worked to align himself with Enzo Ferrari in order to run a mooted Ferrari Indycar in 1987. Nevertheless, with or without Newey, the team continued to field the most competitive of Marches as team manager Steve Horne and resident engineer Grant Newbury plied the team's notebooks.

The team weathered a very real tragedy in the immediate aftermath of winning Indianapolis when Jim Trueman died following a relentless, two-year fight against cancer. Trueman was in Rahal's pit on race day at Indianapolis, and it was obvious to anyone that he had very few days to live. He joined Rahal in the pace car for the victory lap and passed away eleven days later.

Michael Andretti ran his third full Indycar season driving as ever for the Kraco Stereos team. Owned and operated by Kraco boss Maurice Kraines, the team was established in 1981 and quickly became one of March's leading customers. Last year the team replaced TrueSports as the 'factory' outfit with Newey working as race engineer for the first half of the season and appearing strictly on a weekend basis at a few end-of-season races. Managed by Barry Green, the team was substantially changed from previous years and certainly showed the more established teams a thing or two about going motor racing.

To increase the appeal of the Indycar championship to the public and media, CART have been trying hard over the past few years to capture some of the incandescent atmosphere and spectacle of the Indianapolis 500. Impossible as it may be

to equal the sheer size of that historic race, CART have attempted to recreate some of its flavour by experimenting with new races and tracks. Most of these have been road races on both permanent and temporary circuits. Some have been duds (such as Las Vegas and the woebegone Meadowlands in New Jersey adjacent to Manhattan), others have survived and some (Long Beach, Portland in Oregon, Mid-Ohio and Laguna Seca) have flourished. A important point is that the CART schedule seems at last to be stablising with all but one or two of the current races resting on a strong footing.

There was much discussion about rising costs and slimming fields as success inevitably brought problems. Dissatisfaction was expressed about the standard of officiation, particularly concerning the effective use and deployment of the pace car and lap scoring at oval races. Another bone of contention was the eternal, elusive search for methods of restraining increases in lap speeds at Indianapolis in particular and all tracks in general. A positive sign as far as 'selling the product' came near the end of the year in the shape of a new television package for 1987. Included were many more major network races (on ABC and NBC) as well as live rather than tape-delay telecasts, with CART planning to produce a handful of the television shows as well as selling the advertising time.

LOOKING TO THE FUTURE

America's secondary formulae experienced some upheaval in 1986 as CART searched for a more spectacular training category than Super-Vee. With USAC and the SCCA having failed miserably over the years to act as competent sanctioning bodies, the whole spectrum of American single-seat motor racing has fallen into anarchic disorder. Sprint car racing, once the prime training ground for Indycar drivers, has faded drastically in national prominence. Formula Atlantic, spawning ground for Rahal, Sullivan, Andretti Jnr, Cogan and many more of today's Indycar drivers, has been totally neglected by every major sanctioning body in the United States, primarily because the category has never carried with it any self-underwriting corporate sponsor. Certainly, Super-Vee has thrived because of the backing of Volkswagen and the Robert Bosch Corporation but at the end of 1985 CART co-founder Pat Patrick decided that March boss Robin Herd had a better idea in a 3·5 litre, normally-aspirated Buick V6-powered 'spec car' version of F3000.

Called the American Racing Series, Patrick's new formula debuted this year and survived a shaky start with twelve-car fields at most races. Prime contenders for the championship were Italian Fabrizio Barbazza, Argentinian Juan-Manuel Fangio II, Kiwi Steve Millen, Irishman Tommy Byrne and Americans Jeff Andretti (Michael's younger brother) and Mike Groff. Many Indycar races were accompanied by both ARS and Super-Vee races and the top drivers in the more traditional, less powerful VW-engined formula were Belgian Didier Theys and Americans Steve and Cary Bren, Mike Groff (the same),

195

Rick Mears was still recuperating but he returned to increasing competitiveness with the March/Cosworth (pictured) and the PC15-Chevrolet.

A.J. Foyt (left) and Tom Sneva: two members of the senior establishment in Indycar racing (bottom).

Scott Atchison, Tom Knapp and Dave Kudrave. Formula Atlantic operated on a much less visible level with separate regional championships on east and west coasts. Top men in the category were Americans Ted Prappas and Dan Marvin, Canadian Scott Goodyear and Englishman Calvin Fish.

HOLBERT PREVAILS

American sports car racing has become the property of John Bishop's IMSA organisation over the past half-decade. After seventeen years in business IMSA has taken virtually all of the SCCA's marbles. Top billing at any IMSA race meeting is the Camel cigarettes-sponsored prototype sports car category known as GTP which featured fleets of Porsche 962s and a variety of Jaguar XJR6s, Lola-Chevrolets, March-BMWs, March-Buicks and Ford Probes.

Porsche continued to rule the roost with American Porschemeister Al Holbert winning his fourth IMSA title, ably assisted by Derek Bell and Al Unser Jnr. Even though Porsche tended to dominate the show, particularly in the longer races, there was a lot of variety in victory circle. Driven primarily by South African Sarel van der Merwe, the 'Corvette GTP' (actually a turbo Chevy V6-powered Lola) was often very fast and even hung together to win one race. The Jaguars were simply out-horsepowered, as were the still-unreliable Ford Probes, but the new BMW-powered Marches were coming on strong in the latter part of the season with a powerful driving team consisting of John Watson, David Hobbs, Davy Jones and John Andretti (Mario's nephew).

IMSA's small-capacity prototype category continued for a second year in 1986, sponsored by Camel Light cirgarettes and known formally by the same name. Over the course of the year the category grew steadily in strength and helped give IMSA's fields much more depth than Group C. Another increasingly strong IMSA category is known as GTO. Featuring cars like Chevrolet Camaros and Mercury Capris, GTO operated as a powerful rival to the SCCA's TransAm with similar cars and drivers. Top man in GTO was talented youngster Scott Pruett, while the TransAm saw Wally Dallenbach Jnr battling with the likes of Pete Halsmer, Chris Kneifel, Gregg Pickett, Elliott Forbes-Robinson and occasionally Paul Newman. Between an unsuccessful attempt to establish a career in NASCAR, Willy T. Ribbs also appeared with success in GTO and TransAm cars.

IRONHEAD

And so to NASCAR and stock car racing in general. Ah NASCAR! Such a tightly organised, audience-conscious, made-for-TV game they have. And so tidily and comprehensively marketed. Not a single type of motor racing anywhere in the world can compare to NASCAR when it comes to the depth and breadth of commercial sponsorship. There are so many associate and contingency sponsors that the inducements to new teams and drivers are far ahead of any other major category.

Sponsored by Winston cigarettes for sixteen years, NASCAR's top category is known as the

Tim Richmond (left) and Ricky Rudd; winners in another highly competitive NASCAR season (left).

Keeping it in the family. Bobby Unser came out of retirement to smash the Pikes' Peak record in a factory Audi Quattro rally car.

Waltrip's apparent *bêtes noires* were Dale Earnhardt and Tim Richmond. Earnhardt was champion in 1980 and has driven for the past three years for Richard Childress's Wrangler Jeans-backed team, while Richmond is part of a two-car team fielded by Rick Hendrick. The latter is one of America's largest Chevrolet dealers who started his NASCAR team two years ago and next year will field a three-car team, each run from separate workshops with Waltrip leaving Johnson's legendary team to join existing team-mates Richmond and Geoff Bodine in Hendrick's stable!

Hendrick also fielded the 'Corvette GTP' car in IMSA and his strong Chevrolet connection could not have been more obvious last year as his pair of stock cars shared pole position at no fewer than 13 of the 26 Winston Cup races run at the time of writing. Bodine was on the pole eight times and scored a big win at the season-opening Daytona 500 but it was Richmond who threatened Waltrip and Earnhardt for the championship. Rookie-of-the-year at Indianapolis in 1980, Richmond subsequently destroyed five Indycars in successive races and quickly pulled out of single-seaters to try his hand at stock cars. He soon became a front-runner and occasional winner but his aggressive style often got him into trouble. Richmond continued to use a rather more polished version of the same style this year and was more competitive than ever, winning six races, on all types of track, from June through to September.

In the end, however, it was Earnhardt and Waltrip who disputed NASCAR's '86 title. Earnhardt had won four races and Waltrip three by mid-October. Both men boasted ruggedly persistent finishing records among the top three or four places. Earnhardt is as aggressive as any driver in stock car racing (which is saying something!) and he and Richmond enjoyed a number of friendly, spectator-pleasing, fender-leaning battles last year. Known as 'Ironhead', Earnhardt needed to finish only tenth or better in each of the season's final three races run beyond the *Autocourse* press date in order to take the title away from triple champion Waltrip. Other Winston Cup race-winners in 1986 included Bodine, Elliott, Ricky Rudd (in a Ford), Rusty Wallace (Pontiac), Kyle Petty (Ford), Terry Labonte (Chevrolet), Morgan Shepherd (Buick), Bobby Allison (Buick) and first-timer Bobby Hillin Jnr (Buick). Amongst the active former champions who failed to win a race in '86 were Richard Petty, Cale Yarborough, David Pearson and Benny Parsons.

OLD MAN OF THE MOUNTAIN

A notable moment in American motor sport history took place at Pikes' Peak in Colorado on 12 July 1986. At the 64th running of America's second-oldest (after the Indianapolis 500) motor sporting event, three-times Indy 500 winner Bobby Unser came out of retirement to win the 12·4-mile hill climb for the tenth time. Unser drove a factory Audi Quattro short-wheelbase rally car, breaking Michèle Mounton's record with a similar car in 1985 by 16 seconds and marking the fifteenth time since 1934 that Bobby, brother Al, uncle Louie or nephew Al Jnr have held the record.

Winston Cup (the traditional moniker of Grand National racing was dropped from the formal title in 1986). The formula for NASCAR's top category has been unchanged for more than a decade consisting essentially of sheet metal-bodied, tube-frame cars weighing 3700 lb and powered by carburetted, 5·8 litre 'stock-block' V8s, all running on identical Goodyear tyres. There are just three or four chassis builders for these cars and regular fine-tuning of the rules keeps the various cars extremely similar in performance.

Always very strong, NASCAR's top class has boomed over the past five or six years with new drivers and teams proving the equal of the established runners. Forty cars regularly turn up for each of the 29 championship races and the bigger races at Daytona, Charlotte, Darlington and Talladega attract massive 70-car fields!

In 1985 the Elliott brothers emerged in the national eye by dominating the super-speedway portion (tracks with banked turns of one mile and more) of the Winston Cup schedule. Tall, gangling and red-headed, Bill Elliott won twelve races

aboard the Elliott brothers' Ford Thunderbird and for the '86 season NASCAR tightened the restriction on the Ford's carburettor throat diameter. The result was that Elliott struggled to be competitive. He won only twice, in June and August, both times at the super-fast, high-banked Michigan International Speedway outside Detroit. In the championship stakes Elliott was a no-hoper.

Elliott had been beaten to the Winston Cup Championship in 1985 by Darrell Waltrip and Junior Johnson's all-powerful Chevrolet team. Waltrip beat Elliott by thrashing him in most short-track races (unbanked half-mile and five-eighths of a mile ovals, all located in or near the mountains of the Carolinas, Virginia and Tennessee) and also with the aid of first-rate reliability and a gnawingly persistent style of driving. In 1986 Waltrip and Johnson found themselves locked in a more difficult struggle with two younger but very aggressive driver/team combinations, both of them Chevrolet-equipped like Waltrip and Johnson.

The Top Ten of 1986 in Indycars

1
BOBBY RAHAL

2
MICHAEL ANDRETTI

3
AL UNSER JNR

4
MARIO ANDRETTI

5
DANNY SULLIVAN

6
RICK MEARS

7
EMERSON FITTIPALDI

8
KEVIN COGAN

9
ROBERTO GUERRERO

10
JOHNNY RUTHERFORD

The moment of a lifetime. Jim Trueman (left)
savours Bobby Rahal's win for the TrueSports team
at Indy. Eleven days later, the team owner
succumbed to cancer.

1 BOBBY RAHAL

There were three races still to be run in the 1986 Indycar championship when the deadline arrived for this section of *Autocourse*. At the time five drivers still had hopes of winning the American national driving championship but there was no doubt in your American Editor's mind that, for the second year in a row, Bobby Rahal was the top driver in the USA. At his fifth attempt, Rahal finally won the Indianapolis 500, and in race after race he was consistently the most competitive Indycar driver.

Rahal won three races in a row in August and September and there were only two races in which he didn't figure as a potential winner. Capable of leading and winning on any type of track, Rahal last year became more than ever a polished, thinking man's driver. On the fast, crowded oval tracks Rahal was able to avoid trouble and accidents, turning luck to his favour. All this enhanced confidence in the man who continues to race occasionally in IMSA GTP cars and has also been a strong competitor in the IROC series over the past two years. One could add that he became the first Indycar driver ever to win $1 million in a single season, but the main point was that week in, week out, Rahal and the TrueSports team – with whom he has spent every one of his five seasons aboard Indycars – were the combination to beat.

2 MICHAEL ANDRETTI

There was no doubt, either, that Michael Andretti deserved to be ranked second. Michael celebrated his 24th birthday on 5 October, but this was really the year in which he came of age. He made an excellent start, leading powerfully at Phoenix and winning at Long Beach, but then went through a barren patch in the middle of the season. At year's end he was making a big comeback, however, putting heavy pressure on points-leader Rahal.

There were times, at Indianapolis and elsewhere, when Michael was blindingly fast, and it must be said that when everything was working properly he was the most stirring performer in the game. After fourteen races Michael had led more than a quarter of the season's total laps (532 of 2021 laps compared to Rahal's laps-led tally of 318) and was entirely capable of beating Rahal to the championship. If he failed to do so it was due primarily to reliability shortcomings in the Kraco team (mostly engines) and also to a small excess of youthful *brio*, if not good old Andretti family impetuousity. At the same time, every ounce of the family talent, application and drive to succeed is there, too.

3 AL UNSER JNR

Although Al Unser Jnr's 1986 season did not equal his down-to-the-wire battle with his father for the '85 Indycar title, it did reveal a tremendously strong spirit of perseverence. There were times this year when Al Jnr's car was simply off the pace – fearfully so on occasions at the big ovals – yet he kept plugging on, giving his all regardless of circumstances. He finished in the points (down to twelfth place in Indycars) in thirteen of the first fourteen races and when his car was right he was capable of racing aggressively for the lead. He did so at Long Beach, the Meadowlands, Toronto and Sanair, but by press date Unser had failed to win a race in 1986.

Young Unser emphasised his persistent approach by driving in two races a week apart with a separated shoulder sustained in an accident at Elkhart Lake in September. Like Andretti Jnr, he has not only considerable talent and a native understanding for the sport but also possesses an ability to assess situations coolly and to pump himself up for sustained attacks, at maximum aggression and concentration. He also won the 1986 IROC title, the youngest man ever to do so, winning two of the four championship rounds.

4 MARIO ANDRETTI

Here he is, down in fourth place, and maybe even lower in the final points table. The man was eclipsed by his oldest son in 1986 and for the second year in a row it was often a frustrated, brow-knitted Mario Andretti we met in the pit lane. Like Unser Jnr and other Lola-mounted drivers, the elder Andretti suffered from a high-speed aerodynamic performance disadvantage *vis-à-vis* the March-equipped majority. But there was more to it than that. In several races Mario dropped out because of mechanical failure within sight of the chequered flag, or perhaps lost a lap or two with a trifling problem in the middle of the race. He won the Pocono 500 (a long-sought, deserved victory at his 'home' track) as well as a road race at Portland, Oregon (a lucky win), and he was on the front row four times, but in general his cars were neither competitive enough nor reliable enough nor was Mario's personal luck up to championship-winning snuff.

5 DANNY SULLIVAN

Something of an enigma: Indy 500 winner in 1985, a race-winner again in 1986 and sometimes the fastest road racer in the Indycar business, Sullivan often struggled to be even close to the pace on oval tracks. He did not enjoy a single, truly competitive oval race in 1986 and was an also-ran at Indianapolis and elsewhere. By contrast, he led every road race run before our deadline, won two of them, and was ranked third in points, still with a good chance of winning the championship for Penske Racing. In his second year with the dominant team of Indycar racing, it was possible at presstime that Sullivan could have overhauled Rahal and Andretti Jnr for the title, but if so the honour would not have been truly deserved.

6 RICK MEARS

The breaks just didn't go Rick Mears' way in 1986. While still not 100 per cent recuperated from the accident that broke his feet in September 1984, Mears continued to be the fastest oval racer in the game. He was on the pole at Indianapolis and again at the Michigan 500 where he set a remarkable qualifying record of 223·401 mph! Mears finished third at Indianapolis, less than two seconds behind the victor, and led more laps than anyone save Andretti Jnr and Rahal. Yet, at the time of writing, he had not managed to finish any race better than third.

Nevertheless, by the end of the season he was beginning to find excellent form in road races and was also successfully race-testing the Ilmor/Chevrolet engine. He gave every sign of getting ready for a big season in 1987. . .

7 EMERSON FITTIPALDI

Tremendously unlucky through the middle of the season, Emerson Fittipaldi was never a factor in last year's championship. However, the Brazilian frequently mixed it with the likes of Rahal and Sullivan in road races and had two or three 'should haves' taken away by mechanical failure. Less consistently competitive on ovals, Fittipaldi has still developed a keen appreciation for the technical and tactical niceties of speedway racing having fully established himself after three years of his comeback as a top-class, all-round Indycar driver. He continues for a second year in 1987 with sponsor Marlboro and for a third year with Patrick Racing.

8 KEVIN COGAN

After a couple of years in the wilderness, Kevin Cogan found himself in much better conditions last year as Fittipaldi's team-mate at Patrick Racing. Cogan won the season-opener at Phoenix – his first Indycar victory – and was beaten at Indianapolis only by Rahal. Thereafter he had no luck at all and it wasn't until late in the season that he again began to qualify and finish near the front. Nevertheless, at 30, Cogan has developed into a mature driver and man with a solid future in Indycars. If Patrick Racing flourishes in 1987, so too will Cogan.

9 ROBERTO GUERRERO

The young Colombian (he's still only 28) had not yet won an Indycar race by copy date but he had come closer than ever and shown himself indisputably to possess the rare combination of being totally competitive on all types of tracks – super-speedways, short ovals and road courses. Guerrero employs a stirring, 'high-groove' technique on super-speedways and although his aggressive passing manoeuvres continued to get him into trouble on occasion last year, he is now recognised as one of the best all-round Indycar drivers with a special talent for going fast on super-speedways. All he needs is a little luck and that elusive first win . . .

10 JOHNNY RUTHERFORD

At 48, the triple Indy 500 winner was the elder statesman of the circuit and he played a similar role on the racetrack. Driving for Alex Morales' small team he was usually on the pace at most oval races and scored a dogged and worthy victory in the Michigan 500. At every road race Rutherford adopted the technique of avoiding any attempts at heroics and drove carefully to finish. It went against his grain, but he finished race after race in the points and kept himself solidly among the top ten in points all year.

There are several other drivers who deserve to be mentioned for this was a series where there were often as many as ten potential winners at any particular race. Among these top contenders at most oval races was Tom Sneva but it looked unlikely that he would find victory in '86, just as he had in '85. Nor did Sneva look like his old self once the races got underway. In road races he was a persistent finisher but nothing more.

Perhaps the most untapped talent in Indycars last year was Roberto Moreno who ran right with the leaders in a number of road races and often looked good on oval tracks. If he continues in the category in 1987 he should develop into a race-winner. In the same category is fellow Brazilian Raul Boesel. Driving for a small, budget-strained team, Boesel impressed with a clean, forceful style that he put to good effect on all types of tracks.

A young driver with considerable Indycar experience who needs to move up to a stronger team is Mexican Josele Garza.

TOM SNEVA

JOSELE GARZA

RAUL BOESEL

ED PIMM

Very quick on occasions, Garza's '86 season was brought to a premature conclusion when he broke a leg in a big accident at Mid-Ohio in August. Another young driver of unrealised potential is Ed Pimm, who also missed races through injury in 1985. Pimm qualified surprisingly well for all three 500-mile races and needs a productive season in '87.

Hard to rate last year was Moreno's team-mate Geoff Brabham who spent most of the year race-testing John Judd's Honda V8. Pancho Carter drove a third Galles entry in some oval races and was third in both Michigan and Pocono 500s. Also difficult to assess were Jacques Villeneuve and Scott Brayton who usually shared a car, Villeneuve specialising in road races and Brayton on ovals. Although both occasionally showed well, neither scored any results. Also without many results was Dutchman Arie Luyendyk who showed a lot of across-the-board abilities in his second Indycar season.

INDYCAR TOP TEN PHOTOS: DAVID HUTSON

A LOST OPPORTUNITY

On the face of it, the 1986 FIA Sports-Prototype World Championships achieved their highest level of competitiveness in the five seasons since the introduction of the Group C class. Almost all the races were hotly contested, featuring a great many memorable battles, and run under such relentless pressure that the series more than justified the change from its former 'Endurance' title, which had been so promotionally damaging.

For the first time, the outcome of the championship was genuinely unpredictable. Victories were achieved not only by the factory Porsche team and its regular army of private entrants, but also by Jaguar and Mercedes, the newcomers who brought back memories of the halcyon days of three decades before. The nine races were won by seven different cars and by sixteen different drivers. There was also strong competition between four tyre companies – Dunlop, Goodyear, Michelin, Yokohama – and the teams were backed

by an impressive array of international sponsors. It was, outwardly, a vibrant and healthy scene.

And yet, and yet . . . there remain nagging doubts about Group C. They stem from a wide variety of factors whose common denominator is the incomprehensible failure of FISA, the governing body, to support its own series with any kind of effective direction. FISA, whose Paris offices are woefully understaffed, is remote from sports-prototype racing. Its top executives are preoccupied with Formula 1, and frequently show that they simply do not understand the needs of the Group C series and its participants. Officially, the latter are able to communicate with their legislative body only through the Sports-Prototype Commission, whose composition leaves a lot to be desired. It is dominated by delegates representing the circuits: there is only one man voting on behalf of the BPICA (the manufacturers' body).

The most damaging result of this unbalanced type of administration is instability. The structure of the power base fails to take into account the modern nature of manufacturer involvement in competition. The financial investments by the all-important manufacturers, whatever the type of motor sports suiting their particular promotional or technical rationale, are such that long term projections are now essential for them. Yet they have little influence on the rules and, in Group C, it seems that FISA can change the rules on little more than a whim. Even under its own legislation to ensure stability, FISA can make fundamental changes with notice of under 15 months – less if it can justify them on safety grounds. As the manufacturers that have been rallying Group B cars can testify, this lead-time has become hopelessly inadequate.

The outcome is that manufacturers are cautious in committing themselves to programmes needed

Opposite page: Derek Bell assumes the worst as transmission problems appear to wreck his championship hopes at Fuji.

The famous Joest Racing 956 (left) ended the season with a victory in Japan.

The Oscar Larrauri/Jesus Pareja Mayo 962 was one prong of a three-car effort which netted Brun Motorsport the Team Championship, thanks in part to a successful liaison with Michelin.

The nimble Ecosse, powered by a race version of the Metro 6R4 rally engine, claimed the Group C2 Championship.

The Porsche AG factory team entered their experimental 961 at Le Mans for René Metge and Claude Ballot-Lena, the four-wheel-drive car finishing seventh on its debut.

to bring about stability and to raise the level of competition. In Group C, this has reduced the influx of new manufacturers to a trickle. Those that are participating are forever looking over their shoulders, wondering what FISA might do next.

FISA steadfastly resists attempts to give the manufacturers a stronger voice in the rule-making process, and this has contributed to the disappointing development of OSCAR, the teams' organisation. When it was established, in April 1985, there were high hopes that OSCAR would flourish and make real progress in the vital areas of management and promotion. In two seasons, however, its development has been restricted and thus far it is little more than an efficient transportation agent. Its President, Chris Parsons, has now been appointed the series co-ordinator and on a personal level has a voice in various areas, including the development of new events. However, he continues to have no vote on the Commission, so that the teams have little power in any confrontation with FISA.

Just as significantly, neither he nor FISA has a budget for promotion, so that the championship as a whole attracts minimal media interest. Crucially, this quality series has failed miserably to grab the giant opportunities offered by in-car television.

Derek Bell and Hans-Joachim Stuck, albeit by a solitary point, claimed their second straight Drivers' title, but this time it was the only trophy won by the factory Porsche team. The Teams' Championship fell to a sustained three-car onslaught by Brun Motorsport with its privateer Porsche. In the Group C2 division, Gordon Spice and Ray Bellm also achieved a double, but their Teams' title was stolen by Ecurie Ecosse.

THE STAGE

As always, the calendar of a dozen races was issued late by FISA, and it included several fixtures that could only be described as fanciful. Four races disappeared in due course and were replaced by a new event at Jerez. What remained was a series of nine races, eight in Europe and only one further afield, in Japan.

All the races counted towards the Drivers' Championships, but the Teams' titles were contested over only five: the established 'classics' at Silverstone, Le Mans, the Nürburgring, Spa-Francorchamps and Fuji. The confusing split has now been stopped and, from 1987, all the races will count towards both championships.

For the first time, events of less than 1000 km distance were permitted as championship rounds, and the 'sprint' format was successfully employed at Monza, the Norisring (a spectacular addition to the series) and Jerez. Silverstone, Brands Hatch (missing an opportunity), the Nürburgring, Spa and Fuji continued with their 1000 km events. The Le Mans 24-Hours maintained its position as the blue riband race of the year.

Again there was no race on the North American continent. FISA appears to have ceased its previous efforts to to make its World Championship genuinely international.

THE PLOT

The progress of Bell and Stuck towards their second successive title began at the series-opener at Monza, the first-ever World Championship Group C race for which the shorter, 360 km distance was used.

The format allows each car a fuel allocation of 190 litres, a slightly generous interpretation of the 510 litres per 1000 km principle on which Group C is based. A mid-race fuel halt and driver change is mandatory.

The 27-car race was dominated by Joest Racing's Porsche until well into the second half. A transmission failure then halted Ludwig and Barilla, and a broken driveshaft coupling stopped the Jaguar of Warwick and Cheever, which had begun to mount a challenge for the lead.

The win was inherited by the factory Porsche of Bell and Stuck, with the solo Lancia of de Cesaris and Nannini second, and the Brun Porsches filling the next three places. The last lap, however, bordered on farce as most of the leading cars ran short of fuel.

Silverstone, the opening Teams' encounter, was won in an utterly dominant performance by the Jaguar team. Once Lancia's challenge had evaporated, Warwick and Cheever were untroubled as they scored the marque's first sports car World Championship victory since the Ecurie Ecosse triumph at Le Mans in 1957. The achievement was greeted with rapturous enthusiasm by the British crowd.

Bell and Stuck were lapped twice by the XJR-6, but finished second and strengthened their grip on the trophy. The event was contested by 32 cars.

Le Mans 1986 resulted in another maximum score for this pairing (sharing the car with IMSA Champion Al Holbert) and Bell secured his fourth victory there. But the race will be remembered, sadly, for the death of Jo Gartner. The Austrian driver had really begun to establish himself as one of the stars of Group C with the Kremer team.

Up to the point where this tragedy occurred, the event, with its varied and competitive field of 50 cars, had featured a thoroughly absorbing, tactical duel between the factory Porsche of the eventual winners and the Joest Racing car. There was nothing to choose between them except Joest's slender fuel consumption advantage. After Gartner's death had been confirmed, however, the famous Joest car was parked and the team

announced that the engine had failed.

This handed a lead of no less than nine laps to the works entry, which was never again challenged. The Jaguars were a little off the top pace, and all three cars failed to finish, the last to go retiring out of a strong second place on the Sunday morning when a tyre burst. The Brun team secured that position, and the second-string Joest car was third. Thus, the leading results were dominated, yet again, by Porsches.

The low spirits of the Group C circus were revived by a memorable race meeting at the Norisring, the little street circuit in the pre-war Nazi stadium in Nuremberg. Run in hot weather in front of a big and enthusiastic crowd, this was to have been a 360 km event in two parts. The track is used only once each year and there are merely temporary pit facilities. The fixture, however, also counted towards the German National Championship, which is contested by almost all the Porsche privateers. They insisted on close adherence to the German rules, and the organisers complied. Therefore the Norisring event became a single, all-out thrash over only 180 km, with only one driver being allowed for each of the 24 cars.

This made a nonsense of the World Cham-

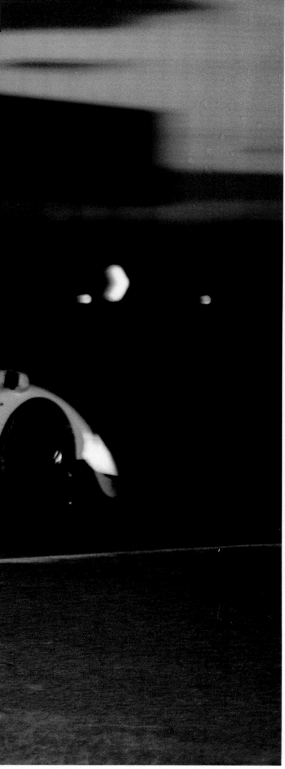

Jaguar enlivened the Group C scene with their splendid XJR-6s but speculation over a successful return to Le Mans by the British team was to be gradually worn down by mechanical problems.

Hans Stuck presses on towards his second successive Drivers' Championship (shared with Derek Bell) in the works Porsche.

pionship and caused all manner of intra-team problems. It was indicative of the political weakness of the World series teams, and of the uncaring attitude of FISA, that the German contest was allowed to take precedence.

The factory Porsche team was also pitching for the National title with a specially built, lightweight sprint car for Stuck, so that Bell had to arrange a drive in a private Porsche in an attempt to add to his own score. Stuck spent some time in passing Ludwig's Joest Porsche, but then established a useful lead. A transmission problem, however, delayed him and, amid much excitement, Ludwig went on to score a fine, narrow victory over the Jaguars of Cheever and Warwick.

Neither Bell nor Stuck, as it happened, scored points. They teamed up again at Brands Hatch in the Norisring-winning car, which was hired for the occasion from the Joest stable. However, the race was won in great style by the RLR team's Porsche, driven by Wollek and Baldi; but Bell and Stuck were second after the Jaguars again failed to finish. Thirty cars started.

Now enjoying a substantial points lead, the Anglo–German pairing gave Jerez a miss. Jaguar responded by sending three cars to Spain, bidding

to place both Warwick and Cheever back in contention for the title. This was another race run over 360 km and one that team should have won with ease. The track suited the cars and the opposition was thin, with a mere 17 entries. Instead, it proved a mightmare for Jaguar from the moment when all three cars spun off in the very first corner, in the silliest incident of the season.

Two of the cars retired in any case, but Warwick, teamed with Lammers, recovered to finish third, keeping his hopes alive. The race, run in oppressive heat, resulted in a 1-2 for Brun Motorsport after a good scrap between the winners, Larrauri and Pareja Mayo, and teammates Brun and Jelinski.

After missing three races, Rothmans Porsche came back at the Nürburgring. The race featured 31 entries and was held in appalling weather conditions, which had disastrous consequences. Eventually, one of the many incidents brought out a pace car but, either due to the dreadful visibility or because of inadequate signalling, the five leading drivers raced on, unaware that the event had been brought under the yellow flag. With a ghastly inevitability, the leaders came up behind the pace car queue. A chain reaction followed and in the massive accident that occurred, both the factory Porsches were destroyed. Stuck and Mass were fortunate to escape unharmed.

The race was stopped (an overdue decision by the organisers), and the restart was run without Porsche's German private teams, Brun, Joest and Kremer. These withdrew their cars in protest at what they saw as organisational irresponsibility. The restart featured a battle between the Sauber-Mercedes of Thackwell and Pescarolo and the Jaguar of Warwick and Lammers. The Sauber was a revelation at this event: having clearly the best package for the very wet conditions, the car had led the first part of the race with ease. The

rain, however, ceased and when the track began to dry out the Jaguar closed the gap and took the lead.

The team then suffered its only engine failure of the season, allowing the Sauber to come through to score an unexpected triumph. That, in itself, gave the series a very welcome boost.

Another came at Spa, where the most thrilling race of the year took place. Five cars disputed the lead throughout and the excitement endured to the final lap. Boutsen, leading with the Brun Porsche co-driven by Jelinski, ran short of fuel and, when his engine faltered, Warwick was on his tail. Coming out of the very last corner, both men dashed for the line, but this time the Jaguar engine died as a result of poor fuel pick-up. Boutsen won by a couple of lengths.

Although virtually out of fuel, Bell lurched across the line in third place. He and Stuck now had the title sewn up unless they could be unplaced in the Fuji finale with Warwick finishing first or second.

Third on the grid, with the Jaguar languishing on the ninth row in the face of the very strong turbo opposition from the Japanese teams, Bell and Stuck had every reason for confidence before the start. In the race, however, they fell far behind the leaders after a driveshaft broke in a pit stop. Meanwhile Warwick, again teamed with Lammers, made startling progress towards the front of the field . . .

Towards the end, the car was in second position which was all they needed to give them not just the the Drivers' crown (to Warwick), but also the Teams' Championship to Jaguar. But then the engine lapsed onto six cylinders when an ignition wire came adrift. Although it was quickly fixed, the pit stop cost the car one place. Third was not enough.

Immediately afterwards, the organisers had the Jaguar still second behind the winning Joest

Porsche of Ghinzani and Barilla, but ahead of the Brun entry of Jelinski and Dickens. On the rostrum, Warwick was even hailed as the new World Champion. But further scrutiny of the scoring computers confirmed that the Jaguar had finished third, to the delight not only of the departed Bell and Stuck, but also Brun Motorsport which thus clinched the Teams' title.

Jaguar team principals alleged that in trying to establish the true result, the organisers had relied on Porsche's computer, so they immediately protested. FISA had not heard the protest when this report was written, but not even Jaguar believed that it would be upheld; the team was making its protest on the point of principle.

THE CAST

Brun Motorsport, owned by Swiss Walter Brun but based in Germany at Gundelfingen, fielded two new Porsche 962C cars (built at its own workshop around monocoques supplied by the factory) plus its ex-Canon Type 956. With impressive sponsorship from Fortuna cigarettes, Torno construction, Jaegermeister tonic drinks and other companies, it contested every race and achieved an impressive reliability record, with 17 finishes from its 25 starts.

With a programme of this size, this highly professional team should, perhaps, have had the championship covered before the final round. But it failed to achieve full competitiveness early in the season. This can be chiefly put down to tyres. In the search for a performance advantage against opposition equipped, in the main, with similar cars, Brun took up an offer from Michelin whose Group C involvement was to be reduced by the partial withdrawal of the works Lancia team. At first, Michelin struggled to produce tyres compatible with the team's Porsches but, as the season progressed, a programme of constant development yielded spectacular rewards.

After being midfield qualifiers, the Brun team cars ended the season with a string of four pole positions and won fine victories at Jerez and Spa. The Teams' Championship, therefore, was won not only through consistency from a three-car effort but also through the late-season pace of strong drivers like Thierry Boutsen, Oscar Larrauri and Frank Jelinski.

Boutsen, although still tending to be unlucky, was outstanding, while Larrauri coped superbly with the relative inexperience and lack of speed of his regular co-driver, Jesus Pareja Mayo. Jelinski was the 'find' of the season, which he started in the cockpit of a Group C2 Gebhardt. Once given the chance in C1, he matured very quickly and finished as team manager Peter Reinisch's most successful driver, with a win, two second places and a third.

The runner-up in the Teams' series, whose top four placings were decided in the final round, was Joest Racing. It fielded its ageing but highly accomplished Porsche 956 cars in the livery of Taka-Q fashion, Blaupunkt hi-fi and Sachs shock absorbers. Based at Abtsteinach and managed by Domingos Piedade, the team centred its programme on Klaus Ludwig and Paolo Barilla with the car that had won Le Mans in 1984-85.

When parked mid-race, this extraordinary car (whose career of 54 races has produced 43 finishes in the top three) was in line to score a hat-trick in the 24-Hours. Then Ludwig took it to victory at the Norisring, whilst in Rothmans colours it brought Bell and Stuck second place at Brands Hatch. The Fuji win by Barilla and Piercarlo Ghinzani ended the season on a high note for Reinhold Joest's team (a Goodyear customer), in which it scored 10 finishes from 14 starts

Third place was shared by Dunlop's runners, the two tobacco-sponsored factory teams of Jaguar and Porsche.

Silk Cut Jaguar Team, run for the Coventry company by Tom Walkinshaw Racing out of Kidlington and managed by Roger Silman, fielded the most impressive line-up of the series. The uprated version of the XJR-6, first raced in August 1985, was a classy race car, generating up to 70 per cent more downforce than the rival Porsches. The atmospheric V12 engine now produced ample horsepower and was on the mark as regards fuel economy.

The drawbacks of the Jaguar engineering package were twofold. First, it was vulnerable to any factor – changeable weather, a longish race period under the yellow – that would release more fuel to the turbocharged cars because these could use higher boost pressure later in the race. Second, the cars were curiously unreliable insofar as a myriad of little things tended to go wrong. Misfires, poor fuel pick-up, minor transmission failures, detached oil lines – all these things stymied the team's promising efforts.

Jaguar had targeted both the Drivers' and the Teams' titles, and TWR ran a full programme of all nine races, taking 12 finishes from 20 starts. In Eddie Cheever, Derek Warwick and Jean-Louis Schlesser, Jaguar had plenty of pace, although Gianfranco Brancatelli was a mite disappointing after winning the European Touring Car title the year before. Other well-known contenders, such as Jan Lammers, Martin Brundle and Win Percy, also drove for Jaguar on occasion.

The high point was obviously its outstanding win at Silverstone, but the team might also have won at Monza, Brands Hatch, Jerez and the Nürburgring. In most cases, mechanical problems of some kind intervened, but in Spain it was the drivers who let the team down: in the first corner, Warwick collided with Brancatelli, also sending Cheever off the road!

Growing rivalry between Warwick and Cheever ultimately proved to be unhealthy for the team. They were split mid-series. Both continued to race well and they finished the season third and fifth respectively in the points table.

Peter Falk's factory Porsche team ran a reduced programme of six events, plus the Norisring with its Blaupunkt-sponsored 'sprint' car. Using two new 962Cs for the longer events, it spent the season experimenting with the dual-clutch, electronically controlled PDK transmission. Designed to allow the driver to make shifts without lifting, this was effective, but added weight and proved to be less reliable than hoped. At the end of the year, an ABS braking system was added to the package.

The 1985 Champions, Derek Bell and Hans-Joachim Stuck were paired again (abbreviated as 'BEST') while Bob Wollek replaced the retired Jacky Ickx as partner to Jochen Mass ('JOB'). BEST had all the luck. JOB finished down the order in two events after being delayed and failed to finish three more. At Fuji, with only Jochen's Le Mans pole to show for their efforts, they were released from their commitment and replaced by Henri Pescarolo and by Al Holbert, the 1986 IMSA Champion who had also shared the BEST entry to win Le Mans.

This was the highlight of the season for Rothmans Porsche, the victory at Monza having been inherited. The low point came at the Nürburgring, where both the team's entries were destroyed in the pace car accident in which it was pure luck that no other cars became involved. The T-car and the converted sprinter had to be used for the last two races.

BEST amassed most of their points in the opening three races, finishing first, second and first. Their last three produced only the out-of-fuel

third placing at Spa. In fact, they would not have won the title had they not personally raised the sponsorship (most of it from Rothmans) to hire Joest Racing's car so as to finish second at Brands Hatch. Theirs is a powerful combination, Derek's guile and experience perfectly complementing Hans-Joachim's pace and aggression. Bell maintains his top pace and, in all his years with the team, has never once seriously crashed a factory Porsche. Stuck, meanwhile, is rated by the team as probably its fastest-ever driver – quicker on his day, perhaps, than even the late and still-lamented Stefan Bellof.

Consistency paid off with fifth place for John Fitzpatrick Racing, whose old-type Porsche 956 was backed by Danone dairy produce for Spaniards Emilio de Villota and Fermin Velez. David Prewitt's charges were never challengers for the lead, but the team did eight events and survived Le Mans in fourth place, following up with a third in the decimated Nürburgring race.

The rain in Germany ideally suited the Kouros-Mercedes fielded in just five races by Peter Sauber. Backed by Yves St Laurent, the Swiss-based car outpaced all comers when the track was at its wettest, thanks to its aerodynamic pack, its Goodyear tyres and the torque of its twin-turbo, low-boost, 5-litre V8 engine. Mike Thackwell and Henri Pescarolo raced as they liked after the Jaguars had wilted, scoring a win that had been wildly unexpected even by the team itself.

For dry conditions, the car needed more power, and elsewhere Sauber's season was disappointing. John Nielsen, Christian Danner and Dieter Quester also drove, but the two-car Le Mans effort was a mechanical *débâcle*.

Richard Lloyd Racing ran its self-built Porsche (with its very rigid honeycomb chassis) for its German sponsor, Liqui Moly additives, using a variety of drivers who included, notably, Bob Wollek (when not committed to the factory team) and Mauro Baldi. This pair, ably managed by Keith Greene, scored a very fine win at Brands Hatch and, with Klaus Niedzwiedz, Baldi was a strong second at the 'Ring.

James Weaver was another RLR team driver, and also raced for Kremer during a season of freelancing. The Kremer brothers were badly affected by poor Jo Gartner's still-unexplained accident at Le Mans, and never fully recovered. Ultimately, the Köln team managed to replace the lost car and ended the year on a note of optimism when Bruno Giacomelli and Volker Weidler came fourth at Fuji. But the team, sponsored by SAT additives, Kenwood hi-fi and others, never improved on the third placing by the highly talented Gartner and Tiff Needell at Silverstone.

The cars described above made the core of the series regulars, along with the Obermaier team's circumspectly run Porsche 956 and the Porsche-engined March entries of the low-budget Cosmik and RC Racing teams (the latter a GTP runner).

Cesare Fiorio's Martini Lancia ran only at Monza and Silverstone, using a new car based on the very quick 1985 LC2 model. Both races were started from the pole, thanks to Andrea de Cesaris. Just before the Norisring event, test driver Giacomo Maggi was killed at Fiat's La Mandria testing circuit, and this ended the programme prematurely.

While team-mate Alessandro Nannini went on to find some drives with the Kremer Porsche team, de Cesaris was invited to co-drive Bruno Giacomelli in a Lancia privately entered by Gianni Mussato, but this inexperienced team only appeared at the Norisring and Brands Hatch. At the end of the year, Giacomelli wrote off the car in an Interserie race at Zeltweg.

The World series suffered, yet again, from the caution of the Japanese manufacturers, especially Nissan and Toyota. Both now have very good Group C cars for their booming national championship, Nissan's built by March Engineering, Toyota by the TOM's team to a Dome design. Unfortunately both manufacturers lost face at Le Mans, and failed to show at the front on home ground at Fuji. No doubt they will continue to defy all efforts to persuade them to mount a more ambitious programme in the FIA series, in which they would be very welcome and would soon become highly competitive with their powerful turbo engines and impressive engineering.

Mazda did Silverstone, Le Mans and Fuji with new, triple-rotary powered GTP entries, backed by Lucky Strike cigarettes. They may expand this participation if a move into Group C1 can be made with competitive machinery.

GROUP C2

Like the championship overall, the 700-kilo, 330-litre division had a highly competitive season with the Teams' title undecided as they went into the finale at Fuji.

The crown was claimed magnificently by Hugh McCaig's Ecurie Ecosse, whose very neat new car was powered by a specially built race version of the Metro 6R4 rally engine, a 3-litre atmospheric V6. Factory interest in the Richard Williams-managed project increased during the season and, after suffering engine problems in the opening races of its programme at Silverstone and Le Mans, Austin Rover's competition engineering

turned the new unit into a torquey, powerful and reliable sports-prototype motor. Indeed, the slippery Ecosse design was never beaten again.

Ray Mallock won at Brands Hatch with David Leslie, and at the Nürburgring, Spa and Fuji with Belgian rally star Marc Duez. The Scottish-owned team won the title by just two points, thanks to a fourth placing at Le Mans with its older Cosworth car, driven by three American rent-a-drivers.

The reigning champions, pipped at the post, had to settle for a repeat of the Drivers' title for Gordon Spice and Ray Bellm. This was a notable effort, for the Jeff Hazell-run Spice Engineering team equipped itself with its first in-house design, called the Spice Fiero as it was based on an IMSA GTP project initiated on behalf of Pontiac. The Cosworth-engined Spice did not show the exceptional reliability of the team's 1985 Tiga, but it did finish all its races. The results were good: wins at Silverstone and Jerez, three seconds, two thirds and a sixth. But in the end it was not enough to resist the late-season charge by Ecosse.

For a while, the series was led by Ian Harrower's highly respected ADA Engineering team with its updated 1984 Gebhardt-Cosworth, the Le Mans winner with team owner Evan Clements aboard with Tom Dodd-Noble. The London team also gained two seconds, a third and two fourths, and recovered well after a heavy accident at Brands Hatch.

The remaining class victories fell to Fritz Gebhardt's own team with its similar 1985 chassis, Frank Jelinski and Stanley Dickens winning at Monza, Dickens in a fine solo effort at the Norisring. The rest of the team's series was half-hearted, however, after its patron had succeeded in getting these drivers into the Brun Porsche C1 team.

The 1985 series-winning car was sold to Italy's Kelmar racing and it ran as reliably as ever, putting its best driver, Pasquale Barberio, into contention for a while. Shortage of funds prevented a stronger effort. Another team that might have done better belonged to Martin Schanche, the rallycross champion running a GTP-type Argo JM-19 fitted with a 1.8 turbo Zakspeed four-cylinder. This quick car, the only Goodyear user in a class dominated by Avon, was a very strong qualifier, and was the only entry to appear in all nine races. Reliability was the problem; the team recovered from Schanche's big practice accident at Silverstone but achieved just three third placings, failing to finish five times.

There were occasional bursts of competitiveness from Roy Baker's semi-works Tiga team, using turbo 1.7 fours from the stillborn Ford RS1700 rally project, especially when Thorkild Thyrring was at the wheel. Will Hoy sometimes drove Hugh Chamberlain's Hart turbo-engined Tiga and made it fly, but otherwise the C2 class was made up of several also-rans. If there was wide variety among the chassis/engine packages, so there was with regard to the relative professionalism of the teams. But the ones at the front were very, very good, well managed and well sponsored. The time may well be near when the C2 category could sustain its own races at the 'supersprint' meetings.

The Martini Lancia of de Cesaris and Nannini
started from pole and finished second at Monza.
Photo: Keith Sutton

ROVER HAS THE LAST BARK

Cliff-hanging finishes are not the sole prerogative of Formula 1 or Sports-Prototype racing. The 1986 Touring Car Championship was not won until the fourteenth and final round. In the end it came down to a duel between two of the nice guys in motor racing. From Dorset came Win Percy – experienced, sympathetic, yet always fast – ranged against the young Venetian, Roberto Ravaglia. He is known within his team as 'Il Gondoliere' and described by BMW Motorsport as 'one of the cornerstones of our success' since he began winning with the 635CSi in 1984 . . . and among the established marques, BMW is itself a cornerstone of touring car racing. When it is not dominating it is waiting in the wings preparing to make an entrance, as it did in 1986. Rover, on the other hand, continues to change in character. The 800 Series has taken over in the marketplace; the V8-engined SD1 is obsolete. The announcement of the withdrawal of Rover from racing shortly before the end of '86 season came as no big surprise – but it made Percy's run for home all the more poignant.

Even without Rover, touring car racing is set to reach greater heights in the future, bringing more variety as more manufacturers take an interest. for, despite the lack of media coverage generally, a cursory look at any Channel 7 video from Mount Panorama is enough to demonstrate the possibilities for the sport at world level.

The secret of success was discovered in 1982, when Group A was introduced. Until then, saloon car formulae had been as flighty as those for sports cars. BMW had had things all its own way in the Group 2 days; Group A racing provides good, competitive events. If it is properly handled from the legislative and administrative point of view, a better set of regulations is hard to imagine. So far, however, there has been little effort to deal promptly with disputes affecting results, so much of the season can pass without anyone being prepared to provide an official championship 'situation report'; in the meantime opportunities to promote a superb series of races are thereby lost.

Despite the lack of coverage in Europe, Group A has heightened World awareness of the possibilities of touring car racing, chiefly because of Australia's adoption of the formula. That 'Down Under' television coverage mentioned earlier (from Bathhurst in particular) has provided exemplary entertainment and it has created folk heroes. Several of the most famous of them were in Europe for the start of the TCC (formerly ETC) season, and Allan Grice gave the series a new look when he took a 5-litre Holden V8 into an early lead at Monza in March. There were other events in which he and his compatriot Peter Brock went ahead of their European rivals, only to lose out later. Nevertheless, the new Australian approach impressed everyone and brought to Europe a breath of fresh air, the like of which had not been felt since battling Bob Jane first crossed the world a quarter of a century ago. (The forceful Grice was to be rewarded for his efforts when he returned home to win the Bathhurst classic.)

The first two races of the 1986 TCC saw the Rover team (run by TWR) in sparkling and confident form; Tom Walkinshaw and Win Percy shared victory at Monza and Donington to move into a healthy lead. But the obsolescent SD1 was to have an increasingly hard time as the season progressed. However, a vital strategic ploy was used in Austria in mid-season when team chief Walkinshaw radioed-in from his stricken car. Promptly, Percy was switched to Armin Hahne's vehicle to maintain the championship lead on his own, and he did so by treating his Rovers wisely despite constant tyre trouble. There was September solace when Jeff Allam and good old Denny Hulme won the TT, the oldest motor race of all, for Rover.

Rüdi Eggenberger led the new Ford assault, with the turbocharged Sierra (Ford's Mustang having never made the grade as a Group A car except in Australia). It was a year of frustration for the talented Swiss driver whose BMWs had been quickest of all in 1984 and who had prepared the champions' Volvos in '85. An end-of-term victory augured well for Ford's 1987 chances.

Volvo's '86 effort was concentrated on the Belgian RAS organisation, and the turbocharged 240 drivers *could* have come out top once again had not the grey areas of the scrutineering bay become quite so dark. Incorrect fuel and oversize fuel tanks led to disqualifications which '85 co-champion Thomas Lindström could ill-afford and which showed that Volvo still lacks judgement in paddock politics. After all, everyone 'stretches' the rules and the more experienced teams are adept at playing this game – but without throwing the ball away as Volvo did.

Apart from a great win at Spa, BMW had experienced a poor 1985 season. Homologation of new components brought the white chargers of Herbert Schnitzer right back into contention, however. The 635 was alive and well again, and whenever the hares – Ford, Holden, Rover or Volvo – tripped up even slightly, the raucous BMW 'tortoises' would take advantage of the situation. With twelve races gone and two to go, BMW had scored four outright victories; Roberto Ravaglia had played a part in three of them, twice with Gerhard Berger and once with Emanuele Pirro's help.

And there was another BMW rearguard action by now. The first few years of Group A had seen almost total domination of the 1.6 to 2.5 litre class by GTV6 drivers who had given Alfa Romeo the Manufacturers' title every time. Although the turbocharged Alfa 75 was making its presence felt towards the end of 1986, the year saw the emergence of the Mercedes-Benz 190E and the BMW 325i as Division Two's leading contenders. BMW experience, and particularly that of Wilfried ('Winnie') Vogt, ensured that the Ludwig Linder-entered 325i took the lion's share of the class wins. Indeed, at this stage of the season, Vogt's points-score was such that the 41-year-old textile businessman from Tiengen *could* have become champion driver. The Manufacturers' title was already settled: Toyota Corollas had taken the sub-1.6 litre class every time – up to now.

Round 13 at Jarama saw the Walkinshaw/Percy Rover Vitesse, so consistently a leading finisher all year, heading for the chequered flag from pole position, when the engine began to cut out intermittently. The car kept going but, shortly before the finish, the Ravaglia/Pirro BMW swooped in to give the Schnitzer team just the 'kill' it needed. Percy still had the most points but, like Mansell in Formula 1, he was having to discard valuable scores. Vogt's chances evaporated, however, when a suspension breakage took him off-course. Nevertheless, it was another Linder 325i which was to take Division Two honours. Division One saw the Toyota teams in trouble and beaten for the first time by an Audi 80.

And so, neck-and-neck, the teams went to Estoril on 19 October, which was to be the day when Ford became the fourth race-winning marque in the 1986 Touring Car Championship. But, above all, it was the greatest day in the fine career of Win Percy, whose second place in the race secured the title for him . . . by just one point!

TWR took a full team of top-rate drivers to back the Walkinshaw/Percy partnership. Dunlop had managed to some extent to overcome the tyre-wear trouble (blamed largely on excessive curing) and the Rover men could afford a little practice gamesmanship *and* take pole position again. 'We just had to go for it, all weekend' said an exhausted Walkinshaw. 'We could have gone ahead in the race, but we had oil surge and, by staying just behind the leaders, we could freewheel the hairpins.' With the BMWs out of the picture and Volvo in trouble again, the Rovers' 2-3-4 finish behind the Soper/Niedzwiedz Sierra made certain that Percy's title was safe. Young Ravaglia's day will come. As for Tom Walkinshaw – winner of more races than anyone since Group A began – it was as though the scales had tipped TWR's way again after its near miss (through Derek Warwick) a little earlier.

Next season will be the 25th for the European Touring Car Championship and the first of the World Touring Car Championship. If FISA and the administrators of Group A racing can bring together the loose ends, ensure that disputes and discontent are not allowed to linger *and* provide a proper record (no matter how provisional) between each race, then European and World class touring car racing must surely be ready for much greater media interest than it has received up till now.

Opposite page: Denny Hulme put his name on the Tourist Trophy one more time.

The 1986 Champion, Win Percy (right), applauds his rival Roberto Ravaglia after a win for the BMW driver, shared with Gerhard Berger (left).

Holden gave the series a new look; Rover withdrew at the end of a successful year *(below)*.

Volvo, Mercedes-Benz and BMW highlighted the growing appeal of the series *(bottom)*.

211

THE NEW ROV

Forget the norm, the expected, the lack-lustre. Brush aside all thoughts of compromise.

Instead, feast your eyes on the new Rover Sterling. Stand back and appreciate the timeless elegance and clean lines of the car. And not merely because they please the eye. The pure aerodynamic shape helps to reduce the drag factor to a minimum providing you with a smooth, confident ride as well as a haven of peace and quiet.

Also, the longer you spend at the wheel of the Sterling the more you'll grow to love the relaxed, almost serene atmosphere in the car.

The electronically adjusted Connolly hide seating, complemented by an abundance of walnut, proves that traditional luxury still sits comfortably in today's hi-tech age.

While air-conditioning, an in-car computer and a seat that remembers your ideal driving position all remind you that progress too has its advantages.

Other comforts and refinements include a powered glass sunroof.

ER 800 SERIES

head-lamp power wash and anti-lock braking. And, for your relaxation, there's the eight speaker, stereo radio/cassette with a hi-power amplifier, boasting 20 watts per channel.

Mind you, the Sterling isn't simply luxury on wheels. It's first and foremost a car to be driven.

The 2.5 litre, V6 fuel-injected engine and its twenty four valves see to that. Generating full-blooded power that will take you to over 130 mph.* (Autobahns only, please.)

But the real excitement comes in the way the Sterling handles that power. The front wheel drive, light body weight and double wishbone front suspension all combine to produce handling yet to be achieved by other luxury saloons.

Providing you with mile upon mile of effortless yet exhilarating driving.

The new Rover 800 Series.

Never before has such elegance handled so beautifully.

ROVER

Ivan Capelli and his championship-winning March
86B; a genuine privateer effort.

By IAN PHILLIPS

UP AND RUNNING

Keith Sutton

Last year's first-ever Formula 3000 Review was headlined 'An Encouraging Start'. What could not be appreciated at the time was just how significant that encouragement was. The reality was brought home at the opening race of 1986 when 37 cars appeared, more than double the average 1985 entry of 17. Against most predictions, the pattern continued throughout the season, with 70 drivers racing 41 different cars in 11 races. With grids rather shortsightedly limited to 26 cars, the average of 11 non-qualifiers per event became an embarrassment. The formula was almost too popular among the competitors for its own good.

Nevertheless, Formula 3000 still has a long way to go before the paying public accepts it for what it is – plain, old-fashioned motor racing. Outside Grand Prix racing, the sport is still struggling to attract worthwhile crowds. At $150,000 a race, F3000 cannot be a guaranteed money-maker to promotors in the current economic climate.

The competition this year was close with near-equality of engines and chassis. The racing matched it. The 26-car grids were covered, on average, by 2.2 seconds and in the majority of races the winning margins were less. The victory spoils were shared by seven different drivers.

The outcome of the championship was yet another vindication of the concept of the formula and, to a much greater degree than in 1985, it developed into a driver's series. In Ivan Capelli the title had gone to the best driver and his Genoa Racing team was about as genuine a privateer operation as possible. On a budget just shy of £200,000, their March 86B was virtually unchanged from the day it was delivered. When the team secured the title at the final round, their Heine Mader-prepared Cosworth DFV engine was at its fifth successive race meeting and their Avon tyres were the same as those used by everyone else in the series. By careful and dedicated effort the three-man team simply made best use of materials which were available to every competitor.

The only major change made to the championship rules over the winter stipulated that only one make of tyres would be used. The previous season's competition between Bridgestone and Avon had been healthy in some respects but it had increased costs. FISA wisely decided that it should be a one-make formula from 1986 through to 1988 and awarded the contract to Avon, undisputedly the best supplier of contract tyres in the business.

The 9000 rpm limit was retained and Glen Monk came up with an improved electronic device which performed faultlessly throughout the season.

The championship status was upgraded from European to Intercontinental, although this ultimately meant little as the final three races scheduled for Curaçao and Brazil were cancelled. It is imperative that future calendars are firm; chasing sponsorship money is difficult enough without having to explain away cancelled events, which reflects badly on the administration of the sport.

In the wake of the March 85B's success in 1985, it was not surprising that the Bicester company fulfilled the majority of chassis orders, with 20 of their Andy Brown-designed 86Bs being sold. The car was still based around the 1984 F2 honeycomb/carbon monocoque with detail alterations to the aerodynamics and rear suspension. The opposition came in the form of two clean-sheet designs from Ralt and Lola.

When Ron Tauranac creates a new production line, the world watches with interest. For Formula 3000 he reverted to an aluminium-skinned monocoque with numerous bulkheads to give it strength. This was a potentially heavy construction but the use of the lighter Hewland FT200 gearbox, suitably beefed up, more than compensated and the car was well within the 540 kg minimum weight limit. Tauranac also spent a great deal of time ensuring that he could use a pullrod rear suspension which was the envy of other designers.

Ralph Bellamy had left March long before his 85B design took last year's championship and he erased memories of the dismal 1985 efforts when he resurfaced at Lola to come up with his purposeful T86/50 design. Based around a full carbon-fibre tub, it was Bellamy's update on the 85B which proved less radical than March's own.

As well as fielding two-car factory-based teams, Lola sold six cars and Ralt four. The works Ralt team brought the first alternative to the Cosworth DFV engine into the formula, having exclusive use of a Honda V8 design developed for the purpose by John Judd in England. March again relied on leading customers, specifically the Onyx and Oreca teams, to do their development work.

Nobody else produced a production design but RAM, AGS and Minardi all fielded cars irregularly. The pretty RAM was a development of their F1 car which was really too big; the AGS was an update on the JH20 model which became a strong contender in late-1985; the Minardi was based on the unsuccessful 1984 F2 car and never looked like being any better.

As ever, the season began at Silverstone in a race that was torn apart by bad weather. For this race FISA agreed that 36 cars could start providing they were within the 110 per cent qualification ruling. Lola quickly showed that they meant business this year when Pascal Fabre took pole position for the works teams as the track dried out. Despite crashing very heavily in the warm-up, it was Britain's Russell Spence who led initially but after two laps the rain caused the race to be stopped. At the restart Spence led again in the Eddie Jordan March, then German Volker Weidler took over in the Bromley Ralt, and later Emanuele Pirro in an Onyx March. An accident caused by terrible visibility forced complete abandonment of the race at half-distance. Fabre, second in both parts, was declared the winner ahead of Pirro, but only half championship points were awarded.

The second round was at Vallelunga, this short Italian circuit having previously been limited to 22 cars on the grid. Although the number allowed was upped to 26, it still meant that, with 37 entries, there had to be qualifying. The entry list was divided into odd and even numbers for 40-minute pre-qualifying sessions, the top 13 from each group going through to official qualifying.

Mike Thackwell won at Pau for Ralt-Honda *(right)*.

Luis Sala was the victor of the street race in Birmingham *(below)*.

Below right: The Honda V8 in the works Ralts provided an alternative to the ubiquitous DFV.

Pierluigi Martini; the F1 also-ran made good as an F3000 winner *(centre right)*.

Emanuele Pirro; lost heart mid-season *(far right)*.

Main picture: Formula 3000 proved a popular training ground for F1.

For the remaining races, the odd and even numbers had their own practice and qualifying, with the top 13 in each group starting the race according to their position within the group, so, for example, the fifth-fastest in each group would start on row 5. This was perhaps the fairest arrangement because it at least gave each driver a full day of running, although it was hard to see why at circuits like Spa and the Österreichring which had a capacity for 36 cars, it was not possible for every entrant to race. A way of giving the non-qualifiers some sort of race ought to be found if the numbers remain high in 1987.

Back to round 2. After a disappointing Silverstone, top 1985 rookie Ivan Capelli made his presence felt on home ground, taking pole position and an easy win in his Genoa Racing March. An indication of how close the racing was going to be during the year was made clear in the battle for second place. Fabre eventually pipped Pirro, Mauricio Gugelmin (March) and Satoru Nakajima (Ralt-Honda) with just three seconds covering the four of them.

Next, it was on to the annual Pau round-the-houses event in France. Pirro took his first position of the year and alongside him was his old adversary from the previous year, Mike Thackwell, guesting for the Ralt-Honda team in place of Nakajima. For the second successive year Pirro dominated the event only for a mechanical problem to rob him of this cherished victory. Thackwell was always shadowing him and immediately took advantage of Pirro's problems to give Honda their first victory in this category.

A week later F3000 was supporting a Grand Prix for the first time in the season, the excellent Spa circuit being the venue for this peaceful co-existence. Pirro again led the way but made an uncharacteristic error and spun just as he appeared to be getting away from his pursuers. In a fraught race former RAM F1 driver Philippe Alliot (Oreca-March) took a narrow victory from John Nielsen's Ralt-Honda.

Up to this point, the March had been the dominant chassis with the Ralt just about on terms; after Fabre's early success the Lola had faded. But at Imola Avon introduced their A-specification hard control tyre for the summer races and the pattern changed. Former Minardi F1 driver Pierluigi Martini took delivery of a new Ralt for this race and went from being a no-hoper to winner. Capelli was on pole but Martini led from start to finish, beating his fellow-countryman by less than a second. Pirro retired and Capelli took a five-point championship lead.

At Mugello Martini took pole position and led from start to finish, again with a queue of cars behind him, this time led by Michel Ferté (Oreca March). Capelli was a distant third as Pirro struggled in sixth, plainly not enjoying his drive on the A tyres. With two wins from two races, Martini lay second to Capelli in the title race.

Capelli was on pole at Enna but after being pushed off on the first lap he retired from second place with subsequent engine damage. Spain's Luis Sala gave Ralt their third successive win while team-mate Martini recovered from a first-lap spin to claim second place, which moved him into a slender one-point championship lead over Capelli. Sala, who had scored in every race from Pau onwards, moved into third place in the table. It was a good race for Lola with Fabre in third place heading home three of their cars, having overtaken Pirro in the points table.

Supporting the Austrian GP, Capelli again showed his class with a flag-to-flag win from poleman Nielsen. With Martini, Fabre and Pirro out of the points he established the first meaningful points lead of the year – eight.

One of the highlights of the year was to be the Birmingham street race. Sadly, the event was ruined by rain, and again half points had to be awarded after a premature end. The Pavesi team scored a 1-2 with their Ralts, Sala beating

poleman Martini with Ferté third. Capelli, dreaming of his AGS F1 debut the next weekend and not really concentrating, crashed, as did Pirro.

A month later at the Le Mans Bugatti circuit, Avon reintroduced their B-spec tyre. Pirro, who had been promised an F1 drive while visiting the Portuguese GP the previous weekend if he got some good results, was a happy man again. He put his Onyx March on pole and walked away with the race in a event in which all the leading March runners reasserted themselves. Oreca pairing Ferté and Pierre-Henri Raphael were second and third with Capelli fourth. Martini retired with his first mechanical failure of the year and Capelli was again eight points in the lead.

With the South American races cancelled, Jarama suddenly became the final round of the championship. Capelli only had to finish fifth to take the title; Martini was his only challenger, needing to win at all costs to stand any chance.

Pirro was once more on pole but sustained wing damage early in the race, leaving Martini to battle with the Ralt-Hondas of Nielsen and, for the second time, Thackwell. Martini saw them both off as Capelli struggled around in fourth or fifth place. The race had to be stopped for a rain shower and the Pavesi team ruined their chances by being caught tampering with Martini's car during the interlude. Although he took the restart Martini was disqualified from the results, which gave Pirro a second successive win from Ferté and second place in the championship. Capelli's third place was sufficient to give him the title. It was a slightly unsatisfactory end to what had otherwise been a superb series.

Capelli is a worthy champion although one suspects that if Pirro hadn't lost heart mid-season he might have been pushed harder. Both young Italians are classy performers and will represent the formula well in Grands Prix.

Martini's career was revitalised in F3000; he is still young and a bit wild but is very quick and determined – his day will surely come. Michel Ferté's place of strength within the Oreca team was eroded by Alliot's early-season presence but he came back with real determination at the end. Thackwell confirmed he can beat anybody when he makes his rare appearances, but Nielsen had a tough year and failed to add to his 1985 tally of wins. Best newcomers were Sala and Raphanel.

Of the chassis makers, March and Ralt shared the honours with five wins each, but Lola failed to add to their lone early success. But so close was the competition that the main difference between winning and losing came down to preparation and driver ability. Over the season the Genoa March and Capelli just had the edge but the fact that 39 points (out of a maximum of 99) gave them the championship was indicative of how open the contest had been.

Martin Donnelly (right) won the hard way.

Far right: the anticipated struggle between Sala (left) and Wallace did not materialise.

Below: Andy Wallace and Madgwick Motorsport proved their point.

BY DAVID TREMAYNE

PATIENCE REWARDED

If 1985 was a year of change for Formula 3, with the banning of ground effects, the switch to flat bottoms and the graduation of some significant FF2000 teams, 1986 was a year of consolidation. Across its entire spectrum, the formula went from strength to strength.

In Britain, however, things got off to a mixed start. There was some excellent news, with the announcement (expected ever since he raced in the company's colours a couple of times in 1985) that David Hunt had pulled off a great coup and introduced Cellnet, the mobile telephone concern, as his major backer. Cellnet also ran Keith Fine as his team-mate and backed every pound of its racing budget with a similar amount for promotion. It was a reflection of the formula's marketing appeal and potential.

Less happy, though, was the fact that the first race – postponed due to bad weather – was to take place without an overall sponsor, Marlboro having finally pulled out after a successful run. It wasn't until the fourth round, at Silverstone in April, that the BRDC and the BARC finally managed to find a sponsor, when Lucas moved in.

There had also been a more sombre event. During testing for West Surrey Racing at a cold Goodwood in February, Bertrand Fabi had crashed his Ralt RT30 very heavily and succumbed to his injuries. He was the first fatality in the series for many years. In the aftermath, the team which has won more championships than any other and which had been expected under Dick Bennetts' guidance to have another hot favourite in the very quick Canadian, pulled out in order to concentrate instead on F3000. F3 had just lost a very fine driver and its overall yardstick.

As things transpired, the team that took up WSR's mantle turned out to be Madgwick Motorsport, the butt of countless pit lane jokes the previous year when it graduated from FF2000 with the carbon-fibre Reynard 853 powered by Saab engines. The whole project was something of a disaster, but circumstances brought together team boss Robert Synge and Andy Wallace, and almost straight away a tight relationship was formed.

Synge sought to polish up his team's tarnished image while Wallace had even more to prove. If Reynard hadn't become over-confident in 1985 when it had concentrated its energies elsewhere instead of developing its 853, the Oxford driver could well have been champion. Instead he suffered dignified defeat at Mauricio Gugelmin's hands at the final race. Now he was bouncing back in Madgwick's vastly superior Reynard 863 – this time with Volkswagen power.

An extra edge to his challenge was given by the fact that his major rival was Maurizio Sandro Sala, who lined up in Eddie Jordan Racing's Ralt RT30. Sala, of course, had been with Synge since he came to race in Britain, but opted for the proven Ralt chassis. Later, this would also develop into a battle of the radiator giants, for Sala was backed by Britain's major manufacturer Stelrad, while Wallace picked up backing from Warmastyle Racing for Britain midway through the year (Warmastyle being Britain's major importer).

Sala won three of the first four races while Wallace took the second. However, the first of 1986's fuel controversies arose when the latter finished third with fastest lap at Silverstone in April's fourth round. It was held that his octane rating was illegal after a post-race fuel check, although later it was accepted to have been within tolerance and he was reinstated. But that set the scene for debate and controversy over fuel for the rest of the year. In a nutshell, the relevant Statutory Instrument issued by the government called for pump fuel available in Britian to have a lead content of 0.15 grammes per litre, although the RACMSA Blue Book regulations continued to allow 0.40 g/l fuel – which wasn't available. Running engines with reduced lead content led to detonation problems for many who were reluctant to retard their ignitions, and anger grew. Eventually the RACMSA issued a confused statement implying, but not confirming, that it condoned the use of additives such as toluene. From then on the gloves were off and the situation became very confused, several teams admitting that they used additives and pointing out that there was nothing in the regulations to prevent it. Others, Eddie Jordan Racing in particular, insisted this was outside the law of the land. EJR continued to run pump fuel for a long time.

The net effect was to throw into relief the most important aspect of the year: driver psychology. Poor Sala couldn't handle the manner in which, as he saw it, he was beaten by other drivers running less than legal fuel, and for some time his driving suffered. After one retirement and a couple of second places – one by the fantastically narrow margin of 0.25 seconds to Sala after a brilliant scrap at Silverstone Club in May – Wallace won at Silverstone GP and Zandvoort. He was second twice more at Oulton Park and Donington after making bad starts, finished second in Silverstone's August Bank Holiday washout and then really turned on the heat to win the last four races, at Brands Club, Spa, Zolder and Silverstone GP. By Spa he had done enough to clinch the title, but to rub it in at Silverstone's finale he poled – for the 13th time! – 1.2 seconds clear of the rest. That unleashed a whole new series of accusations about locked diffs, six-speed gearboxes and tyre softening compounds. The team, of course, denied everything and offered to have its car and rubber checked by anyone, insisting the fantastic dominance was due to its development of the car and Andy's confidence in it. Certainly, the 25-year-old Briton looked incredibly smooth and calm all season and was always on the pace. He has that fluid style and unruffled temperament, allied to brilliance as a technical thinker, that marks him out as F1 material, while his relationship with engineer Mick Cook and mechanic Teo de Silva was the formula's most complete.

Sala, one of those really stylish drivers capable of doing impossible things, seemed outpsyched more often than not, and frequently felt victimised, which was a shame since everyone admires his talent and personality. His psychological distress reached its nadir at Zandvoort where he led until he mistook a course car for the pace car and backed off. He was instantly swamped and fell to seventh but then produced a fabulous recovery

ANDY WALLACE – REYNARD VOLKSWAGEN – 1986.

50 No

On a cold wet day at Silverstone Racing Circuit in March 1984, Johnny Dumfries scored the first of a remarkable series of over 50 consecutive Volkswagen wins in British Formula 3 Championship races. The latest of these wins has seen Andy Wallace crowned as British Formula 3 Champion for 1986. These 54 <u>consecutive</u> wins have been achieved using modified Volkswagen Golf GTi engines, and we hope to win many more. But for now, our thanks to:

JOHNNY DUMFRIES – RALT VOLKSWAGEN – 1984.

Out

Johnny Dumfries, Russell Spence, Andy Wallace,
Ross Cheever, Maurizio Sandro Sala,
Martin Donnelly,
Mauricio Gugelmin,
Gerrit van Kouwen,

Dave Scott, Mario Hytten
and Gary Evans.

Volkswagen Motorsport

Damon Hill: a sought-after newcomer (right).

Nicola Larini, Italian Champion (centre right).

David Hunt had to struggle to find success (below).

drive to take him into a very strong second. He won again at Snetterton to regain the championship lead after Wallace's engine blew, but failed to score at Silverstone, Brands, Spa or Zolder and effectively his challenge fell apart in August. It was a pity, since his talent is the equal of Wallace's, but Andy's killer punch was his ability to cope better with the overall pressures of the year.

At one stage it seemed 1986 would provide a Sala versus Wallace version of Senna versus Brundle from '83, but eventually other drivers got in on the act. The best of the bunch was Martin Donnelly, who scored one win less than Sala with his bag of four, each of which was achieved the hard way. He broke his duck at Donington in May, and won again in July when American Dave Simpson was thrown out for running fuel with an illegal octane rating. Donnelly beat Wallace fair and square at Oulton in June and at Silverstone Club's rainstorm in August. At times at the beginning of the year his Frank Nolan/British Telecom Swallow Racing Ralt slipped from the pace but as his experience increased he always posed a major threat and starts 1987 as a pre-season favourite. With Simpson's exclusion, Dutchman Gerrit van Kouwen was the only other driver apart from Wallace, Sala or Donnelly to see a chequered flag first in a race and that was when he triumphed at Thruxton in May. However, by July Pegasus Motorsport had closed its doors and he moved on to Swallow, but somehow he never looked remotely like repeating the 1985 form which brought him three dominant victories. By the end of the year he appeared thoroughly demoralised, and it showed in his driving.

Good news for Britain came in the form of three particular debutants: Damon Hill, Perry McCarthy and Johnny Herbert. Hill was to have partnered Fabi at WSR but was realigned with Murray Taylor and showed flair on many occasions, leading at Oulton Park and Zandvoort. But somehow the late-season races were less kind to him and the anticipated breakthrough never came. McCarthy partnered Wallace at Madgwick, courtesy of Hawtal Whiting, and frankly was a surprise. Few expected much of him after his sporadic FF1600 forays, but he always looked smooth in the Reynard and even a nerve injury which lost him several mid-season races failed to daunt him. His best result was an excellent second to Wallace at Spa, and on several testing occasions he was very close to Andy's pace. Herbert debuted at Donington in July in Mike Rowe's Ralt, through Warmastyle Racing for Britain, finished a sensational fourth, and was soon snapped up by Glenn Waters at Cellnet. Quiet, almost to the point of being monosyllabic, Herbert's smooth graduation guaranteed that with Hill he is one of the most sought-after newcomers.

Another trio of Brits also had their moments in 1986. Julian Bailey ran most of the season, with Swallow Racing, and although his self-confidence veered from one extreme to the other, he proved that he has the basic talent to win. He took the lead in Zandvoort but ultimately had to settle for third. He repeated that result at the other two continental events, at Spa (where he was best Ralt

in superb style) and Zolder, as well as at the wet Silverstone Club in August. When he has the right frame of mind he can win. Tim Davies, in his second season of F3, began well with his Terropol Promotions Ralt but inevitably suffered from the low budget. With the right backing and the right car he can still run with the best, as he proved in the works Reynard 863 at Zolder. Ross Hockenhull, who ran Class B a couple of times in 1985, showed promise in Richard Dutton's Ralt. He began slowly and didn't score any points until Oulton in June where he was sixth, but he also ran well at Zandvoort and came an excellent fifth at Spa. There he led home new sensation Thomas Danielsson, who hauled his Madgwick Reynard from 33rd on the grid to sixth. By finishing fourth at Zolder and reaching second (to Wallace) in the finale, the Swede indicated that he is likely to prove a strong contender in 1987.

Gary Brabham made his long-awaited series debut, and showed that he has all it takes to succeed bar money, while David Hunt, who had fewer worries about that particular commodity, found that F3 is still a very tough nut to crack. Around mid-season he really looked on the brink of a breakthrough, like Hill, but it never quite materialised. Team-mate Fine showed well early on before losing interest and eventually giving up his drive to Herbert. David Scott initially ran the works Reynard via David Price Racing. He finished second to Wallace at Brands in May but left the team shortly afterwards, feeling that he wasn't furthering his career. New Zealander Paul Radisich had a generally disappointing time for Murray Taylor, with a third as his best result, while Ross Cheever, a pace-setter in '84 and '85, had a dreadful time whenever he appeared in a third Cellnet Ralt and quit with only a point to his name; a sad waste.

Class B again ran well throughout the year, providing some fascinating racing, and here seven

drivers shared the wins. Steve Kempton emerged a deserving champion after an excellent year in his Tony Trevor-run Ralt, while Sean Walker, Gary Dunn, Gary Ward, Alastair Lyall, Paul Stott and Andy King all had their share of glory. Steve Pettit, John Roinson and American Lee Perkinson all showed promise at times although none did the full season. Sadly, the year's second tragedy saw Class B runner Dick Parsons die at the wheel of his Solar Racing Reynard at Silverstone in qualifying for the June meeting, after the highly popular Englishman's machine failed to negotiate Woodcote.

On the technical front the confrontation between Reynard and Ralt made for some interesting clashes, with Ralt winning ten races to Reynard's eight, but the latter deservedly winning the title. The fact that this is the first time since 1979 that Ralt has been deposed indicates just how effective Ron Tauranac's cars have been in the Eighties. Chiefly, the torsionally stiffer Reynard seemed to respond better to changes than did the Ralt, which made it easier to set up. It also explained in part why most Ralt runners had some patchy stages through the year, with even Sala and Donnelly dropping off the pace at times. Next year the two manufacturers will be at it again, while there may be more than the one TOM's Toyota which challenged Volkswagen's might as the German engine headed for and achieved its 53rd consecutive win. The TOM's engine was run in one of the Cellnet cars and looks a useful challenger, while we are also promised a very strong Alfa Romeo challenge from Novamotor via JQF Engineering. FF1600 graduate Phil Andrews is set to use this powerplant in a new Reynard 873. The project should also introduce a new gearbox, offering Mike Hewland's astonishingly successful Mk 9 unit some competition at last.

In some ways 1986 was a sad year, not just for

Stefano Modena flew the flag for Reynard in Italy *(left)*.

Yannick Dalmas, French Champion *(below)*.

the deaths of two fine sportsmen, but also for the sight of the RACMSA blundering its way through the minefield of fuel legislation and proving unequal to the task, to the detriment of the series. Next year there will be plenty of Brits to cheer, some paid-for drives to give the impecunious a chance, and some hot FF2000 and FF1600 graduates anxious to make their mark. The signs are that the fuel regulations have finally been altered sensibly, but the otherwise healthy formula really needs to ensure that it is policed properly. Perhaps some people *were* cheating in 1986, as many alleged; maybe they weren't. Whatever the truth of the allegations, it's long past time for the RACMSA, BRDC and BARC to grasp this particular bull by the horns and wring its neck once and for all.

Healthy abroad, too

It wasn't just the Lucas British F3 Championship that was in super-healthy state, numerically and in terms of the level of competition. In both France and Italy in particular F3 had a bumper year, Yannick Dalmas and Nicola Larini proving the men to beat and clinching their respective titles.

Dalmas drove for Hughes de Chaunac's Oreca team, the WSR of France, and proved a consistent pacesetter, even with the likes of Michel Trollé as his team-mate, and the Martini MK49s proved a match for the Ralt RT30s most of the time. Frédéric Delavallade managed to beat them at Rouen but the only other time they were seriously challenged was in the final stages of the year when Jean Alesi's electrifying talent was finally rewarded with two dominant victories in the SNPE Dallara 386. Both Dalmas and Alesi clearly have big futures.

In Italy, Larini and Enzo Coloni team-mate Marco Apicella split most of the spoils between them in their Dallaras, but although Marco began the year the more favoured of the two, Nicola reversed that by the end to win the series with five wins to Apicella's three. Stefano Modena flew the flag for Reynard with three wins, even though he disgraced himself at the Cellnet Superprix at Brands Hatch in August when he bent Dave Price's 863 twice in four laps. Alex Caffi, the former Coloni driver who switched to the Venturini team and debuted so well in the Italian GP at Monza, scored a couple of good wins in his Dallara to maintain his reputation as a man to watch.

In Germany, Dane Kris Nissen finally struck gold in his Volkswagen Motorsport Ralt RT30, but given his experience in the formula his was hardly a walkover. Victories also went to Spaniard Alfonso García de Vinuesa, Argentinian Victor Rosso (a former UK F3 runner), Swiss Gregor Foitek and Hans-Peter Kaufmann and German Bernd Schneider.

Of all the championships, the Italian is undoubtedly the closest fought, with the British and French not too far behind. EFDA boss Dan Partel currently has plans to establish a six-race European Championship. If all the significant teams from each country can afford to fit it into their already hectic schedules and *if* the hotshots in each series have the courage to risk their reputations (many didn't with the Cellnet Superprix), it could be a fascinating venture.

NO STANDING STILL

by David Tremayne

'He breeds ferrets, you know. Go and ask him if you don't believe me!'

Most people in F3 know that when Madgwick Motorsport's Paul Haigh is in that kind of mood anything could be true – or false! But the one thing about Andy Wallace (pictured) over which no doubt hangs is the manner in which he has grasped his opportunity in the Lucas British Championship this season.

A year ago he had just completed his first season in Formula 3, and been pipped literally at the post by Brazilian Mauricio Gugelmin in the fight for the last Marlboro British Championship. By all standards, the newcomer from Oxford had a sensational year, stepping up from FF2000, in which he was considered by most to be a capable but not outstanding driver. He won the runner-up prize in the 1984 Grovewood Awards, regarded as motor racing's Oscars, but he was not universally rated. That didn't bother him. He kept his head down, ignored the pundits and quickly made the most of his chance in Swallow Racing's brand new carbon-fibre-chassised Reynard 853, powered by Volkswagen. He went to the first round at Silverstone, qualified on pole and walked away to a comfortable debut victory that left rivals open-mouthed in his wake. Two more equally polished victories followed at Donington and Thruxton, and Wallace could be relied on to bring his mount home in a good position at other venues until Reynard began to concentrate its efforts elsewhere. The upshot was a mid-season slump from which the team only recovered in the final races, by which time it was just too late. Gugelmin won the title by eight points. He and Wallace's other great rival, Russell Spence, moved on to Formula 3000 for 1986.

Wallace, a former gas fitter, was left in Formula 3. *That* didn't worry him either. In a year in which driver psychology played a tremendously important role, quite simply he proved the best. The combination of Madgwick Motorsport's organisational and technical ability, Reynard's Volkswagen-powered 863 and Wallace's driving proved irresistible. He made a good start to the year, survived a slight performance dip that might have had other drivers outpsyched, and came back stronger than ever. Eight wins were the result. The man who had emulated Jonathan Palmer's feat by

winning his first F3 race, repeated the Doc's other achievement by wrapping up the Lucas British title well before the final race. On the way he had also placed strongly in all the races he finished but didn't win, and even in adversity maintained that cool, calculating approach. Not for him the fiery tantrums or deep depressions of some of his rivals.

Further to underline his point, he annexed both Cellnet non-championship races and proved devastatingly quick earlier in the year when he tested an F3000 March. Now, naturally, he looks to that formula for 1987, while hoping desperately for the big break into Formula 1.

How good is Andy Wallace? Good enough to win from the front as he did at Spa-Francorchamps, or to fight through, as he did at Zandvoort and Zolder . . . or to annihilate the opposition as he did at Silverstone on October. 'He's a little technician', says designer/constructor Adrian Reynard with undisguised respect. 'He understands more about his car and what makes it work than anyone else out there.' On top of which, he's fast and smooth. Watch out for him!

Who will take over Wallace's mantle for 1987? Two names that most naturally spring to mind are Damon Hill and Julian Bailey. From winning motor cycle championships and dabbling in FF2200, the man who is always known to the mass media as 'Graham Hill's boy' showed serious form in FF1600 and made the step up to F3 for 1986 in a

Murray Taylor Racing Ralt RT30 Volkswagen. Immediately he showed flair and promise, to the point where by mid-season he was a good outside bet for victory. Like Bailey, his best race was at Zandvoort, where he looked a strong contender until outfoxed in the closing stages. Without doubt, the potential is there to win next season.

Bailey, as complex a character as ever sat in a racing car, was sometimes right on the pace, sometimes monosyllabically off it. His Swallow Racing Ralt RT30 Volkswagen was always beautifully prepared, yet somehow there were times when he didn't extract its best. Yet at the times when his fluctuating self-confidence was strong, he looked a real threat. He proved it in Holland and both Belgian races, at Spa and Zolder. At Francorchamps in particular he was far and away the leading Ralt driver. If he can believe in himself more, and be more the character at races that he can be *away* from the tracks, he has all the car control and basic speed to mature into next year's champion.

Besides their nationality and basic talent, the other common point to all three drivers is the Volkswagen engine which is based on the Golf GTi unit. Despite being introduced as long ago as July 1981, it was not finally accepted by the Establishment until 1984, when Johnny Dumfries so convincingly won the Marlboro British title. But since then it has amassed an

extraordinary string of wins. It has taken championships in Britain, France and Germany, and by the Silverstone meeting on 5 October had recorded an amazing 57 victories in the British series alone (61 if you include the qualification races held in 1986). No fewer than 53 have been consecutive.

Volkswagen has been closely associated with many young British drivers, including Johnny Dumfries, Russell Spence, Andy Wallace, Andrew Gilbert-Scott, Damon Hill, Julian Bailey, Dave Scott and Martin Brundle and there is every indication that their backing for up-and-coming British talent will continue in 1987.

Lighter and more compact, yet as powerful as its Japanese and Italian rivals, the Engine Developments unit is now almost universal in Britain. Nevertheless, the man behind it is under no illusions. 'In this game you can never afford to be complacent', says John Judd. 'When that happens, sooner or later you stop winning, and when that happens the phone stops ringing and you don't sell engines!'

Accordingly, development continues. The unit is based on the famous injected four-cylinder, single-cam engine from Volkswagen's Golf GTi, the hot hatch that is the choice of so many people on the racing scene. In Germany, Volkswagen Motorsport's head is Klaus-Peter Rosorius. In Great Britain this position is fulfilled by Nigel Walker as Product Manager of the Volkswagen Group, who says, 'The Golf GTi already has a very sporting image – you only have to look in a motor racing paddock to see that. We feel Formula 3 allows us to project an ideal image for our sporting products in Great Britain.'

Road car engines are reaching high levels of sophistication and race units are following suit. Towards the end of 1986 Engine Developments worked in close collaboration with Zytek Engineering in Birmingham, which had developed an advanced electronic engine management system. Already it has proved a great success, and will be available to customers for the new season. It provides superior control of the engine's functions, enhances already impressive reliability and makes it even more efficient. Engine Developments, like Volkswagen itself, has never been a company to stand still.

1986 RESULTS

During 1986, 32 drivers from fourteen countries participated in the season's sixteen Formula 1 races (there were no non-championship events). They were seen in fourteen different makes of car powered by ten makes of engine. Sixteen drivers took part in all 16 races. Alain Prost scored points 13 times, Nigel Mansell 12, Nelson Piquet 11 and Ayrton Senna 10. Senna took eight pole positions, Piquet, Fabi and Mansell winning two each with Rosberg and Prost taking one each. Piquet set the fastest lap seven times, Mansell four, Berger and Prost two while Fabi claimed one.

Driver	Nat.	Date of birth	Car	Rio de Janeiro	Jerez	Imola	Monte Carlo	Spa-Francorchamps	Montreal	Detroit	Paul Ricard	Brands Hatch	Hockenheim	Budapest	Österreichring	Monza	Estoril	Mexico City	Adelaide	World Championship points	No. of Grands Prix started	1st	2nd	3rd	No. of Grand Prix pole positions
Michele Alboreto	I	23/12/56	Ferrari	R	R	10*	R	4	8	4	8	R	R	R	2	R	5	R	R	14	89	5	7	4	2
Philippe Alliot	F	24/7/54	Ligier-Renault	–	–	–	–	–	–	–	–	R	9	R	R	R	6	8		1	33	–	–	–	–
Elio de Angelis†	I	26/3/58	Brabham-BMW	8	R	R	R	R												0	108	2	2	5	3
René Arnoux	F	4/7/48	Ligier-Renault	4	R	R	5	R	6	R	5	4	4	R	10	R	7	15*	7	14	112	7	9	6	18
Allen Berg	CDN	1/8/61	Osella-Alfa Romeo	–	–	–	–	–	–	R	R	DNS²	12	R	R	–	13	16	NC	0	8	–	–	–	–
Gerhard Berger	A	27/8/59	Benetton-BMW	6	6	3	R	10	R	R	R	R	10	R	7	5	R	1	R	17	36	1	–	1	–
Thierry Boutsen	B	13/7/57	Arrows-BMW	R	7	7	8	R	R	NC	NC	R	R	R	7	10	7	R	R	0	57	–	1	–	–
Martin Brundle	GB	1/6/59	Tyrrell-Renault	5	R	8	R	R	9	R	10	5	R	6	R	10	R	11	4	8	38				
Alex Caffi	I	18/3/64	Osella-Alfa Romeo	–	–	–	–	–	–	–	–	–	–	–	NC	–	–	–	–	0	1				
Ivan Capelli	I	24/5/63	AGS-MM	–	–	–	–	–	–	–	–	–	–	–	–	R	R	–	–	0	4				
Andrea de Cesaris	I	31/5/59	Minardi-MM	R	R	R	NQ	R	R	R	R	R	R	R	R	R	R	8	R	0	88	–	2	1	1
Eddie Cheever	USA	10/1/58	Lola-Ford	–	–	–	–	–	–	R	–	–	–	–	–	–	–	–	–	0	86	–	2	5	–
Christian Danner	D	4/4/58	Osella-Alfa Romeo / Arrows-BMW	R	R	R	NQ	R	R	R	11	DNS²	R	R	6	8	11	9	R	1	16				
Johnny Dumfries	GB	26/4/58	Lotus-Renault	9	R	R	NQ	R	R	7	R	7	R	5	R	R	9	R	6	3	15				
Teo Fabi	I	9/3/55	Benetton-BMW	10	5	R	R	7	R	R	R	R	R	R	R	R	8	R	10	2	48	–	–	1	3
Piercarlo Ghinzani	I	16/1/52	Osella-Alfa Romeo	R	R	R	NQ	R	R	R	R	DNS²	R	R	11	R	R	R	R	0	50				
Stefan Johansson	S	8/9/56	Ferrari	R	R	4	10	3	R	R	11*	4	3	3	6	12*	3			23	44	–	2	4	–
Alan Jones	AUS	2/11/46	Lola-Hart / Lola-Ford	R	R		R	R	11*	10	R	R	R	9	R	4	6	R	R	R	4	116	12	7	5	6
Jacques Laffite	F	21/11/43	Ligier-Renault	3	R	R	6	5	7	2	6	DNS²	–	–	–	–	–	–	–	14	175	6	10	16	7
Nigel Mansell	GB	8/8/54	Williams-Honda	R	2	R	4	1	1	5	1	3	3	R	2	1	5	R		70	90	7	3	7	4
Alessandro Nannini	I	7/7/59	Minardi-MM	R	R	R	NQ	R	R	R	R	R	R	R	R	R	NC	14		0	15	–	–	–	–
Jonathan Palmer	GB	7/11/56	Zakspeed	R	R	R	12	13	R	8	R	9	R	10	R	R	12	10*	9	0	39				
Riccardo Patrese	I	17/4/54	Brabham-BMW	R	R	6*	R	8	R	6	7	R	R	R	R	R	13*	R		2	144	2	4	4	2
Nelson Piquet	BR	17/8/52	Williams-Honda	1	R	2	R	R	3	R	3	2	1	1	R	1	3	4	2	69	126	17	12	10	20
Alain Prost	F	24/2/55	McLaren-TAG	R	3	1	1	6	2	3	2	3	6*	R	1	D	2	2	1	72	105	25	13	10	16
Keke Rosberg	SF	6/12/48	McLaren-TAG	R	4	5*	2	2	4	4	R	5*	R	9*	4	R	R	R	R	22	114	5	8	4	5
Huub Rothengatter	NL	8/10/54	Zakspeed	–	–	R	NQ	R	12	DNS³	R	R	R	R	8	R	DNS	R		0	25	–	–	–	–
Ayrton Senna	BR	21/3/60	Lotus-Renault	2	1	R	3	2	5	1	R	R	2	2	R	4	3	R		55	46	4	7	6	15
Philippe Streiff	F	26/6/55	Tyrrell-Renault	7	R	R	11	12	11	9	R	6	R	8	R	9	R	R	5*	3	22	–	–	1	–
Marc Surer	CH	18/9/51	Arrows-BMW	R	R	9	9	9	–	–	–	–	–	–	–	–	–	–	–	0	82				
Patrick Tambay	F	25/6/49	Lola-Hart / Lola-Ford	R	8	R	R	R	DNS	–	R	R	8	7	5	R	NC	R	R	2	114	2	4	5	5
Derek Warwick	GB	27/8/54	Brabham-BMW	–	–	–	–	–	R	10	9	8	7	R	DNS	R	R	R	R	0	68	–	2	2	–

†   Deceased
*   Retired but classified as a finisher
D   Disqualified
DNS   Qualified, did not start
DNS²   Start declared null and void; unable to take second start
DNS³   Broke down on final parade lap; did not take start
NC   Running at finish, not classified
NQ   Did not qualify
R   Retired

GRAND PRIX SUPER GRID

by John Taylor

This year's Grand Prix Super Grid circuit has a length of 47·323 miles/76·159 km. This is arrived at by adding together the length of all circuits used in the 1986 World Championship. This season a total of 21 drivers achieved a practice time in all the events, thus earning a place on the Super Grid. Once again, Ayrton Senna has gained pole position after setting fastest practice time on no less than eight occasions.

Nigel Mansell (Williams FW11)
22m 45·915s, 124·724 mph/200·723 km/h

Ayrton Senna (Lotus 98T)
22m 40·959s, 125·178 mph/201·454 km/h

Alain Prost (McLaren MP4/2C)
22m 53·552s, 124·031 mph/199·608 km/h

Nelson Piquet (Williams FW11)
22m 47·439s, 124·585 mph/200·450 km/h

Gerhard Berger (Benetton B186)
23m 05·276s, 122·981 mph/197·918 km/h

Keke Rosberg (McLaren MP4/2C)
23m 00·262s, 123·428 mph/198·638 km/h

Teo Fabi (Benetton B186)
23m 15·582s, 122·073 mph/196·457 km/h

René Arnoux (Ligier JS27)
23m 08·874s, 122·662 mph/197·405 km/h

Stefan Johansson (Ferrari F1/86)
23m 21·571s, 121·551 mph/195·617 km/h

Michele Alboreto (Ferrari F1/86)
23m 16·389s, 122·002 mph/196·343 km/h

Johnny Dumfries (Lotus 98T)
23m 35·649s, 120·342 mph/193·671 km/h

Riccardo Patrese (Brabham BT54/BT55)
23m 21·683s, 121·541 mph/195·601 km/h

Alan Jones (Lola THL-1/THL-2)
23m 48·012s, 119·300 mph/191·994 km/h

Martin Brundle (Tyrrell 014/015)
23m 39·842s, 119·987 mph/193·100 km/h

Philippe Streiff (Tyrrell 014/015)
23m 54·045s, 118·799 mph/191·188 km/h

Thierry Boutsen (Arrows A8/A9)
23m 48·218s, 119·283 mph/191·967 km/h

Andrea de Cesaris (Minardi M/85B/M/86)
24m 13·921s, 117·175 mph/188·574 km/h

Jonathan Palmer (Zakspeed 861)
24m 02·415s, 118·109 mph/190·078 km/h

Christian Danner (Osella FA1G/Arrows A8/A9)
24m 30·032s, 115·890 mph/186·506 km/h

Alessandro Nannini (Minardi M/85B/M/86)
24m 15·667s, 117·034 mph/188·347 km/h

Piercarlo Ghinzani (Osella FA1F/FA1G/FA1H)
24m 51·182s, 114·247 mph/183·862 km/h

Laps led (drivers)

Driver	Races led	Laps led (no./per cent)	Miles (to nearest mile)	Km (to nearest km)
Nigel Mansell	8	310 (29·69)	841	1353
Nelson Piquet	10	244 (23·37)	755	1215
Alain Prost	9	185 (17·72)	521	838
Ayrton Senna	8	135 (12·93)	355	571
Keke Rosberg	4	86 (8·24)	246	396
Gerhard Berger	2	58 (5·56)	183	295
Jacques Laffite	1	13 (1·25)	33	53
Teo Fabi	1	8 (0·77)	29	47
René Arnoux	1	3 (0·29)	8	13
Stefan Johansson	1	2 (0·19)	9	14

Laps led (manufacturers)

Manufacturer	Races led	Laps led (no./per cent)	Miles (to nearest mile)	Km (to nearest km)
Williams	15	554 (53·07)	1597	2570
McLaren	9	271 (25·96)	767	1234
Lotus	8	135 (12·93)	355	571
Benetton	3	66 (6·32)	212	341
Ligier	1	16 (1·53)	40	64
Ferrari	1	2 (0·19)	9	14

Total laps/miles/km in season = 1044/2980/4794 km

Points per start average (season)

Position	Name	Nationality	Starts	Points	1st	2nd	3rd	4th	5th	6th	Pole	F. lap	Points average
1	Alain Prost	F	16	74	4	4	3	—	—	2	1	2	4·625
2	Nigel Mansell	GB	16	72	5	2	2	1	2	—	2	4	4·500
3	Nelson Piquet	BR	16	69	4	3	3	1	—	—	2	7	4·313
4	Ayrton Senna	BR	16	55	2	4	2	1	1	—	8	—	3·438
5	Jacques Laffite	F	8	14	—	1	1	—	1	2	—	—	1·750
6	Stefan Johansson	S	16	23	—	—	4	2	—	1	—	—	1·438
7	Keke Rosberg	SF	16	22	—	1	—	4	2	—	1	1	1·375
8	Gerhard Berger	A	16	17	1	—	1	—	1	2	—	2	1·063
9=	René Arnoux	F	16	14	—	—	—	3	2	1	—	—	0·875
9=	Michele Alboreto	I	16	14	—	1	—	2	1	—	—	—	0·875
11	Martin Brundle	GB	16	8	—	—	—	2	—	—	—	—	0·500
12	Alan Jones	AUS	16	4	—	—	—	1	—	1	—	—	0·250
13	Johnny Dumfries	GB	15	3	—	—	—	—	1	1	—	—	0·200
14	Philippe Streiff	F	16	3	—	—	—	—	1	1	—	—	0·188
15	Philippe Alliot	F	7	1	—	—	—	—	—	1	—	—	0·143
16	Patrick Tambay	F	15	2	—	—	—	—	1	—	—	—	0·133
17=	Riccardo Patrese	I	16	2	—	—	—	—	—	2	—	—	0·125
17=	Teo Fabi	I	16	2	—	—	—	—	1	—	—	—	0·125
19	Christian Danner	D	14	1	—	—	—	—	—	1	—	—	0·071

Points per start average (career)

Position	Name	Nationality	Starts	Points	1st	2nd	3rd	4th	5th	6th	Pole	F. lap	Points average
1	Alain Prost	F	105	360·5	25	13	10	4	2	6	16	17	3·433
2	Nelson Piquet	BR	126	305	17	12	10	9	5	3	20	20	2·421
3	Ayrton Senna	BR	46	106	4	7	6	1	1	2	15	4	2·304
4	Alan Jones	AUS	116	206	12	7	5	8	5	2	6	13	1·776
5	René Arnoux	F	112	178	7	9	7	6	7	4	18	12	1·589
6	Nigel Mansell	GB	90	141	7	3	7	5	4	8	4	6	1·567
7	Michele Alboreto	I	89	132·5	5	7	3	7	3	3	2	5	1·489
8	Keke Rosberg	SF	114	159·5	5	8	4	11	9	1	5	3	1·399
9	Jacques Laffite	F	175	228	6	10	16	7	9	10	7	6	1·303
10	Stefan Johansson	S	44	52	—	2	4	6	2	2	—	—	1·182
11	Elio de Angelis	I	107	122	2	2	5	11	17	6	3	—	1·140
12	Patrick Tambay	F	115	103	2	4	5	6	8	7	5	2	0·896
13	Ivan Capelli	I	4	3	—	—	—	—	1	—	—	—	0·750
14	Gerhard Berger	A	36	21	1	—	1	—	2	4	—	2	0·583
15	Eddie Cheever	USA	86	50	—	2	5	3	3	3	—	1	0·581
16	Derek Warwick	GB	69	37	—	2	2	3	3	2	—	1	0·536
17	Riccardo Patrese	I	142	75	2	4	3	2	2	7	2	4	0·528
18	Philippe Streiff	F	22	7	—	1	—	—	1	1	—	—	0·318
19	Andrea de Cesaris	I	88	27	—	2	1	1	2	1	3	1	0·307
20	Thierry Boutsen	B	57	16	—	—	1	—	1	4	—	1	0·281
21	Teo Fabi	I	48	11	—	—	1	—	1	2	3	1	0·229
22	Martin Brundle	GB	38	8	—	—	—	2	—	2	—	—	0·211
23	Marc Surer	CH	81	17	—	1	—	2	1	3	—	1	0·210
24	Johnny Dumfries	GB	15	3	—	—	—	—	1	1	—	—	0·200
25	Christian Danner	D	16	1	—	—	—	—	—	1	—	—	0·071
26	Piercarlo Ghinzani	I	50	2	—	—	—	—	2	—	—	—	0·040
27	Philippe Alliot	F	33	1	—	—	—	—	—	1	—	—	0·030

CHASSIS

AGS

Produced a Formula 1 car, based largely on the redundant Renault patterns and accessories.

JH21C
01 New for Capelli at Monza. For Capelli at Estoril.

ARROWS

Began the season with three 1985 A8 models.

A8
2 For Surer at Rio, Jerez, Imola, Monaco and Spa. For Danner at Montreal (briefly!), Detroit, Paul Ricard and Brands Hatch. Not seen again.
4 For Boutsen at Rio, Jerez, Imola, Monaco, Spa, Montreal, Detroit, Paul Ricard and Brands Hatch (written off).
5 For Boutsen at Hockenheim. For Danner at Budapest (raced by Boutsen). For Boutsen at the Österreichring, Monza and Estoril. For Danner at Mexico City and Adelaide.
6 Not seen before. Spare car at Rio, Jerez, Imola, Monaco, Spa, Montreal, Detroit, Paul Ricard (raced by Danner), Brands Hatch (raced by Boutsen), Hockenheim, Budapest and the Österreichring. For Danner at Monza and Estoril. For Boutsen in Mexico City and Adelaide.
Introduced A9 at Hockenheim.

A9
1 For Danner at Hockenheim. For Boutsen at Budapest (raced by Danner) and the Österreichring. Spare car at Monza, Estoril, Mexico City and Adelaide.

BENETTON

Three new cars ready for start of season, the final chassis completed during the week before Rio and tested by Maurizio Sandro Sala.

B186
1 New for Rio (spare car). Spare car at Jerez (raced by Berger), Imola, Monaco, (raced by Fabi), Spa, Montreal (raced by Fabi) and Detroit.
2 New for Berger at Rio. For Berger at Jerez, Imola, Monaco and Spa. Brought to Montreal to replace '4 written off by Fabi. For Fabi at Detroit. Spare car at Paul Ricard, Brands Hatch, Hockenheim, Budapest, the Österreichring, Monza, Estoril, Mexico City and Adelaide (raced by Fabi).
3 New for Fabi at Rio. For Fabi at Jerez, Imola and Monaco. Spare car at Brands Hatch. Not seen again.
4 New for Fabi at Spa. For Fabi at Montreal (written off during practice).
5 New for Berger at Montreal. For Berger at Detroit, Paul Ricard, Brands Hatch, Hockenheim, Budapest, the Österreichring and Monza.
6 New for Fabi at Paul Ricard. For Fabi at Brands Hatch, Hockenheim, Budapest, the Österreichring, Monza, Estoril, Mexico City and Adelaide.
7 New for Berger at Estoril. For Berger at Mexico City and Adelaide.

BRABHAM

Brought old BT54 out of retirement from Donington Collection.

BT54
9 Raced at Brands Hatch by Patrese.
Three new cars ready for start of season.

BT55
1 Seen during testing but found to be unsuitable. Design then considerably modified.
2 New at Rio (spare car). Spare car at Jerez and Imola. Written off during testing at Paul Ricard on 14 May.
3 New for de Angelis at Rio. For de Angelis at Jerez and Imola. Spare car at Monaco. For Warwick at Spa. Spare car at Montreal, Detroit, Paul Ricard and Brands Hatch. For Patrese at Hockenheim, Budapest and the Österreichring. Spare car at Monza and Estoril.
4 New for Patrese at Rio. For Patrese at Jerez, Imola, Monaco, Spa, Montreal, Detroit and Paul Ricard. Spare car at Hockenheim, Budapest (raced by Patrese) and the Österreichring.
5 New for de Angelis at Monaco. Written off during testing at Donington.
6 New for Warwick at Montreal. For Warwick at Detroit, Paul Ricard, Brands Hatch, Hockenheim, Budapest, the Österreichring, Monza, Estoril, Mexico City and Adelaide.
7 New for Patrese at Monza. For Patrese at Estoril, Mexico City and Adelaide.
8 New (spare car) at Mexico City. Spare car at Adelaide.

FERRARI

Introduced F1/86 in New Year. Continued chassis numbering sequence form 1985 156/85 series.

156/85
85 Spare car at Rio.
86 Found to have a structural problem. Broken up before start of season. Rebuilt later in the year as 1986-spec F1/86. For Johansson in Detroit (as replacement for '91 damaged during race in Montreal).

F1/86
87 New for Johansson at Rio. For Johansson at Jerez (crashed).
88 New for Alboreto at Rio. For Alboreto at Jerez, Imola and Monte Carlo. Spare car at Budapest, the Österreichring and Monza.
89 New at Jerez (spare car). Spare car at Imola and Monaco. For Alboreto at Spa. Spare car at Paul Ricard, Brands Hatch, the Österreichring (raced by Johansson). Tub taken to Adelaide; built up after Alboreto had crashed '92 during practice. Raced by Alboreto.
90 New for Johansson at Imola. For Johansson at Monaco and Spa. Spare car at Montreal, Detroit and Hockenheim. For Johansson at Budapest and the Österreichring (damaged during practice).
91 New (spare car) at Spa. For Johansson at Montreal (crashed).
92 Tub taken to Monaco but not used. For Alboreto at Montreal, Detroit, Paul Ricard, Brands Hatch, Hockenheim, Budapest, the Österreichring, Monza, Estoril, Mexico City and Adelaide (crashed during practice).
93 New for Johansson at Paul Ricard. For Johansson at Brands Hatch, Hockenheim, Monza, Estoril, Mexico City and Adelaide (crashed during practice).
94 New (spare car) at Estoril. Spare car at Mexico City and Adelaide (raced by Johansson).

HAAS-LOLA

Cars designed and built by FORCE. Began season with 1985-spec cars, some of which were modified to accept 1986-spec Hart engine.

THL-1
001 Spare car at Rio, Jerez, and Imola.
002 For Jones at Rio and Jerez. For Tambay at Imola.
003 Not seen before. For Tambay at Rio and Jerez.
Introduced THL-2 to accept Ford Cosworth turbo engine.

THL-2
001 Spare car at Imola and Monaco (raced by Tambay; crashed).
002 New for Jones at Monaco. For Tambay at Spa and Montreal (written off).
003 New for Jones at Imola. For Tambay at Monaco. Spare car at Spa, Montreal, Detroit, Paul Ricard, Brands Hatch, Hockenheim (raced by Jones), Budapest, the Österreichring, Monza, Estoril, Mexico City and Adelaide.
004 New for Jones at Spa. For Cheever at Detroit. For Jones at Paul Ricard, Brands Hatch, Hockenheim, Budapest, the Österreichring, Monza, Estoril, Mexico City and Adelaide.
005 New for Tambay at Paul Ricard. For Tambay at Brands Hatch, Hockenheim, Budapest, the Österreichring, Monza, Estoril, Mexico City and Adelaide.

LOG BOOK

LIGIER

Three completely new cars ready for Rio.

JS27
01 New for Laffite at Rio. For Laffite at Jerez, Imola, Monaco, Spa, Montreal, Detroit, Paul Ricard and Brands Hatch (crashed).
02 New for Arnoux at Rio. For Arnoux at Jerez, Imola, Monaco, Brands Hatch, Hockenheim, Budapest and the Österreichring.
03 New at Rio (spare car). Spare car at Jerez, Imola, Monaco (raced by Laffite), Spa, Montreal, Detroit, Paul Ricard, Brands Hatch, Budapest, the Österreichring, Monza, Estoril, Mexico City and Adelaide.
04 New for Arnoux at Spa. For Arnoux at Paul Ricard. For Alliot at Hockenheim, Budapest, the Österreichring, Monza, Estoril, Mexico City and Adelaide.
05 New for Arnoux at Montreal. For Arnoux at Detroit, Monza, Estoril, Mexico City and Adelaide.

LOTUS

Three new 98Ts ready for Brazil.

98T
1 New for winter testing. Spare car at Rio, Jerez, Imola, Monaco, Spa, Montreal (raced by Dumfries), Detroit, Paul Ricard, Brands Hatch, (raced by Senna), Hockenheim, Budapest, the Österreichring, Monza, Estoril, Mexico City and Adelaide.
2 New for Dumfries at Rio. For Dumfries at Jerez, Imola, Monaco, Spa, Montreal, Detroit, Paul Ricard, Brands Hatch, Hockenheim, Budapest, the Österreichring, Monza, Estoril, Mexico City and Adelaide.
3 New for Senna at Rio. For Senna at Jerez, Imola, Monaco, Spa, Montreal, Detroit and Paul Ricard (crashed).
4 New for Senna at Brands Hatch. For Senna at Hockenheim, Budapest, the Österreichring, Monza, Estoril, Mexico City and Adelaide.

McLAREN

Produced three completely new chassis for Rio.

MP4/2C
1 Spare car at Rio, Jerez, Imola, Monaco, the Österreichring, Monza, Estoril, (raced by Prost), Mexico City and Adelaide.
2 New for Rosberg at Rio. For Rosberg at Jerez, Imola, Monaco, Spa, Montreal, Detroit, Paul Ricard, Brands Hatch, Hockenheim, Budapest, the Österreichring, Monza, Estoril, Mexico City and Adelaide.
3 New for Prost at Rio. For Prost at Jerez, Imola, Monaco, Spa, Montreal, Detroit, Paul Ricard, Brands Hatch, Hockenheim, Budapest, the Österreichring and Monza.
4 New (spare car) at Spa. Spare car at Montreal, Detroit, Paul Ricard, Brands Hatch, Hockenheim, Budapest (raced by Prost and damaged).
5 New for Prost at Estoril. For Prost at Mexico City and Adelaide.

MINARDI

New cars, based on 1985 M/85 design.

M/85
4 Spare car at Rio, Jerez, Imola, Monaco, Spa, Montreal, Detroit, Paul Ricard, Brands Hatch (raced by de Cesaris), Hockenheim, Budapest and the Österreichring.

M/85B
1 New for de Cesaris at Rio. For de Cesaris at Jerez, Imola, Monaco, Spa, Montreal, Detroit, Paul Ricard, Brands Hatch, Hockenheim and the Österreichring. For Nannini at Monza, Estoril, Mexico City and Adelaide.
2 New for Nannini at Rio. For Nannini at Jerez, Imola, Monaco, Spa, Montreal, Detroit, Paul Ricard, Brands Hatch, Hockenheim and Budapest. Spare car at Monza, Estoril, Mexico City and Adelaide.
New model M/86 introduced at Budapest.

M/86
1 New for de Cesaris at Budapest. For Nannini at the Österreichring. For de Cesaris at Monza, Estoril, Mexico City and Adelaide.

OSELLA

Continued with 1985 models.

FA1F
01 For Ghinzani at Rio, Jerez, Imola, Monaco, Spa, Montreal and Detroit. Spare car at Paul Ricard. For Berg at Hockenheim, Budapest and the Österreichring. For Caffi at Monza. For Berg at Estoril, Mexico City and Adelaide.

FA1G
01 For Danner at Rio, Jerez, Imola and Monaco. Spare car at Spa. For Berg at Paul Ricard and Brands Hatch. For Ghinzani at Hockenheim, Budapest, the Österreichring, Monza, Estoril, Mexico City and Adelaide.
Introduced new design (FA1H) in Belgium.

FA1H
01 New for Danner at Spa. For Danner at Montreal. For Berg at Detroit. For Ghinzani at Paul Ricard and Brands Hatch (crashed and written off).

TYRRELL

Continued with 1985-spec 014 cars while waiting for completion of 015.

014
2 For Streiff at Rio, Jerez, Imola and Montreal. Spare car at Detroit, Paul Ricard and Brands Hatch.
3 Spare car at Rio, Jerez, (raced by Brundle), Imola, Monaco and Spa.
4 For Brundle at Rio.

015
1 New for Brundle at Jerez. For Brundle at Imola, Monaco, Spa, Montreal, Detroit, Paul Ricard and Brands Hatch. Spare car at Hockenheim, Budapest, the Österreichring, Monza, Estoril, Mexico City and Adelaide.
2 New for Streiff at Monaco. For Streiff at Spa.
3 New (spare car) at Montreal. For Streiff at Detroit, Paul Ricard, Brands Hatch, Hockenheim, Budapest, the Österreichring, Monza, Estoril, Mexico City and Adelaide.
4 New for Brundle at Hockenheim. For Brundle at Budapest, the Österreichring, Monza, Estoril and Mexico City.
5 New for Brundle at Adelaide.

WILLIAMS

Prepared three 1986 FW11 cars for start of season.

FW11
1 New for Piquet at Rio. For Piquet at Jerez. Spare car for Mansell at Monaco.
2 New for Mansell at Rio. For Mansell at Jerez, Imola, Monaco, Spa, Montreal, Detroit, Paul Ricard, Brands Hatch and Hockenheim. Spare car for Mansell at Estoril, Mexico City and Adelaide.
3 New at Rio (spare car). Spare car at Jerez, Imola, Monaco, (Piquet), Spa, Montreal, Detroit, Paul Ricard, Brands Hatch (raced by Mansell), Hockenheim, Budapest, the Österreichring and Monza. Spare car for Piquet at Estoril, Mexico City and Adelaide.
4 New for Piquet at Imola. For Piquet at Monaco, Spa, Montreal and Detroit (crashed).
5 New for Piquet at Paul Ricard. For Piquet at Brands Hatch, Hockenheim, Budapest, the Österreichring, Monza, Estoril, Mexico City and Adelaide.
6 New for Mansell at Budapest. For Mansell at the Österreichring, Monza, Estoril, Mexico City and Adelaide.

ZAKSPEED

Two new cars ready for Rio.

ZAK 861
1 New at Rio (spare car, raced by Palmer). Spare car at Jerez. For Rothengatter at Imola, Monaco, Spa, Montreal, Detroit, Paul Ricard, Brands Hatch, Hockenheim, Budapest, the Österreichring, Monza, Estoril and Mexico City (crashed during practice).
2 New for Palmer at Rio. For Palmer at Jerez, Imola, Monaco, Spa, Montreal, Detroit, Paul Ricard, Brands Hatch, Hockenheim, Budapest, the Österreichring, Monza, Estoril, Mexico City and Adelaide.
3 New (spare car and raced by Palmer) at Monaco. Spare car at Spa, Montreal, Detroit, Paul Ricard, Brands Hatch (raced by Palmer), Hockenheim, Budapest, the Österreichring, Monza and Estoril. For Rothengatter at Adelaide.

ENTRIES AND PRACTICE TIMES

No.	Driver	Nat.	Car	Tyre	Engine	Entrant	Practice 1	Practice 2	Warm-up
1	Alain Prost	F	Marlboro McLAREN MP4/2C	G	TAG PO1 (TTE PO1)	Marlboro McLaren International	1m 28·467s	1m 28·099s	1m 33·230s
2	Keke Rosberg	SF	Marlboro McLAREN MP4/2C	G	TAG PO1 (TTE PO1)	Marlboro McLaren International	1m 28·763s	1m 27·705s	1m 35·894s
3	Martin Brundle	GB	Data General TYRRELL 014	G	Renault EF15	Data General Team Tyrrell	1m 32·983s	1m 32·009s	1m 38·527s
4	Philippe Streiff	F	Data General TYRRELL 014	G	Renault EF15	Data General Team Tyrrell	1m 35·669s	1m 32·388s	1m 40·353s
5	Nigel Mansell	GB	WILLIAMS FW11	G	Honda RA166-E	Canon Williams Honda Team	1m 27·046s	1m 26·749s	1m 34·006s
6	Nelson Piquet	BR	WILLIAMS FW11	G	Honda RA166-E	Canon Williams Honda Team	1m 26·266s	1m 26·755s	1m 35·071s
7	Riccardo Patrese	I	Olivetti BRABHAM BT55	P	BMW M12/13/1	Motor Racing Developments Ltd		1m 29·294s	1m 34·910s
8	Elio de Angelis	I	Olivetti BRABHAM BT55	P	BMW M12/13/1	Motor Racing Developments Ltd	1m 31·682s	1m 31·074s	1m 34·731s
11	Johnny Dumfries	GB	John Player Special LOTUS 98T	G	Renault EF15	John Player Special Team Lotus	1m 30·452s	1m 29·503s	1m 37·507s
12	Ayrton Senna	BR	John Player Special LOTUS 98T	G	Renault EF15B	John Player Special Team Lotus	1m 26·983s	1m 25·501s	1m 36·556s
14	Jonathan Palmer	GB	West ZAKSPEED ZAK 861	G	Zakspeed	West Zakspeed Racing	1m 35·119s	1m 33·784s	1m 38·974s
15	Alan Jones	AUS	Beatrice LOLA THL-1	G	Hart 415T	Team Haas (USA) Ltd	1m 33·664s	1m 33·236s	1m 38·705s
16	Patrick Tambay	F	Beatrice LOLA THL-1	G	Hart 415T	Team Haas (USA) Ltd	1m 31·429s	1m 30·594s	1m 36·719s
17	Marc Surer	CH	ARROWS A8	G	BMW M12/13	Barclay Arrows BMW	1m 33·781s	1m 34·144s	1m 38·836s
18	Thierry Boutsen	B	ARROWS A8	G	BMW M12/13	Barclay Arrows BMW	1m 32·911s	1m 31·244s	1m 39·154s
19	Teo Fabi	I	BENETTON B186	P	BMW M12/13	Benetton Formula Ltd	1m 31·138s	1m 29·748s	1m 35·655s
20	Gerhard Berger	A	BENETTON B186	P	BMW M12/13	Benetton Formula Ltd	1m 31·653s	1m 31·313s	1m 34·747s
21	Piercarlo Ghinzani	I	OSELLA FA1G	P	Alfa Romeo 185T	Osella Squadra Corse	1m 38·165s	1m 35·988s	2m 52·922s
22	Christian Danner	D	OSELLA FA1F	P	Alfa Romeo 185T	Osella Squadra Corse	1m 39·389s	1m 36·558s	1m 44·015s
23	Andrea de Cesaris	I	Simod MINARDI M/85B	P	Motori Moderni	Minardi Team	1m 37·835s	1m 34·646s	1m 39·328s
24	Alessandro Nannini	I	Simod MINARDI M/85B	P	Motori Moderni	Minardi Team	1m 40·739s	1m 37·466s	1m 43·487s
25	René Arnoux	F	Gitanes LIGIER JS27	P	Renault EF15	Equipe Ligier	1m 30·563s	1m 27·133s	1m 36·710s
26	Jacques Laffite	F	Gitanes LIGIER JS27	P	Renault EF15	Equipe Ligier	1m 30·175s	1m 27·190s	1m 37·494s
27	Michele Alboreto	I	Fiat FERRARI F1/86	G	Ferrari 126C	Scuderia Ferrari SpA	1m 30·363s	1m 27·485s	1m 36·893s
28	Stefan Johansson	S	Fiat FERRARI F1/86	G	Ferrari 126C	Scuderia Ferrari SpA	1m 30·363s	1m 27·711s	1m 35·928s

Friday morning, Saturday morning and Sunday morning practice sessions not officially recorded.

G – Goodyear, P – Pirelli

Fri p.m. Hot, dry, cloudy
Sat p.m. Hot, dry, sunny
Sun a.m. Hot, dry, sunny

STARTING GRID

12 SENNA (1m 25·501s)
Lotus

6 PIQUET (1m 26·266s)
Williams

5 MANSELL (1m 26·749s)
Williams

25 ARNOUX (1m 27·133s)
Ligier

26 LAFFITE (1m 27·190s)
Ligier

27 ALBORETO (1m 27·485s)
Ferrari

2 ROSBERG (1m 27·705s)
McLaren

28 JOHANSSON (1m 27·711s)
Ferrari

1 PROST (1m 28·099s)
McLaren

7 PATRESE (1m 29·294s)
Brabham

11 DUMFRIES (1m 29·503s)
Lotus

19 FABI (1m 29·748s)
Benetton

16 TAMBAY (1m 30·594s)
Lola

8 DE ANGELIS (1m 31·074s)
Brabham

18 BOUTSEN (1m 31·244s)
Arrows

20 BERGER (1m 31·313s)
Benetton

3 BRUNDLE (1m 32·009s)
Tyrrell

4 STREIFF (1m 32·388s)
Tyrrell

15 JONES (1m 33·236s)
Lola

17 SURER (1m 33·781s)
Arrows

14 PALMER (1m 33·784s)
Zakspeed

23 DE CESARIS (1m 34·646s)
Minardi

21 GHINZANI (1m 35·988s)
Osella

22 DANNER (1m 36·558s)
Osella

24 NANNINI (1m 37·466s)
Minardi

RESULTS AND RETIREMENTS

Place	Driver	Car	Laps	Time and speed (mph/km/h)/Retirement	
1	Nelson Piquet	Williams-Honda V6	61	1h 39m 32·583s	114·941/184·980
2	Ayrton Senna	Lotus-Renault V6	61	1h 40m 07·410s	114·274/183·907
3	Jacques Laffite	Ligier-Renault V6	61	1h 40m 32·342s	113·802/183·147
4	René Arnoux	Ligier-Renault V6	61	1h 41m 01·012s	113·263/182·281
5	Martin Brundle	Tyrrell-Renault V6	60		
6	Gerhard Berger	Benetton-BMW 4	59		
7	Philippe Streiff	Tyrrell-Renault V6	59		
8	Elio de Angelis	Brabham-BMW 4	58		
9	Johnny Dumfries	Lotus-Renault V6	58		
10	Teo Fabi	Benetton-BMW 4	56		
	Thierry Boutsen	Arrows-BMW 4	37	Broken exhaust	
	Michele Alboreto	Ferrari V6	35	Fuel pump	
	Alain Prost	McLaren-TAG V6	30	Engine	
	Christian Danner	Osella-Alfa Romeo V8	29	Engine	
	Stefan Johansson	Ferrari V6	26	Brakes/spun off	
	Patrick Tambay	Lola-Hart 4	24	Flat battery	
	Riccardo Patrese	Brabham-BMW 4	21	Split water pipe	
	Jonathan Palmer	Zakspeed 4	20	Cracked airbox	
	Marc Surer	Arrows-BMW 4	19	Engine	
	Alessandro Nannini	Minardi-MM V6	18	Clutch	
	Andrea de Cesaris	Minardi-MM V6	16	Turbo	
	Piercarlo Ghinzani	Osella-Alfa Romeo V8	16	Engine	
	Keke Rosberg	McLaren-TAG V6	6	Engine	
	Alan Jones	Lola-Hart 4	5	Distributor rotor arm	
	Nigel Mansell	Williams-Honda V6	0	Accident with Senna	

Fastest lap: Piquet, on lap 46, 1m 33·546s, 120·305 mph/193·612 km/h (record).
Previous lap record: Alain Prost (F1 McLaren MP4/2-TAG t/c), 1m 36·499s, 116·622 mph/187·686 km/h (1984).

PAST WINNERS

Year	Driver	Nat	Car	Circuit	Distance miles/km	Speed mph/km/h
1972*	Carlos Reutemann	RA	3·0 Brabham BT34-Ford	Interlagos	183·01/294·53	112·89/181·68
1973	Emerson Fittipaldi	BR	3·0 JPS/Lotus 72-Ford	Interlagos	197·85/318·42	114·23/183·83
1974	Emerson Fittipaldi	BR	3·0 McLaren M23-Ford	Interlagos	158·28/254·73	112·23/180·62
1975	Carlos Pace	BR	3·0 Brabham BT44B-Ford	Interlagos	197·85/318·42	113·40/182·50
1976	Niki Lauda	A	3·0 Ferrari 312T/76	Interlagos	197·85/318·42	112·76/181·47
1977	Carlos Reutemann	RA	3·0 Ferrari 312T-2/77	Interlagos	197·85/318·42	112·92/181·73
1978	Carlos Reutemann	RA	3·0 Ferrari 312T-2/78	Rio de Janeiro	196·95/316·95	107·43/172·89
1979	Jacques Laffite	F	3·0 Ligier JS11-Ford	Interlagos	197·85/318·42	117·23/188·67
1980	René Arnoux	F	1·5 Renault RS t/c	Interlagos	195·70/314·95	117·40/188·93
1981	Carlos Reutemann	RA	3·0 Williams FW07C-Ford	Rio de Janeiro	193·82/311·92	96·59/155·45
1982	Alain Prost	F	1·5 Renault RE t/c	Rio de Janeiro	196·95/316·95	112·97/181·80
1983	Nelson Piquet	BR	1·5 Brabham BT52-BMW t/c	Rio de Janeiro	196·95/316·95	108·93/175·30
1984	Alain Prost	F	1·5 McLaren MP4/2-TAG t/c	Rio de Janeiro	190·69/306·89	111·54/179·51
1985	Alain Prost	F	1·5 McLaren MP4/2B-TAG t/c	Rio de Janeiro	190·69/306·89	112·79/181·53
1986	Nelson Piquet	BR	1·5 Williams FW11-Honda t/c	Rio de Janeiro	190·69/306·89	114·94/184·98

*Non-championship

LAP CHART

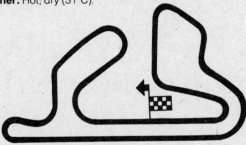

1st Lap Order	Lap progression (laps 1–61)	Running order
12 A. Senna	12 12 6 6 6 6 6 6 6 6 6 6 6 6 6 6 6 6 6 12 1 1 1 1 1 1 6 6 6 6 6 6 6 6 6 6 6 6 6 6 12 6 6 6 6 6 6 6 6 6 6 6 6 6 6 6 6 6 6 6 6	1
6 N. Piquet	6 6 12 12 12 12 12 12 12 12 12 12 12 12 12 12 1 12 6 6 6 6 6 1 12 12 12 12 12 12 12 12 12 12 12 6 12 12 12 12 6 12 12 12 12 12 12 12 12 12 12 12 12 12 12 12 12 12 12 12 12	2
25 R. Arnoux	25 25 27 27 27 27 27 27 27 27 27 27 27 27 1 1 6 6 25 25 12 12 12 12 1 25 25 25 25 25 25 25 25 25 25 25 25 25 25 25 25 25 26 26 25 25 26 26 26 26 26 26 26 26 26 26 26 26 26 26 26	3
27 M. Alboreto	27 27 25 25 25 25 25 25 25 1 1 1 1 27 27 27 6 6 25 25 12 12 12 12 26 26 26 26 26 26 26 26 26 26 26 26 26 26 25 25 25 25 25 25 25 25 25 25 25 25 25 25 25 25 25 25 25 25 25 25 25	4
2 K. Rosberg	2 2 2 2 28 28 28 1 1 25 25 25 25 25 25 26 26 26 26 26 26 26 25 25 25 26 11 11 11 11 11 11 11 20 20 20 20 20 3 3 3 3 3 3 3 3 3 3 3 3 3 3 3 3 3 3 3 3 3 3 3	5
28 S. Johansson	28 28 28 28 28 7 7 1 28 28 28 28 28 28 23 26 16 16 16 16 16 28 28 3 3 11 3 27 27 27 27 20 20 20 3 3 3 3 3 3 20 20 20 20 20 20 20 20 20 20 20 20 20 20 20 20 20 20 20 20 20	6
7 R. Patrese	7 7 7 7 7 1 1 7 7 26 26 26 26 23 26 7 7 11 11 11 28 16 11 11 18 18 11 3 18 3 18 20 20 3 3 3 4 4 4 4 4 4 4 4 4 4 4 4 4 4 4 4 4 4 4 4 4 4 4 4 4	7
26 J. Laffite	26 26 26 26 26 26 26 26 7 7 7 23 26 7 16 16 28 28 28 11 11 3 3 11 11 18 18 27 18 3 18 4 4 11 8 8 8 8 8 8 8 8 8 8 8 8 8 8 8 8 8 8 8 8 8 8 8 8 8 8 8	8
15 A. Jones	15 15 15 15 1 16 16 16 23 23 23 23 7 28 11 11 20 7 20 20 20 3 18 27 27 27 20 20 3 8 8 8 11 11 11 11 11 11 11 11 11 11 11 11 11 11 11 11 11 11 11 11 11 11 11 11	9
16 P. Tambay	16 16 16 1 16 18 23 23 16 16 16 16 16 16 16 20 20 7 20 3 3 18 27 27 20 20 20 20 4 4 4 4 19 19 19 19 19 19 19 19 19 19 19 19 19 19 19 19 19 19 19 19 19 19 19 19	10
1 A. Prost	1 1 1 16 15 23 18 18 18 18 18 18 11 11 28 3 3 18 18 27 20 20 4 4 4 8 8 8 8 18 18	11
18 T. Boutsen	18 18 18 18 18 2 11 11 11 11 11 11 11 18 18 20 18 8 27 18 7 4 4 20 4 4 8 8 8 19 19 19 19	12
11 J. Dumfries	11 11 11 11 3 11 3 3 3 3 3 3 3 20 18 17 3 18 4 4 27 27 4 8 8 22 22 22 19	13
3 M. Brundle	3 3 3 11 3 8 8 8 8 8 8 8 20 3 17 8 17 4 27 27 8 8 22 22 19 19 19	14
8 E. de Angelis	8 8 8 8 8 20 20 20 20 20 20 20 8 17 8 3 18 24 14 22 22 22 22 19 19	15
20 G. Berger	20 20 20 20 20 17 17 17 17 17 17 17 8 3 4 4 17 22 8 19 19 19	16
19 T. Fabi	19 19 19 19 17 17 14 14 14 14 4 4 4 4 4 4 14 14 14 8 19	17
4 P. Streiff	4 14 14 14 14 14 4 4 4 14 14 14 14 14 14 22 22 8 19	18
17 M. Surer	17 4 4 17 4 4 24 24 21 21 21 21 21 21 21 24 19 22	19
14 J. Palmer	14 17 17 4 24 24 21 21 22 22 22 22 22 22 22 19 24 19	20
23 A. de Cesaris	23 24 24 24 22 22 22 22 24 24 24 24 24 24	21
22 C. Danner	22 23 22 22 21 21 19 19 19 19 19 19 19 19 19	22
24 A. Nannini	24 22 21 21 19 19	23
21 P. Ghinzani	21 21	24

CIRCUIT DATA

Autodromo Internacional do Rio de Janeiro, Baixada de Jacarepaguá

Circuit length: 3·126 miles/5·031 km
Race distance: 61 laps, 190·692 miles/306·889 km
Race weather: Hot, dry (31°C).

FASTEST LAPS

Driver	Time	Lap
Nelson Piquet	1m 33·546s	46
Teo Fabi	1m 33·998s	49
Ayrton Senna	1m 34·785s	46
Johnny Dumfries	1m 35·033s	50
Elio de Angelis	1m 35·121s	22
Alain Prost	1m 35·381s	12
Michele Alboreto	1m 35·532s	23
Jacques Laffite	1m 35·767s	39
René Arnoux	1m 36·414s	39
Andrea de Cesaris	1m 36·475s	12
Gerhard Berger	1m 36·958s	30
Stefan Johansson	1m 36·983s	21
Martin Brundle	1m 37·869s	17
Keke Rosberg	1m 38·027s	5
Riccardo Patrese	1m 38·409s	7
Thierry Boutsen	1m 38·591s	23
Patrick Tambay	1m 38·674s	9
Alan Jones	1m 38·710s	2
Philippe Streiff	1m 39·651s	38
Marc Surer	1m 39·970s	6
Alessandro Nannini	1m 40·461s	12
Jonathan Palmer	1m 41·849s	4
Piercarlo Ghinzani	1m 43·412s	8
Christian Danner	1m 43·712s	29

POINTS

WORLD CHAMPIONSHIP OF DRIVERS

1	Nelson Piquet	9 pts
2	Ayrton Senna	6
3	Jacques Laffite	4
4	René Arnoux	3
5	Martin Brundle	2
6	Gerhard Berger	1

CONSTRUCTORS' CUP

1	Williams	9 pts
2	Ligier	7
3	Lotus	6
4	Tyrrell	2
5	Benetton	1

ENTRIES AND PRACTICE TIMES

No.	Driver	Nat.	Car	Tyre	Engine	Entrant	Practice 1	Practice 2	Warm-up
1	Alain Prost	F	Marlboro McLAREN MP4/2C	G	TAG PO1 (TTE PO1)	Marlboro McLaren International	1m 23·702s	**1m 22·886s**	1m 27·390s
2	Keke Rosberg	SF	Marlboro McLAREN MP4/2C	G	TAG PO1 (TTE PO1)	Marlboro McLaren International	1m 23·948s	**1m 23·004s**	1m 28·213s
3	Martin Brundle	GB	Data General TYRRELL 015	G	Renault EF15B	Data General Team Tyrrell	**1m 25·831s**	1m 41·631s	1m 33·152s
4	Philippe Streiff	F	Data General TYRRELL 014	G	Renault EF15	Data General Team Tyrrell	**1m 27·637s**	1m 28·086s	1m 34·347s
5	Nigel Mansell	GB	WILLIAMS FW11	G	Honda RA166—E	Canon Williams Honda Team	1m 23·024s	**1m 22·576s**	1m 29·199s
6	Nelson Piquet	BR	WILLIAMS FW11	G	Honda RA166—E	Canon Williams Honda Team	1m 23·097s	**1m 22·431s**	1m 28·965s
7	Riccardo Patrese	I	Olivetti BRABHAM BT55	P	BMW M12/13/1	Motor Racing Developments Ltd	**1m 26·231s**	1m 29·911s	1m 30·781s
8	Elio de Angelis	I	Olivetti BRABHAM BT55	P	BMW M12/13/1	Motor Racing Developments Ltd	1m 27·300s	**1m 26·550s**	1m 29·349s
11	Johnny Dumfries	GB	John Player Special LOTUS 98T	G	Renault EF15	John Player Special Team Lotus	1m 29·093s	**1m 25·107s**	1m 35·349s
12	Ayrton Senna	BR	John Player Special LOTUS 98T	G	Renault EF15B	John Player Special Team Lotus	**1m 21·605s**	1m 21·924s	1m 28·964s
14	Jonathan Palmer	GB	West ZAKSPEED ZAK 861	G	Zakspeed	West Zakspeed Racing	1m 27·600s	**1m 26·918s**	1m 32·551s
15	Alan Jones	AUS	Beatrice LOLA THL-1	G	Hart 415T	Team Haas (USA) Ltd	1m 28·645s	**1m 26·946s**	1m 31·293s
16	Patrick Tambay	F	Beatrice LOLA THL-1	G	Hart 415T	Team Haas (USA) Ltd	1m 27·045s	**1m 26·992s**	1m 32·753s
17	Marc Surer	CH	ARROWS A8	G	BMW M12/13	Barclay Arrows BMW	1m 28·803s	**1m 28·443s**	1m 38·926s
18	Thierry Boutsen	B	ARROWS A8	G	BMW M12/13	Barclay Arrows BMW	1m 28·112s	**1m 27·169s**	1m 33·141s
19	Teo Fabi	I	BENETTON B186	P	BMW M12/13	Benetton Formula Ltd	**1m 25·052s**	1m 26·196s	1m 29·964s
20	Gerhard Berger	A	BENETTON B186	P	BMW M12/13	Benetton Formula Ltd	1m 24·501s	**1m 25·235s**	1m 40·391s
21	Piercarlo Ghinzani	I	OSELLA FA1G	P	Alfa Romeo 185T	Osella Squadra Corse	1m 28·894s	**1m 28·423s**	1m 34·773s
22	Christian Danner	D	OSELLA FA1F	P	Alfa Romeo 185T	Osella Squadra Corse	1m 29·046s		1m 38·726s
23	Andrea de Cesaris	I	Simod MINARDI M/85B	P	Motori Moderni	Minardi Team	**1m 29·195s**		
24	Alessandro Nannini	I	Simod MINARDI M/85B	P	Motori Moderni	Minardi Team	—	**1m 30·062s**	1m 47·727s
25	René Arnoux	F	Gitanes LIGIER JS27	P	Renault EF15	Equipe Ligier	1m 24·566s	**1m 24·274s**	1m 31·304s
26	Jacques Laffite	F	Gitanes LIGIER JS27	P	Renault EF15B	Equipe Ligier	1m 24·817s	1m 25·863s	1m 31·844s
27	Michele Alboreto	I	Fiat FERRARI F1/86	G	Ferrari 126C	Scuderia Ferrari SpA	1m 26·554s	**1m 26·094s**	1m 29·161s
28	Stefan Johansson	S	Fiat FERRARI F1/86	G	Ferrari 126C	Scuderia Ferrari SpA	**1m 25·466s**	1m 25·655s	1m 32·990s

Thursday afternoon, Friday morning, Saturday morning and Sunday morning practice sessions not officially recorded.

G – Goodyear, P – Pirelli.

Fri p.m.	Sat p.m.	Sun a.m.
Warm, dry, sunny	Cool, dry, cloudy	Warm, dry, sunny

STARTING GRID

	12 SENNA (1m 21·605s) Lotus
6 PIQUET (1m 22·431s) Williams	
	5 MANSELL (1m 22·576s) Williams
1 PROST (1m 22·886s) McLaren	
	2 ROSBERG (1m 23·004s) McLaren
25 ARNOUX (1m 24·274s) Ligier	
	20 BERGER (1m 24·501s) Benetton
26 LAFFITE (1m 24·817s) Ligier	
	19 FABI (1m 25·052s) Benetton
11 DUMFRIES (1m 25·107s) Lotus	
	28 JOHANSSON (1m 25·466s) Ferrari
3 BRUNDLE (1m 25·831s) Tyrrell	
	27 ALBORETO (1m 26·094s) Ferrari
7 PATRESE (1m 26·231s) Brabham	
	8 DE ANGELIS (1m 26·550s) Brabham
14 PALMER (1m 26·918s) Zakspeed	
	15 JONES (1m 26·946s) Lola
16 TAMBAY (1m 26·992s) Lola	
	18 BOUTSEN (1m 27·169s) Arrows
4 STREIFF (1m 27·637s) Tyrrell	
	21 GHINZANI (1m 28·423s) Osella
17 SURER (1m 28·443s) Arrows	
	22 DANNER (1m 29·046s) Osella
23 DE CESARIS (1m 29·195s) Minardi	
	*24 NANNINI (1m 30·062s) Minardi

* Did not take the start.

RESULTS AND RETIREMENTS

Place	Driver	Car	Laps	Time and speed (mph/km/h)/Retirement	
1	Ayrton Senna	Lotus-Renault V6	72	1h 48m 47·735s	104·070/167·486
2	Nigel Mansell	Williams-Honda V6	72	1h 48m 47·749s	104·070/167·486
3	Alain Prost	McLaren-TAG V6	72	1h 49m 09·287s	103·728/166·935
4	Keke Rosberg	McLaren-TAG V6	71		
5	Teo Fabi	Benetton-BMW 4	71		
6	Gerhard Berger	Benetton-BMW 4	71		
7	Thierry Boutsen	Arrows-BMW 4	68		
8	Patrick Tambay	Lola-Hart 4	66		
	Johnny Dumfries	Lotus-Renault V6	52	Gearbox	
	Martin Brundle	Tyrrell-Renault V6	41	Engine lost its oil	
	Jacques Laffite	Ligier-Renault V6	40	Driveshaft	
	Nelson Piquet	Williams-Honda V6	39	Overheating/engine	
	Marc Surer	Arrows-BMW 4	39	Fuel system	
	Elio de Angelis	Brabham-BMW 4	29	Gearbox	
	René Arnoux	Ligier-Renault V6	29	Driveshaft	
	Michele Alboreto	Ferrari V6	22	Wheel bearing	
	Philippe Streiff	Tyrrell-Renault V6	22	Engine lost its oil	
	Christian Danner	Osella-Alfa Romeo V8	14	Engine	
	Stefan Johansson	Ferrari V6	11	Brakes/accident	
	Piercarlo Ghinzani	Osella-Alfa Romeo V8	10	Engine	
	Riccardo Patrese	Brabham-BMW 4	8	Gearbox	
	Andrea de Cesaris	Minardi-MM V6	1	Differential	
	Alan Jones	Lola-Hart 4	0	Accident with Palmer	
	Jonathan Palmer	Zakspeed 4	0	Accident with Jones	
	Alessandro Nannini	Minardi-MM V6	0	Differential (on final parade lap)	

Fastest lap: Mansell, on lap 65, 1m 27·176s, 108·234 mph/174·186 km/h (established record for new circuit).

PAST WINNERS

Year	Driver	Nat.	Car	Circuit	Distance miles/km	Speed mph/km/h
1913	Carlos de Salamanca	E	7·4 Rolls-Royce	Guadarrama	191·00/307·38	54·00/ 86·90
1923	Albert Divo	F	2·0 Sunbeam	Sitges-Terramar	248·00/399·12	96·91/155·96
1926	Meo Costantini	I	2·0 Bugatti T35	San Sebastian	420·00/675·92	76·88/123·73
1927	Robert Benoist	F	1·5 Delage s/c	San Sebastian	429·91/691·87	80·52/129·58
1929	Louis Chiron	F	2·0 Bugatti T35C s/c	San Sebastian	161·00/259·10	78·92/116·52
1929	Louis Chiron	F	2·0 Bugatti T35C s/c	San Sebastian		72·40/116·52
1930	Achille Varzi	I	2·5 Maserati 8C s/c	San Sebastian	302·23/486·40	86·82/139·72
1933	Louis Chiron	F	2·6 Alfa Romeo P3 s/c	San Sebastian	302·23/486·40	83·32/134·09
1934	Luigi Fagioli	I	3·7 Mercedes-Benz W25 s/c	San Sebastian	302·23/486·40	91·13/146·66
1935	Rudi Caracciola	D	4·0 Mercedes-Benz W25 s/c	San Sebastian	302·23/486·40	101·92/164·02
1951	Juan Manuel Fangio	RA	1·5 Alfa Romeo 159M s/c	Pedralbes	274·72/442·12	98·79/158·99
1954	Mike Hawthorn	GB	2·5 Ferrari 553	Pedralbes	313·97/505·28	97·05/156·19
1967*	Jim Clark	GB	3·0 Lotus 49-Ford	Jarama	126·92/204·26	83·59/134·53
1968	Graham Hill	GB	3·0 Lotus 49-Ford	Jarama	190·38/306·39	84·41/135·84
1969	Jackie Stewart	GB	3·0 Matra MS80-Ford	Montjuich	211·95/341·10	92·91/149·52
1970	Jackie Stewart	GB	3·0 March 701B-Ford	Jarama	190·38/306·39	87·22/140·36
1971	Jackie Stewart	GB	3·0 Tyrrell 003-Ford	Montjuich	176·62/284·24	97·19/156·41
1972	Emerson Fittipaldi	BR	3·0 JPS/Lotus 72-Ford	Jarama	190·38/306·39	92·35/148·63
1973	Emerson Fittipaldi	BR	3·0 JPS/Lotus 72-Ford	Montjuich	176·62/284·24	97·86/157·49
1974	Niki Lauda	A	3·0 Ferrari 312B-3/74	Jarama	177·69/285·96	88·48/142·40
1975	Jochen Mass	D	3·0 McLaren M23-Ford	Montjuich	68·31/109·93	95·54/153·76
1976	James Hunt	GB	3·0 McLaren M23-Ford	Jarama	158·65/255·32	93·01/149·69
1977	Mario Andretti	USA	3·0 JPS/Lotus 78-Ford	Jarama	158·65/255·32	91·79/147·73
1978	Mario Andretti	USA	3·0 JPS/Lotus 79-Ford	Jarama	158·65/255·32	93·52/150·51
1979	Patrick Depailler	F	3·0 Ligier JS11-Ford	Jarama	158·65/255·32	95·97/154·45
1980	Alan Jones	AUS	3·0 Williams FW07B-Ford	Jarama	164·64/264·96	95·69/154·00
1981	Gilles Villeneuve	CDN	1·5 Ferrari 126CK t/c	Jarama	164·64/264·96	92·66/149·16
1986	Ayrton Senna	BR	1·5 Lotus 98T-Renault t/c	Jerez	188·71/303·70	104·07/167·49

* Non-championship since 1950

LAP CHART

1st LAP ORDER	Lap sequence (1–72)	Finish
12 A. Senna	12 12 12 12 12 12 12 12 12 12 12 12 12 12 12 12 12 12 12 12 12 12 12 12 12 12 12 12 12 12 12 12 12 12 12 12 12 12 12 12 12 5 5 5 5 5 5 5 5 5 5 5 5 5 5 5 5 5 5 5 5 5 12 12 12 12 12 12 12 12 12 12	1
6 N. Piquet	6 6 6 6 6 6 6 6 6 6 6 6 6 6 6 6 6 6 6 6 6 6 6 6 6 6 6 6 6 6 6 6 6 6 6 6 6 6 6 5 5 5 5 5 12 12 12 12 12 12 12 12 12 12 12 12 12 12 12 12 12 1 1 1 1 1 1 5 5 5 5	2
5 N. Mansell	5 2 2 2 2 2 2 2 2 2 2 2 2 2 2 2 2 2 2 2 2 2 2 2 2 2 2 5 5 5 6 6 6 6 6 6 6 6 1 1 1 1 1 1 1 1 1 1 1 1 1 1 1 1 1 1 1 1 1 1 1 1 1 1 1 5 5 5 5 5 1 1 1	3
2 K. Rosberg	2 5 5 5 5 1 1 1 1 1 1 1 1 1 1 1 1 1 1 1 1 5 5 5 5 5 5 5 5 5 5 5 5 5 2 2 2 2 1 1 1 1 2 2 2 2 2 2 2 2 2 2 2 2 2 2 2 2 2 2 2 2 2 2 2 2 2 2 2 2 2 2	4
1 A. Prost	1 1 1 1 5 5 5 5 5 5 5 5 5 5 5 5 5 5 1 1 1 1 1 1 1 1 1 1 1 1 1 1 2 2 2 2 26 20 20 20 11 11 20 20 19 19 19 19 19 19 19 19 19 19 19 19 19 19 19 19 19 19 19 19 19 19 19 19 19 19 19 19	5
25 R. Arnoux	25 25 25 25 25 25 25 25 25 25 25 25 25 25 25 25 25 25 25 26 26 26 26 26 26 26 26 26 26 26 26 26 26 26 26 3 11 11 11 20 20 20 20 20 11 19 19 19 20 20 20 20 20 20 20 20 20 20 20 20 20 20 20 20 20 20 20 20 20 20 20	6
26 J. Laffite	26 26 26 26 26 26 26 26 26 26 26 26 26 26 26 26 26 26 26 20 20 20 20 20 20 20 20 20 20 20 20 20 20 20 3 11 19 19 19 19 19 19 19 19 18 18 18 18 18 18 18 18 18 18 18 18 18 18 18	7
11 J. Dumfries	11 28 28 28 28 28 28 28 28 28 27 27 27 27 27 27 27 27 27 20 3 3 3 3 3 3 3 3 3 3 3 3 3 3 11 19 18 18 18 18 18 18 18 18 16 16 16 16 16 16 16 16 16 16 16 16 16 16 16	8
28 S. Johansson	28 11 27 27 27 27 27 27 27 20 20 20 20 20 20 20 20 20 3 11 11 11 11 11 11 11 11 11 11 11 11 11 11 11 17 18 16 16 16 16 16 16 16 16 16	9
27 M. Alboreto	27 27 20 20 20 20 20 20 20 11 11 11 11 11 11 11 11 3 3 11 18 18 18 18 18 17 17 17 17 17 17 17 17 19 16	10
3 M. Brundle	3 20 11 11 11 11 11 11 11 11 3 3 3 3 3 3 3 11 11 18 17 17 17 17 17 17 19 19 19 19 19 19 19 19 18	11
20 G. Berger	20 3 3 7 7 7 7 3 3 3 18 18 18 18 18 18 18 18 17 19 19 19 19 18 18 18 18 18 18 18 18 18 16	12
16 P. Tambay	16 7 7 16 3 3 3 7 18 18 17 17 17 17 17 17 17 19 8 8 8 8 8 16 16 16 16 16 16 16 16 16	13
17 M. Surer	17 16 16 3 16 16 16 16 17 17 4 4 4 4 4 4 4 4 8 16 16 16 16 16	14
7 R. Patrese	7 17 18 18 18 18 18 18 4 4 8 8 8 19 19 19 19 19 16 25 25 25 25 25	15
18 T. Boutsen	18 18 17 17 17 17 17 8 8 8 19 19 19 8 8 8 8 8 8	16
23 A. de Cesaris	23 4 4 4 4 4 4 21 21 19 22 22 22 16 16 16 16 16 16 16	17
4 P. Streiff	4 21 21 8 8 8 8 22 19 22 16 16 16	18
21 P. Ghinzani	21 8 8 21 21 21 21 21 19 22 16	19
8 E. de Angelis	8 22 22 22 22 22 22 22 16 16	20
22 C. Danner	22 19 19 19 19 19 19 19	21
19 T. Fabi	19	22

FASTEST LAPS

Driver	Time	Lap
Nigel Mansell	1m 27·176s	65
Keke Rosberg	1m 27·991s	61
Teo Fabi	1m 28·235s	49
René Arnoux	1m 28·332s	26
Alain Prost	1m 28·497s	45
Jacques Laffite	1m 28·504s	35
Ayrton Senna	1m 28·801s	45
Nelson Piquet	1m 29·182s	39
Gerhard Berger	1m 29·690s	54
Elio de Angelis	1m 29·885s	23
Michele Alboreto	1m 30·201s	5
Stefan Johansson	1m 30·467s	11
Johnny Dumfries	1m 30·962s	31
Martin Brundle	1m 31·236s	34
Thierry Boutsen	1m 31·457s	38
Patrick Tambay	1m 31·512s	31
Marc Surer	1m 32·230s	11
Philippe Streiff	1m 32·240s	14
Riccardo Patrese	1m 33·212s	7
Piercarlo Ghinzani	1m 34·027s	8
Christian Danner	1m 35·273s	4
Andrea de Cesaris	1m 52·175s	1

CIRCUIT DATA

Circuito de Jerez, Jerez de la Frontera
Circuit length: 2·6209 miles/4·218 km
Race distance: 72 laps, 188·708 miles/303·696 km
Race weather: Dry, warm, sunny (16°C).

POINTS

WORLD CHAMPIONSHIP OF DRIVERS

	Driver	Points
1	Ayrton Senna	15 pts
2	Nelson Piquet	9
3	Nigel Mansell	6
4=	Jacques Laffite	4
4=	Alain Prost	4
6=	René Arnoux	3
6=	Keke Rosberg	3
8=	Martin Brundle	2
8=	Teo Fabi	2
8=	Gerhard Berger	2

CONSTRUCTORS' CUP

		Points
1=	Lotus	15 pts
1=	Williams	15
3=	Ligier	7
3=	McLaren	7
5	Benetton	4
6	Tyrrell	2

Hazel Chapman congratulates Ayrton Senna on winning the 100th pole position for Team Lotus.

ENTRIES AND PRACTICE TIMES

No.	Driver	Nat.	Car	Tyre	Engine	Entrant	Practice 1	Practice 2	Warm-up
1	Alain Prost	F	Marlboro McLAREN MP4/2C	G	TAG PO1 (TTE PO1)	Marlboro McLaren International	1m 26·273s	**1m 26·176s**	1m 33·078s
2	Keke Rosberg	SF	Marlboro McLAREN MP4/2C	G	TAG PO1 (TTE PO1)	Marlboro McLaren International	1m 26·956s	**1m 26·385s**	1m 32·188s
3	Martin Brundle	GB	Data General TYRRELL 015	G	Renault EF15B	Data General Team Tyrrell	1m 29·687s	**1m 28·329s**	1m 36·873s
4	Philippe Streiff	F	Data General TYRRELL 014	G	Renault EF15B	Data General Team Tyrrell	**1m 30·123s**	1m 32·358s	2m 51·270s
5	Nigel Mansell	GB	WILLIAMS FW11	G	Honda RA166–E	Canon Williams Honda Team	1m 26·752s	**1m 26·159s**	1m 33·457s
6	Nelson Piquet	BR	WILLIAMS FW11	G	Honda RA166–E	Canon Williams Honda Team	1m 25·890s	**1m 25·569s**	1m 34·588s
7	Riccardo Patrese	I	Olivetti BRABHAM BT55	P	BMW M12/13/1	Motor Racing Developments Ltd	1m 30·341s	**1m 29·713s**	1m 34·413s
8	Elio de Angelis	I	Olivetti BRABHAM BT55	P	BMW M12/13/1	Motor Racing Developments Ltd	1m 30·881s	**1m 29·713s**	1m 36·002s
11	Johnny Dumfries	GB	John Player Special LOTUS 98T	G	Renault EF15B	John Player Special Team Lotus	**1m 29·244s**	1m 29·607s	1m 44·764s
12	Ayrton Senna	BR	John Player Special LOTUS 98T	G	Renault EF15B	John Player Special Team Lotus	**1m 25·050s**	1m 25·286s	1m 32·225s
14	Jonathan Palmer	GB	West ZAKSPEED ZAK 861	G	Zakspeed	West Zakspeed Racing	1m 33·352s	**1m 30·024s**	1m 39·888s
15	Alan Jones	AUS	Beatrice LOLA THL-2	G	Ford-Cosworth	Team Haas (USA) Ltd	**1m 30·087s**	1m 30·517s	1m 38·832s
16	Patrick Tambay	F	Beatrice LOLA THL-1	G	Hart 415T	Team Haas (USA) Ltd	1m 29·665s	**1m 27·860s**	1m 34·721s
17	Marc Surer	CH	ARROWS A8	G	BMW M12/13	Barclay Arrows BMW	1m 30·156s	**1m 28·637s**	1m 50·971s
18	Thierry Boutsen	B	ARROWS A8	G	BMW M12/13	Barclay Arrows BMW	1m 29·931s	**1m 28·022s**	1m 36·193s
19	Teo Fabi	I	BENETTON B186	P	BMW M12/13	Benetton Formula Ltd	1m 29·328s	**1m 27·538s**	1m 35·693s
20	Gerhard Berger	A	BENETTON B186	P	BMW M12/13	Benetton Formula Ltd	1m 28·559s	**1m 27·444s**	1m 33·278s
21	Piercarlo Ghinzani	I	OSELLA FA1G	P	Alfa Romeo 185T	Osella Squadra Corse	**1m 34·461s**	–	1m 38·227s
22	Christian Danner	D	OSELLA FA1F	P	Alfa Romeo 185T	Osella Squadra Corse	1m 37·485s	**1m 33·806s**	1m 36·743s
23	Andrea de Cesaris	I	Simod MINARDI M/85B	P	Motori Moderni	Minardi Team	1m 30·956s	**1m 30·131s**	1m 38·594s
24	Alessandro Nannini	I	Simod MINARDI M/85B	P	Motori Moderni	Minardi Team	1m 29·985s	**1m 29·244s**	1m 37·382s
25	René Arnoux	F	Gitanes LIGIER JS27	P	Renault EF15B	Equipe Ligier	1m 28·362s	**1m 27·403s**	1m 35·336s
26	Jacques Laffite	F	Gitanes LIGIER JS27	P	Renault EF15B	Equipe Ligier	1m 28·411s	**1m 28·389s**	1m 52·436s
27	Michele Alboreto	I	Fiat FERRARI F1/86	G	Ferrari 126C	Scuderia Ferrari SpA	1m 26·428s	**1m 26·263s**	1m 35·164s
28	Stefan Johansson	S	Fiat FERRARI F1/86	G	Ferrari 126C	Scuderia Ferrari SpA	1m 27·497s	**1m 27·009s**	1m 35·852s
29	Huub Rothengatter	NL	West ZAKSPEED ZAK 861	G	Zakspeed	West Zakspeed Racing	1m 40·903s	**1m 31·953s**	1m 39·867s

Friday morning, Saturday morning and Sunday morning practice sessions not officially recorded.

G – Goodyear, P – Pirelli

Fri p.m. Cool, dry, cloudy	Sat p.m. Warm, dry, cloudy	Sun a.m. Cool, damp, cloudy

STARTING GRID

12 SENNA (1m 25·050s)
Lotus

6 PIQUET (1m 25·569s)
Williams

5 MANSELL (1m 26·159s)
Williams

1 PROST (1m 26·176s)
McLaren

27 ALBORETO (1m 26·263s)
Ferrari

2 ROSBERG (1m 26·385s)
McLaren

28 JOHANSSON (1m 27·009s)
Ferrari

25 ARNOUX (1m 27·403s)
Ligier

20 BERGER (1m 27·444s)
Benetton

19 FABI (1m 27·538s)
Benetton

16 TAMBAY (1m 27·860s)
Lola

18 BOUTSEN (1m 28·022s)
Arrows

*3 BRUNDLE (1m 28·329s)
Tyrrell

26 LAFFITE (1m 28·389s)
Ligier

17 SURER (1m 28·637s)
Arrows

7 PATRESE (1m 28·828s)
Brabham

11 DUMFRIES (1m 29·244s)
Lotus

24 NANNINI (1m 29·244s)
Minardi

8 DE ANGELIS (1m 29·713s)
Brabham

**14 PALMER (1m 30·024s)
Zakspeed

15 JONES (1m 30·087s)
Lola

4 STREIFF (1m 30·123s)
Tyrrell

23 DE CESARIS (1m 30·131s)
Minardi

29 ROTHENGATTER (1m 31·953s)
Zakspeed

22 DANNER (1m 33·806s)
Osella

21 GHINZANI (1m 34·461s)
Osella

* Raced spare Tyrrell 014 after crashing 015 on warm-up lap.
** Started from pit lane.

RESULTS AND RETIREMENTS

Place	Driver	Car	Laps	Time and speed (mph/km/h)/Retirement	
1	Alain Prost	McLaren-TAG V6	60	1h 32m 28·408s	121·918/196·208
2	Nelson Piquet	Williams-Honda V6	60	1h 32m 36·053s	121·750/195·938
3	Gerhard Berger	Benetton-BMW 4	59		
4	Stefan Johansson	Ferrari V6	59		
5	Keke Rosberg	McLaren-TAG V6	58	Out of fuel	
6	Riccardo Patrese	Brabham-BMW 4	58	Out of fuel	
7	Thierry Boutsen	Arrows-BMW 4	58		
8	Martin Brundle	Tyrrell-Renault V6	58		
9	Marc Surer	Arrows-BMW 4	57		
10	Michele Alboreto	Ferrari V6	56	Turbocharger	
	Piercarlo Ghinzani	Osella-Alfa Romeo V8	52	Out of fuel	
	René Arnoux	Ligier-Renault V6	46	Lost wheel	
	Philippe Streiff	Tyrrell-Renault V6	41	Transmission	
	Teo Fabi	Benetton-BMW 4	39	Engine	
	Jonathan Palmer	Zakspeed 4	38	Brakes	
	Christian Danner	Osella-Alfa Romeo V8	31	Electrics	
	Alan Jones	Lola-Ford V6	28	Radiator/overheating	
	Andrea de Cesaris	Minardi-MM V6	20	Engine	
	Elio de Angelis	Brabham-BMW 4	19	Engine	
	Jacques Laffite	Ligier-Renault V6	14	Transmission	
	Ayrton Senna	Lotus-Renault V6	11	Wheel bearing	
	Nigel Mansell	Williams-Honda V6	8	Engine	
	Johnny Dumfries	Lotus-Renault V6	8	Wheel bearing	
	Huub Rothengatter	Zakspeed 4	7	Turbo	
	Patrick Tambay	Lola-Hart 4	5	Engine	
	Alessandro Nannini	Minardi-MM V6	0	Accident	

Fastest lap: Piquet, on lap 57, 1m 28·667s, 127·151 mph/204·631 km/h (record).
Previous lap record: Michele Alboreto (F1 Ferrari 156/85 t/c V6), 1m 30·961s, 123·945 mph/199·47 km/h (1985).

PAST WINNERS

Year	Driver	Nat.	Car	Circuit	Distance miles/km	Speed mph/km/h
1981	Nelson Piquet	BR	3·0 Brabham BT49C-Ford	Imola	187·90/302·40	101·20/162·87
1982	Didier Pironi	F	1·5 Ferrari 126C2 t/c V6	Imola	187·90/302·40	116·63/187·70
1983	Patrick Tambay	F	1·5 Ferrari 126C2/B t/c V6	Imola	187·90/302·40	115·25/185·48
1984	Alain Prost	F	1·5 McLaren MP4/2-TAG t/c	Imola	187·90/302·40	116·35/187·25
1985	Elio de Angelis	I	1·5 Lotus 97T-Renault t/c V6	Imola	187·90/302·40	119·17/191·79
1986	Alain Prost	F	1·5 McLaren MP4/2C-TAG t/c V6	Imola	187·90/302·40	121·92/196·21

'S'mine!' Nelson Piquet keeps his trophy out of Alain Prost's reach. Gerhard Berger is simply happy to be on the rostrum for the first time.

LAP CHART

1st Lap Order	Lap progression (laps 1–60)	Running order
6 N. Piquet	6 6 6 6 6 6 6 6 6 6 6 6 6 6 6 6 6 6 6 6 6 6 6 6 6 6 6 6 6 6 6 2 2 2 2 1 1 1 1 1 1 1 1 1 1 1 1 1 1 1 1 1 1 1 1 1 1 1 1 1	1
12 A. Senna	12 12 12 1 2 2 2 2 2 2 1 2 2 2 2 2 2 2 2 2 2 2 2 2 2 2 2 2 2 1 1 1 1 2 2 2 2 2 2 2 2 2 2 2 2 2 2 2 2 2 2 2 2 2 2 2 6 6	2
1 A. Prost	1 1 1 2 1 1 1 1 1 1 1 1 2 1 1 1 1 1 1 1 1 1 1 1 1 1 1 1 6 6 6 6 6 6 6 6 6 6 6 6 6 6 6 6 6 6 6 6 6 6 6 6 6 6 6 6 6 20	3
2 K. Rosberg	2 2 2 12 12 12 12 12 12 12 27 27 27 27 27 27 27 27 27 27 27 27 27 27 27 27 27 27 27 27 27 27 27 27 27 27 27 27 27 27 27 27 27 27 27 27 27 27 27 27 27 27 27 7 7 28	4
5 N. Mansell	5 5 27 27 27 27 27 27 27 25 19 19 19 19 19 20 20 20 20 20 20 20 20 20 25 25 25 25 25 25 25 25 7 7 7 7 7 7 7 7 20 20	5
27 M. Alboreto	27 27 25 25 25 25 25 25 25 19 20 20 20 20 19 19 19 19 25 25 25 25 25 25 25 20 7 7 7 7 7 7 7 7 7 7 28 28 28 28 28 28 28 20 20 28 28	6
25 R. Arnoux	25 25 28 28 28 28 19 19 19 19 19 26 28 28 28 28 28 25 19 19 19 19 19 19 7 7 7 7 20 20 20 18 28 28 28 28 28 20 20 20 20 20 28 28 18 18	7
28 S. Johansson	28 28 16 16 19 19 28 20 20 20 26 28 7 7 7 7 7 25 7 7 7 7 7 7 19 19 19 19 19 19 20 19 20 20 20 20 20 18 18 18 18 18 18 18 18 18 17 3	8
16 P. Tambay	16 16 19 19 16 20 20 28 28 26 26 7 15 18 25 25 25 7 18 18 18 17 17 28 28 28 28 28 28 28 28 20 18 18 18 18 17 17 17 17 17 17 17 17 17 3	9
19 T. Fabi	19 19 20 20 20 7 7 7 26 28 28 7 15 18 25 18 18 18 17 17 28 28 17 18 18 18 18 18 18 18 18 17 17 17 17 17 3 3 3 3 3 3 3 3 3	10
20 G. Berger	20 20 18 7 7 26 26 7 7 7 15 18 17 17 17 17 17 28 28 18 18 18 17 17 17 17 17 17 17 17 17 17 3 3 3 3 3 21 21 21 21 21 21	11
18 T. Boutsen	18 18 7 18 26 18 18 18 18 15 18 25 25 8 8 8 8 3 3 3 3 3 3 3 3 3 3 3 3 3 3 3 3 3 3 3 3 4 4 21 21 21 21	12
11 J. Dumfries	11 7 26 26 18 11 15 15 15 18 17 17 8 3 3 3 3 4 4 4 4 4 4 21 21 21 21 21 21 21 21 21 21 21 21	13
7 R. Patrese	7 11 11 11 11 11 15 11 17 17 17 8 8 3 4 4 4 4 21 21 21 21 21 21 4 4 4 4 4 4 4 4 4 4 4	14
26 J. Laffite	26 26 17 15 15 17 17 8 8 8 8 3 3 4 21 21 21 21 14 14 14 14 14 14 14 14 14 14 14 14 14 14 14 14 14	15
17 M. Surer	17 17 15 17 17 8 8 3 3 3 3 21 4 21 14 14 14 14 22 22 22 22 22 22 22 22 22 22 22 22 22	16
23 A. de Cesaris	23 15 21 21 21 3 3 21 21 21 21 4 21 26 23 23 22 22 22 23 15 15 15 15 15 15 15 15	17
15 A. Jones	15 21 3 3 3 21 21 4 4 4 4 14 14 14 22 22 23 23 23 15	18
21 P. Ghinzani	21 3 8 8 8 4 4 14 14 14 23 23 15 15 15 15 15	19
3 M. Brundle	3 22 4 4 29 29 5 23 23 23 22 22 22	20
22 C. Danner	22 4 29 29 14 14 11 22 22 22	21
4 P. Streiff	4 8 5 5 5 5 5 23	22
8 E. de Angelis	8 29 14 14 14 23 23 22	23
29 H. Rothengatter	29 14 23 23 22 22	24
14 J. Palmer	14 23 22 22 22	25

CIRCUIT DATA

Autodromo Dino Ferrari, Imola, Italy
Circuit length: 3·132 miles/5·040 km
Race distance: 60 laps, 187·90 miles/302·40 km
Race weather: Warm, dry (17°C).

FASTEST LAPS

Driver	Time	Lap
Nelson Piquet	1m 28·667s	57
Gerhard Berger	1m 29·141s	58
Alain Prost	1m 29·464s	41
Keke Rosberg	1m 29·652s	58
Michele Alboreto	1m 30·316s	43
Stefan Johansson	1m 30·768s	53
René Arnoux	1m 31·435s	42
Riccardo Patrese	1m 31·842s	58
Ayrton Senna	1m 31·999s	6
Nigel Mansell	1m 32·145s	8
Teo Fabi	1m 32·246s	20
Elio de Angelis	1m 32·544s	19
Alan Jones	1m 32·615s	22
Jacques Laffite	1m 33·223s	12
Jonathan Palmer	1m 33·406s	37
Thierry Boutsen	1m 33·435s	54
Marc Surer	1m 33·565s	49
Martin Brundle	1m 34·022s	51
Andrea de Cesaris	1m 34·134s	19
Patrick Tambay	1m 34·321s	4
Johnny Dumfries	1m 34·540s	5
Christian Danner	1m 34·558s	24
Philippe Streiff	1m 34·811s	22
Piercarlo Ghinzani	1m 35·748s	23
Huub Rothengatter	1m 36·263s	7

POINTS

WORLD CHAMPIONSHIP OF DRIVERS

1	Alain Prost	22 pts
2	Ayrton Senna	19
3	Nelson Piquet	15
4	Keke Rosberg	11
5	Nigel Mansell	9
6	Gerhard Berger	6
7=	Jacques Laffite	5
7=	René Arnoux	5
9	Stefan Johansson	3
10=	Martin Brundle	2
10=	Teo Fabi	2
12	Riccardo Patrese	1

CONSTRUCTORS' CUP

1	McLaren	33 pts
2	Williams	24
3	Lotus	19
4	Ligier	10
5	Benetton	8
6	Ferrari	3
7	Tyrrell	2
8	Brabham	1

ENTRIES AND PRACTICE TIMES

No.	Driver	Nat.	Car	Tyre	Engine	Entrant	Practice 1	Practice 2	Warm-up
1	Alain Prost	F	Marlboro McLAREN MP4/2C	G	TAG PO1 (TTE PO1)	Marlboro McLaren International	1m 26·059s	**1m 22·627s**	1m 26·316s
2	Keke Rosberg	SF	Marlboro McLAREN MP4/2C	G	TAG PO1 (TTE PO1)	Marlboro McLaren International	1m 25·662s	**1m 24·701s**	1m 27·797s
3	Martin Brundle	GB	Data General TYRRELL 015	G	Renault EF15B	Data General Team Tyrrell	1m 28·564s	**1m 24·860s**	1m 31·611s
4	Philippe Streiff	F	Data General TYRRELL 015	G	Renault EF15B	Data General Team Tyrrell	1m 32·646s	**1m 25·720s**	1m 36·263s
5	Nigel Mansell	GB	WILLIAMS FW11	G	Honda RA166–E	Canon Williams Honda Team	1m 30·919s	**1m 23·047s**	1m 28·406s
6	Nelson Piquet	BR	WILLIAMS FW11	G	Honda RA166–E	Canon Williams Honda Team	1m 27·919s	**1m 25·287s**	1m 28·395s
7	Riccardo Patrese	I	Olivetti BRABHAM BT55	P	BMW M12/13/1	Motor Racing Developments Ltd	1m 26·872s	**1m 24·102s**	1m 27·154s
8	Elio de Angelis	I	Olivetti BRABHAM BT55	P	BMW M12/13/1	Motor Racing Developments Ltd	**1m 27·191s**	1m 28·191s	1m 28·214s
11	Johnny Dumfries	GB	John Player Special LOTUS 98T	G	Renault EF15B	John Player Special Team Lotus	1m 35·027s	**1m 27·826s**	—
12	Ayrton Senna	BR	John Player Special LOTUS 98T	G	Renault EF15B	John Player Special Team Lotus	1m 25·222s	**1m 23·175s**	1m 28·376s
14	Jonathan Palmer	GB	West ZAKSPEED ZAK 861	G	Zakspeed	West Zakspeed Racing	1m 30·152s	**1m 26·644s**	1m 30·492s
15	Alan Jones	AUS	LOLA THL-2	G	Ford-Cosworth	Team Haas (USA) Ltd	1m 26·663s	**1m 26·456s**	1m 30·042s
16	Patrick Tambay	F	LOLA THL-2	G	Ford-Cosworth	Team Haas (USA) Ltd	1m 27·038s	**1m 24·686s**	1m 28·552s
17	Marc Surer	CH	ARROWS A8	G	BMW M12/13	Barclay Arrows BMW	1m 28·878s	**1m 26·300s**	1m 31·119s
18	Thierry Boutsen	B	ARROWS A8	G	BMW M12/13	Barclay Arrows BMW	1m 29·244s	**1m 25·832s**	1m 30·592s
19	Teo Fabi	I	BENETTON B186	P	BMW M12/13	Benetton Formula Ltd	1m 29·397s	**1m 25·962s**	1m 35·310s
20	Gerhard Berger	A	BENETTON B186	P	BMW M12/13	Benetton Formula Ltd	1m 26·280s	**1m 23·960s**	1m 29·052s
21	Piercarlo Ghinzani	I	OSELLA FA1G	P	Alfa Romeo 185T	Osella Squadra Corse	1m 29·282s	**1m 27·288s**	—
22	Christian Danner	D	OSELLA FA1F	P	Alfa Romeo 185T	Osella Squadra Corse	1m 30·986s	**1m 28·132s**	—
23	Andrea de Cesaris	I	Simod MINARDI M/85B	P	Motori Moderni	Minardi Team	1m 28·962s	2m 22·479s	—
24	Alessandro Nannini	I	Simod MINARDI M/85B	P	Motori Moderni	Minardi Team	**1m 29·447s**	2m 27·098s	—
25	René Arnoux	F	Gitanes LIGIER JS27	P	Renault EF15B	Equipe Ligier	1m 25·900s	**1m 25·538s**	1m 27·777s
26	Jacques Laffite	F	Gitanes LIGIER JS27	P	Renault EF15B	Equipe Ligier	1m 26·702s	**1m 24·402s**	1m 28·625s
27	Michele Alboreto	I	Fiat FERRARI F1/86	G	Ferrari 126C	Scuderia Ferrari SpA	1m 26·839s	**1m 23·904s**	1m 29·013s
28	Stefan Johansson	S	Fiat FERRARI F1/86	G	Ferrari 126C	Scuderia Ferrari SpA	1m 27·005s	**1m 25·907s**	1m 29·190s
29	Huub Rothengatter	NL	West ZAKSPEED ZAK 861	G	Zakspeed	West Zakspeed Racing	1m 36·814s	**1m 28·060s**	—

Thursday morning, Saturday morning and Sunday morning practice sessions not officially recorded.

G – Goodyear, P – Pirelli

Thur p.m.	Sat p.m.	Sun a.m.
Warm, dry, cloudy	Hot, dry, sunny	Hot, dry, sunny

STARTING GRID

	1 PROST (1m 22·627s) McLaren
5 MANSELL (1m 23·047s) Williams	
	12 SENNA (1m 23·175s) Lotus
27 ALBORETO (1m 23·904s) Ferrari	
	20 BERGER (1m 23·960s) Benetton
7 PATRESE (1m 24·102s) Brabham	
	*26 LAFFITE (1m 24·402s) Ligier
16 TAMBAY (1m 24·686s) Lola	
	2 ROSBERG (1m 24·701s) McLaren
3 BRUNDLE (1m 24·860s) Tyrrell	
	6 PIQUET (1m 25·287s) Williams
25 ARNOUX (1m 25·538s) Ligier	
	4 STREIFF (1m 25·720s) Tyrrell
18 BOUTSEN (1m 25·832s) Arrows	
	28 JOHANSSON (1m 25·907s) Ferrari
19 FABI (1m 25·926s) Benetton	
	17 SURER (1m 26·300s) Arrows
15 JONES (1m 26·456s) Lola	
	14 PALMER (1m 26·644s) Zakspeed
8 DE ANGELIS (1m 27·191s) Brabham	

* Started from back of grid.
Did not start:
21 Ghinzani (Osella), 1m 27·288s, did not qualify.
11 Dumfries (Lotus), 1m 27·826, did not qualify.
29 Rothengatter (Zakspeed), 1m 28·060s, did not qualify.
22 Danner (Osella), 1m 28·132s, did not qualify.
23 de Cesaris (Minardi), 1m 28·962s, did not qualify.
24 Nannini (Minardi), 1m 29·447s, did not qualify.

RESULTS AND RETIREMENTS

Place	Driver	Car	Laps	Time and speed (mph/km/h)/Retirement	
1	Alain Prost	McLaren-TAG V6	78	1h 55m 41·060s	83·657/134·634
2	Keke Rosberg	McLaren-TAG V6	78	1h 56m 06·082s	83·357/134·150
3	Ayrton Senna	Lotus-Renault V6	78	1h 56m 34·706s	83·016/133·601
4	Nigel Mansell	Williams-Honda V6	78	1h 56m 52·462s	82·806/133·263
5	René Arnoux	Ligier-Renault V6	77		
6	Jacques Laffite	Ligier-Renault V6	77		
7	Nelson Piquet	Williams-Honda V6	77		
8	Thierry Boutsen	Arrows-BMW 4	75		
9	Marc Surer	Arrows-BMW 4	75		
10	Stefan Johansson	Ferrari V6	75		
11	Philippe Streiff	Tyrrell-Renault V6	74		
12	Jonathan Palmer	Zakspeed 4	74		
	Martin Brundle	Tyrrell-Renault V6	67	Accident with Tambay	
	Patrick Tambay	Lola-Ford V6	67	Accident with Brundle	
	Gerhard Berger	Benetton-BMW 4	42	Wheel drive pegs	
	Michele Alboreto	Ferrari V6	38	Turbo	
	Riccardo Patrese	Brabham-BMW 4	38	Fuel pump	
	Elio de Angelis	Brabham-BMW 4	31	Engine	
	Teo Fabi	Benetton-BMW 4	17	Brakes	
	Alan Jones	Lola-Ford V6	2	Incident with Streiff; could not restart	

Fastest lap: Prost, on lap 51, 1m 26·607s, 85·957 mph/138·335 km/h (lap record for revised 2·068 mile/3·328 km circuit).
Previous lap record (for 2·058 mile/3·312 km circuit): Michele Alboreto (F1 Ferrari 156/85t/c V6), 1m 22·637s, 89·654 mph/144·284 km/h (1985).

PAST WINNERS

Year	Driver	Nat.	Car	Circuit	Distance miles/km	Speed mph/km/h
1950	Juan Manuel Fangio	RA	1·5 Alfa Romeo 158 s/c	Monte Carlo	197·60/318·01	61·33/98·70
1952*	Vittorio Marzotto	I	2·7 Ferrari 225MM	Monte Carlo	195·42/314·50	58·20/93·66
1955	Maurice Trintignant	F	2·5 Ferrari 625	Monte Carlo	195·42/314·50	65·81/105·91
1956	Stirling Moss	GB	2·5 Maserati 250F	Monte Carlo	195·42/314·50	64·94/104·51
1957	Juan Manuel Fangio	RA	2·5 Maserati 250F	Monte Carlo	205·19/330·22	64·72/104·16
1958	Maurice Trintignant	F	2·0 Cooper T45-Climax	Monte Carlo	195·42/314·50	67·99/109·41
1959	Jack Brabham	AUS	2·5 Cooper T51-Climax	Monte Carlo	195·42/314·50	66·71/107·36
1960	Stirling Moss	GB	2·5 Lotus 18-Climax	Monte Carlo	195·42/314·50	67·48/108·60
1961	Stirling Moss	GB	1·5 Lotus 18-Climax	Monte Carlo	195·42/314·50	70·70/113·79
1962	Bruce McLaren	NZ	1·5 Cooper T60-Climax	Monte Carlo	195·42/314·50	70·46/113·40
1963	Graham Hill	GB	1·5 BRM P57	Monte Carlo	195·42/314·50	72·43/116·56
1964	Graham Hill	GB	1·5 BRM P261	Monte Carlo	195·42/314·50	72·64/116·91
1965	Graham Hill	GB	1·5 BRM P261	Monte Carlo	195·42/314·50	74·34/119·64
1966	Jackie Stewart	GB	1·9 BRM P261	Monte Carlo	195·42/314·50	76·51/123·14
1967	Denny Hulme	NZ	3·0 Brabham BT20-Repco	Monte Carlo	195·42/314·50	75·90/122·14
1968	Graham Hill	GB	3·0 Lotus 49B-Ford	Monte Carlo	156·34/251·60	77·82/125·24
1969	Graham Hill	GB	3·0 Lotus 49B-Ford	Monte Carlo	156·34/251·60	80·18/129·04
1970	Jochen Rindt	A	3·0 Lotus 49C-Ford	Monte Carlo	156·34/251·60	81·85/131·72
1971	Jackie Stewart	GB	3·0 Tyrrell 003-Ford	Monte Carlo	156·34/251·60	83·49/134·36
1972	Jean-Pierre Beltoise	F	3·0 BRM P160B	Monte Carlo	156·34/251·60	63·85/102·75
1973	Jackie Stewart	GB	3·0 Tyrrell 006-Ford	Monte Carlo	158·87/255·68	80·96/130·29
1974	Ronnie Peterson	S	3·0 JPS/Lotus 72-Ford	Monte Carlo	158·87/255·68	80·74/129·94
1975	Niki Lauda	A	3·0 Ferrari 312T/75	Monte Carlo	152·76/245·84	75·53/121·55
1976	Niki Lauda	A	3·0 Ferrari 312T-2/76	Monte Carlo	160·52/258·34	80·36/129·32
1977	Jody Scheckter	ZA	3·0 Wolf WR1-Ford	Monte Carlo	156·41/251·71	79·61/128·12
1978	Patrick Depailler	F	3·0 Tyrrell 008-Ford	Monte Carlo	154·35/248·40	80·36/129·33
1979	Jody Scheckter	ZA	3·0 Ferrari 312T-4	Monte Carlo	156·41/251·71	81·34/130·90
1980	Carlos Reutemann	RA	3·0 Williams FW07B-Ford	Monte Carlo	156·41/251·71	81·20/130·68
1981	Gilles Villeneuve	CDN	1·5 Ferrari 126CK	Monte Carlo	156·41/251·71	82·04/132·03
1982	Riccardo Patrese	I	3·0 Brabham BT49D-Ford	Monte Carlo	156·41/251·71	82·21/132·30
1983	Keke Rosberg	SF	3·0 Williams FW08C-Ford	Monte Carlo	156·41/251·71	80·52/129·59
1984	Alain Prost	F	1·5 McLaren MP4/2-TAG t/c	Monte Carlo	63·80/102·67	62·62/100·77
1985	Alain Prost	F	1·5 McLaren MP4/2B-TAG t/c	Monte Carlo	160·52/258·34	86·02/138·30
1986	Alain Prost	F	1·5 McLaren MP4/2C-TAG t/c	Monte Carlo	161·30/259·58	83·66/134·63

*Non-championship (sports cars)

LAP CHART

1st LAP ORDER	Lap-by-lap positions (1 → 78)	Running order
1 A. Prost	leads throughout (1)	1
12 A. Senna	12 … rises to 2	2
5 N. Mansell	5 … 2 … 12	3
27 M. Alboreto	27 … 2 … 5	4
2 K. Rosberg	2 … 5 … 25	5
20 G. Berger	20 … 7 … 25 … 20 … 6 … 26	6
7 R. Patrese	7 … 20 … 6 … 26 … 3 … 6	7
3 M. Brundle	3 … 25 … 3 … 6 … 16 … 6 … 18	8
16 P. Tambay	16 … 3 … 16 … 6 … 16 … 17	9
6 N. Piquet	6 … 25 … 16 … 6 … 26 … 3 … 28	10
18 T. Boutsen	18 … 25 … 6 … 26 … 28 … 16 … 18 … 17 … 4	11
25 R. Arnoux	25 … 18 … 28 … 26 … 16 … 18 … 17 … 28 … 14	12
28 S. Johansson	28 … 18 … 26 … 28 … 17 … 14 … 4	13
4 P. Streiff	4 … 17 … 26 … 18 … 17 … 14	14
15 A. Jones	15 … 26 … 17 … 14 … 4	15
17 M. Surer	17 … 8 … 14 … 4	16
26 J. Laffite	26 … 14 … 4 … 7	17
8 E. de Angelis	8 … 4 … 8	18
14 J. Palmer	14 … 19 … 19	19
19 T. Fabi	19 19	20

FASTEST LAPS

Driver	Time	Lap
Alain Prost	1m 26·607s	51
Ayrton Senna	1m 26·843s	68
Keke Rosberg	1m 26·971s	56
Nigel Mansell	1m 27·405s	58
Riccardo Patrese	1m 27·585s	36
Patrick Tambay	1m 27·769s	62
Nelson Piquet	1m 27·797s	68
Jacques Laffite	1m 27·873s	28
René Arnoux	1m 27·988s	26
Martin Brundle	1m 28·649s	62
Michele Alboreto	1m 28·776s	25
Gerhard Berger	1m 28·944s	25
Stefan Johansson	1m 29·305s	68
Marc Surer	1m 30·509s	47
Thierry Boutsen	1m 30·621s	53
Philippe Streiff	1m 31·098s	65
Elio de Angelis	1m 31·236s	13
Teo Fabi	1m 31·647s	5
Jonathan Palmer	1m 31·679s	47
Alan Jones	1m 35·510s	2

CIRCUIT DATA

Circuit de Monaco, Monte Carlo
Circuit length: 2·068 miles/3·328 km
Race distance: 78 laps, 161·298 miles/259·584 km
Race weather: Warm, dry, sunny (18°C).

POINTS

WORLD CHAMPIONSHIP OF DRIVERS

1=	Ayrton Senna	15 pts
1=	Nelson Piquet	15
3	Alain Prost	13
4=	Nigel Mansell	6
4=	Gerhard Berger	6
6	Keke Rosberg	5
7	Jacques Laffite	4
8=	René Arnoux	3
8=	Stefan Johansson	3
10=	Martin Brundle	2
10=	Teo Fabi	2
12	Riccardo Patrese	1

CONSTRUCTORS' CUP

1	Williams	21 pts
2	McLaren	18
3	Lotus	15
4	Benetton	8
5	Ligier	7
6	Ferrari	3
7	Tyrrell	2
8	Brabham	1

ENTRIES AND PRACTICE TIMES

No.	Driver	Nat.	Car	Tyre	Engine	Entrant	Practice 1	Practice 2	Warm-up
1	Alain Prost	F	Marlboro McLAREN MP4/2C	G	TAG PO1 (TTE PO1)	Marlboro McLaren International	1m 55·039s	**1m 54·501s**	1m 59·601s
2	Keke Rosberg	SF	Marlboro McLAREN MP4/2C	G	TAG PO1 (TTE PO1)	Marlboro McLaren International	1m 56·354s	**1m 55·662s**	1m 59·590s
3	Martin Brundle	GB	Data General TYRRELL 015	G	Renault EF15/EF15B	Data General Team Tyrrell	1m 57·797s	**1m 56·537s**	2m 03·390s
4	Philippe Streiff	F	Data General TYRRELL 015	G	Renault EF15/EF15B	Data General Team Tyrrell	1m 59·347s	**1m 58·603s**	2m 05·821s
5	Nigel Mansell	GB	WILLIAMS FW11	G	Honda RA166—E	Canon Williams Honda Team	1m 55·345s	**1m 54·582s**	2m 00·054s
6	Nelson Piquet	BR	WILLIAMS FW11	G	Honda RA166—E	Canon Williams Honda Team	1m 54·637s	**1m 54·331s**	2m 00·256s
7	Riccardo Patrese	I	Olivetti BRABHAM BT55	G	BMW M12/13/1	Motor Racing Developments Ltd	2m 00·357s	**1m 57·612s**	2m 04·191s
11	Johnny Dumfries	GB	John Player Special LOTUS 98T	G	Renault EF15/EF15B	John Player Special Team Lotus	1m 58·619s	**1m 57·462s**	2m 04·684s
12	Ayrton Senna	BR	John Player Special LOTUS 98T	G	Renault EF15/EF15B	John Player Special Team Lotus	1m 55·776s	**1m 54·576s**	2m 01·950s
14	Jonathan Palmer	GB	West ZAKSPEED ZAK 861	G	Zakspeed	West Zakspeed Racing	2m 02·307s	**2m 00·148s**	2m 14·177s
15	Alan Jones	AUS	LOLA THL-2	G	Ford-Cosworth	Team Haas (USA) Ltd	1m 59·180s	**1m 57·815s**	
16	Patrick Tambay	F	LOLA THL-2	G	Ford-Cosworth	Team Haas (USA) Ltd	1m 58·574s	**1m 56·309s**	2m 00·724s
17	Marc Surer	CH	ARROWS A8	G	BMW M12/13	Barclay Arrows BMW	**2m 01·320s**	2m 01·415s	2m 07·480s
18	Thierry Boutsen	B	ARROWS A8	G	BMW M12/13	Barclay Arrows BMW	1m 57·918s	**1m 57·612s**	2m 03·399s
19	Teo Fabi	I	BENETTON B186	P	BMW M12/13	Benetton Formula Ltd	1m 57·440s	**1m 54·765s**	2m 01·732s
20	Gerhard Berger	A	BENETTON B186	P	BMW M12/13	Benetton Formula Ltd	**1m 54·468s**	1m 54·939s	2m 02·151s
21	Piercarlo Ghinzani	I	OSELLA FA1G	P	Alfa Romeo 185T	Osella Squadra Corse	**2m 05·092s**	3m 38·767s	2m 14·573s
22	Christian Danner	D	OSELLA FA1F	P	Alfa Romeo 185T	Osella Squadra Corse	2m 09·465s	**2m 06·219s**	—
23	Andrea de Cesaris	I	Simod MINARDI M/85B	P	Motori Moderni	Minardi Team	2m 00·984s	**1m 59·960s**	2m 07·262s
24	Alessandro Nannini	I	Simod MINARDI M/85B	P	Motori Moderni	Minardi Team	2m 01·528s	**2m 01·354s**	2m 09·402s
25	René Arnoux	F	Gitanes LIGIER JS27	P	Renault EF15/EF15B	Equipe Ligier	1m 57·269s	**1m 55·576s**	2m 01·743s
26	Jacques Laffite	F	Gitanes LIGIER JS27	P	Renault EF15/EF15B	Equipe Ligier	**1m 58·238s**	2m 27·817s	2m 05·233s
27	Michele Alboreto	I	Fiat FERRARI F1/86	G	Ferrari 126C	Scuderia Ferrari SpA	1m 56·294s	**1m 56·242s**	2m 01·902s
28	Stefan Johansson	S	Fiat FERRARI F1/86	G	Ferrari 126C	Scuderia Ferrari SpA	1m 57·697s	**1m 56·496s**	2m 01·428s
29	Huub Rothengatter	NL	West ZAKSPEED ZAK 861	G	Zakspeed	West Zakspeed Racing	2m 06·006s	**2m 03·842s**	2m 08·572s

Friday morning, Saturday morning and Sunday morning practice sessions not officially recorded.

G – Goodyear, P – Pirelli

Fri p.m. Cool, dry, cloudy	Sat p.m. Cool, dry, cloudy	Sun a.m. Hot, dry, sunny

STARTING GRID

	6 PIQUET (1m 54·331s) Williams
20 BERGER (1m 54·468s) Benetton	
	1 PROST (1m 54·501s) McLaren
12 SENNA (1m 54·576s) Lotus	
	5 MANSELL (1m 54·582s) Williams
19 FABI (1m 54·765s) Benetton	
	25 ARNOUX (1m 55·576s) Ligier
2 ROSBERG (1m 55·662s) McLaren	
	27 ALBORETO (1m 56·242s) Ferrari
16 TAMBAY (1m 56·309s) Lola	
	28 JOHANSSON (1m 56·496s) Ferrari
3 BRUNDLE (1m 56·537s) Tyrrell	
	11 DUMFRIES (1m 57·462s) Lotus
18 BOUTSEN (1m 57·612s) Arrows	
	*7 PATRESE (1m 57·612s) Brabham
15 JONES (1m 57·815s) Lola	
	26 LAFFITE (1m 58·238s) Ligier
4 STREIFF (1m 58·603s) Tyrrell	
	23 DE CESARIS (1m 59·960s) Minardi
14 PALMER (2m 00·148s) Zakspeed	
	17 SURER (2m 01·320s) Arrows
24 NANNINI (2m 01·354s) Minardi	
	29 ROTHENGATTER (2m 03·842s) Zakspeed
21 GHINZANI (2m 05·092s) Osella	
	*22 DANNER (2m 06·219s) Osella

* Went into pit lane at end of parade lap.

RESULTS AND RETIREMENTS

Place	Driver	Car	Laps	Time and speed (mph/km/h)/Retirement	
1	Nigel Mansell	Williams-Honda V6	43	1h 27m 57·925s	126·479/203·548
2	Ayrton Senna	Lotus-Renault V6	43	1h 28m 17·752s	126·005/202·786
3	Stefan Johansson	Ferrari V6	43	1h 28m 24·517s	125·845/202·528
4	Michele Alboreto	Ferrari V6	43	1h 28m 27·559s	125·773/202·412
5	Jacques Laffite	Ligier-Renault V6	43	1h 29m 08·615s	124·807/200·858
6	Alain Prost	McLaren-TAG V6	43	1h 30m 15·697s	123·261/198·370
7	Teo Fabi	Benetton-BMW 4	42		
8	Riccardo Patrese	Brabham-BMW 4	42		
9	Marc Surer	Arrows-BMW 4	41		
10	Gerhard Berger	Benetton-BMW 4	41		
11	Alan Jones	Lola-Ford V6	40	Out of fuel	
12	Philippe Streiff	Tyrrell-Renault V6	40		
13	Jonathan Palmer	Zakspeed 4	38		
	Andrea de Cesaris	Minardi-MM V6	35	Out of fuel	
	Martin Brundle	Tyrrell-Renault V6	25	Gearbox	
	Huub Rothengatter	Zakspeed 4	25	Alternator/battery	
	Alessandro Nannini	Minardi-MM V6	24	Gearbox	
	René Arnoux	Ligier-Renault V6	23	Engine	
	Nelson Piquet	Williams-Honda V6	16	Turbo boost control	
	Thierry Boutsen	Arrows-BMW 4	7	Electrics	
	Johnny Dumfries	Lotus-Renault V6	7	Spun off/holed radiator	
	Keke Rosberg	McLaren-TAG V6	6	Engine	
	Piercarlo Ghinzani	Osella-Alfa Romeo V8	3	Engine	
	Christian Danner	Osella-Alfa Romeo V8	2	Engine	
	Patrick Tambay	Lola-Ford V6	0	Accident damage	

Fastest lap: Prost, on lap 31, 1m 59·282s, 130·148 mph/209·453 km/h (record).
Previous lap record: Alain Prost (F1 McLaren MP4/2B-TAG t/c), 2m 01·730s, 127·531 mph/205·241 km/h (1985).

PAST WINNERS

Year	Driver	Nat.	Car	Circuit	Distance miles/km	Speed mph/km/h
1950	Juan Manuel Fangio	RA	1·5 Alfa Romeo 158 s/c	Francorchamps	307·08/494·20	110·04/177·09
1951	Giuseppe Farina	I	1·5 Alfa Romeo 159 s/c	Francorchamps	315·85/508·31	114·32/183·99
1952	Alberto Ascari	I	2·0 Ferrari 500	Francorchamps	315·85/508·31	103·13/165·96
1953	Alberto Ascari	I	2·0 Ferrari 500	Francorchamps	315·85/508·31	112·47/181·00
1954	Juan Manuel Fangio	RA	2·5 Maserati 250F	Francorchamps	315·85/508·31	115·06/185·17
1955	Juan Manuel Fangio	RA	2·5 Mercedes-Benz W196	Francorchamps	315·85/508·31	118·83/191·24
1956	Peter Collins	GB	2·5 Lancia-Ferrari D50	Francorchamps	315·85/508·31	118·44/190·61
1958	Tony Brooks	GB	2·5 Vanwall	Francorchamps	210·27/338·40	129·92/209·09
1960	Jack Brabham	AUS	2·5 Cooper T53-Climax	Francorchamps	315·41/507·60	133·63/215·06
1961	Phil Hill	USA	1·5 Ferrari Dino 156	Francorchamps	262·84/423·00	128·15/206·24
1962	Jim Clark	GB	1·5 Lotus 25-Climax	Francorchamps	280·36/451·19	131·90/212·27
1963	Jim Clark	GB	1·5 Lotus 25-Climax	Francorchamps	280·36/451·19	114·10/183·63
1964	Jim Clark	GB	1·5 Lotus 25-Climax	Francorchamps	280·36/451·19	132·79/213·71
1965	Jim Clark	GB	1·5 Lotus 33-Climax	Francorchamps	280·36/451·19	117·16/188·55
1966	John Surtees	GB	3·0 Ferrari 312/66	Francorchamps	245·32/394·80	113·93/183·36
1967	Dan Gurney	USA	3·0 Eagle T1G-Gurney-Weslake	Francorchamps	245·32/394·80	145·99/234·95
1968	Bruce McLaren	NZ	3·0 McLaren M7A-Ford	Francorchamps	245·32/394·80	147·14/236·80
1970	Pedro Rodriguez	MEX	3·0 BRM P153	Francorchamps	245·32/394·80	149·97/241·36
1972	Emerson Fittipaldi	BR	3·0 JPS/Lotus 72-Ford	Nivelles-Baulers	196·69/316·54	113·35/182·42
1973	Jackie Stewart	GB	3·0 Tyrrell 006-Ford	Zolder	183·55/295·39	107·74/173·38
1974	Emerson Fittipaldi	BR	3·0 McLaren M23-Ford	Nivelles-Baulers	196·69/316·54	113·10/182·02
1975	Niki Lauda	A	3·0 Ferrari 312T/75	Zolder	185·38/298·34	107·05/172·28
1976	Niki Lauda	A	3·0 Ferrari 312T/76	Zolder	185·38/298·34	108·11/173·98
1977	Gunnar Nilsson	S	3·0 JPS/Lotus 78-Ford	Zolder	185·38/298·34	96·64/155·53
1978	Mario Andretti	USA	3·0 JPS/Lotus 79-Ford	Zolder	185·38/298·34	111·38/179·24
1979	Jody Scheckter	ZA	3·0 Ferrari 312T-4	Zolder	185·38/298·34	111·24/179·02
1980	Didier Pironi	F	3·0 Ligier JS11/15-Ford	Zolder	190·66/306·86	115·82/186·40
1981	Carlos Reutemann	RA	3·0 Williams FW07C-Ford	Zolder	143·01/230·15	112·12/180·44
1982	John Watson	GB	3·0 McLaren MP4B-Ford	Zolder	185·38/298·34	116·19/187·00
1983	Alain Prost	F	1·5 Renault RE40 t/c	Francorchamps	173·13/278·62	119·14/191·73
1984	Michele Alboreto	I	1·5 Ferrari 126C4 t/c	Zolder	185·38/298·34	115·22/185·43
1985	Ayrton Senna	BR	1·5 Lotus 97T-Renault t/c	Francorchamps	185·67/298·81	117·94/189·81
1986	Nigel Mansell	GB	1·5 Williams FW11-Honda t/c	Francorchamps	185·43/298·42	126·48/203·55

LAP CHART

1st LAP ORDER	1	2	3	4	5	6	7	8	9	10	11	12	13	14	15	16	17	18	19	20	21	22	23	24	25	26	27	28	29	30	31	32	33	34	35	36	37	38	39	40	41	42	43	Race Position
6 N. Piquet	6	6	6	6	6	6	6	6	6	6	6	6	6	6	6	6	12	12	12	12	28	28	5	5	5	5	5	5	5	5	5	5	5	5	5	5	5	5	5	5	5	5	5	1
12 A. Senna	12	12	5	5	12	12	12	12	12	12	12	12	12	12	12	5	5	5	28	5	5	12	12	12	12	12	12	12	12	12	12	12	12	12	12	12	12	12	12	12	12	12	12	2
5 N. Mansell	5	5	12	12	28	28	28	28	28	28	28	28	28	28	5	28	28	28	5	12	12	27	27	27	27	27	27	27	27	27	27	27	27	27	27	28	28	28	28	28	28	28	28	3
28 S. Johansson	28	28	28	28	5	5	5	5	5	5	5	5	5	28	27	27	27	27	28	27	27	28	28	28	28	28	28	28	27	27	27	27	27											4
11 J. Dumfries	1†	11	11	11	11	11	27	27	27	27	27	27	27	25	3	26	26	26	26	26	26	26	26	26	26	26	26	26	26	26	26	26	26	26	26	26	26	26	26	26	26	26	26	5
26 J. Laffite	26	26	15	15	15	27	26	26	25	25	25	25	25	26	3	3	3	3	15	15	15	15	15	15	1	1	1	1	1	1	1	1	1	1	1	1	1	1						6
15 A. Jones	15	15	26	26	27	15	3	3	25	26	26	26	26	3	25	19	19	15	15	15	15	1	1	1	1	15	15	15	15	15	15	15	15	19	19									7
18 T. Boutsen	18	18	18	27	26	26	18	25	3	3	3	3	3	19	19	15	15	1	1	1	19	19	19	19	19	19	19	19	19	19	19	19	19	19	17	7								8
27 M. Alboreto	27	27	27	18	18	2	25	4	4	19	19	19	19	15	1	1	23	19	19	3	17	17	17	17	17	17	17	17	17	17	17	17	7											9
3 M. Brundle	3	3	3	2	18	4	19	19	15	15	15	15	23	1	23	19	23	17	17	7	7	23	23	23	23	23	23	7	7	7	7	20												10
4 P. Streiff	4	4	4	2	3	3	15	23	23	23	23	23	1	23	17	17	17	7	7	7	23	23	7	7	7	7	7	20	20	20	20													11
25 R. Arnoux	25	25	2	4	25	19	15	23	29	17	17	17	17	17	7	7	7	23	23	23	20	20	20	20	20	20	20	4	4	4	4													12
2 K. Rosberg	2	2	25	25	25	4	11	29	17	29	29	29	29	1	29	7	29	29	29	29	20	4	4	4	4	4	4	4	14	14														13
23 A. de Cesaris	23	19	19	19	19	19	23	17	24	24	24	1	29	29	7	29	24	24	24	24	4	14	14	14	14	14	14	14	14	14														14
29 H. Rothengatter	29	23	23	23	23	29	24	24	7	7	7	24	24	7	24	20	20	20	20	20	4	14																						15
19 T. Fabi	19	29	29	29	29	29	7	7	1	1	1	7	24	20	20	4	4	4	4	14	29																							16
24 A. Nannini	24	24	24	24	24	7	24	1	4	4	4	4	4	4	14	25	25	25	25	24																								17
17 M. Surer	17	17	17	17	7	24	17	20	20	20	20	20	20	14	14	25	14	14	14																									18
7 R. Patrese	7	7	7	7	17	17	1	14	14	14	14	14	14	14																														19
20 G. Berger	20	14	14	14	1	1	20																																					20
22 C. Danner	22	22	1	1	20	20	14																																					21
14 J. Palmer	14	1	20	20	14	14																																						22
1 A. Prost	1	20	21																																									23
21 P. Ghinzani	21	21																																										24

CIRCUIT DATA

Circuit de Spa-Francorchamps, Francorchamps

Circuit length: 4·3123 miles/6·940 km (circuit length officially revised by RACB)
Race distance: 43 laps, 185·429 miles/298·420 km
Race weather: Dry, hot, sunny (24°C).

FASTEST LAPS

Driver	Time	Lap
Alain Prost	1m 59·282s	31
Ayrton Senna	1m 59·867s	28
Nigel Mansell	1m 59·879s	40
Stefan Johansson	2m 00·221s	34
René Arnoux	2m 00·751s	20
Michele Alboreto	2m 00·828s	32
Gerhard Berger	2m 00·877s	25
Teo Fabi	2m 01·204s	23
Riccardo Patrese	2m 01·241s	30
Martin Brundle	2m 01·555s	22
Alan Jones	2m 01·584s	36
Jacques Laffite	2m 01·655s	35
Nelson Piquet	2m 01·663s	4
Philippe Streiff	2m 03·183s	35
Andrea de Cesaris	2m 03·916s	27
Jonathan Palmer	2m 04·287s	28
Marc Surer	2m 04·435s	36
Keke Rosberg	2m 04·546s	2
Johnny Dumfries	2m 04·781s	6
Thierry Boutsen	2m 05·545s	2
Alessandro Nannini	2m 07·875s	19
Huub Rothengatter	2m 08·018s	7
Piercarlo Ghinzani	2m 17·068s	3
Christian Danner	2m 34·035s	2

POINTS

WORLD CHAMPIONSHIP OF DRIVERS

1	Ayrton Senna	25 Pts
2	Alain Prost	23
3	Nigel Mansell	18
4	Nelson Piquet	15
5	Keke Rosberg	11
6=	Jacques Laffite	7
6=	Stefan Johansson	7
8	Gerhard Berger	6
9	René Arnoux	5
10	Michele Alboreto	3
11=	Martin Brundle	2
11=	Teo Fabi	2
13	Riccardo Patrese	1

CONSTRUCTORS' CUP

1	McLaren	34 pts
2	Williams	33
3	Lotus	25
4	Ligier	12
5	Ferrari	10
6	Benetton	8
7	Tyrrell	2
8	Brabham	1

ENTRIES AND PRACTICE TIMES

No.	Driver	Nat.	Car	Tyre	Engine	Entrant	Practice 1	Practice 2	Warm-up
1	Alain Prost	F	Marlboro McLAREN MP4/2C	G	TAG PO1 (TTE PO1)	Marlboro McLaren International	1m 29·541s	**1m 25·192s**	1m 27·599s
2	Keke Rosberg	SF	Marlboro McLAREN MP4/2C	G	TAG PO1 (TTE PO1)	Marlboro McLaren International	1m 29·348s	**1m 25·533s**	1m 27·310s
3	Martin Brundle	GB	Data General TYRRELL 014	G	Renault EF15/EF15B	Data General Team Tyrrell	1m 34·233s	**1m 29·111s**	1m 31·036s
4	Philippe Streiff	F	Data General TYRRELL 017	G	Renault EF15/EF15B	Data General Team Tyrrell	1m 32·307s	**1m 28·639s**	1m 31·807s
5	Nigel Mansell	GB	WILLIAMS FW11	G	Honda RA166—E	Canon Williams Honda Team	1m 28·889s	**1m 24·118s**	1m 27·927s
6	Nelson Piquet	BR	WILLIAMS FW11	G	Honda RA166—E	Canon Williams Honda Team	1m 28·588s	**1m 24·384s**	1m 28·519s
7	Riccardo Patrese	I	Olivetti BRABHAM BT55	P	BMW M12/13/1	Motor Racing Developments Ltd	1m 32·692s	**1m 26·483s**	1m 30·305s
8	Derek Warwick	GB	Olivetti BRABHAM BT55	P	BMW M12/13/1	Motor Racing Developments Ltd	1m 33·231s	**1m 27·413s**	1m 30·569s
11	Johnny Dumfries	GB	John Player Special LOTUS 98T	G	Renault EF15/EF15B	John Player Special Team Lotus	1m 32·144s	**1m 28·521s**	1m 32·656s
12	Ayrton Senna	BR	John Player Special LOTUS 98T	G	Renault EF15/EF15B	John Player Special Team Lotus	1m 27·422s	**1m 24·188s**	1m 30·168s
14	Jonathan Palmer	GB	West ZAKSPEED ZAK 861	G	Zakspeed	West Zakspeed Racing	1m 31·856s	**1m 30·005s**	1m 33·520s
15	Alan Jones	AUS	LOLA THL-2	G	Ford-Cosworth	Team Haas (USA) Ltd	1m 33·291s	**1m 28·058s**	1m 31·187s
16	Patrick Tambay	F	LOLA THL-2	G	Ford-Cosworth	Team Haas (USA) Ltd	1m 31·487s	**1m 28·095s**	1m 31·960s
17	*Christian Danner	D	ARROWS A8	G	BMW M12/13	Barclay Arrows BMW			
18	Thierry Boutsen	B	ARROWS A8	G	BMW M12/13	Barclay Arrows BMW	1m 35·843s	**1m 27·614s**	1m 31·665s
19	Teo Fabi	I	BENETTON B186	P	BMW M12/13	Benetton Formula Ltd	1m 51·056s	**1m 28·102s**	1m 30·602s
20	Gerhard Berger	A	BENETTON B186	P	BMW M12/13	Benetton Formula Ltd	1m 29·471s	**1m 26·439s**	1m 30·104s
21	Piercarlo Ghinzani	I	OSELLA FA1G	P	Alfa Romeo 185T	Osella Squadra Corse	1m 36·575s	**1m 31·479s**	1m 32·569s
22	Christian Danner	D	OSELLA FA1F	P	Alfa Romeo 185T	Osella Squadra Corse	**1m 41·436s**	—	1m 37·508s
23	Andrea de Cesaris	I	Simod MINARDI M/85B	P	Motori Moderni	Minardi Team	1m 32·619s	**1m 29·854s**	1m 31·370s
24	Alessandro Nannini	I	Simod MINARDI M/85B	P	Motori Moderni	Minardi Team	1m 35·789s	**1m 29·653s**	1m 34·735s
25	René Arnoux	F	Gitanes LIGIER JS27	P	Renault EF15/EF15B	Equipe Ligier	1m 30·200s	**1m 25·224s**	1m 28·610s
26	Jacques Laffite	F	Gitanes LIGIER JS27	P	Renault EF15/EF15B	Equipe Ligier	1m 30·171s	**1m 26·447s**	1m 29·793s
27	Michele Alboreto	I	Fiat FERRARI F1/86	G	Ferrari 126C	Scuderia Ferrari SpA	1m 42·740s	**1m 27·495s**	1m 29·772s
28	Stefan Johansson	S	Fiat FERRARI F1/86	G	Ferrari 126C	Scuderia Ferrari SpA	**1m 28·881s**	1m 29·078s	1m 29·130s
29	Huub Rothengatter	NL	West ZAKSPEED ZAK 861	G	Zakspeed	West Zakspeed Racing	1m 46·280s	**1m 32·113s**	1m 33·010s

Friday morning, Saturday morning and Sunday morning practice sessions not officially recorded.
G – Goodyear, P – Pirelli
*Danner's late entry by Arrows and contractual difficulties with Osella meant he continued to drive for Osella.

Fri p.m. Cool, damp, cloudy	Sat p.m. Hot, dry, sunny	Sun a.m. Hot, dry, sunny

STARTING GRID

12 SENNA (1m 24·188s)
Lotus

5 MANSELL (1m 24·118s)
Williams

1 PROST (1m 25·192s)
McLaren

6 PIQUET (1m 24·384s)
Williams

2 ROSBERG (1m 25·533s)
McLaren

25 ARNOUX (1m 25·224s)
Ligier

26 LAFFITE (1m 26·447s)
Ligier

20 BERGER (1m 26·439s)
Benetton

8 WARWICK (1m 27·413s)
Brabham

7 PATRESE (1m 26·483s)
Brabham

18 BOUTSEN (1m 27·614s)
Arrows

27 ALBORETO (1m 27·495s)
Ferrari

16 TAMBAY (1m 28·095s)
Lola

15 JONES (1m 28·058s)
Lola

11 DUMFRIES (1m 28·521s)
Lotus

19 FABI (1m 28·102s)
Benetton

28 JOHANSSON (1m 28·881s)
Ferrari

4 STREIFF (1m 28·639s)
Tyrrell

24 NANNINI (1m 29·653s)
Minardi

3 BRUNDLE (1m 29·111s)
Tyrrell

*14 PALMER (1m 30·005s)
Zakspeed

23 DE CESARIS (1m 29·854s)
Minardi

29 ROTHENGATTER (1m 32·113s)
Zakspeed

21 GHINZANI (1m 31·479s)
Osella

*22 DANNER (1m 41·436s)
Osella

* Started from pit lane.
Did not start:
Tambay (Lola), accident during warm-up on race morning.

RESULTS AND RETIREMENTS

Place	Driver	Car	Laps	Time and speed (mph/km/h)/Retirement	
1	Nigel Mansell	Williams-Honda V6	69	1h 42m 26·415s	110·744/178·225
2	Alain Prost	McLaren-TAG V6	69	1h 42m 47·074s	110·373/177·628
3	Nelson Piquet	Williams-Honda V6	69	1h 43m 02·677s	110·094/177·180
4	Keke Rosberg	McLaren-TAG V6	69	1h 44m 02·088s	109·046/175·493
5	Ayrton Senna	Lotus-Renault V6	68		
6	René Arnoux	Ligier-Renault V6	68		
7	Jacques Laffite	Ligier-Renault V6	68		
8	Michele Alboreto	Ferrari V6	68		
9	Martin Brundle	Tyrrell-Renault V6	67		
10	Alan Jones	Lola-Ford V6	66		
11	Philippe Streiff	Tyrrell-Renault V6	65		
12	Huub Rothengatter	Zakspeed 4	63		
	Riccardo Patrese	Brabham-BMW 4	44	Turbo	
	Piercarlo Ghinzani	Osella-Alfa Romeo V8	43	Gearbox	
	Andrea de Cesaris	Minardi-MM V6	40	Gearbox	
	Thierry Boutsen	Arrows-BMW 4	38	Electrics	
	Gerhard Berger	Benetton-BMW 4	34	Turbo	
	Stefan Johansson	Ferrari V6	29	Accident with Dumfries	
	Johnny Dumfries	Lotus-Renault V6	28	Accident with Johansson	
	Jonathan Palmer	Zakspeed 4	24	Engine	
	Derek Warwick	Brabham-BMW 4	20	Engine	
	Alessandro Nannini	Minardi-MM V6	17	Turbo	
	Teo Fabi	Benetton-BMW 4	13	Battery	
	Christian Danner	Osella-Alfa Romeo V8	6	Turbo	

Fastest lap: Piquet, on lap 63, 1m 25·443s, 115·455 mph/185·808 km/h (record).
Previous lap record: Ayrton Senna (F1 Lotus 97T-Renault t/c), 1m 27·445s, 112·812 mph/181·554 km/h (1985).

PAST WINNERS

Year	Driver	Nat.	Car	Circuit	Distance miles/km	Speed mph/km/h
1961*	Pete Ryan	CDN	2·5 Lotus 19-Climax	Mosport Park	245·90/395·74	88·38/142·23
1962*	Masten Gregory	USA	2·5 Lotus 19-Climax	Mosport Park	245·90/395·74	88·52/142·46
1963*	Pedro Rodriguez	MEX	3·0 Ferrari 250P	Mosport Park	245·90/395·74	91·55/147·34
1964*	Pedro Rodriguez	MEX	4·0 Ferrari 330P	Mosport Park	245·90/395·74	94·36/151·86
1965*	Jim Hall	USA	5·4 Chaparral 2B-Chevrolet	Mosport Park	245·90/395·74	93·78/150·92
1966*	Mark Donohue	USA	6·0 Lola T70 Mk 2-Chevrolet	Mosport Park	209·02/336·38	101·87/163·94
1967	Jack Brabham	AUS	3·0 Brabham BT24-Repco	Mosport Park	221·31/356·16	82·99/133·56
1968	Denny Hulme	NZ	3·0 McLaren M7A-Ford	St Jovite	238·50/383·83	97·22/156·47
1969	Jacky Ickx	B	3·0 Brabham BT26A-Ford	Mosport Park	221·31/356·16	111·19/179·93
1970	Jacky Ickx	B	3·0 Ferrari 312B/70	St Jovite	238·50/383·83	101·27/162·98
1971	Jackie Stewart	GB	3·0 Tyrrell 003-Ford	Mosport Park	157·38/253·27	81·96/131·90
1972	Jackie Stewart	GB	3·0 Tyrrell 005-Ford	Mosport Park	196·72/316·59	114·28/183·92
1973	Peter Revson	USA	3·0 McLaren M23-Ford	Mosport Park	196·72/316·59	99·13/159·53
1974	Emerson Fittipaldi	BR	3·0 McLaren M23-Ford	Mosport Park	196·72/316·59	117·52/189·13
1976	James Hunt	GB	3·0 McLaren M23-Ford	Mosport Park	196·72/316·59	117·84/189·65
1977	Jody Scheckter	ZA	3·0 Wolf WR1-Ford	Mosport Park	196·72/316·59	118·03/189·95
1978	Gilles Villeneuve	CDN	3·0 Ferrari 312T-3/78	Ile Notre-Dame	195·72/314·98	99·67/160·40
1979	Alan Jones	AUS	3·0 Williams FW07-Ford	Ile Notre-Dame	197·28/317·52	105·35/169·54
1980	Alan Jones	AUS	3·0 Williams FW07B-Ford	Ile Notre-Dame	191·82/308·70	110·00/177·03
1981	Jacques Laffite	F	3·0 Ligier JS17-Matra	Ile Notre-Dame	172·62/277·83	85·31/137·29
1982	Nelson Piquet	BR	1·5 Brabham BT50-BMW t/c	Ile Notre-Dame	191·82/308·70	107·93/173·70
1983	René Arnoux	F	1·5 Ferrari 126C2/B t/c	Ile Notre-Dame	191·82/308·70	106·04/170·66
1984	Nelson Piquet	BR	1·5 Brabham BT53-BMW t/c	Ile Notre-Dame	191·82/308·70	108·17/174·08
1985	Michele Alboreto	I	1·5 Ferrari 156/85 t/c	Ile Notre-Dame	191·82/308·70	108·54/174·68
1986	Nigel Mansell	GB	1·5 Williams FW11-Honda t/c	Ile Notre-Dame	189·07/304·29	110·74/178·22

* Non-championship (sports cars)

LAP CHART

1st LAP ORDER	1 2 3 4 5 6 7 8 9 10 11 12 13 14 15 16 17 18 19 20 21 22 23 24 25 26 27 28 29 30 31 32 33 34 35 36 37 38 39 40 41 42 43 44 45 46 47 48 49 50 51 52 53 54 55 56 57 58 59 60 61 62 63 64 65 66 67 68 69	Running order
5 N. Mansell	5 5 5 5 5 5 5 5 5 5 5 5 5 5 5 5 5 5 2 2 2 2 2 5 5 5 5 5 5 5 1 5 5 5 5 5 5 5 5 5 5 5 5 5 5 6 5 5 5 5 5 5 5 5 6 5 5 5 5 5 5 5 5 5 5 5 5 5 5	1
12 A. Senna	12 12 12 12 1 1 1 1 1 1 1 2 2 2 5 5 5 5 2 2 2 2 2 1 1 5 6 6 6 2 2 2 2 2 2 2 2 2 2 2 2 2 2 2 2 2 6 6 6 6 1 1 1 1 1 1 1 1 1 1 1	2
1 A. Prost	1 1 1 1 2 2 2 2 2 2 2 2 1 1 1 1 1 1 1 1 1 1 1 1 1 2 6 2 2 2 2 1 1 1 1 1 1 1 1 1 1 1 1 6 6 6 6 6 6 2 1 1 1 1 2 6 6 6 6 6 6 6 6	3
6 N. Piquet	6 6 2 2 6 6 6 6 6 6 6 6 6 6 6 6 6 6 6 6 6 6 6 6 2 2 12 12 1 1 6 6 6 6 6 6 6 6 6 6 6 6 6 1 1 1 1 1 1 2 2 2 2 2 6 2 2 2 2 2 2 2 2 2	4
2 K. Rosberg	2 2 6 6 25 25 25 25 25 25 12 12 12 12 12 12 12 12 12 12 12 12 12 1 1 25 25 25 25 25 25 25 25 12 12 12 12 12 12 12 12 12 12 12 12 12 12 12 12 12 12 12 12 12 12 12 12 12 12 12 12 12 12	5
25 R. Arnoux	25 25 25 25 12 12 12 12 12 12 25 25 25 25 25 25 25 25 25 25 25 25 25 25 12 12 12 12 12 12 12 12 12 12 12 12 12 12 12 12 12 12 12 12 12 12 25 25 25 25 25 25 25 25 25	6
20 G. Berger	20 20 20 20 20 20 20 28 28 28 28 28 28 28 28 28 28 28 28 28 28 28 28 27 26 26 26 26 26 26 27 27 27 27 27 27 27 27 27 27 27 27 27 27 27 27 27 27 27 27 27 27 26 26 26 26 26 26	7
7 R. Patrese	7 7 7 7 7 7 27 20 27 27 27 27 27 27 27 27 27 27 27 27 27 27 26 26 26 26 7 7 7 7 7 26 26 26 26 26 26 26 26 26 26 26 26 26 27 27 27 27 27 27	8
27 M. Alboreto	27 27 27 27 27 28 28 27 20 26 26 26 26 26 26 26 26 26 26 26 26 26 20 20 20 7 7 7 7 26 26 26 26 3 3 3 3 3 3 3 3 3 3 3 3 3 3 3 3 3 3 3	9
26 J. Laffite	26 26 26 26 18 28 26 26 26 20 20 20 20 20 7 7 7 7 7 7 20 20 20 7 7 7 7 18 18 18 3 3 3 3 4 4 4 4 4 4 15 15 15 15 15 15 15 15 15 15 15	10
8 D. Warwick	8 8 28 28 26 26 7 7 7 7 7 7 7 7 7 7 7 20 20 20 20 20 7 7 7 3 3 3 3 3 3 3 3 4 4 4 15 15 15 15 15 15 15 4 4 4 4 4 4 4	11
15 A. Jones	15 15 28 8 8 8 8 8 8 8 8 8 8 8 8 8 3 3 3 3 3 3 18 18 18 18 4 4 15 15 15 15 29 29 29 29 29 29 29 29 29 29 29 29 29 29	12
28 S. Johansson	28 28 15 15 15 18 18 18 3 3 3 3 3 3 3 11 11 11 11 11 11 11 18 4 4 4 21 21 15 15 21 21 21 21 29	13
18 T. Boutsen	18 18 18 18 18 3 3 3 11 11 11 11 11 11 11 11 18 18 18 18 4 21 21 21 15 15 21 23 29 29	14
3 M. Brundle	3 3 3 3 3 11 11 11 11 4 4 4 4 4 4 4 4 4 4 4 4 21 29 15 15 15 23 23 23 23 29	15
11 J. Dumfries	11 11 11 11 11 11 15 23 23 4 19 19 19 18 18 18 18 21 21 21 21 21 21 29 15 29 29 23 23 29 29 29	16
23 A. de Cesaris	23 23 23 23 23 23 4 4 19 23 24 18 24 24 21 21 29 29 29 29 29 29 29 15 23 23 23 29	17
4 P. Streiff	4 4 4 4 4 4 19 23 24 18 24 21 21 21 29 14 14 14 14 14 15 15 15 23	18
19 T. Fabi	19 19 19 19 19 19 24 24 24 18 21 21 29 29 14 14 14 15 15 15 15 15 23 23	19
24 A. Nannini	24 24 24 24 24 24 21 21 21 29 29 14 14 14 23 23 23 23 23 23 23	20
21 P. Ghinzani	21 21 21 21 21 21 29 29 29 14 14 14 23 23 23 15 15 15	21
29 H. Rothengatter	29 29 29 29 29 29 29 14 14 14 14 23 23 23 15 15 15	22
14 J. Palmer	14 14 14 14 14 14 14 15 15 15 15 15 15	23
22 C. Danner	22 22 22 22 22 22 22 22	24

CIRCUIT DATA

Circuit Gilles Villeneuve, Ile Notre Dame, Montreal, Quebec
Circuit length: 2·74 miles/4·41 km
Race distance: 69 laps, 189·07 miles/304·29 km
Race weather: Hot, dry (25°C).

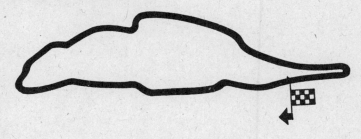

FASTEST LAPS

Driver	Time	Lap
Nelson Piquet	1m 25·443s	63
Nigel Mansell	1m 26·552s	33
Alain Prost	1m 26·859s	63
Keke Rosberg	1m 27·479s	19
Ayrton Senna	1m 27·503s	63
Jacques Laffite	1m 27·742s	60
René Arnoux	1m 27·981s	63
Michele Alboreto	1m 28·408s	37
Stefan Johansson	1m 28·853s	27
Alan Jones	1m 29·366s	58
Martin Brundle	1m 29·553s	57
Gerhard Berger	1m 30·361s	34
Andrea de Cesaris	1m 30·514s	37
Piercarlo Ghinzani	1m 33·598s	19
Riccardo Patrese	1m 30·731s	15
Thierry Boutsen	1m 30·975s	28
Derek Warwick	1m 31·139s	18
Johnny Dumfries	1m 31·623s	6
Philippe Streiff	1m 32·209s	55
Teo Fabi	1m 32·317s	11
Alessandro Nannini	1m 33·173s	5
Huub Rothengatter	1m 33·568s	8
Jonathan Palmer	1m 33·764s	7
Christian Danner	1m 37·444s	4

POINTS

WORLD CHAMPIONSHIP OF DRIVERS

1	Alain Prost	29 pts
2=	Nigel Mansell	27
2=	Ayrton Senna	27
4	Nelson Piquet	19
5	Keke Rosberg	14
6=	Stefan Johansson	7
6=	Jacques Laffite	7
8=	Gerhard Berger	6
8=	René Arnoux	6
10	Michele Alboreto	3
11=	Teo Fabi	2
11=	Martin Brundle	2
13	Riccardo Patrese	1

CONSTRUCTORS' CUP

1	Williams	46 pts
2	McLaren	43
3	Lotus	27
4	Ligier	13
5	Ferrari	10
6	Benetton	8
7	Tyrrell	2
8	Brabham	1

ENTRIES AND PRACTICE TIMES

No.	Driver	Nat.	Car	Tyre	Engine	Entrant	Practice 1	Practice 2	Warm-up
1	Alain Prost	F	Marlboro McLAREN MP4/2C	G	TAG PO1 (TTE PO1)	Marlboro McLaren International	1m 43·368s	**1m 40·715s**	1m 42·841s
2	Keke Rosberg	SF	Marlboro McLAREN MP4/2C	G	TAG PO1 (TTE PO1)	Marlboro McLaren International	1m 43·732s	**1m 40·848s**	1m 42·912s
3	Martin Brundle	GB	Data General TYRRELL 015	G	Renault EF15/EF15B	Data General Team Tyrrell	1m 45·250s	**1m 42·815s**	1m 45·684s
4	Philippe Streiff	F	Data General TYRRELL 014/015	G	Renault EF15/EF15B	Data General Team Tyrrell	1m 47·478s	**1m 43·796s**	1m 51·017s
5	Nigel Mansell	GB	WILLIAMS FW11	G	Honda RA166–E	Canon Williams Honda Team	1m 39·490s	**1m 38·839s**	1m 41·987s
6	Nelson Piquet	BR	WILLIAMS FW11	G	Honda RA166–E	Canon Williams Honda Team	1m 41·510s	**1m 39·076s**	1m 42·974s
7	Riccardo Patrese	I	Olivetti BRABHAM BT55	P	BMW M12/13/1	Motor Racing Developments Ltd	1m 43·664s	**1m 40·819s**	1m 42·518s
8	Derek Warwick	GB	Olivetti BRABHAM BT55	P	BMW M12/13/1	Motor Racing Developments Ltd	1m 44·890s	**1m 42·558s**	1m 43·965s
11	Johnny Dumfries	GB	John Player Special LOTUS 98T	G	Renault EF15/EF15B	John Player Special Team Lotus	1m 45·846s	**1m 42·511s**	1m 44·759s
12	Ayrton Senna	BR	John Player Special LOTUS 98T	G	Renault EF15/EF15B	John Player Special Team Lotus	1m 40·301s	**1m 38·301s**	1m 42·499s
14	Jonathan Palmer	GB	West ZAKSPEED ZAK 861	G	Zakspeed	West Zakspeed Racing	1m 49·812s	**1m 44·401s**	1m 48·459s
15	Alan Jones	AUS	LOLA THL-2	G	Ford-Cosworth	Team Haas (USA) Ltd	1m 45·421s	**1m 44·450s**	1m 44·161s
16	Eddie Cheever	USA	LOLA THL-2	G	Ford-Cosworth	Team Haas (USA) Ltd	1m 46·499s	**1m 41·540s**	1m 44·662s
17	Christian Danner	D	ARROWS A8	G	BMW M12/13	Barclay Arrows BMW	1m 48·855s	**1m 44·259s**	1m 48·256s
18	Thierry Boutsen	B	ARROWS A8	G	BMW M12/13	Barclay Arrows BMW	1m 45·711s	**1m 42·279s**	1m 45·790s
19	Teo Fabi	I	BENETTON B186	P	BMW M12/13	Benetton Formula Ltd	1m 48·912s	**1m 43·658s**	1m 44·852s
20	Gerhard Berger	A	BENETTON B186	P	BMW M12/13	Benetton Formula Ltd	1m 43·759s	**1m 41·836s**	1m 43·792s
21	Piercarlo Ghinzani	I	OSELLA FA1G	P	Alfa Romeo 185T	Osella Squadra Corse	1m 49·067s	**1m 45·059s**	1m 49·857s
22	Allen Berg	CDN	OSELLA FA1F	P	Alfa Romeo 185T	Osella Squadra Corse	1m 56·741s	**1m 48·682s**	1m 49·774s
23	Andrea de Cesaris	I	Simod MINARDI M/85B	P	Motori Moderni	Minardi Team	1m 47·359s	**1m 46·705s**	1m 48·844s
24	Alessandro Nannini	I	Simod MINARDI M/85B	P	Motori Moderni	Minardi Team	**1m 47·230s**	—	1m 48·908s
25	René Arnoux	F	Gitanes LIGIER JS27	P	Renault EF15/EF15B	Equipe Ligier	1m 43·166s	**1m 39·689s**	1m 42·227s
26	Jacques Laffite	F	Gitanes LIGIER JS27	P	Renault EF15/EF15B	Equipe Ligier	1m 45·236s	**1m 40·676s**	1m 44·972s
27	Michele Alboreto	I	Fiat FERRARI F1/86	G	Ferrari 126C	Scuderia Ferrari SpA	1m 44·296s	**1m 41·606s**	1m 43·656s
28	Stefan Johansson	S	Fiat FERRARI F1/86	G	Ferrari 126C	Scuderia Ferrari SpA	1m 42·989s	**1m 40·312s**	1m 43·053s
29	Huub Rothengatter	NL	West ZAKSPEED ZAK 861	G	Zakspeed	West Zakspeed Racing	**1m 49·680s**	—	1m 48·735s

Friday morning, Saturday morning and Sunday morning practice sessions not officially recorded.

G – Goodyear, P – Pirelli

Fri p.m. Hot, dry, sunny | Sat p.m. Hot, dry, sunny | Sun a.m. Hot, dry, sunny

STARTING GRID

12 SENNA (1m 38·301s) Lotus

    5 MANSELL (1m 18·839s) Williams

6 PIQUET (1m 39·076s) Williams

    25 ARNOUX (1m 39·689s) Ligier

28 JOHANSSON (1m 40·312s) Ferrari

    26 LAFFITE (1m 40·676s) Ligier

1 PROST (1m 40·715s) McLaren

    7 PATRESE (1m 40·819s) Brabham

2 ROSBERG (1m 40·848s) McLaren

    16 CHEEVER (1m 41·540s) Lola

27 ALBORETO (1m 41·606s) Ferrari

    20 BERGER (1m 41·836s) Benetton

18 BOUTSEN (1m 42·279s) Arrows

    11 DUMFRIES (1m 42·511s) Lotus

8 WARWICK (1m 42·558s) Brabham

    3 BRUNDLE (1m 42·815s) Tyrrell

19 FABI (1m 43·658s) Benetton

    4 STREIFF (1m 43·796s) Tyrrell

17 DANNER (1m 44·259s) Arrows

    14 PALMER (1m 44·401s) Zakspeed

15 JONES (1m 44·450s) Lola

    21 GHINZANI (1m 45·059s) Osella

23 DE CESARIS (1m 46·705s) Minardi

    24 NANNINI (1m 47·230s) Minardi

22 BERG (1m 48·682s) Osella

    *29 ROTHENGATTER (1m 49·680s) Zakspeed

* Did not start; electrical malfunction on warm-up lap.

RESULTS AND RETIREMENTS

Place	Driver	Car	Laps	Time and speed (mph/km/h)/Retirement	
1	Ayrton Senna	Lotus-Renault V6	63	1h 51m 12·847s	84·971/136·748
2	Jacques Laffite	Ligier-Renault V6	63	1h 51m 43·864s	84·578/136·115
3	Alain Prost	McLaren-TAG V6	63	1h 51m 44·671s	84·568/136·009
4	Michele Alboreto	Ferrari V6	63	1h 52m 43·783s	83·829/134·910
5	Nigel Mansell	Williams-Honda V6	62		
6	Riccardo Patrese	Brabham-BMW 4	62		
7	Johnny Dumfries	Lotus-Renault V6	61		
8	Jonathan Palmer	Zakspeed 4	61		
9	Philippe Streiff	Tyrrell-Renault V6	61		
10	Derek Warwick	Brabham-BMW 4	60		
	Christian Danner	Arrows-BMW 4	51	Electrics	
	René Arnoux	Ligier-Renault V6	46	Accident	
	Thierry Boutsen	Arrows-BMW 4	44	Accident	
	Andrea de Cesaris	Minardi-MM V6	43	Gearbox	
	Nelson Piquet	Williams-Honda V6	41	Accident	
	Stefan Johansson	Ferrari V6	40	Electrics	
	Teo Fabi	Benetton-BMW 4	38	Gearbox	
	Eddie Cheever	Lola-Ford V6	37	Drive pegs	
	Alan Jones	Lola-Ford V6	33	Drive pegs	
	Allen Berg	Osella-Alfa Romeo V8	28	Electrics	
	Martin Brundle	Tyrrell-Renault V6	15	Electrics	
	Piercarlo Ghinzani	Osella-Alfa Romeo V8	14	Turbo	
	Keke Rosberg	McLaren-TAG V6	12	Transmission	
	Gerhard Berger	Benetton-BMW 4	8	Engine cut-out	
	Alessandro Nannini	Minardi-MM V6	3	Turbo	
	Huub Rothengatter	Zakspeed 4	0	Did not start – electrical trouble	

Fastest lap: Piquet, on lap 41, 1m 41·233s, 88·904 mph/143·077 km/h (record).
Previous lap record: Ayrton Senna (F1 Lotus 97T-Renault t/c V6), 1m 45·612s, 85·2175 mph/137·144 km/h (1985).

PAST WINNERS

Year	Driver	Nat.	Car	Circuit	Distance miles/km	Speed mph/km/h
1982	John Watson	GB	3·0 McLaren MP4B-Ford	Detroit	154·57/248·75	78·20/128·85
1983	Michele Alboreto	I	3·0 Tyrrell 011-Ford	Detroit	150·00/241·40	81·16/130·61
1984	Nelson Piquet	BR	1·5 Brabham BT53-BMW t/c	Detroit	157·50/253·47	81·68/131·45
1985	Keke Rosberg	SF	1·5 Williams FW10-Honda t/c	Detroit	157·50/253·47	81·70/131·48
1986	Ayrton Senna	BR	1·5 Lotus 98T-Renault t/c	Detroit	157·50/253·47	84·97/136·75

LAP CHART

1st LAP ORDER	1 2 3 4 5 6 7 8 9 10 11 12 13 14 15 16 17 18 19 20 21 22 23 24 25 26 27 28 29 30 31 32 33 34 35 36 37 38 39 40 41 42 43 44 45 46 47 48 49 50 51 52 53 54 55 56 57 58 59 60 61 62 63	Running order
12 A. Senna	12 12 5 5 5 5 5 12 12 12 12 12 12 12 25 25 26 26 26 26 26 26 26 26 26 26 26 26 6 6 6 6 6 6 6 6 6 12 12 12 12 12 6 6 26 26 25 1 1 1 1 1 1 1 26 26 26 26 26 26 26 12 12	1
5 N. Mansell	5 5 12 12 12 12 12 5 5 25 25 26 26 26 26 26 25 25 25 25 5 5 5 6 6 12 12 12 12 6 6 25 25 25 1 1 1 1 1 1 1 26 26 26 26 26 26 26	2
25 R. Arnoux	25 25 25 25 25 25 5 5 5 26 26 5 5 5 5 5 5 5 5 5 6 6 12 26 1 1 1 1 1 1 1 25 1 1 1 26 26 26 26 26 26 1 1 1 1 1 1 1	3
6 N. Piquet	6 6 6 6 6 6 6 6 26 26 5 5 5 1 1 1 1 1 1 1 1 1 1 12 12 5 5 25 25 25 1 26 26 26 5 5 5 5 5 5 5 27 27 27 27	4
28 S. Johansson	28 28 28 28 28 28 26 26 6 6 1 1 6 6 6 6 6 6 6 6 6 1 1 1 25 26 26 26 26 26 26 7 5 5 5 27 27 27 27 27 27 27 27 25 5 5 5	5
1 A. Prost	1 1 26 26 26 28 28 28 1 1 6 27 27 27 12 12 12 12 12 25 25 25 26 5 7 5 5 5 28 28 28 7 27 27 27 7 7 7 7 7 7 7 7 7 7 7 7 7	6
26 J. Laffite	26 26 26 27 1 1 1 1 27 27 27 27 28 28 12 27 27 27 27 27 27 25 27 27 7 5 7 28 28 5 7 7 7 7 11 11 11 11 11 11 11 11 11 11 11 11 11	7
27 M. Alboreto	27 27 27 1 27 27 27 27 28 28 12 12 28 28 28 28 28 28 28 16 7 28 28 28 7 7 27 5 11 11 11 14 14 14 14 14 14 14 14 14 14 14 14	8
16 E. Cheever	16 16 2 2 2 20 20 16 16 16 16 16 16 16 16 16 16 16 7 28 27 27 27 27 5 28 14 14 14 14 4 4 4 4 4 4 4 4 4 4 4	9
2 K. Rosberg	2 2 16 20 20 20 2 2 7 7 7 7 7 7 7 7 7 7 7 7 28 28 16 16 16 18 18 14 14 18 18 4 8 8 8 8 8 8 8 8 8 8 8 8	10
20 G. Berger	20 20 20 16 16 16 16 18 18 18 18 18 18 18 18 18 18 18 18 11 11 11 18 16 14 11 11 4 4 8 17 17 17 17	11
7 R. Patrese	7 7 7 7 7 7 7 2 3 3 3 3 15 15 15 15 15 11 11 11 11 11 11 11 18 18 18 11 14 11 18 18 23 23 17 17 17	12
18 T. Boutsen	18 18 18 18 18 18 18 3 15 15 15 11 11 11 11 11 11 15 15 15 15 15 15 14 14 11 19 19 4 4 4 17 17 8	13
3 M. Brundle	3 3 3 3 3 3 15 19 19 2 19 19 19 19 19 19 19 19 19 19 19 19 14 14 14 19 19 4 4 23 23 23 8 8	14
15 A. Jones	15 15 15 15 15 15 19 2 2 19 11 11 11 4 4 4 4 14 14 14 14 14 14 19 19 4 4 16 23 23 17 17 17	15
8 D. Warwick	8 8 23 23 4 19 19 11 11 11 11 2 4 14 14 14 14 14 14 4 4 4 17 17 17 4 23 23 23 23 17 8 8 8	16
11 J. Dumfries	11 23 8 4 19 4 11 4 4 4 14 14 17 17 17 17 17 17 17 17 17 4 4 4 17 23 17 17 17 8	17
23 A. de Cesaris	23 11 4 19 23 11 11 4 14 14 14 14 17 8 8 8 8 8 8 8 8 8 23 23 23 23 17 8 8 8 8	18
4 P. Streiff	4 4 11 11 11 23 14 17 17 17 17 8 8 23 23 23 23 23 23 23 23 23 8 8 8 8 8	19
19 T. Fabi	19 19 19 21 14 14 17 21 8 8 8 23 23 22 22 22 22 22 22 22 22 22 22 22 22	20
21 P. Ghinzani	21 21 21 14 14 17 17 21 22 22 22 23 22 22	21
24 A. Nannini	24 24 24 17 17 21 21 22 8 23 23 23 22 22 21 21	22
14 J. Palmer	14 14 14 22 22 22 22 8 23 21 21 21 21	23
17 C. Danner	17 17 17 8 8 8 8 23	24
22 A. Berg	22 22 22	25

CIRCUIT DATA

Detroit Grand Prix Circuit, Detroit, Michigan
Circuit length: 2·50 miles/4·0233 km
Race distance: 63 laps, 157·500 miles/253·471 km
Race weather: Hot, dry, strong breeze (26°C).

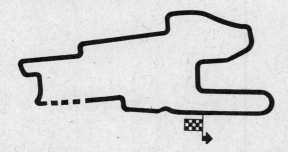

FASTEST LAPS

Driver	Time	Lap
Nelson Piquet	1m 41·233s	41
Ayrton Senna	1m 41·981s	42
René Arnoux	1m 42·921s	46
Nigel Mansell	1m 43·051s	29
Alain Prost	1m 43·293s	39
Jacques Laffite	1m 43·416s	40
Michele Alboreto	1m 43·619s	54
Riccardo Patrese	1m 44·698s	23
Stefan Johansson	1m 44·864s	21
Keke Rosberg	1m 45·254s	12
Johnny Dumfries	1m 45·434s	38
Eddie Cheever	1m 45·836s	52
Gerhard Berger	1m 45·914s	4
Derek Warwick	1m 46·136s	52
Alan Jones	1m 46·579s	19
Andrea de Cesaris	1m 46·621s	36
Jonathan Palmer	1m 46·756s	52
Philippe Streiff	1m 46·869s	47
Thierry Boutsen	1m 47·005s	40
Teo Fabi	1m 47·122s	7
Martin Brundle	1m 47·819s	12
Christian Danner	1m 49·499s	18
Piercarlo Ghinzani	1m 51·711s	5
Alessandro Nannini	1m 53·122s	2
Allen Berg	1m 53·507s	4

POINTS

WORLD CHAMPIONSHIP OF DRIVERS

1	Ayrton Senna	36 pts
2	Alain Prost	33
3	Nigel Mansell	29
4	Nelson Piquet	19
5	Keke Rosberg	14
6	Jacques Laffite	13
7	Stefan Johansson	7
8=	Gerhard Berger	6
8=	Michele Alboreto	6
8=	René Arnoux	6
11=	Teo Fabi	2
11=	Martin Brundle	2
11=	Riccardo Patrese	2

CONSTRUCTORS' CUP

1	Williams	48 pts
2	McLaren	47
3	Lotus	36
4	Ligier	19
5	Ferrari	13
6	Benetton	8
7=	Tyrrell	2
7=	Brabham	2

The Ligier team of Arnoux and Laffite led several laps at Detroit. Gérard Larrousse (left) and Michel Tétu, the designer of the JS27, discuss tactics.

ENTRIES AND PRACTICE TIMES

No.	Driver	Nat.	Car	Tyre	Engine	Entrant	Practice 1	Practice 2	Warm-up
1	Alain Prost	F	Marlboro McLAREN MP4/2C	G	TAG PO1 (TTE PO1)	Marlboro McLaren International	1m 07·270s	**1m 07·266s**	1m 11·148s
2	Keke Rosberg	SF	Marlboro McLAREN MP4/2C	G	TAG PO1 (TTE PO1)	Marlboro McLaren International	**1m 07·545s**	1m 08·175s	1m 10·968s
3	Martin Brundle	GB	Data General TYRRELL 015	G	Renault EF15B	Data General Team Tyrrell	**1m 09·044s**	1m 10·293s	1m 14·226s
4	Philippe Streiff	F	Data General TYRRELL 015	G	Renault EF15B	Data General Team Tyrrell	1m 09·935s	**1m 09·700s**	1m 14·696s
5	Nigel Mansell	GB	WILLIAMS FW11	G	Honda RA166–E	Canon Williams Honda Team	**1m 06·755s**	1m 09·819s	1m 11·257s
6	Nelson Piquet	BR	WILLIAMS FW11	G	Honda RA166–E	Canon Williams Honda Team	**1m 06·797s**	1m 07·184s	1m 11·911s
7	Riccardo Patrese	I	Olivetti BRABHAM BT55	P	BMW M12/13/1	Motor Racing Developments Ltd	1m 09·624s	**1m 09·436s**	1m 12·704s
8	Derek Warwick	GB	Olivetti BRABHAM BT55	P	BMW M12/13/1	Motor Racing Developments Ltd	1m 09·471s	**1m 08·905s**	1m 12·875s
11	Johnny Dumfries	GB	John Player Special LOTUS 98T	G	Renault EF15B	John Player Special Team Lotus	1m 09·477s	**1m 08·544s**	1m 13·881s
12	Ayrton Senna	BR	John Player Special LOTUS 98T	G	Renault EF15B/EF15C	John Player Special Team Lotus	1m 06·807s	**1m 06·526s**	1m 11·982s
14	Jonathan Palmer	GB	West ZAKSPEED ZAK 861	G	Zakspeed	West Zakspeed Racing	**1m 10·305s**	1m 10·511s	1m 15·590s
15	Alan Jones	AUS	LOLA THL-2	G	Ford-Cosworth	Team Haas (USA) Ltd	**1m 09·929s**	1m 10·733s	1m 14·338s
16	Patrick Tambay	F	LOLA THL-2	G	Ford-Cosworth	Team Haas (USA) Ltd	1m 09·108s	**1m 08·616s**	1m 13·283s
17	Christian Danner	D	ARROWS A8	G	BMW M12/13	Barclay Arrows BMW	**1m 09·737s**	1m 10·614s	1m 15·222s
18	Thierry Boutsen	B	ARROWS A8	G	BMW M12/13	Barclay Arrows BMW	**1m 09·987s**	1m 28·882s	1m 14·222s
19	Teo Fabi	I	BENETTON B186	P	BMW M12/13	Benetton Formula Ltd	1m 08·703s	**1m 07·818s**	1m 12·692s
20	Gerhard Berger	A	BENETTON B186	P	BMW M12/13	Benetton Formula Ltd	1m 07·835s	**1m 07·554s**	1m 19·030s
21	Piercarlo Ghinzani	I	OSELLA FA1H	P	Alfa Romeo 185T	Osella Squadra Corse	1m 13·997s	**1m 12·443s**	1m 15·442s
22	Allen Berg	CDN	OSELLA FA1G	P	Alfa Romeo 185T	Osella Squadra Corse	2m 58·486s	**1m 14·264s**	1m 16·809s
23	Andrea de Cesaris	I	Simod MINARDI M/85B	P	Motori Moderni	Minardi Team	**1m 11·483s**	1m 21·859s	1m 15·907s
24	Alessandro Nannini	I	Simod MINARDI M/85B	P	Motori Moderni	Minardi Team	**1m 09·792s**	1m 10·630s	1m 15·019s
25	René Arnoux	F	Gitanes LIGIER JS27	P	Renault EF15B	Equipe Ligier	1m 07·114s	**1m 07·075s**	1m 11·696s
26	Jacques Laffite	F	Gitanes LIGIER JS27	P	Renault EF15B	Equipe Ligier	**1m 07·913s**	1m 08·288s	1m 13·402s
27	Michele Alboreto	I	Fiat FERRARI F1/86	G	Ferrari 126C	Scuderia Ferrari SpA	**1m 07·365s**	1m 09·161s	1m 13·032s
28	Stefan Johansson	S	Fiat FERRARI F1/86	G	Ferrari 126C	Scuderia Ferrari SpA	**1m 07·874s**	1m 08·881s	1m 13·163s
29	Huub Rothengatter	NL	West ZAKSPEED ZAK 861	G	Zakspeed	West Zakspeed Racing	1m 12·940s	**1m 12·163s**	1m 15·333s

Friday morning, Saturday morning and Sunday morning practice sessions not officially recorded.

G – Goodyear, P – Pirelli

Fri p.m.	Sat p.m.	Sun a.m.
Hot, dry,	Hot, dry,	Warm, dry,
sunny	sunny	cloudy

STARTING GRID

	12 SENNA (1m 06·526s) Lotus
5 MANSELL (1m 06·755s) Williams	
	6 PIQUET (1m 06·797s) Williams
25 ARNOUX (1m 07·075s) Ligier	
	1 PROST (1m 07·266s) McLaren
27 ALBORETO (1m 07·365s) Ferrari	
	2 ROSBERG (1m 07·545s) McLaren
20 BERGER (1m 07·554s) Benetton	
	19 FABI (1m 07·818s) Benetton
28 JOHANSSON (1m 07·874s) Ferrari	
	26 LAFFITE (1m 07·913s) Ligier
11 DUMFRIES (1m 08·544s) Lotus	
	16 TAMBAY (1m 08·616s) Lola
8 WARWICK (1m 08·905s) Brabham	
	3 BRUNDLE (1m 09·044s) Tyrrell
7 PATRESE (1m 09·436s) Brabham	
	4 STREIFF (1m 09·700s) Tyrrell
17 DANNER (1m 09·737s) Arrows	
	24 NANNINI (1m 09·792s) Minardi
15 JONES (1m 09·929s) Lola	
	18 BOUTSEN (1m 09·987s) Arrows
14 PALMER (1m 10·305s) Zakspeed	
	23 DE CESARIS (1m 11·483s) Minardi
29 ROTHENGATTER (1m 12·443s) Zakspeed	
	21 GHINZANI (1m 12·443s) Osella
22 BERG (1m 14·264s) Osella	

RESULTS AND RETIREMENTS

Place	Driver	Car	Laps	Time and speed (mph/km/h)/Retirement	
1	Nigel Mansell	Williams-Honda V6	80	1h 37m 19·272s	116·856/188·062
2	Alain Prost	McLaren-TAG V6	80	1h 37m 36·400s	116·514/187·512
3	Nelson Piquet	Williams-Honda V6	80	1h 37m 56·817s	116·109/186·860
4	Keke Rosberg	McLaren-TAG V6	80	1h 38m 07·975s	115·889/186·506
5	René Arnoux	Ligier-Renault V6	79		
6	Jacques Laffite	Ligier-Renault V6	79		
7	Riccardo Patrese	Brabham-BMW 4	78		
8	Michele Alboreto	Ferrari V6	78		
9	Derek Warwick	Brabham-BMW 4	77		
10	Martin Brundle	Tyrrell-Renault V6	77		
11	Christian Danner	Arrows-BMW 4	76		
	Thierry Boutsen	Arrows-BMW 4	67	Running but not classified	
	Patrick Tambay	Lola-Ford V6	64	Brakes	
	Johnny Dumfries	Lotus-Renault V6	56	Engine	
	Jonathan Palmer	Zakspeed 4	46	Engine	
	Philippe Streiff	Tyrrell-Renault V6	43	Fuel leak/fire	
	Huub Rothengatter	Zakspeed 4	32	Accident	
	Allen Berg	Osella-Alfa Romeo V8	25	Turbo	
	Gerhard Berger	Benetton-BMW 4	22	Gearbox	
	Teo Fabi	Benetton-BMW 4	7	Engine/misfire	
	Stefan Johansson	Ferrari V6	5	Turbo	
	Ayrton Senna	Lotus-Renault V6	3	Accident	
	Piercarlo Ghinzani	Osella-Alfa Romeo V8	3	Accident with Nannini	
	Alessandro Nannini	Minardi-MM V6	3	Accident with Ghinzani	
	Andrea de Cesaris	Minardi-MM V6	3	Turbo	
	Alan Jones	Lola-Ford V6	2	Accident	

Fastest lap: Mansell, on lap 57, 1m 09·993s, 121·861 mph/196·117 km/h (record for 2·369 mile/3·813 km circuit).

PAST WINNERS

Year	Driver	Nat.	Car	Circuit	Distance miles/km	Speed mph/km/h
1950	Juan Manuel Fangio	RA	1·5 Alfa Romeo 158 s/c	Reims-Gueux	310·81/500·20	104·84/168·72
1951	Luigi Fagioli/	I				
	Juan Manuel Fangio	RA	1·5 Alfa Romeo 159 s/c	Reims-Gueux	373·94/601·80	110·97/178·59
1952	Alberto Ascari	I	2·0 Ferrari 500	Rouen-les-Essarts	240·39/386·88	80·13/128·96
1953	Mike Hawthorn	GB	2·0 Ferrari 500	Reims	314·56/506·23	113·64/182·89
1954	Juan Manuel Fangio	RA	2·5 Mercedes-Benz W196	Reims	314·64/506·36	115·97/186·64
1956	Peter Collins	GB	2·5 Lancia-Ferrari D50	Reims	314·64/506·36	122·29/196·80
1957	Juan Manuel Fangio	RA	2·5 Maserati 250F	Rouen-les-Essarts	313·01/503·74	100·02/160·96
1958	Mike Hawthorn	GB	2·4 Ferrari Dino 246	Reims	257·90/415·05	125·45/201·90
1959	Tony Brooks	GB	2·4 Ferrari Dino 246	Reims	257·90/415·05	127·43/205·08
1960	Jack Brabham	AUS	2·5 Cooper T53-Climax	Reims	257·90/415·05	131·80/212·11
1961	Giancarlo Baghetti	I	1·5 Ferrari Dino 156	Reims	268·22/431·66	119·85/192·87
1962	Dan Gurney	USA	1·5 Porsche 804	Rouen-les-Essarts	219·51/353·27	101·84/163·89
1963	Jim Clark	GB	1·5 Lotus 25-Climax	Reims	273·37/439·95	125·31/201·67
1964	Dan Gurney	USA	1·5 Brabham BT7-Climax	Rouen-les-Essarts	231·71/372·90	108·77/175·04
1965	Jim Clark	GB	1·5 Lotus 25-Climax	Clermont-Ferrand	200·21/322·21	89·22/143·58
1966	Jack Brabham	AUS	3·0 Brabham BT19-Repco	Reims	247·58/398·44	136·90/220·32
1967	Jack Brabham	AUS	3·0 Brabham BT24-Repco	Bugatti au Mans	219·82/353·77	98·90/159·16
1968	Jacky Ickx	B	3·0 Ferrari 312/66	Rouen-les-Essarts	243·90/392·52	100·45/161·66
1969	Jackie Stewart	GB	3·0 Matra MS80-Ford	Clermont-Ferrand	190·20/306·10	97·71/157·25
1970	Jochen Rindt	A	3·0 Lotus 72-Ford	Clermont-Ferrand	190·20/306·10	98·42/158·39
1971	Jackie Stewart	GB	3·0 Tyrrell 003-Ford	Paul Ricard	198·56/319·55	111·66/179·70
1972	Jackie Stewart	GB	3·0 Tyrrell 003-Ford	Clermont-Ferrand	190·20/306·10	101·56/163·44
1973	Ronnie Peterson	S	3·0 JPS/Lotus 72-Ford	Paul Ricard	194·95/313·74	115·12/185·26
1974	Ronnie Peterson	S	3·0 JPS/Lotus 72-Ford	Dijon-Prenois	163·49/263·11	119·75/192·72
1975	Niki Lauda	A	3·0 Ferrari 312T/75	Paul Ricard	194·95/313·74	116·60/187·65
1976	James Hunt	GB	3·0 McLaren M23-Ford	Paul Ricard	194·95/313·74	115·84/186·42
1977	Mario Andretti	USA	3·0 JPS/Lotus 78-Ford	Dijon-Prenois	188·90/304·00	113·72/183·01
1978	Mario Andretti	USA	3·0 JPS/Lotus 79-Ford	Paul Ricard	194·95/313·74	118·31/190·40
1979	Jean-Pierre Jabouille	F	1·5 Renault RS t/c	Dijon-Prenois	188·88/304·00	118·88/191·32
1980	Alan Jones	AUS	3·0 Williams FW07B-Ford	Paul Ricard	194·95/313·74	126·15/203·02
1981	Alain Prost	F	1·5 Renault RE t/c	Dijon-Prenois	188·88/304·00	118·30/190·39
1982	René Arnoux	F	1·5 Renault RE t/c	Paul Ricard	194·95/313·74	125·02/201·20
1983	Alain Prost	F	1·5 Renault RE t/c	Paul Ricard	194·95/313·74	124·19/199·87
1984	Niki Lauda	A	1·5 McLaren MP4/2-TAG t/c	Dijon-Prenois	186·53/300·20	125·53/202·02
1985	Nelson Piquet	BR	1·5 Brabham BT54-BMW t/c	Paul Ricard	191·34/307·93	125·09/201·32
1986	Nigel Mansell	GB	1·5 Williams FW11-Honda t/c	Paul Ricard	189·54/305·04	116·86/188·06

LAP CHART

1st LAP ORDER	1 2 3 4 5 6 7 8 9 10 11 12 13 14 15 16 17 18 19 20 21 22 23 24 25 26 27 28 29 30 31 32 33 34 35 36 37 38 39 40 41 42 43 44 45 46 47 48 49 50 51 52 53 54 55 56 57 58 59 60 61 62 63 64 65 66 67 68 69 70 71 72 73 74 75 76 77 78 79 80	Running order
5 N. Mansell	5 5 5 5 5 5 5 5 5 5 5 5 5 5 5 5 5 5 5 5 5 5 5 5 5 1 1 1 1 1 1 1 1 1 1 1 1 1 1 1 5 5 5 5 5 5 5 5 5 5 5 5 5 5 5 5 5 5 1 1 1 1 5 5 5 5 5 5 5 5 5 5 5 5 5 5 5 5 5 5	1
12 A. Senna	12 12 12 25 25 25 25 25 25 25 25 25 25 1 1 1 1 1 1 1 1 1 2 2 2 2 2 5 5 5 5 5 1 1 1 1 1 1 1 1 1 1 1 1 1 1 1 1 1 1 1 1 1 5 5 5 5 1 1 1 1 1 1 1 1 1 1 1 1 1 1 1 1 1 1 1 1 1 1	2
25 R. Arnoux	25 25 25 20 20 20 20 20 1 1 1 1 25 25 2 2 2 2 2 2 2 5 5 5 5 6 6 6 6 6 6 6 6 6 6 6 6 2 2 2 2 2 2 2 2 2 2 2 2 2 2 2 2 2 2 2 2 2 2 2 2 2 2 2 2 2 2 6 6 6 6 6 6 6 6	3
20 G. Berger	20 20 20 1 1 1 1 1 20 2 2 2 2 2 2 25 6 6 6 26 26 26 26 6 6 6 2 2 2 2 2 2 2 2 2 2 6 6 6 6 6 6 6 6 6 6 6 6 6 6 6 6 6 6 6 6 6 6 6 6 6 6 6 6 6 6 6 6 6 6 6 2 2 2 2 2	4
1 A. Prost	1 1 1 6 2 2 2 2 20 6 6 6 6 6 6 26 26 26 26 6 6 6 25 25 25 25 25 25 25 25 25 25 25 25 25 25 25 25 25 25 25 25 25 25 25 25 25 25 25 25 25 25 25 25 25 25 25 25 25 25 25 25 25 25 25 25 25 25 25 25 25 25 25 25 25 25	5
11 J. Dumfries	11 6 6 2 6 6 6 6 6 26 26 26 26 26 26 11 11 11 25 25 25 25 11 11 16 26 26 26 26 26 26 26 26 26 26 26 26 26 26 26 26 26 26 26 26 26 26 26 26 26 26 26 26 26 26 26 26 26 26 26 26 26 26 26 26 26	6
6 N. Piquet	6 11 2 11 26 26 26 26 26 11 11 11 11 11 11 11 7 7 11 11 11 11 11 11 16 16 26 16 16 16 16 16 16 7 7 7 7 7 7 7 7 7 27 16 16 16 16 16 16 16 16 16 16 16 3 3 3 7 7 7 7 7 7 7 7 7 7 7 7 7 7	7
2 K. Rosberg	2 2 11 26 11 11 11 11 11 16 7 7 7 7 7 16 25 25 7 7 16 16 26 26 11 7 7 7 27 16 27 27 27 27 27 27 27 16 27 3 3 3 3 3 3 3 3 3 7 7 3 3 3 3 3 8 27 27 27 27 27	8
26 J. Laffite	26 26 26 16 16 16 16 16 16 7 16 16 16 16 25 16 16 16 16 7 27 3 7 7 7 3 3 3 3 7 27 16 16 16 16 16 16 3 3 7 7 7 7 7 7 7 7 7 16 8 8 8 8 8 8 8 27 8 8 8 8 8	9
16 P. Tambay	16 16 16 7 7 7 7 7 7 20 3 3 3 3 3 27 27 27 27 27 27 3 7 3 3 3 4 4 4 27 4 4 3 3 3 3 3 3 7 7 11 11 11 11 11 11 8 8 8 8 8 27 27 27 27 27 27 3 3 3 3 3	10
3 M. Brundle	3 3 3 3 3 3 3 3 3 3 4 4 4 27 3 3 3 3 3 3 7 4 4 27 27 27 4 3 4 4 4 4 4 8 11 11 11 11 8 8 8 8 8 27 27 27 27 16 17 17 17 17 17 17 17 17 17 17 17 17 17	11
28 S. Johansson	28 7 7 4 4 4 4 4 4 4 27 27 27 4 4 4 4 4 4 4 27 27 27 11 11 11 11 8 8 8 8 8 8 8 11 8 8 8 8 27 27 27 27 17 17 17 17 17 17 17 17 18 18 18	12
7 R. Patrese	7 4 18 14 14 14 14 14 14 14 14 14 14 14 14 14 14 14 8 8 8 8 8 8 11 11 11 11 11 11 11 11 11 14 14 14 17 17 17 17 17 17 18 18 18 18 18 18	13
4 P. Streiff	4 18 4 27 27 27 27 27 27 8 8 8 8 8 8 8 8 8 8 14 14 14 14 14 14 14 14 14 14 14 14 14 17 17 17 18 18 18 18 18 18 18	14
14 J. Palmer	14 14 14 17 17 17 17 17 8 8 17 17 17 17 20 20 20 20 20 17 17 17 17 17 17 17 17 17 17 17 17 17 17 18 18 18	15
18 T. Boutsen	18 23 21 8 8 8 8 8 17 20 20 20 20 20 17 17 17 17 29 29 29 29 29 29 29 29 18 18 18 18 18 18 18 18	16
15 A. Jones	15 15 24 29 29 29 29 29 29 29 29 29 29 29 29 29 29 22 18 18 18 18 18 18	17
23 A. de Cesaris	23 21 27 19 19 19 19 18 22 22 22 22 22 22 22 22 22 22 18 18	18
21 P. Ghinzani	21 24 17 18 18 18 22 18 18 18 18 18 18 18 18 18 18 18	19
24 A. Nannini	24 27 23 28 28 28 22	20
27 M. Alboreto	27 17 8 22 22 22 22	21
29 H. Rothengatter	29 28 29	22
8 D. Warwick	8 29 19	23
17 C. Danner	17 8 28	24
19 T. Fabi	19 19 22	25
22 A. Berg	22 22	26

CIRCUIT DATA

ASA Paul Ricard, near Marseilles
Circuit length: 2·369 miles/3·813 km
Race distance: 80 laps, 189·543 miles/305·04 km
Race weather: Warm, dry (28°C).

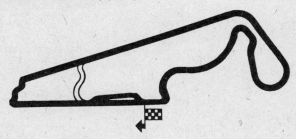

FASTEST LAPS

Driver	Time	Lap
Nigel Mansell	1m 09·993s	57
René Arnoux	1m 10·227s	47
Nelson Piquet	1m 10·582s	66
Alain Prost	1m 10·859s	68
Jacques Laffite	1m 11·220s	58
Keke Rosberg	1m 11·402s	39
Michele Alboreto	1m 11·747s	62
Gerhard Berger	1m 12·436s	16
Patrick Tambay	1m 12·472s	48
Johnny Dumfries	1m 12·572s	43
Riccardo Patrese	1m 12·702s	48
Thierry Boutsen	1m 12·847s	58
Ayrton Senna	1m 12·882s	3
Derek Warwick	1m 12·976s	60
Martin Brundle	1m 12·998s	64
Philippe Streiff	1m 13·810s	43
Christian Danner	1m 14·208s	40
Jonathan Palmer	1m 14·689s	36
Huub Rothengatter	1m 17·441s	25
Andrea de Cesaris	1m 17·683s	2
Alan Jones	1m 17·860s	2
Alessandro Nannini	1m 17·795s	2
Piercarlo Ghinzani	1m 17·832s	2
Teo Fabi	1m 18·154s	6
Allen Berg	1m 19·574s	11
Stefan Johansson	1m 21·581s	4

POINTS

WORLD CHAMPIONSHIP OF DRIVERS

1	Alain Prost	39 pts
2	Nigel Mansell	38
3	Ayrton Senna	36
4	Nelson Piquet	23
5	Keke Rosberg	17
6	Jacques Laffite	14
7	René Arnoux	8
8	Stefan Johansson	7
9=	Gerhard Berger	6
9=	Michele Alboreto	6
11=	Teo Fabi	2
11=	Martin Brundle	2
11=	Riccardo Patrese	2

CONSTRUCTORS' CUP

1	Williams	61 pts
2	McLaren	56
3	Lotus	36
4	Ligier	22
5	Ferrari	13
6	Benetton	8
7=	Tyrrell	2
7=	Brabham	2

ENTRIES AND PRACTICE TIMES

No.	Driver	Nat.	Car	Tyre	Engine	Entrant	Practice 1	Practice 2	Warm-up
1	Alain Prost	F	Marlboro McLAREN MP4/2C	G	TAG PO1 (TTE PO1)	Marlboro McLaren International	1m 09·779s	**1m 09·334s**	1m 12·617s
2	Keke Rosberg	SF	Marlboro McLAREN MP4/2C	G	TAG PO1 (TTE PO1)	Marlboro McLaren International	1m 09·479s	**1m 08·477s**	1m 11·733s
3	Martin Brundle	GB	Data General TYRRELL 015	G	Renault EF15B	Data General Team Tyrrell	1m 11·432s	**1m 10·334s**	1m 15·769s
4	Philippe Streiff	F	Data General TYRRELL 015	G	Renault EF15B	Data General Team Tyrrell	1m 11·682s	**1m 11·450s**	1m 16·436s
5	Nigel Mansell	GB	WILLIAMS FW11	G	Honda RA166–E	Canon Williams Honda Team	1m 08·818s	**1m 07·399s**	1m 11·993s
6	Nelson Piquet	BR	WILLIAMS FW11	G	Honda RA166–E	Canon Williams Honda Team	1m 07·690s	**1m 06·961s**	1m 20·226s
7	Riccardo Patrese	I	Olivetti BRABHAM BT54	P	BMW M12/13/1	Motor Racing Developments Ltd	1m 12·513s	**1m 11·267s**	1m 13·274s
8	Derek Warwick	GB	Olivetti BRABHAM BT55	P	BMW M12/13/1	Motor Racing Developments Ltd	1m 11·430s	**1m 10·209s**	1m 13·934s
11	Johnny Dumfries	GB	John Player Special LOTUS 98T	G	Renault EF15B	John Player Special Team Lotus	**1m 10·304s**	1m 10·583s	1m 15·096s
12	Ayrton Senna	BR	John Player Special LOTUS 98T	G	Renault EF15B/EF15C	John Player Special Team Lotus	1m 09·042s	**1m 07·524s**	1m 13·095s
14	Jonathan Palmer	GB	West ZAKSPEED ZAK 861	G	Zakspeed	West Zakspeed Racing	1m 14·678s	**1m 13·009s**	1m 17·857s
15	Alan Jones	AUS	LOLA THL-2	G	Ford-Cosworth	Team Haas (USA) Ltd	1m 12·060s	**1m 11·121s**	1m 14·854s
16	Patrick Tambay	F	LOLA THL-2	G	Ford-Cosworth	Team Haas (USA) Ltd	1m 13·376s	**1m 11·458s**	1m 14·469s
17	Christian Danner	D	ARROWS A8	G	BMW M12/13	Barclay Arrows BMW	**1m 13·261s**	1m 13·421s	1m 16·904s
18	Thierry Boutsen	B	ARROWS A8	G	BMW M12/13	Barclay Arrows BMW	1m 12·333s	**1m 10·941s**	1m 21·305s
19	Teo Fabi	I	BENETTON B186	P	BMW M12/13	Benetton Formula Ltd	1m 11·819s	**1m 09·409s**	1m 13·826s
20	Gerhard Berger	A	BENETTON B186	P	BMW M12/13	Benetton Formula Ltd	**1m 08·196s**	1m 09·008s	1m 13·561s
21	Piercarlo Ghinzani	I	OSELLA FA1G	P	Alfa Romeo 185T	Osella Squadra Corse	1m 16·440s	**1m 16·134s**	1m 18·385s
22	Allen Berg	CDN	OSELLA FA1H	P	Alfa Romeo 185T	Osella Squadra Corse	**1m 18·319s**	—	6m 26·393s
23	Andrea de Cesaris	I	Simod MINARDI M/85B	P	Motori Moderni	Minardi Team	1m 14·366s	**1m 12·980s**	1m 16·397s
24	Alessandro Nannini	I	Simod MINARDI M/85B	P	Motori Moderni	Minardi Team	1m 13·496s	**1m 12·848s**	1m 16·927s
25	René Arnoux	F	Gitanes LIGIER JS27	P	Renault EF15B	Equipe Ligier	1m 09·971s	**1m 09·543s**	1m 14·242s
26	Jacques Laffite	F	Gitanes LIGIER JS27	P	Renault EF15B	Equipe Ligier	1m 12·715s	**1m 12·281s**	1m 15·005s
27	Michele Alboreto	I	Fiat FERRARI F1/86	G	Ferrari 126C	Scuderia Ferrari SpA	1m 11·662s	**1m 10·338s**	1m 13·913s
28	Stefan Johansson	S	Fiat FERRARI F1/86	G	Ferrari 126C	Scuderia Ferrari SpA	1m 11·568s	**1m 11·500s**	1m 14·209s
29	Huub Rothengatter	NL	West ZAKSPEED ZAK 861	G	Zakspeed	West Zakspeed Racing	**1m 16·854s**	—	1m 23·274s

Friday morning, Saturday morning and Sunday morning practice sessions not officially recorded.

G – Goodyear, P – Pirelli

Fri p.m. Warm, dry, sunny	Sat p.m. Warm, dry, cloudy	Sun a.m. Cool, dry, cloudy

STARTING GRID

	6 PIQUET (1m 06·961s) Williams
5 MANSELL (1m 07·399s) Williams	
	12 SENNA (1m 07·524s) Lotus
20 BERGER (1m 08·196s) Benetton	
	2 ROSBERG (1m 08·477s) McLaren
1 PROST (1m 09·334s) McLaren	
	19 FABI (1m 09·409s) Benetton
25 ARNOUX (1m 09·543s) Ligier	
	8 WARWICK (1m 10·209s) Brabham
11 DUMFRIES (1m 10·304s) Lotus	
	3 BRUNDLE (1m 10·334s) Tyrrell
27 ALBORETO (1m 10·338s) Ferrari	
	18 BOUTSEN (1m 10·941s) Arrows
15 JONES (1m 11·121s) Lola	
	7 PATRESE (1m 11·267s) Brabham
4 STREIFF (1m 11·450s) Tyrrell	
	16 TAMBAY (1m 11·458s) Lola
28 JOHANSSON (1m 11·500s) Ferrari	
	†26 LAFFITE (1m 12·281s) Ligier
*24 NANNINI (1m 12·848s) Minardi	
	23 DE CESARIS (1m 12·980s) Minardi
14 PALMER (1m 13·009s) Zakspeed	
	†17 DANNER (1m 13·261s) Arrows
†21 GHINZANI (1m 16·134s) Osella	
	29 ROTHENGATTER (1m 16·854s) Zakspeed
†22 BERG (1m 18·319s) Osella	

* Started from pit lane.
† Did not take restart.

RESULTS AND RETIREMENTS

Place	Driver	Car	Laps	Time and speed (mph/km/h)/Retirement	
1	Nigel Mansell	Williams-Honda V6	75	1h 30m 38·471s	129·775/208·853
2	Nelson Piquet	Williams-Honda V6	75	1h 30m 44·045s	129·643/208·640
3	Alain Prost	McLaren-TAG V6	74		
4	René Arnoux	Ligier-Renault V6	73		
5	Martin Brundle	Tyrrell-Renault V6	72		
6	Philippe Streiff	Tyrrell-Renault V6	72		
7	Johnny Dumfries	Lotus-Renault V6	72		
8	Derek Warwick	Brabham-BMW 4	72		
9	Jonathan Palmer	Zakspeed 4	69		
	Thierry Boutsen	Arrows-BMW 4	62	Running but not classified	
	Patrick Tambay	Lola-Ford V6	60	Gearbox	
	Michele Alboreto	Ferrari V6	51	Turbo	
	Alessandro Nannini	Minardi-MM V6	50	Driveshaft	
	Teo Fabi	Benetton-BMW 4	45	Fuel system	
	Riccardo Patrese	Brabham-BMW 4	39	Engine	
	Ayrton Senna	Lotus-Renault V6	27	Gearbox	
	Huub Rothengatter	Zakspeed 4	24	Engine	
	Andrea de Cesaris	Minardi-MM V6	23	Electrics	
	Gerhard Berger	Benetton-BMW 4	22	Electrics	
	Alan Jones	Lola-Ford V6	22	Throttle linkage	
	Stefan Johansson	Ferrari V6	20	Engine	
	Keke Rosberg	McLaren-TAG V6	7	Gearbox	

Fastest lap: Mansell, on lap 69, 1m 09·593s, 135·220 mph/217·616 km/h (record).
Previous lap record: Jacques Laffite (F1 Ligier JS25-Renault t/c), 1m 11·526s, 131·566 mph/211·734 km/h (1985).

PAST WINNERS

Year	Driver	Nat.	Car	Circuit	Distance miles/km	Speed mph/km/h
1952	Alberto Ascari	I	2·0 Ferrari 500	Silverstone	248·80/400·40	90·92/146·32
1953	Alberto Ascari	I	2·0 Ferrari 500	Silverstone	263·43/423·95	92·97/149·62
1954	Froilán González	RA	2·5 Ferrari 625	Silverstone	263·43/423·95	89·69/144·34
1955	Stirling Moss	GB	2·5 Mercedes-Benz W196	Aintree	270·00/434·52	86·47/139·16
1956	Juan Manuel Fangio	RA	2·5 Lancia-Ferrari D50	Silverstone	295·63/475·77	98·65/158·76
1957	Tony Brooks/	GB				
	Stirling Moss	GB	2·5 Vanwall	Aintree	270·00/434·52	86·80/139·69
1958	Peter Collins	GB	2·4 Ferrari Dino 246	Silverstone	219·53/353·30	102·05/164·23
1959	Jack Brabham	AUS	2·5 Cooper T51-Climax	Aintree	225·00/362·10	98·88/159·13
1960	Jack Brabham	AUS	2·5 Cooper T53-Climax	Silverstone	225·00/362·10	108·69/174·92
1961	Wolfgang von Trips	D	1·5 Ferrari Dino 156	Aintree	225·00/362·10	83·91/135·04
1962	Jim Clark	GB	1·5 Lotus 25-Climax	Aintree	225·00/362·10	92·25/148·46
1963	Jim Clark	GB	1·5 Lotus 25-Climax	Silverstone	240·00/386·25	107·75/173·41
1964	Jim Clark	GB	1·5 Lotus 25-Climax	Brands Hatch	212·00/341·18	94·14/151·50
1965	Jim Clark	GB	1·5 Lotus 33-Climax	Silverstone	240·00/386·25	112·02/180·28
1966	Jack Brabham	AUS	3·0 Brabham BT19-Repco	Brands Hatch	212·00/341·18	95·48/153·66
1967	Jim Clark	GB	3·0 Lotus 49-Ford	Silverstone	240·00/386·25	117·64/189·32
1968	Jo Siffert	CH	3·0 Lotus 49B-Ford	Brands Hatch	212·00/341·18	104·83/168·71
1969	Jackie Stewart	GB	3·0 Matra MS80-Ford	Silverstone	245·87/395·69	127·25/204·79
1970	Jochen Rindt	A	3·0 Lotus 72-Ford	Brands Hatch	212·00/341·18	108·69/174·92
1971	Jackie Stewart	GB	3·0 Tyrrell 003-Ford	Silverstone	199·04/320·32	130·48/209·99
1972	Emerson Fittipaldi	BR	3·0 JPS/Lotus 72-Ford	Brands Hatch	201·40/324·12	112·06/180·34
1973	Peter Revson	USA	3·0 McLaren M23-Ford	Silverstone	196·11/315·61	131·75/212·03
1974	Jody Scheckter	ZA	3·0 Tyrrell 007-Ford	Brands Hatch	198·75/319·86	115·74/186·26
1975	Emerson Fittipaldi	BR	3·0 McLaren M23-Ford	Silverstone	164·19/264·24	120·02/193·15
1976	Niki Lauda	A	3·0 Ferrari 312T-2/76	Brands Hatch	198·63/319·67	114·24/183·85
1977	James Hunt	GB	3·0 McLaren M26-Ford	Silverstone	199·38/320·88	130·36/209·79
1978	Carlos Reutemann	RA	3·0 Ferrari 312T-3/78	Brands Hatch	198·63/319·67	116·61/187·66
1979	Clay Regazzoni	CH	3·0 Williams FW07-Ford	Silverstone	199·38/320·88	138·80/223·37
1980	Alan Jones	AUS	3·0 Williams FW07B-Ford	Brands Hatch	198·63/319·67	125·69/202·28
1981	John Watson	GB	3·0 McLaren MP4-Ford	Silverstone	199·38/320·88	137·64/221·51
1982	Niki Lauda	A	3·0 McLaren MP4B-Ford	Brands Hatch	198·63/319·67	124·70/200·68
1983	Alain Prost	F	1·5 Renault RE40 t/c	Silverstone	196·44/316·17	139·62/224·05
1984	Niki Lauda	A	1·5 McLaren MP4/2-TAG t/c	Brands Hatch	185·57/298·64	124·41/200·21
1985	Alain Prost	F	1·5 McLaren MP4/2B-TAG	Silverstone	190·58/306·71	146·27/235·40
1986	Nigel Mansell	GB	1·5 Williams FW11-Honda t/c	Brands Hatch	196·05/315·51	129·77/208·85

LAP CHART

Brands Hatch — 1st lap order, driver, lap-by-lap running positions (laps 1–75), and final running order.

1st Lap Order	Lap positions (1→75)	Running order
6 N. Piquet	6 6 6 6 6 6 6 6 6 6 6 6 6 6 6 6 6 6 6 6 6 6 6 6 5 5 5 5 5 5 5 5 5 5 5 5 5 5 5 5 5 5 5 5 5 5 5 5 5 5 5 5 5 5 5 5 5 5 5 5 5 5 5 5 5 5 5 5 5 5 5 5 5 5 5	1
20 G. Berger	20 20 5 5 5 5 5 5 5 5 5 5 5 5 5 5 5 5 5 5 5 5 5 5 6 6 6 6 6 6 6 6 6 6 6 6 6 6 6 6 6 6 6 6 6 6 6 6 6 6 6 6 6 6 6 6 6 6 6 6 6 6 6 6 6 6 6 6 6 6 6 6 6 6 6	2
5 N. Mansell	5 5 20 20 20 20 20 20 20 20 20 20 20 20 20 20 20 20 20 20 12 12 12 27 27 27 25 25 25 25 25 1 1 1 1 1 1 1 1 1 1 1 1 1 1 1 1 1 1 1 1 1 1 1 1 1 1 1 1 1 1 1 1 1 1 1 1 1 1 1 1 1 1 1 1	3
12 A. Senna	12 12 12 12 12 12 12 12 12 12 12 12 12 12 12 12 12 27 27 27 25 25 25 25 8 1 1 1 1 1 27 27 27 27 27 27 25 25 25 8 8 25 25 25 25 25 25 25 25 25 25 25 25 25 25 25 25 25 25 25 25 25 25 25 25 25 25 25 25 25 25 25 25 25 25	4
2 K. Rosberg	2 2 2 2 2 2 1 1 1 1 1 1 1 1 27 27 27 25 25 25 27 25 25 8 8 8 8 8 1 8 27 27 27 25 25 25 25 25 27 8 25 8 8 8 8 8 8 8 8 8 8 8 8 8 8 8 8 8 8 8 8 8 8 8 8 3	5
1 A. Prost	1 1 1 1 1 1 1 19 19 19 19 19 27 27 25 25 25 25 25 25 8 8 8 8 7 7 7 7 1 27 8 8 8 8 8 8 8 19 19 19 8 8 8 8 8 16 16 16 16 3 3 3 3 3 3 3 3 3 3 3 3 3 3 3 4	6
19 T. Fabi	19 19 19 19 19 19 19 27 27 27 27 25 15 15 15 15 8 8 7 7 7 7 1 1 1 11 11 11 19 19 19 19 19 19 19 8 8 8 16 16 16 16 3 3 3 3 16 16 16 4 4 4 4 4 4 4 4 4 11	7
27 M. Alboreto	27 27 27 27 27 27 25 25 25 25 15 15 15 8 8 8 7 7 1 1 1 11 11 11 11 4 19 11 11 16 16 16 16 16 16 3 3 3 3 4 4 4 4 4 11 11 11 11 11 11 11 11 11 11 11 8	8
25 R. Arnoux	25 25 25 25 25 25 15 15 15 15 15 8 8 1 7 7 7 1 1 11 11 11 11 3 3 3 4 19 16 16 16 3 3 3 3 3 3 3 4 4 11 11 11 11 11 14 14 14 14 14 14 14 14 14	9
15 A. Jones	15 15 15 15 15 15 15 8 8 8 8 8 11 7 7 7 1 1 15 15 3 3 3 4 4 19 16 3 3 11 4 4 4 4 4 11 11 11 11 14 14 14 14 14 14 14 14 18 18	10
8 D. Warwick	8 8 8 8 8 8 8 8 11 11 11 11 11 7 11 11 11 11 4 4 4 19 19 19 16 3 3 4 4 4 11 11 11 11 11 14 14 14 18 18 18 18 18 18 18 18 18	11
11 J. Dumfries	11 11 11 11 11 11 11 3 3 3 3 7 3 3 3 3 3 3 19 19 19 16 16 3 7 7 7 7 7 7 7 14 14 14 24 24 24 24 18	12
3 M. Brundle	3 3 3 3 3 3 7 7 7 7 7 3 4 4 4 4 4 4 16 16 14 14 14 14 14 14 14 14 14 14 24 24 24 24 18 18 18 18	13
4 P. Streiff	4 4 7 7 7 7 7 4 4 4 4 28 28 28 28 28 28 19 19 14 14 14 24 24 24 24 24 24 24 24 24 18 18 18 18	14
7 R. Patrese	7 7 4 4 4 4 4 28 28 28 28 28 16 16 16 16 16 19 16 23 24 24 12 18 18 18 18 18 18 18 18 18	15
16 P. Tambay	16 16 16 16 16 16 16 16 16 16 16 19 19 19 19 19 16 14 14 29 18 18 18	16
18 T. Boutsen	18 28 28 28 28 28 28 14 14 14 14 14 14 14 14 14 14 14 24 24 29 18	17
28 S. Johansson	28 18 14 14 14 14 14 18 18 18 18 18 18 18 24 24 24 24 24 23 23 18	18
14 J. Palmer	14 14 18 18 18 18 18 24 24 24 24 24 24 23 23 23 23 23 23 29 29	19
29 H. Rothengatter	29 29 24 24 24 24 24 29 29 23 23 23 23 29 29 29 29 29 29 18 18	20
24 A. Nannini	24 24 29 29 29 29 29 23 29 29 29 29 29 18 18 18 18 18 18	21
23 A. de Cesaris	23 23 23 23 23 23 23	22

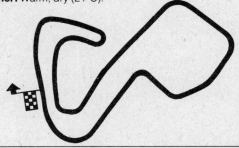

CIRCUIT DATA

Brands Hatch Grand Prix Circuit, Fawkham, Kent
Circuit length: 2·6136 miles/4·206 km
Race distance: 75 laps, 196·050 miles/315·511 km
Race weather: Warm, dry (21°C).

FASTEST LAPS

Driver	Time	Lap
Nigel Mansell	1m 09·593s	69
Nelson Piquet	1m 09·805s	68
Alain Prost	1m 10·827s	54
Riccardo Patrese	1m 12·422s	39
Teo Fabi	1m 12·644s	45
Michele Alboreto	1m 12·741s	38
René Arnoux	1m 12·790s	56
Derek Warwick	1m 12·926s	37
Johnny Dumfries	1m 13·077s	71
Gerhard Berger	1m 13·247s	19
Martin Brundle	1m 13·386s	65
Patrick Tambay	1m 13·460s	48
Philippe Streiff	1m 13·553s	70
Ayrton Senna	1m 14·024s	23
Keke Rosberg	1m 14·639s	5
Alan Jones	1m 14·992s	19
Stefan Johansson	1m 15·490s	9
Andrea de Cesaris	1m 16·380s	22
Alessandro Nannini	1m 16·427s	35
Jonathan Palmer	1m 16·985s	37
Thierry Boutsen	1m 17·103s	57
Huub Rothengatter	1m 17·814s	21

POINTS

WORLD CHAMPIONSHIP OF DRIVERS

1	Nigel Mansell	47 pts
2	Alain Prost	43
3	Ayrton Senna	36
4	Nelson Piquet	29
5	Keke Rosberg	17
6	Jacques Laffite	14
7	René Arnoux	11
8	Stefan Johansson	7
9=	Gerhard Berger	6
9=	Michele Alboreto	6
11	Martin Brundle	4
12=	Teo Fabi	2
12=	Riccardo Patrese	2
14	Philippe Streiff	1

CONSTRUCTORS' CUP

	Constructor	Points
1	Williams	76 pts
2	McLaren	60
3	Lotus	36
4	Ligier	25
5	Ferrari	13
6	Benetton	8
7	Tyrrell	5
8	Brabham	2

GIVE 'EM HELL NIGEL — Nº1

FIRE POINT

ENTRIES AND PRACTICE TIMES

No.	Driver	Nat.	Car	Tyre	Engine	Entrant	Practice 1	Practice 2	Warm-up
1	Alain Prost	F	Marlboro McLAREN MP4/2C	G	TAG PO1 (TTE PO1)	Marlboro McLaren International	1m 43·373s	**1m 42·166s**	1m 49·383s
2	Keke Rosberg	SF	Marlboro McLAREN MP4/2C	G	TAG PO1 (TTE PO1)	Marlboro McLaren International	1m 42·478s	**1m 42·013s**	1m 51·314s
3	Martin Brundle	GB	Data General TYRRELL 015	G	Renault EF15B	Data General Team Tyrrell	1m 49·406s	**1m 45·432s**	1m 52·361s
4	Philippe Streiff	F	Data General TYRRELL 015	G	Renault EF15	Data General Team Tyrrell	**1m 47·371s**	1m 48·397s	1m 53·403s
5	Nigel Mansell	GB	WILLIAMS FW11	G	Honda RA166–E	Canon Williams Honda Team	**1m 42·696s**	1m 43·086s	1m 49·353s
6	Nelson Piquet	BR	WILLIAMS FW11	G	Honda RA166–E	Canon Williams Honda Team	1m 43·852s	**1m 42·545s**	1m 49·759s
7	Riccardo Patrese	I	Olivetti BRABHAM BT55	G	BMW M12/13	Motor Racing Developments Ltd	1m 46·094s	**1m 43·348s**	1m 46·321s
8	Derek Warwick	GB	Olivetti BRABHAM BT55	P	BMW M12/13/1	Motor Racing Developments Ltd	**1m 48·206s**	—	1m 53·270s
11	Johnny Dumfries	GB	John Player Special LOTUS 98T	G	Renault EF15B	John Player Special Team Lotus	1m 47·845s	**1m 44·768s**	1m 54·543s
12	Ayrton Senna	BR	John Player Special LOTUS 98T	G	Renault EF15B/EF15C	John Player Special Team Lotus	1m 45·212s	**1m 42·329s**	1m 51·863s
14	Jonathan Palmer	GB	West ZAKSPEED ZAK 861	G	Zakspeed	West Zakspeed Racing	1m 47·167s	**1m 45·887s**	1m 55·142s
15	Alan Jones	AUS	LOLA THL-2	G	Ford-Cosworth	Team Haas (USA) Ltd	1m 51·918s	**1m 47·518s**	1m 53·460s
16	Patrick Tambay	F	LOLA THL-2	G	Ford-Cosworth	Team Haas (USA) Ltd	1m 47·221s	**1m 44·979s**	1m 51·645s
17	Christian Danner	D	ARROWS A8	G	BMW M12/13	Barclay Arrows BMW	1m 49·439s	**1m 46·355s**	1m 54·497s
18	Thierry Boutsen	B	ARROWS A9	G	BMW M12/13	Barclay Arrows BMW	**1m 49·240s**	2m 03·702s	1m 55·292s
19	Teo Fabi	I	BENETTON B186	P	BMW M12/13	Benetton Formula Ltd	—	**1m 44·001s**	1m 52·114s
20	Gerhard Berger	A	BENETTON B186	P	BMW M12/13	Benetton Formula Ltd	1m 44·493s	**1m 42·541s**	1m 50·946s
21	Piercarlo Ghinzani	I	OSELLA FA1G	P	Alfa Romeo 185T	Osella Squadra Corse	—	**1m 56·468s**	1m 59·659s
22	Allen Berg	CDN	OSELLA FA1F	P	Alfa Romeo 185T	Osella Squadra Corse	**1m 56·959s**	—	2m 00·276s
23	Andrea de Cesaris	I	Simod MINARDI M/85B	P	Motori Moderni	Minardi Team	1m 50·900s	**1m 50·066s**	1m 56·106s
24	Alessandro Nannini	I	Simod MINARDI M/85B	P	Motori Moderni	Minardi Team	1m 50·221s	**1m 49·369s**	1m 56·224s
25	René Arnoux	F	Gitanes LIGIER JS27	P	Renault EF15B/EF15C	Equipe Ligier	1m 43·991s	**1m 43·693s**	1m 51·452s
26	Philippe Alliot	F	Gitanes LIGIER JS27	P	Renault EF15B	Equipe Ligier	**1m 45·047s**	1m 45·905s	1m 53·457s
27	Michele Alboreto	I	Fiat FERRARI F1/86	G	Ferrari 126C	Scuderia Ferrari SpA	1m 46·319s	**1m 44·308s**	1m 52·031s
28	Stefan Johansson	S	Fiat FERRARI F1/86	G	Ferrari 126C	Scuderia Ferrari SpA	1m 46·847s	**1m 44·346s**	1m 52·191s
29	Huub Rothengatter	NL	West ZAKSPEED ZAK 861	G	Zakspeed	West Zakspeed Racing	1m 52·461s	**1m 50·918s**	1m 56·244s

Friday morning, Saturday morning and Sunday morning practice sessions not officially recorded.

G – Goodyear, P – Pirelli

Fri p.m.	Sat p.m.	Sun a.m.
Warm, dry, cloudy	Warm, dry, cloudy	Warm, dry, cloudy

STARTING GRID

1 PROST (1m 42·166s)
McLaren

    2 ROSBERG (1m 42·013s)
    McLaren

20 BERGER (1m 42·541s)
Benetton

    12 SENNA (1m 42·329s)
    Lotus

5 MANSELL (1m 42·696s)
Williams

    6 PIQUET (1m 42·545s)
    Williams

25 ARNOUX (1m 43·693s)
Ligier

    7 PATRESE (1m 43·348s)
    Brabham

27 ALBORETO (1m 44·308s)
Ferrari

    19 FABI (1m 44·001s)
    Benetton

11 DUMFRIES (1m 44·768s)
Lotus

    28 JOHANSSON (1m 44·346s)
    Ferrari

26 ALLIOT (1m 45·047s)
Ligier

    16 TAMBAY (1m 44·979s)
    Lola

14 PALMER (1m 45·887s)
Zakspeed

    3 BRUNDLE (1m 45·432s)
    Tyrrell

4 STREIFF (1m 47·371s)
Tyrrell

    17 DANNER (1m 46·355s)
    Arrows

8 WARWICK (1m 48·206s)
Brabham

    *15 JONES (1m 47·518s)
    Lola

24 NANNINI (1m 49·369s)
Minardi

    18 BOUTSEN (1m 49·240s)
    Arrows

29 ROTHENGATTER (1m 50·918s)
Zakspeed

    23 DE CESARIS (1m 50·066s)
    Minardi

22 BERG (1m 56·959s)
Osella

    21 GHINZANI (1m 56·468s)
    Osella

* Started from back of grid

RESULTS AND RETIREMENTS

Place	Driver	Car	Laps	Time and speed (mph/km/h)/Retirement	
1	Nelson Piquet	Williams-Honda V6	44	1h 22m 08·263s	135·746/218·463
2	Ayrton Senna	Lotus-Renault V6	44	1h 22m 23·700s	135·322/217·781
3	Nigel Mansell	Williams-Honda V6	44	1h 22m 52·843s	134·530/216·505
4	René Arnoux	Ligier-Renault V6	44	1h 23m 23·439s	133·707/215·181
5	Keke Rosberg	McLaren-TAG V6	43	Not running (out of fuel)	
6	Alain Prost	McLaren-TAG V6	43	Not running (out of fuel)	
7	Derek Warwick	Brabham-BMW BT55	43		
8	Patrick Tambay	Lola-Ford V6	43		
9	Alan Jones	Lola-Ford V6	42		
10	Gerhard Berger	Benetton-BMW 4	42		
11	Stefan Johansson	Ferrari V6	41	Not running (broken rear wing)	
12	Allen Berg	Osella-Alfa Romeo V8	40		
	Christian Danner	Arrows-BMW 4	38	Turbo	
	Huub Rothengatter	Zakspeed 4	38	Gearbox	
	Jonathan Palmer	Zakspeed 4	37	Engine	
	Martin Brundle	Tyrrell-Renault V6	34	Electrics	
	Riccardo Patrese	Brabham-BMW 4	22	Turbo	
	Andrea de Cesaris	Minardi-MM V6	20	Gearbox	
	Alessandro Nannini	Minardi-MM V6	19	Overheating	
	Johnny Dumfries	Lotus-Renault V6	17	Holed water radiator	
	Thierry Boutsen	Arrows-BMW 4	13	Turbo	
	Philippe Alliot	Ligier-Renault V6	11	Engine	
	Piercarlo Ghinzani	Osella-Alfa Romeo V8	10	Clutch	
	Philippe Streiff	Tyrrell-Renault V6	7	Engine	
	Michele Alboreto	Ferrari V6	6	Transmission	
	Teo Fabi	Benetton-BMW 4	0	Accident	

Fastest lap: Berger, on lap 35, 1m 46·604s, 142·625 mph/229·534 km/h (record).
Previous lap record: Alain Prost (F1 McLaren MP4/2-TAG t/c V6), 1m 53·538s, 133·915 mph/215·515 km/h (1984).

PAST WINNERS

Year	Driver	Nat.	Car	Circuit	Distance miles/km	Speed mph/km/h
1950*	Alberto Ascari	I	2·0 Ferrari 166	Nürburgring North	266·78/364·96	77·75/125·13
1951	Alberto Ascari	I	4·5 Ferrari 375	Nürburgring North	283·47/456·20	83·76/134·80
1952	Alberto Ascari	I	2·0 Ferrari 500	Nürburgring North	255·12/410·58	82·20/132·29
1953	Giuseppe Farina	I	2·0 Ferrari 500	Nürburgring North	255·12/410·58	83·91/135·04
1954	Juan Manuel Fangio	RA	2·5 Mercedes-Benz W196	Nürburgring North	311·82/501·82	82·87/133·37
1956	Juan Manuel Fangio	RA	2·5 Lancia-Ferrari D50	Nürburgring North	311·82/501·82	85·45/137·52
1957	Juan Manuel Fangio	RA	2·5 Maserati 250F	Nürburgring North	311·82/501·82	88·82/142·94
1958	Tony Brooks	GB	2·5 Vanwall	Nürburgring North	212·60/342·15	90·31/145·34
1959	Tony Brooks	GB	2·4 Ferrari Dino 256	Avus	309·44/498·00	145·35/230·70
1960*	Jo Bonnier	S	1·5 Porsche 718	Nürburgring South	154·04/247·90	80·23/129·12
1961	Stirling Moss	GB	1·5 Lotus 18/21-Climax	Nürburgring North	212·60/342·15	92·30/148·54
1962	Graham Hill	GB	1·5 BRM P57	Nürburgring North	212·60/342·15	80·35/129·31
1963	John Surtees	GB	1·5 Ferrari 156	Nürburgring North	212·60/342·15	95·83/154·22
1964	John Surtees	GB	1·5 Ferrari 158	Nürburgring North	212·60/342·15	96·58/155·43
1965	Jim Clark	GB	1·5 Lotus 33-Climax	Nürburgring North	212·60/342·15	96·76/160·55
1966	Jack Brabham	AUS	3·0 Brabham BT19-Repco	Nürburgring North	212·60/342·15	86·75/139·61
1967	Denny Hulme	NZ	3·0 Brabham BT24-Repco	Nürburgring North	212·60/342·15	101·41/163·20
1968	Jackie Stewart	GB	3·0 Matra MS10-Ford	Nürburgring North	198·65/319·69	85·71/137·94
1969	Jacky Ickx	B	3·0 Brabham BT26A-Ford	Nürburgring North	198·65/319·69	108·43/174·50
1970	Jochen Rindt	A	3·0 Lotus 72-Ford	Hockenheim	210·92/339·44	124·07/199·67
1971	Jackie Stewart	GB	3·0 Tyrrell 003-Ford	Nürburgring North	170·27/274·02	114·45/184·19
1972	Jacky Ickx	B	3·0 Ferrari 312B-2/72	Nürburgring North	198·65/319·69	116·62/187·68
1973	Jackie Stewart	GB	3·0 Tyrrell 006-Ford	Nürburgring North	198·65/319·69	116·79/187·95
1974	Clay Regazzoni	CH	3·0 Ferrari 312B-3/74	Nürburgring North	198·65/319·69	117·33/188·82
1975	Carlos Reutemann	RA	3·0 Brabham BT44B-bford	Nürburgring North	198·65/319·69	117·73/189·47
1976	James Hunt	GB	3·0 McLaren M23-Ford	Nürburgring North	198·65/319·69	117·18/188·59
1977	Niki Lauda	A	3·0 Ferrari 312T-2/77	Hockenheim	198·27/319·08	129·57/208·53
1978	Mario Andretti	USA	3·0 JPS Lotus 79-Ford	Hockenheim	189·83/305·51	129·41/208·26
1979	Alan Jones	AUS	3·0 Williams FW07-Ford	Hockenheim	189·83/305·51	134·27/216·09
1980	Jacques Laffite	F	3·0 Ligier JS11/15-Ford	Hockenheim	189·83/305·51	137·22/220·83
1981	Nelson Piquet	BR	3·0 Brabham BT49C-Ford	Hockenheim	189·83/305·51	132·53/213·29
1982	Patrick Tambay	F	1·5 Ferrari 126C2 t/c	Hockenheim	190·05/305·86	130·43/209·90
1983	René Arnoux	F	1·5 Ferrari 126C3 t/c	Hockenheim	190·05/305·86	130·81/210·52
1984	Alain Prost	F	1·5 McLaren MP4/2-TAG t/c	Hockenheim	185·83/299·07	131·61/211·80
1985	Michele Alboreto	I	1·5 Ferrari 156/85 t/c	New Nürburgring	189·09/304·31	118·77/191·15
1986	Nelson Piquet	BR	1·5 Williams FW11-Honda t/c	Hockenheim	185·83/299·07	135·75/218·46

* Non-championship (Formula 2)

LAP CHART

1st LAP ORDER	1	2	3	4	5	6	7	8	9	10	11	12	13	14	15	16	17	18	19	20	21	22	23	24	25	26	27	28	29	30	31	32	33	34	35	36	37	38	39	40	41	42	43	44	Running order
12 A. Senna	12	2	2	2	2	6	6	6	6	6	6	6	6	6	2	2	2	2	2	1	6	6	6	6	6	6	6	2	2	2	2	2	2	2	2	2	2	6	6	6	6	6	6	6	1
20 G. Berger	20	12	6	6	6	2	2	2	2	2	2	2	2	1	1	1	1	1	6	12	2	2	2	2	2	2	1	1	6	6	6	6	6	6	6	6	2	2	2	2	2	2	2	12	2
2 K. Rosberg	2	20	12	12	1	1	1	1	1	1	1	1	1	6	12	12	12	12	12	2	1	1	1	1	1	1	6	6	1	1	1	1	1	1	1	1	1	1	1	1	1	1	12	5	3
6 N. Piquet	6	6	20	1	12	12	12	12	12	12	12	12	12	6	6	6	2	1	12	12	12	12	12	12	12	12	12	12	12	12	12	12	12	12	12	12	12	12	1	25					4
1 A. Prost	1	1	1	5	5	25	25	25	25	25	25	25	25	25	25	25	25	25	7	5	25	25	25	25	25	25	25	25	25	25	25	25	25	25	5	5	5	5	5						5
5 N. Mansell	5	5	5	20	27	27	5	5	5	5	5	5	5	5	5	7	7	25	25	5	5	5	5	5	5	5	5	5	5	5	5	5	5	5	25	25	25	25							6
7 R. Patrese	7	27	27	27	25	11	11	11	11	11	11	11	11	11	11	7	7	5	5	5	7	7	8	8	8	8	8	8	8	8	8	8	8	8	8	8	8	8	8	8	8	8	8	8	7
27 M. Alboreto	27	7	25	25	7	7	4	8	8	8	7	7	7	7	11	11	8	8	8	8	15	15	15	15	15	15	16	16	16	16	16	16	16	16	16	16	16	16	16						8
25 R. Arnoux	25	25	7	7	11	11	8	15	15	7	7	8	3	3	8	8	16	16	16	15	15	16	16	16	16	16	15	15	15	28	28	28	28	28	28	15									9
11 J. Dumfries	11	11	11	11	16	8	7	7	7	15	3	15	16	16	16	16	16	16	28	28	28	28	28	28	28	28	28	15	15	15	15	15	15	20											10
8 D. Warwick	8	8	8	16	8	4	15	3	3	3	15	23	8	8	15	17	23	17	17	28	17	17	17	17	17	17	17	17	17	17	17	17	17	20	20										11
16 P. Tambay	16	16	16	8	4	16	3	23	23	23	23	8	23	16	17	23	17	23	28	14	14	14	14	14	14	14	14	14	14	20	22	22													12
4 P. Streiff	4	4	4	4	20	15	23	18	18	17	17	17	16	17	23	14	14	14	14	20	20	20	20	20	20	20	20	20	20	22															13
23 A. de Cesaris	23	23	23	23	15	23	18	17	17	18	14	16	17	17	23	14	14	24	24	28	20	22	22	22	22	22	22	22	22	22	22	22	22	29											14
14 J. Palmer	14	14	14	15	23	3	14	14	14	24	14	14	14	24	28	28	22	22	29	29	29	29	29	29	29	29	29	29	29	29	29	29	29												15
15 A. Jones	15	15	15	18	18	18	17	24	24	16	24	24	24	3	28	22	22	20	29	29	3	3	3	3	3	3	3	3	3	3	3														16
18 T. Boutsen	18	18	18	14	3	14	24	29	29	29	18	22	29	29	29	29	29	29	3	3																									17
24 A. Nannini	24	24	24	24	14	24	29	16	16	16	18	22	29	28	28	28	22	20	20	3																									18
29 H. Rothengatter	29	29	29	3	24	17	16	22	22	22	22	29	28	22	22	22	3	3	3																										19
17 C. Danner	17	17	17	29	19	17	22	22	21	21	28	18	20	20	20	20																													20
21 P. Ghinzani	21	3	3	17	29	22	21	21	28	28	28	26	20	20																															21
3 M. Brundle	3	21	21	22	22	21	28	26	26	26	20																																		22
22 A. Berg	22	22	22	21	21	28	26	20	20	20																																			23
28 S. Johansson	28	26	26	26	28	26	20																																						24
26 P. Alliot	26	28	28	28	26	20																																							25

FASTEST LAPS

Driver	Time	Lap
Gerhard Berger	1m 46·604s	35
Nelson Piquet	1m 47·721s	34
Nigel Mansell	1m 47·899s	37
Ayrton Senna	1m 49·424s	39
Keke Rosberg	1m 49·552s	25
Alain Prost	1m 49·649s	26
René Arnoux	1m 50·374s	27
Stefan Johansson	1m 50·932s	30
Patrick Tambay	1m 51·629s	23
Michele Alboreto	1m 52·570s	5
Alan Jones	1m 52·577s	18
Riccardo Patrese	1m 52·818s	11
Derek Warwick	1m 52·955s	30
Martin Brundle	1m 53·682s	21
Johnny Dumfries	1m 53·756s	7
Philippe Streiff	1m 54·025s	7
Philippe Alliot	1m 54·145s	7
Andrea de Cesaris	1m 54·826s	17
Christian Danner	1m 54·975s	28
Jonathan Palmer	1m 56·145s	23
Huub Rothengatter	1m 56·401s	13
Alessandro Nannini	1m 56·721s	3
Thierry Boutsen	1m 56·803s	12
Allen Berg	1m 58·449s	23
Piercarlo Ghinzani	2m 00·492s	7

POINTS

WORLD CHAMPIONSHIP OF DRIVERS

1	Nigel Mansell	51 pts
2	Alain Prost	44
3	Ayrton Senna	42
4	Nelson Piquet	38
5	Keke Rosberg	19
6=	Jacques Laffite	14
6=	René Arnoux	14
8	Stefan Johansson	7
9=	Gerhard Berger	6
9=	Michele Alboreto	6
11	Martin Brundle	4
12=	Teo Fabi	2
12=	Riccardo Patrese	2
14	Philippe Streiff	1

CONSTRUCTORS' CUP

1	Williams	89 pts
2	McLaren	63
3	Lotus	42
4	Ligier	28
5	Ferrari	13
6	Benetton	8
7	Tyrrell	5
8	Brabham	2

Nelson Piquet makes fun of the FISA regulation requiring trophies to be small and light enough for elderly officials to handle. Senna enjoys the Brazilian humour; Mansell reflects on his extraordinary good fortune to be on the rostrum at all.

CIRCUIT DATA

Hockenheimring, near Heidelberg
Circuit length: 4·2234 miles/6·797 km
Race distance: 44 laps, 185·83 miles/299·068 km
Race weather: Hot, dry, sunny (27°C).

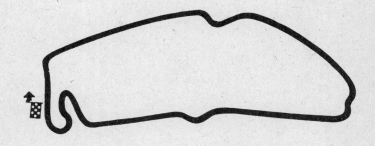

ENTRIES AND PRACTICE TIMES

No.	Driver	Nat.	Car	Tyre	Engine	Entrant	Practice 1	Practice 2	Warm-up
1	Alain Prost	F	Marlboro McLAREN MP4/2C	G	TAG PO1 (TTE PO1)	Marlboro McLaren International	1m 33·113s	**1m 29·945s**	1m 31·709s
2	Keke Rosberg	SF	Marlboro McLAREN MP4/2C	G	TAG PO1 (TTE PO1)	Marlboro McLaren International	1m 34·146s	**1m 30·628s**	1m 32·835s
3	Martin Brundle	GB	Data General TYRRELL 015	G	Renault EF15B	Data General Team Tyrrell	1m 34·725s	**1m 33·368s**	1m 35·566s
4	Philippe Streiff	F	Data General TYRRELL 015	G	Renault EF15B	Data General Team Tyrrell	1m 35·831s	**1m 34·414s**	1m 38·575s
5	Nigel Mansell	GB	WILLIAMS FW11	G	Honda RA166–E	Canon Williams Honda Team	1m 30·516s	**1m 30·072s**	1m 33·205s
6	Nelson Piquet	BR	WILLIAMS FW11	G	Honda RA166–E	Canon Williams Honda Team	1m 31·417s	**1m 29·785s**	1m 34·305s
7	Riccardo Patrese	I	Olivetti BRABHAM BT55	P	BMW M12/13	Motor Racing Developments Ltd	1m 35·337s	**1m 32·956s**	1m 36·553s
8	Derek Warwick	GB	Olivetti BRABHAM BT55	P	BMW M12/13/1	Motor Racing Developments Ltd	1m 34·561s	**1m 34·502s**	1m 36·368s
11	Johnny Dumfries	GB	John Player Special LOTUS 98T	G	Renault EF15B	John Player Special Team Lotus	1m 36·108s	**1m 31·886s**	1m 36·724s
12	Ayrton Senna	BR	John Player Special LOTUS 98T	G	Renault EF15B/EF15C	John Player Special Team Lotus	1m 32·281s	**1m 29·450s**	1m 35·048s
14	Jonathan Palmer	GB	West ZAKSPEED ZAK 861	G	Zakspeed	West Zakspeed Racing	1m 37·937s	**1m 36·485s**	1m 38·714s
15	Alan Jones	AUS	LOLA THL-2	G	Ford-Cosworth	Team Haas (USA) Ltd	1m 33·737s	**1m 32·401s**	1m 34·531s
16	Patrick Tambay	F	LOLA THL-2	G	Ford-Cosworth	Team Haas (USA) Ltd	1m 34·187s	**1m 31·715s**	1m 35·529s
17	Christian Danner	D	ARROWS A8/A9	G	BMW M12/13	Barclay Arrows BMW	1m 36·540s	**1m 35·294s**	1m 38·733s
18	Thierry Boutsen	B	ARROWS A8/A9	G	BMW M12/13	Barclay Arrows BMW	1m 37·260s	**1m 35·392s**	1m 37·881s
19	Teo Fabi	I	BENETTON B186	P	BMW M12/13	Benetton Formula Ltd	1m 35·265s	**1m 32·707s**	1m 36·182s
20	Gerhard Berger	A	BENETTON B186	P	BMW M12/13	Benetton Formula Ltd	1m 32·886s	**1m 32·491s**	1m 35·877s
21	Piercarlo Ghinzani	I	OSELLA FA1G	P	Alfa Romeo 185T	Osella Squadra Corse	1m 39·564s	**1m 36·232s**	1m 40·485s
22	Allen Berg	CDN	OSELLA FA1F	P	Alfa Romeo 185T	Osella Squadra Corse	**1m 40·984s**		1m 41·426s
23	Andrea de Cesaris	I	Simod MINARDI M/86	P	Motori Moderni	Minardi Team	1m 37·796s	**1m 34·670s**	1m 38·602s
24	Alessandro Nannini	I	Simod MINARDI M/85B	P	Motori Moderni	Minardi Team	1m 36·266s	**1m 33·656s**	1m 38·076s
25	René Arnoux	F	Gitanes LIGIER JS27	P	Renault EF15B/EF15C	Equipe Ligier	1m 36·552s	**1m 31·970s**	1m 42·374s
26	Philippe Alliot	F	Gitanes LIGIER JS27	P	Renault EF15B	Equipe Ligier	1m 35·129s	**1m 32·575s**	1m 36·837s
27	Michele Alboreto	I	Fiat FERRARI F1/86	G	Ferrari 126C	Scuderia Ferrari SpA	1m 34·255s	**1m 33·063s**	1m 35·892s
28	Stefan Johansson	S	Fiat FERRARI F1/86	G	Ferrari 126C	Scuderia Ferrari SpA	1m 35·092s	**1m 31·850s**	1m 35·553s
29	Huub Rothengatter	NL	West ZAKSPEED ZAK 861	G	Zakspeed	West Zakspeed Racing	1m 42·736s	**1m 38·527s**	1m 40·209s

Thursday afternoon, Friday morning, Saturday morning and Sunday morning practice sessions not officially recorded.

G – Goodyear, P – Pirelli

Fri p.m.	Sat p.m.	Sun a.m.
Hot, dry, sunny	Hot, dry, sunny	Hot, dry, sunny

STARTING GRID

	12 SENNA (1m 29·450s) Lotus
6 PIQUET (1m 29·785s) Williams	
	1 PROST (1m 29·945s) McLaren
5 MANSELL (1m 30·072s) Williams	
	2 ROSBERG (1m 30·628s) McLaren
16 TAMBAY (1m 31·715s) Lola	
	28 JOHANSSON (1m 31·850s) Ferrari
11 DUMFRIES (1m 31·886s) Lotus	
	25 ARNOUX (1m 31·970s) Ligier
15 JONES (1m 32·401s) Lola	
	20 BERGER (1m 32·491s) Benetton
26 ALLIOT (1m 32·575s) Ligier	
	19 FABI (1m 32·707s) Benetton
7 PATRESE (1m 32·956s) Brabham	
	27 ALBORETO (1m 33·063s) Ferrari
3 BRUNDLE (1m 33·368s) Tyrrell	
	24 NANNINI (1m 33·656s) Minardi
4 STREIFF (1m 34·414s) Tyrrell	
	8 WARWICK (1m 34·502s) Brabham
23 DE CESARIS (1m 34·670s) Minardi	
	17 DANNER (1m 35·294s) Arrows
18 BOUTSEN (1m 35·392s) Arrows	
	21 GHINZANI (1m 36·232s) Osella
14 PALMER (1m 36·485s) Zakspeed	
	29 ROTHENGATTER (1m 38·527s) Zakspeed
22 BERG (1m 40·984s) Osella	

RESULTS AND RETIREMENTS

Place	Driver	Car	Laps	Time and speed (mph/km/h)/Retirement	
1	Nelson Piquet	Williams-Honda V6	76	2h 00m 34·508s	94·326/151·804
2	Ayrton Senna	Lotus-Renault V6	76	2h 00m 52·181s	94·097/151·435
3	Nigel Mansell	Williams-Honda V6	75		
4	Stefan Johansson	Ferrari V6	75		
5	Johnny Dumfries	Lotus-Renault V6	74		
6	Martin Brundle	Tyrrell-Renault V6	74		
7	Patrick Tambay	Lola-Ford V6	74		
8	Philippe Streiff	Tyrrell-Renault V6	74		
9	Philippe Alliot	Ligier-Renault V6	73		
10	Jonathan Palmer	Zakspeed 4	70		
	René Arnoux	Ligier-Renault V6	48	Engine	
	Alan Jones	Lola-Ford V6	46	Differential	
	Gerhard Berger	Benetton-BMW 4	44	Fuel leak/transmission	
	Thierry Boutsen	Arrows-BMW 4	40	Electrics	
	Keke Rosberg	McLaren-TAG V6	34	Rear suspension	
	Teo Fabi	Benetton-BMW 4	32	Spun off/transmission	
	Alessandro Nannini	Minardi-MM V6	30	Engine	
	Michele Alboreto	Ferrari V6	29	Accident with Warwick	
	Derek Warwick	Brabham-BMW 4	28	Accident with Alboreto	
	Alain Prost	McLaren-TAG V6	23	Accident with Arnoux	
	Piercarlo Ghinzani	Osella-Alfa Romeo V8	15	Rear suspension	
	Christian Danner	Arrows-BMW 4	7	Rear suspension	
	Riccardo Patrese	Brabham-BMW 4	5	Spun off/gearbox	
	Andrea de Cesaris	Minardi-MM V6	5	Engine	
	Huub Rothengatter	Zakspeed 4	2	Oil radiator	
	Allen Berg	Osella-Alfa Romeo V8	1	Turbo	

Fastest lap: Piquet, on lap 73, 1m 31·001s, 98·669 mph/158·794 km/h (lap record for new 2·495 mile/4·013 km circuit).

PAST WINNERS

Year	Driver	Nat.	Car	Circuit	Distance miles/km	Speed mph/km/h
1936	Tazio Nuvolari	I	3·8 Alfa Romeo	Budapest Népliget	155·00/249·45	69·5 /111·85
1986	Nelson Piquet	BR	1·5 Williams FW11-Honda t/c	Hungaroring	189·55/305·06	94·33/151·80

LAP CHART

1st LAP ORDER	1	2	3	4	5	6	7	8	9	10	11	12	13	14	15	16	17	18	19	20	21	22	23	24	25	26	27	28	29	30	31	32	33	34	35	36	37	38	39	40	41	42	43	44	45	46	47	48	49	50	51	52	53	54	55	56	57	58	59	60	61	62	63	64	65	66	67	68	69	70	71	72	73	74	75	76	Running order
12 A. Senna	12	12	12	12	12	12	12	12	12	12	6	6	6	6	6	6	6	6	6	6	6	6	6	6	6	6	6	6	6	6	6	6	6	6	6	6	6	12	12	12	12	12	12	12	12	12	12	12	12	12	12	12	12	12	12	12	12	6	6	6	6	6	6	6	6	6	6	6	6	6	6	6	6	6	6	6	1
5 N. Mansell	5	5	6	6	6	6	6	6	6	6	12	12	12	12	12	12	12	12	12	12	12	12	12	12	12	12	12	12	12	6	6	6	6	6	6	6	6	6	6	6	6	6	6	6	6	6	6	6	6	6	12	12	12	12	12	12	12	12	12	12	12	12	12	12	12	12	12	12	12	12	12	12	12	12	12	12	2
6 N. Piquet	6	6	5	5	5	5	5	5	5	5	1	1	1	1	1	5	5	5	5	5	5	5	5	5	5	5	5	5	5	5	5	5	5	5	5	5	5	5	5	5	5	5	5	5	5	5	5	5	5	5	5	5	5	5	5	5	5	5	5	5	5	5	5	5	5	5	5	5	5	5	5	5	5	5	5	5	3
16 P. Tambay	16	16	16	16	16	1	1	1	1	1	5	5	5	5	5	11	11	11	11	11	11	11	20	20	20	20	20	20	20	20	20	20	20	20	20	20	20	28	28	28	28	28	28	28	28	28	28	28	28	28	28	28	28	28	28	28	28	28	28	28	28	28	28	28	28	28	28	28	28	28	28	28	28	28	28	28	4
1 A. Prost	1	1	1	1	16	16	15	15	15	2	2	2	2	2	2	2	27	20	20	20	11	11	11	11	11	11	11	11	11	11	11	11	3	3	3	28	28	28	28	20	11	11	11	11	11	11	11	11	11	11	11	11	11	11	11	11	11	11	11	11	11	11	11	11	11	11	11	11	11	11	11	11	11	11	11	11	5
15 A. Jones	15	15	15	15	15	15	2	2	2	11	11	11	11	11	11	27	20	27	8	8	2	2	2	8	8	8	8	3	3	3	3	28	28	28	28	11	11	11	11	11	3	3	3	3	3	3	3	3	3	3	3	3	3	3	3	3	3	3	3	3	3	3	3	3	3	3	3	3	3	3	3	3	3	3	3	3	6
11 J. Dumfries	11	11	11	11	11	2	16	11	11	16	16	16	16	16	27	20	8	8	3	2	8	8	8	3	27	4	4	4	28	11	11	11	11	3	3	3	3	3	3	3	4	4	4	4	4	4	4	4	4	4	4	4	4	4	16	16	16	16	16	16	16	16	16	16	16	16	16	16	16	16	16	16	16	16	16	16	7
25 R. Arnoux	25	2	2	2	2	11	11	16	16	15	27	27	27	27	20	8	3	2	2	3	3	3	27	27	3	27	28	28	24	4	4	4	4	4	4	4	16	16	16	16	16	16	16	16	16	16	16	16	16	16	16	16	16	16	4	4	4	4	4	4	4	4	4	4	4	4	4	4	4	4	4	4	4	4	4	4	8
2 K. Rosberg	2	28	28	28	28	28	28	28	28	27	19	19	19	19	19	16	3	2	2	4	27	27	4	4	4	28	16	16	16	16	16	26	26	26	26	26	26	26	26	26	26	26	26	26	25	25	26	26	26	26	26	26	26	26	26	26	26	26	26	26	26	26	26	26	26	26	26	26	26	26	26	26	26	26	26	26	9
28 S. Johansson	28	7	7	7	7	27	27	27	27	28	20	20	20	20	8	4	4	4	27	27	4	4	2	16	16	16	25	26	26	26	26	16	16	16	16	16	16	16	26	26	25	25	26	14	14	14	14	14	14	14	14	14	14	14	14	14	14	14	14	14	14	14	14	14	14	14	14	14	14	14	14	14	14	14	14	14	10
7 R. Patrese	7	27	27	27	27	20	19	19	19	19	3	3	3	3	3	28	28	28	28	16	16	16	16	28	28	28	26	25	19	2	25	25	25	25	25	25	25	25	19	15	15	14	14																																		11
26 P. Alliot	26	20	20	20	20	19	20	20	20	20	28	8	8	8	19	16	16	16	28	28	28	28	28	26	26	25	26	19	19	2	25	18	18	18	18	18	15	15	15	15	15	14	14																																		12
27 M. Alboreto	27	26	26	26	26	3	3	3	3	8	4	4	4	4	4	18	26	28	26	26	26	26	26	25	25	26	19	18	2	25	18	2	15	15	15	15	18	14	14	14	14																																			13
20 G. Berger	20	3	19	19	4	4	4	4	4	26	28	28	28	26	18	14	14	25	25	25	19	19	18	2	18	18	15	15	14	14	14	14	14																																												14
3 M. Brundle	3	19	3	3	8	8	8	8	8	26	18	18	18	18	14	14	25	25	25	14	14	14	14	2	15	15	15	14																																																			15
19 T. Fabi	19	4	4	4	26	26	26	26	18	28	26	26	26	25	25	18	18	19	19	19	19	18	18	15	24	14	14																																																			16
4 P. Streiff	4	24	24	24	8	24	24	18	18	14	14	14	14	14	19	19	19	19	19	18	18	18	18	2	2	2	14																																																				17
8 D. Warwick	8	8	8	8	24	18	18	24	14	14	25	25	25	25	24	24	24	24	24	24	24	24	24	24	15	14																																																				18
24 A. Nannini	24	18	18	18	18	17	14	14	24	25	21	24	24	24	21	24	15	15	15	15	15	15	15	15	15	24																																																				19
18 T. Boutsen	18	23	23	23	23	14	21	25	25	21	24	21	24	21	24	15	1	1	1	1	1	1	1																																																					20
23 A. de Cesaris	23	14	14	14	14	21	25	21	21	24	15	15	15	15																																																														21
29 H. Rothengatter	29	21	17	17	17	25	17																																																																								22
14 J. Palmer	14	17	21	21	21																																																																											23
21 P. Ghinzani	21	29	25	25	25																																																																									24
17 C. Danner	17	25																																																																													25
22 A. Berg	22																																																																															26

CIRCUIT DATA

Hungaroring, Mogyoród, Budapest
Circuit length: 2·495 miles/4·013 km
Race distance: 76 laps, 189·557 miles/305·064 km
(Scheduled to run for 78 laps but, in accordance with the rules, the race was stopped once the two-hour mark had been reached.)
Race weather: Hot, dry, sunny (35°C).

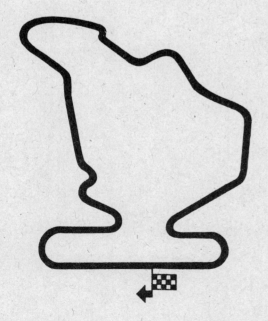

FASTEST LAPS

Driver	Time	Lap
Nelson Piquet	1m 31·001s	73
Ayrton Senna	1m 31·261s	72
Keke Rosberg	1m 32·684s	27
Nigel Mansell	1m 32·965s	51
Alain Prost	1m 33·422s	23
Stefan Johansson	1m 33·474s	66
Patrick Tambay	1m 33·840s	57
Alan Jones	1m 33·896s	39
Martin Brundle	1m 34·633s	64
Michele Alboreto	1m 34·846s	23
Philippe Alliot	1m 35·042s	69
René Arnoux	1m 35·144s	44
Johnny Dumfries	1m 35·414s	73
Gerhard Berger	1m 35·501s	37
Philippe Streiff	1m 35·832s	37
Teo Fabi	1m 35·887s	18
Derek Warwick	1m 36·084s	15
Riccardo Patrese	1m 37·263s	4
Jonathan Palmer	1m 38·091s	59
Christian Danner	1m 38·631s	5
Thierry Boutsen	1m 39·022s	15
Alessandro Nannini	1m 39·204s	4
Andrea de Cesaris	1m 40·570s	5
Piercarlo Ghinzani	1m 43·280s	9
Huub Rothengatter	1m 57·208s	2
Allen Berg	3m 00·202s	1

POINTS

WORLD CHAMPIONSHIP OF DRIVERS

1	Nigel Mansell	55 pts
2	Ayrton Senna	48
3	Nelson Piquet	47
4	Alain Prost	44
5	Keke Rosberg	19
6=	Jacques Laffite	14
6=	René Arnoux	14
8	Stefan Johansson	10
9=	Gerhard Berger	6
9=	Michele Alboreto	6
11	Martin Brundle	5
12=	Teo Fabi	2
12=	Riccardo Patrese	2
12=	Johnny Dumfries	2
15	Philippe Streiff	1

CONSTRUCTORS' CUP

1	Williams	102 pts
2	McLaren	63
3	Lotus	50
4	Ligier	28
5	Ferrari	16
6	Benetton	8
7	Tyrrell	6
8	Brabham	2

ENTRIES AND PRACTICE TIMES

No.	Driver	Nat.	Car	Tyre	Engine	Entrant	Practice 1	Practice 2	Warm-up
1	Alain Prost	F	Marlboro McLAREN MP4/2C	G	TAG PO1 (TTE PO1)	Marlboro McLaren International	**1m 24·346s**	1m 25·285s	1m 30·570s
2	Keke Rosberg	SF	Marlboro McLAREN MP4/2C	G	TAG PO1 (TTE PO1)	Marlboro McLaren International	1m 23·956s	**1m 23·903s**	1m 29·974s
3	Martin Brundle	GB	Data General TYRRELL 015	G	Renault EF15B	Data General Team Tyrrell	1m 28·572s	**1m 28·018s**	1m 32·375s
4	Philippe Streiff	F	Data General TYRRELL 015	G	Renault EF15B	Data General Team Tyrrell	1m 31·455s	**1m 28·951s**	1m 33·949s
5	Nigel Mansell	GB	WILLIAMS FW11	G	Honda RA166–E	Canon Williams Honda Team	1m 25·515s	**1m 24·635s**	1m 29·372s
6	Nelson Piquet	BR	WILLIAMS FW11	G	Honda RA166–E	Canon Williams Honda Team	1m 25·090s	**1m 24·697s**	1m 30·339s
7	Riccardo Patrese	I	Olivetti BRABHAM BT55	P	BMW M12/13/1	Motor Racing Developments Ltd	1m 26·648s	**1m 24·044s**	1m 29·680s
8	Derek Warwick	GB	Olivetti BRABHAM BT55	P	BMW M12/13/1	Motor Racing Developments Ltd	1m 26·892s	**1m 25·726s**	1m 31·782s
11	Johnny Dumfries	GB	John Player Special LOTUS 98T	G	Renault EF15B	John Player Special Team Lotus	**1m 27·212s**	1m 27·833s	1m 33·832s
12	Ayrton Senna	BR	John Player Special LOTUS 98T	G	Renault EF15B/EF15C	John Player Special Team Lotus	1m 26·650s	**1m 25·249s**	1m 31·824s
14	Jonathan Palmer	GB	West ZAKSPEED ZAK 861	G	Zakspeed	West Zakspeed Racing	**1m 29·073s**	1m 29·583s	1m 34·380s
15	Alan Jones	AUS	LOLA THL-2	G	Ford-Cosworth	Team Haas (USA) Ltd	**1m 27·420s**	1m 27·476s	1m 32·403s
16	Patrick Tambay	F	LOLA THL-2	G	Ford-Cosworth	Team Haas (USA) Ltd	1m 27·628s	**1m 26·489s**	1m 33·081s
17	Christian Danner	D	ARROWS A8	G	BMW M12/13	Barclay Arrows BMW	**1m 29·430s**	1m 40·236s	1m 33·973s
18	Thierry Boutsen	B	ARROWS A8/A9	G	BMW M12/13	Barclay Arrows BMW	1m 29·155s	**1m 28·598s**	1m 35·681s
19	Teo Fabi	I	BENETTON B186	P	BMW M12/13	Benetton Formula Ltd	1m 26·421s	**1m 23·549s**	1m 30·302s
20	Gerhard Berger	A	BENETTON B186	P	BMW M12/13	Benetton Formula Ltd	1m 25·638s	**1m 23·743s**	1m 29·689s
21	Piercarlo Ghinzani	I	OSELLA FA1G	P	Alfa Romeo 185T	Osella Squadra Corse	1m 35·070s	**1m 33·988s**	1m 37·293s
22	Allen Berg	CDN	OSELLA FA1F	P	Alfa Romeo 185T	Osella Squadra Corse	1m 38·731s	**1m 36·150s**	1m 38·386s
23	Andrea de Cesaris	I	Simod MINARDI M/85B	P	Motori Moderni	Minardi Team	1m 33·263s	**1m 29·615s**	1m 35·523s
24	Alessandro Nannini	I	Simod MINARDI M/86	P	Motori Moderni	Minardi Team	1m 31·974s	**1m 28·645s**	1m 35·095s
25	René Arnoux	F	Gitanes LIGIER JS27	P	Renault EF15B/EF15C	Equipe Ligier	1m 26·999s	**1m 25·917s**	1m 31·072s
26	Philippe Alliot	F	Gitanes LIGIER JS27	P	Renault EF15B	Equipe Ligier	1m 26·152s	**1m 25·561s**	1m 32·059s
27	Michele Alboreto	I	Fiat FERRARI F1/86	G	Ferrari 126C	Scuderia Ferrari SpA	1m 27·263s	**1m 26·646s**	1m 31·601s
28	Stefan Johansson	S	Fiat FERRARI F1/86	G	Ferrari 126C	Scuderia Ferrari SpA	1m 27·263s	**1m 26·646s**	1m 31·601s
29	Huub Rothengatter	NL	West ZAKSPEED ZAK 861	G	Zakspeed	West Zakspeed Racing	2m 21·202s	**1m 32·512s**	1m 35·199s

Friday morning, Saturday morning and Sunday morning practice sessions not officially recorded.

G – Goodyear, P – Pirelli

Fri p.m. Hot, dry, sunny
Sat p.m. Hot, dry, sunny
Sun a.m. Hot, dry, sunny

STARTING GRID

19 FABI (1m 23·549s)
Benetton

    20 BERGER (1m 23·743s)
    Benetton

2 ROSBERG (1m 23·903s)
McLaren

    7 PATRESE (1m 24·044s)
    Brabham

1 PROST (1m 24·346s)
McLaren

    5 MANSELL (1m 24·635s)
    Williams

6 PIQUET (1m 25·249s)
Williams

    12 SENNA (1m 25·249s)
    Lotus

27 ALBORETO (1m 25·561s)
Ferrari

    *8 WARWICK (1m 25·726s)
    Brabham

26 ALLIOT (1m 25·917s)
Ligier

    25 ARNOUX (1m 26·312s)
    Ligier

16 TAMBAY (1m 26·489s)
Lola

    28 JOHANSSON (1m 26·646s)
    Ferrari

11 DUMFRIES (1m 27·212s)
Lotus

    15 JONES (1m 27·420s)
    Lola

3 BRUNDLE (1m 28·018s)
Tyrrell

    18 BOUTSEN (1m 28·598s)
    Arrows

24 NANNINI (1m 28·645s)
Minardi

    4 STREIFF (1m 28·951s)
    Tyrrell

14 PALMER (1m 29·073s)
Zakspeed

    17 DANNER (1m 29·430s)
    Arrows

23 DE CESARIS (1m 29·615s)
Minardi

    29 ROTHENGATTER (1m 32·512s)
    Zakspeed

21 GHINZANI (1m 33·988s)
Osella

    22 BERG (1m 36·150s)
    Osella

* Did not start

RESULTS AND RETIREMENTS

Place	Driver	Car	Laps	Time and speed (mph/km/h)/Retirement	
1	Alain Prost	McLaren-TAG V6	52	1h 21m 22·531s	141·561/227·821
2	Michele Alboreto	Ferrari V6	51		
3	Stefan Johansson	Ferrari V6	50		
4	Alan Jones	Lola-Ford V6	50		
5	Patrick Tambay	Lola-Ford V6	50		
6	Christian Danner	Arrows-BMW 4	49		
7	Gerhard Berger	Benetton-BMW 4	49		
8	Huub Rothengatter	Zakspeed 4	48		
9	Keke Rosberg	McLaren-TAG V6	47	Not running (electrics)	
10	René Arnoux	Ligier-Renault V6	47		
11	Piercarlo Ghinzani	Osella-Alfa Romeo V8	46		
	Nigel Mansell	Williams-Honda V6	32	Driveshaft c/v joint	
	Nelson Piquet	Williams-Honda V6	29	Engine	
	Thierry Boutsen	Arrows-BMW 4	25	Turbo	
	Teo Fabi	Benetton-BMW 4	17	Engine	
	Philippe Alliot	Ligier-Renault V6	16	Engine	
	Alessandro Nannini	Minardi-MM V6	13	Suspension/spun off	
	Andrea de Cesaris	Minardi-MM V6	13	Clutch	
	Ayrton Senna	Lotus-Renault V6	13	Engine	
	Martin Brundle	Tyrrell-Renault V6	12	Turbo	
	Philippe Streiff	Tyrrell-Renault V6	10	Engine	
	Johnny Dumfries	Lotus-Renault V6	9	Engine	
	Jonathan Palmer	Zakspeed 861	8	Engine	
	Allen Berg	Osella-Alfa Romeo V8	6	Electrics	
	Riccardo Patrese	Brabham-BMW 4	2	Engine	

Fastest lap: Berger, on lap 49, 1m 29·444s, 148·604 mph/239·157 km/h.
Lap record: Alain Prost (F1 McLaren MP4/2B-TAG t/c V6), 1m 29·241s, 148·943 mph/239·701 km/h (1985).

PAST WINNERS

Year	Driver	Nat.	Car	Circuit	Distance miles/km	Speed mph/km/h
1963*	Jack Brabham	AUS	1·5 Brabham BT7-Climax	Zeltweg	159·07/256·00	96·34/115·04
1964	Lorenzo Bandini	I	1·5 Ferrari 156	Zeltweg	208·78/336·00	99·20/159·65
1965†	Jochen Rindt	A	3·3 Ferrari 250LM	Zeltweg	198·84/320·00	97·13/156·32
1966†	Gerhard Mitter/	D				
	Hans Herrmann	D	2·0 Porsche 906	Zeltweg	312·18/502·40	99·68/160·42
1967†	Paul Hawkins	AUS	4·7 Ford GT40	Zeltweg	312·18/502·40	95·29/153·35
1968†	Jo Siffert	CH	3·0 Porsche 908/02 Spyder	Zeltweg	312·18/502·40	106·86/171·97
1969†	Jo Siffert/	CH				
	Kurt Ahrens	D	4·5 Porsche 917	Österreichring	624·40/1004·87	115·78/186·33
1970	Jacky Ickx	B	3·0 Ferrari 312B-1/70	Österreichring	220·38/354·67	129·27/208·04
1971	Jo Siffert	CH	3·0 BRM P160	Österreichring	198·34/319·20	131·64/211·85
1972	Emerson Fittipaldi	BR	3·0 JPS/Lotus 72-Ford	Österreichring	198·34/319·20	133·29/214·51
1973	Ronnie Peterson	S	3·0 JPS/Lotus 72-Ford	Österreichring	198·34/319·20	133·99/215·64
1974	Carlos Reutemann	RA	3·0 Brabham BT44-Ford	Österreichring	198·34/319·20	134·09/215·80
1975	Vittorio Brambilla	I	3·0 March 751-Ford	Österreichring	106·12/170·78	110·30/177·51
1976	John Watson	GB	3·0 Penske PC4-Ford	Österreichring	198·29/319·11	132·00/212·41
1977	Alan Jones	AUS	3·0 Shadow DN8-Ford	Österreichring	199·39/320·89	122·98/197·91
1978	Ronnie Peterson	S	3·0 JPS/Lotus 79-Ford	Österreichring	199·39/320·89	118·03/189·95
1979	Alan Jones	AUS	3·0 Williams FW07-Ford	Österreichring	199·39/320·89	136·52/219·71
1980	Jean-Pierre Jabouille	F	1·5 Renault RS t/c	Österreichring	199·39/320·89	138·69/223·20
1981	Jacques Laffite	F	3·0 Ligier JS17-Matra	Österreichring	195·70/314·95	134·03/215·70
1982	Elio de Angelis	I	3·0 Lotus 91-Ford	Österreichring	195·70/314·95	138·07/222·20
1983	Alain Prost	F	1·5 Renault RE40 t/c	Österreichring	195·70/314·95	138·87/223·49
1984	Niki Lauda	A	1·5 McLaren MP4/2 t/c	Österreichring	188·31/303·06	139·11/223·88
1985	Alain Prost	F	1·5 McLaren MP4/2B t/c	Österreichring	191·99/308·98	143·62/231·13
1986	Alain Prost	F	1·5 McLaren MP4/2C t/c	Österreichring	191·99/308·98	141·56/227·82

* Non-championship (Formula 1)
† Sports car race

LAP CHART

1st LAP ORDER	Lap-by-lap car positions (laps 1–52)	Running order
20 G. Berger	20 20 20 20 20 20 20 20 20 20 20 20 20 20 20 20 20 20 20 20 20 20 20 20 20 20 5 5 5 1 1 1 1 1 1 1 1 1 1 1 1 1 1 1 1 1 1 1 1 1 1 1	1
19 T. Fabi	19 19 19 19 19 19 19 19 19 19 19 19 19 19 1 1 1 5 5 5 5 5 1 1 5 5 5 5 2 2 2 2 2 2 2 2 2 2 2 2 2 2 2 2 27 27 27	2
1 A. Prost	1 1 1 1 1 1 1 1 1 1 1 1 1 1 5 5 5 5 1 2 2 1 25 25 2 2 2 2 27 27 27 27 27 27 27 27 27 27 27 27 27 27 28 28	3
5 N. Mansell	5 5 5 5 5 5 5 5 5 5 5 5 5 5 2 2 2 2 1 25 25 6 6 6 27 27 27 15 15 15 15 15 15 15 15 15 15 15 28 15 15 15	4
6 N. Piquet	6 6 6 6 6 6 6 6 6 6 6 6 2 2 6 25 25 25 25 6 6 2 27 15 15 16 16 16 16 16 28 28 28 28 28 28 15 16 16 16	5
2 K. Rosberg	2 2 2 2 2 2 2 2 2 2 2 6 19 6 6 6 6 6 2 2 27 27 15 17 16 28 28 28 28 28 16 16 16 16 16 16 16 17 17	6
12 A. Senna	12 12 12 12 12 12 25 25 25 25 25 25 25 25 28 28 28 27 27 15 15 17 16 17 17 17 17 17 17 17 17 17 17 17 17 29 20	7
25 R. Arnoux	25 25 25 25 25 25 26 26 26 26 26 27 27 28 15 15 27 15 28 28 17 16 28 17 29 29 29 29 29 29 29 29 29 29 29 20	8
26 P. Alliot	26 26 26 26 26 27 27 27 27 27 27 28 28 15 15 27 15 28 15 16 16 28 29 29 21 20 20 20 20 20 20 20 20 20 20	9
27 M. Alboreto	27 27 27 27 27 27 12 28 28 28 28 28 28 15 15 18 18 17 17 17 16 28 29 25 21 20 20 21 21 21 21 21 25 25 25 25 25	10
7 R. Patrese	7 16 16 16 16 28 28 15 15 15 15 15 15 18 17 17 18 18 18 18 18 29 29 25 21 25 25 25 25 25 25 21 21 21 21 21 21	11
16 P. Tambay	16 15 15 15 15 28 15 15 3 3 3 3 24 18 18 17 17 16 16 16 16 16 18 21 21 21 20 20 25	12
15 A. Jones	15 28 28 28 28 15 3 3 24 24 24 24 18 17 17 26 16 21 21 21 29 29 29 29 29 20 20 20 20	13
28 S. Johansson	28 3 3 3 3 24 24 4 18 18 18 17 29 29 16 21 29 21 21 21 21	14
3 M. Brundle	3 24 24 24 24 4 4 4 18 23 23 23 29 16 16 29 29	15
24 A. Nannini	24 4 4 4 4 18 18 23 17 17 23 21 21 21	16
4 P. Streiff	4 18 18 18 18 16 23 12 29 29 29 16	17
18 T. Boutsen	18 14 14 14 14 14 23 14 17 12 16 16 21	18
14 J. Palmer	14 23 23 23 23 14 17 29 21 21 21 12	19
23 A. de Cesaris	23 17 17 17 17 17 29 21 16 12 12	20
17 C. Danner	17 29 29 29 29 29 29 21 16 4	21
29 H. Rothengatter	29 21 21 21 21 21 21 16 11	22
21 P. Ghinzani	21 22 22 22 22 22 11 11	23
22 A. Berg	22 7 11 11 11 11	24
11 J. Dumfries	11 11	25

FASTEST LAPS

Driver	Time	Lap
Gerhard Berger	1m 29.444s	49
Alain Prost	1m 30.751s	32
René Arnoux	1m 30.958s	47
Teo Fabi	1m 31.522s	10
Keke Rosberg	1m 31.704s	31
Nigel Mansell	1m 31.831s	32
Nelson Piquet	1m 32.633s	26
Stefan Johansson	1m 33.400s	42
Ayrton Senna	1m 33.437s	5
Philippe Alliot	1m 33.845s	13
Michele Alboreto	1m 33.915s	23
Patrick Tambay	1m 34.103s	49
Alan Jones	1m 34.431s	4
Christian Danner	1m 34.844s	30
Martin Brundle	1m 34.997s	4
Alessandro Nannini	1m 35.459s	3
Johnny Dumfries	1m 35.941s	7
Philippe Streiff	1m 35.965s	3
Thierry Boutsen	1m 36.132s	7
Andrea de Cesaris	1m 36.392s	12
Jonathan Palmer	1m 36.560s	3
Huub Rothengatter	1m 36.990s	6
Allen Berg	1m 39.234s	4
Piercarlo Ghinzani	1m 39.607s	3
Riccardo Patrese	1m 46.938s	1

POINTS

WORLD CHAMPIONSHIP OF DRIVERS

1	Nigel Mansell	55 pts
2	Alain Prost	53
3	Ayrton Senna	48
4	Nelson Piquet	47
5	Keke Rosberg	19
6=	Jacques Laffite	14
6=	René Arnoux	14
6=	Stefan Johansson	14
9	Michele Alboreto	12
10	Gerhard Berger	6
11	Martin Brundle	5
12	Alan Jones	3
13=	Teo Fabi	2
13=	Riccardo Patrese	2
13=	Johnny Dumfries	2
13=	Patrick Tambay	2
17=	Philippe Streiff	1
17=	Christian Danner	1

CONSTRUCTORS' CUP

1	Williams	102 pts
2	McLaren	72
3	Lotus	50
4	Ligier	28
5	Ferrari	26
6	Benetton	8
7	Tyrrell	6
8	Lola	5
9	Brabham	2
10	Arrows	1

CIRCUIT DATA

Österreichring, near Knittelfeld
Circuit length: 3.692 miles/5.9424 km
Race distance: 52 laps, 191.993 miles/308.984 km
Race weather: Hot, dry (30°C).

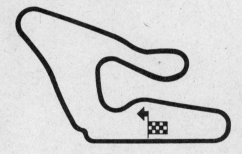

Allen Berg, moving with more consistency than he had been able to achieve with the unreliable Osella, walks back to the pits yet again.

ENTRIES AND PRACTICE TIMES

No.	Driver	Nat.	Car	Tyre	Engine	Entrant	Practice 1	Practice 2	Warm-up
1	Alain Prost	F	Marlboro McLAREN MP4/2C	G	TAG PO1 (TTE PO1)	Marlboro McLaren International	1m 26·885s	**1m 24·514s**	1m 29·465s
2	Keke Rosberg	SF	Marlboro McLAREN MP4/2C	G	TAG PO1 (TTE PO1)	Marlboro McLaren International	1m 26·742s	**1m 25·378s**	1m 30·186s
3	Martin Brundle	GB	Data General TYRRELL 015	G	Renault EF15B	Data General Team Tyrrell	1m 31·266s	**1m 29·125s**	1m 33·531s
4	Philippe Streiff	F	Data General TYRRELL 015	G	Renault EF15B	Data General Team Tyrrell	**1m 30·199s**	1m 30·976s	1m 33·101s
5	Nigel Mansell	GB	WILLIAMS FW11	G	Honda RA166–E	Canon Williams Honda Team	1m 26·181s	**1m 24·882s**	1m 29·495s
6	Nelson Piquet	BR	WILLIAMS FW11	G	Honda RA166–E	Canon Williams Honda Team	1m 26·614s	**1m 25·137s**	1m 30·302s
7	Riccardo Patrese	I	Olivetti BRABHAM BT55	P	BMW M12/13/1	Motor Racing Developments Ltd	1m 27·348s	**1m 26·111s**	1m 28·922s
8	Derek Warwick	GB	Olivetti BRABHAM BT55	P	BMW M12/13/1	Motor Racing Developments Ltd	7m 12·970s	**1m 25·175s**	1m 33·336s
11	Johnny Dumfries	GB	John Player Special LOTUS 98T	G	Renault EF15B	John Player Special Team Lotus	1m 28·857s	**1m 28·024s**	1m 32·331s
12	Ayrton Senna	BR	John Player Special LOTUS 98T	G	Renault EF15B/EF15C	John Player Special Team Lotus	1m 25·363s	**1m 24·916s**	1m 30·482s
14	Jonathan Palmer	GB	West ZAKSPEED ZAK 861	G	Zakspeed	West Zakspeed Racing	1m 32·064s	**1m 29·659s**	1m 35·424s
15	Alan Jones	AUS	LOLA THL-2	G	Ford-Cosworth	Team Haas (USA) Ltd	7m 40·132s	**1m 28·043s**	1m 30·272s
16	Patrick Tambay	F	LOLA THL-2	G	Ford-Cosworth	Team Haas (USA) Ltd	1m 29·744s	**1m 27·808s**	1m 31·458s
17	Christian Danner	D	ARROWS A8	G	BMW M12/13	Barclay Arrows BMW	1m 30·397s	**1m 27·923s**	1m 33·877s
18	Thierry Boutsen	B	ARROWS A8	G	BMW M12/13	Barclay Arrows BMW	1m 28·051s	**1m 26·754s**	1m 32·837s
19	Teo Fabi	I	BENETTON B186	P	BMW M12/13	Benetton Formula Ltd	1m 26·019s	**1m 24·078s**	1m 30·719s
20	Gerhard Berger	A	BENETTON B186	P	BMW M12/13	Benetton Formula Ltd	1m 25·580s	**1m 24·885s**	1m 29·770s
21	Piercarlo Ghinzani	I	OSELLA FA1G	P	Alfa Romeo 185T	Osella Squadra Corse	1m 36·128s	1m 36·334s	1m 36·248s
22	Alex Caffi	I	OSELLA FA1F	P	Alfa Romeo 185T	Osella Squadra Corse	**1m 36·900s**	1m 38·493s	1m 40·310s
23	Andrea de Cesaris	I	Simod MINARDI M/86	P	Motori Moderni	Minardi Team	1m 31·375s	**1m 29·561s**	1m 33·446s
24	Alessandro Nannini	I	Simod MINARDI M/85B	P	Motori Moderni	Minardi Team	1m 29·239s	**1m 28·690s**	1m 34·193s
25	René Arnoux	F	Gitanes LIGIER JS27	P	Renault EF15B/EF15C	Equipe Ligier	1m 27·928s	**1m 26·187s**	1m 30·422s
26	Philippe Alliot	F	Gitanes LIGIER JS27	P	Renault EF15B	Equipe Ligier	1m 27·287s	**1m 27·269s**	1m 32·100s
27	Michele Alboreto	I	Fiat FERRARI F1/86	G	Ferrari 126C	Scuderia Ferrari SpA	—	**1m 25·549s**	1m 29·401s
28	Stefan Johansson	S	Fiat FERRARI F1/86	G	Ferrari 126C	Scuderia Ferrari SpA	1m 26·517s	**1m 26·422s**	1m 30·645s
29	Huub Rothengatter	NL	West ZAKSPEED ZAK 861	G	Zakspeed	West Zakspeed Racing	1m 32·726s	**1m 30·904s**	1m 34·969s
31	Ivan Capelli	I	Charro AGS JH21C	P	Motori Moderni	Jolly Club SpA	—	**1m 33·844s**	1m 36·450s

Friday morning, Saturday morning and Sunday morning practice sessions not officially recorded.

G – Goodyear, P – Pirelli

Fri p.m.	Sat p.m.	Sun a.m.
Hot, dry, sunny	Hot, dry, sunny	Hot, dry, sunny

STARTING GRID

*19 FABI (1m 24·078s)
Benetton

    **1 PROST (1m 24·514s)
    McLaren

5 MANSELL (1m 24·882s)
Williams

    20 BERGER (1m 24·885s)
    Benetton

12 SENNA (1m 24·916s)
Lotus

    6 PIQUET (1m 25·137s)
    Williams

8 WARWICK (1m 25·175s)
Brabham

    2 ROSBERG (1m 25·378s)
    McLaren

27 ALBORETO (1m 25·549s)
Ferrari

    7 PATRESE (1m 26·111s)
    Brabham

25 ARNOUX (1m 26·187s)
Ligier

    28 JOHANSSON (1m 26·422s)
    Ferrari

18 BOUTSEN (1m 26·754s)
Arrows

    26 ALLIOT (1m 27·269s)
    Ligier

16 TAMBAY (1m 27·808s)
Lola

    17 DANNER (1m 27·923s)
    Arrows

11 DUMFRIES (1m 28·024s)
Lotus

    15 JONES (1m 28·043s)
    Lola

24 NANNINI (1m 28·690s)
Minardi

    3 BRUNDLE (1m 29·125s)
    Tyrrell

23 DE CESARIS (1m 29·561s)
Minardi

    14 PALMER (1m 29·659s)
    Zakspeed

4 STREIFF (1m 30·199s)
Tyrrell

    29 ROTHENGATTER (1m 30·904s)
    Zakspeed

31 CAPELLI (1m 33·844s)
AGS

    21 GHINZANI (1m 36·128s)
    Osella

22 CAFFI (1m 36·900s)
Osella

* Started from back of grid
** Started from pit lane

RESULTS AND RETIREMENTS

Place	Driver	Car	Laps	Time and speed (mph/km/h)/Retirement	
1	Nelson Piquet	Williams-Honda V6	51	1h 17m 42·889s	141·904/228·373
2	Nigel Mansell	Williams-Honda V6	51	1h 17m 52·717s	141·605/227·893
3	Stefan Johansson	Ferrari V6	51	1h 18m 05·804s	141·210/227·257
4	Keke Rosberg	McLaren-TAG V6	51	1h 18m 36·698s	140·285/225·768
5	Gerhard Berger	Benetton-BMW 4	50		
6	Alan Jones	Lola-Ford V6	49		
7	Thierry Boutsen	Arrows-BMW 4	49		
8	Christian Danner	Arrows-BMW 4	49		
9	Philippe Streiff	Tyrrell-Renault V6	49		
10	Martin Brundle	Tyrrell-Renault V6	49		
	Alex Caffi	Osella-Alfa Romeo V8	45	Running, not classified	
	Teo Fabi	Benetton-BMW 4	44	Puncture	
	Michele Alboreto	Ferrari V6	33	Engine	
	Andrea de Cesaris	Minardi-MM V6	33	Engine	
	Ivan Capelli	AGS-MM V6	31	Puncture	
	René Arnoux	Ligier-Renault V6	30	Gearbox	
	Alain Prost	McLaren-TAG V6	27	Disqualified	
	Jonathan Palmer	Zakspeed 4	27	Engine	
	Philippe Alliot	Ligier-Renault V6	22	Engine	
	Johnny Dumfries	Lotus-Renault V6	19	Gearbox	
	Derek Warwick	Brabham-BMW 4	16	Spun off	
	Alessandro Nannini	Minardi-MM V6	15	Electrics	
	Piercarlo Ghinzani	Osella-Alfa Romeo V8	12	Broken suspension/spun off	
	Patrick Tambay	Lola-Ford V6	2	Accident with Patrese	
	Riccardo Patrese	Brabham-BMW 4	2	Accident with Tambay	
	Huub Rothengatter	Zakspeed 4	1	Engine	
	Ayrton Senna	Lotus-Renault V6	0	Transmission	

Fastest lap: Fabi, on lap 35, 1m 28·099s, 147·268 mph/237·006 km/h (record).
Previous lap record: Nigel Mansell (F1 Williams FW10-Honda t/c), 1m 28·283s, 146·961 mph/236·512 km/h (1985).

PAST WINNERS

Year	Driver	Nat.	Car	Circuit	Distance miles/km	Speed mph/km/h
1950	Giuseppe Farina	I	1·5 Alfa Romeo 158 s/c	Monza	313·17/504·00	109·70/176·54
1951	Alberto Ascari	I	4·5 Ferrari 375	Monza	313·17/504·00	115·52/185·92
1952	Alberto Ascari	I	2·0 Ferrari 500	Monza	313·17/504·00	110·04/177·09
1953	Juan Manuel Fangio	RA	2·0 Maserati A6SSG	Monza	313·17/504·00	110·68/178·13
1954	Juan Manuel Fangio	RA	2·5 Mercedes-Benz W196	Monza	313·17/504·00	111·98/180·22
1955	Juan Manuel Fangio	RA	2·0 Mercedes-Benz W196	Monza	310·69/500·00	128·49/206·79
1956	Stirling Moss	GB	2·5 Maserati 250F	Monza	310·69/500·00	129·73/208·79
1957	Stirling Moss	GB	2·5 Vanwall	Monza	310·84/500·25	129·73/208·79
1958	Tony Brooks	GB	2·5 Vanwall	Monza	250·10/402·50	121·21/195·08
1959	Stirling Moss	GB	2·5 Cooper T45-Climax	Monza	257·25/414·00	124·38/200·18
1960	Phil Hill	USA	2·4 Ferrari Dino 246	Monza	310·69/500·00	132·06/212·53
1961	Phil Hill	USA	1·5 Ferrari Dino 156	Monza	267·19/430·00	130·11/209·39
1962	Graham Hill	GB	1·5 BRM P57	Monza	307·27/494·50	123·62/198·94
1963	Jim Clark	GB	1·5 Lotus 25-Climax	Monza	302·27/494·50	127·74/205·58
1964	John Surtees	GB	1·5 Ferrari 158	Monza	278·68/448·50	127·77/205·63
1965	Jackie Stewart	GB	1·5 BRM P261	Monza	271·54/437·00	130·46/209·96
1966	Ludovico Scarfiotti	I	3·0 Ferrari 312/66	Monza	242·96/391·00	135·92/218·75
1967	John Surtees	GB	3·9 Honda RA300	Monza	242·96/391·00	140·50/226·12
1968	Denny Hulme	NZ	3·0 McLaren M7A-Ford	Monza	242·96/391·00	145·41/234·02
1969	Jackie Stewart	GB	3·0 Matra MS80-Ford	Monza	242·96/391·00	146·97/236·52
1970	Clay Regazzoni	CH	3·0 Ferrari 312B-1/70	Monza	242·96/391·00	147·08/236·67
1971	Peter Gethin	GB	3·0 BRM P160	Monza	196·51/316·25	150·75/242·62
1972	Emerson Fittipaldi	BR	3·0 JPS/Lotus 72-Ford	Monza	197·36/317·63	131·61/211·81
1973	Ronnie Peterson	S	3·0 JPS/Lotus 72-Ford	Monza	197·36/317·63	132·63/213·45
1974	Ronnie Peterson	S	3·0 JPS/Lotus 72-Ford	Monza	186·76/300·56	135·10/217·42
1975	Clay Regazzoni	CH	3·0 Ferrari 312T/75	Monza	186·76/300·56	135·48/218·03
1976	Ronnie Peterson	S	3·0 March 761-Ford	Monza	187·41/301·60	124·12/199·75
1977	Mario Andretti	USA	3·0 JPS/Lotus 78-Ford	Monza	187·41/301·60	128·01/206·02
1978	Niki Lauda	A	3·0 Brabham BT46-Alfa Romeo	Monza	144·16/232·00	128·95/207·53
1979	Jody Scheckter	ZA	3·0 Ferrari 312T-4	Monza	180·20/290·00	131·85/212·18
1980	Nelson Piquet	BR	3·0 Brabham BT49-Ford	Imola	186·41/300·00	113·98/183·44
1981	Alain Prost	F	1·5 Renault RE30 t/c	Monza	187·40/301·60	129·87/209·00
1982	René Arnoux	F	1·5 Renault RE30B t/c	Monza	187·40/301·60	136·39/219·50
1983	Nelson Piquet	BR	1·5 Brabham BT52B-BMW t/c	Monza	187·40/301·60	136·18/217·55
1984	Niki Lauda	A	1·5 McLaren MP4/2-TAG t/c	Monza	183·80/295·80	137·02/220·51
1985	Alain Prost	F	1·5 McLaren MP4/2B-TAG t/c	Monza	183·80/295·80	141·40/227·56
1986	Nelson Piquet	BR	1·5 Williams FW11-Honda t/c	Monza	183·80/295·80	141·90/228·37

1st LAP ORDER	1	2	3	4	5	6	7	8	9	10	11	12	13	14	15	16	17	18	19	20	21	22	23	24	25	26	27	28	29	30	31	32	33	34	35	36	37	38	39	40	41	42	43	44	45	46	47	48	49	50	51	Running order
20 G. Berger	20	20	20	20	20	20	5	5	5	5	5	5	5	5	5	5	5	5	5	5	5	5	5	5	5	20	20	5	5	5	5	5	5	5	5	5	6	6	6	6	6	6	6	6	6	6	6	6	6	6	6	1
5 N. Mansell	5	5	5	5	5	20	6	6	6	6	6	6	6	6	6	6	6	6	6	20	20	5	5	25	25	6	6	6	6	6	6	6	6	6	6	6	5	5	5	5	5	5	5	5	5	5	5	5	5	5	5	2
6 N. Piquet	6	6	6	6	6	6	27	27	27	27	27	27	27	20	20	20	28	28	28	25	25	6	6	20	20	20	20	20	20	20	20	20	20	20	28	28	28	28	28	28	28	28	28	28	28	28	28	28	28	28	28	3
25 R. Arnoux	25	25	27	27	27	27	20	20	20	20	20	20	20	28	28	28	2	25	6	6	20	20	28	28	28	28	28	28	28	28	28	28	28	28	20	20	20	20	20	20	2	2	2	4
2 K. Rosberg	2	27	25	25	25	28	28	28	28	28	28	28	2	2	2	1	6	19	28	28	28	27	27	2	2	2	2	2	2	2	2	2	2	2	2	20	20	20	5
27 M. Alboreto	27	2	2	2	28	25	25	25	25	2	2	2	2	2	25	1	1	1	2	25	6	2	27	27	27	2	2	2	27	18	18	18	18	18	18	18	18	15	15	15	15	15	6
26 P. Alliot	26	28	28	28	2	2	2	2	25	25	25	25	25	1	25	25	25	19	2	27	2	2	2	19	18	18	3	15	15	15	15	15	15	15	15	18	18	18	18	7
28 S. Johansson	28	8	8	8	8	8	19	19	19	19	1	1	1	19	19	19	27	19	19	19	15	18	3	3	15	3	3	3	3	3	17	17	17	17	17	17	17	8
8 D. Warwick	8	26	26	26	11	11	11	11	11	1	1	1	19	19	11	26	26	26	1	1	1	1	15	3	15	15	15	17	17	17	17	17	17	17	3	3	3	3	3	4	9
11 J. Dumfries	11	11	11	11	26	26	19	8	8	1	1	11	11	11	11	11	27	26	27	27	15	15	18	18	18	18	3	15	17	17	4	4	4	4	4	4	4	4	4	4	4	3	3	10
18 T. Boutsen	18	16	19	19	19	19	26	26	1	8	8	8	8	8	8	26	27	15	15	1	18	15	15	15	3	17	4	4	19	19	19	19	19	19	19	19	19	19	22	11
16 P. Tambay	16	7	18	15	15	15	15	1	26	26	26	26	26	15	18	18	18	3	3	3	3	3	17	4	23	23	22	22	22	22	22	22	22	22	22	12
3 M. Brundle	3	19	15	18	18	1	1	15	15	15	15	15	15	18	3	3	18	17	17	17	17	4	23	23	31	19	19	13
7 R. Patrese	7	18	3	3	1	18	18	18	18	18	18	18	18	3	17	17	17	4	4	4	23	31	31	19	22	22	14
15 A. Jones	15	15	23	1	3	3	3	3	3	3	3	3	3	17	4	4	4	23	23	23	23	21	22	22	22	15
23 A. de Cesaris	23	3	4	23	23	4	24	24	24	24	24	17	14	14	31	23	31	31	31	31	22	25	25	16
19 T. Fabi	19	23	1	4	4	24	17	17	17	17	17	14	4	23	23	31	31	22	22	22	22	17
14 J. Palmer	14	14	14	24	24	14	17	14	14	14	14	14	31	31	22	22	22	14	14	14	14	18
4 P. Streiff	4	4	24	17	14	17	31	31	31	31	31	31	4	23	23	14	14	14	14	19
17 C. Danner	17	17	17	17	14	17	31	21	21	21	21	21	4	4	4	23	22	22	20
24 A. Nannini	24	24	21	31	21	22	22	22	22	4	4	23	23	23	22	21
21 P. Ghinzani	21	1	31	21	21	22	4	4	4	22	22	22	23	22	22
31 I. Capelli	31	21	22	22	22	22	23	23	23	23	23	23
1 A. Prost	1	31
29 H. Rothengatter	29	22
22 A. Caffi	22

Driver	Time	Lap
Teo Fabi	1m 28·099s	35
Nelson Piquet	1m 28·173s	35
Gerhard Berger	1m 28·191s	43
Stefan Johansson	1m 28·625s	43
Nigel Mansell	1m 28·803s	41
Keke Rosberg	1m 29·221s	47
Alain Prost	1m 29·501s	16
Michele Alboreto	1m 30·141s	11
Alan Jones	1m 31·050s	43
René Arnoux	1m 31·514s	21
Christian Danner	1m 32·224s	41
Philippe Alliot	1m 32·244s	21
Derek Warwick	1m 32·444s	12
Johnny Dumfries	1m 32·605s	10
Thierry Boutsen	1m 32·934s	30
Martin Brundle	1m 33·391s	14
Philippe Streiff	1m 33·625s	40
Andrea de Cesaris	1m 33·776s	20
Alessandro Nannini	1m 34·401s	12
Patrick Tambay	1m 34·443s	2
Riccardo Patrese	1m 34·972s	2
Jonathan Palmer	1m 35·845s	6
Ivan Capelli	1m 36·290s	10
Piercarlo Ghinzani	1m 37·179s	11
Alex Caffi	1m 39·818s	7
Huub Rothengatter	1m 58·761s	1

POINTS

WORLD CHAMPIONSHIP OF DRIVERS

1	Nigel Mansell	61 pts
2	Nelson Piquet	56
3	Alain Prost	53
4	Ayrton Senna	48
5	Keke Rosberg	22
6	Stefan Johansson	18
7=	Jacques Laffite	14
7=	René Arnoux	14
9	Michele Alboreto	12
10	Gerhard Berger	8
11	Martin Brundle	5
12	Alan Jones	4
13=	Teo Fabi	2
13=	Riccardo Patrese	2
13=	Johnny Dumfries	2
13=	Patrick Tambay	2
17=	Philippe Streiff	1
17=	Christian Danner	1

CONSTRUCTORS' CUP

1	Williams	117 pts
2	McLaren	75
3	Lotus	50
4	Ferrari	30
5	Ligier	28
6	Benetton	10
7=	Tyrrell	6
7=	Lola	6
9	Brabham	2
10	Arrows	1

CIRCUIT DATA

Autodromo Nazionale di Monza, near Milan

Circuit length: 3·6039 miles/5·80 km
Race distance: 51 laps, 183·801 miles/295·800 km
Race weather: Hot, dry (25°C).

On yer bike. Ayrton Senna was able to make an early exit after his Lotus broke down at the start. A motor bike, normally the only way to travel to Monza, was not essential equipment in 1986 in view of the relatively small crowd.

ENTRIES AND PRACTICE TIMES

No.	Driver	Nat.	Car	Tyre	Engine	Entrant	Practice 1	Practice 2	Warm-up
1	Alain Prost	F	Marlboro McLAREN MP4/2C	G	TAG PO1 (TTE PO1)	Marlboro McLaren International	1m 19·692s	**1m 17·710s**	1m 20·403s
2	Keke Rosberg	SF	Marlboro McLAREN MP4/2C	G	TAG PO1 (TTE PO1)	Marlboro McLaren International	1m 20·556s	**1m 18·360s**	1m 22·231s
3	Martin Brundle	GB	Data General TYRRELL 015	G	Renault EF15B	Data General Team Tyrrell	1m 25·114s	**1m 21·835s**	1m 24·725s
4	Philippe Streiff	F	Data General TYRRELL 015	G	Renault EF15B	Data General Team Tyrrell	1m 23·895s	**1m 22·388s**	1m 26·572s
5	Nigel Mansell	GB	WILLIAMS FW11	G	Honda RA166–E	Canon Williams Honda Team	1m 19·047s	**1m 17·489s**	1m 22·295s
6	Nelson Piquet	BR	WILLIAMS FW11	G	Honda RA166–E	Canon Williams Honda Team	1m 19·410s	**1m 18·180s**	1m 23·750s
7	Riccardo Patrese	I	Olivetti BRABHAM BT55	P	BMW M12/13/1	Motor Racing Developments Ltd	1m 21·257s	**1m 19·637s**	1m 24·515s
8	Derek Warwick	GB	Olivetti BRABHAM BT55	P	BMW M12/13/1	Motor Racing Developments Ltd	1m 23·455s	**1m 19·882s**	1m 25·079s
11	Johnny Dumfries	GB	John Player Special LOTUS 98T	G	Renault EF15B	John Player Special Team Lotus	1m 23·778s	**1m 21·594s**	1m 26·197s
12	Ayrton Senna	BR	John Player Special LOTUS 98T	G	Renault EF15B/EF15C	John Player Special Team Lotus	1m 19·943s	**1m 16·673s**	1m 22·844s
14	Jonathan Palmer	GB	West ZAKSPEED ZAK 861	G	Zakspeed	West Zakspeed Racing	1m 23·941s	**1m 21·929s**	1m 25·144s
15	Alan Jones	AUS	LOLA THL-2	G	Ford-Cosworth	Team Haas (USA) Ltd	1m 22·612s	**1m 21·646s**	1m 24·244s
16	Patrick Tambay	F	LOLA THL-2	G	Ford-Cosworth	Team Haas (USA) Ltd	1m 22·396s	**1m 20·761s**	1m 24·206s
17	Christian Danner	D	ARROWS A8	G	BMW M12/13	Barclay Arrows BMW	1m 24·665s	**1m 22·274s**	1m 26·252s
18	Thierry Boutsen	B	ARROWS A8	G	BMW M12/13	Barclay Arrows BMW	1m 23·412s	**1m 22·068s**	1m 25·649s
19	Teo Fabi	I	BENETTON B186	P	BMW M12/13	Benetton Formula Ltd	1m 20·957s	**1m 18·071s**	1m 24·326s
20	Gerhard Berger	A	BENETTON B186	P	BMW M12/13	Benetton Formula Ltd	1m 19·923s	**1m 17·742s**	1m 23·313s
21	Piercarlo Ghinzani	I	OSELLA FA1G	P	Alfa Romeo 185T	Osella Squadra Corse	1m 26·552s	**1m 23·566s**	1m 29·122s
22	Allen Berg	CDN	OSELLA FA1F	P	Alfa Romeo 185T	Osella Squadra Corse	1m 29·724s	**1m 26·861s**	1m 30·590s
23	Andrea de Cesaris	I	Simod MINARDI M/86	P	Motori Moderni	Minardi Team	1m 23·361s	**1m 21·611s**	1m 27·365s
24	Alessandro Nannini	I	Simod MINARDI M/85B	P	Motori Moderni	Minardi Team	1m 24·724s	**1m 21·702s**	1m 27·581s
25	René Arnoux	F	Gitanes LIGIER JS27	P	Renault EF15B/EF15C	Equipe Ligier	1m 21·876s	**1m 19·657s**	1m 25·211s
26	Philippe Alliot	F	Gitanes LIGIER JS27	P	Renault EF15B	Equipe Ligier	1m 21·693s	**1m 19·769s**	1m 24·627s
27	Michele Alboreto	I	Fiat FERRARI F1/86	G	Ferrari 126C	Scuderia Ferrari SpA	1m 21·123s	**1m 20·019s**	1m 23·698s
28	Stefan Johansson	S	Fiat FERRARI F1/86	G	Ferrari 126C	Scuderia Ferrari SpA	1m 21·621s	**1m 19·332s**	1m 23·996s
29	Huub Rothengatter	NL	West ZAKSPEED ZAK 861	G	Zakspeed	West Zakspeed Racing	1m 25·928s	**1m 24·105s**	1m 27·804s
31	Ivan Capelli	I	Charro AGS JH21C	P	Motori Moderni	Jolly Club SpA	1m 25·795s	**1m 23·987s**	1m 27·952s

Friday morning, Saturday morning and Sunday morning practice sessions not officially recorded.

G – Goodyear, P – Pirelli

Fri p.m. Hot, dry, sunny
Sat p.m. Hot, dry, sunny
Sun a.m. Warm, dry, cloudy

STARTING GRID

12 SENNA (1m 16·673s)
Lotus

5 MANSELL (1m 17·489s)
Williams

1 PROST (1m 17·710s)
McLaren

20 BERGER (1m 17·742s)
Benetton

19 FABI (1m 18·071s)
Benetton

6 PIQUET (1m 18·180s)
Williams

2 ROSBERG (1m 18·360s)
McLaren

28 JOHANSSON (1m 19·332s)
Farrari

7 PATRESE (1m 19·637s)
Brabham

25 ARNOUX (1m 19·657s)
Ligier

26 ALLIOT (1m 19·769s)
Ligier

8 WARWICK (1m 19·882s)
Brabham

27 ALBORETO (1m 20·019s)
Ferrari

16 TAMBAY (1m 20·761s)
Lola

11 DUMFRIES (1m 21·594s)
Lotus

23 DE CESARIS (1m 21·611s)
Minardi

15 JONES (1m 21·646s)
Lola

24 NANINNI (1m 21·702s)
Minardi

3 BRUNDLE (1m 21·835s)
Tyrrell

14 PALMER (1m 21·929s)
Zakspeed

18 BOUTSEN (1m 22·068s)
Arrows

17 DANNER (1m 22·274s)
Arrows

4 STREIFF (1m 22·388s)
Tyrrell

21 GHINZANI (1m 23·566s)
Osella

31 CAPELLI (1m 23·987s)
AGS

29 ROTHENGATTER (1m 24·105s)
Zakspeed

22 BERG (1m 26·861s)
Osella

RESULTS AND RETIREMENTS

Place	Driver	Car	Laps	Time and speed (mph/km/h)/Retirement	
1	Nigel Mansell	Williams-Honda V6	70	1h 37m 21·900s	116·596/187·644
2	Alain Prost	McLaren-TAG V6	70	1h 37m 40·672s	187·043/116·223
3	Nelson Piquet	Williams-Honda V6	70	1h 38m 11·174s	115·621/186·075
4	Ayrton Senna	Lotus-Renault V6	69		
5	Michele Alboreto	Ferrari V6	69		
6	Stefan Johansson	Ferrari V6	69		
7	René Arnoux	Ligier-Renault V6	69		
8	Teo Fabi	Benetton-BMW 4	68	Not running but classified	
9	Johnny Dumfries	Lotus-Renault V6	68		
10	Thierry Boutsen	Arrows-BMW 4	67		
11	Christian Danner	Arrows-BMW 4	67		
12	Jonathan Palmer	Zakspeed 4	67		
13	Allen Berg	Osella-Alfa Romeo V8	63		
	Riccardo Patrese	Brabham-BMW 4	62	Engine	
	Patrick Tambay	Lola-Ford V6	62	Running, not classified	
	Alessandro Nannini	Minardi-MM V6	60	Running, not classified	
	Gerhard Berger	Benetton-BMW 4	44	Spun off/incident with Johansson	
	Andrea de Cesaris	Minardi-MM V6	43	Spun off	
	Keke Rosberg	McLaren-TAG V6	41	Engine	
	Derek Warwick	Brabham-BMW 4	41	Electrics	
	Philippe Alliot	Ligier-Renault V6	39	Engine	
	Philippe Streiff	Tyrrell-Renault V6	28	Engine	
	Martin Brundle	Tyrrell-Renault V6	18	Engine	
	Alan Jones	Lola-Ford V6	10	Spun off/brakes	
	Huub Rothengatter	Zakspeed 4	9	Transmission	
	Piercarlo Ghinzani	Osella-Alfa Romeo V8	8	Engine	
	Ivan Capelli	AGS-MM V6	6	Transmission	

Fastest lap: Mansell, on lap 53, 1m 20·943s, 120·216 mph/193·469 km/h (record).
Previous lap record: Niki Lauda (F1 McLaren MP4/2-TAG t/c), 1m 22·996s, 117·242 mph/188·683 km/h (1984).

PAST WINNERS

Year	Driver	Nat.	Car	Circuit	Distance miles/km	Speed mph/km/h
1958	Stirling Moss	GB	2·5 Vanwall	Oporto	233·01/375·00	105·03/169·03
1959	Stirling Moss	GB	2·5 Cooper T51-Climax	Monsanto	209·00/336·35	95·32/153·40
1960	Jack Brabham	AUS	2·5 Cooper T53-Climax	Oporto	256·31/412·50	109·27/175·85
1984	Alain Prost	F	1·5 McLaren MP4/2-TAG t/c	Estoril	189·21/304·50	112·18/180·54
1985	Ayrton Senna	BR	1·5 Lotus 97T-Renault t/c	Estoril	181·09/291·45	90·19/145·16
1986	Nigel Mansell	GB	1·5 Williams FW11-Honda t/c	Estoril	189·21/304·50	116·59/187·64

LAP CHART

1st LAP ORDER	1	2	3	4	5	6	7	8	9	10	11	12	13	14	15	16	17	18	19	20	21	22	23	24	25	26	27	28	29	30	31	32	33	34	35	36	37	38	39	40	41	42	43	44	45	46	47	48	49	50	51	52	53	54	55	56	57	58	59	60	61	62	63	64	65	66	67	68	69	70	Running order
5 N. Mansell	5	5	5	5	5	5	5	5	5	5	5	5	5	5	5	5	5	5	5	5	5	5	5	5	5	5	5	5	5	5	5	5	5	5	5	5	5	5	5	5	5	5	5	5	5	5	5	5	5	5	5	5	5	5	5	5	5	5	5	5	5	5	5	5	5	5	5	5	5	5	1
12 A. Senna	12	12	12	12	12	12	12	12	12	12	12	12	12	12	12	12	12	12	12	12	1	12	12	12	12	12	12	12	12	12	12	12	12	12	12	12	12	12	12	12	12	12	12	12	12	12	12	12	12	12	12	12	12	12	12	12	12	12	12	12	12	12	12	12	12	12	12	12	12	1	2
20 G. Berger	20	20	20	20	20	20	20	6	6	6	6	6	6	6	6	6	6	6	6	6	6	6	6	6	6	6	6	6	6	1	1	12	1	6	6	6	6	6	6	6	6	6	6	6	6	6	6	6	6	6	6	6	6	6	6	6	6	6	6	6	1	1	1	1	1	6					3
6 N. Piquet	6	6	6	6	6	6	20	1	1	1	1	1	1	1	1	1	1	1	1	1	1	1	1	1	1	1	1	1	1	6	6	6	1	1	1	1	1	1	1	1	1	1	1	1	1	1	1	1	1	1	1	1	1	1	1	1	1	1	1	1	6	6	6	6	6	6	12				4
1 A. Prost	1	1	1	1	1	1	1	20	2	2	2	2	2	2	2	2	2	2	2	2	2	2	2	2	2	2	2	28	28	28	2	2	2	2	2	20	20	20	27	27	27	27	27	27	27	27	27	27	27	27	27	27	27	27	27	27	27	27	27	27	27	27	27	27	27	27					5
19 T. Fabi	19	19	19	19	19	19	19	2	2	20	20	20	20	20	20	20	20	19	28	28	28	28	28	28	28	28	28	19	2	19	20	20	20	20	28	28	28	28	28	28	28	28	28	28	28	28	28	28	28	28	28	28	28	28	28	28	28	28	28	28	28	28	28	28	28	28					6
2 K. Rosberg	2	2	2	2	2	2	19	19	19	19	19	19	19	19	19	28	28	19	19	19	19	19	19	19	19	19	2	2	19	20	19	19	19	19	19	19	19	19	19	19	19	19	19	19	19	19	19	19	19	19	19	19	19	19	19	19	19	19	19	19	19	19	19	19	19	25					7
28 S. Johansson	28	28	28	28	28	28	28	28	28	28	28	28	28	28	28	19	20	20	27	27	27	27	27	27	20	20	20	20	20	28	28	28	28	27	27	27	25	19	25	25	25	25	25	25	25	25	25	25	25	25	25	25	25	25	25	25	25	25	25	25	25	25	25	25	25	25					8
25 R. Arnoux	25	25	25	25	27	27	27	27	27	27	27	27	27	27	27	27	27	27	20	20	20	20	20	20	27	27	27	27	27	27	27	27	27	25	25	25	19	25	11	11	11	11	11	11	11	11	11	11	11	11	11	11	11	11	11	11	11	11	11	11	11	11	11	11	11	11					9
27 M. Alboreto	27	27	27	27	25	25	25	25	25	25	25	25	25	25	25	25	25	25	25	25	25	25	25	25	25	25	25	25	25	25	19	19	19	19	7	7	7	7	7	7	7	7	7	7	7	7	7	7	7	7	7	7	7	7	7	7	7	7	7	18	18	18	18	18						10
26 P. Alliot	26	26	26	26	26	26	26	26	26	26	26	26	26	26	26	26	26	26	26	26	7	7	7	7	7	7	7	7	26	26	26	26	7	7	11	11	11	11	18	18	18	18	18	18	18	18	18	18	18	18	18	18	18	18	18	18	17	17	17	17										11
7 R. Patrese	7	7	7	7	7	7	7	7	7	7	7	7	7	7	7	7	7	7	7	7	26	26	26	26	26	26	26	26	11	11	7	7	18	18	18	18	17	17	17	17	17	17	17	17	17	17	17	17	17	17	17	17	17	17	17	14	14	14	14	14										12
23 A. de Cesaris	23	23	23	8	8	8	8	8	8	8	8	8	8	8	8	8	8	8	8	8	8	8	11	11	11	11	11	11	7	7	11	11	26	8	17	17	14	14	14	14	14	14	14	14	14	14	14	14	14	14	14	14	14	14	22	22														13
11 J. Dumfries	11	11	11	11	11	11	11	11	11	11	11	11	11	11	11	11	11	11	11	11	8	18	18	18	8	8	8	8	8	8	18	14	24	24	24	24	24	24	24	24	24	24	24	24	24	24	24	24	24	24	24	24	24	22															14
8 D. Warwick	8	8	23	15	15	15	15	15	16	16	16	16	16	16	16	16	16	16	16	16	16	16	16	16	16	16	16	8	18	18	18	18	18	18	23	17	23	23	22	22	22	22	22	22	22	22	22	22	22	22	22	22	22	16	16	16														15
15 A. Jones	15	15	15	15	23	16	16	16	18	18	18	18	18	18	18	18	18	18	18	18	18	18	8	8	23	23	23	23	23	23	23	17	14	14	22	16	16	16	16	16	16	16	16	16	16	16	16	16	16	16	16	16	16																	16
16 P. Tambay	16	16	16	16	16	16	23	23	18	23	23	23	23	23	23	23	23	23	4	4	4	4	23	23	14	14	14	14	14	17	17	17	14	23	22	22	16																															17
3 M. Brundle	3	3	3	3	18	18	18	18	23	3	3	3	3	3	3	3	4	4	4	23	23	23	23	23	14	17	17	17	17	14	14	14	22	24	16	16																																	18
18 T. Boutsen	18	18	18	18	3	3	3	3	3	4	4	4	4	4	14	14	14	14	14	14	14	14	17	17	16	16	16	24	24	24	24	24	22																																				19
4 P. Streiff	4	4	4	4	4	4	4	14	14	14	14	14	14	14	17	17	17	17	17	17	17	17	24	24	24	24	24	22	22	22	22	22	16	16																																					20
24 A. Nannini	24	24	24	24	24	24	14	14	17	17	17	17	17	17	24	24	24	24	24	24	22	22	22	22	16	16	16	16	16	16																																										21
14 J. Palmer	14	14	14	14	14	14	24	17	24	24	24	24	24	24	22	22	22	22	22	22	22																																																		22
17 C. Danner	17	17	17	17	17	17	17	17	24	22	22	22	22	22	22	22																																																									23
31 A. Capelli	31	31	31	31	31	31	29	29	22	22																																																																24
29 H. Rothengatter	29	29	29	29	29	29	22	22	29																																																																			25
21 P. Ghinzani	21	21	21	21	22	22	21	21																																																																				26
22 A. Berg	22	22	22	22	21	21																																																																						27

CIRCUIT DATA

Autodromo do Estoril

Circuit length: 2·703 miles/4·350 km
Race distance: 70 laps, 189·207 miles/304·50 km
Race weather: Hot, dry, sunny (27°C).

Murray Walker receives unsolicited assistance whilst preparing a broadcast for BBC television.

POINTS

WORLD CHAMPIONSHIP OF DRIVERS

1	Nigel Mansell	70 pts
2	Nelson Piquet	60
3	Alain Prost	59
4	Ayrton Senna	51
5	Keke Rosberg	22
6	Stefan Johansson	19
7=	Jacques Laffite	14
7=	René Arnoux	14
7=	Michele Alboreto	14
10	Gerhard Berger	8
11	Martin Brundle	5
12	Alan Jones	4
13=	Teo Fabi	2
13=	Riccardo Patrese	2
13=	Johnny Dumfries	2
13=	Patrick Tambay	2
17=	Philippe Streiff	1
17=	Christian Danner	1

CONSTRUCTORS' CUP

1	Williams	130 pts
2	McLaren	81
3	Lotus	53
4	Ferrari	33
5	Ligier	28
6	Benetton	10
7=	Tyrrell	6
7=	Lola	6
9	Brabham	2
10	Arrows	1

FASTEST LAPS

Driver	Time	Lap
Nigel Mansell	1m 20·943s	53
Alain Prost	1m 21·092s	61
Nelson Piquet	1m 21·100s	60
Ayrton Senna	1m 21·283s	60
Michele Alboreto	1m 22·073s	58
Keke Rosberg	1m 22·242s	36
Stefan Johansson	1m 22·347s	50
Teo Fabi	1m 22·999s	53
Johnny Dumfries	1m 23·737s	49
Gerhard Berger	1m 23·850s	26
Patrick Tambay	1m 23·889s	59
Riccardo Patrese	1m 24·243s	36
Christian Danner	1m 24·268s	64
Thierry Boutsen	1m 24·350s	52
René Arnoux	1m 24·356s	53
Philippe Alliot	1m 24·516s	38
Jonathan Palmer	1m 24·947s	37
Derek Warwick	1m 25·113s	18
Alan Jones	1m 25·681s	6
Andrea de Cesaris	1m 26·034s	28
Philippe Streiff	1m 26·242s	27
Martin Brundle	1m 26·612s	15
Ivan Capelli	1m 27·861s	6
Alessandro Nannini	1m 27·910s	4
Huub Rothengatter	1m 28·397s	7
Piercarlo Ghinzani	1m 30·016s	3
Allen Berg	1m 30·477s	34

ENTRIES AND PRACTICE TIMES

No.	Driver	Nat.	Car	Tyre	Engine	Entrant	Practice 1	Practice 2	Warm-up
1	Alain Prost	F	Marlboro McLAREN MP4/2C	G	TAG PO1 (TTE PO1)	Marlboro McLaren International	1m 19·294s	**1m 18·421s**	1m 20·928s
2	Keke Rosberg	SF	Marlboro McLAREN MP4/2C	G	TAG PO1 (TTE PO1)	Marlboro McLaren International	—	**1m 19·342s**	1m 21·280s
3	Martin Brundle	GB	Data General TYRRELL 015	G	Renault EF15B/EF15C	Data General Team Tyrrell	1m 21·587s	**1m 20·198s**	1m 23·360s
4	Philippe Streiff	F	Data General TYRRELL 015	G	Renault EF15B/EF15C	Data General Team Tyrrell	**1m 20·946s**	1m 21·174s	1m 23·688s
5	Nigel Mansell	GB	WILLIAMS FW11	G	Honda RA166–E	Canon Williams Honda Team	1m 18·269s	**1m 17·514s**	1m 21·226s
6	Nelson Piquet	BR	WILLIAMS FW11	G	Honda RA166–E	Canon Williams Honda Team	1m 18·037s	**1m 17·279s**	1m 21·852s
7	Riccardo Patrese	I	Olivetti BRABHAM BT55	P	BMW M12/13/1	Motor Racing Developments Ltd	1m 21·241s	**1m 18·285s**	1m 21·407s
8	Derek Warwick	GB	Olivetti BRABHAM BT55	P	BMW M12/13/1	Motor Racing Developments Ltd	1m 19·713s	**1m 18·527s**	1m 22·017s
11	Johnny Dumfries	GB	John Player Special LOTUS 98T	G	Renault EF15B/EF15C	John Player Special Team Lotus	**1m 20·479s**	1m 21·491s	1m 22·503s
12	Ayrton Senna	BR	John Player Special LOTUS 98T	G	Renault EF15B/EF15C	John Player Special Team Lotus	1m 18·367s	**1m 16·990s**	1m 20·962s
14	Jonathan Palmer	GB	West ZAKSPEED ZAK 861	G	Zakspeed	West Zakspeed Racing	1m 21·154s	**1m 20·668s**	1m 24·019s
15	Alan Jones	AUS	LOLA THL-2	G	Ford-Cosworth	Team Haas (USA) Ltd	1m 20·525s	**1m 20·090s**	1m 21·268s
16	Patrick Tambay	F	LOLA THL-2	G	Ford-Cosworth	Team Haas (USA) Ltd	1m 20·492s	**1m 18·839s**	1m 22·268s
17	Christian Danner	D	ARROWS A8	G	BMW M12/13	Barclay Arrows BMW	**1m 21·069s**	1m 21·461s	1m 25·273s
18	Thierry Boutsen	B	ARROWS A8	G	BMW M12/13	Barclay Arrows BMW	**1m 21·171s**	1m 21·361s	1m 23·619s
19	Teo Fabi	I	BENETTON B186	P	BMW M12/13	Benetton Formula Ltd	1m 18·971s	**1m 18·893s**	1m 22·150s
20	Gerhard Berger	A	BENETTON B186	P	BMW M12/13	Benetton Formula Ltd	1m 17·780s	**1m 17·609s**	1m 20·465s
21	Piercarlo Ghinzani	I	OSELLA FA1G	P	Alfa Romeo 185T	Osella Squadra Corse	1m 25·767s	**1m 24·176s**	1m 27·296s
22	Allen Berg	CDN	OSELLA FA1F	P	Alfa Romeo 185T	Osella Squadra Corse	**1m 26·573s**	1m 27·209s	1m 28·249s
23	Andrea de Cesaris	I	Simod MINARDI M/86	P	Motori Moderni	Minardi Team	**1m 22·470s**	1m 22·521s	1m 25·705s
24	Alessandro Nannini	I	Simod MINARDI M/85B	P	Motori Moderni	Minardi Team	1m 25·179s	**1m 23·457s**	1m 25·390s
25	René Arnoux	F	Gitanes LIGIER JS27	P	Renault EF15B/EF15C	Equipe Ligier	**1m 19·624s**	1m 20·458s	1m 22·123s
26	Philippe Alliot	F	Gitanes LIGIER JS27	P	Renault EF15B/EF15C	Equipe Ligier	1m 20·372s	**1m 19·257s**	1m 21·954s
27	Michele Alboreto	I	Fiat FERRARI F1/86	G	Ferrari 126C	Scuderia Ferrari SpA	1m 19·628s	**1m 19·388s**	1m 22·366s
28	Stefan Johansson	S	Fiat FERRARI F1/86	G	Ferrari 126C	Scuderia Ferrari SpA	1m 20·303s	**1m 19·769s**	1m 21·089s
29	Huub Rothengatter	NL	West ZAKSPEED ZAK 861	G	Zakspeed	West Zakspeed Racing	1m 23·812s	**1m 22·524s**	—

Thursday, Friday morning, Saturday morning and Sunday morning practice sessions not officially recorded.

G – Goodyear, P – Pirelli

Fri p.m.	Sat p.m.	Sun a.m.
Warm, dry, hazy	Warm, dry, hazy	Hot, dry, sunny

STARTING GRID

12 SENNA (1m 16·990s)
Lotus

6 PIQUET (1m 17·279s)
Williams

5 MANSELL (1m 17·514s)
Williams

20 BERGER (1m 17·609s)
Benetton

7 PATRESE (1m 18·285s)
Brabham

1 PROST (1m 18·421s)
McLaren

8 WARWICK (1m 18·527s)
Brabham

16 TAMBAY (1m 18·839s)
Lola

19 FABI (1m 18·893s)
Benetton

26 ALLIOT (1m 19·257s)
Ligier

2 ROSBERG (1m 19·342s)
McLaren

27 ALBORETO (1m 19·388s)
Ferrari

25 ARNOUX (1m 19·624s)
Ligier

28 JOHANSSON (1m 19·769s)
Ferrari

*15 JONES (1m 20·090s)
Lola

3 BRUNDLE (1m 20·198s)
Tyrrell

11 DUMFRIES (1m 20·479s)
Lotus

14 PALMER (1m 20·668s)
Zakspeed

4 STREIFF (1m 20·946s)
Tyrrell

17 DANNER (1m 21·069s)
Arrows

18 BOUTSEN (1m 21·171s)
Arrows

23 DE CESARIS (1m 22·470s)
Minardi

**29 ROTHENGATTER (1m 22·524s)
Zakspeed

24 NANNINI (1m 23·457s)
Minardi

21 GHINZANI (1m 24·176s)
Osella

22 BERG (1m 26·573s)
Osella

* Started from back of grid
** Did not start; crashed during practice, no spare car available.

RESULTS AND RETIREMENTS

Place	Driver	Car	Laps	Time and speed (mph/km/h)/Retirement	
1	Gerhard Berger	Benetton-BMW 4	68	1h 33m 18·700s	120·114/193·306
2	Alain Prost	McLaren-TAG V6	68	1h 33m 44·138s	119·570/192·431
3	Ayrton Senna	Lotus-Renault V6	68	1h 34m 11·213s	118·997/191·509
4	Nelson Piquet	Williams-Honda V6	67		
5	Nigel Mansell	Williams-Honda V6	67		
6	Philippe Alliot	Ligier-Renault V6	67		
7	Thierry Boutsen	Arrows-BMW 4	66		
8	Andrea de Cesaris	Minardi-MM V6	66		
9	Christian Danner	Arrows-BMW 4	66		
10	Jonathan Palmer	Zakspeed 4	65	Out of fuel	
11	Martin Brundle	Tyrrell-Renault V6	65		
12	Stefan Johansson	Ferrari V6	64	Turbo	
13	Riccardo Patrese	Brabham-BMW 4	64	Spun off	
14	Alessandro Nannini	Minardi-MM V6	64		
15	René Arnoux	Ligier-Renault V6	63	Engine	
16	Allen Berg	Osella-Alfa Romeo V8	61		
	Johnny Dumfries	Lotus-Renault V6	53	Electrics	
	Derek Warwick	Brabham-BMW 4	37	Engine	
	Alan Jones	Lola-Ford V6	35	Tyres	
	Keke Rosberg	McLaren-TAG V6	32	Puncture	
	Michele Alboreto	Ferrari V6	10	Turbo	
	Philippe Streiff	Tyrrell-Renault V6	8	Turbo	
	Piercarlo Ghinzani	Osella-Alfa Romeo V8	8	Turbo	
	Teo Fabi	Benetton-BMW 4	4	Engine	
	Patrick Tambay	Lola-Ford V6	0	Accident	

Fastest lap: Piquet, on lap 64, 1m 19·360s, 124·615 mph/200·549 km/h (record for revised 2·747-mile/4·421-km circuit).

PAST WINNERS

Year	Driver	Nat.	Car	Circuit	Distance miles/km	Speed mph/km/h
1962*	Jim Clark	GB	1·5 Lotus 25-Climax	Mexico City	186·40/299·98	90·31/145·34
	Trevor Taylor	GB				
1963	Jim Clark	GB	1·5 Lotus 25-Climax	Mexico City	201·93/324·97	93·28/150·12
1964	Dan Gurney	USA	1·5 Brabham BT7-Climax	Mexico City	201·93/324·97	93·33/150·20
1965	Richie Ginther	USA	1·5 Honda RA272	Mexico City	201·93/324·97	94·26/151·70
1966	John Surtees	GB	3·0 Cooper T81-Maserati	Mexico City	201·93/324·97	95·72/154·05
1967	Jim Clark	GB	3·0 Lotus 49-Ford	Mexico City	201·93/324·97	101·42/163·22
1968	Graham Hill	GB	3·0 Lotus 49B-Ford	Mexico City	201·93/324·97	103·80/167·05
1969	Denny Hulme	NZ	3·0 McLaren M7A-Ford	Mexico City	201·93/324·97	106·15/170·83
1970	Jacky Ickx	B	3·0 Ferrari 312B	Mexico City	201·93/324·97	106·78/171·85
1986	Gerhard Berger	A	1·5 Benetton B186-BMW t/c	Mexico City	186·80/300·62	120·11/193·30

*Non-championship

CIRCUIT DATA

Autodromo Hermanos Rodriguez, Magdalena Mixhuca, Mexico City

Circuit length: 2·747 miles/4·421 km
Race distance: 68 laps, 186·801 miles/300·628 km
Race weather: Hot, dry, humid (25°C).

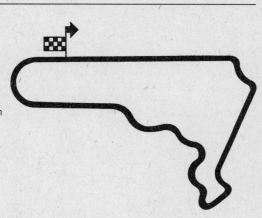

LAP CHART

1st LAP ORDER	1	2	3	4	5	6	7	8	9	10	11	12	13	14	15	16	17	18	19	20	21	22	23	24	25	26	27	28	29	30	31	32	33	34	35	36	37	38	39	40	41	42	43	44	45	46	47	48	49	50	51	52	53	54	55	56	57	58	59	60	61	62	63	64	65	66	67	68	Running order
6 N. Piquet	6	6	6	6	6	6	6	6	6	6	6	6	6	6	6	6	6	6	6	6	6	6	6	6	6	6	6	6	6	6	6	12	12	12	20	20	20	20	20	20	20	20	20	20	20	20	20	20	20	20	20	20	20	20	20	20	20	20	20	20	20	20	20	20	20	20	20	20	*1*
12 A. Senna	12	12	12	12	12	12	12	12	12	12	12	12	12	12	12	12	12	12	12	12	12	12	12	12	12	12	12	20	20	12	12	12	12	12	12	12	12	12	1	1	1	1	1	1	1	1	1	1	1	1	1	1	1	1	1	1	1	1	1	1	1	1	1	1	1	1	1	1	*2*
20 G. Berger	20	20	20	20	20	20	1	1	1	1	1	1	1	1	1	1	1	1	1	1	1	1	1	1	1	1	1	1	1	1	1	20	20	6	28	28	28	6	6	6	6	6	6	1	1	12	12	12	12	12	12	12	12	12	12	12	12	12	12	12	12	12	12	12	12	12	12	12	*3*
1 A. Prost	1	1	1	1	1	1	20	20	20	20	20	20	20	20	20	20	20	20	20	20	20	20	20	28	28	28	6	6	1	1	1	1	1	1	6	28	28	28	28	28	28	28	28	28	28	28	28	28	28	28	28	28	28	28	28	28	28	28	28	28	28	28	28	28	28	6	6	6	*4*
27 M. Alboreto	27	27	27	27	27	27	27	27	27	27	26	26	26	26	28	28	28	28	28	28	28	28	28	28	2	2	1	1	1	28	8	28	28	28	28	6	6	6	6	6	6	6	6	7	7	7	7	7	7	7	7	7	7	7	7	7	7	7	7	7	7	7	5	5	5	5	5	5	*5*
26 P. Alliot	26	26	26	26	26	26	26	26	26	26	3	28	28	28	26	26	2	2	2	2	2	2	2	2	2	2	2	1	1	8	8	8	8	28	7	7	7	7	7	7	7	7	7	7	7	7	7	7	7	6	6	6	6	6	6	6	6	6	6	6	6	6	26	26	26				*6*
3 M. Brundle	3	3	3	3	3	3	3	3	3	28	3	2	2	2	26	26	26	26	26	26	8	8	8	8	8	8	8	2	7	7	7	7	26	26	26	26	26	26	26	26	26	26	26	26	26	26	26	5	5	5	5	5	5	5	5	5	5	5	5	5	5	14	18						*7*
7 R. Patrese	7	11	11	11	11	11	11	11	11	28	28	2	2	3	3	3	3	3	3	3	3	3	3	3	7	7	7	7	7	7	5	5	26	26	5	5	5	5	5	5	5	5	5	5	5	5	26	26	26	26	26	26	26	26	26	26	26	23	23									*8*
11 J. Dumfries	11	7	28	28	28	28	28	28	2	2	5	11	11	11	11	11	8	8	8	8	8	8	8	7	5	5	5	5	5	26	26	26	5	17	14	14	14	14	14	14	14	14	14	14	14	14	14	14	14	14	14	14	14	14	14	14	14	18	17									*9*
8 D. Warwick	8	28	7	7	7	2	2	2	11	5	11	7	7	7	8	8	11	18	18	18	18	5	18	18	18	14	14	26	17	17	17	5	23	23	23	23	23	23	23	23	23	23	23	23	23	18	18	18	18	18	18	25	25	23	17													*10*
28 S. Johansson	28	25	25	25	2	5	5	5	5	11	7	8	8	8	25	25	25	7	7	7	7	7	5	18	14	14	18	26	26	17	3	3	14	14	25	25	25	25	25	25	18	18	18	18	18	25	25	25	25	25	18	18	18	18	3													*11*
25 R. Arnoux	25	8	2	2	25	7	7	7	7	7	8	25	25	18	18	14	14	14	14	5	5	18	26	26	26	26	17	17	3	14	14	23	23	18	18	18	18	18	18	25	25	25	25	25	25	23	23	23	23	23	23	23	23	23	17													*12*
2 K. Rosberg	2	2	8	5	5	25	25	25	25	25	18	18	18	7	7	7	5	5	5	14	14	14	3	17	17	3	3	14	23	23	25	25	17	17	17	3	3	11	11	11	11	11	11	11	11	11	11	3	3	3	17	17	17	17	17	17	17	17	3									*13*
19 T. Fabi	19	19	19	8	8	8	8	8	8	18	14	14	14	14	14	17	17	17	17	17	17	17	17	3	3	18	23	23	25	25	18	18	3	3	3	17	11	3	3	3	3	3	3	3	3	3	17	17	3	3	3	3	3	3	3	24												*14*
4 P. Streiff	4	5	5	19	4	4	4	4	18	18	14	5	17	17	17	17	11	11	11	11	11	11	23	11	25	18	18	3	3	3	11	11	11	11	11	17	17	17	17	17	17	17	17	17	24	24	24	24	24	24	24	24	24														*15*
14 J. Palmer	14	4	4	4	18	18	18	15	15	23	23	23	5	5	23	11	11	11	18	24	24	24	11	24	24	24	24	24	24	24	24	24	24	24	24	24	24	24	24	22	22	22	22	22	22	22	22	22	22																*16*
18 T. Boutsen	18	18	18	18	15	15	15	14	14	17	17	5	23	23	25	25	25	25	25	25	25	25	25	25	11	11	11	11	11	24	22	22	22	22	22	22	22	22	22	22	22	22	22	22																							*17*
5 N. Mansell	5	14	14	15	14	14	14	23	24	24	24	15	15	15	24	24	24	24	24	24	24	24	24	24	24	24	24	24	15	15	15	22	22																																		*18*
23 A. de Cesaris	23	15	15	14	23	23	23	17	17	15	15	15	24	24	24	15	15	15	15	15	15	15	15	15	15	15	15	15	22	22	22																																					*19*
24 A. Nannini	24	23	23	23	17	17	17	24	24	22	22	22	22	22	22	22	22	22	22	22	22	22	22	22	22	22	22	22																																							*20*
15 A. Jones	15	24	17	17	24	24	24	24	22	22																																																									*21*
17 C. Danner	17	17	24	24	22	22	22	22																																																												*22*
21 P. Ghinzani	21	22	22	22	21	21	21	21																																																												*23*
22 A. Berg	22	21	21	21																																																																*24*

FASTEST LAPS

Driver	Time	Lap
Nelson Piquet	1m 19·360s	64
Nigel Mansell	1m 19·441s	63
Stefan Johansson	1m 20·182s	52
Ayrton Senna	1m 20·237s	64
Alain Prost	1m 20·357s	37
Gerhard Berger	1m 20·543s	42
Riccardo Patrese	1m 21·060s	60
Keke Rosberg	1m 21·298s	19
Philippe Alliot	1m 21·630s	62
Jonathan Palmer	1m 21·732s	62
Derek Warwick	1m 21·890s	32
René Arnoux	1m 22·020s	57
Alan Jones	1m 22·024s	26
Johnny Dumfries	1m 22·036s	22
Thierry Boutsen	1m 22·315s	54
Andrea de Cesaris	1m 22·430s	48
Michele Alboreto	1m 22·546s	9
Martin Brundle	1m 23·337s	7
Christian Danner	1m 23·551s	30
Philippe Streiff	1m 24·525s	6
Alessandro Nannini	1m 24·978s	46
Teo Fabi	1m 25·615s	3
Allen Berg	1m 28·736s	53
Piercarlo Ghinzani	1m 30·412s	5

POINTS

WORLD CHAMPIONSHIP OF DRIVERS

1	Nigel Mansell	*70 pts (72)
2	Alain Prost	*64 (65)
3	Nelson Piquet	63
4	Ayrton Senna	55
5	Keke Rosberg	22
6	Stefan Johansson	19
7	Gerhard Berger	17
8=	Jacques Laffite	14
8=	René Arnoux	14
8=	Michele Alboreto	14
11	Martin Brundle	5
12	Alan Jones	4
13=	Teo Fabi	2
13=	Riccardo Patrese	2
13=	Johnny Dumfries	2
13=	Patrick Tambay	2
17=	Philippe Streiff	1
17=	Christian Danner	1
17=	Philippe Alliot	1

CONSTRUCTORS' CUP

1	Williams	135 pts
2	McLaren	87
3	Lotus	57
4	Ferrari	33
5	Ligier	29
6	Benetton	19
7=	Tyrrell	6
7=	Lola	6
9	Brabham	2
10	Arrows	1

* Best 11 results

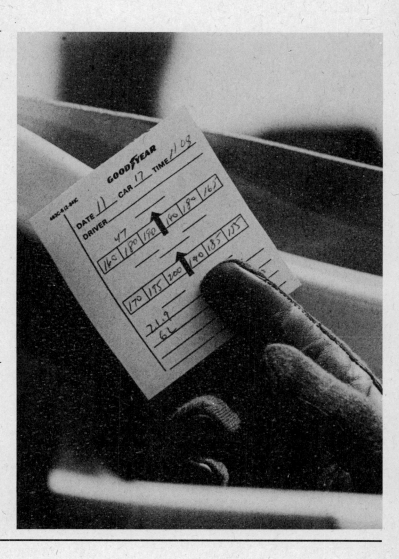

Rubberwear. Christian Danner (car 17) examines the tyre temperature check for his Arrows during unofficial practice on Saturday morning in Mexico. Every time the car stops, a Goodyear technician probes the rubber to take readings on the inner, middle and outer areas of the tread, thus giving the team an indication of temperature variations and the effectiveness of the car's set-up.

ENTRIES AND PRACTICE TIMES

No.	Driver	Nat.	Car	Tyre	Engine	Entrant	Practice 1	Practice 2	Warm-up
1	Alain Prost	F	Marlboro McLAREN MP4/2C	G	TAG PO1 (TTE PO1)	Marlboro McLaren International	1m 19·785s	**1m 19·654s**	1m 23·247s
2	Keke Rosberg	SF	Marlboro McLAREN MP4/2C	G	TAG PO1 (TTE PO1)	Marlboro McLaren International	1m 21·295s	**1m 20·778s**	1m 25·044s
3	Martin Brundle	GB	Data General TYRRELL 015	G	Renault EF15B/EF15C	Data General Team Tyrrell	1m 24·061s	**1m 23·004s**	1m 25·968s
4	Philippe Streiff	F	Data General TYRRELL 015	G	Renault EF15B/EF15C	Data General Team Tyrrell	1m 23·262s	**1m 21·720s**	1m 26·567s
5	Nigel Mansell	GB	WILLIAMS FW11	G	Honda RA166-E	Canon Williams Honda Team	1m 19·255s	**1m 18·403s**	1m 23·300s
6	Nelson Piquet	BR	WILLIAMS FW11	G	Honda RA166-E	Canon Williams Honda Team	1m 20·088s	**1m 18·714s**	1m 23·691s
7	Riccardo Patrese	I	Olivetti BRABHAM BT55	P	BMW M12/13/1	Motor Racing Developments Ltd	1m 23·396s	**1m 23·230s**	1m 24·705s
8	Derek Warwick	GB	Olivetti BRABHAM BT55	P	BMW M12/13/1	Motor Racing Developments Ltd	1m 23·552s	**1m 23·313s**	1m 25·357s
11	Johnny Dumfries	GB	John Player Special LOTUS 98T	G	Renault EF15B/EF15C	John Player Special Team Lotus	1m 23·786s	**1m 22·664s**	1m 25·269s
12	Ayrton Senna	BR	John Player Special LOTUS 98T	G	Renault EF15B/EF15C	John Player Special Team Lotus	1m 21·302s	**1m 18·906s**	1m 22·698s
14	Jonathan Palmer	GB	West ZAKSPEED ZAK 861	G	Zakspeed	West Zakspeed Racing	1m 24·509s	**1m 23·476s**	1m 26·300s
15	Alan Jones	AUS	LOLA THL-2	G	Ford-Cosworth	Team Haas (USA) Ltd		**1m 22·796s**	1m 25·158s
16	Patrick Tambay	F	LOLA THL-2	G	Ford-Cosworth	Team Haas (USA) Ltd	1m 24·584s	**1m 23·008s**	1m 25·763s
17	Christian Danner	D	ARROWS A8	G	BMW M12/13	Barclay Arrows BMW	1m 25·296s	**1m 25·233s**	1m 28·181s
18	Thierry Boutsen	B	ARROWS A8	G	BMW M12/13	Barclay Arrows BMW	1m 24·768s	**1m 24·295s**	1m 27·735s
19	Teo Fabi	I	BENETTON B186	P	BMW M12/13	Benetton Formula Ltd	1m 22·584s	**1m 22·129s**	1m 27·447s
20	Gerhard Berger	A	BENETTON B186	P	BMW M12/13	Benetton Formula Ltd	1m 22·260s	**1m 20·554s**	1m 23·940s
21	Piercarlo Ghinzani	I	OSELLA FA1G	P	Alfa Romeo 185T	Osella Squadra Corse	3m 03·680s	**1m 25·257s**	1m 27·594s
22	Allen Berg	CDN	OSELLA FA1F	P	Alfa Romeo 185T	Osella Squadra Corse	1m 28·912s	**1m 27·208s**	1m 28·350s
23	Andrea de Cesaris	I	Simod MINARDI M/86	P	Motori Moderni	Minardi Team	1m 23·476s	**1m 22·012s**	1m 26·119s
24	Alessandro Nannini	I	Simod MINARDI M/85B	P	Motori Moderni	Minardi Team	1m 25·953s	**1m 23·052s**	1m 27·687s
25	René Arnoux	F	Gitanes LIGIER JS27	P	Renault EF15B/EF15C	Equipe Ligier	1m 20·491s	**1m 19·976s**	1m 24·481s
26	Philippe Alliot	F	Gitanes LIGIER JS27	P	Renault EF15B/EF15C	Equipe Ligier	1m 22·765s	**1m 20·981s**	1m 26·976s
27	Michele Alboreto	I	Fiat FERRARI F1/86	G	Ferrari 126C	Scuderia Ferrari SpA	**1m 21·709s**	1m 21·747s	1m 24·414s
28	Stefan Johansson	S	Fiat FERRARI F1/86	G	Ferrari 126C	Scuderia Ferrari SpA	**1m 22·050s**	1m 22·309s	1m 25·219s
29	Huub Rothengatter	NL	West ZAKSPEED ZAK 861	G	Zakspeed	West Zakspeed Racing	1m 24·859s	**1m 25·181s**	1m 27·795s

Friday morning, Saturday morning and Sunday morning practice sessions not officially recorded.

G – Goodyear, P – Pirelli

Fri p.m. Cool, dry, cloudy, then wet.	Sat p.m. Warm, dry, sunny	Sun a.m. Warm, dry, sunny

STARTING GRID

5 MANSELL (1m 18·403s)
Williams

    6 PIQUET (1m 18·714s)
    Williams

12 SENNA (1m 18·906s)
Lotus

    1 PROST (1m 19·654s)
    McLaren

25 ARNOUX (1m 19·976s)
Ligier

    20 BERGER (1m 20·554s)
    Benetton

2 ROSBERG (1m 20·778s)
McLaren

    26 ALLIOT (1m 20·981s)
    Ligier

27 ALBORETO (1m 21·709s)
Ferrari

    4 STREIFF (1m 21·720s)
    Tyrrell

23 DE CESARIS (1m 22·012s)
Minardi

    28 JOHANSSON (1m 22·050s)
    Ferrari

19 FABI (1m 22·129s)
Benetton

    11 DUMFRIES (1m 22·664s)
    Lotus

15 JONES (1m 22·796s)
Lola

    3 BRUNDLE (1m 23·004s)
    Tyrrell

16 TAMBAY (1m 23·008s)
Lola

    24 NANNINI (1m 23·052s)
    Minardi

7 PATRESE (1m 23·230s)
Brabham

    8 WARWICK (1m 23·313s)
    Brabham

14 PALMER (1m 23·476s)
Zakspeed

    18 BOUTSEN (1m 24·295s)
    Arrows

29 ROTHENGATTER (1m 25·181s)
Zakspeed

    17 DANNER (1m 25·233s)
    Arrows

21 GHINZANI (1m 25·257s)
Osella

    *22 BERG (1m 27·208s)
    Osella

* Started from the pits.

RESULTS AND RETIREMENTS

Place	Driver	Car	Laps	Time and speed (mph/km/h)/Retirement	
1	Alain Prost	McLaren-TAG V6	82	1h 54m 20·388s	101·040/162·609
2	Nelson Piquet	Williams-Honda V6	82	1h 54m 24·593s	100·978/162·509
3	Stefan Johansson	Ferrari V6	81		
4	Martin Brundle	Tyrrell-Renault V6	81		
5	Philippe Streiff	Tyrrell-Renault V6	80	Out of fuel	
6	Johnny Dumfries	Lotus-Renault V6	80		
7	René Arnoux	Ligier-Renault V6	79		
8	Philippe Alliot	Ligier-Renault V6	79		
9	Jonathan Palmer	Zakspeed 4	77		
10	Teo Fabi	Benetton-BMW 4	77		
	Patrick Tambay	Lola-Ford V6	70	Running, not classified	
	Nigel Mansell	Williams-Honda V6	63	Tyre failure	
	Riccardo Patrese	Brabham-BMW 4	63	Electrics/engine	
	Keke Rosberg	McLaren-TAG V6	60	Tyre failure	
	Allen Berg	Osella-Alfa Romeo V8	61	Running, not classified	
	Derek Warwick	Brabham-BMW 4	57	Brakes	
	Christian Danner	Arrows-BMW 4	52	Engine	
	Thierry Boutsen	Arrows-BMW 4	50	Throttle spring	
	Ayrton Senna	Lotus-Renault V6	43	Engine	
	Gerhard Berger	Benetton-BMW 4	40	Clutch/engine	
	Andrea de Cesaris	Minardi-MM V6	40	Fire extinguisher	
	Huub Rothengatter	Zakspeed 4	29	Rear suspension	
	Alan Jones	Lola-Ford V6	16	Engine	
	Alessandro Nannini	Minardi-MM V6	10	Accident	
	Piercarlo Ghinzani	Osella-Alfa Romeo V8	2	Transmission	
	Michele Alboreto	Ferrari V6	0	Startline accident	

Fastest lap: Piquet, on lap 82, 1m 20·787s, 104·637 mph/168·398 km/h (record).
Previous lap record: Keke Rosberg (F1 Williams FW10-Honda t/c), 1m 23·758s, 100·899 mph/162·382 km/h (1985).

PAST WINNERS

Year	Driver	Nat.	Car	Circuit	Distance miles/km		Speed mph/km/h
1950	Doug Whiteford	AUS	Ford Special	Nuriootpa	104/	167	72·00/115·87
1951	F. W. Pratley	AUS	Ford Special	Narrogin	102/	164	61·40/ 98·81
1952	Doug Whiteford	AUS	4·5 Lago-Talbot	Bathurst	150/	241	76·80/123·60
1953	Doug Whiteford	AUS	4·5 Lago-Talbot	Albert Park	200/	322	81·80/131·64
1954	Lex Davison	AUS	2·4 HWM-Jaguar	Southport	154/	248	83·70/134·70
1955	Jack Brabham	AUS	2·0 Cooper T23-Bristol	Port Wakefield	104/	167	71·90/115·71
1956	Stirling Moss	GB	2·5 Maserati 250F	Albert Park	250/	402	95·90/154·34
1957	Lex Davison	AUS	3·8 Ferrari 500/750	Caversham	154/	248	—
1958	Lex Davison	AUS	3·8 Ferrari 500/750	Bathurst	178/	286	—
1959	Stan Jones	AUS	2·5 Maserati 250F	Longford	112/	180	—
1960	Alex Mildren	AUS	2·5 Cooper T45-Maserati	Lowood	102/	164	94·50/152·08
1961	Lex Davison	AUS	2·5 Cooper T51-Climax	Adelaide	102/	164	—
1962	Bruce McLaren	NZ	2·7 Cooper T62-Climax	Caversham	122/	196	89·30/143·71
1963	Jack Brabham	AUS	2·7 Brabham BT4-Climax	Warwick Farm	101/	163	79·34/127·69
1964	Jack Brabham	AUS	2·5 Brabham BT7A-Climax	Sandown Park	120/	193	96·48/155·27
1965	Bruce McLaren	NZ	2·5 Cooper T79-Climax	Longford	117/	188	114·72/184·62
1966	Graham Hill	GB	2·1 BRM P261	Lakeside	99/	159	94·90/152·73
1967	Jackie Stewart	GB	2·1 BRM P261	Warwick Farm	101/	163	87·67/141·09
1968	Jim Clark	GB	2·5 Lotus 49T-Cosworth	Sandown Park	106/	171	101·90/163·99
1969	Chris Amon	NZ	2·4 Ferrari Dino 246	Lakeside	100/	161	100·18/161·22
1970	Frank Matich	AUS	5·0 McLaren M10A-Repco	Warwick Farm	100/	161	95·52/153·72
1971	Frank Matich	AUS	5·0 Matich A50-Repco	Warwick Farm	101/	163	93·24/150·06
1972	Graham McRae	NZ	5·0 Leda LT27/GM1-Chevrolet	Sandown Park	100/	161	109·48/176·19
1973	Graham McRae	NZ	5·0 McRae GM1-Chevrolet	Sandown Park	100/	161	103·87/167·16
1974	Max Stewart	AUS	5·0 Lola T330-Chevrolet	Oran Park	94/	151	—
1975	Max Stewart	AUS	5·0 Lola T400-Chevrolet	Surfers Paradise	—		—
1976	John Goss	AUS	5·0 Matich A53-Repco	Sandown Park	—		—
1977	Warwick Brown	AUS	5·0 Lola T430-Chevrolet	Oran Park	94/	151	86·17/138·68
1978	Graham McRae	NZ	5·0 McRae GM3-Chevrolet	Sandown Park	—		—
1979	John Walker	AUS	5·0 Lola T332-Chevrolet	Wanneroo Park	97/	156	—
1980	Alan Jones	AUS	3·0 Williams FW07-Cosworth	Calder Park	95/	153	—
1981	Roberto Moreno	BR	1·6 Ralt RT4-Ford	Calder Park	100/	161	88·73/142·80
1982	Alain Prost	F	1·6 Ralt RT4-Ford	Calder Park	100/	161	89·14/143·46
1983	Roberto Moreno	BR	1·6 Ralt RT4-Ford	Calder Park	100/	161	88·99/143·22
1984	Roberto Moreno	BR	1·6 Ralt RT4-Ford	Calder Park	100/	161	84·68/136·28
1985	Keke Rosberg	SF	1·5 Williams FW10-Honda t/c	Adelaide	192·50/309·80		95·71/154·03
1986	Alain Prost	F	1·5 McLaren MP4/2C-TAG t/c	Adelaide	192·50/309·80		101·04/162·61

Note: all races up to and including 1984 were non-championship.

LAP CHART

1st LAP ORDER	1 2 3 4 5 6 7 8 9 10 11 12 13 14 15 16 17 18 19 20 21 22 23 24 25 26 27 28 29 30 31 32 33 34 35 36 37 38 39 40 41 42 43 44 45 46 47 48 49 50 51 52 53 54 55 56 57 58 59 60 61 62 63 64 65 66 67 68 69 70 71 72 73 74 75 76 77 78 79 80 81 82	Running order
6 N. Piquet	6 6 6 6 6 6 2 2 2 2 2 2 2 2 2 2 2 2 2 2 22 22 2 2 2 2 2 2 2 2 2 2 2 2 2 2 2 2 2 2 2 2 2 2 2 2 2 2 2 2 2 2 2 2 2 2 2 2 2 2 2 2 6 6 1 1 1 1 1 1 1 1 1 1 1 1 1 1 1 1 1 1	1
12 A. Senna	12 2 2 2 2 2 6 6 6 6 6 6 6 6 6 6 6 6 6 6 6 1 1 1 1 1 1 1 1 1 5 5 5 5 5 5 5 5 5 6 6 6 6 6 6 6 6 6 6 6 1 1 1 1 1 1 1 1 1 1 1 1 1 1 1 1	2
2 K. Rosberg	2 12 12 5 5 5 5 5 5 5 1 1 1 1 1 1 1 1 1 1 5 5 5 5 5 5 5 6 6 6 6 6 6 6 6 6 5 5 5 5 5 5 5 5 5 5 5 5 5 5 5 28 4 4 4 4 4 4 4 4 4 4 4 3 28	3
5 N. Mansell	5 5 5 12 12 12 1 1 1 5 5 5 5 5 5 5 5 5 6 6 6 6 6 6 6 6 6 1 1 1 1 1 1 1 1 1 1 28 4 3 3 3 3 3 3 3 3 3 3 3 3 3 3 28 3	4
1 A. Prost	1 1 1 1 1 12 12 12 12 12 12 12 12 12 12 12 12 12 12 12 12 12 28 28 28 7 7 7 7 7 7 7 7 28 28 28 28 28 28 4 3 28 28 28 28 28 28 28 28 4	5
20 G. Berger	20 20 20 20 20 20 20 20 20 20 20 28 28 28 28 28 28 28 28 28 28 28 28 28 28 28 28 12 7 7 7 7 28 28 28 28 28 28 7 4 4 25 11 11 11 11 11 11 11 11 11 11 11 11 11 11 11	6
4 P. Streiff	4 4 4 28 28 28 28 28 28 28 28 20 20 20 20 4 4 4 4 4 4 4 7 7 7 7 7 7 7 7 7 7 7 4 4 4 4 4 4 3 7 11 25 25 25 25 25 25 25 25 25	7
26 P. Alliot	26 26 26 28 4 4 4 4 4 15 15 15 15 4 20 7 7 7 7 7 7 7 7 4 4 4 4 4 3 3 3 3 3 3 3 3 3 7 11 26 26 26 26 26 26 26 26 26 26	8
28 S. Johansson	28 28 29 19 15 15 15 15 15 4 4 4 7 7 7 7 20 20 3 3 3 3 3 3 3 3 3 3 3 8 8 8 8 8 8 8 8 25 25 18 19 19 19 19 14 14 14 14 14	9
15 A. Jones	15 15 15 15 19 19 19 19 19 11 11 7 7 3 3 3 3 20 20 20 20 20 8 8 8 8 8 8 8 25 25 25 25 25 25 11 11 25 26 14 14 14 14 14 19 19 19 19 19	10
19 T. Fabi	19 19 19 26 11 11 11 11 11 19 7 3 3 8 8 8 8 8 8 8 20 20 20 20 20 25 25 11 11 11 11 11 11 11 14 14 26 26 16 16 16 16 16	11
11 J. Dumfries	11 11 11 11 3 3 3 7 7 7 3 11 11 26 26 26 26 26 26 26 25 25 25 25 25 25 25 25 11 11 18 18 26 18 26 18 14 14 14 26 26 19 19 14	12
3 M. Brundle	3 3 3 26 26 26 7 3 3 3 19 8 8 18 18 18 18 18 18 18 25 26 18 18 18 18 11 11 11 18 26 26 18 26 26 14 26 26 19 19 14 14 16	13
16 P. Tambay	16 16 16 7 7 7 26 26 26 26 8 19 26 23 14 14 14 14 14 25 25 18 18 26 11 11 11 11 11 26 14 14 14 14 17 17 19 19 19 16 16 16 16	14
23 A. de Cesaris	23 23 23 7 16 23 8 8 8 8 26 18 14 23 23 11 11 11 25 11 11 11 11 11 26 26 26 14 14 17 17 17 17 17 19 16 16 16 16 22 22 22 22	15
24 A. Nannini	24 24 7 23 23 8 8 23 16 16 16 16 16 23 11 11 11 25 25 25 14 14 14 14 14 14 17 17 19 19 19 19 16 16 16 22 22 22 22	16
14 J. Palmer	14 7 24 8 16 16 23 23 18 18 18 14 29 29 25 25 23 29 29 29 29 17 17 17 17 17 17 19 19 16 16 16 16 16 22 22	17
7 R. Patrese	7 14 8 24 24 24 18 18 18 18 23 23 29 17 17 17 17 17 19 19 19 23 23 23 23 16 16 22 22 22 22 22	18
18 T. Boutsen	18 8 14 14 14 18 24 14 14 14 14 29 17 25 17 19 19 19 19 19 23 23 23 23 19 19 19 22 22	19
8 D. Warwick	8 18 18 18 18 14 14 24 24 24 17 17 25 19 19 19 23 23 23 23 23 16 16 16 16 16 16 16	20
17 C. Danner	17 17 17 17 17 17 17 17 17 29 29 29 25 19 16 16 16 16 16 16 22 22 22 22 22 22 16 16	21
29 H. Rothengatter	29 29 29 29 29 29 29 29 25 25 25 16 22 22 22 22 22 22 22 22 22	22
21 P. Ghinzani	21 21 25 25 25 25 25 25 22 22 22 22 22 22	23
25 R. Arnoux	25 25 22 22 22 22 22 22 22 22	24
22 A. Berg	22 22	25

CIRCUIT DATA

Adelaide Grand Prix Circuit, Adelaide, South Australia
Circuit length: 2·347 miles/3·778 km
Race distance: 82 laps, 192·498 miles/309·796 km
Race weather: Warm, dry (19°C).

FASTEST LAPS

Driver	Time	Lap
Nelson Piquet	1m 20·787s	82
Alain Prost	1m 20·979s	69
Nigel Mansell	1m 21·194s	58
Keke Rosberg	1m 21·900s	62
Stefan Johansson	1m 22·136s	74
Johnny Dumfries	1m 22·464s	69
Philippe Streiff	1m 22·681s	63
Martin Brundle	1m 22·950s	63
René Arnoux	1m 22·955s	68
Riccardo Patrese	1m 23·095s	55
Derek Warwick	1m 23·695s	40
Jonathan Palmer	1m 23·866s	68
Ayrton Senna	1m 24·149s	6
Patrick Tambay	1m 24·182s	42
Alan Jones	1m 24·585s	15
Gerhard Berger	1m 24·807s	29
Thierry Boutsen	1m 25·351s	48
Christian Danner	1m 25·635s	50
Philippe Alliot	1m 25·798s	78
Teo Fabi	1m 25·895s	47
Huub Rothengatter	1m 26·479s	29
Andrea de Cesaris	1m 26·591s	27
Alessandro Nannini	1m 27·821s	9
Allen Berg	1m 33·172s	26
Piercarlo Ghinzani	1m 34·172s	2

POINTS

WORLD CHAMPIONSHIP OF DRIVERS

1	Alain Prost	*72 pts (74)
2	Nigel Mansell	*70 (72)
3	Nelson Piquet	69
4	Ayrton Senna	55
5	Stefan Johansson	23
6	Keke Rosberg	22
7	Gerhard Berger	17
8=	Jacques Laffite	14
8=	René Arnoux	14
8=	Michele Alboreto	14
11	Martin Brundle	8
12	Alan Jones	4
13=	Johnny Dumfries	3
13=	Philippe Streiff	3
15=	Teo Fabi	2
15=	Riccardo Patrese	2
15=	Patrick Tambay	2
18=	Christian Danner	1
18=	Philippe Alliot	1

CONSTRUCTORS' CUP

1	Williams	141 pts
2	McLaren	96
3	Lotus	58
4	Ferrari	37
5	Ligier	29
6	Benetton	19
7	Tyrrell	11
8	Lola	6
9	Brabham	2
10	Arrows	1

* Best 11 results

1986 RESULTS

A DETAILED SUMMARY OF THE SEASON

FIA Formula 3000 International Championship

DAILY EXPRESS INTERNATIONAL TROPHY, Silverstone Grand Prix Circuit, Great Britain, 13 April. FIA Formula 3000 International Championship, round 1. Aggregate of 1 x 2-lap and 1 x 22-lap parts of the 2·932-mile/4·719-km circuit, 24 laps, 70·37 miles/113·26 km (race stopped due to accident in heavy rain).
1 Pascal Fabre, F (Lola T86/50-Cosworth DFV), 35m 33·97s, 118·71 mph/191·04 km/h.
2 Emanuele Pirro, I (March 86B-Cosworth DFV), 35m 35·19s.
3 John Nielsen, DK (Ralt RT20-Honda), 24 laps.
4 Mike Thackwell, NZ (Lola T86/50-Cosworth DFV), 24.
5 Tomas Kaiser, S (Lola T86/50-Cosworth DFV), 24.
6 Alessandro Santin, I (Lola T86/50-Cosworth DFV), 24.
7 Gary Evans, GB (Lola T86/50-Cosworth DFV), 24; **8** Jeff MacPherson, USA (March 86B-Cosworth DFV), 24; **9** Michel Ferté, F (March 86B-Cosworth DFV), 24; **10** Volker Weidler, D (Ralt RT20-Cosworth DFV), 24; **11** Lamberto Leoni, I (March 86B-Cosworth DFV), 24; **12** Luis Sala, E (Ralt RT20-Cosworth DFV), 24; **13** Alain Ferté, F (March 86B-Cosworth DFV), 24; **14** Mauricio Gugelmin, BR (March 86B-Cosworth DFV), 24; **15** Mario Hytten, CH (March 85B-Cosworth DFV), 24; **16** Adrian Campos, E (March 86B-Cosworth DFV), 24; **17** Franco Scapini, I (March 86B-Cosworth DFV), 24; **18** Russell Spence, GB (March 86B-Cosworth DFV), 23 (DNF, accident damage); **19** Pierluigi Martini, I (Ralt RB20-Cosworth DFV), 23; **20** John Jones, CDN (March 86B-Cosworth DFV), 23; **21** Cary Bren, USA (March 86B-Cosworth DFV), 23; **22** Thierry Tassin, B (March 86B-Cosworth DFV), 23 (DNF, accident); **23** Altfried Heger, D (March 85B-Cosworth DFV), 21; **24** Dominique Delestre, F (March 85B-Cosworth DFV), 20 (DNF, accident); **25** Philippe Alliot, F (March 86B-Cosworth DFV), 17 (DNF, engine); **26** Pierre-Henri Raphanel, F (March 86B-Cosworth DFV), 16 (DNF, overheating); **27** Ivan Capelli, I (March 86B-Cosworth DFV), 12 (DNF, exhaust); **28** Jari Nurminen, SF (March 86B-Cosworth DFV), 11; **29** Andrew Gilbert-Scott, GB (Lola T86/50-Cosworth DFV), 9 (DNF, accident); **30** Ken Johnson, USA (Lola T86/50-Cosworth DFV), 3 (DNF, accident); **31** Satoru Nakajima, J (Ralt RT20-Honda), 2 (DNF, accident).
Fastest lap: Fabre, 1m 26·65s, 121·81 mph/196·03 km/h (record).
Did not start: Cor Euser, NL (March 85B-Cosworth DFV), did not qualify; Claudio Antonioli, I (March 86B-Cosworth DFV), did not qualify; Guido Daccò, I (March 86B-Cosworth DFV), did not qualify; Steven Andskar, S (March 85B-Cosworth DFV), did not qualify; Jean-Pierre Frey, CH (March 85B-Cosworth DFV), did not qualify; James Weaver, GB (RAM 04-Cosworth DFV), time not allowed, car underweight.
Championship points: 1 Fabre, 4.5; **2** Pirro, 3; **3** Nielsen, 2; **4** Thackwell, 1.5; **5** Kaiser, 1; **6** Santin, 0.5.

FIA FORMULA 3000 INTERNATIONAL CHAMPIONSHIP RACE, Autodromo di Vallelunga, Italy, 4 May. FIA Formula 3000 International Championship, round 2. 64 laps of the 1·988-mile/3·200-km circuit, 127·23 miles/204·80 km.
1 Ivan Capelli, I (March 86B-Cosworth DFV), 1h 14m 24·22s, 102·60 mph/165·12 km/h.
2 Pascal Fabre, F (Lola T86/50-Cosworth DFV), 1h 14m 42·88s.
3 Emanuele Pirro, I (March 86B-Cosworth DFV), 64 laps.
4 Mauricio Gugelmin, BR (March 86B-Cosworth DFV), 64.
5 Saturo Nakajima, J (Ralt RT20-Honda), 64.
6 Alessandro Santin, I (Lola T86/50-Cosworth DFV), 64.
7 Volker Weidler, D (Ralt RT20-Cosworth DFV), 64; **8** Philippe Alliot, F (March 86B-Cosworth DFV), 63; **9** Ken Johnson, USA (Lola T86/50-Cosworth DFV), 63; **10** Pierluigi Martini, I (Ralt RB20-Cosworth DFV), 63; **11** Eliseo Salazar, RCH (RAM 04-Cosworth DFV), 63; **12** Michel Ferté, F (March 86B-Cosworth DFV), 63; **13** Gabriele Tarquini, I (March 85B-Cosworth DFV), 63; **14** Pierre-Henri Raphanel, F (March 86B-Cosworth DFV), 63; **15** Guido Daccò, I (Lola T86/50-Cosworth DFV), 63; **16** Gary Evans, GB (Lola T86/50-Cosworth DFV), 62; **17** Claudio Antonioli, I (March 86B-Cosworth DFV), 62; **18** Tomas Kaiser, S (Lola T86/50-Cosworth DFV), 61; **19** Mario Hytten, CH (March 85B-Cosworth DFV), 56 (DNF, electrics); **20** Lamberto Leoni, I (March 86B-Cosworth DFV), 35 (DNF, accident); **21** Franco Scapini, I (March 86B-Cosworth DFV), 35 (DNF, puncture); **22** Andrew Gilbert-Scott, GB (Lola T86/50-Cosworth DFV), 34 (DNF, drive-train); **23** Alain Ferté, F (March 86B-Cosworth DFV), 29 (DNF, engine); **24** Pierre Chauvet, A (March 86B-Cosworth DFV), 29 (DNF, engine); **25** Luis Sala, E (Ralt RT20-Cosworth DFV), 26 (DNF, battery); **26** John Nielsen, DK (Ralt RT20-Honda), 0 (DNF, differential).
Fastest lap: Capelli, 1m 08·27s, 104·83 mph/168·71 km/h (record).
Did not start: John Jones, CDN (March 86B-Cosworth DFV), did not qualify; Jeff MacPherson, USA (March 86B-Cosworth DFV), did not qualify; Russell Spence, GB (March 86B-Cosworth DFV), did not qualify; Franco Tacchino, I (March 85B-Cosworth DFV), did not qualify; Jari Numinen, SF (March 86B-Cosworth DFV), did not qualify; Cary Bren, USA (March 86B-Cosworth DFV), did not qualify; Altfried Heger, D (March 85B-Cosworth DFV), did not qualify; Aldo Bertuzzi, I (Minardi M3085-Cosworth DFV), did not qualify; Jean-Pierre Frey, CH (March 85B-Cosworth DFV), did not qualify; Adrian Campos, E (March 86B-Cosworth DFV), did not qualify; Franco Forini, CH (March 85B-Cosworth DFV), did not qualify.
Championship points: 1 Fabre, 10.5; **2** Capelli, 9; **3** Pirro, 7; **4** Gugelmin, 3; **5** Nielsen and Nakajima, 2.

46 GRAND PRIX de PAU, Circuit de Pau, France, 19 May. FIA Formula 3000 International Championship, round 3. 73 laps of the 1·715-mile/2·760-km circuit, 125·20 miles/201·48 km.
1 Mike Thackwell, NZ (Ralt RT20-Honda), 1h 31m 17·92s, 82·28 mph/132·42 km/h.
2 Emanuele Pirro, I (March 86B-Cosworth DFV), 1h 32m 11·07s.
3 Michel Ferté, F (March 86B-Cosworth DFV), 73 laps.
4 Richard Dallest, F (AGS JH20B/86-Cosworth DFV), 72.
5 Luis Sala, E (Ralt RT20-Cosworth DFV), 72.
6 John Jones, CDN (March 86B-Cosworth DFV), 71.
7 Lamberto Leoni, I (March 86B-Cosworth DFV), 71; **8** Pierre-Henri Raphanel, F (March 86B-Cosworth DFV), 51 (DNF, gearbox); **9** Tomas Kaiser, S (Lola T86/50-Cosworth DFV), 51 (DNF, driveshaft); **10** Ivan Capelli, I (March 86B-Cosworth DFV), 35 (DNF, spun off); **11** Alain Ferté, F (March 86B-Cosworth DFV), 29 (DNF, engine); **12** Philippe Alliot, F (March 86B-Cosworth DFV), 21 (DNF, accident); **13** Pascal Fabre, F (Lola T86/50-Cosworth DFV), 20 (DNF, throttle); **14** Adrian Campos, E (March 86B-Cosworth DFV), 17 (DNF, accident); **15** Gabriele Tarquini, I (March 85B-Cosworth DFV), 6 (DNF, wheel bearing); **16** John Nielsen, DK (Ralt RT20-Honda), 2 (DNF, electrics); **17** Alessandro Santin, I (Lola T86/50-Cosworth DFV), 1 (DNF, accident); **18** Volker Weidler, D (Ralt RT20-Cosworth DFV), 0 (DNF, accident); **19** Russell Spence, GB (March 86B-Cosworth DFV, 0 (DNF, accident); **20** Mario Hytten, CH (March 85B-Cosworth DFV), 0 (DNF, accident).
Fastest lap: Pirro, 1m 13·70s, 83·77 mph/134·81 km/h.
Did not start: Mauricio Gugelmin, BR (March 86B-Cosworth DFV), accident in practice; Marcel Tarrès, F (March 85B-Cosworth DFV), did not qualify; Ken Johnson, USA (Lola T86/50-Cosworth DFV), did not qualify; Jeff MacPherson, USA (March 85B-Cosworth DFV), did not qualify; Pierluigi Martini, I (Ralt RB20-Cosworth DFV), did not qualify; Andrew Gilbert-Scott, GB (Lola T86/50-Cosworth DFV), did not qualify; Gary Evans, GB (Lola T86/50-Cosworth DFV), did not qualify; Eliseo Salazar, RCH (RAM 04-Cosworth DFV), did not qualify; Claudio Antonioli, I (March 86B-Cosworth DFV), did not qualify; Jari Nurminen, SF (March 86B-Cosworth DFV), did not qualify; Aldo Bertuzzi, I (Minardi M3085-Cosworth DFV), did not qualify; Pierre Chauvet, A (March 86B-Cosworth DFV), did not qualify; Cathy Muller, F (Lola T86/50-Cosworth DFV), did not qualify; Franco Tacchino, I (March 85B-Cosworth DFV), did not qualify; Altfried Heger, D (March 85B-Cosworth DFV), did not qualify; Franco Scapini, I (March 86B-Cosworth DFV), did not qualify; Cary Bren, USA (March 86B-Cosworth DFV), did not qualify; Jean-Pierre Frey (March 85B-Cosworth DFV), did not qualify.
Championship points: 1 Pirro, 13; **2** Thackwell and Fabre, 10.5; **4** Capelli, 9; **5** Ferté (Michel), 4; **6** Gugelmin and Dallest, 3.

GRAND PRIX DE BELGIQUE DE F3000, Spa-Francorchamps Circuit, Belgium, 24 May. FIA Formula 3000 International Championship, round 4. 28 laps of the 4·3179-mile/6·9490-km circuit, 120·90 miles/194·57 km.
1 Philippe Alliot, F (March 86B-Cosworth DFV), 1h 02m 03·562s, 117·42 mph/188·97 km/h.
2 John Nielsen, DK (Ralt RT20-Honda), 1h 02m 06·078s.
3 Ivan Capelli, I (March 86B-Cosworth DFV), 28 laps.
4 Luis Sala, E (Ralt RT20-Cosworth DFV), 28.
5 Michel Ferté, F (March 86B-Cosworth DFV), 28.
6 Pierre-Henri Raphanel, F (March 86B-Cosworth DFV), 28.
7 Mauricio Gugelmin, BR (March 86B-Cosworth DFV), 28; **8** Gabriele Tarquini, I (March 85B-Cosworth DFV), 28; **9** Pascal Fabre, F (Lola T86/50-Cosworth DFV), 28; **10** Alessandro Santin, I (Lola T86/50-Cosworth DFV), 28. **11** Pierluigi Martini, I (Ralt RB20-Cosworth DFV), 28; **12** Tomas Kaiser, S (Lola T86/50-Cosworth DFV), 28; **13** Richard Dallest, F (AGS JH20B-Cosworth DFV), 28; **14** Alain Ferté, F (March 86B-Cosworth DFV), 28; **15** Russell Spence, GB (March 86B-Cosworth DFV), 28; **16** Andrew Gilbert-Scott, GB (Lola T86/50-Cosworth DFV), 28; **17** Cathy Muller, F (Lola T86/50-Cosworth DFV), 28; **18** Ken Johnson, USA (Lola T86/50-Cosworth DFV), 28; **19** Emanuele Pirro, I (March 86B-Cosworth DFV), 27; **20** Gary Evans, GB (Lola T86/50-Cosworth DFV), 27; **21** Eliseo Salazar, RCH (Ram 04-Cosworth DFV), 27; **22** John Jones, CDN (March 86B-Cosworth DFV), 25 (DNF, electrics); **23** Lamberto Leoni, I (March 86B-Cosworth DFV), 24 (DNF accident); **24** Pierre Chauvet, A (March 86B-Cosworth DFV), 7 (DNF, transmission); **25** James Weaver, GB (Ralt RT20-Honda), 0 (DNF, accident).
Fastest lap: Nielsen, 2m 11·139s, 119·07 mph/191·624 km/h (record).
Did not start: Altfried Heger, D (March 86B-Cosworth DFV), accident in warm-up; Franco Tacchino, I (March 85B-Cosworth DFV), did not qualify; Jeff MacPherson, USA (March 86B-Cosworth DFV), did not qualify; Guido Daccò, I (March 86B-Cosworth DFV), did not qualify; Volker Weidler, D (Ralt RT20-Cosworth DFV), did not qualify; Franco Scapini, I (March 86B-Cosworth DFV), did not qualify; Jari Nurminen, SF (March 86B-Cosworth DFV), did not qualify; Adrian Campos, E (March 86B-Cosworth DFV), did not qualify; Cary Bren, USA (March 86B-Cosworth DFV), did not qualify; Claudio Antonioli, I (March 86B-Cosworth DFV), did not qualify; Jean-Pierre Frey, CH (March 85B-Cosworth DFV), did not qualify.
Championship points: 1 Capelli and Pirro, 13; **3** Fabre and Thackwell, 10.5; **5** Alliot, 9; **6** Nielsen, 8.

TROFEO ELIO DE ANGELIS, Autodromo Dino Ferrari, Imola, Italy, 8 June. FIA Formula 3000 International Championship, round 5. 39 laps of the 3·132-mile/5·040-km circuit, 122·15 miles/196·56 km.
1 Pierluigi Martini, I (Ralt RT20-Cosworth DFV), 1h 05m 48·56s, 111·37 mph/179·23 km/h.
2 Ivan Capelli, I (March 86B-Cosworth DFV), 1h 05m 49·37s.
3 Alain Ferté, F (March 86B-Cosworth DFV), 39 laps.
4 Gabriele Tarquini, I (March 85B-Cosworth DFV), 39.
5 Luis Sala, E (Ralt RT20-Cosworth DFV), 39.
6 Franco Forini, CH (March 86B-Cosworth DFV), 39.
7 Alessandro Santin, I (Lola T86/50-Cosworth DFV), 39; **8** Satoru Nakajima, J (Ralt RT20-Honda), 39; **9** Lamberto Leoni, I (March 86B-Cosworth DFV), 39; **10** Pascal Fabre, F (Lola T86/50-Cosworth DFV), 39; **11** Marco Lucchinelli, I (Lola T86/50-Cosworth DFV), 39; **12** Michel Ferté, F (March 86B-Cosworth DFV), 39; **13** Philippe Alliot, F (March 86B-Cosworth DFV), 38; **14** Guido Daccò, I (March 85B-Cosworth DFV), 37; **15** Pierre-Henri Raphanel, F (March 85B-Cosworth DFV), 37; **16** John Nielsen, DK (Ralt RT20-Honda), 33 (DNF, accident); **17** Altfried Heger, D (March 85B-Cosworth DFV), 30 (DNF, throttle cable); **18** Adrian Campos, E (March 86B-Cosworth DFV), 13 (DNF, spin); **19** Mauricio Gugelmin, BR (March 86B-Cosworth DFV), 4 (DNF, accident); **20** Cathy Muller, F (Lola T86/50-Cosworth DFV), 3 (DNF, accident); **21** Emanuele Pirro, I (March 86B-Cosworth DFV), 3 (DNF, engine); **22** Pierre Chauvet, A (March 86B-Cosworth DFV), 1 (DNF, accident); **23** Russell Spence, GB (March 86B-Cosworth DFV), 1 (DNF, accident); **24** Tomas Kaiser, S (Lola T86/50-Cosworth DFV), 1 (DNF, accident); **25** Eliseo Salazar, RCH (RAM 04-Cosworth DFV), 0 (DNF, accident); **26** Jeff MacPherson, USA (March 86B-Cosworth DFV), 0 (DNF, accident).
Fastest lap: Ferté (Michel), 1m 39·60s, 113·20 mph/182·18 km/h (record).
Did not start: Jari Nurminen, SF (March 86B-Cosworth DFV), did not qualify; Ken Johnson, USA (Lola T86/50-Cosworth DFV), did not qualify; Franco Scapini, I (March 86B-Cosworth DFV), did not qualify; Andrew Gilbert-Scott, GB (Lola T86/50-Cosworth DFV), did not qualify; Gary Evans, GB (Lola T86/50-Cosworth DFV), did not qualify; John Jones, CDN (March 86B-Cosworth DFV), did not qualify; Franco Tacchino, I (March 86B-Cosworth DFV), did not qualify; Jean-Pierre Frey, CH (March 85B-Cosworth DFV), did not qualify; Aldo Bertuzzi, I (March 85B-Cosworth DFV), did not qualify; Fulvio Ballabio, I (Monte Carlo 001-Cosworth DFV), did not qualify.
Championship points: 1 Capelli, 19; **2** Pirro, 13; **3** Fabre and Thackwell, 10.5; **5** Alliot and Martini, 9.

FIA FORMULA 3000 INTERNATIONAL CHAMPIONSHIP RACE, Autodromo Internazionale del Mugello, Italy, 29 June. FIA Formula 3000 International Championship, round 6. 38 laps of the 3·259-mile/5·245-km circuit, 123·84 miles/199·31 km.
1 Pierluigi Martini, I (Ralt RT20-Cosworth DFV), 1h 10m 48·43s, 104·94 mph/168·88 km/h.
2 Michel Ferté, F (March 86B-Cosworth DFV), 1h 10m 48·85s.
3 Ivan Capelli, I (March 86B-Cosworth DFV), 38 laps.
4 Olivier Grouillard, F (Lola T86/50-Cosworth DFV), 38.
5 Satoru Nakajima, J (Ralt RT20-Honda), 38.
6 Emanuele Pirro, I (March 86B-Cosworth DFV), 38.
7 Alain Ferté, F (March 86B-Cosworth DFV), 38; **8** Pierre-Henri Raphanel, F (March 86B-Cosworth DFV), 38; **9** Claudio Langes, I (Lola T86/50-Cosworth DFV), 38; **10** Gary Evans, GB (Lola T86/50-Cosworth DFV), 38; **11** Tomas Kaiser, S (Lola T86/50-Cosworth DFV), 38; **12** John Jones, CDN (March 86B-Cosworth DFV), 38; **13** Altfried Heger, D (Ralt RT20-Cosworth DFV), 38; **14** Franco Forini, CH (March 86B-Cosworth DFV), 38; **15** Andrew Gilbert-Scott, GB (Lola T86/50-Cosworth DFV), 38; **16** Volker Weidler, D (Ralt RT20-Cosworth DFV), 38; **17** Cathy Muller, F (Lola T86/50-Cosworth DFV), 37; **18** Pierre Chauvet, A (March 86B-Cosworth DFV), 37; **19** Philippe Alliot, F (March 86B-Cosworth DFV), 34 (DNF, accident); **20** John Nielsen, DK (Ralt RT20-Honda), 28 (DNF, electrics); **21** Alessandro Santin, I (Lola T86/50-Cosworth DFV), 18 (DNF, gearbox); **22** Jeff MacPherson, USA (March 86B-Cosworth DFV), 11 (DNF, accident); **23** Franco Tacchino, I (March 85B-Cosworth DFV), 11 (DNF, accident); **24** Pascal Fabre, F (Lola T86/50-Cosworth DFV), 8 (DNF, suspension); **25** Gabriele Tarquini, I (March 85B-Cosworth DFV), 7 (DNF, electrics).
Fastest lap: Martini, 1m 49·35s, 107·29 mph/172·67 km/h (record).
Did not start: Adrian Campos, E (March 86B-Cosworth DFV), driver ill; Guido Daccò, I (March 85B-Cosworth DFV), did not qualify; Russell Spence, GB (March 86B-Cosworth DFV), did not qualify; Lamberto Leoni, I (March 86B-Cosworth DFV), did not qualify; Jari Nurminen, SF (March 86B-Cosworth DFV), did not qualify; Eliseo Salazar, RCH (RAM 04-Cosworth DFV), did not qualify; Steven Andskar, S (March 85B-Cosworth DFV), did not qualify; Aldo Bertuzzi, I (March 85B-Cosworth DFV), did not qualify; Jean-Pierre Frey, CH (March 85B-Cosworth DFV), did not qualify; Luis Sala, E (Ralt RT20-Cosworth DFV), did not qualify; Mauricio Gugelmin, BR (March 86B-Cosworth DFV), did not qualify.
Championship points: 1 Capelli, 23; **2** Martini, 18; **3** Pirro 14; **4** Ferté (Michel), 12; **5** Fabre and Thackwell, 10.5.

24 GRAN PREMIO del MEDITERRANEO, Ente Autodromo di Pergusa, Enna, Sicily, 20 July. FIA Formula 3000 International Championship, round 7. 40 laps of the 3·076-mile/4·950-km circuit, 123·04 miles/198·00 km.
1 Luis Sala, E (Ralt RT20-Cosworth DFV), 1h 01m 42·72s, 119·62 mph/192·51 km/h.
2 Pierluigi Martini, I (Ralt RT20-Cosworth DFV), 1h 01m 49·52s.
3 Pascal Fabre, F (Lola T86/50-Cosworth DFV), 40 laps.
4 Tomas Kaiser, S (Lola T86/50-Cosworth DFV), 40.
5 Claudio Langes, I (Lola T86/50-Cosworth DFV), 40.
6 John Nielsen, DK (Ralt RT20-Honda), 40.
7 Pierre-Henri Raphanel, F (March 86B-Cosworth DFV), 40; **8** Alessandro Santin, I (March 86B-

Cosworth DFV), 40; **9** Mike Thackwell, NZ (Lola T86/50-Cosworth DFV), 40; **10** Gary Evans, GB (Lola T86/50-Cosworth DFV), 40; **11** John Jones, CDN (March 86B-Cosworth DFV), 40; **12** Michel Ferté, F (March 86B-Cosworth DFV), 40; **13** Emanuele Pirro, (March 86B-Cosworth DFV), 40; **14** Jeff MacPherson, USA (March 86B-Cosworth DFV), 40; **15** Lamberto Leoni, I (March 86B-Cosworth DFV), 40; **16** Guido Daccò, I (March 85B-Cosworth DFV), 40; **17** Andrew Gilbert-Scott, GB (Lola T86/50-Cosworth DFV), 39; **18** Alain Ferté, F (March 86B-Cosworth DFV), 39; **19** Franco Tacchino, I (March 85B-Cosworth DFV), 39; **20** Ivan Capelli, I (March 86B-Cosworth DFV), 35 (DNF, overheating); **21** Mauricio Gugelmin, BR (March 86B-Cosworth DFV), 29 (DNF, spin); **22** Russell Spence, GB (March 86B-Cosworth DFV), 15 (DNF, accident); **23** Nicola Larini, I (March 85B-Cosworth DFV), 5 (DNF, accident); **24** Gabriele Tarquini, I (March 85B-Cosworth DFV), 2 (DNF, accident); **25** Satoru Nakajima, J (Ralt RT20-Honda), 0 (DNF, accident); **26** Franco Scapini, I (Lola T86/50-Cosworth DFV), 0 (DNF, accident).

Fastest lap: Thackwell, 1m 30·92s, 120·62 mph/194·12 km/h (record).

Did not start: Eliseo Salazar, RCH (RAM 04-Cosworth DFV), did not qualify; Franco Forini, CH (March 86B-Cosworth DFV), did not qualify; Cathy Muller, F (Lola T86/50-Cosworth DFV), did not qualify; Adrian Campos, E (March 86B-Cosworth DFV), did not qualify; Volker Weidler, D (Ralt RT20-Cosworth DFV), did not qualify; Altfried Heger, D (Ralt RT20-Cosworth DFV), did not qualify; Mario Hytten, CH (Ralt RT20-Cosworth DFV), did not qualify; Jari Nurminen, SF (March 86B-Cosworth DFV), did not qualify; Wayne Taylor, ZA (March 86B-Cosworth DFV), did not qualify; Jean-Pierre Frey, CH (March 86B-Cosworth DFV), did not qualify.

Championship points: 1 Martini, 24; **2** Capelli, 23; **3** Sala, 16; **4** Fabre, 14.5; **5** Pirro, 14; **6** Ferté (Michel), 12.

FIA FORMULA 3000 INTERNATIONAL CHAMPIONSHIP RACE, Österreichring, Austria, 16 August. FIA Formula 3000 International Championship, round 8. 34 laps of the 3·6920-mile/5·9424-km circuit, 125·53 miles/202·04 km.

1 Ivan Capelli, I (March 86B-Cosworth DFV), 58m 47·530s, 128·037 mph/206·055 km/h.

2 John Nielsen, DK (Ralt RT20-Honda), 58m 49·688s.

3 Gabriele Tarquini, I (March 85B-Cosworth DFV), 34 laps.

4 Satoru Nakajima, J (Ralt RT20-Honda), 34.

5 Luis Sala, E (Ralt RT20-Cosworth DFV), 34.

6 Olivier Grouillard, F (Lola T86/50-Cosworth DFV), 34.

7 Pierluigi Martini, I (Ralt RT20-Cosworth DFV), 34; **8** Mauricio Gugelmin, BR (March 86B-Cosworth DFV); **9** Volker Weidler, D (Ralt RT20-Cosworth DFV), 34; **10** Gary Evans, GB (Lola T86/50-Cosworth DFV), 34; **11** Russell Spence, GB (March 86B-Cosworth DFV), 34; **12** Pierre-Henri Raphanel, F (March 86B-Cosworth DFV), 34; **13** Franco Scapini, I (Lola T86/50-Cosworth DFV), 34; **14** John Jones, CDN (March 86B-Cosworth DFV), 33; **15** Jari Nurminen, SF (March 86B-Cosworth DFV), 33; **16** Guido Daccò, I (March 86B-Cosworth DFV), 33; **17** Alessandro Santin, I (March 85B-Cosworth DFV), 32; **18** Pascal Fabre, F (Lola T86/50-Cosworth DFV), 26 (DNF, electrics); **19** Emanuele Pirro, I (March 86B-Cosworth DFV), 26 (DNF, fuel system); **20** Michel Ferté, F (March 86B-Cosworth DFV), 25 (DNF, throttle); **21** Kenny Acheson, GB (March 86B-Cosworth DFV), 22 (DNF, accident); **22** Claudio Langes, I (Lola T86/50-Cosworth DFV), 20 (DNF, engine); **23** Mario Hytten, CH (Ralt RT20-Cosworth DFV), 12 (DNF, accident); **24** Tomas Kaiser, S (Lola T86/50-Cosworth DFV), 3 (DNF, engine); **25** Bernard Santal, F (Lola T86/50-Cosworth DFV), 1 (DNF, accident).

Fastest lap: Nielsen, 1m 42·704s, 129·342 mph/208·155 km/h.

Did not start: Lamberto Leoni, I (March 86B-Cosworth DFV), accident in practice; Altfried Heger, D (Ralt RT20-Cosworth DFV), did not qualify; Pierre Chauvet, A (March 86B-Cosworth DFV), did not qualify; Cathy Muller, F (March 86B-Cosworth DFV), did not qualify; Oscar Pedersoli, I (March 85B-Cosworth DFV), did not qualify; Steven Andskar, S (March 85B-Cosworth DFV), did not qualify; Franco Forini, CH (March 86B-Cosworth DFV), did not qualify; Bruno Corradi, I (Minardi M3085-Cosworth DFV) did not qualify; Jean-Pierre Frey, CH (March 86B-Cosworth DFV), did not qualify; Andrew Gilbert-Scott, GB (Lola T86/50-Cosworth DFV), did not qualify.

Championship points: 1 Capelli, 32; **2** Martini, 24; **3** Sala, 18; **4** Nielsen, 15; **5** Fabre, 14.5; **6** Pirro, 14.

HALFORDS BIRMINGHAM SUPERPRIX, Birmingham Street Circuit, Great Britain, 25 August. FIA Formula 3000 International Championship, round 9. 24 laps of the 2·470-mile/3·975-km circuit, 59·28 miles/95·40 km. Race stopped due to heavy rain and accidents.

1 Luis Sala, E (Ralt RT20-Cosworth DFV) 42m 24·40s, 83·87 mph/134·98 km/h.

2 Pierluigi Martini, I (Ralt RT20-Cosworth DFV), 42m 27·72s.

3 Michel Ferté, F (March 86B-Cosworth DFV), 24 laps.

4 Eliseo Salazar, RCH (Lola T86/50-Cosworth DFV), 24.

5 Pascal Fabre, F (Lola T86/50-Cosworth DFV), 24.

6 Russell Spence, GB (March 86B-Cosworth DFV), 24.

7 John Jones, CDN (March 86B-Cosworth DFV), 24; **8** Satoru Nakajima, J (Ralt RT20-Honda) 24; **9** Tomas Kaiser, S (Lola T86/50-Cosworth DFV), 24; **10** Roberto Moreno, BR (Ralt RT20-Cosworth DFV), 24; **11** John Nielsen, DK (Ralt RT20-Honda), 24; **12** Alessandro Santin, I (March 85B-Cosworth DFV), 24; **13** Gabriele Tarquini, I (March 85B-Cosworth DFV), 24; **14** Mauricio Gugelmin, BR (March 86B-Cosworth DFV), 23; **15** Tommy Byrne, IRL (March 86B-Cosworth DFV), 23; **16** Gary Evans, GB (Lola T86/50-Cosworth DFV), 23; **17** Andrew Gilbert-Scott, GB (Lola T86/50-Cosworth DFV), 21 (DNF, accident); **18** Olivier Grouillard, F (Lola T86/50-Cosworth DFV), 18 (DNF, accident); **19** Claudio Langes, I (Lola T86/50-Cosworth DFV), 17 (DNF, accident); **20** Altfried Heger, D (March 85B-Cosworth DFV), 17 (DNF, accident); **21** Emanuele Pirro, I (March 86B-Cosworth DFV), 14 (DNF, accident); **22** Alain Ferté, F (March 86B-Cosworth DFV), 11 (DNF, accident); **23** Pierre-Henri Raphanel, F (March 86B-Cosworth DFV), 9 (DNF, handling); **24** Marcel Tarrès, F (March 85B-Cosworth DFV), 2 (DNF, accident); **25** Tim Davies, GB (March 86B-Cosworth DFV), 2 (DNF, accident); **26** Ivan Capelli, I (March 86B-Cosworth DFV), 0 (DNF, accident).

Fastest lap: Salazar, 1m 42·62s, 86·64 mph/139·43 km/h (record).

Did not start: Guido Daccò, I (March 86B-Cosworth DFV), did not qualify; Franco Tacchino, I (March 86B-Cosworth DFV), did not qualify; Mario Hytten, CH (Ralt RT20-Cosworth DFV), did not qualify; Franco Forini, CH (March 86B-Cosworth DFV), did not qualify; Jari Nurminen, SF (March 86B-Cosworth DFV), did not qualify; Dave Scott, GB (March 86B-Cosworth DFV), did not qualify; Ross Cheever, USA (March 86B-Cosworth DFV), did not qualify; Jean-Pierre Frey, CH (March 85B-Cosworth DFV), did not qualify.

Championship points: 1 Capelli, 32; **2** Martini, 27; **3** Sala, 22.5; **4** Fabre, 15.5; **5** Nielsen, 15; **6** Pirro and Ferté (Michel), 14.

FIA FORMULA 3000 INTERNATIONAL CHAMPIONSHIP RACE, Bugatti Circuit, Le Mans, France, 28 September. FIA Formula 3000 International Championship, round 10. 47 laps of the 2·635-mile/4·240-km circuit, 123·845 miles/199·28 km.

1 Emanuele Pirro, I (March 86B-Cosworth DFV), 1h 10m 36·43s, 105·658 mph/170·040 km/h.

2 Michel Ferté, F (March 86B-Cosworth DFV), 1h 10m 42·95s.

3 Pierre-Henri Raphanel, F (March 86B-Cosworth DFV), 47 laps.

4 Ivan Capelli, I (March 86B-Cosworth DFV), 47.

5 Luis Sala, E (Ralt RT20-Cosworth DFV), 47.

6 Claudio Langes, I (Lola T86/50-Cosworth DFV), 47.

7 John Nielsen, DK (Ralt RT20-Honda), 47; **8** James Weaver, GB (Ralt RT20-Honda), 47; **9** Mauricio Gugelmin, BR (March 86B-Cosworth DFV), 47; **10** Russell Spence, GB (March 86B-Cosworth DFV), 47; **11** Jan Lammers, NL (March 86B-Cosworth DFV), 47; **12** Eliseo Salazar, RCH (Lola T86/50-Cosworth DFV), 47; **13** Tomas Kaiser, S (Lola T86/50-Cosworth DFV), 46; **14** Pierre Chauvet, A (March 86B-Cosworth DFV), 46; **15** John Jones, CDN (March 86B-Cosworth DFV), 46; **16** Guido Daccò, I (March 86B-Cosworth DFV), 46; **17** Cathy Muller, F (March 86B-Cosworth DFV), 45; **18** Adrian Campos, E (Lola T86/50-Cosworth DFV), 39 (DNF, out of fuel); **19** Altfried Heger, D (Ralt RT20-Cosworth DFV), 33 (DNF, gearbox); **20** Pierluigi Martini, I (Ralt RT20-Cosworth DFV), 16 (DNF, throttle cable); **21** Richard Dallest, F (AGS JH20-Cosworth DFV), 14 (DNF, throttle slides); **22** Gabriele Tarquini, I (March 85B-Cosworth DFV), 1 (DNF, accident); **23** Alessandro Santin, I (March 86B-Cosworth DFV), 1 (DNF, accident); **24** Andrew Gilbert-Scott, GB (Lola T86/50-Cosworth DFV), 1 (DNF, accident); **25** Yannick Dalmas, F (March 86B-Cosworth DFV), 1 (DNF, accident); **26** Alain Ferté, F (AGS JH20-Cosworth DFV), 1 (DNF, accident).

Fastest lap: Pirro, 1m 29·20s, 106·767 mph/171·824 km/h (record).

Did not start: Gary Evans, GB (Lola T86/50-Cosworth DFV), did not qualify; Jari Nurminen, SF (March 86B-Cosworth DFV), did not qualify; Beppe Gabbiani, I (March 86B-Cosworth DFV), did not qualify; Beniot Morand, CH (Lola T86/50-Cosworth DFV), did not qualify; Nicola Tesini, I (March 85B-Cosworth DFV), did not qualify; Mark Galvin, IRL (March 86B-Cosworth DFV), did not qualify; Paolo Barilla, I (March 85B-Cosworth DFV), did not qualify; Marcel Tarrès, F (March 85B-Cosworth DFV), did not qualify; Jean-Pierre Frey, CH (March 86B-Cosworth DFV), did not qualify; Steven Andskar, S (March 85B-Cosworth DFV), did not qualify; Aldo Bertuzzi, I (March 85B-Cosworth DFV), did not qualify.

Championship points: 1 Capelli, 35; **2** Martini, 27; **3** Sala, 24.5; **4** Pirro, 23; **5** Ferté (Michel), 20; **6** Fabre, 15.5.

FIA FORMULA 3000 INTERNATIONAL CHAMPIONSHIP RACE, Circuito Permanente del Jarama, Spain, 5 October. FIA Formula 3000 International Championship, round 11. Aggregate of 1 x 43-lap and 1 x 15-lap heats of the 2·058-mile/3·312-km circuit, 58 laps, 119·36 miles/192·10 km.

1 Emanuele Pirro, I (March 86B-Cosworth DFV), 1h 18m 05·49s, 91·71 mph/147·59 km/h.

2 Michel Ferté, F (March 86B-Cosworth DFV), 1h 18m 15·92s.

3 Ivan Capelli, I (March 86B-Cosworth DFV), 58 laps.

4 John Nielsen, DK (Ralt RT20-Honda), 58.

5 Mauricio Gugelmin, BR (March 86B-Cosworth DFV), 58.

6 Adrian Campos, E (Lola T86/50-Cosworth DFV), 58.

7 Luis Sala, E (Ralt RT20-Cosworth DFV), 58; **8** Olivier Grouillard, F (Lola T86/50-Cosworth DFV), 58; **9** Tomas Kaiser, S (Lola T86/50-Cosworth DFV), 58; **10** John Jones, CDN (March 86B-Cosworth DFV), 58; **11** Claudio Langes, I (Lola T86/50-Cosworth DFV), 58; **12** Altfried Heger, D (Ralt RT20-Cosworth DFV), 58; **13** Gabriele Tarquini, I (Lola T86/50-Cosworth DFV), 58; **14** Pierre-Henri Raphanel, F (March 86B-Cosworth DFV), 54; **15** Eliseo Salazar, RCH (Lola T86/50-Cosworth DFV), 44 (DNF, accident); **16** Pierre Chauvet, A (March 86B-Cosworth DFV), 44 (DNF, accident); **17** Alfonso García de Vinuesa, E (March 86B-Cosworth DFV), 43 (DNF, accident); **18** Mike Thackwell, NZ, (Ralt RT20-Honda), 42 (DNF, accident); **19** Gary Evans, GB (Lola T86/50-Cosworth DFV), 44 (DNF, electrics); **20** Cor Euser, NL (March 86B-Cosworth DFV), 24 (DNF, spun off); **21** Russell Spence, GB (March 86B-Cosworth DFV), 13 (DNF, accident); **22** Alain Ferté, F (AGS JH20B-Cosworth DFV), 9 (DNF, broken hub); **23** Andrew Gilbert-Scott, GB (March 85B-Cosworth DFV), 1 (DNF, accident); **24** Alessandro Santin, I (March 86B-Cosworth DFV), 1 (DNF, accident); **25** Gregor Foitek, CH (Lola T86/50-Cosworth DFV), 0 (DNF, accident).

Disqualified: Pierluigi Martini, I (Ralt RT20-Cosworth DFV) finished 1st on the road but was disqualified as team worked on the car between heats.

Fastest lap: Ferté (Michel), 1m 19·51s, 93·18 mph/149·96 km/h (record).

Did not start: Bernard Santal, F (March 86B-Cosworth DFV), did not qualify; Cathy Muller, F (March 86B-Cosworth DFV), did not qualify; Jari Nurminen, SF (March 86B-Cosworth DFV), did not qualify; Mario Hytten, CH (Ralt RT20-Cosworth DFV), did not qualify; Guido Daccò, I (March 86B-Cosworth DFV), did not qualify; Marco Romano, I (March 86B-Cosworth DFV), did not qualify; Nicola Tesini, I (March 85B-Cosworth DFV), did not qualify; Aldo Bertuzzi, I (March 85B-Cosworth DFV), did not qualify; Jean-Pierre Frey, CH (March 86B-Cosworth DFV), did not qualify.

Final Championship points

1 Ivan Capelli, I	39
2 Emanuele Pirro, I	32
3 Pierluigi Martini, I	27
4 Michel Ferté, F	26
5 Luis Sala, E	24.5
6 John Nielsen, DK	18

7 Pascal Fabre, F 15.5; **8** Mike Thackwell, NZ, 10.5; **9** Philippe Alliot, F, 9; **10** Satoru Nakajima, J and Gabriele Tarquini, I, 7; **12** Mauricio Gugelmin, BR and Pierre-Henri Raphanel, F, 5; **14** Olivier Grouillard, F, Alain Ferté, F and Tomas Kaiser, S, 4; **17** Richard Dallest, F and Claudio Langes, I, 3; **19** Eliseo Salazar, RCH and Alessandro Santin, I, 1.5; **21** Adrian Campos, E, Franco Forini, CH and John Jones, CDN, 1; **24** Russell Spence, GB, 0.5.

FORMULA 3

LUCAS BRITISH FORMULA 3 CHAMPIONSHIP RACE, Thruxton Circuit, Great Britain, 9 March. Lucas British Formula 3 Championship, round 1. 15 laps of the 2·356-mile/3·792-km circuit, 35·34 miles/56·88 km.

1 Maurizio Sandro Sala, BR (Ralt RT30/86-VW), 20m 46·19s, 101·65 mph/163.59 km/h (1st class A).

2 Andy Wallace, GB (Reynard 863-VW), 20m 51·37s.

3 Martin Donnelly, GB (Ralt RT30/86-VW), 15 laps.

4 Tim Davies, GB (Ralt RT30/86-VW), 15.

5 Graham de Zille, GB (Ralt RT30/86-VW), 15.

6 Gerrit van Kouwen, NL (Ralt RT30/86-VW), 15.

7 Mark Galvin, IRL (Ralt RT30/86-VW), 15; **8** Dave Scott, GB (Reynard 863-VW), 15; **9** Ross Hockenhull, GB (Ralt RT30/86-VW), 15; **10** Keith Fine, GB (Ralt RT30/86-Toyota), 15.

Fastest lap: Galvin, 1m 21·20s, 104·00 mph/167·37 km/h.

Class B winner: Gary Dunn, GB (Ralt RT30/85-VW), 15.

British Championship points. Class A: 1 Sandro Sala, 9; **2** Wallace, 6; **3** Donnelly, 4; **4** Davies, 3; **5** de Zille, 2; **6** Galvin and van Kouwen, 1. **Class B: 1** Dunn, 10; **2** Kempton, 6; **3** Khan, 4.

LUCAS BRITISH FORMULA 3 CHAMPIONSHIP RACE, Silverstone Short Circuit, Great Britain, 23 March. Lucas British Formula 3 Championship, round 2. 20 laps of the 1·608-mile/2·588-km circuit, 32·16 miles/51·76 km.

1 Andy Wallace, GB (Reynard 863-VW), 18m 16·78s, 105·55 mph/169·87 km/h (1st class A).

2 Maurizio Sandro Sala, BR (Ralt RT30/86-VW), 18m 19·77s.

3 Dave Scott, GB (Reynard 863-VW), 20 laps.

4 Tim Davies, GB (Ralt RT30/86-VW), 20.

5 Keith Fine, GB (Ralt RT30/86-Toyota), 20.

6 Gary Brabham, AUS (Ralt RT30/86-VW), 20.

7 Gerrit van Kouwen, NL (Ralt RT30/86-VW), 20; **8** Martin Donnelly, GB (Ralt RT30/86-VW), 20; **9** David Hunt, GB (Ralt RT30/86-VW), 20; **10** Damon Hill, GB (Ralt RT30/86-VW), 20.

Fastest lap: Wallace, 54·22s, 106·76 mph/171·81 km/h.

Class B winner: Andy King, GB (Reynard 853-VW), 20.

British Championship points. Class A: 1 Wallace, 16; **2** Sandro Sala, 15; **3** Davies, 6; **4** Donnelly and Scott, 4; **6** Fine and de Zille, 2. **Class B: 1** Dunn, 12; **2** Kempton, 10; **3** King, 9.

LUCAS BRITISH FORMULA 3 CHAMPIONSHIP RACE, Thruxton Circuit, Great Britain, 31 March. Lucas British Formula 3 Championship, round 3. 20 laps of the 2·356-mile/3·792-km circuit, 47·12 miles/75·84 km.

1 Maurizio Sandro Sala, BR (Ralt RT30/86-VW), 25m 14·97s, 111·97 mph/180·20 km/h (1st class A).

2 Keith Fine, GB (Ralt RT30/86-Toyota), 25m 20·22s.

3 Gerrit van Kouwen, NL (Ralt RT30/86-VW), 20 laps.

4 David Hunt, GB (Ralt RT30/86-VW), 20.

5 Dave Scott, GB (Reynard 863-VW), 20.

6 Tim Davies, GB (Ralt RT30/86-VW), 20.

7 Andy Wallace, GB (Reynard 863-VW), 20; **8** Mark Galvin, IRL (Ralt RT30/86-VW), 20; **9** Graham de Zille, GB (Ralt RT30/86-VW), 20; **10** Perry McCarthy, GB (Reynard 863-VW), 20.

Fastest lap: Sandro Sala, 1m 14·80s, 113·39 mph/182·48 km/h.

Class B winner: Paul Stott, GB (Ralt RT30/85-VW), 20.

British Championship points. Class A: 1 Sandro Sala, 25; **2** Wallace, 16; **3** Fine, 8; **4** Davies, 7; **5** Scott, 6; **6** van Kouwen, 5. **Class B: 1** Stott, 17; **2** Dunn, 15; **3** Kempton, 11.

LUCAS BRITISH FORMULA 3 CHAMPIONSHIP RACE, Silverstone Grand Prix Circuit, Great Britain, 13 April. Lucas British Formula 3 Championship, round 4. 19 laps of the 2·932-mile/4·719-km circuit, 55·71 miles/89·66 km.

1 Maurizio Sandro Sala, BR (Ralt RT30/86-VW), 27m 51·54s, 120·00 mph/193·12 km/h (1st class A).

2 Gary Brabham, AUS (Ralt RT30/86-VW), 27m 51·87s.

3 Andy Wallace, GB (Reynard 863-VW), 19 laps.

4 David Hunt, GB (Ralt RT30/86-VW), 19.

5 Gerrit van Kouwen, NL (Ralt RT30/86-VW), 19.

6 Tim Davies, GB (Ralt RT30/86-VW), 19.

7 Mark Galvin, IRL (Ralt RT30/86-VW), 19; **8** Graham de Zille, GB (Ralt RT30/86-VW), 19; **9** Dave Scott, GB (Reynard 863-VW), 19; **10** Julian Bailey, GB (Ralt RT30/86-VW), 19.

Fastest lap: Wallace, 1m 26·40s, 122·16 mph/196·60 km/h.

Class B winner: Andy King, GB (Reynard 853-VW), 19 (disqualified due to fuel infringement).

British Championship points. Class A: 1 Sandro Sala, 34; **2** Wallace, 21; **3** Davies and Fine, 8; **5** Brabham and van Kouwen, 7. **Class B: 1** Stott, 21; **2** Dunn, 17; **3** Kempton, 14.

LUCAS BRITISH FORMULA 3 CHAMPIONSHIP RACE, Brands Hatch Indy Circuit, Great Britain, 20 April. Lucas British Formula 3 Championship, round 5. 30 laps of the 1·2036-mile/1·9370-km circuit, 36·11 miles/58·11 km.

1 Andy Wallace, GB (Reynard 863-VW), 22m 19·93s, 97·01 mph/156·12 km/h (1st class A).

2 Dave Scott, GB (Reynard 863-VW), 22m 20·17s.

3 Gerrit van Kouwen, NL (Ralt RT30/86-VW), 30 laps.

4 Martin Donnelly, GB (Ralt RT30/86-VW), 30.

5 Gary Brabham, AUS (Ralt RT30/86-VW), 30.

6 Perry McCarthy, GB (Reynard 863-VW), 30.

7 Mark Galvin, IRL (Ralt RT30/86-VW), 30; **8** Tim Davies, GB (Ralt RT30/86-VW), 30; **9** David Hunt, GB (Ralt RT30/86-VW), 30; **10** Graham de Zille, GB (Ralt RT30/86-VW), 30.

Fastest lap: Brabham, 43·95s, 98·58 mph/158·65 km/h (record).

Class B winner: Gary Dunn, GB (Ralt RT30/85-VW), 30.

British Championship points. Class A: 1 Sandro Sala, 34; **2** Wallace, 30; **3** Scott, 12; **4** van Kouwen, 11; **5** Brabham, 10; **6** Davies and Fine, 8. **Class B: 1** Dunn, 26; **2** Stott, 25; **3** Kempton, 20.

LUCAS BRITISH FORMULA 3 CHAMPIONSHIP RACE, Thruxton Circuit, Great Britain, 5 May. Lucas British Formula 3 Championship, round 6. 20 laps of the 2·356-mile/3·792-km circuit, 47·12 miles/75·84 km.

1 Gerrit van Kouwen, NL (Ralt RT30/86-VW), 25m 10·30s, 112·30 mph/180·73 km/h (1st class A).

2 Andy Wallace, GB (Reynard 863-VW), 25m 10·74s.

3 Tim Davies, GB (Ralt RT30/86-VW), 20 laps.

4 Keith Fine, GB (Ralt RT30/86-Toyota), 20.

5 Maurizio Sandro Sala, BR (Ralt RT30/86-VW), 20.

6 Julian Bailey, GB (Ralt RT30/86-VW), 20.

7 Martin Donnelly, GB (Ralt RT30/86-VW), 20; **8** Damon Hill, GB (Ralt RT30/86-VW), 20; **9** Paul Radisich, NZ (Ralt RT30/86-VW), 20; **10** Dave Simpson, USA (Ralt RT30/86-VW), 20.

Fastest lap: Wallace, 1m 14·81s, 113·30 mph/182·34 km/h.

Class B winner: Sean Walker, GB (Ralt RT30/85-VW), 20.

British Championship points. Class A: 1 Wallace, 37; **2** Sandro Sala, 36; **3** van Kouwen, 20; **4** Davies and Scott, 12; **6** Fine, 11; **Class B: 1** Dunn, 30; **2** Kempton, 27; **3** Stott, 26.

28 GRAND PRIX DE MONACO FORMULA 3, Monte Carlo, Monaco, 10 May. 24 laps of the 2·080-mile/3·347-km circuit, 49·92 miles/80·33 km.

1 Yannick Dalmas, F (Martini MK49-VW), 39m 13·421s, 76·36 mph/122·89 km/h.

2 Stefano Modena, I (Reynard 863-Alfa Romeo), 39m 44·568s.

3 Michel Trollé, F (Martini MK49-VW), 24 laps.

4 Nicola Larini, I (Dallara 386-Alfa Romeo), 24.

5 Harald Huysman, N ((Ralt RT30/86-VW), 24.

6 Enrico Bertaggia, I (Dallara 386-Alfa Romeo), 24.

7 Eric Bachelart, B (Martini MK49-Alfa Romeo), 24; **8** Fabien Giroix, F (Reynard 863-VW), 24; **9** Eric Bellefroid, F (Martini MK49-Alfa Romeo), 24; **10** Bernard Santal, CH (Dallara 386-VW), 24.

Fastest lap: Dalmas, 1m 36·664s, 77·46 mph/124·66 km/h.

LUCAS BRITISH FORMULA 3 CHAMPIONSHIP RACE, Donington Park Circuit, Great Britain, 18 May. Lucas British Formula 3 Championship, round 7. 20 laps of the 2·500-mile/4·023-km circuit, 50·00 miles/80·46 km.

1 Martin Donnelly, GB (Ralt RT30/86-VW), 32m 38·22s, 91·69 mph/147·56 km/h (1st class A).

2 Maurizio Sandro Sala, BR (Ralt RT30/86-VW), 32m 43·48s.

3 Gerrit van Kouwen, NL (Ralt RT30/86-VW), 20 laps.

4 Tim Davies, GB (Ralt RT30/86-VW), 20.

5 Damon Hill, GB (Ralt RT30/86-VW), 20.

6 Paul Radisich, NZ (Ralt RT30/86-VW), 20.

7 David Hunt, GB (Ralt RT30/86-VW), 20; **8** Ross Hockenhull, GB (Ralt RT30/86-VW), 20; **9** Julian Bailey, GB (Ralt RT30/86-VW), 20; **10** Gary Brabham, AUS (Ralt RT30/86-VW), 20.

Fastest lap: Donnelly, 1m 36·84s, 92·71 mph/149·20 km/h.

Class B winner: Alastair Lyall, GB (Ralt RT30/85-VW), 20.

British Championship points. Class A: 1 Sandro Sala, 42; **2** Wallace, 37; **3** van Kouwen, 24; **4** Donnelly, 17; **5** Davies, 15; **6** Scott, 12. **Class B: 1** Dunn, 34; **2** Kempton and Walker, 27.

LUCAS BRITISH FORMULA 3 CHAMPIONSHIP RACE, Silverstone Short Circuit, Great Britain, 25 May. Lucas British Formula 3 Championship, round 8. 25 laps of the 1·608-mile/

2·588-km circuit, 40·20 miles/64·70 km.
1 Maurizio Sandro Sala, BR (Ralt RT30/86-VW), 22m 55·43s, 105·21 mph/169·32 km/h (1st class A).
2 Andy Wallace, GB (Reynard 863-VW), 22m 55·60s.
3 Keith Fine, GB (Ralt RT30/86-Toyota), 25 laps.
4 Gary Brabham, AUS (Ralt RT30/86-VW), 25.
5 Paul Radisich, NZ (Ralt RT30/86-VW), 25.
6 Damon Hill, GB (Ralt RT30/86-VW), 25.
7 Dave Simpson, USA (Reynard 863-VW), 25; **8** Sean Walker, GB (Ralt RT30/85-VW), 25 (1st class B); **9** Adrian Willmott, GB (Ralt RT30/85-VW), 25; **10** Gary Ward, GB (Ralt RT30/85-VW), 25.
Fastest lap: Wallace, 54·36s, 106·49 mph/171·38 km/h.
British Championship points. Class A: 1 Sandro Sala, 51; **2** Wallace, 44; **3** van Kouwen, 24; **4** Donnelly, 17; **5** Davies and Fine, 15. **Class B: 1** Walker, 37; **2** Dunn, 34; **3** Kempton, 30.

LUCAS BRITISH FORMULA 3 CHAMPIONSHIP RACE, Silverstone Grand Prix Circuit, Great Britain, 8 June. Lucas British Formula 3 Championship, round 9. 11 laps of the 2·932-mile/4·719-km circuit, 32·25 miles/51·91 km.
1 Andy Wallace, GB (Reynard 863-VW), 16m 00·32s, 120·90 mph/194·57 km/h (1st class A).
2 Mark Galvin, IRL (Ralt RT30/86-VW), 16m 04·07s.
3 Maurizio Sandro Sala, BR (Ralt RT30/86-VW), 11 laps.
4 David Hunt, GB (Ralt RT30/86-VW), 11.
5 Julian Bailey, GB (Ralt RT30/86-VW), 11.
6 Ross Cheever, USA (Ralt RT30/86-VW), 11.
7 Paul Radisich, NZ (Ralt RT30/86-VW), 11; **8** Graham de Zille, GB (Ralt RT30/86-VW), 11; **9** Damon Hill, GB (Ralt RT30/86-VW), 11; **10** Anthony Reid, GB (Ralt RT30/86-Toyota), 11.
Fastest lap: Wallace, 1m 26·43s, 122·12 mph/196·53 km/h.
Class B winner: Gary Ward, GB (Ralt RT30/85-VW), 11.
British Championship points. Class A: 1 Sandro Sala, 55; **2** Wallace, 54; **3** van Kouwen, 24; **4** Donnelly, 17; **5** Davies and Fine, 15. **Class B: 1** Walker, 41; **2** Kempton, 36; **3** Dunn, 34.

LUCAS BRITISH FORMULA 3 CHAMPIONSHIP RACE, Oulton Park Circuit, Great Britain, 21 June. Lucas British Formula 3 Championship, round 10. 25 laps of the 2·356-mile/3·792-km circuit, 58·90 miles/94·80 km.
1 Martin Donnelly, GB (Ralt RT30/86-VW), 32m 28·20s, 108·83 mph/175·14 km/h (1st class A).
2 Andy Wallace, GB (Reynard 863-VW), 32m 28·73s.
3 Maurizio Sandro Sala, BR (Ralt RT30/86-VW), 25 laps.
4 Damon Hill, GB (Ralt RT30/86-VW), 25.
5 David Hunt, GB (Ralt RT30/86-VW), 25.
6 Ross Hockenhull, GB (Ralt RT30/86-VW), 25.
7 Paul Radisich, NZ (Ralt RT30/86-VW), 25; **8** Dave Simpson, USA (Reynard 863-VW), 25; **9** Steve Kempton, GB (Ralt RT30/85-VW), 25 (1st class B); **10** Alastair Lyall, GB (Ralt RT30/85-VW), 25.
Fastest lap: Wallace, 1m 16·88s, 110·32 mph/177·54 km/h.
British Championship points. Class A: 1 Wallace, 61; **2** Sandro Sala, 59; **3** Donnelly, 26; **4** van Kouwen, 24; **5** Davies and Fine, 15. **Class B: 1** Kempton, 46; **2** Walker, 45; **3** Dunn, 37.

LUCAS BRITISH FORMULA 3 CHAMPIONSHIP RACE, Circuit van Zandvoort, Holland, 29 June. Lucas British Formula 3 Championship, round 11. 19 laps of the 2·642-mile/4·252-km circuit, 50·20 miles/80·79 km.
1 Andy Wallace, GB (Reynard 863-VW), 30m 22·68s, 99·14 mph/159·55 km/h (1st class A).
2 Maurizio Sandro Sala, BR (Ralt RT30/86-VW), 30m 25·64s.
3 Julian Bailey, GB (Ralt RT30/86-VW), 19 laps.
4 Martin Donnelly, GB (Ralt RT30/86-VW), 19.
5 Damon Hill, GB (Ralt RT30/86-VW), 19.
6 Ross Hockenhull, GB (Ralt RT30/86-VW), 19.
7 Tim Davies, GB (Ralt RT30/86-VW), 19; **8** Dave Simpson, USA (Reynard 863-VW), 19; **9** Perry McCarthy, GB (Reynard 863-VW), 19; **10** Graham de Zille, GB (Ralt RT30/86-VW), 19.
Fastest lap: Sandro Sala, 1m 34·35s, 100·80 mph/162·22 km/h.
Class B winner: Steve Kempton, GB (Ralt RT30/85-VW), 19.
British Championship points. Class A: 1 Wallace, 70; **2** Sandro Sala, 66; **3** Donnelly, 29; **4** van Kouwen, 24; **5** Davies and Fine, 15. **Class B: 1** Kempton, 55; **2** Walker, 49; **3** Dunn, 37.

CELLNET TROPHY, Brands Hatch Grand Prix Circuit, Great Britain, 13 July. 20 laps of the 2·6136-mile/4·2060-km circuit, 52·27 miles/84·12 km.
1 Andy Wallace, GB (Reynard 863-VW), 28m 38·72s, 109·48 mph/176·19 km/h (1st class A).
2 Gary Brabham, AUS (Ralt RT30/86-VW), 28m 41·58s.
3 Tim Davies, GB (Ralt RT30/86-VW), 20 laps.
4 Julian Bailey, GB (Ralt RT30/86-VW), 20.
5 David Hunt, GB (Ralt RT30/86-VW), 20.
6 Maurizio Sandro Sala, BR (Ralt RT30/86-VW), 20.
7 Ross Hockenhull, GB (Ralt RT30/86-VW), 20; **8** Ross Cheever, USA (Ralt RT30/86-VW), 20; **9** Cor Euser, NL (Ralt RT30/86-VW), 20; **10** Paul Radisich, NZ (Ralt RT30/86-VW), 20.
Fastest lap: Wallace, 1m 24·91s, 110·81 mph/178·33 km/h.
Class B winner: Ian Khan, GB (Ralt RT30/85-VW), 20.

LUCAS BRITISH FORMULA 3 CHAMPIONSHIP RACE, Donington Park Circuit, Great Britain, 20 July. Lucas British Formula 3 Championship, round 12. 25 laps of the 2·500-mile/4·023-km circuit, 62·50 miles/100·58 km.
* Dave Simpson, USA (Reynard 863-VW), 40m 45·15s, 92·01 mph/148·08 km/h (1st class A).
1 Martin Donnelly, GB (Ralt RT30/86-VW), 40m 47·09s.
2 Andy Wallace, GB (Reynard 863-VW), 25 laps.
3 Tim Davies, GB (Ralt RT30/86-VW), 25.
4 Johnny Herbert, GB (Ralt RT30/86-VW), 25.
5 Maurizio Sandro Sala, BR (Ralt RT30/86-VW), 25.
6 David Hunt, GB (Ralt RT30/86-VW), 25; **7** Perry McCarthy, GB (Reynard 863-VW), 25; **8** Julian Bailey, GB (Ralt RT30/86-VW), 25; **9** Ross Hockenhull, GB (Ralt RT30/86-VW), 25; **10** Gerrit van Kouwen, NL (Ralt RT30/86-VW), 25.
Fastest lap: Simpson, 1m 36·82s, 92·95 mph/149·59 km/h (record).
* Disqualified.
Class B winner: Sean Walker, GB (Ralt RT30/85-VW), 25.
British Championship points. Class A: 1 Wallace, 76; **2** Sandro Sala, 69; **3** Donnelly, 38; **4** van Kouwen, 24; **5** Davies, 19; **6** Fine, 15. **Class B: 1** Walker, 58; **2** Kempton, 55; **3** Dunn, 44.

CELLNET SUPERPRIX, Brands Hatch Grand Prix Circuit, Great Britain, 3 August. 30 laps of the 2·6136-mile/4·2060-km circuit, 78·41 miles/126·18 km.
1 Andy Wallace, GB (Reynard 863-VW) 50m 51·93s, 92·48 mph/148·83 km/h (1st class A).
2 Martin Donnelly, GB (Ralt RT30/86-VW), 51m 34·92s.
3 Johnny Herbert, GB (Ralt RT30/86-VW), 30 laps.
4 Perry McCarthy, GB (Reynard 863-VW), 30.
5 Gary Brabham, AUS (Ralt RT30/86-VW), 30.
6 Tim Davies, GB (Ralt RT30/86-VW), 30.
7 Dave Simpson, USA (Reynard 863-VW), 30; **8** Ross Hockenhull, GB (Ralt RT30/86-VW), 30; **9** Keith Fine, GB (Ralt RT30/86-Toyota), 30; **10** Joachim Lindström, S (Ralt RT30/86-VW), 30.
Fastest lap: Brabham, 1m 36·64s, 95·38 mph/153·50 km/h.
Class B winner: Steve Kempton, GB (Ralt RT30/85-VW), 29.

LUCAS BRITISH FORMULA 3 CHAMPIONSHIP RACE, Snetterton Circuit, Great Britain, 10 August. Lucas British Formula 3 Championship, round 13. 25 laps of the 1·917-mile/3·085-km circuit, 47·93 miles/77·13 km.
1 Maurizio Sandro Sala, BR (Ralt RT30/86-VW), 26m 18·53s, 109·29 mph/175·88 km/h (1st class A).
2 Damon Hill, GB (Ralt RT30/86-VW), 26m 20·77s.
3 Paul Radisich, NZ (Ralt RT30/86-VW), 25 laps.
4 David Hunt, GB (Ralt RT30/86-VW), 25.
5 Perry McCarthy, GB (Reynard 863-VW), 25.
6 Tim Davies, GB (Ralt RT30/86-VW), 25.
7 Martin Donnelly, GB (Ralt RT30/86-VW), 25; **8** Dave Simpson, USA (Reynard 863-VW), 25; **9** Ross Hockenhull, GB (Ralt RT30/86-VW), 25; **10** Paul Jackson, GB (Ralt RT30/86-VW), 25.
Fastest lap: Sandro Sala, 1m 02·43s, 110·54 mph/177·90 km/h.
Class B winner: Gary Ward, GB (Ralt RT30/85-VW), 25.
British Championship points. Class A: 1 Sandro Sala, 79; **2** Wallace, 76; **3** Donnelly, 38; **4** van Kouwen, 24; **5** Davies, 20; **6** Fine, 15. **Class B: 1** Walker, 58; **2** Kempton, 56; **3** Dunn, 48.

LUCAS BRITISH FORMULA 3 CHAMPIONSHIP RACE, Silverstone Short Circuit, Great Britain, 25 August. Lucas British Formula 3 Championship, round 14. 24 laps of the 1·608-mile/2·588-km circuit, 38·59 miles/62·11 km.
1 Martin Donnelly, GB (Ralt RT30/86-VW), 24m 41·76s, 93·76 mph/150·89 km/h (1st class A).
2 Andy Wallace, GB (Reynard 863-VW), 24m 46·49s.
3 Julian Bailey, GB (Ralt RT30/86-VW), 24 laps.
4 Johnny Herbert, GB (Ralt RT30/86-VW), 24.
5 Gary Brabham, AUS (Ralt RT30/86-VW), 24.
6 Ross Hockenhull, GB (Ralt RT30/86-VW), 24.
7 Peter Hardman, GB (Reynard 863-VW) 24; **8** Paul Radisich, NZ (Ralt RT30/86-VW), 24; **9** David Hunt, GB (Ralt RT30/86-VW), 23; **10** Andrew King, GB (Reynard 853-VW), 23 (1st class B).
Fastest lap: Wallace, 59·75s, 96·88 mph/155·91 km/h.
British Championship points. Class A: 1 Wallace, 83; **2** Sandro Sala, 79; **3** Donnelly, 47; **4** van Kouwen, 24; **5** Davies, 20; **6** Fine and Brabham, 15. **Class B: 1** Kempton, 60; **2** Walker, 58; **3** Dunn, 48.

LUCAS BRITISH FORMULA 3 CHAMPIONSHIP RACE, Brands Hatch Indy Circuit, Great Britain, 31 August. Lucas British Formula 3 Championship, round 15. 30 laps of the 1·2036-mile/1·9370-km circuit, 36·11 miles/58·11 km.
1 Andy Wallace, GB (Reynard 863-VW) 22m 02·26s, 98·30 mph/158·20 km/h (1st class A).
2 Martin Donnelly, GB (Ralt RT30/86-VW), 22m 05·86s.
3 Mark Galvin, IRL (Ralt RT30/86-VW), 30 laps.
4 Gary Brabham, AUS (Ralt RT30/86-VW), 30.
5 Julian Bailey, GB (Ralt RT30/86-VW), 30.
6 Damon Hill, GB (Ralt RT30/86-VW), 30.
7 Peter Hardman, GB (Reynard 863-VW) 30; **8** David Hunt, GB (Ralt RT30/86-VW), 30; **9** Tim Davies, GB (Ralt RT30/86-VW), 30; **10** Ross Hockenhull, GB (Ralt RT30/86-VW), 30.
Fastest lap: Brabham, 49·55s, 99·49 mph/160·11 km/h (record).
Class B winner: Steve Kempton, GB (Ralt RT30/85-VW), 30.
British Championship points. Class A: 1 Wallace, 92; **2** Sandro Sala, 79; **3** Donnelly, 53; **4** van Kouwen, 24; **5** Davies, 20; **6** Brabham, 19. **Class B: 1** Kempton, 70; **2** Walker, 64; **3** Dunn, 52.

LUCAS BRITISH FORMULA 3 CHAMPIONSHIP RACE, Spa-Francorchamps Circuit, Belgium, 13 September. Lucas British Formula 3 Championship, round 16. 15 laps of the 4·3179-mile/6·9490-km circuit, 64·77 miles/104·24 km.
1 Andy Wallace, GB (Reynard 863-VW) 37m 45·20s, 102·94 mph/165·67 km/h (1st class A).
2 Perry McCarthy, GB (Reynard 863-VW), 38m 08·54s.
3 Julian Bailey, GB (Ralt RT30/86-VW), 15 laps.
4 Neto Jochamowitz, PE (Reynard 863-VW), 15.
5 Ross Hockenhull, GB (Ralt RT30/86-VW), 15.
6 Thomas Danielsson, S (Reynard 863-VW), 15.
7 Tim Davies, GB (Ralt RT30/86-VW), 15; **8** Johnny Herbert, GB (Ralt RT30/86-VW), 15; **9** Harald Huysman, N (Ralt RT30/86-VW), 15; **10** Paul Belmondo, F (Reynard 863-Alfa Romeo), 15.
Fastest lap: Danielsson, 2m 28·51s, 104·67 mph/168·45 km/h.
Class B winner: Steve Kempton, GB (Ralt RT30/85-VW), 15.
British Championship points. Class A: 1 Wallace, 101; **2** Sandro Sala, 79; **3** Donnelly, 53; **4** van Kouwen, 24; **5** Davies, 20; **6** Brabham, 19. **Class B: 1** Kempton, 80; **2** Walker, 67; **3** Dunn, 53.

LUCAS BRITISH FORMULA 3 CHAMPIONSHIP RACE, Omloop van Zolder, Belgium, 28 September. Lucas British Formula 3 Championship, round 17. 20 laps of the 2·621-mile/4·248-km circuit, 52·42 miles/84·96 km.
1 Andy Wallace, GB (Reynard 863-VW), 33m 22·52s, 94·24 mph/151·66 km/h (1st class A).
2 Martin Donnelly, GB (Ralt RT30/86-VW), 33m 24·88s.
3 Julian Bailey, GB (Ralt RT30/86-VW), 20 laps.
4 Thomas Danielsson, S (Reynard 863-VW), 20.
5 Perry McCarthy, GB (Reynard 863-VW), 20.
6 Eric van de Poele, B (Ralt RT30/86-VW), 20.
7 Maurizio Sandro Sala, BR (Reynard 863-VW), 20; **8** Harald Huysman, N (Ralt RT30/86-VW), 20; **9** Neto Jochamowitz, PE (Reynard 863-VW), 20; **10** Johnny Herbert, GB (Ralt RT30/86-VW), 20.
Fastest lap: Wallace, 1m 37·96s, 96·33 mph/155·03 km/h.
Class B winner: Steve Kempton, GB (Ralt RT30/85-VW), 20.
British Championship points. Class A: 1 Wallace, 111; **2** Sandro Sala, 79; **3** Donnelly, 59; **4** van Kouwen, 24; **5** Bailey, 21; **6** Davies, 20. **Class B: 1** Kempton, 89; **2** Walker, 73; **3** Dunn, 53.

LUCAS BRITISH FORMULA 3 CHAMPIONSHIP RACE, Silverstone Grand Prix Circuit, Great Britain, 5 October. Lucas British Formula 3 Championship, round 18. 20 laps of the 2·932-mile/4·719-km circuit, 58·64 miles/94·38 km.
1 Andy Wallace, GB (Reynard 863-VW), 29m 08·28s, 120·74 mph/194·31 km/h (1st class A).
2 Thomas Danielsson, S (Reynard 863-VW), 29m 25·70s.
3 Maurizio Sandro Sala, BR (Reynard 863-VW), 20 laps.
4 Gary Brabham, AUS (Ralt RT30/86-VW), 20.
5 Johnny Herbert, GB (Ralt RT30/86-VW), 20.
6 David Hunt, GB (Ralt RT30/86-Toyota), 20.
7 Ross Hockenhull, GB (Ralt RT30/86-VW), 20; **8** Martin Donnelly, GB (Ralt RT30/86-VW), 20; **9** Tim Davies, GB (Reynard 863-VW), 20; **10** Peter Hardman, GB (Ralt RT30/86-VW), 20.
Fastest lap: Wallace, 1m 25·75s, 123·09 mph/198·09 km/h (record).
Class B winner: Paul Stott, GB (Ralt RT30/85-VW), 20.

Final Lucas British Formula 3 Championship points

Class A

1	Andy Wallace, GB	121
2	Maurizio Sandro Sala, BR	83
3	Martin Donnelly, GB	59
4	Gerrit van Kouwen, NL	24
5	Gary Brabham, AUS	22
6	Julian Bailey, GB	21

7 Tim Davies, GB, 20; **8** David Hunt, GB, 16; **9** Keith Fine, GB and Damon Hill, GB, 15; **11** Dave Scott, GB, 12; **12** Mark Galvin, IRL, Perry McCarthy, GB and Thomas Danielsson, S, 11; **15** Johnny Herbert, GB 8.

Class B

1	Steve Kempton, GB	90
2	Sean Walker, GB	76
3	Gary Dunn, GB	57
4=	Paul Stott, GB	51
4=	Gary Ward, GB	51
6	Alastair Lyall, GB	43

7 Ian Khan, GB, 19; **8** Andy King, GB, 18; **9** Steve Pettitt, GB, 13; **10** Adrian Willmott, 10.

FIA FORMULA 3 NATIONS CUP, Autodromo Dino Ferrari, Imola, Italy, 26 October. 20 laps of the 3·132-mile/5·040-km circuit, 62·64 miles/100·80 km.
1 Stefano Modena, I (Reynard 863-Alfa Romeo), 43m 54·33s, 85·60 mph/137·76 km/h.
2 Alex Caffi, I (Dallara 386-Alfa Romeo), 44m 53·45s.
3 Nicola Larini, I (Dallara 386-Alfa Romeo), 20 laps.
4 Maurizio Sandro Sala, BR (Ralt RT30/86-VW), 20.
5 Neto Jochamowitz, PE (Reynard 863-VW), 20.
6 Michel Trollé, F (Martini MK49-VW), 20.
7 Massimo Monti, I (Ralt RT30/86-VW), 19; **8** Hakan Olausson, S (Ralt RT30/86-VW), 19; **9** Eugenio Visco, I (Dallara 386-Alfa Romeo), 19; **10** Jean Alesi, F (Dallara 386-Alfa Romeo), 19.
Fastest lap: Bernd Schneider, D (Reynard 863-VW), 2m 09·53s, 87·05 mph/140·09 km/h.

World Endurance Championship 1985 Results

The final round of the 1985 World Endurance Championship for Drivers was run after *Autocourse 1985/86* went to press.

SELANGOR 800, Shah Alam Circuit, Malaysia, 1 December. World Endurance Championship for Drivers, round 10. 217 laps of the 2·295-mile/3·693-km circuit, 498·02 miles/801·38 km.
1 Jochen Mass/Jacky Ickx, D/B (2.6 t/c Porsche 962C), 5h 32m 03·34s, 90·18 mph/145·13 km/h (1st Group C).
2 Mike Thackwell/John Nielsen/Jan Lammers, NZ/DK/NL (6.0 Jaguar XJR-6), 5h 33m 25·73s.
3 Vern Schuppan/James Weaver, AUS/GB (2.6 t/c Porsche 956), 208 laps.
4 Franz Konrad/Andrew Miedecke, D/AUS (2.6 t/c Porsche 956), 205.
5 Oscar Larrauri/Massimo Sigala/Frank Jelinski, RA/I/D (2.6 t/c Porsche 956), 195.
6 Richard Piper/Ian Harrower/Evan Clements, GB/GB/GB (3.3 Gebhardt 843-Cosworth DFL), 191 (1st Group C2).
7 Pasquale Barberio/Jean-Pierre Frey/John Nicholson, I/CH/NZ (3.3 Alba AR3-Cosworth DFL), 189; **8** Christian Danner/Costas Los, D/GR (2.6 t/c March 84G-Porsche), 187; **9** David Palmer/Michael Hall, GB/AUS (1.7 t/c Tiga GC285-Ford), 182; **10** Max Payne/David Andrews, GB/GB (2.0 Ceekar 83J-Ford), 175.
Fastest lap: Mass, 1m 24·52s, 97·76 mph/157·33 km/h.

Final Drivers' Championship points

Group C

1=	Derek Bell, GB	117
1=	Hans Stuck, D	117
3=	Jacky Ickx, B	101
3=	Jochen Mass, D	101
5=	Klaus Ludwig, D	58
5=	Bob Wollek, F	58

7 Paolo Barilla, I, 52; **8** Alessandro Nannini, I, 50; **9=** Manfred Winkelhock, D and Marc Surer, CH, 45; **11** Mike Thackwell, NZ, 41; **12** Jonathan Palmer, GB, 39; **13** Mauro Baldi, I; 36; **14** Riccardo Patrese, I, 34; **15** Jan Lammers, NL, 31; **16=** Gordon Spice, GB and Ray Bellm, GB, 30; **18** Oscar Larrauri, RA, 29; **19** James Weaver, GB, 27; **20=** Vern Schuppan, AUS and Massimo Sigala, I, 23.

Group C2

1=	Gordon Spice, GB	130
1=	Ray Bellm, GB	130
3	Ray Mallock, GB	75
4	Mike Wilds, GB	65
5	Max Payne, GB	62
6	David Andrews, GB	54

FIA Sports-Prototype World Championship 1986 Results

KOUROS CUP/TROFEO FILIPPO CARACCIOLA, Autodromo Nazionale di Monza, Italy, 20 April. FIA Sports-Prototype World Championship for Drivers, round 1. 63 laps of the 3·604-mile/5·800-km circuit, 227·05 miles/365·40 km.
1 Hans Stuck/Derek Bell, D/GB (3.0 t/c Porsche 962C), 1h 48m 40·29s, 125·36 mph/201·75 km/h (1st Group C).
2 Andrea de Cesaris/Alessandro Nannini, I/I (3.0 t/c Lancia LC2-86), 1h 49m 29·39s.
3 Massimo Sigala/Walter Brun, I/CH (2.6 t/c Porsche 956), 61 laps.
4 Oscar Larrauri/Jesus Pareja-Mayo, RA/E (2.6 t/c Porsche 962C), 61.
5 Drake Olson/Thierry Boutsen, USA/B (2.6 t/c Porsche 962C), 61.
6 Jochen Mass/Bob Wollek, D/F (3.0 t/c Porsche 962C), 61.
7 Fulvio Ballabio/Richard Hamann, I/D (2.6 t/c Porsche 956), 61; **8** Jo Gartner/Klaus Niedzwiedz, A/D (2.6 t/c Porsche 962C), 60; **9** John Nielsen/Henri Pescarolo, DK/F (5.6 t/c Sauber C8-Mercedes-Benz), 60; **10** Emilio de Villota/Fermin Velez, E/E (2.6 t/c Porsche 956B), 59.
Fastest lap: Nannini, 1m 36·96s, 133·80 mph/215·33 km/h.
Other class winners. Group C2: Frank Jelinski/Stanley Dickens, D/S (3.3 Gebhardt 853-Cosworth DFL), 57. **GTX:** Victor Coggiola/Tony Palma, I/I (2.8 t/c Porsche 935), 52.
Championship points: drivers. Group C: 1 Stuck and Bell, 20; **3** Nannini and de Cesaris, 15; **5** Sigala and Brun, 12. **Group C2: 1** Jelinski and Dickens, 20; **3** Spice and Bellm, 15; **5** Schanche and Dyrstad, 12.

KOUROS 1000, Silverstone Grand Prix Circuit, Great Britain, 5 May. FIA Sports-Prototype World Championship for Teams, round 1. FIA Sports-Prototype World Championship for Drivers, round 2. 212 laps of the 2·932-mile/4·719-km circuit, 621·58 miles/1000·43 km.
1 Derek Warwick/Eddie Cheever, GB/USA (6.0 Jaguar XJR-6), 4h 48m 55·37s, 129·08 mph/207·73 km/h (1st Group C).
2 Derek Bell/Hans Stuck, GB/D (2.6 t/c Porsche 962C), 210 laps.
3 Jo Gartner/Tiff Needell, A/GB (2.6 t/c Porsche 962C), 207.
4 James Weaver/Klaus Niedzwiedz GB/D (2.6 t/c Porsche 956 GTI), 206.
5 Emilio de Villota/Fermin Velez, E/E (2.6 t/c Porsche 956B), 206.
6 George Follmer/John Morton/Paolo Barilla, USA/USA/I (2.6 t/c Porsche 956B), 205.
7 Jean-Louis Schlesser/Gianfranco Brancatelli, F/I (6.0 Jaguar XJR-6), 204; **8** Mike Thackwell/John Nielsen/Henri Pescarolo, NZ/DK/F (5.6 t/c Sauber C8-Mercedes-Benz), 203; **9** Walter Brun/Frank Jelinski, CH/D (2.6 t/c Porsche 956), 203; **10** Oscar Larrauri/Jesus Pareja-Mayo, RA/E (2.6 t/c Porsche 962C), 203.
Fastest lap: Andrea de Cesaris, I (3.0 t/c Lancia LC2-86), 1m 13·95s, 142·73 mph/229·70 km/h (record).
Other class winners. Group C2: Gordon Spice/Ray Bellm, GB/GB (3.3 Spice SC86C-Cosworth DFL), 192. **GTP:** Yoshimi Katayama/Yojiro Terada, J/J (1.3 Mazda 757), 194.

Championship points: drivers. Group C: 1 Bell and Stuck, 35; **3** Warwick and Cheever, 20; **5** Nannini, de Cesaris and Gartner, 15. **Group C2: 1** Spice and Bellm, 35; **3** Barberio, 25; **4** Jelinski and Dickens, 20; **6** Gellini and Nicholson, 15.
Teams. Group C: 1 Silk Cut Jaguar, 20; **2** Rothmans Porsche, 15; **3** Kremer Porsche Racing, 12; **4** Liqui Moly Equipe, 10; **5** Danone Porsche España, 8; **6** Joest Racing, 6. **Group C2: 1** Spice Engineering, 20; **2** Kelmer Racing, 15; **3** ADA, 12; **4** Jens Winther Denmark, 10; **5** ALD, 8.

Le Mans 24 Hours

54 GRAND PRIX D'ENDURANCE, LES 24 HEURES DU MANS, Circuit de la Sarthe, Le Mans, France, 31 May/1 June. FIA Sports-Prototype World Championship for Teams, round 2. FIA Sports-Prototype World Championship for Drivers, round 3. 367 laps of the 8·406-mile/13·528-km circuit, 3085·00 miles/4964·78 km.
1 Hans Stuck/Derek Bell/Al Holbert, D/GB/USA (2.6 t/c Porsche 962C), 367 laps, 128·744 mph/207·193 km/h (1st Group C).
2 Oscar Larrauri/Joel Gouhier/Jesus Pareja-Mayo, RA/F/E (2.6 t/c Porsche 962C), 359 laps.
3 George Follmer/John Morton/Kenper Miller, USA/USA/USA (2.6 t/c Porsche 956), 354.
4 Emilio de Villota/George Fouche/Fermin Velez, E/ZA/E (2.6 t/c Porsche 956), 348.
5 Jürgen Lässig/Fulvio Ballabio/Dudley Wood, D/I/GB (2.6 t/c Porsche 956), 344.
6 Siggi Brun/Ernst Schuster/Rudi Seher, D/D/D (2.8 t/c Porsche 936CJ), 343.
7 René Metge/Claude Ballot-Lena, F/F (2.6 t/c Porsche 961), 320 (1st GTX class); **8** Evan Clements/Ian Harrower/Tom Dodd-Noble, GB/GB/GB (3.3 Gebhardt 843-Cosworth DFL), 317 (1st Group C2); **9** Mauro Baldi/Price Cobb/Rob Dyson, I/USA/USA (2.6 t/c Porsche 956B), 317; **10** Philippe Alliot/Michel Trollé/Paco Romero, F/F/E (2.6 t/c Porsche 956/962), 311; **11** David Mercer/Jens Winther/Lars Viggo GB/DK/DK (3.5 URD C82-BMW), 309; **12** Claude Haldi/Roger Dorchy/Pascal Pessiot, CH/F/F (2.8 t/c WM P84-Peugeot), 300; **13** Marc Menant/Jean-Philippe Grand/Jacques Goudchaux, F/F/F (3.3 Rondeau 482-Cosworth DFL), 298; **14** Lionel Robert/Richard Cleare/Jack Newsum, F/GB/USA (2.8 t/c March 85G-Porsche), 298 (1st GTP Class); **15** Les Delano/Andy Petery/John Hotchkiss, USA/USA/USA (3.3 Ecosse C285-Cosworth DFL), 292; **16** James Weaver/Masahiro Hasemi/Takao Wada, GB/J/J (3.0 t/c March 85G-Nissan), 284; **17** Noel del Bello/Bruno Soty/Lucien Rossiaud, F/F/F (3.0 Rondeau 379-Cosworth DFV), 277; **18** Pierre-Henri Raphanel/Alain de Cadanet/Yves Courage, F/GB/F (2.6 t/c Cougar C12-Porsche), 266; **19** Ray Bellm/Gordon Spice/Jean-Michel Martin, GB/GB/B (3.3 Spice SC86C-Cosworth DFL), 257.
Running not classified: Pascal Wittmeur/Jean-Paul Libert/Michael Krankenbrug, B/B/D (3.5 BMW M1), 264; Nick Adams/Robin Donovan/Richard Jones, GB/GB/GB (3.3 Bardon DB1-Cosworth DFL), 210; Dominique Lecaud/Yvon Tapy/Roland Bassaier, F/F/F (3.5 Sauber C6-BMW), 200.
Retired: Eje Elgh/Beppe Gabbiani/Toshio Suzuki, S/I/J (2.1 t/c Dome 86C-Toyota), 295, turbo fire; Derek Warwick/Eddie Cheever/Jean-Louis Schlesser, GB/USA/F (6.0 Jaguar XJR-6), 239, body damage; Klaus Ludwig/Paolo Barilla/'Johnny Winter', D/I/D (2.6 t/c Porsche 956), 196, engine; David Leslie/Ray Mallock/Mike Wilds, GB/GB/GB (3.0 Ecosse C286-Rover), 181, overheating; Bob Wollek/Jochen Mass/Vern Schuppan, F/D/AUS (2.6 t/c Porsche 962C), 180, accident; Jo Gartner/Sarel van der Merwe/Kunimitsu Takahashi, A/ZA/J (2.6 t/c Porsche 962C), 169, accident; Costas Los/Neil Crang/Raymond Touroul, GR/AUS/F (2.6 t/c March 84G-Porsche), 169, electrics; Hubert Striebig/Pierre Yver/Max Cohen-Olivar, F/F/MOR (2.6 t/c Porsche 956), 160, withdrawn; Gianfranco Brancatelli/Win Percy/Armin Hahne, I/GB/D (6.0 Jaguar XJR-6), 154, driveshaft; David Kennedy/Mark Galvin/Pierre Dieudonné, IRL/IRL/B (1.3 Mazda 757), 137, transmission; François Migault/Jean-Daniel Raulet/Marcel Pignard, F/F/F (2.8 t/c WM P82-Peugeot), 132, engine; Nick Nicholson/Thorkild Thyrring/John Sheldon, USA/DK/GB (1.7 t/c Tiga GC285-Ford), 125, engine; Jean-Claude Justice/Patrick Oudet, F/F (3.3 Rondeau 382-Cosworth DFL), 110, oil pressure; Geoff Lees/Satoru Nakajima/Masanori Sekiya, GB/J/J (2.1 t/c Dome 86C-Toyota), 105, engine; Mike Allison/Val Musetti/Tom Frank, USA/GB/USA (1.7 t/c Tiga GC286-Ford), 95, electrics; Thierry Boutsen/Alain Ferté/Didier Theys, B/F/B (2.6 t/c Porsche 962C), 89, accident; Henri Pescarolo/Christian Danner/Dieter Quester, F/D/A (5.0 t/c Sauber C8-Mercedes-Benz), 86, transmission; Massimo Sigala/Walter Brun/Frank Jelinski, I/CH/D (2.6 t/c Porsche 962C), 75, engine; Luigi Taverna/Tony Palma/Marco Vanoli, I/I/CH (3.3 Alba AR3-Cosworth DFL), 74, driveshaft; Stanley Dickens/Pierre de Thoisy/Jean-François Yvon, S/F/F (3.3 Gebhardt 853-Cosworth DFL), 68, accident; Kazuyoshi Hoshino/Keiji Matsumoto/Aguri Suzuki, J/J/J (3.0 t/c March 86S-Nissan), 64, engine; John Nielsen/Mike Thackwell, DK/NZ (5.0 t/c Sauber C8-Mercedes-Benz), 61, engine; Takashi Yorino/Yojiro Katayama/Yojiro Terada, J/J/J (1.3 Mazda 757), 59, transmission; Hans Heyer/Brian Redman/Hurley Haywood, D/GB/USA (6.0 Jaguar XJR-6), 53, fuel pressure; Vern Schuppan/Drake Olson, AUS/USA (2.6 t/c Porsche 962C), 41, transmission; Jacques Heuclin/Louis Descartes, F/F (3.3 ALD 02-BMW), 41, accident; David Andrews/Mike Hall/Duncan Bain, GB/AUS/GB (1.7 t/c Tiga GC286-Ford), 1, driveshaft; Martin Birrane/Martin Schanche/Torgye Kleppe, IRL/N/N (1.8 t/c Argo JM19-Zakspeed), 1, engine.
Fastest lap: Ludwig/Barilla/Winter, 3m 23·30s, 148·825 mph/239·551 km/h.
Championship points: drivers. Group C: 1 Bell and Stuck, 55; **3** Laurrari and Pareja-Mayo, 26; **5** Cheever, Warwick and Holbert, 20. **Group C2; 1** Bellm and Spice, 41; **3** Clements and Harrower, 32; **5** Mercer, Winther and Barberio, 25.
Teams. Group C: 1 Rothmans Porsche, 35; **2** Silk Cut Jaguar, 20; **3** Joest Racing and Danone Porsche España 18; **5** Brun Motorsport, 17; **6** Kremer Porsche Racing and Liqui Moly Equipe, 12. **Group C2: 1** ADA, 32; **2** Spice Engineering, 26; **3** Jens Winther Denmark, 25; **4** Kelmer Racing, 15; **5** Secateva, 12; **6** Ecurie Ecosse, 10.

200 MEILEN VON NÜRNBERG, Norisring, German Federal Republic, 29 June. FIA Sports-Prototype World Championship for Drivers, round 4. 79 laps of the 1·429-mile/2·300-km circuit, 112·89 miles/181·70 km.
1 Klaus Ludwig, D (2·8 t/c Porsche 962), 1h 07m 00·36s, 101·09 mph/162·69 km/h (1st Group C).
2 Eddie Cheever, USA (6·0 Jaguar XJR-6), 1h 07m 08·03s.
3 Derek Warwick, GB (6·0 Jaguar XJR-6), 79 laps.
4 Frank Jelinski, D (2·8 t/c Porsche 962), 78.
5 James Weaver, GB (2·8 t/c Porsche 962), 78.
6 Walter Brun, CH (2·8 t/c Porsche 962), 78.
7 Jürgen Lässig, D (2·6 t/c Porsche 956), 77; **8** 'Johnny Winter', D (2·8 t/c Porsche 956), 76; **9** Danny Ongais, USA (2·8 t/c Porsche 962), 76 (1st GTP class); **10** Thierry Boutsen, B (2·8 t/c Porsche 956), 76.
Fastest lap: Hans Stuck, D (3·0 t/c Porsche 962), 48·28s, 106·55 mph/171·48 km/h (record).
Other class winners. Group C2: Stanley Dickens, S (3·3 Gebhardt 853-Cosworth DFL), 73.
Championship points: Drivers. Group C: 1 Stuck and Bell, 55; **3** Cheever, 35; **4** Warwick, 32; **5** Larrauri and Pareja-Mayo, 26. **Group C2: 1** Spice and Bellm, 41; **3** Dickens, 40; **4** Clements and Harrower, 32; **6** Barberio, Mercer and Winther, 25.

SHELL GEMINI 1000, Brands Hatch Grand Prix Circuit, Great Britain, 20 July. FIA Sports-Prototype World Championship for Drivers, round 5. 236 laps of the 2·6136-mile/4·2060-km circuit, 616·81 miles/992·62 km.
1 Bob Wollek/Mauro Baldi, F/I (2·8 t/c Porsche 956 GTI), 5h 53m 44·43s, 104·62 mph/168·37 km/h (1st Group C).
2 Hans Stuck/Derek Bell/Klaus Ludwig, D/GB/D (2·8 t/c Porsche 956), 232 laps.
3 Thierry Boutsen/Frank Jelinski, B/D (2·8 t/c Porsche 956), 231.
4 Derek Warwick/Jean-Louis Schlesser, GB/F (6·0 Jaguar XJR-6), 231.
5 Paolo Barilla/'Johnny Winter'/Klaus Ludwig, I/D/D (2·8 t/c Porsche 956), 230.
6 Eddie Cheever/Gianfranco Brancatelli, USA/I (6·0 Jaguar XJR-6), 230.
7 Ray Mallock/David Leslie, GB/GB (3·0 Ecosse C286-Rover), 221 (1st Group C2); **8** Jürgen Lässig/Dudley Wood/Fulvio Ballabio, D/GB/I (2·6 t/c Porsche 956), 220; **9** Tiff Needell/Costas Los, GB/GR (2·6 t/c March 84G-Porsche), 219; **10** John Nicholson/Maurizio Gellini/Pasquale Barberio, NZ/I/I (3·3 Tiga GC85-Cosworth DFL), 209.
Fastest lap: Wollek, 1m 18·68s, 119·58 mph/192·44 km/h (record).
Championship points: Drivers. Group C: 1 Stuck and Bell, 70; **3** Warwick, 42; **4** Cheever, 41; **5** Larrauri, Wollek and Pareja-Mayo, 26. **Group C2: 1** Bellm and Spice, 53; **3** Dickens and Barberio, 40; **5** Mercer and Winther, 35.

TROFEO SILK CUT, Jerez, Spain, 3 August. FIA Sports-Prototype World Championship for Drivers, round 6. 86 laps of the 2·621-mile/4·218-km circuit, 225·41 miles/362·75 km.
1 Oscar Larrauri/Jesus Parejo-Mayo, RA/E (2·8 t/c Porsche 962), 2h 27m 47·34s, 91·51 mph/147·27 km/h (1st Group C).
2 Walter Brun/Frank Jelinski, CH/D (2·8 t/c Porsche 956), 2h 28m 23·24s.
3 Derek Warwick/Jan Lammers, GB/NL (6·0 Jaguar XJR-6), 84 laps.
4 Fulvio Ballabio/Dudley Wood/Jürgen Lässig, I/GB/D (2·6 t/c Porsche 956), 82.
5 Gordon Spice/Ray Bellm, GB/GB (3·3 Spice SF86-Cosworth DFL), 79 (1st Group C2).
6 Evan Clements/Ian Harrower, GB/GB (3·3 Gebhardt 843-Cosworth DFL), 78.
7 Pasquale Barberio/Maurizio Gellini, I/I (3·3 Tiga GC85-Cosworth DFL), 77; **8** Fermin Velez/Emilio de Villota, E/E (2·6 t/c Porsche 956), 76; **9** Tiff Needell/Costas Los, GB/GR (2·6 March 84G-Porsche), 69; **10** Max Cohen-Olivar/David Palmer, MOR/GB (1·7 t/c Tiga GC285-Ford) 64.
Fastest lap: Larrauri, 1m 38·09s, 96·19 mph/154·80 km/h (record).
Championship points: Drivers. Group C: 1 Bell and Stuck, 70; **3** Warwick, 54; **4** Larrauri and Pareja-Mayo, 46; **6** Cheever, 41. **Group C2: 1** Spice and Bellm, 73; **3** Barberio, 52; **4** Harrower and Clements, 47; **6** Gellini, 42.

ADAC KOUROS 1000 KMS, Nürburgring, German Federal Republic, 24 August. FIA Sports-Prototype World Championship for Teams, round 3. FIA Sports-Prototype World Championship for Drivers, round 7. 121 laps of the 2·822-mile/4·542-km circuit, 341·46 miles/549·58 km. (Race stopped after 22 laps due to heavy rain and accidents and restarted for 3 hours.)
1 Mike Thackwell/Henri Pescarolo, NZ/F (5·0 t/c Sauber C8-Mercedes Benz), 3h 42m 30·02s, 92·08 mph/148·19 km/h (1st Group C).
2 Mauro Baldi/Klaus Niedzwiedz, I/D (2·8 t/c Porsche 956 GTI), 119 laps.
3 Emilio de Villota/Fermin Velez, E/E (2·6 t/c Porsche 956), 119.
4 Jürgen Lässig/Fulvio Ballabio/Harald Grohs, D/I/D (2·6 t/c Porsche 956), 115.
5 Ray Mallock/Marc Duez, GB/B (3·0 Ecosse C286-Rover), 115 (1st Group C2).
6 Walter Lechner/Ernst Franzmeier A/A (3·3 Gebhardt 853-Cosworth DFL), 112.
7 Gordon Spice/Ray Bellm, GB/GB (3·3 Spice SF86-Cosworth DFL), 110; **8** Evan Clements/Ian Harrower, GB/GB (3·3 Gebhardt 843-Cosworth DFL), 107; **9** Jens Winther/Angelo Pallavicini, DK/CH (3·5 URD C82-BMW), 107; **10** Volker Weidler/Costas Los, D/GR (2·6 t/c March 84G-Porsche), 106.
Fastest lap: Baldi/Niedzwiedz, 1m 34·82s, 107·14 mph/172·42 km/h.
Championship points: Drivers. Group C: 1 Bell and Stuck, 70; **3** Warwick, 54; **4** Larrauri and Pareja-Mayo, 46; **6** Cheever, 41. **Group C2: 1** Spice and Bellm, 85; **3** Clements and Harrower, 57; **5** Barberio, 52; **6** Winther, 43.
Teams. Group C: 1 Rothmans Porsche, 35; **2** Danone Porsche España, 30; **3** Liqui Moly Equipe, 27; **4** Sauber Kouros, 23; **5** Silk Cut Jaguar, 20; **6** Joest Racing and Obermaier Racing, 18. **Group C2: 1** ADA, 42; **2** Spice Engineering, 38; **3** Jens Winther Denmark, 33; **4** Ecurie Ecosse, 30; **5** Kelmer Racing and Gebhardt Racing, 15.

KOUROS SPA 1000 KMS, Spa-Francorchamps Circuit, Belgium, 15 September. FIA Sports-Prototype World Championship for Teams, round 4. FIA Sports-Prototype World Championship for Drivers, round 8. 145 laps of the 4·3179-mile/6·9490-km circuit, 626·10 miles/1007·61 km.
1 Thierry Boutsen/Frank Jelinski, B/D (2·8 t/c Porsche 962C), 5h 35m 54·54s, 111·83 mph/179·97 km/h (1st Group C).
2 Derek Warwick/Jan Lammers, GB/NL (6·0 Jaguar XJR-6), 5h 35m 55·34s.
3 Derek Bell/Hans Stuck, GB/D (2·8 t/c Porsche 962C), 145 laps.
4 Paolo Barilla/Klaus Ludwig, I/D (2·8 t/c Porsche 956), 144.
5 Eddie Cheever/Jean-Louis Schlesser, USA/F (6·0 Jaguar XJR-6), 143.
6 Mike Thackwell/Henri Pescarolo, NZ/F (5·0 t/c Sauber C8-Mercedes-Benz), 140.
7 Jochen Mass/Bob Wollek, D/F (2·8 t/c Porsche 962C), 140; **8** 'Johnny Winter'/Vern Schuppan/Nils-Kristian Nissen, D/AUS/DK (2·8 t/c Porsche 956), 139; **9** Didier Theys/Massimo Sigala/Walter Brun, B/I/CH (2·8 t/c Porsche 956), 139; **10** Mauro Baldi/James Weaver, I/GB (2·8 t/c Porsche 956 GTI), 135.
Fastest lap: Cheever, 2m 09·38s, 120·15 mph/193·36 km/h (record).
Other class winners. Group C2: Ray Mallock/Marc Duez, GB/B (3·0 Ecosse 286-Rover), 133.
Championship points: Drivers. Group C: 1 Bell and Stuck, 82; **3** Warwick, 69; **4** Jelinski, 59; **5** Cheever, 49; **6** Larrauri and Pareja-Mayo, 46. **Group C2: 1** Spice and Bellm, 100; **3** Harrower and Clements, 69; **5** Mallock, 60; **6** Winther, 53.
Teams. Group C: 1 Rothmans Porsche, 47; **2** Brun Motorsport, 37; **3** Silk Cut Jaguar, 35; **4** Danone Porsche España, 30; **5** Sauber Kouros, 29; **6** Liqui Moly Equipe and Joest Racing, 28. **Group C2: 1** ADA, 54; **2** Spice Engineering, 53; **3** Ecurie Ecosse, 50; **4** Jeans Winther Denmark, 43; **5** Kelmer Racing and Gebhardt Racing, 15.

FUJI 1000 KMS, Fuji International Speedway, Japan, 6 October. FIA Sports-Prototype World Championship for Teams, round 5. FIA Sports-Prototype World Championship for Drivers, round 9. 226 laps of the 2·7404-mile/4·4102-km circuit, 619·33 miles/996·71 km.
1 Paolo Barilla/Piercarlo Ghinzani, I/I (2·8 t/c Porsche 956), 5h 29m 25·332s, 112·80 mph/181·53 km/h (1st Group C).
2 Frank Jelinski/Stanley Dickens, D/S (2·8 t/c Porsche 956), 225 laps.
3 Eddie Cheever/Derek Warwick, USA/GB (6·0 Jaguar XJR-6), 225.
4 Bruno Giacomelli/Volker Weidler, I/D (2·8 t/c Porsche 962), 224.
5 Nils-Kristian Nissen/Harald Grohs/'Johnny Winter', DK/D/D (2·8 t/c Porsche 956), 223.
6 Vern Schuppan/George Fouche/Kelichi Suzuki, AUS/ZA/J (2·8 t/c Porsche 956), 223.
7 Oscar Larrauri/Jesus Pareja-Mayo, RA/E (2·8 t/c Porsche 962), 222; **8** Kunimitsu Takahashi/Kenji Takahashi, J/J (2·8 t/c Porsche 962), 221; **9** Satoru Nakajima/Geoff Lees/Masanori Sekiya, J/GB/J (2·1 t/c Dome 86C-Toyota), 217; **10** Kazuyoshi Hoshino/Osamu Nakako, J/J (3·0 t/c March R86V-Nissan), 216.
Fastest lap: Not given.
Other class winners. Group C2: Ray Mallock/Marc Duez, GB/B (3·0 Ecosse 286-Rover), 210.

Final Championship points

Drivers:
Group C

1=	Derek Bell, GB	82
1=	Hans Stuck, D	82
3	Derek Warwick, GB	81
4	Frank Jelinski, D	74
5	Eddie Cheever, USA	61
6=	Oscar Larrauri, RA	50
6=	Jesus Pareja-Mayo, E	50

8 Paolo Barilla, I, 44; **9** Thierry Boutsen, B, 41; **10** Mauro Baldi, I, 38; **11** Walter Brun, CH, 37; **12**=Fulvio Ballabio, I and Jürgen Lässig, D, 35; **14**=Emilio de Villota, E and Fermin Velez, E, 34; **16** Henri Pescarolo, F, 31; **17** Klaus Ludwig, D, 30; **18** =Bob Wollek, F and Mike Thackwell, NZ, 29; **20** Klaus Niedzwiedz, D, 28.

Group C2

1=	Ray Bellm, GB	105
1=	Gordon Spice, GB	105
3	Ray Mallock, GB	80
4=	Ian Harrower, GB	79
4=	Evan Clements, GB	79
6	Marc Duez, B	60

Teams:
Group C

1	Brun Motorsport,	57
2	Joest Racing	48
3=	Rothmans Porsche	47
3=	Silk Cut Jaguar	47
5	Danone Porsche España	30
6	Sauber Kouros	29

Group C2

1	Ecurie Ecosse	70
2	Spice Engineering	68
3	ADA	64
4	Jens Winther Denmark	43
5=	Kelmer Racing	15
5=	Gebhardt Racing	15

FIA Touring Car Championship

500 KM DI MONZA, Autodromo Nazionale di Monza, Italy, 23 March. FIA Touring Car Championship, round 1. 87 laps of the 3·604-mile/5·800-km circuit, 313·55 miles/504·60 km.
1 Tom Walkinshaw/Win Percy, GB/GB (3.5 Rover Vitesse), 2h 59m 56·55s, 105·13 mph/169·19 km/h (1st over-2500 cc class).
2 Jeff Allam/Eddy Joosen, GB/B (3.5 Rover Vitesse), 2h 59m 13·36s.
3 Dieter Quester/Otto Rensing, A/D (3.5 BMW 635 CSi), 85 laps.
4 Markus Oestreich/Winni Vogt, D/D (2.5 BMW 325i), 84 (1st 1601 cc–2500 cc class).
5 Alain Cudini/Dany Snobeck, F/F (2.3 Mercedes-Benz 190E), 83.
6 Daniele Gasparri/Tony Palma/Giancarlo Naddeo, I/I/I (3.5 BMW 635 CSi), 82.
7 Rolf Göring/Claude Haldi, D/CH (3.5 BMW 635 CSi), 81; **8** Girolama Capra/Giovanni de Schio, I/I (3.5 BMW 635 CSi), 81; **9** Johnny Cecotto/Thomas Lindström, YV/S (2.0 t/c Volvo 240 Turbo), 80; **10** Johannes Wollstadt/Peter Hass, D/D (2.5 BMW 325i), 80.
Fastest lap: Allam/Joosen, 2m 00·17s, 107·96 mph/173·75 km/h.
Other class winners. Up to 1600 cc: Bruno Eichmann/Philippe Muller, CH/CH (1.6 Toyota Corolla), 79.
Championship points. Drivers: 1 Walkinshaw and Percy, 29; **3** Oestreich and Vogt, 23; **5** Allam and Joosen, 21. **Manufacturers: 1** Rover, BMW and Toyota, 20; **4** Mercedes-Benz and Audi, 15; **6** BMW and Alfa Romeo, 12.

DONINGTON 500, Donington Park Circuit, Great Britain, 6 April. FIA Touring Car Championship, round 2. 125 laps of the 2·500-mile/4·023-km circuit, 312·50 miles/502·88 km.
1 Tom Walkinshaw/Win Percy, GB/GB (3.5 Rover Vitesse), 4h 02m 42·09s, 77·06 mph/124·02 km/h (1st over-2500 cc class).
2 Gerhard Berger/Roberto Ravaglia, A/I (3.5 BMW 635 CSi), 4h 03m 51·17s.
3 Anders Olofsson/Ulf Granberg, S/S (2.0 t/c Volvo 240 turbo), 124 laps.
4 Jeff Allam/Gianfranco Brancatelli, GB/I (3.5 Rover Vitesse), 124.
5 Peter Brock/Allan Moffat, AUS/CDN (4.9 Holden Commodore), 124.
6 Markus Oestreich/Winni Vogt, D/D (2.5 BMW 325i), 124 (1st 1601 cc–2500 cc class).
7 Dany Snobeck/Alain Cudini, F/F (2.3 Mercedes-Benz 190E), 124; **8** Sigi Müller Jnr/Pierre Dieudonné, D/B (2.3 t/c Ford Sierra XR4Ti), 124; **9** Andy Rouse/David Sears, GB/GB (2.3 t/c Ford Sierra XR4Ti), 123; **10** Fabien Giroix/Michel Trollé, F/F (3.5 BMW 635 CSi), 123.
Fastest lap: Johnny Cecotto/Thomas Lindström, YV/S (2.0 t/c Volvo 240 Turbo), 1m 47·66s, 83·38 mph/134·19 km/h (record).
Other class winners. Up to 1600 cc: John Nielsen/Erik Hoyer/Kurt Thiim, DK/DK/DK (1.6 Toyota Corolla), 115.
Championship points. Drivers: 1 Walkinshaw and Percy, 58; **3** Oestreich and Vogt, 44; **5** Allam, 34; **6** Snobeck and Cudini, 32.
Manufacturers: 1 Rover, BMW and Toyota, 40; **4** Mercedes-Benz, 30; **5** BMW, 27; **6** Volvo, VW and Alfa Romeo, 18.

FIA TOURING CAR CHAMPIONSHIP RACE, Hockenheimring, German Federal Republic, 13 April. FIA Touring Car Championship, round 3. 74 laps of the 4·2234-mile/6·7970-km circuit, 312·53 miles/502·98 km.
1 Johnny Cecotto/Thomas Lindström, YV/S (2.0 t/c Volvo 240 Turbo), 3h 03m 33·17s, 102·74 mph/165·34 km/h (1st over-2500 cc class).
2 Dieter Quester/Roberto Ravaglia, A/I (3.5 BMW 635 CSi), 3h 05m 11.09s.
3 Klaus Niedzwiedz/Steve Soper, D/GB (2.3 t/c Ford Sierra XR4Ti), 73 laps.
4 Tom Walkinshaw/Win Percy, GB/GB (3.5 Rover Vitesse), 73.
5 Peter Brock/Allan Moffat, AUS/CDN (4.9 Holden Commodore), 73.
6 René Metge/Alain Guyaux, F/F (3.5 BMW 635 CSi), 72.
7 Dany Snobeck/Alain Cudini, F/F (2.3 Mercedes-Benz 190E), 72 (1st 1601 cc–2500 cc class); **8** Anna Cambiaghi/Georges Bosshard, I/CH (3.5 BMW 635 CSi), 71; **9** Tony Palma/Daniele Gasparri, I/I (3.5 BMW 635 CSi), 71; **10** Georg Pacher/Josef Gerold, A/A (2.3 t/c Ford Sierra XR4Ti), 71.
Fastest lap: Allan Grice, AUS (4.9 Holden Commodore), 2m 24·74s, 105·65 mph/170·63 km/h.
Other class winners. Up to 1600 cc: Philippe Muller/Bruno Eichmann, CH/CH (1.6 Toyota Corolla), 67.
Championship points. Drivers: 1 Walkinshaw and Percy, 71; **3** Cudini and Snobeck, 52; **5** Oestreich and Vogt, 44.
Manufacturers: 1 Toyota, 60; **2** BMW, 52; **3** Rover and Mercedes-Benz, 50; **5** BMW, 42; **4** Volvo, 38.

FIA TOURING CAR CHAMPIONSHIP RACE, Autodromo Santamonica, Misano, Italy, 4 May. FIA Touring Car Championship, round 4. 144 laps of the 2·167-mile/3·488-km circuit, 312·05 miles/502·27 km.
1 Gerhard Berger/Roberto Ravaglia, A/I (3.5 BMW 635 CSi), 3h 29m 36·07s, 89·86 mph/144·62 km/h (1st over–2500 cc class).
2 Johnny Cecotto/Anders Olofsson, YV/S (2.0 t/c Volvo 240 Turbo), 144.
3 Tom Walkinshaw/Win Percy, GB/GB (3.5 Rover Vitesse), 143 laps.
4 Dieter Quester/Otto Rensing, A/D (3.5 BMW 635 CSi), 142.
5 Winni Vogt/Markus Oestreich/Massimo Micangeli, D/D/I (2.5 BMW 325i), 142 (1st 1601 cc–2500 cc class).
6 Dany Snobeck/Alain Cudini, F/F (2.3 Mercedes-Benz 190E), 142.

7 Marco Micangeli/Umberto Grano, I/I (3.5 BMW 635 CSi), 141; **8** Ulf Granberg/Thomas Lindström, S/S (2.0 t/c Volvo 240 Turbo), 140; **9** Massimo Micangeli/Christian Danner, I/D (2.5 BMW 325i), 139; **10** Jürgen Hamelmann/Robert Walterscheid-Müller, D/D (2.5 BMW 325i), 139.
Fastest lap: Granberg, 1m 25·29s, 91·46 mph/147·19 km/h.
Other class winners. Up to 1600 cc: Herbert Lingmann/Ludwig Holzl, D/D (1.6 Toyota Corolla), 132.
Championship points. Drivers: 1 Walkinshaw and Percy, 87; **3** Cudini and Snobeck, 68; **5** Vogt, 66; **6** Cecotto, 56.
Manufacturers: 1 Toyota, 80; **2** BMW, 72; **3** Mercedes-Benz, 65; **4** Rover and BMW, 62; **6** Volvo, 53.

FIA TOURING CAR CHAMPIONSHIP RACE, Anderstorp, Sweden, 18 May. FIA Touring Car Championship, round 5. 118 laps of the 2·505-mile/4·031-km circuit, 295·59 miles/475·66 km.
1 Thomas Lindström/Ulf Granberg, S/S (2·0 t/c Volvo 240 Turbo), 3h 31m 06·24s, 84·01 mph/135·20 km/h (1st over-2500 cc class).
2 Armin Hahne/Gianfranco Brancatelli, D/I (3·5 Rover Vitesse), 3h 31m 06·61s.
3 Johnny Cecotto/Anders Olofsson, YV/S (2·0 t/c Volvo 240 Turbo), 118 laps.
4 Tom Walkinshaw/Win Percy, GB/GB (3·5 Rover Vitesse), 118.
5 Denny Hulme/Jeff Allam, NZ/GB (3·5 Rover Vitesse), 118.
6 Marco Micangeli/Carlo Rossi, I/I (3·5 BMW 635 CSi), 116.
7 Marc Surer/Hans Heyer, CH/D (3·5 BMW 635 CSi), 116; **8** Dieter Quester/Otto Rensing, A/D (3·5 BMW 635 CSi), 116; **9** Christian Danner/Winni Vogt, D/D (2·5 BMW 325i), 115 (1st 1601 cc – 2500 cc class); **10** Massimo Micangeli/Johnny Reindl/Christian Danner, I/A/D (2·5 BMW 325i), 113.
Fastest lap: Percy, 1m 44·56s, 86·25 mph/138·81 km/h (record).
Other class winners. Up to 1600 cc: Erik Hoyer/John Nielsen/Kurt Thiim, DK/DK/DK (1·6 Toyota Corolla), 109.
Championship points. Drivers: 1 Walkinshaw and Percy, 100; **3** Vogt, 86; **4** Cecotto, 72; **5** Lindström, 70; **6** Snobeck and Cudini, 68.
Manufacturers: 1 Toyota, 100; **3** BMW, 92; **3** Rover, 77; **4** Mercedes-Benz and Volvo, 73; **6** BMW, 68.

FIA TOURING CAR CHAMPIONSHIP RACE, Brno, Czechoslovakia, 8 May. FIA Touring Car Championship, round 6. 59 laps of the 6·788-mile/10·925-km circuit, 400·49 miles/644·58 km.
1 Thomas Lindström/Ulf Granberg, S/S (2·0 t/c Volvo 240 Turbo), 3h 32m 47·71s, 112·92 mph/181·73 km/h (1st over-2500 cc class).
2 Tom Walkinshaw/Win Percy, GB/GB (3·5 Rover Vitesse), 3h 33m 28·11s.
3 Johnny Cecotto/Anders Olofsson, YV/S (2·0 t/c Volvo 240 Turbo), 59 laps.
4 Armin Hahne/Gianfranco Brancatelli, D/I (3·5 Rover Vitesse), 58.
5 Jeff Allam/Denny Hulme, GB/NZ (3·5 Rover Vitesse), 58.
6 Gerhard Berger/Roberto Ravaglia, A/I (3·5 BMW 635 CSi), 58.
7 Dieter Quester/Otto Rensing, A/D (3·5 BMW 635 CSi), 58; **8** Georges Bosshard/Anna Cambiaghi, CH/I (3·5 BMW 635 CSi), 57; **9** Hans Heyer/Enzo Calderari, D/CH (3·5 BMW 635 CSi), 57; **10** Pierre Dieudonné/Mike Thackwell, B/NZ (2·3 t/c Ford Sierra XR4Ti), 57.
Fastest lap: Olofsson, 3m 32·08s, 115·22 mph/185·83 km/h.
Other class winners. 1601 cc–2500 cc: Christian Danner/Winni Vogt/Bratislav Enge, D/D/CS (2·5 BMW 325i), 56. **Up to 1600 cc:** Ludwig Holzl/Herbert Lingmann, D/D (1·6 Toyota Corolla), 52.
Championship points. Drivers: 1 Walkinshaw and Percy, 121; **3** Vogt, 106; **4** Lindström, 99; **5** Cecotto, 88; **6** Granberg, 80.
Manufacturers: 1 Toyota, 120; **2** BMW, 112; **3** Volvo, 93; **4** Rover, 92; **5** Mercedes-Benz, 83; **6** BMW, 74.

AUSTRIA-TROPHAE, Österreichring, Austria, 15 June. FIA Touring Car Championship, round 7. 100 laps of the 3·692-mile/5·942-km circuit, 369·20 miles/594·20 km.
* Johnny Cecotto/Anders Olofsson, YV/S (2·0 t/c Volvo 240 Turbo), 3h 30m 13·12s, 103·89 mph/167·19 km/h (1st over-2500 cc class).
* Thomas Lindström/Ulf Granberg, S/S (2·0 t/c Volvo 240 Turbo), 3h 30m 15·74s.
* Sigi Müller Jnr/Pierre Dieudonné, D/B (2·3 t/c Ford Sierra XR4Ti), 99 laps.
1 Armin Hahne/Win Percy, D/GB (3·5 Rover Vitesse), 99 laps.
2 Enzo Calderari/Carlo Rossi, CH/I (3·5 BMW 635 CSi), 98.
3 Dieter Quester/Roberto Ravaglia, A/I (3·5 BMW 635 CSi), 97.
4 Ron Dickson/Neville Crichton, AUS/NZ (3·5 Rover Vitesse), 97.
5 Georges Bosshard/Eddy Joosen, CH/B (3·5 BMW 635 CSi), 96.
6 Hans-Jörg Haidacher/Rupert Hofmarcher, A/A (2·3 Mercedes-Benz 190E), 96 (1st 1601 cc – 2500 cc class).
7 René Metge/Alexandre Guyaux, F/F (3·5 BMW 635 CSi), 96; **8** Philippe Haezebrouck/Dominique Fornage, F/F (3·5 BMW 635 CSi), 96; **9** Zdenek Vojtech/Ferdinand de Lesseps, CS/F (2·3 Mercedes-Benz 190E), 96; **10** Jürgen Hamelmann/Robert Walterscheid-Müller, D/D (2·5 BMW 325i), 95.
Fastest lap: Not given.
Other class winners. Up to 1600 cc: John Nielsen/Erik Hoyer/Kurt Thiim, DK/DK/DK (1·6 Toyota Corolla), 92.
* First three all disqualified for various fuel/fuel tank related offences.
Championship points. Drivers: 1 Percy, 150; **2** Walkinshaw, 121; **3** Vogt, 108; **4** Lindström, 99; **5** Cecotto, 88; **6** Hoyer, 81.
Manufacturers: 1 Toyota, 140; **2** BMW, 124; **3** Rover, 112; **4** Mercedes-Benz, 103; **5** Volvo, 93; **6** BMW, 89.

GROSSER PREIS der TOURENWAGEN, Nürburgring, German Federal Republic, 13 July. FIA Touring Car Championship, round 8. 111 laps of the 2·822-mile/4·542-km circuit, 313·24 miles/504·16 km.
1 Roberto Ravaglia/Emanuele Pirro, I/I (3·5 BMW 635 CSi), 3h 31m 09·79s, 89·01 mph/143·25 km/h (1st over-2500 cc class).
2 Sigi Müller Jnr/Pierre Dieudonné, D/B (2·3 t/c Ford Sierra XR4Ti), 3h 32m 30·91s.
3 Armin Hahne/Gianfranco Brancatelli, D/I (3·5 Rover Vitesse), 110 laps.
4 Tom Walkinshaw/Win Percy, GB/GB (3·5 Rover Vitesse), 110.
5 Carlo Rossi/Marco Micangeli, I/I (3·5 BMW 635 CSi), 110.
6 Otto Rensing/Dieter Quester, D/A (3·5 BMW 635 CSi), 109.
7 Jean-Pierre Malcher/Michel Trollé, F/F (3·5 BMW 635 CSi), 109; **8** Volker Weidler/Franz Klammer, D/A (2·3 Mercedes-Benz 109E), 108 (1st 1601 cc – 2500 cc class); **9** Winni Vogt/Altfried Heger, D/D (2·5 BMW 325i), 108; **10** Johnny Cecotto/Anders Olofsson, YV/S (2·0 t/c Volvo 240 Turbo), 108.
Fastest lap: Klaus Niedzwiedz, D (2·3 t/c Ford Sierra XR4Ti), 1m 51·43s, 91·17 mph/146·72 km/h.
Other class winners. Up to 1600 cc: Herbert Lingmann/Ludwig Holzl, D/D (1·6 Toyota Corolla), 102.
Championship points. Drivers: 1 Percy, 163; **2** Walkinshaw, 134; **3** Vogt, 123; **4** Ravaglia, 102; **5** Lindström, 99; **6** Lingmann and Holzl, 97.
Manufacturers: 1 Toyota, 160; **2** BMW, 139; **3** Rover, 124; **4** Mercedes-Benz, 123; **5** BMW, 109; **6** Volvo, 96.

SPA 24 HOURS, Spa-Francorchamps Circuit, Belgium, 2/3 August. FIA Touring Car Championship, round 9. 499 laps of the 4·3179-mile/6·9490-km circuit, 2154·63 miles/3467·55 km.
1 Dieter Quester/Thierry Tassin/Altfried Heger, A/B/D (3·5 BMW 635 CSi), 24h 00m 37·06s, 89·74 mph/144·42 km/h (1st over-2500 cc class).
2 Carlo Rossi/Marco Micangeli/Maurizio Micangeli, I/I/I (3·5 BMW 635 CSi), 494 laps.
3 Gerhard Berger/Roberto Ravaglia/Emanuele Pirro, A/I/I (3·5 BMW 635 CSi), 491.
4 René Metge/Marc Sourd/Philippe Haezebrouck, F/F/F (3·5 BMW 635 CSi), 489.
5 Winni Vogt/Christian Danner/Markus Oestreich, D/D/D (2·5 BMW 325i), 487 (1st 1601 cc – 2500 cc class).
6 Armin Hahne/Jeff Allam/Denny Hulme, D/GB/NZ (3·5 Rover Vitesse), 481.
7 Steve Soper/Klaus Niedzwiedz/Sigi Müller Jnr, GB/D/D (2·3 t/c Ford Sierra XR4Ti), 475; **8** Lella Lombardi/Rinaldo Drovandi/Roberto Castagna, I/I/I (2·5 Alfa Romeo 75), 473; **9** Michel Maillien/Quentin Bovy/'Faustein', B/B/B (2·5 Alfa Romeo GTV6), 461; **10** Georges Cremer/Charles Cremer/Edward Gillessen, B/B/B (2·5 Alfa Romeo GTV6), 461.
Fastest lap: Thomas Lindström, S (2·0 t/c Volvo 240 Turbo), 2m 41·19s, 96·44 mph/155·20 km/h.
Other class winners. Up to 1600 cc: Ludwig Holzl/Hans-Peter Hess/Bruno Eichmann, D/D/CH (1·6 Toyota Corolla), 460.
Championship points. Drivers: 1 Percy, 163; **2** Vogt, 145; **3** Walkinshaw, 134; **4** Ravaglia, 118; **5** Holzl, 117; **6** Quester, 109.
Manufacturers: 1 Toyota, 180; **2** BMW, 159; **3** Rover, 137; **4** Mercedes-Benz, 131; **5** BMW, 129; **6** Volvo, 100.

ISTEL RAC TOURIST TROPHY, Silverstone Grand Prix Circuit, Great Britain, 7 September. FIA Touring Car Championship, round 10. 107 laps of the 2·932-mile/4·719-km circuit, 313·72 miles/504·93 km.
1 Denny Hulme/Jeff Allam, NZ/GB (3·5 Rover Vitesse), 3h 01m 56·72s, 103·45 mph/166·49 km/h (1st over-2500 cc class).
2 Dieter Quester/Roberto Ravaglia, A/I (3·5 BMW 635 CSi), 3h 02m 43·83s.
3 Tom Walkinshaw/Win Percy, GB/GB (3·5 Rover Vitesse), 107 laps.
4 Ulf Granberg/Thomas Lindström, S/S (2·0 t/c Volvo 240 Turbo), 106.
5 Pierre Dieudonné/Sigi Müller Jnr, B/D (2·3 t/c Ford Sierra XR4Ti), 105.
6 Fabien Giroix/René Metge, F/F (3·5 BMW 625 CSi), 105.
7 Umberto Grano/Marcello Cipriani, I/I (3·5 BMW 635 CSi), 104; **8** Winni Vogt/Markus Oestreich, D/D (2·5 BMW 325i), 104 (1st 1601 cc – 2500 cc class); **9** Hans van de Beek/Raymond Coronel, NL/NL (2·0 Mazda 929), 103; **10** Jürgen Hamelmann/Frank Sytner, D/GB (2·5 BMW 325i), 103.
Fastest lap: Steve Soper, GB (2·3 t/c Ford Sierra XR4Ti), 1m 36·97s, 108·85 mph/175·18 km/h (record).
Other class winners. Up to 1600 cc: Chris Hodgetts/Alex Moss, GB/GB (1·6 Toyota Corolla), 98.
Championship points. Drivers: 1 Percy, 179; **2** Vogt, 165; **3** Walkinshaw, 150; **4** Ravaglia, 139; **5** Quester, 130; **6** Holzl, 127.
Manufacturers: 1 Toyota, 200; **3** BMW, 179; **3** Rover, 157; **4** BMW, 144; **5** Mercedes-Benz, 139; **6** Volvo, 110.

GRAND PRIX de NOGARO, Circuit Automobile Paul Armagnac, Nogaro, France, 14 September. FIA Touring Car Championship, round 11. 147 laps of the 1·939-mile/3·120-km circuit, 285·03 miles/458·64 km.
1 Roberto Ravaglia/Gerhard Berger, I/A (3·5 BMW 635 CSi), 3h 30m 12·2s, 81·82 mph/131·68 km/h (1st over-2500 cc class).
2 Johnny Cecotto/Thomas Lindström, YV/S (2·0 t/c Volvo 240 Turbo), 3h 30m 51·9s.
3 Ulf Granberg/Anders Olofsson, S/S (2·0 t/c Volvo 240 Turbo), 147 laps.
4 Klaus Niedzwiedz/Steve Soper, D/GB (2·3 t/c Ford Sierra XR4Ti), 146.
5 Dieter Quester/Ivan Capelli, A/I (3·5 BMW 635 CSi), 146.
6 Pierre Dieudonné/Sigi Müller Jnr, B/D (2·3 Ford Sierra XR4Ti), 146.
7 Alain Cudini/Dany Snobeck, F/F (2·3 Mercedes-Benz 190E), 146 (1st 1601 cc–2500 cc class); **8** Marco Micangeli/Marcello Cipriani, I/I (3·5 BMW 635 CSi), 145; **9** Christian Danner/Winni Vogt, D/D (2·5 BMW 325i), 145; **10** Markus Oestreich/Otto Rensing, D/D (2·5 BMW 325i), 145.
Fastest lap: Win Percy, GB (3·5 Rover Vitesse), 1m 23·4s, 84·17 mph/135·46 km/h.
Other class winners. Up to 1600 cc: Herbert Lingmann/Ludwig Holzl, D/D (1·6 Toyota Corolla), 136.
Championship points. Drivers: 1 Percy, 181; **2** Vogt, 180; **3** Ravaglia, 168; **4** Walkinshaw, 152; **5** Holzl, 147; **6** Quester, 140.
Manufacturers: 1 Toyota, 200 (220); **2** BMW, 182 (194); **3** BMW, 158 (164); **4** Rover, 157 (159); **5** Mercedes-Benz, 151 (159); **6** Volvo, 125.

FIA TOURING CAR CHAMPIONSHIP RACE, Omloop van Zolder, Belgium, 28 September. FIA Touring Car Championship, round 12. 107 laps of the 2·621-mile/4·248-km circuit, 280·45 miles/454·54 km.
1 Johnny Cecotto/Thomas Lindström, YV/S (2·0 t/c Volvo 240 Turbo), 3h 30m 04·12s, 80·10 mph/128·91 km/h (1st over-2500 cc class).
2 Gerhard Berger/Roberto Ravaglia, A/I (3·5 BMW 635 CSi), 106 laps.
3 Tom Walkinshaw/Win Percy, GB/GB (3·5 Rover Vitesse), 106.
4 Eric van de Poele/Hans Heyer, B/D (3·5 BMW 635 CSi), 106.
5 Dieter Quester/Uwe Schafer, A/D (3·5 BMW 635 CSi), 105.
6 Winni Vogt/Markus Oestreich, D/D (2·5 BMW 325i), 105 (1st 1601 cc – 2500 cc class).
7 Per Stureson/Anders Lindberg, S/S (2·0 t/c Volvo 240 Turbo), 105; **8** Georges Bosshard/Jose-Angel Sassiambarrena, CH/I (3·5 BMW 635 CSi), 104; **9** Christian Danner/Otto Rensing, D/D (2·5 BMW 325i), 104; **10** Jürgen Hamelmann/Robert Walterscheid-Müller, D/D (2·5 BMW 325i), 102.
Fastest lap: Cecotto, 1m 50·39s, 85·48 mph/137·57 km/h.
Other class winners. Up to 1600 cc: Erik Hoyer/John Nielsen, DK/DK (1·6 Toyota Corolla), 100.
Championship points. Drivers: 1 Vogt, 199 (201); **2** Percy, 195 (197); **3** Ravaglia, 189; **4** Walkinshaw, 168; **5** Lindström, 162; **6** Holzl, 149.
Manufacturers: 1 Toyota, 200 (240); **2** BMW, 190 (214); **3** BMW, 167 (179); **4** Rover, 157 (169); **5** Mercedes-Benz, 151 (159); **6** Volvo, 142 (145).

FIA TOURING CAR CHAMPIONSHIP RACE, Circuito Permanente del Jarama, Spain, 12 October. FIA Touring Car Championship, round 13. 150 laps of the 2·058-mile/3·312-km circuit, 308·70 miles/496·80 km.
1 Robert Ravaglia/Emanuele Pirro, I/I (3·5 BMW 635 CSi), 4h 05m 09·99s, 75·99 mph/122·29 km/h (1st over-2500 cc class).
2 Tom Walkinshaw/Win Percy, GB/GB (3·5 Rover Vitesse), 4h 05m 33·86s.
3 Johnny Cecotto/Thomas Lindström, YV/S (2·0 t/c Volvo 240 Turbo), 150 laps.
4 Gianfranco Brancatelli/Jeff Allam/Eddy Joosen, I/GB/B (3·5 Rover Vitesse), 149.
5 Pierre Dieudonné/Klaus Ludwig, B/D (2·3 t/c Ford Sierra XR4Ti), 149.
6 Fabien Giroix/Romain Feitler, F/LUX (3·5 BMW 635 CSi), 147.
7 Maurio Baldi/Per-Gunnar Andersson, I/S (2·0 t/c Volvo 240 Turbo)), 147; **8** Otto Rensing/Volker Strycek, D/D (2·5 BMW 325i), 145 (1st 1601 cc – 2500 cc class); **9** Harold Grohs/Joachim Winkelhock, D/D (2·3 t/c Ford Sierra XR4Ti), 145; **10** Zdenek Vojtech/Maurizio Micangeli, CS/I (2·3 Mercedes-Benz 190E), 145.
Fastest lap: Ravaglia/Pirro 1m 33·60s, 79·15 mph/127·38 km/h.
Other class winners. Up to 1600 cc: Peter Seikel/Dagmar Suster, D/YU (1·6 Audi 80), 132.
Championship points (following disqualification of first- and third-place Volvos from round 5 at Anderstorp).
Drivers: 1 Ravaglia, 218; **2** Percy, 211 (226); **3** Vogt, 199 (201); **4** Walkinshaw, 187 (189); **5** Holzl and Lindström, 149.
Manufacturers: 1 Toyota, 200 (255); **2** BMW, 195 (234); **3** BMW, 175 (203); **4** Rover, 167 (189); **5** Mercedes-Benz, 158 (174); **6** Volvo, 132 (135).

FIA TOURING CAR CHAMPIONSHIP RACE, Autodromo do Estoril, Portugal, 19 October. FIA Touring Car Championship, round 14. 115 laps of the 2·703-mile/4·350-km circuit, 310·85 miles/500·25 km.
1 Steve Soper/Klaus Niedzwiedz, GB/D (2·3 t/c Ford Sierra XR4Ti), 3h 33m 20·97s, 87·92 mph/141·49 km/h (1st over-2500 cc class).
2 Tom Walkinshaw/Win Percy, GB/GB (3·5 Rover Vitesse), 3h 34m 16·75s.
3 Armin Hahne/Jeff Allam, D/GB (3·5 Rover Vitesse), 115 laps.
4 Gianfranco Brancatelli/Jean-Louis Schlesser, I/F (3·5 Rover Vitesse), 115.
5 Mauro Baldi/Per-Gunnar Andersson, I/S (2·0 t/c Volvo 240 Turbo), 114.
6 Georges Bosshard/Jose-Angel Sassiambarrena, CH/E (3·5 BMW 635 Ci), 113.
7 Marcello Cipriani/Luciano Lovato, I/I (3·5 BMW 635 CSi), 113; **8** Allan Grice/David Kennedy, AUS/IRL (4·9 Holden Commodore), 113; **9** Ivan Capelli/Roberto Ravaglia, I/I (3·5 BMW 635 CSi), 112; **10** Emanuele Pirro/Dieter Quester, I/A (3·5 BMW 635 CSi), 112.
Fastest lap: Schlesser, 1m 48·78s, 89·97 mph/144·79 km/h.
Other class winners. 1601 cc – 2500 cc: Markus Oestreich/Winni Vogt, D/D (2·5 BMW 325i), 112. **Up to 1600 cc:** Peter Seikel/Dagmar Suster, D/YU (1·6 Audi 80), 102.

Final Championship points (points not confirmed by FIA when *Autocourse 1986/87* went to press):

Drivers

1	Win Percy, GB	219 (239)
2	Roberto Ravaglia, I	218 (220)
3	Winni Vogt, D	206 (221)
4	Tom Walkinshaw, GB	203 (210)
5	Erik Hoyer, DK	153
6=	Thomas Lindström, S	149
6=	Ludwig Holzl, D	149

Manufacturers

1	Toyota	200 (270)
2	BMW	200 (254)
3	BMW	175 (209)
4	Rover	170 (204)
5	Mercedes-Benz	160 (186)
6	Volvo	134 (143)

Note: BMW scored points in both the 1601 cc–2500 cc class and in the over-2500 cc class.

CART PPG Indy Car World Series 1985 Results

The final round of the 1985 CART PPG Indy Car World Series was run after *Autocourse 1985/86* went to press.

BEATRICE INDY CHALLENGE, Tamiami Park Road Circuit, Miami, Florida, United States of America, 9 November. CART PPG Indy Car World Series, round 15. 112 laps of the 1·784-mile/2·871-km circuit, 199·81 miles/321·55 km.
1 Danny Sullivan, USA (March 85C-Cosworth DFX), 2h 04m 59·41s, 95·915 mph/154·360 km/h.
2 Bobby Rahal, USA (March 85C-Cosworth DFX), 2h 05m 15·21s.
3 Al Unser Jnr, USA (Lola T900-Cosworth DFX), 112 laps.
4 Al Unser Snr, USA (March 85C-Cosworth DFX), 112.
5 Roberto Moreno, BR (March 85C-Cosworth DFX), 112.
6 Danny Ongais, USA (March 85C-Cosworth DFX), 110.
7 Arie Luyendyk, NL (Lola T900-Cosworth DFX), 110; **8** Bill Whittington, USA (March 85C-Cosworth DFX), 110; **9** Josele Garza, MEX (March 85C-Cosworth DFX), 109; **10** Rupert Keegan, GB (March 85C-Cosworth DFX), 100; **11** Dominic Dobson, USA (March 85C-Cosworth DFX), 95; **12** Ed Pimm, USA (Eagle 85GC-Cosworth DFX), 95.
Fastest qualifier: Rahal, 56·408s, 113·856 mph/183·233 km/h.

Final Championship points

1	Al Unser Snr, USA	151
2	Al Unser Jnr, USA	150
3	Bobby Rahal, USA	134
4	Danny Sullivan, USA	126
5	Mario Andretti, USA	114
6	Emerson Fittipaldi, BR	104

7 Tom Sneva, USA, 66; **8** Jacques Villeneuve, CDN, 54; **9** Mike Andretti, USA, 53; **10** Rick Mears, USA, 51; **11** Johnny Rutherford, USA, 51; **12** Josele Garza, MEX, 46; **13** Ed Pimm, USA, 45; **14** Kevin Cogan, USA, 44; **15** Geoff Brabham, AUS, 41; **16** Pancho Carter, USA, 37; **17** Roberto Guerrero, COL, 34; **18** Arie Luyendyk, NL, 33; **19** Bruno Giacomelli, I, 32; **20** Jim Crawford, GB, 16.

1986 Results

DANA 200, Phoenix International Raceway, Arizona, United States of America, 6 April. CART PPG Indy Car World Series, round 1. 200 laps of the 1·000-mile/1·609-km circuit, 200·00 miles/321·80 km.
1 Kevin Cogan, USA (March 86C-Cosworth DFX), 1h 39m 42·76s, 120·345 mph/193·676 km/h.
2 Tom Sneva, USA (March 86C-Cosworth DFX), 199 laps.
3 Emerson Fittipaldi, BR (March 86C-Cosworth DFX), 199.
4 Danny Sullivan, USA (March 86C-Cosworth DFX), 198.
5 Johnny Rutherford, USA (March 86C-Cosworth DFX), 198.
6 Arie Luyendyk, NL (Lola T86/00-Cosworth DFX), 196.
7 Mario Andretti, USA (Lola T86/00-Cosworth DFX), 195 (DNF, out of fuel); **8** Roberto Guerrero, COL (March 86C-Cosworth DFX), 195; **9** Jan Lammers, NL (Eagle 86GC-Cosworth DFX), 195; **10** Geoff Brabham, AUS (Lola T86/00-Cosworth DFX), 192; **11** Randy Lanier, USA (March 86C-Cosworth DFX), 189; **12** Al Unser Jnr, USA (Lola T86/00-Cosworth DFX), 188.
Fastest qualifier: Andretti (Mario), 21·716s, 165·776 mph/266·800 km/h.
Championship points: 1 Cogan, 20; **2** Sneva, 16; **3** Fittipaldi, 14; **4** Sullivan, 12; **5** Rutherford, 10; **6** Luyendyk, 8.

TOYOTA GRAND PRIX OF LONG BEACH, Long Beach Circuit, California, United States of America, 13 April. CART PPG Indy Car World Series, round 2. 95 laps of the 1·67-mile/2·69-km circuit, 158·65 miles/255·55 km.
1 Mike Andretti, USA (March 86C-Cosworth DFX), 1h 57m 34·2s, 80·695 mph/129·866 km/h.
2 Al Unser Jnr, USA (Lola T86/00-Cosworth DFX), 1h 57m 34·6s.
3 Geoff Brabham, AUS (Lola T86/00-Cosworth DFX), 95 laps.
4 Tom Sneva, USA (March 86C-Cosworth DFX), 94.
5 Mario Andretti, USA (Lola T86/00-Cosworth DFX), 94.
6 Roberto Moreno, BR (Lola T86/00-Cosworth DFX), 93 (DNF, engine).
7 Josele Garza, MEX (March 85C-Cosworth DFX), 93; **8** Jacques Villeneuve, CDN (March 86C-Cosworth DFX), 90; **9** Johnny Rutherford, USA (March 86C-Cosworth DFX), 89; **10** Randy Lewis, USA (Lola T86/00-Cosworth DFX), 88; **11** Danny Sullivan, USA (March 86C-Cosworth DFX), 86 (DNF, ignition); **12** Dominic Dobson, USA (March 85C-Cosworth DFX), 84.

Fastest qualifier: Sullivan, 1m 06·565, 90·318 mph/145·352 km/h.
Championship points: **1** Sneva, 28; **2** Andretti (Mike), 22; **3** Cogan, 20; **4** Andretti (Mario), Brabham and Unser Jnr, 17.

INDIANAPOLIS 500, Indianapolis Motor Speedway, Indiana, United States of America, 1 June. CART PPG Indy Car World Series, round 3. 200 laps of the 2·500-mile/4·023-km circuit, 500·00 miles/804·57 km.
1 Bobby Rahal, USA (March 86C-Cosworth DFX), 2h 55m 43·480s, 170·722 mph/274·750 km/h.
2 Kevin Cogan, USA (March 86C-Cosworth DFX), 2h 55m 44·921s.
3 Rick Mears, USA (March 86C-Cosworth DFX), 200 laps.
4 Roberto Guerrero, COL (March 86C-Cosworth DFX), 200.
5 Al Unser Jnr, USA (Lola T86/00-Cosworth DFX), 199.
6 Mike Andretti, USA (March 86C-Cosworth DFX), 199.
7 Emerson Fittipaldi, BR (March 86C-Cosworth DFX), 199; **8** Johnny Rutherford, USA (March 86C-Cosworth DFX), 198; **9** Danny Sullivan, USA (March 86C-Cosworth DFX), 197; **10** Randy Lanier, USA (March 86C-Cosworth DFX), 195; **11** Gary Bettenhausen, USA (March 85C-Cosworth DFX), 193; **12** Geoff Brabham, AUS (Lola T86/00-Cosworth DFX), 193; **13** Raul Boesel, BR (Lola T86/00-Cosworth DFX), 192; **14** Dick Simon, USA (Lola T86/00-Cosworth DFX), 189; **15** Arie Luyendyk, NL (Lola T86/00-Cosworth DFX), 188 (DNF, accident); **16** Pancho Carter, USA (Lola T86/00-Cosworth DFX), 179 (DNF, wheel bearing); **17** Ed Pimm, USA (March 86C-Cosworth DFX), 168 (DNF, electrics); **18** Josele Garza, MEX (March 86C-Cosworth DFX), 167; **19** Roberto Moreno, BR (Lola T86/00-Cosworth DFX), 158 (DNF, engine); **20** Jacques Villeneuve, CDN (March 86C-Cosworth DFX), 154 (DNF, engine); **21** Chip Ganassi, USA (March 86C-Cosworth DFX), 151 (DNF, engine); **22** Al Unser Snr, USA (Penske PC15-Chevrolet), 149 (DNF, engine); **23** Danny Ongais, USA (March 86C-Buick), 136 (DNF, ignition); **24** A. J. Foyt, USA (March 86C-Cosworth DFX), 135 (DNF, accident); **25** Rich Vogler, USA (March 86C-Cosworth DFX),132 (DNF, accident); **26** George Snider, USA (March 86C-Cosworth DFX), 110 (DNF, engine); **27** Johnny Parsons, USA (March 86C-Cosworth DFX), 100 (DNF, accident); **28** Tony Bettenhausen, USA (March 86C-Cosworth DFX), 77 (DNF, ignition); **29** Jim Crawford, GB (March 86C-Buick), 70 (DNF, engine); **30** Scott Brayton, USA (March 86C-Cosworth DFX), 69 (DNF, engine); **31** Phil Krueger, USA (March 85C-Cosworth DFX), 67 (DNF, engine); **32** Mario Andretti, USA (Lola T86/00-Cosworth DFX), 19 (DNF, withdrew); **33** Tom Sneva, USA (March 86C-Cosworth DFX), 0 (DNS, accident on warm-up lap).
Fastest qualifier: Mears, 2m 46·030s, 216·828 mph/348·950 km/h (4 laps).
Fastest lap: Rahal, 43·031s, 209·152 mph/336·597 km/h.
Championship points: **1** Cogan, 36; **2** Andretti (Mike), 30; **3** Sneva, 28; **4** Unser Jnr, 27; **5** Rahal and Fittipaldi, 20.

MILLER AMERICAN 200, Wisconsin State Fair Park Speedway, Milwaukee, Wisconsin, United States of America, 8 June. CART PPG Indy Car World Series, round 4. 200 laps of the 1·000-mile/1·609-km circuit, 200·00 miles/321·80 km.
1 Mike Andretti, USA (March 86C-Cosworth DFX), 1h 42m 45·00s, 116·788 mph/187·952 km/h.
2 Tom Sneva, USA (March 86C-Cosworth DFX), 199 laps.
3 Rick Mears, USA (March 86C-Cosworth DFX), 199.
4 Johnny Rutherford, USA (March 86C-Cosworth DFX), 199.
5 Mario Andretti, USA (Lola T86/00-Cosworth DFX), 198.
6 Bobby Rahal, USA (March 86C-Cosworth DFX), 198.
7 Josele Garza, MEX (March 86C-Cosworth DFX), 197; **8** Al Unser Jnr, USA (Lola T86/00-Cosworth DFX), 196 (DNF, out of fuel); **9** Arie Luyendyk, NL (Lola T86/00-Cosworth DFX), 196; **10** Ed Pimm, USA (March 86C-Cosworth DFX), 195; **11** Danny Sullivan, USA (March 86C-Cosworth DFX), 195; **12** Kevin Cogan, USA (March 86C-Cosworth DFX), 194 (DNF, engine).
Fastest qualifier: Andretti (Mike), 23·544s, 152·905 mph/246·076 km/h.
Championship points: **1** Andretti (Mike), 52; **2** Sneva, 44; **3** Cogan, 37; **4** Unser Jnr, 32; **5** Rutherford, 31; **6** Mears, 30.

GI JOE'S 200, Portland International Raceway, Portland, Oregon, United States of America, 15 June. CART PPG Indy Car World Series, round 5. 104 laps of the 1·915-mile/3·082-km circuit, 199·16 miles/320·53 km.
1 Mario Andretti, USA (Lola T86/00-Cosworth DFX), 1h 50m 53·48s, 107·759 mph/173·421 km/h.
2 Mike Andretti, USA (March 86C-Cosworth DFX), 1h 50m 53·55s.
3 Al Unser Jnr, USA (Lola T86/00-Cosworth DFX), 104 laps.
4 Tom Sneva, USA (March 86C-Cosworth DFX), 102 (DNF, accident).
5 Jacques Villeneuve, CDN (March 86C-Cosworth DFX), 102 (DNF, accident).
6 Ed Pimm, USA (March 86C-Cosworth DFX), 101.
7 Geoff Brabham, AUS (Lola T86/00-Honda), 96;
8 Raul Boesel, BR (Lola T86/00-Cosworth DFX), 92; **9** Randy Lanier, USA (March 86C-Cosworth DFX), 92; **10** Mike Nish, USA (March 85C-Cosworth DFX), 91; **11** Danny Sullivan, USA (March 86C-Cosworth DFX), 81 (DNF, accident); **12** Emerson Fittipaldi, BR (March 86C-Cosworth DFX), 80 (DNF, engine).
Fastest qualifier: Fittipaldi, 1m 13·275s, 94·084 mph/151·413 km/h (wet).
Championship points: **1** Andretti (Mike), 69; **2** Sneva, 56; **3** Andretti (Mario), 47; **4** Unser Jnr, 46; **5** Cogan, 37; **6** Rutherford, 31.

CHASE GRAND PRIX, Meadowlands Grand Prix Circuit, New York, United States of America, 29 June. CART PPG Indy Car World Series, round 6. 100 laps of the 1·682-mile/2·707-km circuit, 168·20 miles/270·70 km.
1 Danny Sullivan, USA (March 86C-Cosworth DFX), 1h 49m 17·540s, 92·34 mph/148·61 km/h.
2 Emerson Fittipaldi, BR (March 86C-Cosworth DFX), 1h 49m 28·430s.
3 Bobby Rahal, USA (March 86C-Cosworth DFX), 100 laps.
4 Roberto Guerrero, COL (March 86C-Cosworth DFX), 100.
5 Jacques Villeneuve, CDN (March 86C-Cosworth DFX), 99.
6 Randy Lanier, USA (March 86C-Cosworth DFX), 95.
7 Johnny Rutherford, USA (March 86C-Cosworth DFX), 94; **8** Josele Garza, MEX (March 86C-Cosworth DFX), 94; **9** Al Unser Jnr, USA (Lola T86/00-Cosworth DFX), 93; **10** Randy Lewis, USA (Lola T86/00-Cosworth DFX), 81; **11** Dominic Dobson, USA (March 86C-Cosworth DFX), 80; **12** Ed Pimm, USA (March 86C-Cosworth DFX), 78.
Fastest qualifier: Mike Andretti, USA (March 86C-Cosworth DFX), 1m 00·535s, 100·03 mph/160·98 km/h.
Championship points: **1** Andretti (Mike), 70; **2** Sneva, 56; **3** Unser Jnr, 50; **4** Andretti (Mario), 47; **5** Sullivan, 43; **6** Rahal, 42.

BUDWEISER CLEVELAND GRAND PRIX, Burke Lakefront Airport Circuit, Cleveland, Ohio, United States of America, 6 July. CART PPG Indy Car World Series, round 7. 88 laps of the 2·485-mile/3·999-km circuit, 218·68 miles/351·91 km.
1 Danny Sullivan, USA (March 86C-Cosworth DFX), 1h 43m 01·17s, 127·106 mph/204·557 km/h.
2 Mike Andretti, USA (March 86C-Cosworth DFX), 1h 43m 45·42s.
3 Mario Andretti, USA (Lola T86/00-Cosworth DFX), 88 laps.
4 Rick Mears, USA (March 86C-Cosworth DFX), 88.
5 Tom Sneva, USA (March 86C-Cosworth DFX), 88.
6 Raul Boesel, BR (Lola T86/00-Cosworth DFX), 85.
7 Josele Garza, MEX (March 86C-Cosworth DFX), 84; **8** Al Unser Jnr, USA (Lola T86/00-Cosworth DFX), 84; **9** Randy Lanier, USA (March 86C-Cosworth DFX), 82; **10** Johnny Rutherford, USA (March 86C-Cosworth DFX), 80; **11** Rick Miaskiewicz, USA (March 85C-Cosworth DFX), 78; **12** Dale Coyne, USA (Coyne DC1-Chevrolet), 63 (DNF, camshaft).
Fastest qualifier: Sullivan, 66·063s, 135·144 mph/217·493 km/h.
Championship points: **1** Andretti (Mike), 86; **2** Sneva, 66; **3** Sullivan, 65; **4** Andretti (Mario), 61; **5** Unser Jnr, 55; **6** Mears and Rahal, 42.

MOLSON INDY-TORONTO, Canadian National Exhibition Grounds Circuit, Toronto, Canada, 20 July. CART PPG Indy Car World Series, round 8. 103 laps of the 1·78-mile/2·86-km circuit, 183·34 miles/294·58 km.
1 Bobby Rahal, USA (March 86C-Cosworth DFX), 2h 05m 50·51s, 87·414 mph/140·679 km/h.
2 Danny Sullivan, USA (March 86C-Cosworth DFX), 2h 05m 52·76s.
3 Mario Andretti, USA (Lola T86/00-Cosworth DFX), 103 laps.
4 Al Unser Jnr, USA (Lola T86/00-Cosworth DFX), 103.
5 Kevin Cogan, USA (March 86C-Cosworth DFX), 103.
6 Arie Luyendyk, NL (March 86C-Cosworth DFX), 102.
7 Raul Boesel, BR (Lola T86/00-Cosworth DFX), 101; **8** Rick Mears, USA (March 86C-Cosworth DFX), 100; **9** Tom Sneva, USA (March 86C-Cosworth DFX), 99 (DNF, accident); **10** Johnny Rutherford, USA (March 86C-Cosworth DFX), 97; **11** Randy Lewis, USA (Lola T86/00-Cosworth DFX), 97; **12** John Morton, USA (March 86C-Buick), 97.
Fastest qualifier: Emerson Fittipaldi, BR (March 86C-Cosworth DFX), 1m 00·312s, 106·247 mph/170·988 km/h.
Championship points: **1** Andretti (Mike), 86; **2** Sullivan, 81; **3** Andretti (Mario), 75; **4** Sneva, 70; **5** Unser Jnr, 68; **6** Rahal, 62.

MICHIGAN 500, Michigan International Speedway, Brooklyn, Michigan, United States of America, 2 August. CART PPG Indy Car World Series, round 9. 250 laps of the 2·000-mile/3·219-km circuit, 500·00 miles/804·75 km.
1 Johnny Rutherford, USA (March 86C-Cosworth DFX), 3h 38m 45·32s, 137·139 mph/220·703 km/h.
2 Josele Garza, MEX (March 86C-Cosworth DFX), 3h 38m 47·14s.
3 Pancho Carter, USA (Lola T86/00-Cosworth DFX), 248 laps.
4 Geoff Brabham, AUS (Lola T86/00-Honda), 239 (DNF, accident).
5 Raul Boesel, BR (Lola T86/00-Cosworth DFX), 239.
6 Roberto Moreno, BR (Lola T86/00-Cosworth DFX), 238.
7 Spike Gehlhausen, USA (Lola T900-Cosworth DFX), 237; **8** Al Unser Jnr, USA (Lola T86/00-Cosworth DFX), 235; **9** A.J. Foyt, USA (March 86C-Cosworth DFX), 229 (DNF, engine); **10** Bobby Rahal, USA (March 86C-Cosworth DFX), 219 (DNF, engine); **11** Mike Andretti, USA (March 86C-Cosworth DFX), 195 (DNF, engine); **12** Rick Mears, USA (March 86C-Cosworth DFX), 181 (DNF engine).
Fastest qualifier: Mears, 32·229s, 223·401 mph/359·528 km/h (world record for closed course).
Championship points: **1** Andretti (Mike), 88; **2** Sullivan, 81; **3** Andretti (Mario), 75; **4** Unser Jnr, 73; **5** Sneva, 70; **6** Rahal, 66.

DOMINO'S PIZZA 500, Pocono International Raceway, Pennsylvania, United States of America, 17 August. CART PPG Indy Car World Series, round 10. 200 laps of the 2·500-mile/4·023-km circuit, 500·00 miles/804·60 km.
1 Mario Andretti, USA (Lola T86/00-Cosworth DFX) 3h 17m 13·80s, 152·016 mph/244·645 km/h.
2 Kevin Cogan, USA (March 86C-Cosworth DFX), 199 laps.
3 Pancho Carter, USA (Lola T86/00-Cosworth DFX), 198.
4 A.J. Foyt, USA (March 86C-Cosworth DFX), 197.
5 Raul Boesel, BR (Lola T86/00-Cosworth DFX), 197.
6 Al Unser Jnr, USA (Lola T86/00-Cosworth DFX), 195.
7 Josele Garza, MEX (March 86C-Cosworth DFX), 194; **8** Rick Mears, USA (March 86C-Cosworth DFX), 188; **9** Sammy Swindell, USA (March 86C-Cosworth DFX), 187; **10** Roberto Moreno, BR (Lola T86/00-Cosworth DFX), 186; **11** Mike Andretti, USA (March 86C-Cosworth DFX), 185 (DNF, engine); **12** Geoff Brabham, AUS (Lola T86/00-Honda), 184.
Fastest qualifier: Andretti (Mike), 43·748s, 205·724 mph/331·080 km/h.
Championship points: **1** Andretti (Mario), 96; **2** Andretti (Mike), 91; **3** Unser Jnr and Sullivan, 81; **5** Sneva, 70; **6** Rahal, 66.

ESCORT RADAR WARNING 200, Mid-Ohio Sports Car Course, Lexington, Ohio, United States of America, 31 August. CART PPG Indy Car World Series, round 11. 84 laps of the 2·400-mile/3·863-km circuit, 201·60 miles/324·41 km.
1 Bobby Rahal, USA (March 86C-Cosworth DFX), 1h 56m 18·62s, 103·430 mph/166·454 km/h.
2 Roberto Guerrero, COL (March 86C-Cosworth DFX), 1h 56m 19·44s.
3 Danny Sullivan, USA (March 86C-Cosworth DFX), 84 laps.
4 Kevin Cogan, USA (March 86C-Cosworth DFX), 84.
5 Al Unser Jnr, USA (Lola T86/00-Cosworth DFX), 83.
6 Derek Daly, IRL (March 86C-Cosworth DFX), 82.
7 Raul Boesel, BR (Lola T86/00-Cosworth DFX), 81; **8** Johnny Rutherford, USA (March 86C-Cosworth DFX), 80; **9** Ian Ashley, GB (Lola T86/00-Cosworth DFX), 80; **10** Mike Andretti, USA (March 86C-Cosworth DFX), 79; **11** Jacques Villeneuve, CDN (March 86C-Cosworth DFX), 79; **12** Tom Sneva, USA (March 86C-Cosworth DFX), 78 (DNF, out of fuel).
Fastest qualifier: Mario Andretti, USA (Lola T86/00-Cosworth DFX), 1m 16·237s, 113·331 mph/182·388 km/h.
Championship points: **1** Andretti (Mario), 97; **2** Sullivan, 96; **3** Andretti (Mike), 94; **4** Unser Jnr, 91; **5** Rahal, 86; **6** Cogan, 75.

MOLSON INDY-MONTREAL, Sanair Super Speedway, Montreal, Quebec, Canada, 7 September. CART PPG Indy Car World Series, round 12. 225 laps of the 0·826-mile/1·329-km circuit, 185·85 miles/299·03 km.
1 Bobby Rahal, USA (March 86C-Cosworth DFX), 1h 48m 05·83s, 103·157 mph/166·015 km/h.
2 Al Unser Jnr, USA (Lola T86/00-Cosworth DFX), 1h 48m 19·57s.
3 Emerson Fittipaldi, BR (March 86C-Cosworth DFX), 223 laps.
4 Kevin Cogan, USA (March 86C-Cosworth DFX), 223.
5 Danny Sullivan, USA (March 86C-Cosworth DFX), 221.
6 Mike Andretti, USA (March 86C-Cosworth DFX), 219.
7 Johnny Parsons, USA (March 86C-Cosworth DFX), 219; **8** Mario Andretti, USA (Lola T86/00-Cosworth DFX), 219; **9** Raul Boesel, BR (Lola T86/00-Cosworth DFX), 217; **10** Derek Daly, IRL (March 86C-Cosworth DFX), 216; **11** Geoff Brabham, AUS (Lola T86/00-Cosworth DFX), 210; **12** Dale Coyne, USA (Coyne DC1-Chevrolet), 193.
Fastest qualifier: Rick Mears, USA (Penske PC15-Chevrolet), 20·074s, 148·132 mph/238·395 km/h (record).
Championship points: **1** Unser Jnr and Rahal, 107; **3** Sullivan, 106; **4** Andretti (Mario) and Andretti (Mike), 102; **6** Cogan, 87.

PEPSI-COLA 250, Michigan Speedway, Michigan, United States of America, 28 September. CART PPG Indy Car World Series, round 13. 125 laps of the 2·000-mile/3·219-km circuit, 250·00 miles/402·38 km.
1 Bobby Rahal, USA (March 86C-Cosworth DFX), 1h 22m 33·20s, 181·701 mph/292·419 km/h.
2 Mike Andretti, USA (March 86C-Cosworth DFX) 1h 22m 36·45s.
3 Emerson Fittipaldi, BR (March 86C-Cosworth DFX), 125 laps.
4 Kevin Cogan, USA (March 86C-Cosworth DFX), 125.
5 Tom Sneva, USA (March 86C-Cosworth DFX), 125.
6 Roberto Moreno, BR (Lola T86/00-Cosworth DFX), 124 (DNF, engine).
7 Ed Pimm, USA (March 86C-Cosworth DFX), 124;
8 Rick Mears, USA (March 86C-Chevrolet), 124;
9 Johnny Rutherford, USA (March 86C-Cosworth DFX), 124; **10** Mario Andretti, USA (Lola T86/00-Cosworth DFX), 123 (DNF, engine); **11** Geoff Brabham, AUS (Lola T86/00-Honda), 123; **12** Danny Sullivan, USA (March 86C-Cosworth DFX), 123.
Fastest qualifier: Mears, 32·810s, 219·445 mph/353·162 km/h.
Championship points: **1** Rahal, 128; **2** Andretti (Mike), 119; **3** Sullivan and Unser Jnr, 107; **5** Andretti (Mario), 105; **6** Cogan, 99.

RACE FOR LIFE 200, Road America, Elkhart Lake, Wisconsin, United States of America, 4 October. CART PPG Indy Car World Series, round 14. 50 laps of the 4·000-mile/6·437-km circuit, 200·00 miles/321·85 km.
1 Emerson Fittipaldi, BR (March 86C-Cosworth DFX), 2h 26m 38·4s, 81·80 mph/131·64 km/h.
2 Mike Andretti, USA (March 86C-Cosworth DFX) 2h 26m 38·7s.
3 Rick Mears, USA (March 86C-Chevrolet), 50 laps.
4 Roberto Guerrero, COL (March 86C-Cosworth DFX), 50.
5 Bobby Rahal, USA (March 86C-Cosworth DFX), 50.
6 Danny Sullivan, USA (March 86C-Cosworth DFX), 50.
7 Arie Luyendyk, NL (Lola T86/00-Cosworth DFX), 49; **8** Raul Boesel, BR (Lola T86/00-Cosworth DFX), 49; **9** Mario Andretti, USA (Lola T86/00-Cosworth DFX), 49; **10** Jacques Villeneuve, CDN (March 86C-Cosworth DFX), 48; **11** Al Unser Jnr, USA (Lola T86/00-Cosworth DFX), 48; **12** Tom Sneva, USA (March 86C-Cosworth DFX), 47 (DNF, spun off).
Fastest qualifier: Rahal, 1m 55·829s, 124·321 mph/200·075 km/h.
Championship points: **1** Rahal, 138; **2** Andretti (Mike), 136; **3** Sullivan, 115; **4** Unser Jnr and Andretti (Mario), 109; **6** Cogan, 99.

CHAMPION SPARK PLUG 300, Laguna Seca Raceway, California, United States of America, 12 October. CART PPG Indy Car World Series, round 15. 98 laps of the 1·900-mile/3·056-km circuit, 186·20 miles/299·49 km.
1 Bobby Rahal, USA (March 86C-Cosworth DFX), 1h 33m 20·34s, 119·693 mph/192·627 km/h.
2 Danny Sullivan, USA (March 86C-Cosworth DFX), 1h 33m 21·75s.
3 Mike Andretti, USA (March 86C-Cosworth DFX), 98 laps.
4 Mario Andretti, USA (Lola T86/00-Cosworth DFX), 98.
5 Roberto Guerrero, COL (March 86C-Cosworth DFX), 98.
6 Geoff Brabham, AUS (Lola T86/00-Cosworth DFX), 98.
7 Emerson Fittipaldi, BR (March 86C-Cosworth DFX), 98; **8** Jan Lammers, NL (Eagle GC86C-Cosworth DFX), 96; **9** Kevin Cogan, USA (March 86C-Cosworth DFX), 95; **10** Arie Luyendyk, NL (March 86C-Cosworth DFX), 95; **11** Ed Pimm, USA (March 86C-Cosworth DFX), 94; **12** Johnny Rutherford, USA (March 86C-Cosworth DFX), 93.
Fastest qualifier: Andretti (Mario), 53·036s, 128·969 mph/207·555 km/h.
Championship points: **1** Rahal, 159; **2** Andretti (Mike), 150; **3** Sullivan, 131; **4** Andretti (Mario), 122; **5** Unser Jnr, 109; **6** Cogan, 99.

CIRCLE K FIESTA BOWL 200, Phoenix International Raceway, Arizona, United States of America, 19 October. CART PPG Indy Car World Series, round 16. 200 laps of the 1·000-mile/1·609-km circuit, 200·00 miles/321·80 km.
1 Mike Andretti, USA (March 86C-Cosworth DFX), 1h 29m 06·16s, 134·676 mph/216·739 km/h.
2 Danny Sullivan, USA (March 86C-Cosworth DFX), 1h 29m 26·40s.
3 Bobby Rahal, USA (March 86C-Cosworth DFX), 199 laps.
4 Mario Andretti, USA (Lola T86/00-Cosworth DFX), 199.
5 Emerson Fittipaldi, BR (March 86C-Cosworth DFX), 198.
6 Al Unser Jnr, USA (Lola T86/00-Cosworth DFX), 193.
7 Ed Pimm, USA (March 86C-Cosworth DFX), 192;
8 Geoff Brabham, AUS (Lola T86/00-Cosworth DFX), 188 (DNF, out of fuel); **9** Johnny Rutherford, USA (March 86C-Cosworth DFX), 187 (DNF, oil leak); **10** Roberto Moreno, BR (Lola T86/00-Cosworth DFX), 187; **11** Johnny Parsons, USA (March 86C-Cosworth DFX), 182; **12** Roberto Guerrero, COL (March 86C-Cosworth DFX), 179 (DNF, engine).
Fastest qualifier: Rahal, 22·097s, 162·918 mph/262·190 km/h.

Championship points (prior to last round in November)

1	Bobby Rahal, USA	174
2	Mike Andretti, USA	171
3	Danny Sullivan, USA	147
4	Mario Andretti, USA	134
5	Al Unser Jnr, USA	117
6=	Emerson Fittipaldi, USA	103
6=	Kevin Cogan, USA	103

8 Tom Sneva, USA, 82; **9** Johnny Rutherford, USA, 77; **10** Rick Mears, USA, 72.

Final results will be given in *Autocourse 1987/88*.

IMSA CAMEL GT Championship 1985 Results

The final round of the 1985 IMSA CAMEL GT Championship was run after *Autocourse 1985/86* went to press.

EASTERN AIRLINES 3-HOUR CAMEL GT, Daytona International Speedway, Florida, United States of America, 1 December. IMSA Camel GT Championship, round 17. 89 laps of the 3·560-mile/5·729-km circuit, 316·84 miles/509·88 km/h.
1 Al Holbert/Al Unser Jnr, USA/USA (t/c Porsche 962), 3h 00m 55·13s, 105·077 mph/169·105 km/h (1st GTP class).
2 Brian Redman/Hurley Haywood, GB/USA (Jaguar XJR-5), 3h 01m 03·49s.
3 Pete Halsmer/John Morton, USA/USA (t/c Porsche 962), 88 laps.
4 Bob Tullius/Chip Robinson, USA/USA (Jaguar XJR-7), 87.
5 Randy Lanier/Michael Roe, USA/IRL (March 85G-Chevrolet), 86.
6 Bob Akin/Jo Gartner, USA/A (t/c Porsche 962), 86.
7 John Kalagian/Jim Mullen, USA/USA (t/c March 85G-Porsche), 86; **8** Drake Olson/Bobby Rahal, USA/USA (t/c Porsche 962), 85; **9** John Jones/Lyn St James, CDN/USA (Ford Mustang), 84 (1st GTO

class); **10** Lew Price/Chip Mead/Carson Baird, USA/USA/USA (Chevrolet Corvette GTP), 84.
Fastest lap: Bill Adam, USA (t/c Lola GTP-Chevrolet), 1m 41·546s, 126·209 mph/203·113 km/h (record).
Other class winners. 700 kg: Jim Downing/John Maffucci, USA/USA (Argo JM16-Mazda), 82. **GTU:** Chris Cord, USA (Toyota Celica), 79.

Final Championship points

GTP class

1	Al Holbert, USA	218
2	Derek Bell, GB	154
3	Hurley Haywood, USA	149
4	Pete Halsmer, USA	138
5	Chip Robinson, USA	137
6	Drake Olson, USA	117

7 Brian Redman, GB, 112; **8** Bob Wollek, F, 105; **9** Bob Tullius, USA, 100; **10** Jim Busby, USA, 98.

700 kg class

1	Jim Downing, USA	265
2	John Maffucci, USA	212
3	Kelly Marsh, USA	165
4	Jeff Kline, USA	115
5	Bill Alsup, USA	106
6	Charles Morgan, USA	86

GTO class

1	John Jones, CDN	216
2	Darin Brassfield, USA	115
3	Wally Dallenbach Jnr, USA	110
4	Danny Smith, USA	109
5	Lyn St James, USA	104
6	Roger Mandeville, USA	81

GTU class

1	Jack Baldwin, USA	221
2	Chris Cord, USA	175
3	Amos Johnson, USA	148
4	Bob Earl, USA	130
5	Al Bacon, USA	87
6	Scott Pruett, USA	72

1986 Results

25 SUNBANK DAYTONA 24 HOURS, Daytona International Speedway, Florida, United States of America, 1/2 February. IMSA Camel GT Championship, round 1. 712 laps of the 3·560-mile/5·729-km circuit, 2534·72 miles/4079·05 km.
1 Al Holbert/Derek Bell/Al Unser Jnr, USA/GB/USA (t/c Porsche 962), 24h 01m 45·800s, 105·484 mph/169·760 km/h (1st GTP class).
2 Danny Sullivan/A. J. Foyt/Arie Luyendyk, USA/USA/NL (t/c Porsche 962), 24h 03m 34·950s.
3 Jim Busby/Derek Warwick/Darin Brassfield/Jochen Mass, USA/GB/USA/D (t/c Porsche 962), 711 laps.
4 Lanny Hester/Maurice Hester/Lee Mueller, USA/USA/USA (Ford Mustang), 622 (1st GTO class).
5 Bruce Jenner/Scott Pruett/Klaus Ludwig, USA/USA/D (Ford Mustang), 614.
6 Bob Tullius/Chip Robinson/Claude Ballot-Lena, USA/USA/F (Jaguar XJR-7), 607.
7 Frank Rubino/Ray Mummery/John Schneider, USA/USA/USA (Argo JM19-Mazda), 600 (1st 700 kg class); **8** Amos Johnson/Dennis Shaw/Jack Dunham, USA/USA/USA (Mazda RX-7), 597 (1st GTU class); **9** Mandy Gonzalez/Basilio Davila/Ernesto Soto/Diego Montoya, PR/PR/YV/COL (Royale RP40-Porsche), 579; **10** Bob Reed/Tom Kendall/John Hogdal, USA/USA/USA (Mazda RX-7), 563.
Fastest lap: John Paul Jnr, USA (t/c March 85G-Buick), 1m 42·519s, 125·011 mph/201·185 km/h.
Championship points. GTP: 1 Holbert and Bell, 20; **3** Foyt and Luyendyk, 15; **5** Busby, Mass and Brassfield, 12; **700 kg: 1** Rubino, Mummery and Schneider, 20. **GTO: 1** Hester, Hester and Mueller, 20. **GTU: 1** Johnson, Shaw and Dunham, 20.

LÖWENBRÄU GRAND PRIX OF MIAMI CAMEL GTP, Miami Street/Road Circuit, Miami, Florida, United States of America, 2 March. IMSA Camel GT Championship, round 2. 128 laps of the 1·873-mile/3·014-km circuit, 239·74 miles/385·79 km.
1 Bob Wollek/Paolo Barilla, F/I (t/c Porsche 962), 3h 01m 22·423s, 79·309 mph/127·635 km/h.
2 Danny Sullivan/A. J. Foyt, USA/USA (t/c Porsche 962), 3h 01m 51·597s.
3 Hans Stuck/Jo Gartner, D/A (t/c Porsche 962), 128 laps.
4 Brian Redman/Hurley Haywood, GB/USA (Jaguar XJR-7), 127 (DNF, accident).
5 Klaus Ludwig/Tom Gloy, D/USA (t/c Ford Mustang Probe), 126.
6 Al Holbert/Derek Bell, USA/GB (t/c Porsche 962), 123.
7 Oscar Larrauri/Massimo Sigala, RA/I (t/c Porsche 962), 123; **8** Pete Halsmer/Lyn St James, USA/USA (t/c Ford Mustang Probe), 123; **9** David Hobbs/John Watson, GB/GB (t/c BMW GTP), 122; **10** Tony Adamowicz/Elliott Forbes-Robinson, USA/USA (t/c Nissan GTP ZX-T), 119.
Fastest lap: Larrauri, 1m 17·546s, 86·952 mph/139·935 km/h (record).

MIAMI CAMEL LIGHT GRAND PRIX, Miami Street/Road Circuit, Miami, Florida, United States of America, 23 February. 21 laps of the 1·873-mile/3·014-km circuit, 39·33 miles/63·29 km.
1 Don Bell, USA (Royale RP40-Buick), 30m 54·520s, 76·353 mph/122·878 km/h.
2 Gianpiero Moretti, I (Alba AR2-Ferrari), 31m 01·912s.
3 Jim Downing, USA (Argo JM19-Mazda), 21 laps.
4 Logan Blackburn, USA (Tiga GT285-Mazda), 20.
5 Frank Rubino, USA (Argo JM19-Mazda), 19.
6 Paul Corazzo, USA (Royale RP40-Mazda), 18.
7 Jim Fowells, USA (Argo JM16-Mazda), 18; **8** Tom Hessert, USA (Harrier-Mazda), 18. No other finishers.

Fastest lap: Bell, 1m 24·176s, 80·104 mph/128·915 km/h (record).
Other race winners. GTO: Jack Baldwin, USA (Chevrolet Camaro), 26 laps, 48·69 miles/78·36 km in 45m 55·190s, 63·630 mph/102·402 km/h. **GTU:** Bob Earl, USA (Pontiac Fiero), 31 laps, 58·06 miles/93·43 km in 46m 31·812s, 74·871 mph/120.493 km/h.
Championship points. GTP: 1 Foyt, 30; **2** Holbert and Bell, 26; **4** Wollek, 20; **5** Luyendyk, 15; **6** Busby, Mass, Brassfield, Stuck and Gartner, 12. **700 kg: 1** Rubino, 28; **2** Mummery, Schneider and Bell, 20. **GTO: 1** Jenner, 23; **2** Hassey, Hester, Mueller and Baldwin, 20. **GTU: 1** Johnson, 32; **2** Kendall, 25; **3** Shaw, Dunham and Earl, 20.

COCA-COLA 12 HOURS OF SEBRING CAMEL GT, Sebring International Raceway, Florida, United States of America, 22 March. IMSA Camel GT Championship, round 3. 287 laps of the 4·86-mile/7·82-km circuit, 1394·82 miles/2244·34 km.
1 Bob Akin/Hans Stuck/Jo Gartner, USA/D/A (t/c Porsche 962), 12h 02m 22·989s, 115·852 mph/186·445 km/h (1st GTP class).
2 John Morton/Darin Brassfield/Jim Busby, USA/USA/USA (t/c Porsche 962), 279 laps.
3 Al Holbert/Derek Bell/Al Unser Jnr (t/c Porsche 962), 269.
4 Bruce Jenner/Scott Pruett, USA/USA (Ford Mustang), 265 (1st GTO class).
5 Bill Elliott/Ricky Rudd, USA/USA (Ford Mustang), 265.
6 Jim Rothbarth/Mike Meyer/Jeff Kline, USA/USA/USA (Royale RP40-Mazda), 246 (1st 700 kg class).
7 Ron Grable/John Heinricy/Bobby Carradine, USA/USA/USA (Chevrolet Corvette), 245; **8** Roger Mandeville/Danny Smith, USA/USA (Mazda RX-7), 240 (1st GTU class); **9** Jim Downing/John Maffucci/John O'Steen, USA/USA/USA (Argo JM19-Mazda), 236; **10** Lance van Every/Ash Tisdelle/Rusty Bond, USA/USA/USA (Chevrolet Camaro), 233.
Fastest lap: Bell, 2m 13·857s, 130·707 mph/210·352 km/h (record).
Championship points. GTP: 1 Holbert and Bell, 38; **3** Stuck and Gartner, 32; **5** Foyt, 30; **6** Brassfield, 27. **700 kg: 1** Rubino, Meyer and Kline, 28. **GTO: 1** Jenner, 43; **2** Pruett, 35; **3** Hassey, Hester, Mueller and Baldwin, 20. **GTU: 1** Kendall, 40; **2** Mandeville, 35; **3** Johnson, 32.

ATLANTA JOURNAL/CONSTITUTION CAMEL GT, Road Atlanta, Georgia, United States of America, 6 April. IMSA Camel GT Championship, round 4. 124 laps of the 2·520-mile/4·055-km circuit, 312·48 miles/502·82 km.
1 Sarel van der Merwe/Doc Bundy, ZA/USA (t/c Lola GTP-Chevrolet Corvette), 2h 48m 07·910s, 110·627 mph/178·036 km/h (1st GTP class).
2 John Paul Jnr/Whitney Ganz, USA/USA (t/c March 85G-Buick), 2h 48m 36·990s.
3 Al Holbert/Derek Bell, USA/GB (t/c Porsche 962), 124 laps.
4 Bob Tullius/Chip Robinson, USA/USA (Jaguar XJR-7), 122.
5 John Morton/Jim Busby, USA/USA (t/c Porsche 962), 120.
6 Darin Brassfield/Jochen Mass, USA/D (t/c Porsche 962), 119.
7 Al Leon/Art Leon/Calvin Fish, USA/USA/GB (March 84G-Chevrolet), 116; **8** 'John Winter'/Marc Duez, D/B (t/c Porsche 962), 115; **9** Jim Downing/John Maffucci, USA/USA (Argo JM19-Mazda), 112 (1st 700 kg class); **10** Mike Brockman/Steve Durst, USA/USA (Tiga GT285-Mazda), 111.
Fastest lap: van der Merwe, 1m 14·410s, 120·951 mph/194·651 km/h (record).
Other race/class winners. GTO: Scott Pruett, USA (Ford Mustang), 32 laps, 80·64 miles/129·76 km in 46m 26·905s, 103·340 mph/166·309 km/h. **GTU:** Bob Earl, USA (Pontiac Fiero), 31 laps.
Championship points. GTP: 1 Holbert and Bell, 50; **3** Brassfield, 33; **4** Stuck and Gartner, 32; **6** Morton, 31. **700 kg: 1** Downing, 47; **2** Rubino, 36; **3** Maffucci, 35. **GTO: 1** Pruett, 55; **2** Jenner, 43; **3** Baldwin, 32. **GTU: 1** Kendall, 55; **2** Johnson, 44; **3** Earl and Reed, 40.

LOS ANGELES TIMES/FORD GRAND PRIX OF ENDURANCE, Riverside International Raceway, California, United States of America, 27 April. IMSA Camel GT Championship, round 5. 178 laps of the 3·25-mile/5·23-km circuit, 578·50 miles/930·94 km.
1 Rob Dyson/Price Cobb, USA/USA (t/c Porsche 962), 6h 01m 45·423s, 95·948 mph/154·413 km/h (1st GTP class).
2 Darin Brassfield/Jochen Mass, USA/D (t/c Porsche 962), 177 laps.
3 Bob Wollek/Paolo Barilla, F/I (t/c Porsche 962), 176.
4 Bob Akin/James Weaver, USA/GB (t/c Porsche 962), 170.
5 Jack Baldwin/Jim Miller, USA/USA (Chevrolet Camaro), 168 (1st GTO class).
6 Jim Adams/John Hotchkis, USA/USA (t/c March 83G-Porsche), 168.
7 Scott Pruett/Bruce Jenner, USA/USA (Ford Mustang), 166; **8** Michael Chandler/Steve Cameron/Danny May, USA/USA/USA (Ford Thunderbird), 163; **9** Jim Downing/John Maffucci, USA/USA (Argo JM19-Mazda), 163 (1st 700 kg class); **10** Jim Busby/John Morton, USA/USA (t/c Porsche 962), 162.
Fastest lap: John Paul Jnr, USA (t/c March 85G-Buick), 1m 30·103s, 129·851 mph/208·974 km/h (record).
Other class winners. GTU: Roger Mandeville/Danny Smith, USA/USA (Mazda RX-7), 161.
Championship points. GTP: 1 Holbert and Bell, 54; **3** Brassfield, 48; **4** Mass, 33; **5** Stuck, Gartner and Wollek, 32. **700 kg: 1** Downing, 67; **2** Maffucci, 55; **3** Meyer, 40. **GTO: 1** Pruett, 70; **2** Jenner, 58; **3** Baldwin, 52. **GTU: 1** Kendall, 63; **2** Mandeville, 55; **3** Johnson, 54.

MONTEREY TRIPLE CROWN CAMEL GRAND PRIX, Laguna Seca Raceway, California, United States of America, 4 May. IMSA Camel GT Championship, round 6. 98 laps of the 1·900-mile/3·058-km circuit, 186·20 miles/299·68 km.
1 Klaus Ludwig, D (t/c Ford Mustang Probe), 1h 43m 47·384s, 107·641 mph/173·231 km/h (1st GTP class).
2 Chip Robinson/Hurley Haywood, USA/USA (Jaguar XJR-7), 1h 44m 24·346s.
3 Price Cobb, USA (t/c Porsche 962), 96 laps.
4 Al Holbert, USA (t/c Porsche 962), 95.
5 Pete Halsmer, USA (t/c Ford Mustang Probe), 94.
6 Bob Earl, USA (Pontiac Fiero GTP), 90 (1st 700 kg class).
7 Jim Downing, USA (Argo JM19-Mazda), 90; **8** Don Bell, USA (Argo JM19-Buick), **9** Logan Blackburn, USA (Tiga GT286-Buick), 89; **10** Jim Rothbarth/Mike Meyer, USA/USA (Royale RP40-Mazda), 87.
Fastest lap: Holbert, 58·874s, 116·180 mph/186·973 km/h (record).
Other race/class winners. GTO: 1 Scott Pruett, USA (Ford Mustang), 33 laps, 62·70 miles/100·91 km in 37m 25·497s, 100·521 mph/161·772 km/h. **GTU:** Tom Kendall, USA (Mazda RX-7), 32 laps.
Championship points. GTP: 1 Holbert, 64; **2** Bell, 54; **3** Brassfield, 48; **4** Morton, 37; **5** Robinson, 35; **6** Mass, 33. **700 kg: 1** Downing, 82; **2** Maffucci, 55; **3** Meyer, 48. **GTO: 1** Pruett, 90; **2** Jenner, 64; **3** Baldwin, 52. **GTU: 1** Kendall, 83; **2** Johnson, 69; **3** Mandeville, 68.

CHARLOTTE 500 KM CAMEL GRAND PRIX, Charlotte Motor Speedway, North Carolina, United States of America, 18 May. IMSA Camel GT Championship, round 7. 138 laps of the 2·250-mile/3·621-km circuit, 310·50 miles/499·70 km.
1 Drake Olson/Price Cobb, USA/USA (t/c Porsche 962), 2h 49m 55·575s, 109·636 mph/176·442 km/h (1st GTP class).
2 Bob Akin/Hans Stuck, USA/D (t/c Porsche 962), 136 laps.
3 Whitney Ganz/Bob Lobenberg, USA/USA (t/c March 85G-Buick), 135.
4 Sarel van der Merwe/Doc Bundy, ZA/USA (t/c Lola GTP-Chevrolet Corvette), 135.
5 Darin Brassfield/John Morton, USA/USA (t/c Porsche 962), 131.
6 Bob Earl/Ray Bellm, USA/GB (Pontiac Fiero GTP), 127 (1st 700 kg class).
7 Jim Rothbarth/Mike Meyer, USA/USA (Royale RP40-Mazda), 122; **8** Ron Canizares/Howard Katz, USA/USA (Tiga GT286-Mazda), 121; **9** Colin Trueman/Deborah Gregg/Jeff Kline, USA/USA/USA (Tiga GT286-Porsche), 118; **10** Martino Finotto/Carlo Facetti/Paolo Barilla, I/I/I (t/c Alba AR6-Carma), 115.
Fastest lap: Klaus Ludwig, D (t/c Ford Mustang Probe), 1m 08·468s, 118·303 mph/190·390 km/h (record).
Other race/class winners. GTO: Jack Baldwin, USA (Chevrolet Camaro), 83 laps, 186·75 miles/300·54 km in 2h 09m 26·679s, 86·562 mph/139·308 km/h. **GTU:** Tom Kendall, USA (Mazda RX-7), 81 laps.
Championship points. GTP: 1 Holbert, 64; **2** Brassfield, 56; **3** Bell, 54; **4** Cobb, 52; **5** Stuck, 47; **6** Morton and Akin, 45. **700 kg: 1** Downing, 82; **2** Meyer, 63; **3** Maffucci and Rothbarth, 55. **GTO: 1** Pruett, 102; **2** Jenner, 76; **3** Baldwin, 72. **GTU: 1** Kendall, 103; **2** Johnson, 84; **3** Mandeville, 68.

LIME ROCK 150-LAP CAMEL GRAND PRIX, Lime Rock Park, Connecticut, United States of America, 26 May. IMSA Camel GT Championship, round 8. 150 laps of the 1·53-mile/2·46-km circuit, 229·50 miles/369·00 km.
1 Al Holbert, USA (t/c Porsche 962), 2h 18m 49·858s, 99·185 mph/159·622 km/h (1st GTP class).
2 Drake Olson/Price Cobb, USA/USA (t/c Porsche 962), 2h 19m 09·342s.
3 Bob Wollek/Paolo Barilla, F/I (t/c Porsche 962), 149 laps.
4 Derek Bell, GB (t/c Porsche 962), 149.
5 Bob Tullius/Chip Robinson, USA/USA (Jaguar XJR-7), 147.
6 Bob Akin/Jo Gartner, USA/A (t/c Porsche 962), 146.
7 Sarel van der Merwe/Doc Bundy, ZA/USA (t/c Lola GTP-Chevrolet Corvette), 146; **8** Darin Brassfield/Jochen Mass, USA/D (t/c Porsche 962), 145; **9** David Loring, USA (Mazda GTP), 141 (1st 700 kg class); **10** Pete Halsmer/Tom Gloy, USA/USA (t/c Ford Mustang Probe), 139.
Fastest lap: Olson, 47·470s, 116·031 mph/186·733 km/h (record).
Championship points. GTP: 1 Holbert, 84; **2** Cobb, 67; **3** Bell, 64; **4** Brassfield, 59; **5** Akin, 51; **6** Stuck, 47. **700 kg: 1** Downing, 90; **2** Meyer, 69; **3** Rothbarth, 61.

500 KM MID-OHIO CAMEL GRAND PRIX, Mid-Ohio Sports Car Course, Lexington, Ohio, United States of America, 8 June. IMSA Camel GT Championship, round 9. 129 laps of the 2·400-mile/3·862-km circuit, 309·60 miles/498·20 km.
1 Al Holbert/Derek Bell, USA/GB (t/c Porsche 962), 3h 07m 54·731s, 98·855 mph/159·091 km/h (1st GTP class).
2 Bob Tullius/Chip Robinson, USA/USA (Jaguar XJR-7), 3h 09m 11·272s.
3 Doc Bundy/Sarel van der Merwe, USA/ZA (t/c Lola GTP-Chevrolet Corvette), 128 laps.
4 Bob Wollek/Paolo Barilla, F/I (t/c Porsche 962), 128.
5 Brian Redman/Hurley Haywood, GB/USA (Jaguar XJR-7), 128.
6 Drake Olson/Price Cobb, USA/USA (t/c Porsche 962), 128.
7 Elliott Forbes-Robinson/Ludwig Heimrath Jnr, USA/CDN (t/c Nissan GTP ZX-T), 127; **8** Oscar Larrauri/Massimo Sigala, RA/I (t/c Porsche 962), 126; **9** Darin Brassfield/Jochen Mass, USA/D (t/c Porsche 962), 125; **10** Jim Busby/John Morton, USA/USA (t/c Porsche 962), 124; **11** Mike Brockman/Steve Durst, USA/USA (Tiga GT285-Mazda), 120 (1st 700 kg class).
Fastest lap: Holbert, 1m 23·120s, 103·946 mph/167·284 km/h (record).
Other race/class winners. GTO: Scott Pruett, USA (Ford Mustang), 65 laps, 156.00 miles/251·03 km in 1h 44m 37·307s, 89·465 mph/143·980 km/h. **GTU:** Bob Earl, USA (Pontiac Fiero), 63 laps.
Championship points. GTP: 1 Holbert, 104; **2** Bell, 84; **3** Cobb, 73; **4** Brassfield, 61; **5** Robinson, 58; **6** Wollek, 54. **700 kg: 1** Downing, 105; **2** Meyer, 79; **3** Rothbarth, 71. **GTO: 1** Pruett, 122; **2** Jenner, 91; **3** Baldwin, 84. **GTU: 1** Kendall, 103; **2** Johnson, 96; **3** Mandeville, 83.

3-HOUR GRAND PRIX OF PALM BEACH, West Palm Beach Street Circuit, Florida, United States of America, 22 June. IMSA Camel GT Championship, round 10. 136 laps of the 1·600-mile/2·575-km circuit, 217·60 miles/350·20 km.
1 Sarel van der Merwe/Doc Bundy, ZA/USA (t/c Lola GTP-Chevrolet Corvette) 3h 00m 54·093s, 72·172 mph/116·149 km/h (1st GTP class).
2 Darin Brassfield/Jochen Mass, USA/D (t/c Porsche 962), 3h 00m 54·486s.
3 Brian Redman/Hurley Haywood, GB/USA (Jaguar XJR-7), 136 laps.
4 Derek Bell/Al Holbert, GB/USA (t/c Porsche 962), 136.
5 Jim Busby/John Morton, USA/USA (t/c Porsche 962), 135.
6 Oscar Larrauri/Gianpiero Moretti, RA/I (t/c Porsche 962), 134.
7 Ruggero Melgrati/Carlo Facetti, I/I (t/c Alba AR6-Carma), 131 (1st 700 kg class); **8** Don Bell/Jeff Kline, USA/USA (Argo JM16-Buick), 130; **9** A.J. Foyt/Danny Ongais, USA/USA (t/c Porsche 962), 127; **10** Bob Tullius/Chip Robinson, USA/USA (Jaguar XJR-7), 127.
Fastest lap: Mass, 1m 07·436s, 85·414 mph/137·460 km/h (record).
Other race winners. GTO: Scott Pruett, USA (Ford Mustang), 35 laps, 56·00 miles/90·13 km in 45m 30·506s, 73·832 mph/118·821 km/h. **GTU:** Roger Mandeville, USA (Mazda RX-7), 32 laps, 51·20 miles/82·40 km in 45m 20·069s, 67·763 mph/109·054 km/h.
Championship points. GTP: 1 Holbert, 114; **2** Bell, 94; **3** Brassfield, 76; **4** Cobb, 73; **5** Bundy and van der Merwe, 66. **700 kg: 1** Downing, 105; **2** Meyer, 91; **3** Rothbarth, 83. **GTO: 1** Pruett, 142; **2** Jenner, 99; **3** Baldwin, 84. **GTU: 1** Kendall, 118; **2** Johnson, 108; **3** Mandeville, 103.

CAMEL CONTINENTAL, Watkins Glen International Circuit, New York, United States of America, 6 July. IMSA Camel GT Championship, round 11. 148 laps of the 3·377-mile/5·435-km circuit, 499·80 miles/804·38 km.
1 Al Holbert/Derek Bell, USA/GB (t/c Porsche 962), 4h 37m 08·802s, 108·202 mph/174·134 km/h (1st GTP class).
2 Oscar Larrauri/Gianpiero Moretti, RA/I (t/c Porsche 962), 147 laps.
3 Whitney Ganz/Jim Crawford, USA/GB (t/c March 85G-Buick), 146.
4 Bob Akin/Price Cobb/James Weaver, USA/USA/GB (t/c Porsche 962), 145.
5 Davey Jones/John Andretti, USA/USA (t/c BMW GTP), 144.
6 John Watson/David Hobbs, GB/GB (t/c BMW GTP), 143.
7 Jochen Mass/Darin Brassfield, D/USA (t/c Porsche 962), 143; **8** Jim Adams/John Hotchkiss, USA/USA (t/c Porsche 962), 141; **9** Bob Tullius/Chip Robinson, USA/USA (Jaguar XJR-7), 138; **10** Charles Morgan/Logan Blackburn, USA/USA (Tiga GT286-Buick), 135 (1st 700 kg class).
Fastest lap: Jim Busby, USA (t/c Porsche 962) 1m 41·170s, 120·166 mph/193·388 km/h (record).
Other class winners. GTO: Jack Baldwin/Geoff Bodine, USA/USA (Chevrolet Camaro), 135. **GTU:** Roger Mandeville/Danny Smith, USA/USA (Mazda RX-7), 128.
Championship points. GTP: 1 Holbert, 134; **2** Bell, 114; **3** Cobb, 83; **4** Brassfield, 80; **5** Bundy and van der Merwe, 67. **700 kg: 1** Downing, 117; **2** Meyer, 97; **3** Rothbarth, 89. **GTO: 1** Pruett, 152; **2** Jenner, 114; **3** Baldwin, 104. **GTU: 1** Kendall, 133; **2** Mandeville, 123; **3** Johnson, 111.

GI JOE'S GRAN PRIX, Portland International Raceway, Portland, Oregon, United States of America, 27 July. IMSA Camel GT Championship, round 12. 97 laps of the 1·915-mile/3·082-km circuit, 185·76 miles/289·95 km.
1 Al Holbert, USA (t/c Porsche 962), 1h 42m 54·986s, 108·295 mph/174·283 km/h (1st GTP class).
2 Bob Tullius/Chip Robinson, USA/USA (Jaguar XJR-7), 1h 42m 56·543s.
3 Geoff Brabham, AUS (t/c Nissan GTP ZX-T), 97 laps.
4 John Watson/David Hobbs, GB/GB (t/c BMW GTP), 97.
5 Tom Gloy/Lyn St James, USA/USA (t/c Ford Mustang Probe), 97.
6 Klaus Ludwig/Scott Pruett, D/USA (t/c Ford Mustang Probe), 97.
7 Derek Bell, GB (t/c Porsche 962), 97; **8** Sarel van der Merwe/Doc Bundy, ZA/USA (t/c Lola GTP-Chevrolet Corvette), 97; **9** Brian Redman/Hurley Haywood, GB/USA (Jaguar XJR-7), 96; **10** Bob Wollek, F (t/c Porsche 962), 95.
Fastest lap: van der Merwe, 1m 01·130s, 112·776 mph/181·495 km/h (record).
Other race/class winners. 700 kg: Jim Downing, USA (Argo JM19-Mazda, 87. **GTO:** Bruce Jenner/Scott Pruett, USA/USA (Ford Mustang), 97 laps, 185·76 miles/298·95 km in 1h 55m 25·212s, 96·563 mph/155·403 km/h. **GTU:** Bob Earl, USA (Pontiac Fiero), 92.
Championship points. GTP: 1 Holbert, 154; **2** Bell, 118; **3** Cobb, 83; **4** Brassfield, 80; **5** Robinson, 78; **6** Bundy and van der Merwe, 70. **700 kg: 1** Downing, 137; **2** Meyer, 109; **3** Rothbarth, 101. **GTO: 1** Pruett, 157; **2** Jenner, 134; **3** Baldwin, 114. **GTU: 1** Kendall, 145; **2** Mandeville, 125; **3** Johnson, 111.

SEARS POINT 300-KM GRAND PRIX, Sears Point International Raceway, Sonoma, California, United States of America, 3 August. IMSA Camel GT Championship, round 13. 75 laps of the 2·523-mile/4·060-km circuit, 189·23 miles/304·50 km.

1 Rob Dyson/Price Cobb, USA/USA (t/c Porsche 962), 1h 55m 01·830s, 98·700 mph/158·842 km/h (1st GTP class).
2 Al Holbert/Derek Bell, USA/GB (t/c Porsche 962), 1h 55m 43·010s.
3 Brian Redman/Hurley Haywood, GB/USA (Jaguar XJR-7), 75 laps.
4 Elliott Forbes-Robinson, USA (t/c Nissan GTP ZX-T), 75.
5 John Andretti/Davey Jones, USA/USA (t/c BMW GTP), 75.
6 Paolo Barilla/Bob Wollek, I/F (t/c Porsche 962), 74.
7 Jochen Mass/Darin Brassfield, D/USA (t/c Porsche 962), 72; 8 James Weaver, GB (t/c Porsche 962), 68 (DNF, engine); 9 Jim Downing, USA (Argo JM19-Mazda), 67 (1st 700 kg class); 10 Steve Phillips, USA (Tiga GT285-Chevrolet), 67.
Fastest lap: Klaus Ludwig, D (t/c Ford Mustang Probe), 1m 28·757s, 102·333 mph/164·689 km/h.
Other race/class winners. GTO: Willy T. Ribbs, USA (Chevrolet Camaro), 25 laps, 63·08 miles/101·50 km in 41m 47·720s, 90·548 mph/145·723 km/h. **GTU:** Tom Kendall, USA (Mazda RX-7), 24.
Championship points. GTP: 1 Holbert, 169; 2 Bell, 133; 3 Cobb, 103; 4 Brassfield, 84; 5 Robinson, 78; 6 Bundy and van der Merwe, 71. **700 kg:** 1 Downing, 157; 2 Rothbarth, 113; 3 Meyer, 109. **GTO:** 1 Pruett, 157; 2 Jenner, 140; 3 Baldwin, 114. **GTU:** 1 Kendall, 168; 2 Mandeville, 127; 3 Johnson, 126.

LÖWENBRÄU CLASSIC 500-MILE CAMEL GRAND PRIX, Road America, Elkhart Lake, Wisconsin, United States of America, 24 August. IMSA Camel GT Championship, round 14. 125 laps of the 4·000-mile/6·437-km circuit, 500·00 miles/804·63 km.
1 Al Holbert/Al Unser Jnr, USA/USA (t/c Porsche 962), 4h 35m 57·504s, 108·712 mph/174·955 km/h (1st GTP class).
2 Rob Dyson/Price Cobb, USA/USA (t/c Porsche 962), 120 laps.
3 Rocky Moran/Dennis Aase, USA/USA (t/c Toyota Celica Turbo), 115 (1st GTO class).
4 Scott Pruett/Bruce Jenner, USA/USA (Ford Mustang), 115.
5 Martino Finotto/Ruggero Melgrati, I/I (Alba AR6-Carma), 115 (1st 700 kg class).
6 Bob Akin/Kees Nierop, USA/CDN, (t/c Porsche 962), 114.
7 Chip Ganassi/David Sears, USA/GB (Pontiac Fiero GTP), 113; 8 David Loring/Pierre Honegger USA/USA (Mazda GTP), 113; 9 Jim Downing/John Maffucci, USA/USA (Argo JM19-Mazda), 113; 10 Don Bell/Jeff Kline, USA/USA (Royal GTP-Buick), 112.
Fastest lap: John Watson, GB (t/c BMW GTP), 2m 01·531s, 118·488 mph/190·687 km/h (record).
Other class winners. GTU: Roger Mandeville/Danny Smith, USA/USA (Mazda RX-7), 108.
Championship points. GTP: 1 Holbert, 189; 2 Bell, 133; 3 Cobb, 118; 4 Brassfield, 94; 5 Robinson, 78; 6 Akin, 73. **700 kg:** 1 Downing, 167; 2 Rothbarth, 113; 3 Meyer, 109. **GTO:** 1 Pruett, 172; 2 Jenner, 155; 3 Baldwin, 117. **GTU:** 1 Kendall, 183; 2 Mandeville, 147; 3 Johnson, 130.

KODAK COPIERS 500 CAMEL GRAND PRIX, Watkins Glen Grand Prix Circuit, New York, United States of America, 21 September. IMSA Camel GT Championship, round 15. 92 laps of the 3·377-mile/5·435-km circuit, 310·68 miles/500·02 km.
1 Davey Jones/John Andretti, USA/USA (t/c BMW GTP), 2h 47m 07·813s 111·536 mph/179·499 km/h (1st GTP class).
2 Al Holbert/Derek Bell, USA/GB (t/c Porsche 962), 2h 47m 31·922s.
3 Rob Dyson/Price Cobb, USA/USA (t/c Porsche 962), 92 laps.
4 Sarel van der Merwe/Doc Bundy, ZA/USA (t/c Lola GTP-Chevrolet Corvette), 91.
5 Brian Redman/Hurley Haywood, GB/USA (Jaguar XJR-7), 91.
6 John Hotchkis/Jim Adams, USA/USA (t/c Porsche 962), 90.
7 Chip Ganassi/Bob Earl, USA/USA (Pontiac Fiero GTP), 85 (1st 700 kg class); 8 David Loring, USA (Mazda GTP), 84; 9 Bob Akin/James Weaver, USA/GB (t/c Porsche 962), 83; 10 Skeeter McKitterick/Tim Coconis, USA/USA (Alba AR6-Oldsmobile), 83.
Fastest lap: Jones, 1m 39·200s, 122·552 mph/197·228 km/h (record).
Other race/class winners. GTO: Dennis Aase, USA (t/c Toyota Celica Turbo), 55 laps, 185·74 miles/298·93 km in 1h 47m 09·096s, 104·003 mph/167·376 km/h. **GTU:** Roger Mandeville, USA (Mazda RX-7), 52.
Championship points. GTP: 1 Holbert, 204; 2 Bell, 148; 3 Cobb, 130; 4 Brassfield, 94; 5 Robinson, van der Merwe and Bundy, 81. **700 kg:** 1 Downing, 177; 2 Rothbarth, 119; 3 Meyer, 115. **GTO:** 1 Pruett, 172; 2 Jenner, 163; 3 Baldwin, 149. **GTU:** 1 Kendall, 218; 2 Mandeville, 179; 3 Johnson, 155.

COLUMBUS FORD DEALERS 500 CAMEL GRAND PRIX, Ohio Street Circuit, Columbus, Ohio, United States of America, 5 October. IMSA Camel GT Championship, round 16. 136 laps of the 2·30-mile/3·70-km circuit, 312·80 miles/503·40 km.
1 Bob Wollek/Scott Pruett, F/USA (t/c Porsche 962), 3h 44m 46·050s 83·500 mph/134·380 km/h (1st GTP class).
2 Darin Brassfield/Jochen Mass, USA/D (t/c Porsche 962), 135 laps.
3 Brian Redman/Hurley Haywood, GB/USA (Jaguar XJR-7), 134.
4 Rob Dyson/Price Cobb, USA/USA (t/c Porsche 962), 134.
5 Elliott Forbes-Robinson/Geoff Brabham, USA/AUS (t/c Nissan GTP ZX-T), 134.
6 Jim Busby/John Morton, USA/USA (t/c Porsche 962), 134.
7 John Hotchkis/Jim Adams, USA/USA (t/c Porsche 962), 130; 8 Bruce Leven/Steve Millen, USA/NZ (t/c Porsche 962), 129; 9 Bob Akin/James Weaver, USA/GB (t/c Porsche 962), 127; 10 Steve Shelton/Tom Shelton, USA/USA (t/c Porsche 962), 126; 11 Steve Durst/Michael Brockman, USA/USA (Tiga GT286-Mazda), 123 (1st 700 kg class).
Fastest lap: Brabham, 1m 33·730s, 88·339 mph/142·17 km/h.
Other race/class winners. GTO: Willy T. Ribbs, USA (Chevrolet Camaro), 31 laps, 71·30 miles/114·70 km in 1h 00m 30·905s, 70·693 mph/113·769 km/h. **GTU:** Roger Mandeville, USA (Mazda RX-7), 30.

Championship points (prior to final round at Daytona):
GTP

1	Al Holbert, USA (Champion)	204
2	Derek Bell, GB	148
3	Price Cobb, USA	140
4	Darin Brassfield, USA	109
5	Bob Wollek, F	83

6 Chip Robinson, USA, Sarel van der Merwe, ZA, Doc Bundy, USA and Hurley Haywood, USA, 81; 10 Bob Akin, USA, 79.
700 kg: 1 Jim Downing, USA, 177 (Champion); 2 Jim Rothbarth, USA, 131; 3 Mike Meyer, USA, 127.
GTO: 1 Scott Pruett, USA, 176 (Champion); 2 Bruce Jenner, USA, 163; 3 Jack Baldwin, USA, 149.
GTU: 1 Tom Kendall, USA, 226 (Champion); 2 Roger Mandeville, USA, 199; 3 Amos Johnson, USA, 155.

Final results will be given in *Autocourse 1987/88*.

NASCAR Winston Cup 1985 Results

The final rounds of the 1985 NASCAR Winston Cup were run after *Autocourse 1985/86* went to press.

ATLANTA JOURNAL 500, Atlanta International Raceway, Georgia, United States of America, 3 November. NASCAR Winston Cup, round 27. 328 laps of the 1·552-mile/2·449-km circuit, 499·22 miles/803·41 km.
1 Bill Elliott, USA (Ford), 3h 34m 34s, 139·597 mph/224·659 km/h.
2 Cale Yarborough, USA (Ford), 3h 34m 38·25s.
3 Darrell Waltrip, USA (Chevrolet), 328 laps.
4 Dale Earnhardt, USA (Chevrolet), 328.
5 Morgan Shepherd, USA (Chevrolet), 327.
6 Terry Labonte, USA (Chevrolet), 327.
7 Lake Speed, USA (Pontiac), 327; 8 Harry Gant, USA (Chevrolet), 327; 9 Greg Sacks, USA (Buick), 327; 10 Richard Petty, USA (Pontiac), 326.
Fastest qualifier: Gant, 32·626s, 167·940 mph/270·273 km/h.
Championship points. Drivers: 1 Waltrip, 4141; 2 Elliott, 4121; 3 Gant, 3868; 4 Bonnett, 3732; 5 Bodine, 3707; 6 Rudd, 3677.
Manufacturers: 1 Chevrolet, 190; 2 Ford, 159; 3 Buick, 41; 4 Pontiac, 33; 5 Oldsmobile, 10.

WINSTON WESTERN 500, Riverside International Raceway, California, United States of America, 17 November. NASCAR Winston Cup, round 28. 119 laps of the 2·620-mile/4·216-km circuit, 311·78 miles/501·76 km.
1 Ricky Rudd, USA (Ford), 2h 58m 03s, 105·065 mph/169·085 km/h.
2 Terry Labonte, USA (Chevrolet), 2h 58m 03s (Rudd won by two car lengths).
3 Neil Bonnett, USA (Chevrolet), 119 laps.
4 Harry Gant, USA (Chevrolet), 119.
5 Dale Earnhardt, USA (Chevrolet), 119.
6 Geoff Bodine, USA (Chevrolet), 119.
7 Darrell Waltrip, USA (Chevrolet), 119; 8 Richard Petty, USA (Pontiac), 119; 9 Lake Speed, USA (Pontiac), 118; 10 Ron Bouchard, USA (Buick), 118.
Fastest qualifier: Labonte, 1m 20·658s, 116·938 mph/188·193 km/h.

Final Championship points

Drivers

1	Darrell Waltrip, USA	4292
2	Bill Elliott, USA	4191
3	Harry Gant, USA	4033
4	Neil Bonnett, USA	3902
5	Geoff Bodine, USA	3862
6	Ricky Rudd, USA	3857

7 Terry Labonte, USA, 3683; 8 Dale Earnhardt, USA, 3561; 9 Kyle Petty, USA, 3582; 10 Lake Speed, USA, 3507; 11 Tim Richmond, USA, 3413; 12 Bobby Allison, USA, 3312; 13 Ron Bouchard, USA, 3267; 14 Richard Petty, USA, 3140; 15 Bobby Hillin Jnr, USA, 3091; 16 Ken Schrader, USA, 3024; 17 Buddy Baker, USA, 2986; 18 Dave Marcis, USA, 2871; 19 Rusty Wallace, USA, 2867; 20 Buddy Arrington, USA, 2780.

Manufacturers

1	Chevrolet	196
2	Ford	168
3	Buick	41
4	Pontiac	33
5	Oldsmobile	10

1986 Results

DAYTONA 500, Daytona International Speedway, Florida, United States of America, 16 February. NASCAR Winston Cup, round 1. 200 laps of the 2·500-mile/4·023-km circuit, 500·00 miles/804·67 km.
1 Geoff Bodine, USA (Chevrolet), 3h 22m 32s, 148·124 mph/238·382 km/h.
2 Terry Labonte, USA (Oldsmobile), 3h 22m 43·26s.
3 Darrell Waltrip, USA (Chevrolet), 200 laps.
4 Bobby Hillin Jnr, USA (Chevrolet), 200.
5 Benny Parsons, USA (Oldsmobile), 199.
6 Ron Bouchard, USA (Pontiac), 199.
7 Rick Wilson, USA (Oldsmobile), 199; 8 Rusty Wallace, USA (Pontiac), 199; 9 Sterling Marlin, USA (Chevrolet), 198; 10 Lake Speed, USA (Pontiac), 198.
Fastest qualifier: Bill Elliott, USA (Ford), 43·894s, 205·039 mph/329·977 km/h.
Championship points. Drivers: 1 Bodine, 185; 2 Labonte, 175; 3 Waltrip, 170; 4 Hillin Jnr, 165; 5 Parsons, 155; 6 Bouchard, 150.
Manufacturers: 1 Chevrolet, 9; 2 Oldsmobile, 6; 3 Pontiac, 4; 4 Ford, 3; 5 Buick, 2.

MILLER HIGH LIFE 400, Richmond Fairgrounds Raceway, Virginia, United States of America, 23 February. NASCAR Winston Cup, round 2. 400 laps of the 0·542-mile/0·872-km circuit, 216·80 miles/348·80 km.
1 Kyle Petty, USA (Ford), 3h 02m 54s, 71·078 mph/114·389 km/h.
2 Joe Ruttman, USA (Buick), 3h 02m 58s.
3 Dale Earnhardt, USA (Chevrolet), 400 laps.
4 Bobby Allison, USA (Buick), 399.
5 Darrell Waltrip, USA (Chevrolet), 398.
6 Bobby Hillin Jnr, USA (Buick), 398.
7 Neil Bonnett, USA (Chevrolet), 398; 8 Geoff Bodine, USA (Chevrolet), 397; 9 Dave Marcis, USA (Chevrolet), 397; 10 Rusty Wallace, USA (Pontiac), 395.
Fastest qualifier: Not given.
Championship points. Drivers: 1 Bodine, 332; 2 Waltrip, 330; 3 Hillin Jnr, 315; 4 Earnhardt, 301; 5 Petty, 295; 6 Labonte, 293.
Manufacturers: 1 Chevrolet, 13; 2 Ford, 12; 3 Oldsmobile, 8; 4 Buick, 8; 5 Pontiac, 7.

GOODWRENCH 500, North Carolina Motor Speedway, Rockingham, North Carolina, United States of America, 2 March. NASCAR Winston Cup, round 3. 492 laps of the 1·017-mile/1·637-km circuit, 500·36 miles/805·26 km.
1 Terry Labonte, USA (Oldsmobile), 4h 09m 10s, 120/488 mph/193·906 km/h.
2 Harry Gant, USA (Chevrolet), 4h 09m 11s.
3 Richard Petty, USA (Pontiac), 492 laps.
4 Morgan Shepherd, USA (Buick), 491.
5 Darrell Waltrip, USA (Chevrolet), 491.
6 Cale Yarborough, USA (Ford), 490.
7 Bill Elliott, USA (Ford), 490; 8 Dale Earnhardt, USA (Chevrolet), 490; 9 Neil Bonnett, USA (Chevrolet), 490; 10 Lake Speed, USA (Pontiac), 489.
Fastest qualifier: Labonte, 25·017s, 146·348 mph/235·523 km/h (record).
Championship points. Drivers: 1 Waltrip, 490; 2 Labonte, 478; 3 Earnhardt, 448; 4 Bodine, 440; 5 Petty, 430; 6 Wallace, 408.
Manufacturers: 1 Chevrolet, 19; 2 Oldsmobile, 17; 3 Ford, 14; 4 Buick, 11; 5 Pontiac, 11.

MOTORCRAFT 500, Atlanta International Raceway, Georgia, United States of America, 16 March. NASCAR Winston Cup, round 4. 328 laps of the 1·522-mile/2·449-km circuit, 499·22 miles/803·27 km.
1 Morgan Shepherd, USA (Buick), 3h 46m 41s, 132·126 mph/212·636 km/h.
2 Dale Earnhardt, USA (Chevrolet), 3h 46m 42s.
3 Terry Labonte, USA (Oldsmobile), 328 laps.
4 Darrell Waltrip, USA (Chevrolet), 328.
5 Bill Elliott, USA (Ford), 328.
6 Benny Parsons, USA (Oldsmobile), 328.
7 Tim Richmond, USA (Chevrolet), 328; 8 Rusty Wallace, USA (Pontiac), 327; 9 Bobby Allison, USA (Buick), 327; 10 Geoff Bodine, USA (Chevrolet), 327.
Fastest qualifier: Earnhardt, 32·096s, 170·713 mph/274·735 km/h (record).
Championship points. Drivers: 1 Waltrip, 655; 2 Labonte, 643; 3 Earnhardt, 628; 4 Bodine, 574; 5 Wallace, 550; 6 Elliott, 535.
Manufacturers: 1 Chevrolet, 25; 2 Oldsmobile, 21; 3 Buick, 20; 4 Ford, 17; 5 Pontiac, 13.

VALLEYDALE MEATS 500, Bristol International Raceway, Tennessee, United States of America, 6 April. NASCAR Winston Cup, round 5. 500 laps of the 0·533-mile/0·858-km circuit, 266·50 miles/429·00 km.
1 Rusty Wallace, USA (Pontiac) 2h 58m 14s, 89·747 mph/144·43 km/h.
2 Ricky Rudd, USA (Ford), 2h 58m 24·69s.
3 Darrell Waltrip, USA (Chevrolet), 500 laps.
4 Harry Gant, USA (Chevrolet), 499.
5 Bill Elliott, USA (Ford), 499.
6 Bobby Allison, USA (Buick), 499.
7 Terry Labonte, USA (Oldsmobile), 498; 8 Tim Richmond, USA (Chevrolet), 498; 9 Kyle Petty, USA (Ford), 497; 10 Dale Earnhardt, USA (Chevrolet), 497.
Fastest qualifier: Geoff Bodine, USA (Chevrolet), 16·707s, 114·850 mph/184·83 km/h (record).
Championship points. Drivers: 1 Waltrip, 825; 2 Labonte, 794; 3 Earnhardt, 767; 4 Wallace, 735; 5 Elliott, 690; 6 Bodine, 670.
Manufacturers: 1 Chevrolet, 29; 2 Oldsmobile, 23; 3 Buick, 23; 4 Ford, 23; 5 Pontiac, 22.

TRANSOUTH 500, Darlington International Raceway, South Carolina, United States of America, 13 April. NASCAR Winston Cup, round 6. 367 laps of the 1·366-mile/2·198-km circuit, 501·32 miles/806·67 km.
1 Dale Earnhardt, USA (Chevrolet), 3h 53m 11s, 128·994 mph/207·595 km/h.
2 Darrell Waltrip, USA (Chevrolet), 3h 53m 11s (Earnhardt won by three car lengths).
3 Bobby Allison, USA (Buick), 366 laps.
4 Neil Bonnett, USA (Chevrolet), 366.
5 Tim Richmond, USA (Chevrolet), 364.
6 Rusty Wallace, USA (Pontiac), 364.
7 Richard Petty, USA (Pontiac), 364; 8 Bill Elliott, USA (Ford), 362; 9 Kyle Petty, USA (Ford), 361; 10 Ken Schrader, USA (Ford), 356.
Fastest qualifier: Geoff Bodine, USA (Chevrolet), 30·890s, 159·197 mph/256·202 km/h (record).
Championship points. Drivers: 1 Waltrip, 1000; 2 Earnhardt, 952; 3 Wallace, 885; 4 Labonte, 861; 5 Elliott, 832; 6 Petty (Kyle), 785.
Manufacturers: 1 Chevrolet, 38; 2 Buick, 29; 3 Ford, 26; 4 Pontiac, 26; 5 Oldsmobile, 25.

FIRST UNION 400, North Wilkesboro Speedway, North Carolina, United States of America, 20 April. NASCAR Winston Cup, round 7. 400 laps of the 0·625-mile/1·006-km circuit, 250·00 miles/402·34 km.
1 Dale Earnhardt, USA (Chevrolet), 2h 49m 40s, 88·408 mph/142·28 km/h.
2 Ricky Rudd, USA (Ford), 2h 49m 41s.
3 Geoff Bodine, USA (Chevrolet), 400 laps.
4 Darrell Waltrip, USA (Chevrolet), 400.
5 Joe Ruttman, USA (Buick), 400.
6 Bobby Allison, USA (Buick), 400.
7 Harry Gant, USA (Chevrolet), 400; 8 Kyle Petty, USA (Ford), 400; 9 Bill Elliott, USA (Ford), 400; 10 Rusty Wallace, USA (Pontiac), 399.
Fastest qualifier: Bodine, 112·419 mph/180·920 km/h (two-day average).
Championship points. Drivers: 1 Waltrip, 1160; 2 Earnhardt, 1137; 3 Wallace, 1019; 4 Elliott, 970; 5 Labonte, 948; 6 Petty (Kyle), 927.
Manufacturers: 1 Chevrolet, 47; 2 Buick, 33; 3 Ford, 32; 4 Pontiac, 29; 5 Oldsmobile, 27.

SOVRAN BANK 500, Martinsville Speedway, Virginia, United States of America, 27 April. NASCAR Winston Cup, round 8. 500 laps of the 0·525-mile/0·845-km circuit, 262·50 miles/422·45 km.
1 Ricky Rudd, USA (Ford), 3h 25m 15s, 76·882 mph/123·729 km/h.
2 Joe Ruttman, USA (Buick), 499 laps.
3 Terry Labonte, USA (Oldsmobile), 496.
4 Alan Kulwicki, USA (Ford), 496.
5 Kyle Petty, USA (Ford), 496.
6 Bobby Hillin Jnr, USA (Buick), 495.
7 Ken Schrader, USA (Ford), 493; 8 Bobby Allison, USA (Buick), 492; 9 Derrike Cope, USA (Ford), 489; 10 Jody Ridley, USA (Pontiac), 487.
Fastest qualifier: Tim Richmond, USA (Chevrolet), 20·874s, 90·716 mph/145·993 km/h (record).
Championship points. Drivers: 1 Waltrip, 1247; 2 Earnhardt, 1242; 3 Labonte, 1113; 4 Wallace, 1092; 5 Petty (Kyle), 1082; 6 Elliott, 1040.
Manufacturers: 1 Chevrolet, 49; 2 Ford, 41; 3 Buick, 39; 4 Pontiac, 32; 5 Oldsmobile, 31.

WINSTON 500, Alabama, International Motor Speedway, Talladega, Alabama, United States of America, 4 May. NASCAR Winston Cup, round 9. 188 laps of the 2·660-mile/4·281-km circuit, 500·08 miles/804·80 km.
1 Bobby Allison, USA (Buick), 3h 10m 16s, 157·698 mph/253·790 km/h.
2 Dale Earnhardt, USA (Chevrolet), 3h 10m 16s (Allison won by one car length).
3 Buddy Baker, USA (Oldsmobile), 188 laps.
4 Bobby Hillin Jnr, USA (Buick), 188.
5 Phil Parsons, USA (Oldsmobile), 188.
6 Morgan Shepherd, USA (Buick), 188.
7 Richard Petty, USA (Pontiac), 188; 8 Rick Wilson, USA (Chevrolet), 188; 9 Ron Bouchard, USA (Pontiac), 188; 10 Greg Sacks, USA (Pontiac), 188.
Fastest qualifier: Bill Elliott, USA (Ford), 45·121s, 212·229 mph/341·549 km/h (record).
Championship points. Drivers: 1 Earnhardt, 1417; 2 Waltrip, 1308; 3 Wallace, 1216; 4 Allison, 1198; 5 Labonte, 1189; 6 Petty (Kyle), 1152.
Manufacturers: 1 Chevrolet, 55; 2 Buick, 48; 3 Ford, 43; 4 Oldsmobile, 35; 5 Pontiac, 35.

BUDWEISER 500, Dover Downs International Speedway, Delaware, United States of America, 18 May. NASCAR Winston Cup, round 10. 500 laps of the 1·000-mile/1·609-km circuit, 500·00 miles/804·67 km.
1 Geoff Bodine, USA (Chevrolet), 4h 20m 51s, 115·009 mph/185·089 km/h.
2 Bobby Allison, USA (Buick), 4h 20m 54s.
3 Dale Earnhardt, USA (Chevrolet), 499 laps.
4 Ricky Rudd, USA (Ford), 498.
5 Darrell Waltrip, USA (Chevrolet), 498.
6 Richard Petty, USA (Pontiac), 494.
7 Bill Elliott, USA (Ford), 493; 8 Bobby Hillin Jnr, USA (Buick), 493; 9 Tommy Ellis, USA (Chevrolet), 493; 10 Ken Schrader, USA (Ford), 493.
Fastest qualifier: Rudd, 26·046s, 138·217 mph/222·438 km/h.
Championship points. Drivers: 1 Earnhardt, 1587; 2 Waltrip, 1463; 3 Allison, 1373; 4 Labonte, 1306; 5 Wallace, 1301; 6 Elliott, 1287.
Manufacturers: 1 Chevrolet, 64; 2 Buick, 54; 3 Ford, 47; 4 Pontiac, 38; 5 Oldsmobile. 37.

COCA-COLA 600, Charlotte Motor Speedway, North Carolina, United States of America, 25 May. NASCAR Winston Cup, round 11. 400 laps of the 1·500-mile/2·414-km circuit, 600·00 miles/965·80 km.
1 Dale Earnhardt, USA (Chevrolet), 4h 16m 24s, 140·406 mph/225·961 km/h.
2 Tim Richmond, USA (Chevrolet), 4h 16m 29s.
3 Cale Yarborough, USA (Ford), 400 laps.
4 Harry Gant, USA (Chevrolet), 400.
5 Darrell Waltrip, USA (Chevrolet), 400.
6 Bill Elliott, USA (Ford), 400.
7 Sterling Marlin, USA (Chevrolet), 399; 8 Ricky Rudd, USA (Ford), 399; 9 Morgan Shepherd, USA (Buick), 399; 10 Rusty Wallace, USA (Pontiac), 398.
Fastest qualifier: Geoff Bodine, USA (Chevrolet), 2m 11·298s, 164·511 mph/264·754 km/h (4 laps).
Championship points. Drivers: 1 Earnhardt, 1767; 2 Waltrip, 1623; 3 Allison, 1505; 4 Elliott, 1447; 5 Wallace, 1440; 6 Labonte, 1436.
Manufacturers: 1 Chevrolet, 73; 2 Buick, 58; 3 Ford, 53; 4 Pontiac, 40; 5 Oldsmobile, 39.

BUDWEISER 400, Riverside International Raceway, California, United States of America, 1 June. NASCAR Winston Cup, round 12. 95 laps of the 2·620-mile/4·126-km circuit, 248·90 miles/400·56 km.
1 Darrell Waltrip, USA (Chevrolet), 2h 22m 07s, 105·083 mph/169·114 km/h.
2 Tim Richmond, USA (Chevrolet), 2h 22m 07s (Waltrip won by four feet).
3 Ricky Rudd, USA (Ford), 95 laps.
4 Rusty Wallace, USA (Pontiac), 95.
5 Dale Earnhardt, USA (Chevrolet), 95.

6 Richard Petty, USA (Pontiac), 95.
7 Bobby Allison, USA (Buick), 95; **8** Neil Bonnett, USA (Chevrolet), 95; **9** Harry Gant, USA (Chevrolet), 95; **10** Glen Steurer, USA (Chevrolet), 94.
Fastest qualifier: Waltrip, 1m 20·570s, 117·006 mph/188·302 km/h (record).
Championship points. Drivers: 1 Earnhardt, 1922; **2** Waltrip, 1803; **3** Allison, 1651; **4** Wallace, 1600; **5** Elliott, 1577; **6** Labonte, 1568.
Manufacturers: 1 Chevrolet, 82; **2** Buick, 61; **3** Ford, 59; **4** Pontiac, 44; **5** Oldsmobile, 41.

MILLER HIGH LIFE 500, Pocono International Raceway, Pennsylvania, United States of America, 8 June. NASCAR Winston Cup, round 13. 200 laps of the 2·500-mile/4·023-km circuit, 500·00 miles/804·57 km.
1 Tim Richmond, USA (Chevrolet), 4h 24m 50s, 113·279 mph/182·304 km/h.
2 Dale Earnhardt, USA (Chevrolet), 200 laps (race ended under yellow flag).
3 Cale Yarborough, USA (Ford), 200.
4 Ricky Rudd, USA (Ford), 200.
5 Bill Elliott, USA (Ford), 200.
6 Rusty Wallace, USA (Pontiac), 200.
7 Joe Ruttman, USA (Buick), 200; **8** Kyle Petty, USA (Ford), 200; **9** Geoff Bodine, USA (Chevrolet), 200; **10** Bobby Hillin Jnr, USA (Buick), 199.
Fastest qualifier: Bodine, 58·574s, 153·625 mph/247·235 km/h (record).
Championship points. Drivers: 1 Earnhardt, 2097; **2** Waltrip, 1846; **3** Allison, 1773; **4** Wallace, 1750; **5** Richmond, 1742; **6** Elliott, 1737.
Manufacturers: 1 Chevrolet, 91; **2** Ford, 65; **3** Buick, 64; **4** Pontiac, 48; **5** Oldsmobile, 43.

MILLER AMERICAN 400, Michigan International Speedway, Brooklyn, Michigan, United States of America, 15 June. NASCAR Winston Cup, round 14. 200 laps of the 2·000-mile/3·219-km circuit, 400·00 miles/643·80 km.
1 Bill Elliott, USA (Ford), 2h 53m 21s, 138·851 mph/223·458 km/h.
2 Harry Gant, USA (Chevrolet), 2h 53m 21s (Elliott won by two car lengths).
3 Geoff Bodine, USA (Chevrolet), 200 laps.
4 Buddy Baker, USA (Oldsmobile), 200.
5 Darrell Waltrip, USA (Chevrolet), 200.
6 Dale Earnhardt, USA (Chevrolet), 200.
7 Bobby Hillin Jnr, USA (Buick), 200; **8** Rick Wilson, USA (Oldsmobile), 200; **9** Joe Ruttman, USA (Buick), 200; **10** Ricky Rudd, USA (Ford), 200.
Fastest qualifier: Tim Richmond, USA (Chevrolet), 41·853s, 172·031 mph/276·856 km/h (record).
Championship points. Drivers: 1 Earnhardt, 2252; **2** Waltrip, 2001; **3** Elliott, 1917; **4** Allison, 1910; **5** Richmond, 1865; **6** Wallace, 1861.
Manufacturers: 1 Chevrolet, 97; **2** Ford, 74; **3** Buick, 67; **4** Pontiac, 50; **5** Oldsmobile, 47.

PEPSI FIRECRACKER 400, Daytona International Speedway, Florida, United States of America, 4 July. NASCAR Winston Cup, round 15. 160 laps of the 2·500-mile/4·023-km circuit, 400·00 miles/643·68 km.
1 Tim Richmond, USA (Chevrolet), 3h 01m 54s, 131·916 mph/212·298 km/h.
2 Sterling Marlin, USA (Chevrolet), 3h 01m 54·35s.
3 Bobby Hillin Jnr, USA (Buick), 160 laps.
4 Darrell Waltrip, USA (Chevrolet), 160.
5 Kyle Petty, USA (Ford), 160.
6 Ricky Rudd, USA (Ford), 160.
7 Joe Ruttman, USA (Buick), 160; **8** Rusty Wallace, USA (Pontiac) 160; **9** Phil Parsons, USA (Oldsmobile), 160; **10** Alan Kulwicki, USA (Ford), 160.
Fastest qualifier: Cale Yarborough, USA (Ford), 44·222s, 203·519 mph/327·531 km/h.
Championship points. Drivers: 1 Earnhardt, 2344; **2** Waltrip, 2166; **3** Richmond, 2045; **4** Elliott, 2037; **5** Allison, 2033; **6** Wallace, 2003.
Manufacturers: 1 Chevrolet, 106; **2** Ford, 78; **3** Buick, 73; **4** Pontiac, 53; **5** Oldsmobile, 49.

SUMMER 500, Pocono International Raceway, Pennsylvania, United States of America, 20 July. NASCAR Winston Cup, round 16. 150 laps of the 2·500-mile/4·023-km circuit, 375·00 miles/603·45 km (race shortened due to fog).
1 Tim Richmond, USA (Chevrolet), 2h 41m 08s, 124·218 mph/199·909 km/h.
2 Ricky Rudd, USA (Ford), 2h 41m 08·5s.
3 Geoff Bodine, USA (Chevrolet), 150 laps.
4 Darrell Waltrip, USA (Chevrolet), 150.
5 Bobby Allison, USA (Buick), 150.
6 Terry Labonte, USA (Oldsmobile), 150.
7 Dale Earnhardt, USA (Chevrolet), 150; **8** Kyle Petty, USA (Ford), 149; **9** Tommy Ellis, USA (Chevrolet), 148; **10** Rick Wilson, USA (Oldsmobile, 148.
Fastest qualifier: Harry Gant, USA (Chevrolet), 58·293s, 154·392 mph/248·470 km/h (record).
Championship points. Drivers: 1 Earnhardt, 2490; **2** Waltrip, 2331; **3** Richmond, 2225; **4** Allison, 2188; **5** Rudd, 2128; **6** Elliott, 2095.
Manufacturers: 1 Chevrolet, 115; **2** Ford, 84; **3** Buick, 77; **4** Pontiac, 55; **5** Oldsmobile, 52.

TALLADEGA 500, Alabama International Motor Speedway, Talladega, Alabama, United States of America, 27 July. NASCAR Winston Cup, round 17. 188 laps of the 2·660-mile/4·281-km circuit, 500·08 miles/804·83 km.
1 Bobby Hillin Jnr, USA (Buick), 3h 17m 59s, 151·552 mph/243·899 km/h.
2 Tim Richmond, USA (Chevrolet), 3h 17m 59s (Hillin Jnr won by three car lengths).
3 Ricky Rudd, USA (Ford), 188 laps.
4 Sterling Marlin, USA (Chevrolet), 188.
5 Benny Parsons, USA (Oldsmobile), 188.
6 Morgan Shepherd, USA (Buick), 188.
7 Davey Allison, USA (Chevrolet), 188; **8** Joe Ruttman, USA (Buick), 188; **9** Kyle Petty, USA (Ford), 188; **10** Bobby Allison, USA (Buick), 187.
Fastest qualifier: Bill Elliott, USA (Ford), 45·817s, 209·005 mph/336·360 km/h.
Championship points. Drivers: 1 Earnhardt, 2585; **2** Waltrip, 2424; **3** Richmond, 2400; **4** Allison (Bobby), 2327; **5** Rudd, 2293; **6** Elliott, 2182.
Manufacturers: 1 Chevrolet, 121; **2** Ford, 88; **3** Buick, 86; **4** Pontiac, 56; **5** Oldsmobile, 55.

BUDWEISER AT THE GLEN, Watkins Glen Short Course, New York, United States of America, 10 August. NASCAR Winston Cup, round 18. 90 laps of the 2·428-mile/3·907-km circuit, 218·52 miles/351·63 km.
1 Tim Richmond, USA (Chevrolet), 2h 12m 56s, 90·463 mph/145·586 km/h.
2 Darrell Waltrip, USA (Chevrolet), 2h 12m 57·45s.
3 Dale Earnhardt, USA (Chevrolet), 90 laps.
4 Bill Elliott, USA (Ford), 90.
5 Neil Bonnett, USA (Chevrolet), 90.
6 Rusty Wallace, USA (Pontiac), 90.
7 Ricky Rudd, USA (Ford), 90; **8** Benny Parsons, USA (Oldsmobile), 90; **9** Kyle Petty, USA (Ford), 90; **10** Richard Petty, USA (Pontiac), 90.
Fastest qualifier: Richmond, 1m 14·350s, 117·563 mph/189·199 km/h (record).
Championship points. Drivers: 1 Earnhardt, 2750; **2** Waltrip, 2599; **3** Richmond, 2580; **4** Allison (Bobby), 2454; **5** Rudd, 2439; **6** Elliott, 2347.
Manufacturers: 1 Chevrolet, 130; **2** Ford, 94; **3** Buick, 88; **4** Pontiac, 60; **5** Oldsmobile, 58.

CHAMPION SPARK PLUG 400, Michigan International Speedway, Brooklyn, Michigan, United States of America, 17 August. NASCAR Winston Cup, round 19. 200 laps of the 2·000-mile/3·219-km circuit, 400·00 miles/643·80 km.
1 Bill Elliott, USA (Ford), 2h 57m 28s, 135·376 mph/217·866 km/h.
2 Tim Richmond, USA (Chevrolet), 2h 57m 29.45s.
3 Darrell Waltrip, USA (Chevrolet), 200 laps.
4 Geoff Bodine, USA (Chevrolet), 200.
5 Dale Earnhardt, USA (Chevrolet), 199.
6 Rusty Wallace, USA (Pontiac), 199.
7 Cale Yarborough, USA (Ford), 199; **8** Harry Gant, USA (Chevrolet), 199; **9** Phil Parsons, USA (Oldsmobile), 199; **10** David Pearson, USA (Chevrolet), 199.
Fastest qualifier: Benny Parsons, USA (Oldsmobile), 41·879s, 171·924 mph/276·684 km/h.
Championship points. Drivers: 1 Earnhardt, 2910; **2** Waltrip, 2769; **3** Richmond, 2755; **4** Allison, 2545; **5** Rudd, 2539; **6** Elliott, 2532.
Manufacturers: 1 Chevrolet, 136; **2** Ford, 103; **3** Buick, 90; **4** Pontiac, 64; **5** Oldsmobile, 61.

BUSCH 500, Bristol International Raceway, Tennessee, United States of America, 23 August. NASCAR Winston Cup, round 20. 500 laps of the 0·533-mile/0·858-km circuit, 266·50 miles/429·00 km.
1 Darrell Waltrip, USA (Chevrolet), 3h 03m 55s, 86·934 mph/139·906 km/h.
2 Terry Labonte, USA (Oldsmobile), 3h 04m 03·55s.
3 Geoff Bodine, USA (Chevrolet), 499 laps.
4 Dale Earnhardt, USA (Chevrolet), 499.
5 Harry Gant, USA (Chevrolet), 499.
6 Tim Richmond, USA (Chevrolet), 498.
7 Richard Petty, USA (Pontiac), 497; **8** Bobby Allison, USA (Buick), 496; **9** Bobby Hillin Jnr, USA (Buick), 495; **10** Alan Kulwicki, USA (Ford), 494.
Fastest qualifier: Bodine, 16·734s, 114·665 mph/184·535 km/h.
Championship points. Drivers: 1 Earnhardt, 3075; **2** Waltrip, 2954; **3** Richmond, 2910; **4** Allison, 2692; **5** Elliott, 2638; **6** Rudd, 2633.
Manufacturers: 1 Chevrolet, 145; **2** Ford, 105; **3** Buick, 93; **4** Pontiac, 68; **5** Oldsmobile, 67.

SOUTHERN 500, Darlington International Raceway, South Carolina, United States of America, 31 August. NASCAR Winston Cup, round 21. 367 laps of the 1·366-mile/2·198-km circuit, 501·32 miles/806·67 km.
1 Tim Richmond, USA (Chevrolet), 4h 08m 45s, 121·068 mph/194·840 km/h.
2 Bobby Allison, USA (Buick), 4h 08m 47s.
3 Bill Elliott, USA (Ford), 367 laps.
4 Morgan Shepherd, USA (Buick), 367.
5 Darrell Waltrip, USA (Chevrolet), 367.
6 Ricky Rudd, USA (Ford), 367.
7 Bobby Hillin Jnr, USA (Buick), 367; **8** Geoff Bodine, USA (Chevrolet), 367; **9** Dale Earnhardt, USA (Chevrolet), 366; **10** Cale Yarborough, USA (Ford), 366.
Fastest qualifier: Richmond, 31·028s, 158·489 mph/255·063 km/h.
Championship points. Drivers: 1 Earnhardt, 3218; **2** Waltrip, 3109; **3** Richmond, 3095; **4** Allison, 2867; **5** Elliott, 2808; **6** Rudd, 2783.
Manufacturers: 1 Chevrolet, 145; **2** Ford, 107; **3** Buick, 96; **4** Pontiac, 67; **5** Oldsmobile, 63.

WRANGLER JEANS INDIGO 400, Richmond Fairgrounds Raceway, Virginia, United States of America, 7 September. NASCAR Winston Cup, round 22. 400 laps of the 0·542-mile/0·972-km circuit, 216·80 miles/348·90 km.
1 Tim Richmond, USA (Chevrolet), 3h 05m 24s, 70·161 mph/112·913 km/h.
2 Dale Earnhardt, USA (Chevrolet), 3h 05m 24s (Richmond won by two car lengths).
3 Morgan Shepherd, USA (Pontiac), 400 laps.
4 Richard Petty, USA (Pontiac), 400.
5 Neil Bonnett, USA (Chevrolet), 400.
6 Joe Ruttman, USA (Buick), 400.
7 Harry Gant, USA (Chevrolet), 400; **8** Bobby Allison, USA (Buick), 400; **9** Bill Elliott, USA (Ford), 399; **10** Bobby Hillin Jnr, USA (Buick), 397.
Fastest qualifier: Gant, 20·765s, 93·966 mph/151·223 km/h.
Championship points. Drivers: 1 Earnhardt, 3393; **2** Richmond, 3275; **3** Waltrip, 3185; **4** Allison, 3009; **5** Elliott, 2946; **6** Rudd, 2884.
Manufacturers: 1 Chevrolet, 163; **2** Ford, 113; **3** Buick, 104; **4** Pontiac, 81; **5** Oldsmobile, 67.

DELAWARE 500, Dover Downs International Speedway, Delaware, United States of America, 14 September. NASCAR Winston Cup, round 23. 500 laps of the 1·000-mile/1·609-km circuit, 500·00 miles/804·50 km.
1 Ricky Rudd, USA (Ford), 4h 23m 24s, 114·329 mph/183·994 km/h.
2 Neil Bonnett, USA (Chevrolet), 4h 23m 30s.
3 Kyle Petty, USA (Ford), 500 laps.
4 Buddy Baker, USA (Oldsmobile), 499.
5 Dave Marcis, USA (Chevrolet), 498.
6 Joe Ruttman, USA (Buick), 498.
7 Alan Kulwicki, USA (Ford), 497; **8** Tommy Ellis, USA (Chevrolet), 496; **9** Bobby Hillin Jnr, USA (Buick), 495; **10** Morgan Shepherd, USA (Pontiac) 493.
Fastest qualifier: Geoff Bodine, USA (Chevrolet), 24·623s, 146·205 mph/235·294 km/h (record).
Championship points. Drivers: 1 Earnhardt, 3498; **2** Richmond, 3360; **3** Waltrip, 3306; **4** Allison, 3112; **5** Rudd, 3069; **6** Elliott, 3033.
Manufacturers: 1 Chevrolet, 169; **2** Ford, 122; **3** Buick, 107; **4** Pontiac, 83; **5** Oldsmobile, 71.

GOODY'S 500, Martinsville Speedway, Virginia, United States of America, 21 September. NASCAR Winston Cup, round 24. 500 laps of the 0·526-mile/0·847-km circuit, 263·00 miles/423·50 km.
1 Rusty Wallace, USA (Pontiac), 3h 35m 32s, 73·191 mph/117·789 km/h.
2 Geoff Bodine, USA (Chevrolet), 3h 35m 32s (Wallace won by two car lengths).
3 Harry Gant, USA (Chevrolet), 500 laps.
4 Darrell Waltrip, USA (Chevrolet), 499.
5 Joe Ruttman, USA (Buick), 499.
6 Kyle Petty, USA (Ford), 499.
7 Ken Schrader, USA (Ford), 498; **8** Neil Bonnett, USA (Chevrolet), 497; **9** Dave Marcis, USA (Chevrolet), 497; **10** Tim Richmond, USA (Chevrolet), 496.
Fastest qualifier: Bodine, 20·901s, 90·599 mph/145·805 km/h.
Championship points. Drivers: 1 Earnhardt, 3630; **2** Richmond, 3494; **3** Waltrip, 3471; **4** Allison, 3212; **5** Elliott, 3163; **6** Rudd, 3148.
Manufacturers: 1 Chevrolet, 175; **2** Ford, 125; **3** Buick, 111; **4** Pontiac, 102; **5** Oldsmobile, 73.

HOLLY FARMS 400, North Wilkesboro Speedway, North Carolina, United States of America, 28 September. NASCAR Winston Cup, round 25. 400 laps of the 0·625-mile/1·006-km circuit, 250·00 miles/402·34 km.
1 Darrell Waltrip, USA (Chevrolet), 2h 36m 53s, 95·612 mph/153·872 km/h.
2 Geoff Bodine, USA (Chevrolet), 2h 36m 54·21s.
3 Richard Petty, USA (Pontiac), 400 laps.
4 Rusty Wallace, USA (Pontiac), 400.
5 Harry Gant, USA (Chevrolet), 400.
6 Joe Ruttman, USA (Buick), 399.
7 Ricky Rudd, USA (Ford), 399; **8** Dave Marcis, USA (Chevrolet), 399; **9** Dale Earnhardt, USA (Chevrolet), 398; **10** Terry Labonte, USA (Oldsmobile), 398.
Fastest qualifier: Tim Richmond, USA (Chevrolet), 39·666s, 113·447 mph/182·575 km/h.
Championship points. Drivers: 1 Earnhardt, 3773; **2** Waltrip, 3651; **3** Richmond, 3629; **4** Allison, 3309; **5** Rudd, 3294; **6** Elliott, 3283.
Manufacturers: 1 Chevrolet, 184; **2** Ford, 128; **3** Buick, 115; **4** Pontiac, 108; **5** Oldsmobile, 75.

OAKWOOD HOMES 500, Charlotte Motor Speedway, North Carolina, United States of America, 5 October. NASCAR Winston Cup, round 26. 334 laps of the 1·500-mile/2·414-km circuit, 501·00 miles/806·28 km.
1 Dale Earnhardt, USA (Chevrolet), 3h 47m 02s, 132·403 mph/213·081 km/h.
2 Harry Gant, USA (Chevrolet), 3h 47m 03·9s.
3 Neil Bonnett, USA (Chevrolet), 333 laps.
4 Ricky Rudd, USA (Ford), 333.
5 Buddy Baker, USA (Chevrolet), 333.
6 Geoff Bodine, USA (Chevrolet), 333.
7 Bill Elliott, USA (Ford), 333; **8** Rusty Wallace, USA (Pontiac), 332; **9** Darrell Waltrip, USA (Chevrolet), 332; **10** Phil Parsons, USA (Oldsmobile), 331.
Fastest qualifier: Tim Richmond, USA (Chevrolet), 2m 09·281s, 167·078 mph/268·885 km/h (4 laps).
Championship points. Drivers: 1 Earnhardt, 3953; **2** Waltrip, 3794; **3** Richmond, 3721; **4** Rudd, 3454; **5** Elliott, 3429; **6** Wallace, 3390.
Manufacturers: 1 Chevrolet, 193; **2** Ford, 134; **3** Buick, 117; **4** Pontiac, 111; **5** Oldsmobile, 79.

NATIONWISE 500, North Carolina Motor Speedway, North Carolina, United States of America, 19 October. NASCAR Winston Cup, round 27. 492 laps of the 1·017-mile/1·627-km circuit, 500·36 miles/805·26 km.
1 Neil Bonnett, USA (Chevrolet), 3h 57m 33s, 126·381 mph/203·390 km/h.
2 Ricky Rudd, USA (Ford), 3h 57m 35·53s.
3 Darrell Waltrip, USA (Chevrolet), 492 laps.
4 Harry Gant, USA (Chevrolet), 492.
5 Buddy Baker, USA (Oldsmobile), 492.
6 Dale Earnhardt, USA (Chevrolet), 491.
7 Bill Elliott, USA (Ford), 491; **8** Richard Petty, USA (Pontiac), 491; **9** Joe Ruttman, USA (Buick), 490; **10** Kyle Petty, USA (Ford), 489.
Fastest qualifier: Tim Richmond, USA (Chevrolet), 24·915s, 146·948 mph/236·489 km/h (record).

Championship points (prior to final two rounds in November):
Drivers

1	Dale Earnhardt, USA	4108
2	Darrell Waltrip, USA	3964
3	Tim Richmond, USA	3829
4	Ricky Rudd, USA	3624
5	Bill Elliott, USA	3575
6	Rusty Wallace, USA	3496

7 Geoff Bodine, USA, 3449; **8** Bobby Allison, USA, 3437; **9** Harry Gant, USA, 3362; **10** Bobby Hillin Jnr, USA, 3278; **11** Kyle Petty, USA, 3273; **12** Terry Labonte, USA, 3197; **13** Neil Bonnett, USA, 3071; **14** Richard Petty, USA, 3044; **15** Joe Ruttman, USA, 3002.
Manufacturers

1	Chevrolet	202
2	Ford	140
3	Buick	119
4	Pontiac	114
5	Oldsmobile	83

Final results will be given in *Autocourse 1987/88*.

Bendix Brake Trans-Am Championship 1985 Results

The final rounds of the Bendix Brake Trans-Am Championship was run after *Autocourse 1985/86* went to press.

BENDIX BRAKE TRANS-AM RACE, St Petersburg Grand Prix Circuit, Florida, United States of America, 3 November. Bendix Brake Trans-Am Championship, round 15. 50 laps of the 2·000-mile/3·219-km circuit, 100·00 miles/160·95 km.
1 Willy T. Ribbs, USA (Mercury Capri), 1h 18m 50·329s, 79·910 mph/128·60 km/h.
2 Jim Miller, USA (Mercury Capri), 1h 19m 35·515s.
3 Eppie Wietzes, CDN (Pontiac Firebird), 50 laps.
4 Peter Dus, USA (Pontiac Trans-Am), 48.
5 Rick Dittman, USA (Pontiac Firebird), 47.
6 John Brandt Jnr, USA (Chevrolet Camaro), 47.
7 Patti Moise, USA (Buick Regal Somerset), 47; **8** Richard Kidd, USA (Pontiac Firebird), 46; **9** Del Taylor, USA (Pontiac Firebird), 45; **10** Tom Gloy, USA (Mercury Capri), 44.
Fastest lap: Ribbs, 1m 27·836s, 81·971 mph/131·919 km/h.

Final Championship points

Drivers

1	Wally Dallenbach Jnr, USA	228
2	Willy T. Ribbs, USA	213
3	Tom Gloy, USA	172
4	Elliott Forbes-Robinson, USA	123
5	Chris Kneifel, USA	101
6	Jim Miller, USA	93

7 Paul Miller, USA, 79; **8** Paul Newman, USA, 72; **9** Eppie Wietzes, CDN, 70; **10** Les Lindley, USA, 56; **11** Rob McFarlin, USA, 51; **12** John Brandt Jnr, USA, 50; **13** Bruce Jenner, USA, 44; **14** Jim Derhaag, USA, 44; **15** John Jones, CDN, 39.

Manufacturers

1	Mercury	124
2	Buick	46
3	Pontiac	24
4	Porsche	16
5	Nissan	15
6	Chevrolet	8

1986 Results

BENDIX BRAKE TRANS-AM RACE, Riverside International Raceway, California, United States of America, 18 May. Bendix Brake Trans-Am Championship, round 1. 40 laps of the 2·547-mile/4·099-km circuit, 101·88 miles/163·96 km.
1 Scott Pruett, USA (Mercury Capri), 1h 01m 50·780s, 98·56 mph/158·62 km/h.
2 Pete Halsmer, USA (Mercury Merkur XR4Ti), 1h 01m 54·009s.
3 Chris Kneifel, USA (Mercury Capri), 40 laps.
4 Les Lindley, USA (Chevrolet Camaro), 40.
5 Larry Park, USA (Chevrolet Corvette), 40.
6 Andy Porterfield, USA (Chevrolet Camaro), 40.
7 George Follmer, USA (Chevrolet Corvette), 40; **8** Bill Doyle, USA (Pontiac Trans-Am), 40; **9** Bob Brewer, USA (Chevrolet Camaro), 40; **10** Lee Mueller, USA (Pontiac Trans-Am), 39.
Fastest lap: Pruett, 1m 24·037s, 109·109 mph/175·593 km/h.
Championship points. Drivers: 1 Pruett, 20; **2** Halsmer, 16; **3** Kneifel, 14; **4** Lindley, 12; **5** Park, 11; **6** Porterfield, 10.
Manufacturers: 1 Mercury, 9; **2** Chevrolet, 3.

BENDIX BRAKE TRANS-AM RACE, Sears Point International Raceway, Sonoma, California, United States of America, 1 June. Bendix Brake Trans-Am Championship, round 2. 40 laps of the 2·523-mile/4·060-km circuit, 100·92 miles/162·40 km.
1 Wally Dallenbach Jnr, USA (Chevrolet Camaro), 1h 12m 44·476s, 82·48 mph/132·74 km/h.
2 Chris Kneifel, USA (Mercury Capri), 1h 13m 05·177s.
3 Pete Halsmer, USA (Mercury Merkur XR4Ti) 40 laps.
4 Les Lindley, USA (Chevrolet Camaro), 40.
5 Jim Miller, USA (Chevrolet Camaro), 40.
6 Elliott Forbes-Robinson, USA (Buick Somerset Regal), 40.
7 Mike Miller, USA (Mercury Capri), 40; **8** Paul Newman, USA (Nissan 300ZX Turbo), 40; **9** John Schneider, USA (Buick Somerset Regal), 40; **10** Jim Derhaag, USA (Pontiac Trans-Am), 40.
Fastest lap: Dallenbach Jnr, 1m 40·030s, 90·80 mph/146·13 km/h.
Championship points. Drivers: 1 Halsmer and Kneifel, 30; **3** Lindley, 24; **4** Dallenbach Jnr, 23; **5** Pruett, 20; **6** Park and Doyle, 13.
Manufacturers: 1 Mercury, 15; **2** Chevrolet, 12; **3** Buick, 1.

BENDIX BRAKE TRANS-AM RACE, Portland International Raceway, Oregon, United States of America, 14 June. Bendix Brake Trans-Am Championship, round 3. 53 laps of the 1·915-mile/3·082-km circuit, 101·50 miles/163·35 km.
1 Wally Dallenbach Jnr, USA (Chevrolet Camaro), 1h 06m 00·17s, 92·26 mph/148·48 km/h.
2 Jim Miller, USA (Chevrolet Camaro), 1h 06m 02·95s.
3 Chris Kneifel, USA (Mercury Capri), 53 laps.
4 Elliott Forbes-Robinson, USA (Buick Somerset Regal), 53.
5 Les Lindley, USA (Chevrolet Camaro), 53.
6 Jim Derhaag, USA (Pontiac Trans-Am), 52.

7 David Schroeder, USA (Chevrolet Corvette), 52; **8** John Schneider, USA (Buick Somerset Regal), 52; **9** Larry Park, USA (Chevrolet Corvette), 52; **10** Mike Miller, USA (Mercury Capri), 51.
Fastest lap: Kneifel, 1m 12·07s, 95·66 mph/153·95 km/h.
Championship points. Drivers: 1 Kneifel and Dallenbach Jnr, 44; **3** Lindley, 35; **4** Halsmer, 31; **5** Miller (Jim), 27; **6** Forbes-Robinson, 22.
Manufacturers: 1 Chevrolet, 21; **2** Mercury, 19; **3** Buick, 4; **4** Pontiac, 1.

BENDIX BRAKE TRANS-AM RACE, Detroit Grand Prix Circuit, Michigan, United States of America, 21 June. Bendix Brake Trans-Am Championship, round 4. 40 laps of the 2·500-miles/4·023-km circuit, 100·00 miles/160·92 km.
1 Wally Dallenbach Jnr, USA (Chevrolet Camaro), 1h 39m 43·192s, 60·17 mph/96·83 km/h.
2 Pete Halsmer, USA (Mercury Merkur XR4Ti).
3 Jim Miller, USA (Chevrolet Camaro), 40 laps.
4 Greg Pickett, USA (Chevrolet Camaro), 40.
5 Les Lindley, USA (Chevrolet Camaro), 40.
6 Mike Miller, USA (Mercury Capri), 39.
7 Irv Hoerr, USA (Oldsmobile Toronado), 39; **8** Jim Fitzgerald, USA (Nissan 300ZX Turbo), 39; **9** John Schneider, USA (Buick Somerset Regal), 39; **10** Craig Shafer, USA (Chevrolet Camaro), 39.
Fastest lap: Dallenbach Jnr, 2m 03·623s, 72·80 mph/117·16 km/h.
Championship points. Drivers: 1 Dallenbach Jnr, 65; **2** Halsmer, 47; **3** Lindley, 46; **4** Kneifel, 44; **5** Miller (Jim), 41; **6** Miller (Mike), 25.
Manufacturers: 1 Chevrolet, 30; **2** Mercury, 25; **3** Buick, 4; **4** Pontiac, 1.

BENDIX BRAKE TRANS-AM RACE, Mid-Ohio Sports Car Course, Lexington, Ohio, United States of America, 13 July. Bendix Brake Trans-Am Championship, round 5. 42 laps of the 2·400-mile/3·863-km circuit, 100·80 miles/162·25 km.
1 Greg Pickett, USA (Chevrolet Camaro), 1h 12m 48·781s, 83·06 mph/133·67 km/h.
2 Elliott Forbes-Robinson, USA (Buick Somerset Regal), 1h 13m 27·301s.
3 Eppie Wietzes, CDN (Chevrolet Camaro), 42 laps.
4 Mike Miller, USA (Mercury Merkur XR4Ti), 42.
5 John Schneider, USA (Buick Somerset Regal), 41.
6 Jim Derhaag, USA (Pontiac Trans-Am), 41.
7 Les Lindley, USA (Chevrolet Camaro), 41; **8** Bob Sobey, USA (Pontiac Trans-Am), 41; **9** Jerry Clinton, USA (Mercury Capri), 41; **10** Pete Brallier, USA (Pontiac Trans-Am), 40.
Fastest lap: Tommy Riggins, USA (Buick Somerset Regal), 1m 31·631s, 94·29 mph/151·74 km/h.
Championship points. Drivers: 1 Dallenbach Jnr, 65; **2** Lindley, 55; **3** Halsmer, 47; **4** Kneifel, 44; **5** Miller (Jim), 41; **6** Forbes-Robinson, 39.
Manufacturers: 1 Chevrolet, 39; **2** Mercury, 28; **3** Buick, 10; **4** Pontiac, 2.

BENDIX BRAKE TRANS-AM RACE, Brainerd International Raceway, Minnesota, United States of America, 20 July. Bendix Brake Trans-Am Championship, round 6. 33 laps of the 3·000-mile/4·828-km circuit, 99·00 miles/159·32 km.
1 Greg Pickett, USA (Chevrolet Camaro), 58m 28·78s, 101·57 mph/163·46 km/h.
2 Pete Halsmer, USA (Mercury Merkur XR4Ti), 58m 29·86s.
3 Tommy Riggins, USA (Buick Somerset Regal), 33 laps.
4 Wally Dallenbach Jnr, USA (Chevrolet Camaro), 33.
5 Chris Kneifel, USA (Mercury Merkur XR4Ti), 33.
6 Les Lindley, USA (Chevrolet Camaro), 33.
7 Jim Derhaag, USA (Pontiac Trans-Am), 33; **8** Jim Sanborn, USA (Pontiac Trans-Am), 33; **9** Scott Pruett, USA (Mercury Capri), 32; **10** Jim Miller, USA (Chevrolet Camaro), 32.
Fastest lap: Pruett, 1m 36·086s, 112·40 mph/180·89 km/h (record).
Championship points. Drivers: 1 Dallenbach Jnr, 77; **2** Lindley, 65; **3** Halsmer, 63; **4** Kneifel, 55; **5** Pickett, 52; **6** Miller (Jim), 47.
Manufacturers: 1 Chevrolet, 48; **2** Mercury, 34; **3** Buick, 14; **4** Pontiac, 2.

BENDIX BRAKE TRANS-AM RACE, Road America, Elkhart Lake, Wisconsin, United States of America, 27 July. Bendix Brake Trans-Am Championship, round 7. 25 laps of the 4·000-mile/6·437-km circuit, 100·00 miles/160·93 km.
1 Pete Halsmer, USA (Mercury Merkur XR4Ti), 1h 03m 15·180s, 94·85 mph/152·65 km/h.
2 Wally Dallenbach Jnr, USA (Chevrolet Camaro), 1h 03m 16·409s.
3 Chris Kneifel, USA (Mercury Capri), 25 laps.
4 Jim Fitzgerald, USA (Nissan 300ZX Turbo), 25.
5 Mike Miller, USA (Mercury Merkur XR4Ti), 25.
6 Eppie Wietzes, CDN (Chevrolet Camaro), 25.
7 Rick Dittman, USA (Pontiac Firebird), 25; **8** Jim Derhaag, USA (Pontiac Trans-Am), 25; **9** Les Lindley, USA (Chevrolet Camaro), 25; **10** Elliott Forbes-Robinson, USA (Buick Somerset Regal), 24.
Fastest lap: Halsmer, 2m 17·033s, 105·08 mph/169·11 km/h.
Championship points. Drivers: 1 Dallenbach Jnr, 94; **2** Halsmer, 84; **3** Lindley, 72; **4** Kneifel, 69; **5** Miller (Jim), 53; **6** Pickett, 52.
Manufacturers: 1 Chevrolet, 54; **2** Mercury, 43; **3** Buick, 14; **4** Nissan, 3; **5** Pontiac, 2.

BENDIX BRAKE TRANS-AM RACE, Lime Rock Park, Connecticut, United States of America, 16 August. Bendix Brake Trans-Am Championship, round 8. 66 laps of the 1·53-mile/2·46-km circuit, 100·98 miles/162·36 km.
1 Paul Newman, USA (Nissan 300ZX Turbo), 1h 06m 32·638s, 91·049 mph/146·529 km/h.
2 Elliott Forbes-Robinson, USA (Buick Somerset Regal), 1h 06m 32·966s.
3 Scott Pruett, USA (Mercury Capri),66 laps.
4 Tommy Riggins, USA (Buick Somerset Regal), 66.
5 Chris Kneifel, USA (Mercury Merkur XR4Ti), 66.
6 Mike Miller, USA (Mercury Merkur XR4Ti), 66.
7 Les Lindley, USA (Chevrolet Camaro), 65; **8** Peter Dus, USA (Chevrolet Corvette), 65; **9** Peter Andrighetti, USA (Chevrolet Corvette), 65; **10** John Schneider, USA (Buick Somerset Regal), 65.
Fastest lap: Wally Dallenbach Jnr, USA (Chevrolet Camaro), 52·760s, 104·397 mph/168·010 km/h (record).
Championship points. Drivers: 1 Dallenbach Jnr, 94; **2** Halsmer, 86; **3** Lindley, 81; **4** Kneifel, 80; **5** Miller (Mike), 63; **6** Forbes-Robinson, 61.
Manufacturers: 1 Chevrolet, 54; **2** Mercury, 47; **3** Buick, 20; **4** Nissan, 12; **5** Pontiac, 2.

BENDIX BRAKE TRANS-AM RACE, Mosport Park Circuit, Ontario, Canada, 14 September. Bendix Brake Trans-Am Championship, round 9. 40 laps of the 2·459-mile/3·957-km circuit, 98·36 miles/158·28 km.
1 Scott Pruett, USA (Mercury Capri), 1h 02m 36·970s, 94·250 mph/151·680 km/h.
2 Wally Dallenbach Jnr, USA (Chevrolet Camaro), 1h 02m 37·939s.
3 Greg Pickett, USA (Chevrolet Camaro), 40 laps.
4 Jim Miller, USA (Chevrolet Camaro), 40.
5 Tommy Riggins, USA (Buick Somerset Regal), 40.
6 Mike Miller, USA (Mercury Merkur XR4Ti), 39.
7 Pete Halsmer, USA (Mercury Merkur XR4Ti), 39; **8** John Schneider, USA (Buick Somerset Regal), 39; **9** Jim Derhaag, USA (Pontiac Trans-Am), 39; **10** Jerry Clinton, USA (Mercury Capri), 39.
Fastest lap: Dallenbach Jnr, 1m 21·965s, 108·002 mph/173·812 km/h.
Championship points. Drivers: 1 Dallenbach Jnr, 111; **2** Halsmer, 96; **3** Lindley, 83; **4** Kneifel, 80; **5** Miller (Mike), 73; **6** Pickett, 66.
Manufacturers: 1 Chevrolet, 60; **2** Mercury, 56; **3** Buick, 22; **4** Nissan, 12; **5** Pontiac, 2.

BENDIX BRAKE TRANS-AM RACE, Sears Point International Raceway, Sonoma, California, United States of America, 28 September. Bendix Brake Trans-Am Championship, round 10. 40 laps of the 2·523-mile/4·060-km circuit, 100·92 miles/162·40 km.
1 Wally Dallenbach Jnr, USA (Chevrolet Camaro), 1h 14m 02·883s, 81·774 mph/131·602 km/h.
2 Greg Pickett, USA (Chevrolet Camaro), 1h 14m 03·154s.
3 Scott Pruett, USA (Mercury Capri),40 laps.
4 Elliott Forbes-Robinson, USA (Buick Somerset Regal), 40.
5 Tommy Riggins, USA (Buick Somerset Regal), 40.
6 John Schneider, USA (Buick Somerset Regal), 40.
7 Jim Miller, USA (Chevrolet Camaro), 40; **8** Andy Porterfield, USA (Chevrolet Camaro), 40; **9** Bob Sobey, USA (Pontiac Trans-Am), 40; **10** Jerry Miller, USA (Chevrolet Camaro), 40.
Fastest lap: Pruett, 1m 38·545s, 92·169 mph/148·331 km/h.
Championship points. Drivers: 1 Dallenbach Jnr, 132; **2** Halsmer, 96; **3** Lindley, 83; **4** Pickett, 82; **5** Pruett and Kneifel, 80.
Manufacturers: 1 Chevrolet, 69; **2** Mercury, 60; **3** Buick, 25; **4** Nissan, 12; **5** Pontiac, 2.

BENDIX BRAKE TRANS-AM RACE, Road Atlanta, Georgia, United States of America, 12 October. Bendix Brake Trans-Am Championship, round 11. 40 laps of the 2·520-mile/4·055-km circuit, 100·80 miles/162·24 km.
1 Chris Kneifel, USA (Mercury Merkur XR4Ti), 1h 39m 15·956s, 60·920 mph/98·041 km/h.
2 Elliott Forbes-Robinson, USA (Buick Somerset Regal), 1h 39m 49·706s.
3 Jim Miller, USA (Chevrolet Camaro), 40 laps.
4 Mike Miller, USA (Mercury Merkur XR4Ti), 40.
5 Jerry Miller, USA (Chevrolet Camaro), 39.
6 Wally Dallenbach Jnr, USA (Chevrolet Camaro), 39.
7 Jim Derhaag, USA (Pontiac Trans-Am), 38; **8** Greg Pickett, USA (Chevrolet Camaro), 38; **9** Kerry Hitt, USA (Chevrolet Corvette), 38; **10** Les Lindley, USA (Chevrolet Camaro), 38.
Fastest lap: Kneifel, 1m 35·113s, 95·381 mph/153·500 km/h.

Championship points (prior to final two rounds in November):
Drivers

1	Wally Dallenbach Jnr, USA	143
2	Chris Kneifel, USA	100
3	Pete Halsmer, USA	96
4	Greg Pickett, USA	90
5=	Elliott Forbes-Robinson, USA	89
5=	Les Lindley, USA	89

7 Mike Miller, USA, 85; **8** Jim Miller, USA, 82; **9** Scott Pruett, USA, 80; **10** Jim Derhaag, USA 63; **11** John Schneider, USA, 59; **12** Tommy Riggins, USA, 48; **13** Jerry Miller, USA 30; **14** Paul Newman, USA, 29; **15** Rick Dittman, USA, 28.
Manufacturers

1	Chevrolet	73
2	Mercury	69
3	Buick	31
4	Nissan	12
5	Pontiac	2

Final results will be given in *Autocourse 1987/88.*

Robert Bosch/VW Super Vee Championship

ROBERT BOSCH/VW SUPER VEE RACE, Long Beach Circuit, Long Beach, California, United States of America, 13 April. Robert Bosch/VW Super Vee Championship, round 1. 37 laps of the 1·67-mile/2·69-km circuit, 61·79 miles/99·53 km.
1 Steve Bren, USA (Ralt RT5-VW), 50m 31·72s, 73·37 mph/118·08 km/h.
2 Mike Groff, USA (Ralt RT5-VW), 50m 34·00s.
3 Jeff Andretti, USA (Ralt RT5-VW), 37 laps.
4 Didier Theys, B (Martini MK47-VW), 37.
5 Dennis Vitolo, USA (Ralt RT5-VW), 37.
6 Dave Kudrave, USA (Ralt RT5-VW), 37.
7 Matt McBride, USA (Ralt RT5-VW), 37; **8** Dave Whitney, USA (Ralt RT5-VW), 37; **9** Eddie Jones, GB (Shannon AJ82V-VW), 37; **10** Danny Thompson, USA (Ralt RT5-VW), 36.
Fastest lap: Groff, 1m 14·045s, 81·19 mph/130·66 km/h.
Championship points: 1 Bren, 20; **2** Groff, 16; **3** Andretti, 14; **4** Theys, 12; **5** Vitolo, 11; **6** Kudrave, 10.

ROBERT BOSCH/VW SUPER VEE RACE, Indianapolis Raceway Park, Indianapolis, Indiana, United States of America, 24 May. Robert Bosch/VW Super Vee Championship, round 2. 80 laps of the 0·686-mile/1·104-km circuit, 54·88 miles/88·32 km.
1 Didier Theys, B (Martini MK50-VW), 38m 12·260s, 86·18 mph/138·69 km/h.
2 Johnny O'Connell, USA (Anson PM6-VW), 38m 15·976s.
3 Mike Groff, USA (Ralt RT5-VW), 80 laps.
4 Gary Rubio, USA (Ralt RT5-VW), 79.
5 Steve Thompson, USA (Ralt RT5-VW), 79.
6 Steve Bren, USA (Ralt RT5-VW), 79.
7 Thomas Knapp, USA (Ralt RT5-VW), 79; **8** Scott Atchison, USA (Ralt RT5-VW), 78; **9** Dennis Vitolo, USA (Ralt RT5-VW), 78; **10** Jeff Wilson, USA (Ralt RT5-VW), 78.
Fastest lap: O'Connell, 20·970s, 117·77 mph/189·53 km/h.
Championship points: 1 Theys, 32; **2** Bren and Groff, 30; **4** Vitolo, 18; **5** O'Connell, 16; **6** Andretti, 14.

ROBERT BOSCH/VW SUPER VEE RACE, Wisconsin State Fair Park Speedway, Milwaukee, Wisconsin, United States of America, 7 June. Robert Bosch/VW Super Vee Championship, round 3. 62 laps of the 1·000-mile/1·609-km circuit, 62·00 miles/96·54 km.
1 Mike Groff, USA (Ralt RT5-VW), 33m 45·00s, 110·22 mph/177·38 km/h.
2 Steve Bren, USA (Ralt RT5-VW), 33m 45·21s.
3 Johnny O'Connell, USA (Anson PM6-VW), 61 laps.
4 Matt McBride, USA (Ralt RT5-VW), 61.
5 Tero Palmroth, SF (Ralt RT5-VW), 61.
6 Gary Rubio, USA (Ralt RT5-VW), 61.
7 Dennis Vitolo, USA (Ralt RT5-VW), 61; **8** Steve Thompson, USA (Ralt RT5-VW), 61; **9** Thomas Knapp, USA (Ralt RT5-VW), 61; **10** Scott Atchison, USA (Ralt RT5-VW), 61.
Fastest lap: Not available.
Championship points: 1 Groff, 50; **2** Bren, 46; **3** Theys, 32; **4** O'Connell, 30; **5** Vitolo, 27; **6** Rubio, 22.

ROBERT BOSCH/VW SUPER VEE RACE, Detroit Grand Prix Circuit, Michigan, United States of America, 21 June. Robert Bosch/VW Super Vee Championship, round 4. 24 laps of the 2·500-mile/4·023-km circuit, 60·00 miles/96·55 km.
1 Scott Atchison, USA (Ralt RT5-VW) 49m 10·464s, 73·21 mph/117·82 km/h.
2 Matt McBride, USA (Ralt RT5-VW) 49m 25·540s.
3 Thomas Knapp, USA (Ralt RT5-VW), 24 laps.
4 Tero Palmroth, SF (Ralt RT5-VW), 24.
5 Tony George, USA (Ralt RT5-VW), 24.
6 E.J. Lenzi, USA (Ralt RT5-VW), 24.
7 Charles Wilson, USA (Ralt RT5-VW), 24; **8** Mike Groff, USA (Ralt RT5-VW), 23; **9** Pat Phinny, USA (Ralt RT5-VW), 23; **10** Steve Thompson, USA (Ralt RT5-VW), 23.
Fastest lap: Groff, 1m 57·521s, 76·58 mph/123·24 km/h.
Championship points: 1 Groff, 58; **2** Bren, 46; **3** McBride, 37; **4** Atchison, 34; **5** Theys, 32; **6** O'Connell and Knapp, 30.

ROBERT BOSCH/VW SUPER VEE RACE, Meadowlands Grand Prix Circuit, New York, United States of America, 28 June. Robert Bosch/VW Super Vee Championship, round 5. 33 laps of the 1·682-mile/2·707-km circuit, 55·51 miles/89·33 km.
1 Didier Theys, B (Martini MK50-VW), 38m 12·792s, 87·16 mph/140·27 km/h.
2 Scott Atchison, USA (Ralt RT5-VW), 38m 13·975s.
3 Mike Groff, USA (Ralt RT5-VW), 33 laps.
4 Dave Kudrave, USA (Ralt RT5-VW), 33.
5 Tero Palmroth, SF (Ralt RT5-VW), 33.
6 Matt McBride, USA (Ralt RT5-VW), 33.
7 Charles Wilson, USA (Ralt RT5-VW), 32; **8** Tony George, USA (Ralt RT5-VW), 32; **9** Phil Katzakian, USA (Ralt RT5-VW), 32; **10** Pat Phinny, USA (Ralt RT5-VW), 32.
Fastest lap: Theys, 1m 08·664s, 88·19 mph/141·93 km/h.
Championship points: 1 Groff, 72; **2** Theys, 52; **3** Atchison, 50; **4** McBride, 47; **5** Bren, 46; **6** Palmroth, 39.

ROBERT BOSCH/VW SUPER VEE RACE, Burke Lakefront Airport Circuit, Cleveland, Ohio, United States of America, 6 July, Robert Bosch/VW Super Vee Championship, round 6. 25 laps of the 2·485-mile/3·999-km circuit, 62·13 miles/99·98 km.
1 Didier Theys, B (Martini MK50-VW), 31m 52·77s, 116·93 mph/188·18 km/h.
2 Steve Bren, USA (Ralt RT5-VW), 32m 13·78s.
3 Dave Kudrave, USA (Ralt RT5-VW), 25 laps.
4 Scott Atchison, USA (Ralt RT5-VW), 25.
5 Dave Simpson, USA (Ralt RT5-VW), 25.
6 Matt McBride, USA (Ralt RT5-VW), 25.
7 Cary Bren, USA (Ralt RT5-VW), 25; **8** Tony George, USA (Ralt RT5-VW), 25; **9** Dennis Vitolo, USA (Ralt RT5-VW), 24; **10** Rich Rutherford, USA (Ralt RT5-VW), 24.
Fastest lap: Theys, 1m 15·26s, 118·87 mph/191·30 km/h.
Championship points: 1 Theys and Groff, 72; **3** Bren (Steve) and Atchison, 62; **5** McBride, 57; **6** Palmroth, 39.

ROBERT BOSCH/VW SUPER VEE RACE, Road America, Elkhart Lake, Wisconsin, United States of America, 27 July. Robert Bosch/VW Super Vee Championship, round 7. 15 laps of the 4·000-mile/6·437-km circuit, 60·00 miles/96·56 km.
1 Thomas Knapp, USA (Ralt RT5-VW), 39m 20·650s, 91·50 mph/147·25 km/h.
2 Cary Bren, USA (Ralt RT5-VW), 39m 39·650s.
3 Dave Kudrave, USA (Ralt RT5-VW), 15 laps.
4 Gary Rubio, USA (Ralt RT5-VW), 15.
5 Johnny O'Connell, USA (Anson PM6-VW), 15.
6 Scott Atchison, USA (Ralt RT5-VW), 15.
7 Tero Palmroth, SF (Ralt RT5-VW), 15; **8** Tony George, USA (Ralt RT5-VW), 15; **9** C. T. Hancock, USA (Ralt RT5-VW), 15; **10** Hank Chapman, USA (Ralt RT5-VW), 15.
Fastest lap: Kudrave, 2m 11·708s, 109·33 mph/175·95 km/h.
Championship points: 1 Theys, 75; **2** Groff and Atchison, 72; **4** Bren (Steve), 66; **5** McBride, 57; **6** Knapp and Kudrave, 50.

ROBERT BOSCH/VW SUPER VEE RACE, Mid-Ohio Sports Car Course, Lexington, Ohio, United States of America, 31 August. Robert Bosch/VW Super Vee Championship, round 8. 25 laps of the 2·400-mile/3·863-km circuit, 60·00 miles/96·58 km.
1 Steve Bren, USA (Ralt RT5-VW), 35m 53·462s, 100·30 mph/161·42 km/h.
2 Scott Atchison, USA (Ralt RT5-VW), 36m 11·491s.
3 Dave Kudrave, USA (Ralt RT5-VW), 25 laps.
4 Mike Groff, USA (Ralt RT5-VW), 25.
5 Dennis Vitolo, USA (Ralt RT5-VW), 25.
6 Gary Rubio, USA (Ralt RT5-VW), 25.
7 Cary Bren, USA (Ralt RT5-VW), 25; **8** Didier Theys, B (Martini MK50-VW), 25; **9** Tony George, USA (Ralt RT5-VW), 25; **10** Pat Phinny, USA (Ralt RT5-VW), 25.
Fastest lap: Bren (Steve), 1m 25·020s, 101·62 mph/163·54 km/h.
Championship points:1 Atchison, 88; **2** Bren (Steve), 86; **3** Groff, 84; **4** Theys, 83; **5** Kudrave, 64; **6** McBride, 57.

ROBERT BOSCH/VW SUPER VEE RACE, Road America, Elkhart Lake, Wisconsin, United States of America, 21 September. Robert Bosch/VW Super Vee Championship, round 9. 15 laps of the 4·000-mile/6·437-km circuit, 60·00 miles/96·56 km.
1 Thomas Knapp, USA (Ralt RT5-VW), 39m 43·43s, 90·626 mph/145·848 km/h.
2 Didier Theys, B (Martini MK50-VW), 40m 00·03s.
3 Cary Bren, USA (Ralt RT5-VW), 15 laps.
4 Steve Bren, USA (Ralt RT5-VW) 15.
5 Dave Kudrave, USA (Ralt RT5-VW), 15.
6 Dennis Vitolo USA (Ralt RT5-VW), 15.
7 Mike Groff, USA (Ralt RT5-VW), 15; **8** E.J. Lenzi, USA (Anson SA6-VW), 14; **9** Scott Atchison, USA (Ralt RT5-VW), 14; **10** Mike Follmer, USA (Ralt RT5-VW), 14.
Fastest lap: Theys, 2m 35·32s, 92·712 mph/149·205 km/h.
Championship points: 1 Theys, 99; **2** Bren (Steve), 98; **3** Atchison, 95; **4** Groff, 93; **5** Kudrave, 75; **6** Knapp, 70.

ROBERT BOSCH/VW SUPER VEE RACE, Laguna Seca Raceway, California, United States of America, 12 October. Robert Bosch/VW Super Vee Championship, round 10. 33 laps of the 1·900-mile/3·056-km circuit, 62·70 miles/100·85 km.
1 Steve Bren, USA (Ralt RT5-VW), 37m 00·023s, 101·675 mph/163·630 km/h.
2 Didier Theys, B (Martini MK50-VW), 37m 01·216s.
3 Cary Bren, USA (Ralt RT5-VW), 33 laps.
4 Mike Groff, USA (Ralt RT5-VW), 33.
5 Dennis Vitolo, USA (Ralt RT5-VW), 33.
6 Scott Atchison, USA (Ralt RT5-VW), 33.
7 Gary Rubio, USA (Ralt RT5-VW), 33; **8** Pat Phinny, USA (Ralt RT5-VW), 33; **9** Dave Whitney, USA (Ralt RT5-VW), 33; **10** Jeff Simpson, USA (Ralt RT5-VW), 33.
Fastest lap: Bren (Steve), 1m 01·436s, 111·335 mph/179·176 km/h.
Championship points: 1 Bren (Steve), 118; **2** Theys, 115; **3** Groff and Atchison, 105; **5** Kudrave, 75; **6** Knapp, 70.

ROBERT BOSCH/VW SUPER VEE RACE, Phoenix International Raceway, Arizona, United States of America, 19 October. Robert Bosch/VW Super Vee Championship, round 11. 60 laps of the 1·000-mile/1·609-km circuit, 60·00 miles/96·54 km.
1 Mike Groff, USA (Ralt RT5-VW), 35m 50·021s, 106·455 mph/171·322 km/h.
2 Ken Johnson, USA (Ralt RT5-VW) 60 laps.
3 Steve Bren, USA (Ralt RT5-VW), 60.
4 Dave Kudrave, USA (Ralt RT5-VW), 60.
5 Gary Rubio, USA (Ralt RT5-VW) 60.
6 Mark Smith, USA (Ralt RT5-VW), 60.
7 Pat Phinny, USA (Ralt RT5-VW), 60; **8** Scott Atchison, USA (Ralt RT5-VW), 60; **9** Cary Bren, USA (Ralt RT5-VW), 60; **10** Mike Smith, USA (Ralt RT5-VW), 60.
Fastest lap: Not available.

Championship points (prior to final 2 rounds in November)

1	Steve Bren, USA	132
2	Mike Groff, USA	125
3	Didier Theys, B	115
4	Scott Atchison, USA	113
5	Dave Kudrave, USA	87
6	Gary Rubio, USA	71

7 Thomas Knapp, USA, 70; **8** Cary Bren, USA, 69; **9** Dennis Vitolo, USA, 66; **10** Matt McBride, USA, 57; **11** Tony George, USA, 54; **12** Tero Palmroth, SF, 52; **13** Ken Johnson, USA and Johnny O'Connell, USA, 45; **15** Steve Thompson, USA, 27.

Final results will be given in *Autocourse 1987/88.*